DATE DUE

DE 14 08			
DE 12 06			

DEMCO 38-296

ALSO BY CLIVE PONTING

The Right to Know:
The Inside Story of the Belgrano *Affair*

Whitehall: Tragedy and Farce

Breach of Promise: Labour in Power 1964–1970

Whitehall: Changing the Old Guard

Secrecy in Britain

1940: Myth and Reality

A Green History of the World

Churchill

Armageddon: The Second World War

THE
TWENTIETH
CENTURY

A World History

CLIVE PONTING

A John Macrae Book
Henry Holt and Company / New York

Henry Holt and Company, Inc.
Publishers since 1866
115 West 18th Street
New York, New York 10011

Henry Holt® is a registered trademark
of Henry Holt and Company, Inc.

Copyright © 1998 by Clive Ponting
All rights reserved.
Published in Canada by Fitzhenry & Whiteside Ltd.,
195 Allstate Parkway, Markham, Ontario L3R 4T8.

First published in the United States in 1999
by Henry Holt and Company, Inc.

Originally published in Great Britain in 1998 by
Chatto & Windus under the title *Progress and Barbarism*

Library of Congress Cataloging-in-Publication Data
Ponting, Clive.
[Progress and barbarism]
The twentieth century: a world history / Clive Ponting.—1st
U.S. ed.
p.   cm.
Originally published: Great Britain: Chatto & Windus, 1998 under
the title: Progress and barbarism.
"A John Macrae book."
Includes bibliographical references and index.
ISBN 0-8050-6088-X
1. History, Modern—20th century   I. Title.   II. Title: 20th century
D421.P66   1999   98-37613
909.82—dc21   CIP

Henry Holt books are available for special promotions and
premiums. For details contact: Director, Special Markets.

First American Edition 1999

Printed in the United States of America
All first editions are printed on acid-free paper.∞

1   3   5   7   9   10   8   6   4   2

To Laura

who makes everything possible

CONTENTS

Part One

THE TWENTIETH CENTURY

INTRODUCTION

ANY ATTEMPT to write the history of the world in the twentieth century raises two questions. First, how should it be structured? And, second, is a century a coherent period to study? It would be possible to write a history of the twentieth century on a strictly chronological basis, year by year, but that approach would not help us to understand how world history has been shaped over the last hundred years. It would also be possible to adopt a country-by-country or region-by-region approach, which would give greater coherence than the first option, but would make it more difficult to identify the common themes, problems and forces that have affected all of the world without large amounts of repetition. This book adopts an alternative approach in order to identify the economic, social and political forces operating within twentieth-century history. Each chapter, apart from the first and last, is an individual journey across the landscape of the twentieth century with its own starting and finishing points, and each visits different places en route. Some of the routes cross each other or look across the same landscape from different vantage points. Each chapter is relatively self-contained and can be read on its own, but as the reader progresses through the book the relationships between the various subjects will, I hope, become clearer. The journeys begin in Part Two with the fundamental social and economic factors, move on in Part Three to international issues and then in Part Four to domestic politics. From the table of contents it will be clear that there are major omissions, in particular cultural and religious themes. This was a conscious decision.

All historians would accept that any attempt to divide up the constant flow of events is artificial and bound to produce problems. However, some would question whether the twentieth century is a self-contained period for historical study. Eric Hobsbawm, for example, has argued in favour of the so-called 'Short Twentieth

Century', from 1914 to 1989. Adopting such a framework has certain unavoidable consequences, most important of all it privileges European history. The outbreak of the First World War marked an important transition for some European states, but it had little impact in Latin America, Africa and Asia. Using 1989 as an end date similarly places too much importance on European history. Although the collapse of Communism in Eastern Europe and the end of the Cold War undoubtedly had global effects, the impact of these events outside Europe, North America and the then Soviet Union was surprisingly limited. In addition, using 1989 as an end date almost inevitably leads to an analysis in which the conflict between liberal democracy and Communism (or even a widely defined 'socialism') becomes the main feature of twentieth-century history. The problems with this approach are well illustrated by the arguments in Francis Fukuyama's *The End of History*. Contrary to his assertions, the near-universal adoption of capitalism in the 1990s did not bring history to a halt. It is impossible to reduce the complexities of world history in the twentieth century simply to a conflict between two different economic and political systems. Concentrating on the struggle between these two world-views, important as it was for some states for part of the century, not only ignores vast areas of twentieth-century history and human experience but once again introduces a bias towards a European perspective. The ideas of both liberal capitalism and 'socialism'/ 'communism' emerged in Europe between the late eighteenth and late nineteenth centuries. They were both products of the European experience and way of thinking. From a global perspective their spread and influence were part of the general expansion of Europe and its dominance in the early twentieth century. The fact that one of them was eventually victorious tells us something about world history, but is very far from being the whole story.

A global economic viewpoint would produce a very different chronology from the 'Short Twentieth Century' of 1914–89. From this viewpoint 1914 is of little importance. Much more crucial would be the onset of the world depression between 1929 and 1931, with the collapse of commodity prices which were vital to Latin American, African and Asian economies, and which led to the destruction of nearly all the existing political systems across Latin America. In world economic terms 1989 is far less important than 1973, which marked the end of the economic 'Golden Age' that had begun in 1950, and with the collapse of the global financial system established after the Second World War. The sharp rise in oil prices was one of the factors that produced a return to the economic conditions typical of the rest of the century – low growth and high unemployment.

Finding a single chronological framework for world history is an almost impossible undertaking. Instead, this book is based on the assumption that, handled with care, the twentieth century is a reasonable unit of historical analysis, although neither 1900 nor 2000 should be seen as marking significant transitions. Many of the chapters look back into the late nineteenth century to identify important trends in the early twentieth century and towards the end of Chapter 22 there is an attempt to isolate some of the key trends that are already shaping the early twenty-first century. Each chapter has a chronology suitable to its subject matter. Using the relatively 'neutral' chronological framework of a single century has the advantage of not forcing world history into a Procrustean bed suitable for the history of one geographical area or one type of history whether economic, military, diplomatic or any other variety.

Any attempt to describe the course of twentieth-century world history raises acute problems of terminology. Given the huge changes during the century – the apogee and decline of the colonial empires, and the rise and eventual collapse of the Soviet Union to name but two – it is important to use consistent labels which are applicable across the century. 'East' and 'West' really only existed for part of the Cold War era and the 'Third World' of 'under-developed' countries could only exist when there was a 'Second World' of Communist states. The more recent use of 'North' and 'South' is equally inexact, when the highly 'developed' economies of Australia and New Zealand are in the 'South' and numerous 'developing' ones exist north of the equator. So the organizing framework adopted and the terminology that flows from it are based on the 'world systems theory' developed by Immanuel Wallerstein. This historical approach argues that since the sixteenth century the world economy, the nature of the states in the world and the relationship between them have been moulded by two factors: the expansion of Europe and the creation of a world economy dominated by a few prosperous industrialized states. As a consequence the majority of people in the world and most states have been subordinated to the minority who have wielded economic and political power.

This approach has not been adopted in a strongly theoretical or rigid way, but it does provide a framework that can be applied across the century. It sees the world as dominated by a core of industrialized, wealthy states in Western Europe and North America, which in the last third of the century were joined by Japan. The majority of people and states in the world formed the periphery, which was economically and politically dependent on the core. The periphery was largely confined to producing raw materials and food for the core, for much of the century large parts of it were colonial territories and even after formal independence the dependent relationship was little altered. Between these two areas (in an economic and political but not a geographical sense) was the semi-periphery, made up of the semi-industrialized, middle-income countries in three areas – Latin America, southern Europe and central and eastern Europe. Later in the century they were joined by some of the economies in other areas such as east Asia and the Middle East. The division of the world into three highly unequal parts was no so rigid that some countries could not change their position – Japan was the most notable example of such a development – but most did not. Over the course of the century the differences between the core and the periphery became greater, not smaller.

This economic structure was also broadly reflected in politics. Most democracies were found in the core states, many of those in the semi-periphery fluctuated between semi-democracy, democracy and dictatorships of various kinds. Apart from India, the states of the periphery were either colonies or dictatorships. From this perspective, the struggle between liberal capitalism and Communism could be seen as a highly flawed and failed attempt by parts of the semi-periphery to find a different route to economic development in a situation where political and economic isolation meant few alternatives were available. The collapse of Communism in the Soviet Union in the early 1990s, and the equally important adoption of a semi-capitalist approach in China from the 1980s, did not change the fundamental structure of the world economy. History did not come to a full stop; it continued in a slightly different guise.

Within this general framework the book begins, after a survey of the world in 1900, with the economic forces that shaped the century: the unprecedented rise in population, the phenomenal increase in industrial production, the pace of technological advance, the impact of all these changes on the environment and the growing speed of globalization. It then considers how these changes affected different national economies. The last chapter in Part Two deals with the major social changes of the century, including the nature of work, literacy, urbanization, the changing position of women and aspects of leisure and crime. Part Three examines some of the major themes of international history – the great overseas empires that dominated the world in the first half of the century and their decline, the impact of nationalism, the changing balance of power globally and the nature of conflict in the twentieth century. Part Four considers themes in domestic history. It begins with the survival of traditional political structures and ideas and then looks at the only original twentieth-century 'philosophy' – fascism. Next it examines the varieties of the century's most common form of government – dictatorship. In Chapter 16, on revolution, the experiences of Mexico, Russia and China are compared. Chapters 17 and 18 deal with the important but minority experiences of democracy and social democracy. Chapters 19–21 are about the darker side of twentieth-century history – the growing power of the state to repress (and in extreme cases slaughter) its own citizens, the growth and decline of racial discrimination, and, finally, the worst of the century's crimes – genocide. Chapter 22 examines the balance between the various trends over the course of the century and looks forward to likely developments in the early twenty-first century.

The reader may wonder why some important developments in the twentieth century are not given chapters of their own. For example, it is clear in retrospect that Walter Lippmann's assertion that the twentieth century would be 'The American Century' has been largely correct. For the last hundred years the United States has been the largest economic power and has, to varying degrees, dominated the world's power structure (both military and diplomatic). Many Americans, including some of its most important leaders, from Woodrow Wilson through Franklin Roosevelt and Harry Truman to Ronald Reagan, believed that the role of the United States was to illuminate the path for other states and peoples to follow. In practice, much of its history in the twentieth century was unique and bore little relation to that of even its fellow industrialized countries in the core let alone the majority of the world's population. Although engaged in numerous wars, its mainland territory was not invaded or even attacked. Internally, although wealthier than any other country, it was divided by the greatest disparity in wealth of any of the core states and by extensive racial discrimination. Its political system was unique. Like other states the history of the United States runs through many of the chapters, but given the book's overall structure it is not given special predominance.

Another theme found in many chapters is the decline of European power – the loss of empire, strategic decline compared with the United States and the Soviet Union and, equally important, the loss of European self-confidence, which had been so apparent at the start of the century. In a wider context this decline is part of an even more fundamental trend – the revival of Asia and other areas which were subordinate to western Europe and North America in the first decades of the century. The first signs of this trend were visible at the start of the century with the Chinese nationalist Boxer movement, Filipino resistance to American conquest, growing Indian nationalism and the increasing power of Japan, demonstrated by its defeat of Russia in the war of 1904–5. By the early 1920s the revival was apparent in the Middle East with the emergence of the nationalist state in Turkey and growing opposition to the British in Egypt. After 1945, as the European empires collapsed, the United States was unable to extend its influence into areas that had not been controlled earlier by the Europeans. By the end of the century it was clear that this trend was of wider significance than just the decline of Europe. The first signs were emerging of an end to the 'Atlantic predominance' which had moulded world history for at least the previous 400 years. The countries surrounding the Pacific were increasing in importance and becoming the focus of the world economy. In the longest historical perspective, the most important date in the twentieth century will probably turn out to be 1949 when a reunified China was established with a strong government determined to bring about economic growth and reassert China's status as a major power. Until the seventeenth century China had been not just the largest state in the world but also the most prosperous and most technologically advanced. On current trends China will once again be the largest economy in the world by the second decade of the twenty-first century.

The book's major theme is the struggle between progress and barbarism. For Europeans and many Americans the twentieth century was a narrative of almost unbroken progress. The phenomenal industrialization, urbanization and growing prosperity of the previous century fuelled a massive self-confidence about their position in the world and their ability (indeed right) to rule it. There seemed little reason to believe that their optimism was misplaced or that this progress would not continue throughout the twentieth century. The origin of these views lay deep within European history, in particular in the Enlightenment of the eighteenth century, and was linked to ideas of free trade, capitalism, the development of a rational science, continued technological improvement and the conquest of nature. Similarly, political developments – the end of absolutism and the development of limited government, liberal institutions, partial democracy and the nation state – all seemed successful and unproblematic. All of these European developments were seen as pointing the way for the rest of humanity.

Within twenty years these illusions lay shattered. The First World War and, more importantly, the collapse of the Russian, Austro-Hungarian and German empires in 1917–18 and the seizure of power by the Bolsheviks in Russia, broke the mould of the old European order, which had survived from the nineteenth century. Already conservatives such as Winston Churchill were speaking of 'the terrible twentieth century'. Worse was to follow. The rise of fascism, Nazism and the repressive state in the Soviet Union were only the forerunners of the most dreadful war of the century, in which probably 85 million people died between 1939 and 1945. Six million of them died in the greatest crime of the century – the death camps and the Jewish holocaust. At the end of the war the Japanese were the first to suffer a nuclear attack. Although the world avoided a nuclear war during the remaining decades of the century, tens of millions more died in numerous wars and almost as many at the hands of their own governments: in the 1970s at least a third of the population of Cambodia was killed by Pol Pot's government, which was driven by its Marxist 'philosophy' derived from Europe.

The unparalleled barbarity of these events was not an aberration from the mainstream of European development. The two most destructive political movements of the twentieth century – Communism and Nazism – had their origins deep in European history and ways of thinking. They were part of the much darker side of the European inheritance from the eighteenth-century Enlightenment and the nineteenth century. This period had also seen the development of intolerant revolutionary universalist ideas, increasingly divisive and exclusive nationalism, racism and social Darwinist views about the 'survival of the fittest' (in terms of classes, nations and races) and the right of the successful to rule and dominate others. Economic, scientific and technological progress made it easier to carry out these ideas. By the end of the twentieth century other aspects of the European inheritance were also being questioned increasingly. The modern state as it emerged in Europe seemed to be in decline. Internally it was abandoning functions such as economic regulation and welfare provision that only a few decades earlier had seemed central to its functions. Externally it was losing power with the emergence of global economic and financial forces and, in particular, transnational corporations, none of which it could control. In addition, the view that scientific and technological advances automatically equalled 'progress' was in doubt because of their damaging social and environmental impacts.

However, the belief in progress was not entirely misplaced. The twentieth century witnessed the greatest ever expansion in industrial output, far beyond the wildest dreams of those alive in 1900. New technologies were to transform the lives of hundreds of millions of people – the car, the telephone, radio and, perhaps most important of all, electricity and all the subsidiary inventions which depended upon it. At the start of the century the first primitive aircraft were being built. By the end hundreds of millions of people were flying around the globe every year. Other technologies were still unknown in 1900 – tape recording, television, plastics, photocopying, lasers, satellites, spaceflight and, most important of all, computers, semiconductors, robots and silicon chips.

For those able to afford the products of these new technologies the increase in their standard of living was phenomenal. Over the century everybody became wealthier (at least on average). The problem was that the world's wealth was unequally distributed. Twenty per cent of the world's population enjoyed 80 per cent of its wealth – perhaps the century's greatest barbarity. The overwhelming majority of humanity lived in abject poverty with few material possessions, subject to the continual threat of hunger and starvation and, frequently, war and civil conflict. During the twentieth century worldwide disparities in wealth became greater not smaller. For much of the century the United States, about 5 per cent of the world's people, consumed more than 30 per cent of its resources. Yet within the United States, the differences in wealth and social care were such that the people who lived in inner-city ghettoes had child mortality rates little better than the cities of the periphery.

As a history this book adopts an international framework for each chapter and attempts to assess the varying impacts of various trends in different parts of the world. For some this may be an unsettling perspective and the conclusions that flow from it may be equally unfamiliar. Most readers will probably be educated, middle-class citizens living in the prosperous countries of Western

Europe, North America and Australasia. Their experiences and those of their families are not typical of the majority of the world's population in the twentieth century. The most common human experience is that of being a peasant anywhere outside the economically 'developed' countries, the largest single group in this category being the Chinese peasantry. These people have been subject to starvation, limited education and the ravages of civil war, whereas the states of western Europe were by world standards relatively pleasant places to live in the twentieth century (apart from the two World Wars). Eastern Europe, including the Soviet Union, was a different story.

For example, people born in the Ukraine at the beginning of the century experienced the First World War and German occupation, followed by civil war, mass killings and widespread starvation by the time they were in their twenties. If they survived, they would then have faced the imposition of Soviet rule, the ruthless anti-kulak and collectivization drives, mass starvation on an unprecedented scale and the Stalinist terror. If they were still alive by 1941, they would then have suffered the most ruthless war of the century, forced labour, starvation and the 'anti-partisan' shootings of the second German occupation. If they served in the Soviet army, they would probably have been captured and died in appalling conditions in a German prisoner-of-war camp. If they were Jewish, they would either have been massacred by mobile killing squads or condemned to the horrors of the death camps. By 1944 many of those still alive would have been sent to Germany as slave labour. Those who remained faced war, the reimposition of Soviet rule, terror and possibly being sent to the Gulag. Anybody who survived until old age would have suffered from the consequences of the Chernobyl nuclear disaster.

Any attempt to tell the story of the twentieth century has to face the fact that the chance of a relatively stable and prosperous life has been confined to a very small and lucky minority of the world's people.

This book is an attempt at interpretation and is mainly based, inevitably, on secondary sources, but only a few of these works have been listed as a guide to further reading. I decided not to burden the text with footnotes, which would have been endless. My aim has been to try and develop a different angle of vision through a comparative approach. Carl Burkhardt, the eminent Swiss nineteenth-century historian of the Renaissance in Italy, wrote that no historical view is possible without some organizing generalizations and principles: the same material in the hands of a different historian would produce different conclusions.

I   1900

THE IDEA of the twentieth century is a Western, Christian concept. For most of the world's people 1 January 1900 was not the start of a new century. For many 1 January was not even the start of a new year in their calendars. In China the calendar was still based on the emperor's reign, as it had been for at least two millennia. In the Muslim world the calendar started in the early seventh century of the Christian era. For Jews 1900 was the year 5661, in Thailand 2443 and according to one of the Hindu religious calendars it was the year 5002. Nine out of ten people in the world lived in the countryside as peasants. They had their own rituals and calendars which were often only vaguely based on the official version. Even the western world was not agreed about the calendar. Although purists might argue that the new century did not begin until 1 January 1901, there were differences over what calendar to use. Russia and Greece still kept to the Julian calendar, which was twelve days behind the commonly used Gregorian version and which led to many misunderstandings. The Russian shooting team, for example, arrived too late to take part in the 1908 Olympics in London because they forgot to allow for the different calendar. Russia finally abandoned the Julian calendar during the 1917 Revolution, Greece did so in 1923.

However, the idea of the twentieth century as a significant historical period is justified by the importance of the states of western Europe and North America, not just in 1900, but throughout the century. By 1900 a process that had begun in the early sixteenth century with the expansion of Europe into other regions of the world was almost complete. Until the late eighteenth century there was little difference in the relative wealth of the different parts of the world; indeed, only a few centuries earlier China had been by far the wealthiest and most powerful state in the world. As late as 1800 about two-thirds of the world's industrial output was produced outside Europe and North America.

However, the expansion of Europe and rapidly growing industrialization in western Europe and North America in the nineteenth century had produced a massively unequal world by the early twentieth century. It was a world in which a handful of states dominated a global economy, from which they obtained nearly all the benefits and in which they had gradually restructured the remaining economies and societies so that these were in dependent, subordinate positions. The dominant states also directly controlled a large part of the world as their colonies. For them the nineteenth century had been a period of immense technological, economic and social progress.

The best way to analyse the structure of the world in 1900, and throughout the twentieth century, is to divide it into three very unequal parts – the core, the semi-periphery and the periphery. In 1900, just four major states – the United States, Britain, Germany and France – dominated the core. Between them they had only one-eighth of the world's population, but they produced more than three-quarters of world's industrial output, provided the same proportion of its trade and even more of its foreign investment. They had changed greatly in the nineteenth century. From rural, agricultural societies dominated, in Europe, by a landed elite, they had been transformed into industrial, mainly urban societies with a large working class and a developed infrastructure in which over 90 per cent of the population was literate and enjoyed a standard of living far in advance of the rest of the world. The United States was the most industrialized country in the world, with Britain close behind. The core states controlled over 400 million people (about a quarter of the world's population) directly in their colonies and hundreds of millions more indirectly, through their 'informal empires' of economic influence. Within the core there were also a number of smaller, less powerful, but still wealthy states, such as Belgium, Switzerland, the Netherlands and Sweden.

The semi-periphery was made up of three types of state. The first was in south and eastern Europe – Russia, Spain, Portugal, Italy, Austria-Hungary and the Balkan states. They were still largely agricultural, less wealthy and developed than the core states though often important militarily. Some, like Russia and Italy, appeared to be developing into economies and societies more like the core states, while others, such as Spain, appeared to be in decline. The second type of semi-peripheral state was found outside Europe – the European settlement colonies of Canada, Australia, New Zealand

and parts of Latin America, such as Argentina and Uruguay. These were relatively prosperous societies with economies built on the export of primary products, in particular food, to the core states. They had varying degrees of political independence. The third type consisted of just one state – Japan. It was the only state to have escaped European political control and to have embarked on a process of industrialization. That process had not gone far by 1900 (industrial output per head was one-fifteenth of the level in the United States) but, although still overwhelmingly a rural nation, Japan was already an important regional power capable of challenging the core powers in east Asia.

The overwhelming majority of the world (comprising nearly two-thirds of the world's people) constituted the periphery. Most of Asia and Africa had been divided up by the core states as colonies. Two major states were outside the control of the core – China and the Ottoman empire – but they were in what appeared to be terminal decline and it seemed unlikely that they could survive much longer as independent entities as core pressure on them mounted. Whatever its exact political status, all the periphery was overwhelmingly rural and nearly all its population were illiterate peasants condemned to short lives of grinding poverty. (Industrial output per head in India, one of the more developed peripheral economies, was at 1 per cent of the level in the United States.) Most of the peasants were largely self-sufficient and had little, if any, contact with the wider economy or core values, although colonial authorities everywhere were trying to force them into a money economy. Where they had succeeded peripheral economies were often dominated by a single crop – over 80 per cent of Egypt's exports was raw cotton – and this was the basis for the small modern sector of the economy. A few traders (often foreigners – Lebanese in West Africa, Indians in East and South Africa) and a small urban elite were linked to the culture of the core states (hence the huge opera house built deep in the Amazon jungle at Manaus, the centre of the rubber trade). Such 'development' as there was in the periphery was linked almost entirely to the needs of the core and was therefore highly unbalanced and localized. In Africa and Latin America the interior was linked to the coast in a few places by railways, but there were few, if any, cross-country links. In Brazil the railways in the north-east were a different gauge from those in the south (the coffee-growing area), and although there was a labour surplus in the north it was easier for the coffee producers to attract immigrant labour from Europe. In Colombia it was cheaper to bring goods to Medellin from London than from the capital Bogotá, which, although it was only 200 miles away, was cut off by two mountain ranges.

During 1900 Paris was a major focus of attention in the core states – the Universal Exposition opened on 15 April and attracted 48 million visitors. Three weeks earlier one event seemed to symbolize the industrial power of the core states and the emerging new technology of electricity. Two 275-foot-high chimneys, garlanded in flowers, let out the first smoke from 92 boilers, which drove turbines producing 40,000 horse-power of electricity to power the Exposition: the machines, a train, a 'moving staircase', and a great wheel with 80 cabins. Another major technological achievement took place a few hundred miles to the east. Internal combustion engines had only just begun to power cars (there were only 8,000 vehicles in the whole of the United States), but on 2 July the first Zeppelin airship took off from the German side of Lake Constance for a twenty-minute flight, during which it climbed to nearly a thousand feet. It was clear that aircraft would be flying soon as the power-to-weight ratio of petrol engines steadily increased.

Although the core states were the most advanced in the world industrially, they still had major social problems. At least a third of their populations lived in poverty, often on the margins of subsistence, in poor housing and social conditions. In Britain, the most industrialized country in the world, the census defined 'overcrowded' as a household of at least 2 adults and 4 children living in 2 rooms without their own water supply and sanitation. Even by this restrictive definition 8 per cent of the population were officially designated as being overcrowded and in the areas of the greatest deprivation the figure was far higher: in London the average was 16 per cent, in Glasgow it was 55 per cent and in Dundee it was 63 per cent. On 24 August a Dr Thomas Colvin was called to a family living in one room of a tenement block in Glasgow. One person was already dead and three others were seriously ill with what he thought was enteric fever. The next day the local Belvedere Hospital discovered that they were actually suffering from bubonic plague. Public health measures were able to contain the outbreak, but not before there were 27 cases, half of whom died. At the same time the British army was trying to find recruits for the war against the Boers in South Africa. In Manchester 11,000 men volunteered – all but 1,000 of them were rejected as medically unfit.

For the political, social and intellectual elites in the core states, these social conditions were only one of a series of problems they felt their states and societies had to face. The set of assumptions and opinions they brought to these problems and the solutions they suggested tell us much about the vital trends that were to influence much of the twentieth century. From the eighteenth-century Enlightenment they inherited the idea of progress. In 1793 the Marquis de Condorcet published his *Sketch for a Historical Picture of the Progress of the Human Mind*. It was a statement of his belief in the unlimited scope for human progress:

> The perfectibility of man is truly indefinite; and that the progress of this perfectibility, from now onwards independent of any power that might wish to halt it, has no limit than the duration of the globe upon which nature has cast us . . . this progress . . . will never be reversed as long as the earth occupies its present place in the system of the universe.

Had Condorcet known that he was to die the next year in jail during the period of terror in the French Revolution he might have taken a less sanguine view of human nature and history. The great eighteenth-century historian Edward Gibbon took a similar view. Although he thought that history was 'little more than the register of the crimes, follies and misfortunes of mankind', towards the end of *The Decline and Fall of the Roman Empire* he set out his belief in future progress:

> The experience of four thousand years should enlarge our hopes and diminish our apprehensions: we cannot determine to what height the human species may aspire in their advances towards perfection; but it may safely be assumed that no people, unless the force of nature is changed, will relapse into their original barbarism.

These ideas remained common throughout the nineteenth century. In 1875 *Larousse's* entry for 'Progress' stated:

> Humanity is perfectible and it moves incessantly from less good to better, from ignorance to science, from barbarism to civilization . . . The idea that humanity becomes day by day better and happier is particularly dear to our century. Faith in the law of progress is the true faith of our century.

In 1883 the British historian J. R. Seeley wrote in *The Expansion of*

England, 'No one can long study history without being haunted by the idea of development, of progress.' That most nineteenth-century belief – Marxism – was based on the idea of progress, with the inevitable march of human society from feudalism to capitalism and finally to the material abundance and social harmony of Communism. The idea of progress seemed to be enshrined in the growing scientific, technical and industrial advance of western Europe and the United States. The century saw the development of steam power, the production of iron and steel, the construction of railways, steamships and new forms of communication. By the end of the century newer technologies, in particular electricity, seemed to point the way to even greater progress. Such progress seemed to legitimate the right of Europeans and Americans to rule the rest of the world.

However, it was the beliefs developed in western Europe in the later half of the nineteenth century, such as Marxism and racism, together with those based on long-standing prejudices, such as anti-Semitism, which produced some of the greatest barbarisms of the twentieth century. By the early part of the century it was possible to detect a much darker set of beliefs among the elite of the core states, which existed alongside their belief in progress and their own superiority. It was made up of a number of elements – social Darwinism, eugenics, racism and the fear of degeneration. Social Darwinism marked the final scientific acceptance of Charles Darwin's ideas, published in *The Origin of Species* in 1859 but transformed, mainly by Herbert Spencer and, in Germany, by the zoologist Ernst Haeckel, into a theory about how human societies function. Human life was seen as a struggle for existence in which only the fittest survived – this applied not just to individuals but also to the competition between states. In many ways this doctrine provided a pseudo-scientific justification for the reassertion of power by the old ruling class (the fittest, since they had risen to the top of society), for elitism rather than democracy, and for failing to intervene to save the weakest in society since this could only damage the overall health of the organism. One of the best statements of these beliefs came from Karl Pearson, later a professor at the University of London, in *National Life from the Standpoint of Science* published in 1901:

> the scientific view of the nation is that of the organised whole, kept up
> to a pitch of internal efficiency by insuring that its numbers are

substantially recruited from the better stocks, and kept to a high pitch of external efficiency by contest, chiefly by way of war with inferior races, and with equal races by the struggle for trade routes and for the sources of raw material and of food supply.

Such views were widespread. For example, William Beveridge, then an academic and prominent social reformer but later one of the architects of the British welfare state, told his brother-in-law, the socialist R. H. Tawney: 'The well-to-do represent on the whole a higher level of character and ability than the working class because in the course of time the better stocks have come to the top.' At a conference at the London School of Economics in 1906 he declared that those working in industry should retain all their civic rights, but:

> Those who through general defects are unable to fill such a 'whole' place . . . must become the acknowledged dependants of the state . . . with the complete and permanent loss of all citizen rights – including not only the franchise but civil freedom and fatherhood. To those moreover, if any, who may be born personally efficient, but in excess of the number for whom the country can provide, a clear choice will be offered: loss of independence by entering a public institution, emigration or immediate starvation.

At the time these ideas seemed 'modern' and 'progressive' and they spread widely, not just in the core states but across the world. In China such ideas were introduced by Yan Fu, who had spent two years in Britain and who translated Spencer into Chinese. One of the best examples of social Darwinism's influence on politics came in a speech delivered in Germany at Kulmbach some years into the century:

> The idea of struggle is as old as life itself for life is only preserved because other living things perish through struggle . . . In this struggle the stronger, the more able, win, while the less able, the weak, lose. Struggle is the father of all things . . . It is not by the principles of humanity that man lives or is able to preserve himself above the animal world, but solely by means of the most brutal struggle.

The speaker was Adolf Hitler.

If life both within and between societies was a matter of continuous struggle with only the fittest surviving, then this immediately raised the question of what should be done to ensure success in this competition. A policy was required because many in the elite believed that they were facing a crisis of degeneration. To some extent this attitude was a response to the social changes produced in the core states in the nineteenth century – urbanization, the growth of the working class, poverty, poor economic and social conditions, rising criminality. The French writer Charles Fere, in *Degeneration and Criminality* published in 1888, wrote: 'The impotent, the mad, criminals or decadents of every form, must be considered as the waste-matter of adaptation, the invalids of civilization . . . general utility cannot accommodate the survival of the unproductive.' A decade later the American writer Eugene Talbot published *Degeneracy: Its Signs, Causes and Results*. It contained passages on types of degeneracy such as ethical, intellectual, sensory, nutritive and spinal, together with degeneracy in the negro, giantism, feet degeneracy and juvenile obesity. In addition there were pictures of juvenile criminals who, according to Talbot, were 'puny, sickly, scrofulous, often deformed with peculiar, unnaturally developed heads, sluggish, stupid, liable to fits, mean in figure and defective in vital energy.'

One of the favoured solutions to this problem was found in the 'science' of eugenics, a term coined in 1883 by Francis Galton, Charles Darwin's cousin. He defined it as the science of improving the human stock by giving 'the more suitable races or strains of blood a better chance of prevailing speedily over the less suitable'. He wondered: 'Could not the undesirables be got rid of and desirables multiplied?'

In the United States the leading eugenicist was Charles B. Davenport, whose work was largely funded by the Carnegie Foundation. In 1911 he published *Heredity in Relation to Eugenics*, which argued that, though there were some clearly hereditable defects such as Huntingdon's chorea and haemophilia, other social and mental problems such as insanity, epilepsy, alcoholism, pauperism, criminality and feeble-mindedness also had to be included. This view had also been put forward by the British Royal Commission on the Care and Control of the Feeble-Minded a few years earlier. Like Galton, Davenport identified 'good human stock' with the white middle class and argued that the genetically and socially defective should be stopped from breeding by being sexually segregated or castrated. Starting in Connecticut in 1896, over twenty US states passed laws to prohibit marriage and extra-marital relations to the eugenically unfit. In 1899 Indiana began forcibly sterilizing criminals in prison, a practice which had spread to sixteen states and involved over 36,000 people by 1941. Similar laws were passed by Sweden, Denmark, Finland and some Swiss cantons. It was not until the Nazi accession to power in 1933 that Germany had a similar law, although it was then enforced rigorously – by 1937 225,000 people had been forcibly sterilized. In Canada the practice continued until 1972.

Belief in such ideas was widespread. In Britain leading members of the Labour movement such as H. G. Wells and Sidney and Beatrice Webb were supporters. In Germany Alfred Grotjahn, the Socialist Party appointee as Professor of Social Hygiene at the University of Berlin in 1920, argued for isolation and sterilization to produce a 'respectable' working class by stopping the breeding of the insane, the 'workshy' and alcoholics, among others. When he entered politics Winston Churchill stated: 'The improvement of the British breed is my political aim in life.' As a cabinet minister he wrote to Prime Minister Herbert Asquith to argue for government action:

> The unnatural and increasingly rapid growth of the feeble-minded and insane classes, coupled as it is with a steady restriction among all the thrifty, energetic and superior stocks, constitutes a national and race danger which it is impossible to exaggerate . . . I feel that the source from which the stream of madness is fed should be cut off and sealed up before another year has passed.

Privately Churchill argued strongly for the forcible sterilization of 100,000 people whom he described as 'mental degenerates'. Such ideas remained highly influential. In 1937 an opinion poll in the United States showed that two-thirds of the population favoured forcible sterilization of habitual criminals and mental defectives.

For some people it was not enough to stop 'degenerates' from breeding, sterner measures were required if the efficiency of the nation was to improve. In Germany Ernst Haeckel, a great admirer of the Spartan practice of exposing children at birth to sort out the fit from the sickly, argued in *The Riddle of Life*, published in 1904:

> What profit does humanity derive from the thousands of cripples who are born each year, from the deaf and dumb, from cretins, from those

with incurable hereditary defects? How much of this loss and suffering could be obviated, if one finally decided to liberate the totally incurable from their indescribable suffering with a dose of morphia?

One of the ways in which many of the elite in the core states believed their countries could be tested, in a social Darwinist sense, was against other states in war. It was the ultimate proof of which states were rising and which falling, which were winning the battle of 'efficiency'. Although the World Peace Congress met in Paris in early September 1900, as one of the many meetings linked to the Universal Exposition, it represented only a small minority of people. Increased militarism was evident everywhere in the core societies in the last years of the nineteenth century, from rifle clubs, the growth of the militia and cadet forces, to gymnastics, the scouting movement and the general acceptance of military values. War was widely seen as an acceptable, even desirable, way of settling disputes and by many intellectuals as a source of spiritual salvation and regeneration. In 1899, writing on the ethics of war in the *Nineteenth Century* journal, the Reverend H. I. D. Ryder argued that war evoked 'the best qualities of human nature, giving the spirit predominance over the flesh' for both military and civilians. Just over a decade later the German Youth League called war: 'the noblest and holiest expression of human activity', which was 'beautiful' because 'its august sublimity elevates the human heart beyond the earthly and the common'. Peace was seen as decadent, corrupt and materialistic. William Graham Sumner at Yale University argued that peace was 'selfishness' and war proved that men 'have a deeper horror of falsehood than of bloodshed'. Just after the outbreak of the First World War, a British Professor of History, J. A. Cramb, argued in *Origins and Destiny of Imperial Britain* that universal peace was a 'nightmare' and 'a world sunk in bovine content'.

The realities of modern war were, however, being demonstrated in 1900 in South Africa. On 10 January Field-Marshal Roberts and General Kitchener disembarked at Cape Town to take charge of the defeated and demoralized troops who had lost the opening engagements in a war the British had provoked with the Boer republics of Transvaal and Orange Free State. They quickly succeeded in defeating the small Boer armies and on 5 June British troops entered Pretoria, the capital of Transvaal. The British believed that the war was over. Within days the Boers had begun waging guerrilla warfare and on 16 June the British issued a proclamation. It warned that civilian hostages would be made to travel on trains to prevent Boer attacks, that collective responsibility would be imposed in local areas to recoup the cost of the damage done by the Boer guerrillas and that houses and farms would be destroyed in the areas affected. Farm burning became standard policy where British communications and trains were attacked. By September, as the attacks continued, all farms within a ten-mile radius of an incident (this involved an area of nearly 350 square miles) were cleared of all stock and supplies. The next month villages, as well as farms, were burnt. At the same time the British stopped Boers who surrendered from returning to their homes and instead forced their families to join them, and many of the families of those still fighting, in what were called 'concentration camps' – the first use of what was to become a common twentieth-century expression. Major drives were started to round up civilians and within a few months over 110,000 Boers were in the camps. Disaster struck because the British arrangements for providing food, sanitation and medical care were either poor or non-existent. In total over 28,000 Boers died in the camps, 26,500 of whom were women and children (at its peak the death toll for children was 10 per cent every month). African farms were also burnt and the men rounded up into gangs for forced labour. The women and children were expected to survive on half the rations given to the Boers. Altogether just over 100,000 Africans were sent to the concentration camps and about one in five of them died. The methods adopted by the British were not effective – it was another two years before the Boers finally agreed to make peace. These actions were roundly condemned not just abroad but in Britain too. The leader of the opposition Liberal Party, Sir Henry Campbell-Bannerman, described them as the 'methods of barbarism'.

The separate treatment given by the British to the Africans (they also refused to allow African and Indian troops to take part in what they saw as a 'white man's war') reflected widespread racist beliefs in European and American society in the early twentieth century. These beliefs were deeply embedded, had been apparent for centuries, were accepted almost without question and were to reach a peak in the first half of the century. Nearly all the white members of the core societies saw themselves as being at the summit of humanity, with other people in a clear racial hierarchy of ability which placed blacks at the bottom. For example the 1903 edition of the *Encyclopaedia Britannica* contained the following entry under

'Negro': 'weight of brain, as indicating cranial capacity, 35 ounces (highest gorilla 20, average European 45) . . . thick epidermis . . . emitting a peculiar rancid odour, compared . . . to that of a buck goat'. The entry went on to explain that in negroes the brain stopped growing at an early age:

> To this premature ossification of the skull . . . many pathologists have attributed the inherent mental inferiority of the blacks . . . the development of the Negro and white proceeds on different lines. It is more correct to say of the Negro that he is nonmoral than immoral. All the social institutions are at the same low level . . . Slavery continues everywhere to prevail . . . where not checked by European governments [sic] . . . No full-blood Negro has ever been distinguished as a man of science, a poet or an artist, and the fundamental equality claimed for him by ignorant philanthropists is belied by the whole history of the race throughout the historic period.

In 1900 *The Living Races of Mankind* was published in Britain in eighteen fortnightly parts. It told its readers that the muscular development of the black races was 'good' and that in work which 'depends only on muscle they excel the average European; but in anything requiring judgement they are easily beaten. The nervous system is not very sensitive, and the appreciation of pain is dull. Operations can be conducted without anaesthetic.' School text-books reinforced the same message. The British *The World and Its Peoples* of 1907 described the African as 'an overgrown child, vain, self-indulgent and fond of idleness'. Four years later the author and poet Rudyard Kipling published *A School History of England*, in which he told pupils that the African slaves taken to the West Indies were

> lazy, vicious and incapable of any serious improvement, or work except under compulsion . . . In such a climate a few bananas will sustain the life of a negro quite sufficiently; why should he work to get more than this? He is quite happy and quite useless, and spends any extra wages which he may earn upon finery.

The deep-rooted racist thinking found among Europeans and Americans was, at the beginning of the twentieth century, heightened by empire. The conquest and control of large parts of the globe were taken as vindicating white superiority. Jules Harmand, one of the main advocates of French imperialism, said:

there is a hierarchy of races and civilizations and we belong to the
superior race and civilization . . . The basic legitimation of conquest over
native peoples is the conviction of our superiority, not merely our
mechanical, economic and military superiority, but our moral
superiority.

The former ruler of Egypt, Lord Cromer, wrote on the question of
'Subject Races' in the *Edinburgh Review* in 1908. He argued that
'free institutions' in any colony had to be kept in check because logic
was something 'the existence of which the Oriental is disposed
altogether to ignore'. The colonial peoples therefore needed to
understand their limitations and 'endeavour to find, in the
contentment of the subject race, a more worthy and, it may be
hoped, a stronger bond of union between the rulers and the ruled'.
In dealing with 'Indians, or Egyptians, or Shilluks or Zulus', it was
necessary to take into account what was in their own best interests,
but this was, of course, determined 'by the light of Western
knowledge and experience' and what 'we conscientiously think is
best for the subject race'. Such policies would inculcate 'the respect
always accorded to superior talents and unselfish conduct'.

In the United States the sudden conquest of an empire at the end
of the nineteenth century produced similar sentiments. In 1898 the
Nation spoke of the 8 million 'people of the colored races' now
under American control as 'a varied assortment of inferior races
which, of course, could not be allowed to vote'. The *Atlantic
Monthly* drew the implications for the United States itself: 'If the
stronger and cleverer race is free to impose its will upon "new-
caught, sullen peoples" on the other side of the globe, why not in
South Carolina and Mississippi?' Racism in the United States
needed no encouragement, given its past history. Indeed discrimination and segregation were on the increase at the turn of the
century, based on the official acceptance of the 'separate but equal'
doctrine and removal from blacks of the right to vote. Widespread
and deeply held views about white superiority were reinforced by
numerous academic works. Professor Paul B. Barringer of the
University of Virginia wrote in 1900, 'The negro race is essentially a
race of peasant farmers and laborers . . . As a source of cheap labor
for a warm climate he is beyond competition; everywhere else he is
a foreordained failure.' Other books published at the time give a
clear picture of prevailing views: Charles Carroll, *The Negro a Beast*
(1900); William P. Calhoun, *The Caucasian and the Negro in the*

United States (1902); William B. Smith, *The Color Line: A Brief in Behalf of the Unborn* (1905) and Robert W. Shufelt, *The Negro: A Menace to American Civilization* (1907).

Such racist thinking was widespread and unquestioned, affecting not just Africans and Asians but also gradations within other groups. It was, for example, accepted almost without demur that nationalities such as the Irish or Italians constituted separate races with separate characteristics. At the top of this tree were the Anglo-Saxon or Aryan races, who were responsible for all of European civilization from the ancient Greeks to the nineteenth century. As Winston Churchill put it: 'Why be apologetic about Anglo-Saxon superiority. We are superior.' European struggles were also seen in racial terms. The German Emperor Wilhelm II thought a future European war would be 'the last battle between Teutons and Slavs'. He felt that a diplomatic solution was impossible because: 'it is not a question of high politics, but one of *race* . . . for what is at issue is whether the Germanic race is to be or not to be in Europe'. In 1915 the French doctor, Edgar Berillon, made the widely believed 'discovery' that Germans had intestines nine feet longer than all other humans and were therefore prone to excessive defecation and body odour. As a result he was able to unmask German spies and Germans posing as Frenchmen from Alsace.

The idea that race determined character, behaviour, even political institutions, was widespread. In 1903 the Argentine writer Carlos Octavio Bunge published *Our America*, an attack on political life and institutions in Latin America. He argued: 'the republic is a severely European institution belonging only to the purest of European races'. A republic could therefore work in North America because the people 'possessed a certain republican individualism in their ideas, in their customs, in their institutions and in their blood dating back to Caesar and Hamilcar, even to prehistoric times'. Such institutions, he argued, could not work in Latin America because of the racial mixing of whites, blacks and Indians, which produced 'resignation, sadness, laziness and decadence'. This produced a society of 'collective sloth' and a preference for rule by the *caudillo* or strongman because 'the rabble' were 'too apathetic to think and act for themselves'.

These attitudes were one element behind the widespread anti-Semitism in European society. In the early twentieth century this was found less in Germany, where the prosperous Jewish community was quite strongly assimilated, than in France and eastern

Europe, particularly in Poland and Russia. However, it seems remarkable that, in a throwback to the medieval world, on 14 November 1900 a Czech jury could find a Jew, Leopold Hilsner, guilty not just of the murder but of the ritual murder of two Christian children (Agnes Hruza and Marie Klima). The Zionist movement had developed in the 1890s, partly in response to this anti-Semitism – the fourth Zionist Congress was held in London on 13 August 1900. The movement, however, was still relatively weak – only half the money necessary to set up the Colonial Trust to finance Jewish settlement in Palestine had been subscribed by the time of the fourth Congress. However, the attempt to build a Jewish state in Palestine also partly rested on the acceptance of European racial concepts. One of the leaders of the Zionist movement, Chaim Weizmann, told Arthur Balfour (one of its strongest British supporters) of 'the treacherous nature of the Arabs'. He questioned whether there was 'an Arab people in Palestine' and argued that an Arab state there could not come about because 'the fellah is at least four centuries behind the times and the effendi is dishonest, uneducated, greedy, and as unpatriotic as he is inefficient'.

Although in 1900 Western Europe and the United States dominated the globe economically and politically, there were the first signs of a growing revolt against such domination, which was to be one of the major themes of the twentieth century. On 10 January 1900 the Young Turks' manifesto was published in Cairo. It called for Turkey's revitalization and an end to ineffective Ottoman rule, to set the country on a path of 'modernization' that would lead to a reassertion of nationhood – a policy they started to implement before the decade was over. Later in 1900 the first Pan-African Congress was held in London but it was a low-key affair which attracted almost no attention. It was perhaps symbolic of Africa's condition that, although there were delegates from the Caribbean, the United States and Britain, there were none from the continent itself.

Even more significant, though, were the events that took place in China in 1900. On the penultimate day of 1899 a British missionary was murdered near Tsinan. As retribution the British consul in Shanghai ordered that three Chinese should be beheaded, one strangled, one sentenced to life imprisonment, one to ten years in jail, one banished and that three village elders in the area should be flogged. The fact that a British diplomat was in a position to take such action says much about China's decline during the nineteenth century. The Chinese, ruled since the mid-seventeenth century by the foreign Manchu Qing dynasty, saw themselves not as part of Asia or the Far East but as the 'Middle Kingdom', the embodiment of civilization in opposition to the foreign barbarians. However, in the nineteenth century a conjunction of crises brought the Chinese state to the brink of dissolution. A near doubling of the population between 1770 and 1840, linked to very slow increase in the amount of cultivated land, produced major social strains. The government was increasingly marred by corruption and inefficiency and the growth of secret societies led to numerous revolts against the Manchu. Until 1840 the Chinese were just able to maintain the 'closed door' against western influence, but then following the 'Opium' and other wars they were forced to make fundamental concessions. Trade was opened up through the 'Treaty Ports', all foreigners were removed from Chinese jurisdiction, concession areas in the ports were taken over by foreigners and external control of the Chinese Customs Service was established. By 1860, with three major rebellions – the Taiping in the south, the Nian in the north and the Muslim in the west – China seemed on the edge of disintegration. However, there was a limited revival and a series of conservative reforms was implemented, though not on the scale of the contemporaneous Meiji restoration in Japan.

By the 1890s no fundamental changes had occurred and Chinese defeat in the 1894–5 war with Japan precipitated what seemed to be the final crisis. Although the European powers forced Japan to give back Liaodong, they exploited the situation for their own benefit and the last five years of the century saw a greater expansion of western power in China than the previous fifty. In return for loans to fund the war indemnity to Japan (which took up a third of Chinese government revenue), British and French influence was vastly expanded and concessions were made to Germany, Japan and Russia, which had previously held none.

Following the murder of two German missionaries in 1897 the Chinese were forced to concede a German naval base at Qingdao on a ninety-nine year lease with full German sovereignty; a fifty-kilometre zone around the base, subject to German occupation, nominally still under Chinese sovereignty but where they could take no action without German consent; the building of three railway lines in the area and the ceding of all mining rights for fifteen kilometres on either side of these lines. A year later the Russians, who had already obtained the concession for the Trans-Manchurian railway, took Port Arthur (Lüshun) as a naval base, the French established their primacy in Yunan, Guangdong and Guangxi and the British leased the 'New Territories' on the mainland opposite Hong Kong and obtained the port of Weihaiwei to block any move south from Port Arthur by the Russians. In 1899 the Americans sent the 'Open Door' diplomatic note to the other major powers arguing for equal western access to China. This was not a defence of China, since it admitted the validity of all the existing concessions. It was merely an attempt to secure American interests in a situation where they had few concessions themselves. By the end of the nineteenth century it seemed possible that China might be partitioned between the western powers and Japan. However, no state had the power to conquer China and all were wary of the others. For the moment they could obtain most of what they wanted from the existing system and were content to manipulate the decaying Chinese government.

The most important reaction to this combination of internal decay and external control, particularly in terms of twentieth-century history, came from within China. It took the form of a nationalist revival and a widespread movement against western influence, in particular the Christian missions and the Chinese who had converted to Christianity. Drawing on support from the peasants, who were alienated from an agricultural system in crisis, and the long tradition of Chinese secret societies, a new movement, the 'Boxers', emerged at the end of the nineteenth century. Their exact origins are unclear but they may have been linked to the Yihequain (The Righteous and Harmonious Fists), who had been banned in 1808. The movement took different forms in different parts of the country – it was known as the 'Big Sword Society' in the south-west, for example – but developed strongly in areas such as Qingdao, which was controlled by the Germans. Recruits were attracted through public exhibitions of 'boxing', in reality a series of invulnerability rituals which involved spirit possession, followed by secret initiation into the society and adherence to its strict rules. There were separate organizations for women recruits. From 1898 the Boxers obtained increasing, though surreptitious, support from the government – they became the Yihetuan (The Righteous and Harmonious Militia).

Punitive measures taken by the British in Shanghai in early 1900 caused the Boxer movement to grow rapidly: by March the Boxers controlled the whole of the Tientsin region and were beginning to infiltrate the capital. They received increasingly open support from the government in their attempts to remove foreign influence from China. The position of the Boxers as both anti-western and pro-Manchu was shown in their songs:

> We are only afraid of being like India, unable to defend our land;
> We are only afraid of being like Annam, of having no hope of reviving,
> We Chinese have no part in this China of ours . . .
> When at last all the Foreign Devils
> Are expelled to the very last man,
> The Great Qing, united, together
> Will bring peace to our land.

By mid-June the Boxers controlled Peking and a member of the Japanese legation was shot. In Tientsin western troops from the legations, trying to rescue Chinese Christians, killed over forty Boxers and seized the Chinese forts in the city. In Peking the government asked all the foreign embassies to leave. On 20 June the German minister was murdered, the Europeans withdrew into the legation area, fighting started and the Chinese declared war. About 470 foreigners and 3,000 Chinese Christians were besieged for fifty-five days, although the fighting was hardly intense – the Chinese only fired 4,000 shells in the entire period and more of the besiegers than the besieged died. Across China about 200 missionaries and over 30,000 Chinese Christians were killed.

All the European states and Japan regarded this as a clear challenge by inferiors to their position in China and, sinking their differences, agreed on a joint response. Germany took a strong lead with the Emperor Wilhelm II declaring:

> Peking should be razed to the ground. Show no mercy! Take no prisoners! A thousand years ago [sic], the Huns of King Attila made a name for themselves which is still considered formidable in history and legend. Thus may you impose the name of Germany in China for a thousand years, in such a way that no Chinese will ever dare to look askance at a German again.

On 4 August a hurriedly assembled, 20,000 strong, 'western' force (over half were Japanese troops) set out from Tientsin and, after two minor skirmishes, eleven days later arrived in Peking to lift the siege. Despite the lack of resistance the passage of the western troops was marked by wholesale rape and slaughter of the population, and the destruction of villages. Peking itself was sacked, looted and thousands more Chinese killed. The Russians committed similar atrocities as they took advantage of the situation to move their troops through Manchuria.

The western powers exacted their revenge through the protocol the Chinese government was forced to sign in January 1901. They secured a massive indemnity by taking control of all revenues from the Chinese customs and the salt tax. Examinations to the Chinese civil service were stopped for five years to ensure no Boxers were recruited; the Chinese were prohibited from importing arms for two years; the legation area in Peking was expanded and no Chinese was allowed to live there; foreign troops were to guard the legation area and all Chinese forts in Peking were to be destroyed.

Although the Chinese were defeated and forced to accept humiliating terms, their reaction was simply to increase pressure for radical national reform as a basis for reasserting Chinese rights and status. The beginnings of a similar nationalist reaction against western dominance could be seen elsewhere in Asia. In 1896 the Philippines had revolted against Spanish control and, although the outcome was the imposition of American rule by 1900, they engaged in a long guerrilla war against their new rulers. Elsewhere nationalist leaders were emerging – in India Tilak and Gokhale of the Indian National Congress, in Indonesia Tjoakraminoto and Sudironusodo, and in Burma U Ba Pe. These were the seeds of the more general revolt against the west later in the century.

For the elites in the core states in 1900 these external pressures were still small clouds on the horizon of what seemed likely to be a continuing expansion of their influence and control. Powers like Germany and the United States were still confident about their rise to world power. This attitude was made clear in Germany in 1900 when Admiral Tirpitz submitted a new naval law to the Reichstag which was designed to challenge the predominance of British naval power and in the United States by a sixfold expansion of the navy. Only the British as a relatively weak status quo power were, at least in private, less confident about their ability to sustain their position in the face of such challenges. Joseph Chamberlain, a convinced imperialist, told the conference of colonial prime ministers, 'The weary Titan staggers under the too vast orb of its fate.' However, many in the elites thought the main challenge at the beginning of the twentieth century came less from abroad than from various forces at home.

None of the core states were full democracies. None allowed women to vote and most still restricted the number of males who could vote – for example only 60 per cent could do so in Britain. In the United States vigorous and successful efforts were being made to end voting by blacks, especially in the southern states. The social and economic changes brought about by industrialization and urbanization seemed to challenge elite, in particular landed elite, control. State machineries were still limited in their activities, confined mainly to defence and foreign affairs with only exceptional interventions in the economic field (mainly tariffs) and very small welfare programmes (primarily in Germany). Even the repressive powers of the state were still limited. States elsewhere in the world were even more limited in their functions and in some places such as Latin America had little impact on their societies.

To the elites of the core states a growing working class and socialist movement seemed a major threat. Imperialism and war abroad and the pursuit of 'national efficiency' at home were ways of trying to divert the energies of the masses into less threatening areas. In 1906 Wilhelm II wrote to his Chancellor, von Bülow: 'Shoot down, behead and eliminate the Socialists first, if need be, by a blood-bath, then war abroad. But not before, and not *a tempo* [at the same time].' On 23 September 1900 the fifth Congress of the Socialist Second International met in the Salle Wagram in Paris. Of the 1,300 delegates 1,000 came from France, with the next largest delegation being from Britain, with 95 members. Only 6 delegates came from the Americas and the only Japanese representative was unable to afford the boat fare. The socialist movement was still in the early stages of its development, still divided between those who believed that no compromise with capitalist society and its institutions was possible and those who believed that a united working class might be able to gain power through the electoral system once universal suffrage was achieved. However, even in a very moderate Labour movement such as that in Britain only the first tentative steps in the latter direction were being taken. In 1900 the Labour Representation Committee (the forerunner of the Labour Party) was set up as the first step in securing separately organized Labour MPs. Until then they had been a small group within the Liberal Party. Few people would have noticed the first publication in Leipzig on Christmas Eve 1900 of *Iskra*, an obscure Russian emigré newspaper under the control of Vladimir Ilyich Ulyanov (known to his fellow revolutionaries as Lenin). In July he

had left Siberian exile and began the newspaper as part of his
campaign to form a more hard-line group within the Social
Democrats.

Many did not possess the socialist and Marxist belief that progress
was inevitable and foresaw growing barbarism. Two men, both of
whom believed that the twentieth century did not begin until 1901,
mused in their diaries about the future as the new century dawned.
In central Europe, Simon Dubnow, a Jewish opponent of Zionism,
wrote:

> We are entering the twentieth century. What does it have in store for
> humanity, and for Jewry in particular? To judge by the last few decades,
> it seems as if humanity might be entering a new Dark Age with
> horrifying wars and national struggles. But the mind refuses to believe it.

Dubnow went on to become a major contributor to the *Jewish
Encyclopaedia* and also wrote a ten-volume *History of the Jews*. He
was battered to death by a drunken Lithuanian Nazi in Vilnius in
1941.

In Britain the writer, commentator, man about town and friend of
the famous, Wilfred Scawen Blunt, wrote in his diary just before
Christmas 1900:

> All the nations of Europe are making the same hell on earth in China,
> massacring and pillaging and raping in the captured cities as
> outrageously as in the Middle Ages. The Emperor of Germany gives the
> word for slaughter and the Pope looks on and approves. In South Africa
> our troops are burning farms under Kitchener's command and the
> Queen and the two Houses of Parliament and the bench of bishops
> thank God publicly and vote money for the work. The Americans are
> spending fifty millions a year on slaughtering Filipinos; the King of the
> Belgians has invested his whole fortune on the Congo, where he is
> brutalising the negroes to fill his pockets. The French and the Italians for
> the moment are playing a less prominent part in the slaughter, but their
> inactivity grieves them. The whole white race is revelling openly in
> violence as though it had never pretended to be Christian. God's equal
> curses on them all! So ends the famous nineteenth century into which we
> were so proud to have been born.

Part Two

ECONOMIC AND SOCIAL HISTORY

2 PEOPLE

THE WORLD became a much more crowded place in the twentieth century. For every person alive in 1900 there were four people alive by the end of the century. This unprecedented increase had a huge impact on how people lived and on the demand for resources, from food and water to minerals and energy. However, the rise was not steady. Between 1900 and 1950 the world population rose by just over half. In the next fifty years it more than doubled. By the 1990s about 95 million extra people were being added to the world's population every year. The rise was also spread unevenly across the globe. The population of Europe did not quite double in the twentieth century – Africa's rose eight-fold and Latin America's eleven-fold. In 1900 Europe accounted for over a quarter of the world's population, but by the end of the century it was only an eighth of the total. Throughout the century six out of ten people in the world lived in Asia.

The rate of population growth is largely determined by the relationship between life expectancy and the birth rate. These two factors are also central to the quality of life which individuals experience. Both changed dramatically during the century. However, the experiences of the core and the periphery were fundamentally different. For the minority of the world's population in the core states, the twentieth century brought declining death rates, increasing lifespans, major changes in the causes of death and a generally declining birth rate. (Most countries in the semi-periphery followed the same trends but slightly later.) The majority of the world's population in the periphery also experienced declining mortality, but this was combined with a very high birth rate except in a few states during the last part of the century.

In the core states death rates began to fall substantially in the latter part of the nineteenth century and that fall was maintained in the twentieth century, though generally at a slower pace. The biggest fall was in the infant death rate – child mortality in Sweden in the 1980s was one-fortieth of the rate in 1900 and similar, though less dramatic, falls occurred in the other core countries. The result was a major increase in life expectancy at birth but a much smaller increase once adulthood was achieved. At the beginning of the century a British male could expect, at birth, to live to the age of forty-five. By the end of the century this had increased to seventy-three. However, for a male who survived to forty-five, his increase in life expectancy was much less. At the start of the century a British male could expect to live another twenty-three years, by the 1990s this had only risen by five years. The trends were similar for women.

The increase in life expectancy in the core countries was largely achieved by conquering childhood diseases. The major part of the decline in mortality stemmed from the virtual elimination of death by air-borne diseases such as tuberculosis, bronchitis and pneumonia. Less important was the end of water- and food-borne diseases such as cholera and dysentery, and a general reduction in infectious diseases. These reductions are often supposed to stem from better medical treatment, but in practice this played only a minor role. Tuberculosis, for example, was in drastic decline long before any effective medical treatment was possible or the bacillus responsible was even identified. By the time a vaccination was available the death rate was one-sixteenth of that experienced in the 1840s. For water-borne diseases such as cholera the crucial factor was not medical treatment but improved sanitation in cities. In some cases, such as scarlet fever, the disease appears to have become less virulent and in others, such as measles, the population appears to have become more resistant – over 80 per cent of the fall in the death rate from measles in the twentieth century was achieved before any treatment was available. With pneumonia some treatment was available from the late 1930s with the introduction of the new sulphonamide drugs, but by then the death rate from the disease was only half that at the start of the century. In a few cases, medical treatment was important – the introduction of vaccination against polio in the early 1950s reduced the incidence of the disease in Britain from about 4,000 cases a year to a mere handful.

During the twentieth century the scourge of infectious diseases was largely eliminated in the core countries. Only in one case was there a substantial death toll – the influenza epidemic that swept the world in the two years after 1918 and killed about 20 million people. However, at the end of the century there were signs that economic and social decay in parts of the core states were creating conditions for the resurgence of infectious diseases. In the last half of the 1980s there was a 25 per cent rise in tuberculosis cases in the United States and western Europe and in some inner cities the increase was much steeper – in New York City in the 1980s it more than doubled, primarily among the poor and homeless.

The most significant change in the causes of death in the core countries was the consequence of alterations to lifestyle. A richer diet – higher fat intake largely in the form of dairy products and more processed food – together with lack of exercise, vastly greater levels of smoking and increased pollution, led to huge increases in the number of deaths from heart disease and cancer. In the early twentieth century heart disease was largely confined to the very wealthy, who were able to afford a high-fat diet. Even in 1930 coronary heart disease was responsible for only 1 per cent of British deaths. By the mid-1990s this figure had risen to just over 30 per cent. Overall in the core countries by the end of the twentieth century heart disease was responsible for 40 per cent of the male and 20 per cent of the female death rate and the figure was continuing to rise. About a fifth of these deaths were directly attributable to smoking, which was also a major determinant of the rise in cancer rates. In 1900 cancer affected one in every twenty-seven Americans. In 1980 it affected one in three with one in four Americans dying from the disease. Deaths from lung cancer in the core countries – primarily caused by smoking – rose by 78 per cent in the twenty years after 1960 and continued to rise for the rest of the century. Both heart disease and cancer are 'diseases of civilization' – European cancer rates at the end of the century were ten times higher than those in West Africa.

The decline in death rates and the increase in life expectancy were greater in the periphery during the twentieth century than in the core, but this largely reflects the fact that the situation was so bad at the beginning of the century. In 1900 male life expectancy at birth in the periphery was slightly more than twenty-five years – just over half the average for the core countries. By 1985 this had more than doubled to sixty-three years, which was about 85 per cent of that for the core states. Unlike the core countries, this major improvement was largely brought about by medical advances and not by a general improvement in social and economic conditions. The introduction from the late 1940s of vaccinations, antibiotics and chemical spraying of mosquito breeding grounds to control malaria produced unprecedentedly sharp reductions in death rates. In Mauritius, for example, the death rate fell by 80 per cent between the mid-1940s and the mid-1950s – a similar decline took over 150 years to achieve in Europe. Falls on a similar scale occurred elsewhere – in Costa Rica and El Salvador, for example – though over a slightly longer period. The incidence of some diseases was altered fundamentally. Smallpox was eradicated from the world and polio had been eliminated in 145 countries by the end of the century.

However, by the 1970s the fall in death rates in the periphery was slowing down and in some countries went into reverse. This probably reflected the limits of medical intervention in the face of major social and economic problems – in particular malnutrition, poor water supply and sanitation and the concentration of medical facilities in the cities. In many parts of the periphery by the end of the century infectious diseases were on the increase, partly because resistant strains were increasing. The number of malaria cases in India rose from 100,000 in 1965 to 10 million in 1977. Yellow fever killed a few hundred people a year in Africa in the 1940s, but over 200,000 a year by 1990. Bubonic plague re-emerged in several outbreaks in India at the end of the century. In 1900 tuberculosis killed 2 million people a year; by 1990 this was over 3 million a year across the globe. Cholera also spread from Asia into Latin America for the first time since the nineteenth century. New infectious diseases emerged, such as ebola in Africa. The sudden outbreak of AIDS in the 1980s also primarily affected the periphery. By the end of the century about 40 million people were infected – 90 per cent in the periphery with the overwhelming majority of those in Africa, where one in five of the population in some regions were affected. Due to changes in lifestyle the periphery also began to see the emergence of those diseases usually associated with the core states. Before 1940 rising blood pressure with age was unknown in Kenya and Uganda – by the 1980s it was common, as were diabetes, obesity and hypertension. The first cases of coronary heart disease were noted in Uganda in 1956 and in Kenya a decade later. The increasingly widespread habit of smoking was producing the first substantial increases in cancer cases by the 1990s.

By the end of the century there were still substantial differences in death rates and life expectancy between the core and the periphery. Infant mortality remained much higher in the periphery – the chances of a child born in Sierra Leone dying before the age of five were thirty-three times greater than for a child born in Iceland.

Deaths below the age of five constituted about 1 per cent of the total in the core countries but nearly half of all deaths in Bangladesh. However, there were also large differences within the periphery – child mortality in Togo and Benin was 40 per 1,000 – the same level as Sweden in 1800. In parts of Latin America it was 20 per 1,000 – the same level as in Britain in the 1920s. There were also major differences within the core: infant mortality in Northern Ireland in the 1990s was nearly three times the level in Iceland.

The substantial differences in life expectancy found in 1900 were still apparent at the end of the century. Even though in all areas people had a greater chance of surviving childhood and then living longer, the differences remained fundamental. They were not simply the result of relative levels of income and wealth – social infra-structure was also important. For example, life expectancy in Sri Lanka was only five years less than in Britain even though per capita income was less than a thirtieth of the British level. Nor was a continuous increase in life expectancy guaranteed. In some areas, in particular across sub-Saharan Africa, life expectancy at the end of the twentieth century was falling. Similarly in Russia after the collapse of the Soviet Union life expectancy fell rapidly and drastically from sixty-five years in 1987 to fifty-nine years in 1993, reflecting economic and social disruption and increasing levels of alcoholism. By the end of the century life expectancy in Russia was little better than in 1900.

Throughout the twentieth century there were differences in life expectancy not just between countries but within countries, reflecting racial discrimination, differing access to medical facilities and different income levels. In South Africa, for example, the tuberculosis mortality rate for blacks was vastly higher than for whites. By the 1990s the life expectancy of a white child in the United States was six years greater than that of a black child, partly reflecting a black infant mortality rate twice that of whites. In some inner-city areas infant mortality rates were as high as in some countries of the periphery. During the rapid urbanization of Europe and North America in the nineteenth and early twentieth centuries death rates were far higher in the cities, but in the periphery in the twentieth century rapid urbanization produced lower death rates in the cities. The concentration of medical facilities in urban areas and the conscious priority given by elites to the needs of the cities over rural areas were both factors in this. Throughout the core states there were substantial differences between social groups and these differences often widened during the century. In the early 1930s manual workers in Britain had a mortality rate about 25 per cent higher than professional groups; by the early 1980s it was 150 per cent higher. These differences reflected higher occupational risks, poorer access to health care, and lifestyle differences such as higher rates of smoking. By the late twentieth century the child of professional parents could expect to live seven years longer than the child of a manual labourer.

The general reduction in death rates was a key determinant of the rapid rise in world population. Equally important, though, was the birth rate and in this area the experiences of the core states and the periphery were fundamentally different. There is some evidence to suggest that during industrialization the birth rate in the core states rose, but by the late nineteenth century birth rates were in decline. The decline continued and by the 1930s birth rates in the core states had fallen by over a third compared with the 1890s. This was the beginning of one of the most important social revolutions of the twentieth century: its impact was at least as great as that of industrialization and urbanization in the nineteenth century. Yet it is probably the least understood of all the major revolutions and there is very little evidence about how and why human actions and attitudes changed.

To some extent birth rates had always been low in western Europe (and later in their settlement colonies of North America and Australasia), reflecting long-established social patterns, in particular late marriage. Very low birth rates were apparent in France and the Netherlands from the early nineteenth century. However, the decline which became apparent in Belgium, Germany, Australia and New Zealand in the 1880s and in most of the rest of western Europe in the 1900s, was fundamentally different from earlier fluctuations in the birth rate. It reflected the complex interaction of a number of factors – class, gender, community, beliefs and costs – which produced a new attitude to the number of children couples thought appropriate and a conscious decision to regulate family size. Class was an important factor – the decline began among the upper and middle classes who could, if they so chose, afford mechanical methods of contraception. However, the use of contraception, *coitus interruptus*, greater abstinence or abortion (the last was more common among working-class families) all required conscious choice and such choices reflected changing views of motherhood, relations between the sexes, ideas about what made a 'good' wife or husband and notions of personal identity. Easy access to the contraceptive pill from the mid-1960s (one of the most fundamental social changes of the century) produced further major alterations in human attitudes and behaviour that have proved difficult to analyse. Although little is known about the interplay of these factors, it is clear that they are not simplistically related to levels of industrialization and income and are not reproducible from one society to another.

By the 1930s birth rates in the core countries were at historically low levels. They rose sharply everywhere after the end of the Second World War in a short 'baby boom' that was over by the mid- to late-1950s. In Japan the birth rate fell by a half in the 1950s – the most concentrated reduction ever achieved in any country. By the early 1960s birth rates in the core states were between a third and a quarter below the already low levels of the 1930s and continued to fall, with only occasional very short-term rises for the rest of the century. By the 1990s in nearly every core country the fertility rate was near or below the population replacement rate of 2·1 children per couple, in some cases substantially below – about 1·5 children per couple in Austria, Belgium, Italy, Luxemburg, Switzerland and Germany. Throughout the century there were major differences within the core states reflecting class, religious and racial differences. In most states birth rates were higher among the working class – nearly a quarter higher among manual labourers than professional groups in Britain in the 1980s. In the United States black fertility was higher than white throughout the twentieth century, usually by about a quarter.

Religion also had an impact. The Mormon state of Utah had a birth rate twice that of the rest of the United States and the birth rate among Catholics in Northern Ireland at the end of the century was the highest in any core states. On the other hand, the Catholic minority in Quebec had one of the lowest fertility rates in the world, as did both Italy and France.

The fertility pattern in the periphery was fundamentally different from the core, reflecting different social and economic conditions and different decisions about priorities. In peripheral countries a large family was a rational choice for couples since children initially provided a source of labour and later security in old age. Social and economic changes slowly altered this pattern in some countries, such as Singapore, but the argument often expressed in the 1960s that 'economic development' would automatically lead to a reduction in family size, just as it had done in the core states, was clearly much too simplistic. Sometimes social and economic changes increased fertility levels, as they did in Latin America and the Caribbean in the 1950s, following a decrease in the age of marriage.

In general in the states of the periphery there were few falls in the birth rate until the mid-1960s (Singapore and Taiwan were the main exceptions) and therefore the rapid falls in mortality produced a large rise in the population. After the mid-1960s the situation changed quickly and within a decade significant reductions were apparent in a number of states, but particularly across Asia and Latin America regardless of the different levels of 'development'. Overall in the thirty years after 1955 the birth rate in Asia and Latin America fell by a third, with some countries such as Singapore, Taiwan and South Korea experiencing even bigger falls. By the end of the twentieth century the birth rate in some countries of the periphery was approaching that of the core – for example, Mauritius, China, Thailand, Indonesia and Cuba. The major exceptions to this trend were most of Africa, the Middle East and other Muslim states such as Pakistan and Bangladesh. In Africa, birth rates only fell by about 10 per cent in the thirty years after 1955. In part, this was because three-quarters of the population still lived in rural areas where children were an important economic asset. In the Middle East, however, the crucial factor seemed to be less the level of development than the continuation of social ideas emphasizing the subordinate role of women. These very high birth rates, combined with a fall in child mortality, produced a huge increase in the child population. By 1990 in most countries across Africa over half the population was aged under fourteen.

Throughout the century governments of very different political persuasions tried, with marginal success, to influence this most personal aspect of human behaviour. In the core states these efforts usually involved attempts to reverse the decline in the birth rate. French governments since the mid-nineteenth century had worried about the problem, particularly because of its impact on the size of the army they could maintain in relation to Germany. But they had only limited success in changing behaviour. Between 1920 and 1967 abortion was prohibited, as were the sale of contraceptives and the provision of information about contraception. Family allowances were introduced and extra payments were made to mothers who stayed at home, so that by the 1950s state allowances for a three-child family were higher than the average wage. In practice this policy had little impact and France's birth rate followed the same pattern of decline as those of other core states. In Nazi Germany similar policies were introduced: suppression of abortions, a tax on unmarried adults, a state loan on marriage that was written off when the first child was born, and tax and housing concessions for large families. Although the birth rate rose by a third between 1933 and 1938 it is not clear whether this represented an increase in family size or couples choosing earlier births to take advantage of the inducements. Fascist Italy had similar policies after 1926 but with equally limited results.

One of the most determined efforts to increase the birth rate came in Romania in the late 1960s. Across eastern Europe easy access to abortion under the post-1945 Communist regimes had by the early 1960s produced the lowest birth rates in the world. In 1966, to combat the threat of a declining population, the Romanian government made abortion and the manufacture or import of contraceptive devices illegal. Married women under the age of forty were subjected to a monthly examination to ensure that a pregnancy had not been terminated. President Ceauşescu declared, 'The foetus is the socialist property of the whole society. Giving birth is a patriotic duty.' These measures had an immediate impact – within a year the birth rate doubled – but made little long-term difference as the birth rate later fell back towards the low levels of the early 1960s.

Government campaigns to reduce the birth rate, which in the second half of the century were largely confined to the states of the periphery, were equally problematic but slightly more successful. Until the mid-1960s only a handful of states such as India, South Korea, Fiji and China had birth-control programmes and these were at a low level. The initial fall in the birth rate in the periphery mostly took place without intervention. By the mid-1970s, under strong pressure from core governments and international institutions, sixty-three states in the periphery had introduced birth-control programmes. These were mainly in Asia and Latin America – in Africa, apart from Egypt, little was done. The policies introduced by Singapore in 1970 were typical of those in many Asian states. Income tax relief was restricted to the first three children, paid maternity leave was made available only for the first two, charges at maternity hospitals increased for each birth and no priority was given to large families in allocating scarce housing. More drastic measures such as the sterilization and quota programme in India were highly unpopular and were a major reason for the defeat of

Indira Gandhi's government in the 1977 elections. However, it is far from clear whether these campaigns had as much impact as changes in human attitudes. After 1979 the Chinese government introduced a complex series of incentives for couples to have only one child, which they combined with strong social pressure and monitoring to reinforce the guidance. In fact the birth rate had already fallen by a half in the previous decade. In practice, social and economic changes were just as important as government pressure. The birth rate fell most in countries such as Costa Rica and Sri Lanka, where income distribution became more equal and far less in countries such as Brazil and India, where income inequalities were either stable or increased.

By the end of the century highly complex alterations in human attitudes and behaviour, social and economic changes, improved medical facilities and easier contraceptive methods had produced a different balance between births and deaths across the globe. In the core states reductions in the death rate had been compensated by reductions in the birth rate to produce very low population growth. In the periphery even larger reductions in the death rate had not been matched by equally large decreases in the birth rate. Overall, by the end of the century world population was growing at almost 2 per cent a year, nearly four times the rate in 1900, but that increase was very unevenly spread across the globe. In Europe the population was almost stable, with a growth rate of just 0.3 per cent a year. Apart from the core countries, Asia had the next lowest growth at about 2 per cent a year. Latin America was only marginally higher, but in Africa population was increasing at nearly 3 per cent a year – ten times the rate in Europe.

The distribution of people across the globe in the twentieth century reflected not just different population patterns but also migration. Humans moved between countries in an unprecedented wave of voluntary migrations involving over 200 million people. In the early twentieth century the movement of people between states was almost entirely uncontrolled. The largest movement was within the core states – outward from Europe mainly to the United States, but also to the semi-periphery, in particular Brazil, Argentina and Australasia. The period between 1891 and 1920 marked the greatest-ever outflow from Europe, when just over 27 million people emigrated, mainly from the rural states of Ireland, Italy, Spain and eastern Europe, although 1.6 million people also left highly industrialized Britain. Immigration remained central to the population growth of states such as Australia and the United States: in 1920 nearly one in seven of the American population were foreign born. At the same time there was also considerable movement within Europe, mainly from the marginal areas into the wealthy states such as Britain, France and Germany. Over half of all Italian emigrants moved within Europe, primarily to France, Germany and Switzerland. Elsewhere the Irish moved to Britain and the Poles to Germany. The imperial states in Europe were also operating schemes of indentured labour (semi-free workers, who agreed to work for a period in return for free transport and minimal wages) which resulted in the movement of huge numbers of people around the globe and affected over forty countries. The British, for example, recruited over 30 million Indians and moved them to Trinidad, Guyana and Fiji as agricultural labourers. Indentured labour was not abolished in the Dutch empire until 1941.

After the First World War, in a period of generally low economic growth and high unemployment, migration declined and restrictions on immigration were introduced. Emigration from Europe fell by over a third from its pre-war level to about 300,000 a year on average with the largest number of migrants coming from Britain (mainly to Australasia, although government-sponsored schemes to increase the rate proved ineffective). In Europe only France had a major immigration scheme, to compensate for its low population growth. A state recruitment organization negotiated agreements with many countries in Eastern Europe to provide workers who would be tied to specific work contracts with only very restricted rights to change their job and subject to special identity cards to regulate their movements. During the 1920s over 2 million people moved to France on these special contracts and by 1931 overseas workers made up over 6 per cent of the French population. As the depression began to bite, immigration quotas and new laws were introduced so that foreign workers could be sacked and deported from areas of high unemployment. Germany had a similar but much smaller scheme for state recruitment during the 1920s.

After 1945 the pattern of world migration changed markedly. Emigration from Europe doubled from inter-war levels to about 600,000 a year. A total of about 10 million people had left by 1963. In Italy 1·2 million people emigrated in the fifteen years after the war and in Britain levels returned to the pre-1914 peak. The destinations of European emigrants remained, as before, primarily the United States, Australasia, Brazil and Argentina. This movement was vital to many states – in the quarter century after 1945 over half the growth in the Australian labour force came from immigration. At the same time nearly all west European states came to rely on immigrant labour on an increasing scale – over 30 million people moved to western Europe in the thirty years after 1945. By 1975 on average one in seven of all manual workers was an immigrant.

Part of the post-1945 movement was unregulated – in particular the movement from colonial and ex-colonial territories to countries such as Britain, France and the Netherlands from the Caribbean, Africa and parts of Asia. The majority, though, came from government-sponsored schemes and involved not ex-colonies but semi-skilled and unskilled workers from the poorer countries of Europe's semi-periphery. The key to all these schemes was that the workers were given limited rights in the host country and were subject to easy deportation. The first schemes began immediately after the Second World War. In Britain a 'European Voluntary Worker' scheme was introduced in 1945, under which 90,000 workers were tied to designated jobs, not allowed to bring their families with them and subject to immediate deportation for any form of indiscipline. Belgium ran a similar scheme until 1963, utilizing mainly Italian workers. The three largest schemes were in France, Switzerland and West Germany. In France the state-run ONI bureau had recruited 2 million workers and their dependants by 1970. Switzerland allowed recruitment by private employers under state control, in which the 'guestworkers' were not allowed to change their jobs, settle permanently or be joined by their families. By the early 1970s they made up nearly a third of the workforce and over 15 per cent of the population. West Germany had a highly organized state-run system from the late 1950s. The Federal Labour Office (BFA) operated recruitment centres in the Mediterranean area which selected workers and took them to Germany, where employers provided initial accommodation. Work permits were issued only for specific jobs and loss of a permit meant immediate expulsion. The number of foreign workers in West Germany rose from 95,000 in 1956 to 2,600,000 in 1973. In theory dependants were not allowed into Germany, but in practice employers recruited them as workers and with the birth of children the immigrant population in West Germany rose to just over 4 million (or 7 per cent of the population) by the mid-1970s.

In the last quarter of the century the pattern of migration (involving over 80 million people) changed again. Decline in economic growth and permanent high levels of unemployment in western Europe reduced the demand for labour. Most 'guestworker' schemes were halted and some workers, especially in Switzerland, were deported. However, a large minority population of some 18 million people remained. The countries of southern Europe, in particular Italy, switched, for the first time, from being long-term exporters of labour to being importers. By the late 1980s Italy had a legal foreign population of about 800,000 plus about 250,000 illegal immigrants. During the 1980s the United States continued its historically high levels of immigration – about 800,000 a year. Nearly half came from Asia and only one in ten from Europe (the exact reverse of the proportions in the 1950s). In addition there were at least 4 million (and, some estimates indicate, perhaps twice that number) illegal immigrant workers, mainly from Mexico.

The major change in the period was the emergence of migration on a major scale in other parts of the world. In Latin America about 1·5 million Bolivian and Paraguayan workers emigrated to Argentina, while Venezuela had 3·5 million illegal residents (mainly from Colombia) in a population of just over 13 million. Until the mid-1980s the Dominican government paid Haiti about $2 million a year to provide workers for the sugar harvest, where they were held in conditions described as 'slavery'. In Asia about 12 million workers were migrants. The main labour-importing countries were Japan, Singapore, Taiwan and Brunei. Some countries, such as Thailand and South Korea, imported some types of labour and exported others; the main exporting countries were the Philippines, Bangladesh, Sri Lanka and Pakistan. Many workers moved to the Middle East, where the newly rich oil-producing states became major importers of labour. Most moved as contract labourers with no civil or political rights and lived segregated in barracks without the right of reunion with their families. Many women became domestic servants and were heavily exploited. By the early 1980s over half the labour force in states such as Saudi Arabia, Libya, Bahrein, Oman, Qatar and Kuwait were immigrants on contract labour schemes. There was also considerable movement within the Arab states, totalling about 3 million people by 1980. Egypt exported over 700,000 workers and in countries such as Jordan and Yemen as much as 40 per cent of the labour force was working abroad and providing the biggest single source of foreign exchange earnings for the country.

The quadrupling of the world's population during the twentieth century produced a major problem in feeding the extra numbers. The century was characterized by major problems of hunger and famine. In the core states malnutrition was in decline by the early part of the century, although neither it nor its associated deficiency diseases disappeared until after 1945. Rickets, caused by lack of Vitamin D, was common in Britain and the United States until the 1930s. Pellagra, caused by lack of niacin, was found in areas where maize constituted a large part of the diet. Even as late as the 1930s it was officially calculated that, because of the high levels of unemployment, a third of the British population was too poor to buy the minimum diet that the League of Nations thought essential to maintain health. On average, though, the number of calories consumed per person per day in the core states (about 3,000) did not change greatly during the century. What did change was the composition of the diet, with a major shift from cereals and root crops to animal foods (meat and dairy products): in France in 1900 animal foods provided just one-fifth of the total calorie intake; by 1965 this had risen to a third and continued to rise for the rest of the century. One consequence of the improved diet was that children became taller – in Sweden between 1883 and 1971 the average height of eighteen year olds rose by 6 per cent, the onset of menarche also fell by two years.

There are no statistics available on the scale of world hunger before the 1930s, but the earliest figures show a pattern that prevailed throughout the century, with the worst problems concentrated in Africa, Latin America and parts of Asia. In the 1930s probably about 1 billion individuals (half the people in the world) suffered from malnutrition. By the early 1950s this had risen to about six out of ten people in the world – over 1·5 billion individuals. During the 1950s the proportion of the world's population who were malnourished fell only slightly, but because of the rapid rise in the population the numbers affected reached nearly 2 billion. From the early 1960s the situation improved and by 1980 about a quarter of the world's population suffered from malnutrition. However, because of the continuing population rise the number of people affected remained well above 1 billion, the same as in 1950. During the last two decades of the century the situation worsened steadily; as well as the more than 1 billion who suffered from chronic malnutrition, at least as many again had a grossly inadequate diet. For all the century and for the vast majority of people in the world, life revolved around trying to find enough food every day simply to stay alive – hundreds of millions lived under constant threat of starvation. An inadequate diet led inevitably to greater susceptibility to disease and early death. Throughout the century lack of food produced enormous human suffering. By the late 1990s about 40 million people a year were dying from hunger and its related diseases.

For much of the century the problem was not an overall lack of food in the world but its maldistribution both within countries and between countries. In Britain in 1900 the poorest members of society ate just half the number of calories of the middle and upper classes. The situation improved slightly during the century in the core states, but in the periphery average food-consumption figures continued to disguise huge differences within society. In the 1980s in Brazil, one of the richer countries of the semi-periphery, over two-thirds of the population had a diet below the minimum judged by the World Health Organization to be necessary to sustain a healthy life. On average in the twentieth century a person living in the core states had far more food available to eat (and a greater variety) than someone living in the periphery. By the early 1980s grain consumption per head in the United States was five times higher than that in sub-Saharan Africa and the disparity in protein consumption was even greater. A domestic cat in the United States ate more meat than people living in most parts of the periphery. By the end of the century the average diet in the core states had become too rich in animal products, fats and sugar, which caused major health problems, while in the periphery people continued to die of starvation on a massive scale.

The twentieth century was marked not just by high and continuing levels of poor diet and severe malnutrition but also by periodic famines and mass starvation. In the core states such events were restricted to Europe and were associated with the social and economic dislocation brought on by war and civil war – Belgium in the First World War, Germany at the end of that war as the British blockade tightened, western Russia in the civil war, Leningrad in the Second World War (where over 1 million people died) and Holland in the winter of 1944. In the periphery famine was widespread throughout the century. The number of dead in the first half of the century is unknown: often the colonial authorities took little interest. In 1908 there was a major famine in northern Nigeria, but even the authorities in the capital Lagos knew nothing about it until they read the annual report of the officer in Kano. He wrote that mortality had been 'considerable' but he hoped 'not so great as the natives allege' and continued that 'we had no remedy at the time and therefore as little was said about it as possible'. In French West Africa there were major famines across the Sahel in 1913–14 and again in 1931. During the second famine the French laid the blame on African 'idleness', 'apathy' and 'fatalism' and throughout it the government continued to requisition grain. Before 1950 there were other major famines in Niger (1942), Bengal (1943–4) where about 3 million people died and in Henan province in China (1942) where another 3 million died.

After 1950 there is more detailed evidence about famines, although it is still necessary to estimate the number who died. The worst famine was in China between 1958 and 1961 during the chaos produced by the 'Great Leap Forward' – the Chinese authorities officially admitted to 16 million deaths, but the true total is probably nearer to 30 million. Later in the century there were major famines in Bangladesh (1975), across the Sahel in the 1970s, Ethiopia (1984–5) and in Somalia in the early 1990s. In all of these, as well as those who died, tens of millions of people were affected by the famine and had to struggle to survive. In every case famine resulted not from a simple shortage of food (in Bengal the famine of 1943 followed the largest ever rice crop) but from lack of available land, poverty and rising food prices, which left many people unable either to grow enough food to survive or earn enough money to buy it. In every case the poor and most marginal members of society suffered most.

Exactly how many people died in the famines of the twentieth century is unknown. A conservative estimate would suggest at least 100 million. The number affected by famine conditions might be ten times that number. The number affected by a lifetime of hunger and semi-starvation amounts to tens of billions. These are terrible statistics and illustrate how, throughout the century, for the majority of people in the world, progress was limited and life remained barbaric, precarious, difficult and often extremely short.

3 PRODUCTION

FOR MANY people living in the core states in the nineteenth century the increase in industrial output and the growing pace of technological change were clear signs of progress and confirmation of their position at the summit of humanity. The twentieth century continued those trends and was marked not just by the largest-ever growth in population but also by the greatest-ever increase in output in every economic area – industrial production, energy, materials and food. Like population growth, that increase was not evenly spread across the century: growth after 1950 was twice as fast as in the first fifty years. By the 1990s the annual growth in the world economy was at such a level that every two years it added to current world output the equivalent of the *total* world output in 1900.

The growth in industrial output was even greater and on a scale that would have been unimaginable at the start of the century. In the nineteenth century, in the early stages of world industrialization, industrial output tripled. In the twentieth century it rose about 35-fold. Once again the real burst in growth occurred after the early 1950s. Such was the pace of change that world industrial output in the twenty years after 1953 was equivalent to the *total* industrial output of the previous 150 years.

Industrial production was not spread evenly across the globe. In the first decades of the century over 90 per cent came from the core states of north-west Europe and North America. That proportion was reduced by the industrialization of the Soviet Union after 1930, and Japan and eastern Europe after 1945, but it was only slightly reduced by the so-called 'newly industrializing countries' of Asia after 1960. By the end of the twentieth century half the world's industrial production took place in just three countries – the United States, Japan and Russia. Three-quarters of world production came from seven countries, those three plus China, Germany, France and Britain. Most of the rest came from the other industrialized core countries such as Sweden, Belgium, the Netherlands and Italy. The impact of other countries was minimal. Of the newly industrializing countries of the semi-periphery Brazil was the most important, but it contributed less than 2 per cent of world industrial output. For both South Korea and Taiwan the figure was less than 1 per cent. Most countries, especially those in the periphery in Africa and Latin America, saw their share of world industrial output fall during the century.

Productivity growth and technological change were at the heart of this huge growth in industrial production. They led to the development of completely new industries and major increases in output per worker. An American factory worker in the 1990s produced over six times more than his counterpart in 1900. In the core states this process, combined with increases in agricultural productivity, meant that far more people could be employed in other sectors of the economy such as finance, advertising, tourism, education and healthcare. In the core countries in 1900 about a third of overall output came from agriculture and slightly more from industry. By the end of the century, despite large increases in agricultural output and even bigger increases in industrial production, agriculture contributed just over 3 per cent of total output, industry about 35 per cent and over 60 per cent came from services. The same transition took place in other parts of the world, but at a much slower pace and from a baseline in which agriculture was of overwhelming importance in 1900. By the end of the century the proportion of total output from the three sectors in Asia was roughly at the levels found in the core at the beginning of the century.

Technological change, through the development of new products, methods of production and transport and the creation of new markets, was vital for economic growth in the twentieth century. Much of the innovation was incremental, with products such as the car being modified progressively throughout the twentieth century. Radical innovation usually required a cluster of inventions to produce a new industry, but deep transformations in an economy normally depended upon a major new technology. The effort devoted to research and development increased dramatically in the twentieth century: in 1920 there were 20,000 research workers in American industry; by 1970 there were over 1·5 million. Increasingly, industrial firms came to dominate this area. In 1906 individual inventors accounted for about four out of five of all American patents, by 1957 this figure had halved. However, world research-and-development expenditure remained concentrated in a few states. In the late 1980s nearly three-quarters of it was accounted for by the core states and most of the rest by the Soviet Union.

Technology did not exist in a vacuum. Its social and economic contexts were equally, if not more, important. Which inventions were taken up and the ways in which they were applied were largely determined by existing structures and organizations within society, in particular firms and, after the 1950s, transnational corporations. The full adoption of new technology by a society required not just an enclave economy, as in many parts of the periphery, but education and adaptation throughout society. In nearly every case new technologies began in the core states and were restricted to them or their large corporations until they were later diffused into the semi-periphery.

Technological change occurred in a series of 'waves'. New technologies were adopted, creating new markets and rapid growth, but were followed by market saturation and slowed growth before another wave developed. In the nineteenth century the first wave of technical change was dominated by steam power, mass production of textiles and the widespread use of iron. This had faded by mid-century, and the second wave of railway construction and the adoption of steel was also fading by the turn of the century. In 1900 a 'third wave' was emerging, which was to dominate the core economies in the first half of the twentieth century. It was based on the increasing use of electricity (the first easily distributed form of energy), the bringing together of a number of new technologies to create the motor vehicle industry and new processes in the chemical industry.

The widespread use of electricity began in the last quarter of the nineteenth century. At first it was used to provide light rather than power. By the end of the nineteenth century in the major cities of the core states important public places such as theatres, restaurants, shops and banks had installed electric lighting. However, less than 1 per cent of homes had electricity and lighting was still provided mainly by gas or candles. Gradually, new technologies developed, such as the more reliable tungsten filament light bulb and larger and more reliable generators, as well as distribution networks on local, regional and eventually national levels. Electricity then became the foundation for much subsequent technological advance. Factories were powered by electricity rather than steam, new industries such as aluminium production (which required vast quantities of electricity) were established and new markets opened up, particularly in providing products for the home. (In the twentieth century electricity consumption increased twice as fast as the very high rate of growth in overall energy consumption.) In the 1920s the United States was the first country to go down this road, first in urban areas and a decade later in the countryside. In Europe the countryside did not generally receive electricity until the 1950s. This phasing largely determined the emergence of consumer-durable industries supplying new products, such as refrigerators and washing machines, which took place in the United States in the 1920s, Western Europe in the 1950s and Japan in the 1960s. By the end of the twentieth century the availability of electricity varied hugely across the world. In the core states about 99 per cent of homes had electricity. In the states of the semi-periphery, such as Uruguay and Venezuela, this figure was about 80 per cent. In the periphery it was much lower – 4 per cent in Haiti, less than 1 per cent in Ivory Coast. By the 1990s each person in Norway used 2,805 times as much electricity as someone living in Burundi.

The key production industry for much of the twentieth century was vehicles – not just the manufacture of cars and lorries, but also the ancillary industries of vehicle maintenance, road building and fuel provision. In the 1880s and 1890s the development of the internal combustion engine and the pneumatic tyre made possible the evolution of the first primitive cars. In 1899 just 2,500 vehicles were sold in the United States (and most of those were electric or steam driven). By 1909 this figure had risen to 120,000 and by 1922 to 2,270,000. The number of vehicles on the road in the United States rose from about 80,000 in 1905 to over 10 million by 1921 and to 30 million by 1938. The United States became the first society to be dominated by the car and the impact on its industries was fundamental. By 1938 vehicle production was taking up half of all steel production, four-fifths of rubber output, two-thirds of plate-glass production and about a third of nickel and lead output. Similar trends did not occur in western Europe until the 1950s, when car production rose over five-fold, and in Japan until the 1960s. The impact of vehicle production can be judged by the fact that world output of cars in 1900 was a few tens of thousands but by the 1990s it had risen to over 35 million a year and car ownership worldwide rose from about 100,000 to nearly 600 million.

The chemical industry had only a slightly less spectacular impact on the world economy through the production of a wide range of new materials. The first synthetic fibre, rayon, was manufactured before the First World War, but the real boom came in the 1920s when it could be produced for a quarter of the price of silk. World output increased seventy-fold in the two decades after 1918. This was followed by a whole range of other fibres, starting with nylon (invented in 1938), and by the end of the century over half the world's output of textile fibres came from synthetic materials. New methods were developed for fixing atmospheric nitrogen, which by the 1920s led to a range of artificial fertilizers that transformed the world's food output. New methods of oil-refining led to the production of an increasingly diverse range of plastics, which went into major production after 1945. In the second half of the century world production of plastics on average doubled every twelve years and by the 1970s it already exceeded the combined production of aluminium, copper, lead and zinc. Aluminium was itself another of the twentieth century's new industries. In 1895 world production was just 223 tons. A wide range of uses was developed, from household utensils to aeroplane parts to cans, and by the late twentieth century nearly 25 million tons of aluminium were being produced a year.

By the late 1960s there were signs in the core economies that the impetus provided by the vehicle and chemical industries was decreasing. It was gradually replaced by a 'fourth wave' of technological change based on electronics and communications, a process that was still gathering momentum at the end of the century. In the late nineteenth century the development of electrical technology through the invention of the cable and the telephone broke the direct link between transport and communication and meant for the first time that the latter could be faster than the former, whether by ship, road, rail or air. Cable-laying in the last decades of the nineteenth century and the development of radio after 1901 provided a worldwide communication system, but major inventions took a long time to develop. Some of the most important changes came in the period 1935–50 with the invention of radar, the tape recorder, television and, most important, the transistor, in 1948, which replaced the valve and started the process of miniaturization. In communications further major changes came in the early 1960s, with the development of geostationary satellites capable of transmitting multiple circuits. At first they were on a small scale. Intelsat I, launched in 1965, could carry 120 simultaneous telephone circuits and two TV channels. By the 1990s satellites could carry 120,000 bi-directional circuits and the cost of a circuit fell from $60,000 a year to less than $10,000. On telephone circuits the telex was replaced by fax machines in the 1980s, and by the end of the century over two-thirds of the telephone traffic across the Pacific was between fax machines. The 1980s saw the rapid development of the portable telephone.

Even more remarkable was the speed of development in the miniaturization of electronics. The first primitive electro-mechanical computers were developed during the Second World War. The introduction of the transistor did not bring about a rapid revolution in computers, which remained slow and cumbersome. That revolution depended on the invention of the integrated circuit (a huge number of highly miniaturized transistors on a 'chip' of silicon) followed by the microprocessor (a huge number of solid-state circuits on a 'chip' the size of a fingernail – in effect a computer on a chip). A highly sophisticated industry developed to manufacture silicon chips of rapidly escalating capacity, as did a software industry to create the programs to process information.

The pace of miniaturization was nothing short of spectacular. In 1965 the Atlas supercomputer cost the equivalent of £30 million (at mid-1990s prices) and could carry out 500,000 calculations a second, but took up space equivalent to four large living rooms. By 1995 a supercomputer the size of a refrigerator costing £250,000 could do 1·6 billion calculations a second. Even more important, though, was the development, from the early 1980s, of the personal computer and its linking into networks capable of handling vast amounts of data. This transformed all industries, especially the service industries and, together with the improvements in communications, made possible the rapid worldwide transmission and processing of large quantities of data. Increasingly, towards the end of the century, the combination of new technologies produced even newer tech-nologies and industries. A simple example from the 1980s was the combination of micro-electronics and lasers to produce the compact disc, which was used both to store large quantities of data and to reproduce music for a new domestic consumer industry, largely replacing the long-playing record, which had been invented in 1948. The application of computers to other industries transformed production methods. The introduction of industrial robots into the vehicle industry from the 1980s onwards not only reduced the amount of labour needed but also enabled a multiplicity of models to be made on one production line. The number of industrial robots in Japan increased from 14,000 in 1981 to nearly 330,000 by the end of the decade.

The unprecedented increase in industrial production across the world, the even faster growth in electricity consumption and the development of new industries all depended upon a massive increase in energy consumption. The transition to economies dependent on fossil fuels began in Europe in the sixteenth century, although it was not until the onset of major industrialization in the nineteenth century that consumption rose rapidly. Until the early twentieth century industrialization was based almost entirely upon the use of coal, except in the United States, where wood remained central until late in the nineteenth century. In the twentieth century world energy consumption increased over thirty-fold. This increase was mainly based on oil – world production rose from 10 million tons a year in 1890 to over 3,000 million tons a year by the early 1990s. In 1900 coal provided nine-tenths of the world's energy, by the end of the century it provided less than a third (although total output still increased six-fold). Despite this vast increase in consumption, the core states became more energy efficient during the twentieth century. By the late 1980s the energy required to produce a unit of gross domestic product had fallen by about a half since the 1890s. Nevertheless, an average American in the early 1990s used three and half times as much energy as his predecessor a century earlier. World energy consumption was highly inequitable – the overwhelming majority of it was used by the industries and population of the core states. As early as 1929 an American used over seven times as much energy as the world average. By the end of the century the United States, with about 5 per cent of the world's population, used a third of all the energy consumed in the world. The average American used twice as much energy as a European and thirty times more than a person living in India.

World energy production went through a number of phases in the twentieth century. The first lasted until about 1920 and marked the last period of coal's domination. Coal still provided over three-quarters of the world's energy and was essential in running the crucial iron and steel industries as well as providing domestic heating and, indirectly through gas, lighting. World coal production was dominated by Europe (over half the total) and the United States. It was one of the major industrial employers, though most production came from small-scale firms with the export market mainly confined to Europe, and dominated by Britain. Oil provided no more than 5 per cent of the world's energy (wood was far more important). In 1900 about 80 per cent of the oil produced was refined into kerosene to provided illuminating oil, most of the rest went to make lubricants – gasoline remained a minority product of the industry until after 1920. In 1900 the world's main producer of oil was Russia, although its share declined rapidly to less than a fifth by 1914 with the development of new fields in Mexico, Romania and the Dutch East Indies and the continued importance of American production at about two-fifths of the world total.

Energy production in the second phase, between 1920 and 1950, was marked by three trends: first, the relative decline of coal, partly through the increasing use of electricity in factories. Excess capacity in the industry resulted, over the two decades after 1920, in the closure of a third of the mines in Britain and America and chronic industrial disputes as owners tried to cut costs by cutting wages. The level of coal exports fell by half, with Germany and Poland replacing Britain as the main source of this predominantly intra-European trade. Nevertheless, in Europe coal still provided nearly 90 per cent of energy needs in 1950. The second trend occurred in the United States, where coal was replaced by oil as the main source of energy by the late 1930s. This oil came from relatively cheap domestic sources with the development of new fields in Oklahoma and especially east Texas. The Texan field was only discovered in 1930, yet within three years it was providing half of American output. The third trend was the domination of world oil production by the United States. Between 1920 and 1950 it never produced less than half the world's output, most of the time the figure was over 60 per cent. The next most important producer was Venezuela, with just over 10 per cent of world output. However, the world trade in oil remained relatively small: over half of all oil produced was consumed in the country of production.

Between 1950 and 1973 the third phase of world energy production was marked by four major trends. First, the very rapid shift in western Europe in the 1950s from coal to oil, which resulted in large-scale mine closures. Western Europe came to rely on imports of relatively cheap oil for over two-thirds of its energy requirements. Only in eastern Europe was coal still providing over 80 per cent of energy in the late 1960s. The second trend was the rapid development of oil production in the Middle East. In 1950 the region provided less than a tenth of the world's oil; by 1973 the figure was about 33 per cent and the region had nearly two-thirds of the world's proven reserves. The result, combined with a continuing rise in demand, produced the third trend. The US share of world production fell from a half to about a fifth and the United States shifted from being a net exporter of oil to being a large-scale importer. The final trend was the development of natural gas as a major energy source. Although it had been used locally near American oilfields from the beginning of the century, its widespread use depended on improvements in pipeline technology, which made possible the pumping of gas over long distances under high pressure. This was achieved in the United States in the 1930s, but not until the 1960s did its use become widespread in western Europe, with the development of the Groningen field in the Netherlands. By 1970 natural gas accounted for over a fifth of world energy consumption.

The fourth phase, in the last quarter of the century, was characterized by a diversification of energy sources. The major oil-price rises of 1973–4 and 1979–80 had important short-term impacts, but their long-term effects were limited (by the late 1990s oil prices had, allowing for inflation, fallen back to the levels of the early 1970s). The impact of new fields in the North Sea, Nigeria and Alaska was limited, but the oil-producing states in the Middle East were, for a variety of practical and political reasons, unable to control the market. The production of oil became even more diversified – the largest single producer in the late 1980s was the Soviet Union with about 20 per cent of world output, the United States was second at 15 per cent and Saudi Arabia third with 8 per cent. World coal production continued to increase, especially in China but also in the United States. The use of natural gas continued to expand dramatically – by the end of the century gas provided over half the energy needs of the Netherlands and about a third of Britain's. Major fields were also developed in Algeria and Siberia, with imports into western Europe accounting for half the world's trade. Hydro-electricity provided over a fifth of the world's electricity after steady development through the century. In the 1950s the new technology of nuclear power seemed to provide a route to cheap electricity. By the end of the century it provided about 10 per cent of the world's electricity, but only 45 new stations were under construction and over 80 had already been closed down. None of the electricity generated was cheaper than that obtained from conventional sources. Other renewable sources of energy –

solar, wind, tidal and geothermal – remained insignificant.

These major energy trends, although important for the world economy, only affected a minority of the world's population – those in the core states, the handful of exporter states in the Middle East and states such as Venezuela and Mexico. The majority of the world's population in the periphery continued to follow traditional patterns of energy use. Some states such as China and India could develop their coal resources and Brazil had alternative sources of fuel, but lack of wealth and limited foreign exchange meant that only small quantities of relatively expensive oil could be imported. Most of the population remained dependent on organic fuels, in particular wood and dried cow dung. Although Indonesia was an oil exporter, over three-quarters of its domestic energy needs came from these traditional sources. In India the proportion was even higher – over 90 per cent. For most people in the world energy came not from turning on a switch in their houses but from hard labour – gathering wood and, particularly when this was not available, drying dung which could have been better used as fertilizer on their fields.

The huge increases in industrial output also demanded a major increase in mineral extraction. World consumption of metals rose about sixteen-fold. In the first sixty years of the century alone more metals were mined than in all previous human history. Some of the increases were even greater. Development of the electrical industries and car production relied heavily on copper. World output rose from about 150,000 tons at the end of the nineteenth century to over 9 million tons a century later. Production of nickel (mainly used to harden steel) increased over seventy-fold. Part of this increase in output was obtained by improvements in technology, which allowed lower-grade ores to be used. In 1900 the lowest workable grade of copper ore was about 3 per cent – by the end of the century this had fallen to 0·35 per cent. However, exploiting this ore involved breaking, transporting and milling over 300 tons of rock and then removing it as waste in order to obtain a ton of copper. The amounts of energy involved in this process were immense and were the main constraint on exploiting such low-grade ore. In the second half of the twentieth century over a fifth of US energy consumption was used to extract and process minerals.

Unlike oil, mineral production in the twentieth century remained concentrated in a few areas. Nearly three-quarters of the world's metal production came from just 170 mines – half of world production of molybdenum came from just one mine in Colorado. Over half the world's metal-ore production was concentrated in five countries – the United States, the Soviet Union, Canada, Australia and South Africa. Only for a few metals were other countries important: bauxite (Jamaica), copper (Chile and Zambia), tin (Malaysia and Bolivia) and cobalt (Zaire). The core states, which consumed nearly all the metals produced, were able to control exploration and concentrate it in those countries which they regarded as stable.

World food production also expanded considerably: how much is difficult to estimate because statistics for the first half of the century are unreliable. Overall it probably tripled, though this was less than the rate of population increase. Production was increased in three ways – by bringing more land into agriculture, by increasing mechanization and through using more artificial inputs in the form of fertilizers, herbicides and pesticides. By 1900 one of the major revolutions in world agriculture was already well under way – the huge expansion of cultivated areas in Canada, Argentina and Australia to supply the population of the core states with cheap food and with the more exotic products which their growing wealth enabled them to buy. This expansion depended on the political and economic power of the core states and demonstrated their ability to remake the economies of the semi-periphery and periphery. Originally the food trade was limited to grain, but in the last two decades of the nineteenth century the development of ships with refrigerated and frozen compartments enabled meat and dairy products to be brought to Europe from the Americas and Australasia. A symbolic moment came in 1901 when the first refrigerated banana boat brought fruit from Jamaica to Britain.

The consequence of this growing trade was two-fold. The first was a long period of stagnation in western European agriculture, which lasted until after the Second World War. Output increased only slowly and for long periods actually fell under competition from cheaper imported food. Second, in other parts of the world the expansion of the area under cultivation continued. In the United States this process ended by 1930, but in the first five decades of the century the area under cropland tripled in Canada and quadrupled in Argentina and Australia. After 1950 this process began to slow down everywhere – the total amount of arable land in the world had only increased by a further 16 per cent by 1980. After 1980 the rate of increase fell even further to just 0·3 per cent a year and in Africa the area under cultivation started to decline.

The revolution in the agriculture of the core states occurred after 1950. Although the amount of agricultural land continued to decline (in western Europe in 1985 it was back to the same acreage as in 1860) and the labour force fell even more quickly (by two-thirds in the thirty years after 1950), output more than doubled. This was possible for three reasons: massive government support and protection, mechanization, and high levels of inputs. Extensive support for agriculture began in the 1930s but developed rapidly after 1950, so that by the later decades of the century over 40 per cent of the output of British farms was the result of subsidies. In the United States the large-scale use of machines such as tractors and combine harvesters began in the 1920s, but not in Europe until the 1950s. (As late as 1950 Germany still used over 2 million horses on its farms.) Electric milking machines were introduced in New Zealand in 1920, but in western Europe in 1950 only 3 per cent of cows were machine milked. Within twenty years, however, western European agriculture was almost entirely mechanized. Elsewhere the mechanization process continued apace. In 1965 just 1 per cent of the Californian tomato crop was picked by machines; within three years only 5 per cent was picked by hand. The revolution in inputs began in the 1920s with the development of artificial nitrogen fertilizers. In the late 1920s British agriculture used just 50,000 tons a year. Fifty years later consumption was over 1 million tons a year. After 1950 the chemical industry invented a wide range of artificial compounds which acted as either pesticides or herbicides. Their use in the core states rose fifteen-fold in the twenty-five years after 1953.

Agriculture in the periphery presented a very different picture. Because of core political and economic control increasing amounts of land were devoted to growing crops for export. In addition land was very unequally distributed – in Latin America in the late twentieth century two-thirds of the land was owned by less than 2 per cent of the population. In Africa three-quarters of the agricultural population owned just 4 per cent of the land. In general, the large landholdings were less productive than the small, peasant plots. When combined with a rapidly rising population, the consequence was a fall in the amount of arable land per head of population. The only way enough food could be grown was by increasing productivity. After 1950 the so-called 'green revolution' (the use of high-yielding varieties of rice and wheat) seemed to provide an answer and where they were adopted yields often doubled in a decade. However, these varieties required high levels of both fertilizers and pesticides which could only be afforded by relatively wealthy farmers, so existing social inequalities were intensified and more peasants were driven into becoming landless labourers.

The history of agriculture in Africa in the twentieth century was even bleaker. The continent faced a number of almost insuperable problems – low-fertility soils, high rainfall but also droughts, high levels of animal and human disease and a terrain that made the construction of a reasonable transport network very difficult. These problems were exacerbated by government policies in both the colonial and independence periods. High tariffs increased costs to farmers and state marketing schemes reduced their incomes significantly. In 1900 the plough was still unknown south of the Sahara; throughout the century four-fifths of the energy input came from humans. Until about 1960 agriculture was just able to keep pace with population growth, but after this the situation worsened dramatically in a manner not found elsewhere. Even in a relatively prosperous country like Kenya, in the 1970s population grew by 4 per cent a year but food output at only half that rate. Nearly everywhere in tropical Africa the amount of food available per person fell after 1960. By 1980 it was clear that supplies were no longer adequate and only imports could sustain even a basic diet.

4 ENVIRONMENT

THE UNPRECEDENTED growth in population, the enormous increase in industrial production and the expansion of cropland had a fundamental impact on the earth's environment in the twentieth century. Many of the problems that emerged were not new, but the increasing scale on which they were happening, from local to regional and then to global levels, together with their growing complexity, was. The types of problem encountered and their causes were not the same across the globe. In the periphery, where population pressure was greatest and most people still lived on the land, the major problems were the expansion of cropland into unsuitable areas, deforestation, desertification and only marginally the pollution caused by industry. In the core states, although they were indirectly responsible for many of the problems in the periphery, the major environmental impacts came from the pollution caused by increased industrial output and energy use.

Two basic environmental requirements for humans are a supply of clean water and a sewerage system that does not pollute drinking water. Throughout the twentieth century the overwhelming majority of the world's people had neither. In 1900 even one of the most prosperous countries in the world, Britain, had only a rudimentary water supply and sanitation system. In Manchester less than half the houses had their own lavatory. Dundee in 1910 had only three hotels and two houses with water closets and even then they only worked with buckets of water. The rest of the town had to use about 1,000 privately owned privies and fourteen public conveniences. Numerous local authorities across the country still dried and sold human excrement to local farmers. In Paris, in 1925, half the houses were not connected to a sewerage system and until the 1960s half of the city's sewage went into the Seine untreated. Only with the destruction of much inner-city housing in mid-century did nearly all the population of the core states come to have their own sanitation and clean-water systems. Even by the end of the century much waste was still simply dumped at sea, much of it near to bathing beaches.

If in the early twentieth century the wealthiest states in the world still had very primitive systems, it is hardly surprising that elsewhere conditions were even worse. In Moscow the first sewer was not constructed until 1898 and by 1917 only eighteen cities in the century had even a basic system. As late as 1960 two-thirds of urban homes in the Soviet Union were not connected to a sewer and throughout the century most of Moscow's sewage was put untreated into the Moscow River. The picture was much the same in Japan. Not until 1912 was construction of a primitive sewerage system in Tokyo started and sixty years later over half the country did not have mains drainage.

Conditions in the states of the periphery were even worse. The colonial authorities usually showed little interest in building sewerage systems for the native inhabitants. Governor Lugard of the Gold Coast summed up this attitude: 'Such a community has no desire for municipal improvement. It neither appreciates nor desires clean water, sanitation or good roads or streets.' The white rulers therefore imposed strict residential segregation and limited street cleaning and piped water supply to the European areas. After independence most countries in the periphery lacked the capital to construct effective water and sewerage systems and the rapid growth of urban populations made a difficult situation worse. A report on Hyderabad in the 1950s was typical of conditions in much of the periphery: 'A high majority of the citizens commit nuisance promiscuously in open spaces . . . Public latrines are few and far between . . . [and] are not kept clean by the scavengers, and it is an annoying sight to see many a scavenger emptying his bucket full at some street corner.' Without even a primitive sewerage system local rivers became open sewers: in Manila in the 1970s the Pasig River was, by volume, 70 per cent raw sewage. By the end of the century four out of five people who lived in the periphery (in other words the overwhelming majority of the world's population) had no sanitary facilities.

The major expansion of agricultural land in the twentieth century, whether for pasture or arable, inevitably meant the destruction of the natural environment, especially forest clearance. In the temperate areas of north-west Europe and eastern North America the environmental impact was limited because of the nature of the soils and the climate. Elsewhere the impact could be devastating. Cropland expansion in the United States and the Soviet Union produced two of the major ecological disasters of the century. Until the late nineteenth century the settlers pushing westward across the American continent generally avoided ploughing up the Great Plains. However, the development of the heavy steel plough pulled by teams of up to a dozen oxen made it technically feasible, even though most of the area was extremely marginal for cereal cultivation: the climate was semi-arid with rainfall of about twenty inches a year and the thin topsoil was only held together by the grass. In 1909 the US Bureau of Soils claimed (in defiance of all ecological principles) that 'the soil is the one indestructible, immutable asset that the nation possesses. It is the one resource that cannot be exhausted.' The events of the next decades were to demonstrate in a terrible way the fallacy of that statement.

The last large Indian territory, Oklahoma, was opened for settlement in 1889 and in the next forty years about 40 million acres of virgin land were ploughed up and cultivated with new forms of drought-resistant wheat. The early 1930s brought one of the periodic droughts that regularly affect the Great Plains. The loose, fragile, dry soil, which had lost its protective grass cover, was blown away by the high winds, creating huge dust storms across the region. The first major storm picked up about 350 million tons of topsoil and deposited it over the eastern United States (it was even detected on ships 300 miles out in the Atlantic). Frequent storms followed – between January and May 1935 Amarillo in Texas experienced seven of them, which caused zero visibility in the town. By 1938 10 million acres of land had lost the top five inches of soil and another 13 million acres the top two-and-a-half inches. Over 3 million people abandoned farms in the area, Oklahoma lost a fifth of its population and in some counties almost half the people left.

This huge ecological and social disaster, through the creation of the 'dust bowl', forced the American government to survey the full extent of soil erosion in the country. The results, published in 1938, showed an alarming situation and demonstrated just how destructive modern farming practices could be. Even in a prime agricultural area like Illinois, a third of the land was found to be damaged by soil erosion. In total an area as large as the state of South Carolina had been eroded away, an area the size of Oklahoma and Alabama combined had been seriously damaged and the amount of sand and gravel washed down by the rivers would have covered an area as big as Maryland. The situation deteriorated still further in the rest of the century. The 'dust bowl' returned in large areas of the Great Plains in 1952–7 and again in the 1970s. By then a third of the topsoil of the United States had been lost and over 200 million acres of cropland had been ruined or made highly marginal for cultivation. Over 700,000 acres of productive land were being lost every year and soil-loss rates were six times higher than in 1900.

In the Soviet Union the major agricultural catastrophe came in the 1950s with the 'virgin lands' programme – the drive to open up the marginal grasslands of areas such as Kazakhstan. In total about 100 million acres were ploughed up between 1954 and 1960. Yields peaked in 1956 and then fell steadily. Practices such as deep ploughing and leaving the soil bare during fallow periods, and a severe drought in 1963, led to major soil erosion. In just three years 40 million acres of land were lost to cultivation so that within a decade half the new land was already out of production. Losses continued at about a million acres a year after the mid-1960s. Similar problems occurred elsewhere. In 1984 it was estimated that half of Australia's agricultural land was affected by soil degradation. In the middle of the century China was losing about a million acres of agricultural land a year to soil erosion which, combined with high losses in the past, meant that a seventh of the vast land surface of China was affected by erosion. The dust caused by spring ploughing could be detected in Hawaii more than 5,000 miles away. Modern agricultural practices in the core states during the great period of production expansion after 1950 caused other forms of environmental destruction. Britain, for example, lost nearly all its lowland meadows, two-thirds of its lowland heaths, half its ancient lowland woodlands, bogs and wetlands and a quarter of all its hedgerows.

Far greater problems of environmental destruction through agriculture were apparent in the countries of the periphery, particularly in tropical areas. Rapidly rising populations meant that more and more land had to be brought into cultivation. This process was intensified by the highly inequitable nature of landholding, which meant that settlements moved into the most marginal and ecologically vulnerable areas. In many areas the traditional agricultural system had been 'swidden' or 'slash and burn', in which farmers cleared an area of forest for cultivation by burning, planted crops for a few years until weeds re-established themselves and then abandoned the land for a new site until the forest had regrown. This highly efficient system limited environmental destruction. However, under population pressure the clearance time tended to shorten until permanent cultivation was established and the 'swidden' system was pushed further into virgin forests. Permanent clearance of tropical forests produced major ecological problems. Although tropical forests are immensely productive ecosystems, most of the nutrients are held not in the soil but in the trees and plants. When these are cleared the nutrients, apart from some ash, are destroyed and since the underlying soils are thin they provide a poor base for crops and grass. They also erode easily once they are exposed to wind and rain. The inevitable consequence of permanent forest clearance was that farmers found they could only grow crops for a couple of seasons until the soil was exhausted. They then had to convert it to poor-quality grassland which had only limited productivity. The pressure for forest clearance was reinforced by the demands of the core countries for tropical timber. In many cases logging companies opened up the forests and the dirt roads they created acted as a magnet for settlement by poor farmers. In some countries, in particular Brazil, the government encouraged settlement in the vast Amazon region for strategic and developmental reasons and also to lessen the pressure for land reform in the settled areas of the country.

The result was widespread destruction of the tropical forests in the second half of the century. About half of the world's tropical forests were destroyed after 1950 and about three-quarters of that destruction was done to provide land for agriculture. Much of the loss was concentrated in West Africa, where about three-quarters of all the forests had been destroyed by the end of the century. After 1975 the losses in the Amazon began to mount rapidly as settlements increased. Here and in Central America much of the clearance was to provide large-scale cattle ranches to supply the United States. Many of them only lasted for a short while until the land could not even support grazing cattle: nearly all the ranches established in the Amazon area before 1978 had been abandoned within a decade.

Another contributory factor in increasing rates of deforestation and soil erosion was overgrazing by pastoral groups in marginal areas of Africa, the Near East and Central Asia. Their lifestyle required large amounts of land and resources to avoid overstressing the environment. In the twentieth century they came under pressure from two sources – a rise in their numbers, but also increasing pressure from farmers moving into their traditional grazing areas, which pushed them into even more marginal land. Attempts to restrict the movements of pastoralists or turn them into sedentary groups by building deep water holes only concentrated the destructive effects of grazing, as did a switch to large herds of a single type of animal.

The destruction of tropical forests and soil erosion had a number of other effects. The removal of vegetation cover increased temperatures, dried out the soil, created dust and tended to stop rain clouds forming. Once about 100,000 acres have been cleared these effects are noticeable on a significant scale. In the twentieth century four times this area was cleared in West Africa. By the last quarter of the century constantly low rainfall was being experienced across the region and average rainfall was a third less than at the start of the century. Soil erosion caused vast quantities of silt to be washed down the rivers. In the Himalayas, one of the areas worst affected by deforestation, the beds of the region's great rivers were rising at six inches a year by the late twentieth century, causing widespread flooding and a rapid expansion of the already large deltas. In Bangladesh, in particular, this created extensive areas of very vulnerable land on which the rapidly rising population was forced to settle but was exposed to constant 'natural' disasters such as flooding. By the end of the century almost an eighth of the world's population lived in areas affected by the flooding caused by deforestation in the Himalayas.

The most extreme form of soil loss is desertification – the permanent loss of land to deserts. The twentieth century saw the steady advance of deserts into once productive areas. By the 1990s these conditions were particularly apparent in the south-west of the United States, northern Mexico, North Africa, the Sahel, Australia and large parts of South Africa. Between 1925 and 1975 the Sahara desert grew by about 250,000 square miles along its southern edge. In Sudan and Chile the Sahara and Atacama deserts were expanding by about two square miles a year by the end of the century, and overall about 650 million people in the world lived in arid and semi-arid areas threatened by the further encroachment of deserts.

The expansion of world food production led to a vast increase in the amount of irrigated land, particularly in Asia. In 1900 there were about 100 million acres in the world under irrigation, but by the end of the century this had increased more than five-fold. Although, in the right conditions, irrigation can dramatically increase crop yields it has many drawbacks. It uses large quantities of an increasingly scarce resource – water. By the end of the century over three-quarters of the world's water was used for irrigation and most of that was used very inefficiently: in India and China two-thirds of the water was lost through evaporation and seepage and even in the United States half of the water was lost. The major problem, though, occurs in areas with high temperatures when waterlogging of the soil and evaporation from the surface eventually leave a crust of salt which makes it impossible to grow crops. By the 1980s such effects were found in half of all the irrigated land in Syria and Iraq and in some places, for example the Punjab, the figure reached 80 per cent. Overall, as much irrigated land was being abandoned as was being brought into cultivation.

The worst environmental disaster caused by irrigation occurred in the Soviet Union around the Aral Sea. This large inland sea in southern Kazakhstan was unusual: although two rivers flowed into it, none flowed out and the lake was maintained in size by very high evaporation rates. In the early 1970s the Soviet authorities implemented a grandiose scheme to use the two rivers to irrigate over 18 million acres so cotton and rice could be grown in highly unsuitable climates and soils. Predictably this major diversion of water caused the Aral Sea to shrink rapidly. By the late 1980s two-thirds of it had dried up, exposing the seabed across an area of over 12,000 square miles. Major climatic changes resulted – temperatures rose and rainfall fell. The effects locally were devastating. Nearly all the species of fish in the sea became extinct, the fishing industry collapsed and large numbers of villages were abandoned. The salinity of the Aral tripled; salt-dust storms swept the area; the water table fell, causing the sewerage system to collapse, with the result that typhoid rates rose thirty-fold, and nine out of ten children were diagnosed as being permanently ill. In 1990 there was an outbreak of bubonic plague. By the early twenty-first century the Aral Sea is unlikely to exist.

The environmental problems created by unprecedented industrial expansion were, to some extent, confined to smaller areas than the problems caused by agriculture, but their impact was much greater. Industrialization in the core states in the nineteenth century was essentially unregulated and by the early twentieth century had created huge amounts of pollutants in areas such as the Ruhr in Germany, Limburg in Belgium, the Black Country of the English

Midlands and the Monongahela valley near Pittsburgh. The last had 14,000 smokestacks belching fumes into the atmosphere. Some areas were turned into poisoned wastelands by the fumes and residues: a century of copper and other metal production in the Swansea valley in Wales led to the destruction of most of the vegetation and the creation of soils that poisoned nearly all plants. Everywhere rivers were treated as an easy way of disposing of a lethal cocktail of chemical wastes, leaving them incapable of supporting life and a danger to the human population. Only slowly during the twentieth century did a few governments begin to restrict the output of pollutants.

The process of industrialization elsewhere in the world in the twentieth century replicated the conditions in Europe and North America in the previous century. This was particularly the case in the Communist states which put a high priority on industrialization. One of the most devastated areas was in East Germany, north Bohemia and Upper Silesia and, in particular, the areas around the towns of Most in Czechoslovakia and Katowice in Poland. The large concentration of iron and steel plants, metal industries and chemical plants, nearly all using poor quality and highly polluting lignite coal, produced an environmental disaster zone. By the 1980s in Most sulphur dioxide emissions were twenty times higher than the maximum recommended by the World Health Organization (WHO) and schoolchildren often had to use portable respirators. Around Katowice two-thirds of the food produced was so contaminated that it was unfit for human consumption and three-quarters of the water could not be drunk. A third of all rivers had no life in them and the Vistula was unfit even for industrial use for over two-thirds of its length because it was so corrosive. In the Baltic an area of 100,000 square miles was biologically dead because of the poisons brought down by the rivers. Basic industrialization in the periphery produced a similar picture. In China by the end of the century sulphur dioxide levels in the industrial cities were over seven times higher than WHO-recommended levels. In Brazil the Cubatão area near São Paulo became the most polluted on earth. Air pollution was at twice the level considered lethal by the WHO, there was no fish in the rivers and nearly all the local flora was destroyed.

After 1945 in the core states, and later elsewhere, there was a major change in industrial processes; in particular the number of synthetic chemicals produced rose. In the first half of the century pollution came overwhelmingly from two main sources, coal-burning and heavy industrial production. The new synthetic chemicals, such as plastic compounds and pesticides, were often highly toxic even in minute quantities and were resistant to degradation by natural processes, so they accumulated in the environment. US synthetic chemical production rose 400-fold in the forty years after 1945. By the 1980s there were about 70,000 chemicals in use, with new ones being added at a rate of about 1,000 a year and the overwhelming majority had not been tested for safety.

Two cases, pesticides and polychlorinated biphenyls (PCBs), show the impact of some of these new chemicals. Before the middle of the twentieth century farmers relied on natural products such as pyrethrum or chemicals with no long-term damaging effects such as 'Bordeaux' and 'Burgundy' mixtures for pest control. After 1945 pesticide production became a major industry – its output increased 33-fold by the mid-1980s and output continued to grow at over 12 per cent a year. Because only about 1 per cent of the pesticide sprayed hit the pests, it had to be highly toxic even in minute quantities. The first pesticides were organo-chlorines such as DDT, followed in the early 1950s by organo-phosphates, which were far more toxic but slightly less persistent. Many of these compounds were carcinogenic and about 1 million people suffered serious health effects as a result of their use. For decades there were few controls over their use and only a handful such as DDT were banned in the core states, although they were still used in the periphery. By the end of the century a third of all US pesticide exports were of types banned domestically. The increasing use of pesticides did not even reduce crop losses. Pests rapidly developed immunity and crop losses actually rose in the United States after the 1940s.

PCBs are chlorinated hydrocarbons, closely related to DDT, and some of the most carcinogenic compounds known to science. Their manufacture began in the 1930s and they were used as insulators in electrical products, particularly transformers, additives in paint and in 'carbonless' carbon paper. As early as 1936 chloracne (a very serious skin complaint) was identified in people who handled PCBs and special procedures were introduced for its manufacture but not its disposal. Production continued for four decades until it was banned in the United States and Japan in the 1970s and the European Community in the 1980s. By then about 2 million tons had been made and two-thirds was still in use. The one-third that went for disposal was dumped in the oceans or left to rot in toxic-waste dumps, where it polluted water supplies. PCBs tend to accumulate in animal fatty tissue and even minute quantities cause birth defects. By the late twentieth century contamination had been found in human milk across the core states, in penguins in the Antarctic, and in the Wadden Sea off the Netherlands half the seals were sterile because of contamination.

Chemical accidents also caused disasters in some areas. In 1976 an explosion at Seveso in northern Italy resulted in the release of the highly toxic chemical dioxin. Nearly a thousand people had to be evacuated and many suffered from disfiguring skin diseases. The top eight inches of soil over an area covering seven square miles was so badly contaminated that they had to be removed and buried. In 1984 at Bhopal in central India thirty tons of methyl isocyanate escaped from a storage tank into an adjoining slum area where 200,000 people lived. The best estimate of the death toll is about 10,000 and at least twice that number were severely disabled. Two years later a fire at the Sandoz chemical plant at Basel resulted in thirty tons of pesticides, fungicides and dyes being released into the River Rhine. No life survived in the river for 120 miles downstream. The vast increase in the use of chemicals and increased industrial output produced major problems in waste disposal. In the 1940s the United States produced about 1 million tons of hazardous waste, by the 1990s this had risen to over 250 million tons, which was two-thirds of the world total. Much of this waste was simply placed in dumps with few, if any, controls. At Love Canal near the Great Lakes the firm responsible for the site in the 1940s sold it for one dollar with an indemnity against any future liability. In 1978 the area was declared a disaster zone by the federal government and the population was evacuated.

Despite some minimal environmental controls rivers and oceans were still used as dumps. Many rivers became so full of chemicals and wastes that they caught fire – for example the Iset near Sverdlovsk (1965), the Ganges (1968), the Cuyahoga at Cleveland (1969) and the Volga (1970). By the last quarter of the century New York was dumping 9 million tons of waste a year in the Atlantic off the mouth of the Hudson River. The result was an area of black toxic waste sludge covering about 100 square kilometres which supported no marine life at all. In total the United States was dumping 67 million tons of toxic waste at sea every year and in the North Sea a number of states were incinerating over 100,000 tons a year.

Although theoretical calculations showed that the chances of a nuclear disaster were remote, in practice nuclear power suffered from serious accidents throughout its life. In 1957 a fire in a reactor core at Windscale in north-west England released radioactivity across much of the country and over 2 million litres of contaminated milk had to be destroyed. In the Soviet Union in the 1950s the area around Kyshytm became a radioactive wasteland. In 1949 the Soviet authorities had released liquid nuclear waste into the Techna River. Within three years it reached Lake Karachai near Kyshytm, where the heat from the decaying radioactive material dried out the lake. The radioactive lake-bed had to be covered in concrete to stop the wind spreading the pollution any further. In 1957 there was an explosion in a nuclear waste dump near Kyshytm which killed about 10,000 people, contaminated an area of about 150 square miles and led to the evacuation of 270,000 people. In the United States over 400,000 gallons of radioactive material leaked out of storage tanks at the Hanford site in the thirty years after 1945. In 1979 one of the reactors at the Three Mile Island plant in Pennsylvania suffered a partial core meltdown and a catastrophic accident was only just avoided. Such an accident did occur seven years later at Chernobyl in the Ukraine. An explosion in one of the reactors released a gigantic cloud of radioactive debris which spread across Scandinavia and western Europe. Vegetable, fruit and animal sales were stopped across a wide area and many of the reindeer in Lapland were slaughtered because they had eaten large quantities of contaminated lichen. In the Ukraine over 200 villages had to be abandoned and another 600 decontaminated. Over 150,000 people were evacuated from the worst-affected areas, though millions of others remained in the less heavily contaminated areas. The health of hundreds of thousands of people was put at risk for decades.

Another major source of pollution was the growing number of vehicles in cities. Even before the internal combustion engine the cities of the world were swamped by the pollution caused by horse-drawn traffic. The nineteenth century saw a huge increase in the number of horses in the core states. In 1900 Britain had about 3·5 million horses, about a third of which worked in cities. London had 3,700 horse-drawn omnibuses (each drawn by two horses and needing about ten horses a day to keep one bus operational), and over 11,000 vehicles for hire. The railway companies used 6,000 horses to distribute goods from their depots and coal merchants another 8,000. New York had over 200,000 horses. The result was that the streets were covered in urine and manure. In 1900 about 10 million tons of manure was deposited on Britain's streets every year, which brought with it an ever-present smell, flies and risk of disease. Most of the horses were grossly overworked and few survived more than a couple of years. In 1900 New York had to clear 15,000 dead horses a year from its streets. These problems were never solved, but disappeared when horses were replaced by cars, buses and lorries, which caused a different type of pollution.

At first, therefore, vehicles were welcomed as a solution to the problem of polluted streets, but further problems emerged as the number of vehicles on the road began to rise. All internal combustion engines produce a range of pollutants – carbon dioxide, carbon monoxide, nitrogen oxides, a range of toxic organic compounds and smoke. Once in the atmosphere, these in turn produce different forms of air pollution including peroxides, which irritate the eyes, and ozone, which makes breathing difficult. In combination they react with sunlight to produce 'photochemical smog'. Vehicle exhausts were also made more polluting by adding lead to fuel. Lead is poisonous and can cause brain damage in children who inhale the fumes. By the 1920s the higher compression engines then coming into production required higher octane fuel to operate correctly. Instead of improving refining techniques the oil companies found it was easier and cheaper to add tetraethyl lead, which produced the same effect. The corporation which manufactured tetraethyl lead in the United States was owned by General Motors, so the temptation was to keep increasing the compression ratios in engines in order to increase the demand for fuel with the additive. In the two decades after 1946 the amount of lead used per vehicle-mile in the United States rose by 80 per cent.

The pollution associated with vehicles was first noticed in the United States, where there were already high levels of car ownership by the 1920s. The Los Angeles valley has a natural inversion layer, which results in air being trapped in the valley for many days in the year, thereby allowing the level of toxic chemicals to increase. The first photochemical smog occurred in 1943 and the situation continued to worsen over the next decades. By the 1950s eye irritation was noticed on half the days of the year and in August 1969 during a particularly bad period doctors had to warn residents not to play golf, jog or do anything that involved deep breathing. By the late 1980s photochemical smog affected over a hundred American cities. As car ownership increased in other countries, the same problems developed. Photochemical smog became serious in Tokyo in the late 1960s, and in Mexico City which, like Los Angeles, has a natural inversion layer in the valley there were 312 days of severe smog in 1988 and in early 1989 schoolchildren had to be kept at home for a month because of the high pollution levels.

No government was prepared to take steps to limit vehicle ownership and controls therefore concentrated on technological fixes aimed at the symptoms rather than the causes. In 1970 with the Clean Air Act the United States started to phase out lead additives, a process that did not begin in the European Community until the mid-1980s. This was relatively simple to achieve in that it merely required the oil companies to produce a slightly modified product and car manufacturers to make adjustments to engines. The reduction of exhaust gases proved more difficult. After 1975 all new cars sold in the United States had to be fitted with catalytic converters, which remove some of the most harmful chemicals in exhausts. Similar controls were also introduced in Japan and in the early 1990s in the European Community. Outside the core states, however, little was done to reduce vehicle pollution. Venezuela experimented with a scheme in Caracas which only allowed vehicles to be driven on alternate days depending on whether their number plates had an odd or an even number. It was a failure – the rich simply bought two cars.

There was some improvement in smoke pollution in the urban environment of the core states. In 1900 coal was almost the only fuel used for domestic heating and cooking. In 1900 central London had nearly 4 million fireplaces all pumping out fumes into the atmosphere. In the winter London came to be typified by 'smogs' – dense clouds of pollutants cutting down visibility and substantially increasing the death toll from lung diseases. Year after year and decade after decade these conditions were replicated, with several thousand people dying every winter. Between 1920 and 1950 the average number of hours of sunshine in central London was 20 per cent less than in the outer areas which were less affected by the smogs. It was the terrible smog of December 1952, when over 4,000 people died, that finally brought about some action. The Clean Air Act of 1956 introduced controls on the types of fuel that could be burnt in the centre of cities and by 1970 the amount of smoke in the air over London had fallen by 80 per cent. General trends in energy consumption were also important – the greater use of electricity, gas and oil for heating and cooking and the introduction of central heating in homes. By the end of the century the problem of air pollution in cities was becoming worse in the peripheral states. Pollution levels were fourteen times higher in Delhi than in London and three times higher in Baghdad than Athens (the worst city in Europe).

All these pollution problems were essentially localized: they produced appalling environmental conditions in concentrated areas, but their wider impact was usually limited. Pollutants might travel down rivers causing problems, but normally only a few miles away from the great industrial cities of the core states conditions began to improve rapidly. In the second half of the century the scale of environmental problems began to change and problems began to be experienced over wider areas, at first at a regional level and then globally.

The phenomenon of acid rain was first identified in British industrial cities in the 1850s. The burning of fossil fuels and the smelting of sulphide iron ores produces sulphur dioxide, which in the atmosphere is altered through a complex series of processes into sulphuric acid which makes rainfall unnaturally acidic. Until well into the twentieth century most factories and power stations had low chimneys, which kept acid rain localized around the main industrial centres. But the ever-greater consumption of fossil fuels and the expansion of industrial output, together with the misguided policy of building very tall chimneys, in an attempt to reduce local pollution levels by dispersing the pollutants, turned acid rain into a major regional problem. Global sulphur dioxide production rose from about 45 million tons at the beginning of the century to about 170 million tons in the 1990s. Over half of these emissions came from the core states and a quarter from only two countries, the United States and Canada. In just ten years in the middle of the century the Sudbury copper and nickel smelter in Ontario emitted more sulphur dioxide than all the volcanoes (the main natural source) in the history of the earth. Downwind from industrial areas and power stations the acidity of rain could mount rapidly: on many occasions across the core states rainfall was as acid as vinegar and once in Wheeling, West Virginia, in the heart of one of the most polluted areas in the United States, rainfall was almost as acid as battery acid.

Acid rain eats away the fabric of buildings – the historic Polish city of Cracow was badly affected by emissions from nearby Katowice – but its most important environmental impact was the gradual acidification of streams, rivers and lakes, causing animal life to die out steadily as acid levels rose. Some of the greatest damage to rivers and lakes occurred in eastern Canada and the north-eastern United States, downwind of the main industrial areas, and in Sweden and Norway downwind of Britain. In the early 1950s Lumsden Lake in the La Cloche mountains in Ontario had eight species of fish, by 1978 all were extinct. In western Sweden by the 1980s the lakes were a hundred times more acidic than they had been fifty years earlier. Across Scandinavia by 1990 over a quarter of the lakes no longer contained any life. At the same time acid rain, combined with other chemicals, produced a lethal cocktail which badly damaged trees, restricted their growth and, in the most extreme cases, killed them. The transmission of pollutants across state boundaries made action difficult because the polluting states were reluctant to take action which involved costs to themselves in order to alleviate environmental problems in another state. No effective agreements were reached until 1984 when the so-called '30 per cent club' was formed among some of the core countries, pledged to reduce emissions by 30 per cent over 1980 levels by 1993. Some states such as Austria and Switzerland did better than this, but in most action was partial and dictated mainly by estimates of the extra costs involved. By the mid-1990s agreement had been reached on further reductions. These agreements alleviated a regional problem, but in global terms their impact was limited. Increasing industrialization, particularly with the use of very high-sulphur-content-coal, meant that in many Chinese cities sulphur dioxide levels in the air were four or five times those in the core states.

In the last quarter of the twentieth century two world-wide problems became apparent – ozone depletion and global warming – both of which threatened the complex global mechanisms that make life on earth possible. The ozone layer in the stratosphere absorbs ultra-violet radiation, which is harmful to nearly all forms of life. In the mid-1970s it was discovered that this layer was being destroyed by artificial chemicals called chlorofluorocarbons (CFCs), which, although present in only minute traces, were extremely potent – one chlorine atom released from a CFC molecule can destroy up to 100,000 ozone molecules. CFCs were invented in the 1920s by Thomas Midgley (the same scientist who suggested tetraethyl lead as an additive in petrol) and at first they seemed a classic example of the beneficial aspects of technological progress. They were non-poisonous, did not burn and did not react with other substances.

They were therefore widely adopted to clean electronic circuit boards, as coolants in refrigerators and air-conditioning systems, to make expanded foam containers and, after 1950, as propellants in spray cans. No precautions were taken to stop them escaping into the atmosphere and emissions rose from 100 tons in 1931 to 650,000 tons a year by the mid-1980s. Nearly all CFCs were used by the core states: American consumption in the 1970s was eight times higher than the world average. Only in the late twentieth century did some of the industrializing states of the periphery begin to make an impact: the number of people owning fridges in Peking rose from 3 per cent of the population to 60 per cent in the ten years before 1985.

The first major fall in ozone levels occurred over the South Pole, where the conditions in winter were ideal for large-scale destruction. By the end of the 1980s about half the ozone over Antarctica was destroyed and the 'hole' created each spring covered an area equivalent in size to the continental United States. Early in the summer the 'hole' drifted northwards over South America, Australia and New Zealand, where ozone levels fell by a quarter. In the early 1990s a severe thinning of the ozone layer was evident in the northern hemisphere in the spring and early summer. Scientific evidence suggested that for every 1 per cent fall in ozone levels the number of human skin cancers increased by 4 per cent and the number of eye cataracts by 1 per cent. It was a long time before any action was taken to deal with the growing problem. CFCs could be removed from spray cans because alternatives were easily available, but the major chemical companies strenuously denied any link between CFCs and ozone destruction and it was not until they were able to make alternatives that governments were prepared to take action. In a series of negotiations in the late 1980s and early 1990s agreement was reached on a worldwide phasing out of CFC production by 1996 and for transferring technology to the countries of the periphery to assist these states in the change-over. The problem with these agreements was that the alternative chemicals HCFCs (hydrochlorofluorocarbons) also destroyed the ozone layer but were less long-lived than CFCs. Although CFC emissions started to fall in the 1980s, atmospheric concentrations continued to rise and it will be several decades into the twenty-first century before ozone levels return to the levels of the mid-twentieth century.

Ozone-layer depletion was an example of the problems caused by a single synthetic chemical, wrongly thought to be benign, which was highly destructive in even minute quantities and able to cause a worldwide problem even though it was emitted from only a few states. The problem could be alleviated and eventually cured by the substitution of alternative chemicals. Global warming, on the other hand, demonstrated the problems caused by processes deeply embedded in modern history – the very rapid consumption of fossil fuels in the twentieth century together with industrial and agricultural expansion. Global warming over and above the natural processes that are essential to maintain life on earth is caused by four gases – carbon dioxide, methane, nitrous oxide and CFCs – which trap heat in the atmosphere. Carbon dioxide is responsible for about two-thirds of the total effect and is released whenever fossil fuels are burnt. The huge increase in energy consumption in the twentieth century was therefore the major and direct cause of global warming. The burning of coal, oil and natural gas by industry, in power stations and most importantly in vehicles, released carbon dioxide. In addition deforestation caused carbon dioxide levels to rise not just through the burning of trees and plants but also because there were fewer plants and trees to absorb carbon dioxide through photosynthesis. About half of all the carbon dioxide produced was not absorbed by various natural 'sinks' (in particular the oceans) but stayed in the atmosphere. Levels of carbon dioxide in the atmosphere began to rise in the nineteenth century with the onset of major industrialization, but over half the total increase between 1750 and 1990 occurred after 1950. The huge growth in the world economy meant that carbon dioxide emissions nearly quadrupled in those forty years and by the end of the century were rising at about 4 per cent a year (equivalent to a doubling every sixteen years).

The second major greenhouse gas is methane, the output of which was closely related to agricultural expansion. The need to feed a rapidly growing population in Asia produced a big increase in the number of paddy fields, each of which produced methane from the decaying vegetation acting as a fertilizer at the bottom of the fields. The number of paddy fields in the world increased at about 1 per cent a year throughout the twentieth century, while the number of cattle in the world doubled between 1960 and 1980 alone. The increase in the number of domesticated animals, which all have bacteria in their guts producing methane as a waste product, was another contributory factor to global warming. Deforestation increased the number of termites eating the dead wood and they also produce methane from their guts. The last two gases involved in global warming were CFCs and the nitrous oxides produced from vehicle exhausts and the greater use of nitrate fertilizers. Although these gases were only present in the atmosphere in minute quantities, they had a major impact: nitrous oxide is 120 times more potent as a greenhouse gas than carbon dioxide.

The potential impact of releasing large quantities of carbon dioxide into the atmosphere through burning fossil fuels was first set out by the Swedish scientist, Svante Arrhenius, in 1896. A hundred years later no effective action had been taken to deal with the problem. An international panel of scientists working for the United Nations agreed in a series of reports issued in the early and mid-1990s that the global rise in temperatures experienced in the twentieth century was caused by human pollution in the atmosphere. By the end of the century global temperatures had risen by 0.5°C. However, most of the greenhouse gases put into the atmosphere in the last decades of the century had still not had any effect on temperatures and a further rise of 0.5°C was therefore inevitable, with a total rise of about 2.5°C by the early decades of the twenty-first century almost certain. This would be the biggest and most rapid rise in temperature in human history. The impact is likely to vary from area to area, with the biggest temperature rises likely in high latitudes. The higher temperatures will alter agricultural patterns, affect water supplies, cause sea-level rises and badly affect natural vegetation, especially forests.

In the 1990s there was a series of international negotiations but no agreement on any binding targets for a major reduction in the output of greenhouse gases. The difficulty in reaching meaningful agreements stemmed from two linked problems. First, the output of greenhouse gases was deeply embedded in the economic and industrial expansion of the twentieth century and, in particular, the growing use of the car. Few people and no politicians seemed willing to confront the very difficult decisions involved in cutting back on the production and use of the car. Second, major questions of equity within the world system were raised. The overwhelming responsibility for the output of greenhouse gases, especially carbon dioxide, lay with the industrialized states of the core, which produced most of the world's output and consumed most of the world's energy. However, any attempt to freeze greenhouse gas output at the emission levels of the 1990s would penalize the industrializing states of the semi-periphery and periphery by restricting their future economic growth when they were the poorest states in the world and had not been the prime cause of the global problem. Yet failure to impose some controls over the industrial expansion and energy consumption of China, which, by the early twenty-first century, will be the largest economy in the world, would mean that any reductions made by the core states would be offset very rapidly. By the end of the 1990s the prospects for dealing with this, the most serious environmental legacy of the twentieth century, looked bleak.

5 GLOBALIZATION

THE TWENTIETH century was marked by the emergence of global economic systems. These involved an increase in world trade, the development of a sophisticated world financial structure, the increasing importance of transnational corporations and the linked internationalization of both production and services. However, this process was not continuous. There were major discontinuities in the world economy, in particular the two World Wars and the great depression of the 1930s, which saw countries either being forced or choosing to adopt greater self-sufficiency. All these developments took place within a highly unequal world system effectively controlled by the core states – a domination they had established before 1900 and which they were not to lose throughout the century.

The first and second halves of the century had very different patterns of world trade. Until 1950 world trade grew at a little over 1 per cent a year, which was less than the overall growth in output. The period was characterized by a tendency towards greater autarky in national economies and the creation of separate trading blocs. After 1950 world trade grew on average at over 6 per cent a year, far faster than the growth in output. By the 1990s world trade was over twelve times greater than in 1950 and taking up about a fifth of the world's total output of goods and services. Throughout the century world trade was dominated by the core countries: they accounted for three-quarters of the total in 1900 and almost exactly the same proportion by the end of the century. However, the nature of that trade had changed. Food fell from about a quarter of the total in 1900 to less than a tenth by the end of the century and the share of manufactured goods doubled to three-quarters. In general, though, the core states became more dependent on trade and imports of raw materials to support their massive growth in output and consumption. In 1900 the core states were net importers of just 1 million tons of iron ore a year, by 1990 Western Europe was a net importer of 65 million tons and Japan of 75 million tons. The same trend can be seen in energy. Until 1957 the United States was, on average, self-sufficient in oil, but thereafter became increasingly dependent on imports. Until 1950 western Europe was a net exporter of energy (coal), but by 1973 was importing over 40 per cent of its needs.

Some countries were much more dependent on trade than others. In the 1980s among the core states, Belgian exports were worth just over 60 per cent of its national output, but for the United States the figure was 5 per cent (less than the Soviet Union). The picture was the same elsewhere in the world – Taiwan exported the equivalent of well over half its national output, India less than 5 per cent. It was widely believed that the great growth in world trade after 1950 was the result of the liberalization of tariffs and other barriers to trade. In fact, world trade became increasingly regionalized in the last half of the century, reflecting, in part, separate trading blocs. In North America the proportion of intra-regional trade rose from 25 per cent in the 1950s to nearly 40 per cent by the 1990s when a quarter of all American manufactured exports went to just one country – Canada. This pattern was even more apparent in western Europe with the creation of the European Economic Community (later the European Union). In the late 1950s less than a third of the trade of members of the EEC was within the community, by the 1990s it was nearly two-thirds.

The huge increase in world trade in the twentieth century required the development of an increasingly large and sophisticated system of world finance. By the last third of the century the changes occurring in national economies, especially the increasing importance of services as opposed to industry, were being replicated on a global scale. The world financial system took off, creating a new world market that was not related to physical trade. Most of these developments in the international economy took place beyond the control of national governments and without any overall design.

In the twentieth century it is possible to discern a number of phases in the development of the world economy. The first, which lasted until 1914, was very closely linked to the pattern established in the late nineteenth century when a world trade and financial system first emerged. The second, from 1914 to 1950, was marked by increasing autarky and an inability to devise a satisfactory system for even minimal regulation of the international economy. The third phase, from 1950 to 1973, was viewed in retrospect as a 'golden age' of rapid growth and stability. However, the way in which the system functioned in this period was, in practice, very different from the myths current at the time. The final phase, after 1973, marked a return to the conditions typical of most of the century but made worse by the increasing scale and complexity of the international monetary and financial system, which placed it beyond any controls. There were some common problems in all these periods. The international economy required some recognized monetary unit for transactions; a method for dealing with trade and therefore monetary balances as some states accumulated surpluses and others deficits; an ability to adjust to shifts in the values of national currencies and a willingness among states to accept the minimal rules of the system and also to make adjustments to their domestic policies as international pressures dictated.

In the period from 1900 to 1914 world trade was dominated by Europe, partly because the United States was almost entirely self-sufficient. Primary products – minerals and food – accounted for nearly two-thirds of all world trade. The mid-nineteenth century regime of low tariffs had long disappeared, with the average American tariff at nearly 60 per cent; most European states, especially Germany, were moving in the same direction. Only Britain, Denmark and the Netherlands were still free trade states (Japan was forced by treaty to be a free trade state until 1911). However, this did not stop world trade growing steadily at a faster rate than output was rising. The period also saw a doubling in international capital movements as states such as Britain and France increased their investments abroad. The biggest share went to other European states, in particular Russia, the white settlement colonies of the British empire and Latin America. For some economies this investment had a major impact. In Argentina in 1913 foreign investments were worth three times its gross national product and the whole of the railway system was owned by the British. The increasing level and complexity of world trade were followed by the evolution of a multilateral payments network, which reduced the need for the physical movement of assets such as gold and silver between countries to pay for trade. By 1914, however, this still covered only a quarter of world trade and the relatively unsophisticated nature of the world financial system can be judged from the fact that all other transactions were settled bilaterally. There was no attempt to produce any formal institutional structure to 'manage' the international economy and financial system.

After the First World War it became an article of faith that the world financial system before 1914 had functioned well because it operated on a Gold Standard. In theory under this system each currency had a fixed gold content and therefore if its value got too far out of line because of a trading deficit or inflation then gold would flow out of the country. This would force the country's central bank to take action either to eliminate the trading deficit or to deflate the economy by raising interest rates in order to restore the value of the currency, thereby keeping the exchange rate between currencies stable. Ideally the system was believed to be a self-regulating and automatic way of ensuring stability in the world system. It worked, it was believed, because of Britain's key role in the financial system, because of sterling's central role as the unit of account in world trade and the fixed relationship between sterling and gold.

In practice the system emerged by accident in the latter part of the nineteenth century, worked for reasons that had little to do with the theory and was already showing signs of strain before 1914. There was no single world financial system before 1914. A gold as opposed to a bimetallic gold and silver standard was not established in western Europe until 1878 and effectively in the United States a year later, although not legally until 1900. However, large parts of the world – China, most of Latin America and parts of Africa – remained on a silver standard. Britain, or rather the financial institutions of the City of London, were at the centre of world finances before 1914. This reflected the position of Britain as the largest trader in the world, its role as the biggest single source of overseas investment and the sophistication and standing of its financial institutions. In practice, though, gold was not used very much to settle international debts and finance trade. This was done mainly by sterling bills of exchange.

The international financial system before 1914 was therefore less a Gold Standard than a sterling–Gold Standard which rested ultimately on the free convertibility of sterling into gold. The problem was that Britain only held a fifth of the world's gold reserves and this was insufficient to back all transactions. The system continued to function for a number of reasons. Britain was in substantial trade deficit with the rest of the world, only partly offset by India's trade surplus and British control of the sub-continent, which enabled them to commandeer Indian resources to bolster their own position. Britain did, however, run a substantial surplus on 'invisible' items such as finance, shipping and insurance, which produced an overall national surplus. This financial surplus was put back into the international financial system by British overseas investment, which kept the international system in rough balance and helped to maintain confidence. Before 1914, however, it was becoming clear, with the emergence of the United States as the biggest economy in the world, that New York was beginning to challenge London as the world's financial centre. Any shift towards a sterling–dollar standard or disruption of the trade-invisibles balance in Britain would be highly disruptive and call into question the delicate and fortuitous circumstances that kept the system functioning. In practice the pre-1914 financial system was not highly stable and worked for the most part because international trade and financial flows were relatively small in relation to the size of national economies and financial reserves and therefore their potential to cause disruption was limited.

The First World War shattered that system for ever. The strain of financing not just its own war effort but also the overseas purchases of its allies ruined Britain's financial position. The national debt rose from £650 million to over £7,400 million so that interest charges took up 40 per cent of the budget after 1919. Although Britain was a creditor of its European allies, Russia repudiated the debt after the 1917 Revolution and Britain had not only sold its assets in the United States but also run up a debt of £1,365 million. The attempt to set up a system whereby German reparations helped to pay off Allied debts to Britain, which then used the money to pay off its debt to the Americans, failed when it became clear as soon as the early 1920s that the massive reparations payments imposed on Germany under the Treaty of Versailles could not be enforced. By the end of the war the United States had accumulated nearly 45 per cent of the world's gold reserves while Britain held less than 10 per cent. Any attempt to create a world financial system after 1919 had to take into account these changes and the increasing importance of New York as a world financial centre.

Trade patterns were also disrupted after 1918, in particular by the introduction in 1922 of the Fordney–McCumber tariff (the highest ever) by the United States. This resulted in a major drop in European exports to the United States and made it much more difficult for European states to earn dollars to pay off their war debts. Because the Americans held so much gold, other countries tried to stabilize their currencies by holding currencies convertible into gold: the pound and the dollar. This meant that both the United

States and Britain needed to hold more gold than was necessary just to back their own financial transactions. The United States could do this, Britain could not (and had not done so before 1914). The British situation was made worse by the decision in 1925 to restore the pre-1914 exchange rate for the pound against the dollar. This was intended to signal that Britain was restoring the pre-1914 financial system and reasserting its predominant role in that system. The result was an overvalued pound, a further decline in British exports and so a further weakening of the British position.

The financial system of the 1920s was only kept afloat by American loans to Europe at a time when the British could no longer play their pre-war role. The system's fragility was demonstrated by the impact of the worldwide depression that began in 1929. Industrial production was already in steep decline in the United States before the stock market crash in September, which undermined the financial system and caused the collapse of a large number of weak, poorly regulated banks. The international financial system magnified the consequences of the collapse across the world, leading to more bank failures in Germany and Austria. In the United States gross domestic product fell by almost a third between 1929 and 1932 and unemployment affected almost a quarter of the workforce. Argentina and Brazil left the Gold Standard by 1930, but the crucial decision came in September 1931 when the British too abandoned it. By the end of 1932 over thirty other countries had followed the British and in April 1933 the Americans also allowed the dollar to float. A rump of European states around France stayed with gold until 1936 when they too finally gave up the struggle.

The weakness of international co-operation in dealing with these problems was symbolized by the failure of the World Economic Conference in London in June 1933. The national actions that were taken only exacerbated the problems. In the 1920s world trade expanded more slowly than the overall growth in output, but the trade restrictions imposed after 1929 made the situation far worse. Tariffs rose sharply, starting with the American Smoot–Hawley Act of 1930. The key decision though was the final abandonment of free trade by the British in 1932 with a general 10 per cent tariff, which was quickly raised to over 30 per cent for key products such as steel and chemicals. Even more damaging was the introduction of physical quotas on imports, started by France in 1932 and spreading to nearly thirty countries by the end of the decade.

These trends were compounded by a series of regional trade

agreements – the Danube group (Hungary, Romania, Yugoslavia and Bulgaria), the 1934 Rome agreement (Italy, Austria and Hungary), the Oslo group (the Nordic and Benelux countries) and, most important of all, the Ottawa agreements of 1932, which established a preferential trade system within the British empire. In some places the normal mechanisms of trade broke down altogether: in 1932 Hungary and Czechoslovakia were reduced to exchanging eggs for coal. In parallel with trade restrictions a series of currency blocs emerged. The sterling area based on London included most of the empire (though not Canada) and some other states with close trading links with Britain. The dollar area was dominated by the United States and included Canada and most of Latin America. The yen area was based on Tokyo and included parts of the Far East. On the continent of Europe there was an exchange control area in east and central Europe, which was dominated by Germany, and a gold bloc of Belgium, France, the Netherlands and Switzerland. Complex trade deals were struck between different blocs, such as the Anglo-American agreement of 1938 and the Anglo-German agreement of 1934, which limited German imports from Britain in any month to 55 per cent of its exports to Britain two months earlier.

One of the worst affected areas was Latin America, which had earlier been able to cope relatively well with the disruption caused by the First World War. After 1929, however, with the massive global decrease in industrial output there was a major decline in the demand for primary products and prices fell sharply, which significantly altered the terms of trade by making imports relatively expensive. For economies largely dependent on the export of primary products this was a massive shock, causing social disruption, and nearly every Latin American political system collapsed under the resulting strain. In addition, the world financial crisis and the emergence of currency blocs which tended to lend money only to their members dried up capital flows from Europe and the United States. The Latin American countries left the Gold Standard and introduced exchange controls, trade discrimination and quantitative restrictions. In the three years after 1929 exports fell by a third and imports by almost two-thirds and neither recovered for the rest of the decade. By the mid-1930s nearly every country in the region had defaulted on its debts, although without retaliation from the lenders.

At the end of the Second World War the victorious allies designed an international trade and finance system – the only time such an attempt was made in the twentieth century. The blueprint that emerged not surprisingly reflected the interests of the United States as the largest economy in the world – it made over half the manufactured goods in the world and held over half the gold reserves. The plan was built around two pillars: an International Monetary Fund to help manage the financial system and an International Trade Organization to promote multilateral free trade and end discriminatory systems. The IMF was to be funded by quotas of gold, dollars and national currency, which were determined by national wealth and importance in world trade. Voting rights were determined by quota, which allowed the Americans to dominate the IMF. The world financial system was to be a multilateral payments system based on the worldwide convertibility of currencies by 1952. There were to be no exchange controls and exchange rates would be stabilized by pegging national currencies to within 2 per cent of the dollar–gold rate. Countries in balance-of-payments deficit would be able to draw resources from the IMF in order to provide support while corrective action was taken. Later mythology holds that the 'golden age' of the world economy from 1950 to 1973 with its rapid growth rates, even faster increase in world trade, low unemployment and relatively low inflation, was the consequence of the regime constructed at the end of the Second World War. However, in practice the system devised in 1944–6 never operated as the theory suggested, most of its aims were not achieved and the exact reasons for the quarter-century of unusually favourable conditions in the world economy remain unclear.

Some of the problems experienced after the First World War were avoided in 1949 when, led by Britain, nineteen countries devalued their currencies by about 30 per cent against the dollar. The IMF was established in 1947, but for a number of reasons was of little importance until the late 1950s. The funds that it had available were less than half those which the United States provided in Marshall Aid for the European recovery programme. However, the United States could not let the IMF operate as intended. For about a decade after the war there was an acute shortage of dollars in the world because of the huge American trade surplus – the United States provided a third of the world's exports but accounted for only a tenth of the imports. Under IMF rules the dollar should have been declared a 'scarce currency', which would then have allowed other countries to impose controls on American exports. This the American government could not accept. Neither did full convertibility of currencies operate. The British maintained the sterling area with free movement of the pound within the bloc but with a single account (controlled in London) for external payments. The British tried full convertibility of sterling for a very short period in 1947 (as required by the Americans), but did not have the currency reserves to allow the countries which held sterling to convert their holdings into dollars. In Western Europe the highly successful European Payments Union provided a mechanism to help national currencies and avoid domination by the dollar.

For only a short period between 1958 and 1964 did the system envisaged at the end of the war operate in anything like the way intended. By the late 1950s the huge American trade surplus disappeared because of the recovery by the European economies and the increasing level of American military spending abroad. This enabled the European states to dismantle their protective currency arrangements and full convertibility of currencies was finally achieved between 1958 and 1961. The dollar was fixed at a gold price of $35 an ounce, which was maintained by central bank co-operation through the London gold pool, producing a system which was much closer to the pre-1914 Gold Standard than had been intended at the end of the war. IMF quotas were also increased in the early 1960s and countries, beginning with Britain during the Suez crisis in 1956, started to borrow from the fund to help cope with balance-of-payments and other financial difficulties.

In retrospect it is clear that the period from 1958 to 1964 was no more than a temporary calm before trends which had been apparent as early as the late 1950s overwhelmed the system. The basic reason for the collapse was that the United States was not prepared to accept the disciplines imposed on it under the post-war system. The continuing American trade deficit combined with high military spending abroad, made worse by the Vietnam War after 1965, provided enough dollars to finance world trade but meant that other states accumulated large quantities of dollars as foreign exchange reserves. By the late 1960s these exceeded the level of American gold holdings and therefore the system could only be maintained as long as other states were prepared not to cash their holdings of dollars. The whole system came to depend on 'confidence' in the United States. However, the United States refused to take action to meet the problem, preferring to print money to finance its geopolitical policies and extensive domestic spending rather than accept the disciplines which lesser states running massive balance-of-payments deficits had to take under the IMF system.

By the late 1960s the strains were showing. The British found that their small reserves and poor economic performance made it difficult to sustain even the limited role sterling had in the international system in that decade. They had to make extensive borrowings from the IMF, negotiate support from the United States and deflate their economy; but it was all to no avail and the pound was devalued in November 1967. Meanwhile the problems caused by the United States continued to worsen. Their balance-of-payments deficit increased and their gold holdings fell by nearly 40 per cent in the 1960s. Japan and West Germany were accumulating vast foreign-exchange reserves because of their trade surpluses, but under IMF rules there was no requirement on them to take any action to correct the situation. The amount of gold available was inadequate to fund the huge increase in world trade and in 1970 the IMF started creating an artificial unit (Special Drawing Rights), but it still only controlled less than a fifth of the world's liquidity.

The post-war system finally collapsed after a series of decisions in the eighteen months following August 1971. First, the United States ended the convertibility of the dollar into gold (in effect, the equivalent of the British coming off the Gold Standard in 1931) and imposed an import surcharge. Both were in violation of IMF rules. In December 1971 the Smithsonian agreement between the ten major core states was supposed to be no more than a temporary realignment of currencies, involving the devaluation of the dollar by 10 per cent and wider bands for currency fluctuation, but the arrangements became permanent. After the Smithsonian meeting the IMF was unable to come up with any long-term reform plan and the Paris agreements in March 1973 marked the end of the post-war system. The dollar had been devalued by another 10 per cent the month before, the West Germans agreed to revalue the mark and a European 'snake' was introduced to keep some rough stability in exchange rates. This was thought necessary because the idea of fixed exchange rates was finally abandoned. The artificial gold price and the gold pool went too: the price of gold rapidly tripled to over $100 an ounce. The IMF was circumvented through reciprocal swap agreements between central banks. Governments were pitched into a new world in which they had little control over international financial markets.

The other supposed pillar of the post-war system – free trade – similarly was never implemented. The Americans' original intention was to create an International Trade Organization (ITO) with the sweeping aim of ending all preferential systems – which would benefit the United States as the world's dominant economy. This proposal was rejected by the Western Europeans and the more modest negotiating body, the General Agreement on Tariffs and Trade (GATT), came into being instead. It had some success as a forum for negotiations and in reducing tariffs between the core states (by the mid-1950s US tariffs were at half their levels of twenty years earlier), but from the start it failed to implement either of the two key elements which would liberalize world trade – the universal application of the Most-Favoured-Nation clause and the no-new-preferences rule. GATT also included three exceptions which provided significant let-outs from free trade. Import quotas could be imposed in times of balance-of-payments difficulties and to protect new industries. Also agricultural products subject to government price support were exempted from free trade. In addition GATT was unable to deal with the emergence of customs unions after 1945, which began with the Benelux countries but by the late 1950s had moved on to the European Economic Community, which was highly discriminatory and produced significant trade diversion. Other trading blocs followed in Central America (although this bloc collapsed in the early 1970s), the Andes after 1969, Central Africa, West Africa and the Caribbean. The expansion of the EEC in 1973 with the admission of Britain, Ireland and Denmark, and later Greece, Spain and Portugal, was followed by the creation of a single market in the early 1990s and the accession of Sweden, Finland and Austria, resulting in the largest trading bloc in the world. The American response was the North American Free Trade Agreement (NAFTA) in 1988, its first clear break with the GATT ideal of multilateralism, with the aim of producing a single US-Canadian market by the end of the twentieth century. Mexico was included after 1993.

GATT's main success was in reducing tariffs on manufactured goods traded between the core states. The so-called Kennedy round of negotiations which ended in 1967 was the most successful, lowering tariffs by about 40 per cent; the following Tokyo round of 1973–9 was much less successful. Nevertheless, by the late 1980s industrial tariffs within the core were low – about 6 per cent at most. However, this figure disguised the parallel growth in non-tariff barriers to trade: anti-dumping regulations; special labelling and packaging regulations; customs procedures and regulations (at one time France required all imported video recorders to pass through a single warehouse in Poitiers) and import quotas. The most significant development was, however, the rise of 'voluntary' export restraint agreements. By the mid-1980s there were over a hundred of these in the world. Nine out of ten of them protected the European Community, the United States and Canada and two-thirds affected exports by Japan and South Korea. The differing importance of tariffs and non-tariff barriers is well illustrated by developments in the world car market. In 1960 Britain and France had a 30 per cent tariff, Japan 40 per cent. Thirty years later the European Community (EC) tariff was 11 per cent, the United States 3 per cent and Japan did not impose one. However, in 1981 the United States forced through a voluntary agreement with Japan, which placed a volume limit on imports and left the Japanese government to allocate shares between its car manufacturers. NAFTA also specifically excluded Japanese cars made in Canada from the free trade provisions, although this did not apply to US cars made in Canada. In the EC the Japanese market share was restricted to 11 per cent in Britain, 3 per cent in France and Italy only allowed in 3,000 vehicles a year.

GATT was dominated by the core states – initially they alone were members, but even growth to a membership of over a hundred countries by the 1980s did not change the structure. GATT made no attempt to deal with the inequitable trade structure in the world and refused to negotiate in the United Nations Conference on Trade and Development (UNCTAD), established in 1964, which was dominated by the states of the periphery as a forum for their demands for a New International Economic Order. Indeed, the Uruguay round of GATT negotiations, which lasted from 1986 to 1994, was largely about opening up markets in the periphery to the service industries of the core. One of the major GATT 'achievements' was to restrict textile exports from the periphery. In 1962–73 the Long Term Agreement Regarding International Trade in Cotton Textiles limited the growth in imports to 5 per cent a year. This agreement was replaced in 1974 by the first of a series of Multi-Fibre Agreements (MFAs) covering all textiles. Although in theory they allowed import growth of 6 per cent a year, in practice each MFA was more restrictive than its predecessor, with more and more tariffs against countries of the periphery but not other core states. Overall MFAs cut the growth in periphery textile exports by three-quarters.

A new phase in the world economy began in 1973 after the collapse of the post-war financial system and the quintupling of the price of oil. It was marked by much slower growth in output, slower growth in world trade, higher levels of unemployment and greater inflation. It also saw an unprecedented increase in world financial transactions, with huge flows of money around the globe, the development of world financial markets, liberalization of those markets and the loss of any remaining government control over their operation. The first signs of this trend came in the early 1960s with the development of the eurodollar market. The growing American payments deficit produced a surplus of dollars in Europe, which investors did not want to move to the United States because of low interest rates and government controls. Instead an unregulated market developed in London which was worth $9 billion in 1964 and $57 billion by the end of the decade. The huge flows of funds to the oil-producing countries after the 1973–4 price rise caused another increase in the eurodollar market because these states feared political interference if they placed their funds in the United States. By 1981 the eurodollar market was worth $661 billion. The growing US trade deficit caused the eurodollar market to more than triple in the 1980s to over $2,800 billion, making it more than thirty times bigger than in the early 1960s. With the removal of all foreign-exchange controls in the core states by the early 1980s, dealings across the world mounted sharply from $100 billion a day in 1979 to four times that level by the end of the decade – an annual turnover of $100 trillion. A global market in equities also emerged in the 1980s worth about $1,000 billion. All these markets were no longer related to the world trade in physical goods. By the late 1980s the London eurodollar market was turning over twenty-five times the level of world trade annually and at the same time foreign exchange markets were ten times bigger than the level of world trade.

Having liberalized markets and accepted floating exchange rates, governments found that they could no longer control international financial markets. Indeed their ability even to influence them was limited by the sheer scale of the money flows and the very limited reserves governments had available. Regular attempts were made – the Plaza and Louvre accords of the late 1980s and regular meetings of heads of government and finance ministers of the G7 (the major core countries) – but they all failed once a short-term adjustment was over. The European Monetary System collapsed under market pressure in 1992–3. Nevertheless some government policies were important, in particular those of the United States. After 1973 the USA, as before, refused to play by the rules of the game. Until 1978 it attempted to deal with its chronic payments deficit and assert its supremacy by devaluing the dollar. When it found states were unwilling to hold dollars, the only alternative was a massive rise in interest rates. This rise, combined with a further increase in oil prices in 1979–80, proved catastrophic for many countries in the periphery, in particular Latin America. Their external debts rose seventeen-fold in the two decades after 1970 and repayments, especially at very high rates of interest, often took up over three-quarters of export earnings. Unlike the situation in the 1930s, the core states were able to stop any widespread default and insist on repayment regardless of the cost. The result was a net flow of funds from the poorest states in the world to the richest of about $30 billion a year by the late 1980s. The United States also continued to run a huge balance-of-payments deficit (in total $763 billion in the last half of the 1980s) and also, after 1980, a huge fiscal deficit of about $200 billion a year. The world financial system was kept afloat by the willingness of West Germany and Japan to provide the United States with extensive credit and to invest there. American net assets abroad of $141 billion in 1982 turned into a debt of $1 trillion a decade later. The chronic American trade and fiscal deficit was financed by the savings of citizens in Japan, Western Europe, South Korea and Taiwan. The problem of American irresponsibility linked to its power to ignore the rules that applied to other states, which originally emerged in the late 1950s, remained unresolved by the end of the century but was by then on a massive scale.

The huge growth in world trade and the creation of an increasingly complex global financial system were two aspects of increasing integration within a world economy dominated by the core states. Another was the rise of the transnational corporation (TNC), a company with a national identity but with operations and assets across the globe. By the end of the century half of the 100 largest economic entities in the world were states and half were corporations. The Exxon oil company in the 1990s had a turnover six times bigger than Morocco's gross national product and General Motors had a turnover twice the GNP of Egypt. Until well into the twentieth century transnational corporations were almost entirely confined to the extractive industries, in particular oil, and agricultural commodities. For example, the American-owned United Fruit Company dominated the economies (and politics) of many Central American states. The major exceptions to this picture were the two American car giants, Ford and General Motors. Ford opened its first overseas plant in Windsor, Ontario as early as 1904 and moved into Europe with the opening of the Trafford Park plant in Manchester in 1911 and a Bordeaux plant in 1913. After the First World War Ford built new plants in Berlin and Cologne and, in 1931, the massive integrated plant at Dagenham in east London. General Motors did not build their own plants, but instead bought up foreign firms, starting with the Canadian firm McLoughlin in 1918 and moving into Europe with the purchase of Vauxhall in 1926 and Opel in 1929.

Until the mid-twentieth century most TNCs followed a relatively simple corporate strategy of allowing largely autonomous subsidiaries to operate in separate national markets with the profits being repatriated to the parent country. Most TNCs were American (the next largest national group was British), but they usually only operated in a small number of countries. In 1950 only three of the top 315 TNCs had manufacturing subsidiaries in more than twenty countries and less than a third of British TNCs operated in more than six countries. In the second half of the century this picture changed radically. By the late 1960s the formation rate of overseas manufacturing subsidiaries by TNCs was running at ten times the rate of the 1920s and the original domination of American firms was changing. Major TNCs emerged in Germany, Japan and, by the end of the century, South Korea. The main areas of TNC operation were, in order of importance, petrochemicals, cars, consumer electronics, tyres, pharmaceuticals, tobacco, soft drinks, fast food, financial consultancies and luxury hotels. Although these firms kept a distinct national ethos, their operations were becoming increasingly international. Over 40 per cent of the assets of IBM and Ford were overseas and for Ford, Unilever, ITT and the Dutch group, Philips, over half of their employment was abroad. TNCs from smaller countries were even more international – the Swiss-Swedish corporation Asea, Brown Boveri and Philips made over four-fifths of their sales overseas. Increasingly TNCs were adopting globally integrated strategies, removing independent local subsidiaries and treating the corporation's activities as a single unit.

By the end of the century the impact of TNCs on national economies was enormous, but variable from country to country. About a quarter of all production in the core states was controlled by TNCs. In international trade the domination was far greater. The old idea of international trade being about a national firm buying or selling in an overseas market was outdated – by the 1980s a third of all world trade took place as transactions within transnational corporations. About a half of all American and Japanese imports and exports was trade within TNCs and about four-fifths of Britain's manufactured exports was made up of intra-firm trade between British enterprises and their foreign affiliates or within foreign-controlled firms operating in Britain. Foreign domination of national economies was apparent in some core countries. In Canada four out of ten workers were employed in, and half of all manufacturing production came from, foreign firms (in Japan the comparative figures were less than 1 per cent for both). Some states tried to influence TNCs to set up operations on their soil through the creation of Export Processing Zones (EPZs) – enclaves outside customs laws and often other national legislation such as labour protection laws. By the early 1990s there were nearly 200 such zones in the world; the largest was along the Mexican border with the United States – the *maquiladoras* or assembly plants which enjoyed free imports as long as their products were exported. They employed over 400,000 people.

In many cases the impact of TNCs, especially in the periphery, was to create 'enclave economies' which had very little relationship with the national economy. For example, the huge iron-ore mines in Mauritania sent their ore to the coast on a company railway to a company-owned port, where it was exported in company-owned ships to be processed by another part of the TNC. Although the exports officially counted as Mauritania's, they had almost no impact on the local economy. Similarly in 1957 the US aluminium corporations outbid the British to develop a bauxite industry in newly independent Ghana. The companies were to build the Volta dam to generate electricity to power the smelter, but they refused to let the Ghanaian government have a stake in the project. The smelter took two-thirds of the electricity generated by the dam so that by 1980 fewer than one in twenty of Ghana's population had access to electricity and the country was reduced to importing electricity from the Ivory Coast. The US companies had a monopoly over bauxite exploitation and the rate of development was determined by their requirements rather than those of the local economy. The companies also received large tax benefits and were able to take their profits out of the country through complex transfer pricing.

EPZs were only one aspect of a general trend towards the internationalization of production, especially among TNCs. A simple example could be found in the car industry. In the early 1960s Ford designed and built the Cortina in Britain for the British market. Twenty years later its replacement, the Escort, was a multinational car designed for the European market, assembled at three plants – Valencia, Saarlouis and Dagenham – but incorporating parts made in fifteen countries. Another example was the Japanese washing-machine manufacturer, Matushita. It had an agreement with a Malaysian manufacturer to supply both domestic markets and exports. The outer case, control unit and drive shaft were made in Japan, the motor in Taiwan, the condenser in Thailand, the valve magnet in South Korea and the rest in Malaysia. But even some of these parts were subdivided so that the motor was put together using parts made in Japan and Canada. Corporations sub-contracted operations around the world in order to take advantage of cheap labour or other cost savings. For example, precision drilling for Swiss watches took place in Mauritius and rapid telecommunications created data-processing industries in low-wage areas such as south-east Asia and the Caribbean. Some corporations 'disintegrated' in order to take advantage of this form of production: by the end of the century the Nike footwear company, which had its headquarters in Oregon, did not own any production facilities but instead sub-contracted manufacture to a number of firms in south-east Asia.

Oil was the greatest example of an industry dominated by transnational corporations. Until the late 1960s the international economic relationships of the industry central to the world economy were administered within corporations and consortia formed by those corporations. They controlled the discovery and exploitation of reserves, the location of refining and distribution, the flow of investment, the structure and level of prices and government revenues. The industry also demonstrated the imbalance of political and economic power between the core and the periphery, especially in the early twentieth century: governments in the periphery, often under severe political pressure from the core states, were forced to grant extensive concessions to the oil companies on highly disadvantageous terms. The governments of the core were able to take a tougher stance – the American government prohibited the foreign ownership of oil resources and, during the development of the North Sea field after the mid-1960s, the British and Norwegian governments insisted on retaining ownership and allocating licences to a multitude of firms.

The modern structure of the industry was set in 1912 when the US government forced the break-up of the Rockefeller-owned Standard Oil Company, which controlled 90 per cent of US sales and made an average annual profit of 25 per cent. However, the outcome left the various Standard Oil subsidiaries in a strong position in an industry dominated by the 'Seven Sisters': Exxon (Standard Oil of New Jersey), Chevron (Standard Oil of California), Mobil (Standard Oil of New York), Gulf Oil, Texaco, British Petroleum (originally Anglo-Persian) and Royal Dutch-Shell. By 1949 the Seven Sisters owned, outside the United States and Soviet Union, over four-fifths of known reserves, nearly nine-tenths of crude oil production, over three-quarters of refining capacity, two-thirds of the oil tanker fleet and nearly all the pipelines. With demand for oil growing steadily and inexorably, the major companies were in a position to dictate nearly every aspect of the industry's operations, prices and profits. Through a complex series of anti-competitive deals they were able, in a way not found in any other industry, to control production, maintain prices, agree and keep to almost fixed market shares in the steadily expanding overall market and stop price discounting on sales. In these circumstances they could hardly fail to make huge profits.

The basis for the Seven Sisters' operation was agreement on exploitation of reserves. Before the First World War the British had forced through a virtual monopoly on Persian oil for the Anglo-Persian company and a dominant position in Kuwait. In 1920, under the San Remo Treaty, the British and French awarded themselves a monopoly of oil concessions in the former Ottoman empire. However, they could not maintain this when vast oilfields were discovered in Iraq; American pressure and threats by Exxon to cut back supplies to Britain, where they controlled half the market, resulted in the so-called 'red-line agreement' of 1928. This carved up the area within the 'red line' of the old Ottoman empire between different consortia (Kuwait was controlled by BP and Gulf). The companies agreed, first, to negotiate as a body within the area and, second, that the three largest companies should be able to exercise a veto. This agreement was maintained as new fields were developed (Saudi Arabia was exploited by the Aramco consortium of Texaco, Chevron, Mobil and Exxon) and as political shifts occurred (American firms took a greater share of Iranian production after the restoration of the Shah in 1953). Because the companies negotiated as a cartel in the Gulf it was almost impossible for the host governments to obtain reasonable terms. The companies were also able to determine the revenues of the Gulf states by altering the rate of extraction and through a price structure which benefited the companies. Since the refining and distribution of crude oil were controlled by the same companies which controlled production, the producer states were unable to break away and market their own oil.

The final parts of the highly anti-competitive agreements to secure the position of the Seven Sisters were the Achnacarry Agreement of 1928 and the London Committee, which was established in 1934. The former controlled marketing by dividing up the world market between the companies in the proportions they held in 1928. In order to control the price, as cheap Middle East oil competed with that from the United States and Venezuela, the companies agreed that the world price would be calculated by adding shipping costs to the Gulf of Mexico price. This meant that in the 1930s oil from Iraq (which cost eight cents a barrel to produce) was sold as though it were US oil (which cost seventy-seven cents a barrel to produce) plus transportation costs. This deal created a completely artificial price and left the oil companies with huge profits. From the early 1930s, after the massive East Texas field came into production, the US price, which was the key to the world price, was also set artificially by the peculiarly named Texas Railroad Commission. The London Committee was empowered to review shifts in market shares and impose 'fines' against companies which exceeded their agreed market share and pay 'compensation' to those who fell short. There were also complex deals between the companies so that those with an excess of crude oil sold it to those who had an excess of refining capacity to ensure that no real market in oil developed which would affect the artificial price created by the companies.

These arrangements were highly disadvantageous to the producer countries and demonstrate the power of both the core states and the oil companies to control the key resource for the growth in output and energy consumption in the core countries. Until the 1950s the host government received a small payment based on the tonnage exported, not the price. After 1950 the oil companies, starting with the Aramco consortium in Saudi Arabia, calculated a notional 'posted price' for crude oil so that they could offset their payments to the host governments against US tax. Deals were struck with the host governments for a 50:50 split of the posted price, but this simply gave the companies an incentive to keep this price as low as possible and make their profits from refining, transporting and marketing. In general the price of oil was maintained at about ten times the marginal cost of production. For example in 1970, of the West European price of oil just 6 per cent went to the producer governments, 42 per cent to the companies and 52 per cent to the governments of the importing countries as tax.

Attempts by producer governments to get better terms began with the creation of state oil companies in Mexico (1938) and Brazil (1940), but they had little impact given the overall control by the major companies. In the early 1950s the companies and the British and American governments were able to defeat Iranian national-ization of the Anglo-Iranian company by organizing a boycott which cut Iranian output by 90 per cent. The situation began to change in 1959–60 when the companies unilaterally cut the price of Middle East and Venezuelan crude so as to reduce revenues to the host governments. This led to the creation of the Organization of Petroleum Exporting Countries (OPEC). At first OPEC could do little more than stop further price reductions, but it was gradually able to develop cohesion and in 1968 asserted the right of the producer states to set prices. It was helped by the growing import-ance of independent oil companies such as Continental in Libya, state firms such as the Italian ENI and the French companies exploiting Algerian oilfields, all of whom were more willing to compromise with the host governments. The key moment came in 1968 after the Libyan revolution, when the new government asserted control over the country's oil and the independent companies accepted the position and continued to market the oil. This emboldened other governments to take the same course, forcing the abandonment of the old concessionary regime and demanding price increases. In 1971 OPEC was able to insist on an immediate 20 per cent national share of production, with a majority share to be reached within a decade as staff gained expertise and state oil companies took over exploitation and production. Once control over production was obtained the producer governments were able to set prices, though they were only able to act as an effective cartel for limited periods – for example in 1973–4 when a quintupling of the price of crude oil was enforced.

By the early 1980s the Seven Sisters had access to less than half of Middle East production, and that was under contract from state companies. In Latin America, Mexico and Venezuela owned and marketed their own oil. The market share of the Seven Sisters fell to less than half. The growing wealth of the oil-producing states brought about a remarkable transformation when, in the late 1980s,

Kuwait became the major shareholder in British Petroleum and began marketing its own oil in Britain. Although these changes corrected some of the huge imbalances in power and influence apparent during the first seventy years of the century it did not mean that the producer states could dominate the market. Political differences meant that the OPEC cartel could not be sustained, particularly given Saudi Arabian willingness to increase production to break the cartel. By the mid-1990s the price of oil was, in real terms, back to the level of the early 1970s. Although the power of the major oil companies was reduced, it was still substantial. They could no longer dictate the price of oil, but they were still a major influence over it and competition was still limited.

Over the century growing world trade, a complex and rapidly expanding global financial system, the greater internationalization of production and the activities of transnational corporations led to greater integration of the world's economies. Over the century most states in the periphery had little control over their economies either as colonies or later as politically independent but economically subordinate states. However, the ability of the core states to exert national control over their economies declined too. In the international financial system before 1914 what control there was came about largely because the level of world trade and financial flows were small, especially in relation to the size of national economies. After 1945, when a concerted effort was made to exert political control over the system, it could not survive the rapid growth in world trade and the development of global financial markets utilizing money that was beyond national control. After 1973 the core states decided to deregulate the system, partly in the mistaken belief that this would increase national growth and wealth. In practice deregulation left them subject to the shocks created by the system and unable to do much more than adjust national policy when it got too far out of line with the demands of the financial markets.

6 ECONOMIES

ALL THE economies in the world in the twentieth century were influenced by the major forces of population growth, technological change, increasing production, greater energy consumption, rising world trade and financial flows and the internationalization of production. However, the way in which they were affected, and their ability to respond to these forces, were very different and depended on their position in the world economy. Over the course of the century one of the most striking facts about the world economy was the stability of the general structure of core, semi-periphery and periphery. There was very little movement within this structure, apart from Japan: the states that made up the core in 1900 were still in the same position at the end of the century, as were nearly all those in the periphery. Every state became wealthier, but the problem faced by many of the less industrialized states was that, although they found it relatively easy to adopt the latest technology, this did not enable them to break the grip that the core states held over the world economy. They became more industrialized and wealthier, but the core states were moving just as fast, if not faster, and had started from a more advanced position. The huge differences in wealth between different states that were apparent in 1900 remained throughout the century, indeed in many cases they grew bigger.

In 1900 the United States was the largest industrialized economy in the world, a position it was to retain throughout the century. It had taken over the leading role from Britain in about 1890 during its period of sustained industrial expansion after 1870, which saw its GDP more than quadruple in the last third of the nineteenth century. In 1900 the United States made about a third of the world's manufactured output, but with its large internal market only about a tenth of the world's manufactured exports, less than a third of the British level. American domination of the world economy increased in the first part of the century: by the late 1920s it made over 40 per cent of the world's manufactured goods. It faltered in the 1930s but reached a peak of nearly 50 per cent in 1950 as the other core economies were still recovering from the Second World War. Some decline from this position was inevitable, but although the American economy continued to grow in the second half of the century, its predominant position was steadily eroded as other states grew. In 1948 US industrial production was ten times that of West Germany, twenty years later it was only four times as big. Its share of world industrial production fell to below 30 per cent by the late 1980s and its share of world trade was back to 1900 levels. In 1950 the United States made over three-quarters of all the cars in the world, by the early 1990s less than a fifth. By the end of the century it was also clear that the United States was losing some of the advantages it had enjoyed for more than a century. Its natural resources had been heavily exploited and therefore costs were rising. Changes in bulk transportation technology allowed Europe and Japan easy access to bigger, low-cost resources. The size of the American internal market was also no longer a unique asset – by the end of the century the European Union was bigger.

The second most dynamic economy in 1900 was that of Germany. Industrialization came late in the nineteenth century, but the economy had moved rapidly from industries typical of early growth (railways, iron and steel) into chemicals and electrical engineering – by 1907 Germany was the world's largest producer of chemicals. During the twentieth century, despite defeat in two world wars and the catastrophic inflation of the early 1920s, Germany enjoyed steady but largely unspectacular growth and maintained its position as one of the top three economies within the core. In 1900 France was still well behind both Britain and Germany in output and wealth, partly because of low population growth and a lack of coal and iron ore, the two key resources for early industrialization. France was, however, able to take advantage of the new technologies – in the early twentieth century it had the largest car industry in Europe – but for the first half of the century growth remained sluggish. In the second half of the century growth was, for much of the time, twice as fast as in Britain and enabled France to maintain its position just behind Germany as one of the major economies in the core.

Of the core economies the one relative failure in the twentieth century was Britain – its rate of growth was consistently slower than that of its rivals, causing it to become relatively poorer. By the late nineteenth century the advantages stemming from early industrialization were being steadily eroded as its industrial output was surpassed by first the United States and then Germany. The British economy made the same transitions as the other core economies – from basic industries into chemicals and cars and then electronics – but for reasons that are far from clear the economy remained less dynamic. Over the century Germany roughly maintained its share of world industrial output, but Britain suffered a clear and, in the later stages, a precipitous decline. In 1900 Britain made 20 per cent of the world's manufactured goods and 10 per cent in the period after the Second World War. By the end of the century this had fallen to about 2 per cent. In 1984 Britain became a net importer of manufactured goods for the first time in over two centuries. Economic growth in Britain was sufficient, on average, to increase wealth per head just over three-fold in the course of the century. However, in 1900 the average Briton was almost as wealthy as an American, by the end of the century average wealth was at less than two-thirds of US levels and well behind that of most other west European states.

Two economies which were only on the fringes of the core in 1900, Sweden and Switzerland, demonstrated that it was possible for relatively small states, with only limited domestic markets and few natural resources, to become some of the wealthiest in the world. Both show that it was not necessary to engage in mass production in every sector (Switzerland never had a car industry of any importance) in order to become technologically advanced economies. Instead they concentrated on a few key areas of expertise: Switzerland on foods, chemicals and pharmaceuticals, together with high-precision items such as watches and scientific instruments; Sweden on heavy trucks, cars, roller bearings and mining equipment. Each produced major transnational corporations – Hoffman-La Roche, Sandoz and Ciba-Geigy in Switzerland and Volvo, Saab-Scania, SKF and Atlas Copco in Sweden. In general they produced high-quality, expensive items for a limited market.

Italy took a different route with a markedly dual economy (industry in the north and a backward agriculture in the south) but a broad-based industrialization. Although in the first half of the century Italy was well behind Britain, France and Germany in national wealth, it was one of the most successful European economies after 1950. Overall its growth rate was three times that of

Britain and higher than France and Germany. By the end of the century it was wealthier than Britain.

The problem for the states of the semi-periphery and periphery was how to develop, grow and industrialize in a world economy which was already dominated by the core economies. These were the most technologically advanced and already made most of the world's industrial output. The economies of the rest of the world were dependent on the core and many were skewed towards producing raw materials and food, often predominantly a single commodity. In an economy which was open to imported industrial goods it was difficult for an indigenous industry to compete with the products of the core states. However, if, in response to this problem, high protective tariff barriers were introduced, they tended to produce an inefficient industry which whilst it could dominate the domestic market had little ability or incentive to export in competition with the core states. And this strategy could only hope to work in a country with a large enough population to provide a reasonable domestic market. A further problem was how to find the capital necessary for initial industrialization, although if this was available then a newly industrializing country did have the advantage of being able to adopt modern technology from the start. A number of different approaches were chosen in the twentieth century, but it was clear that industrialization required a high level of carefully thought-out government planning and support. This was needed to provide the right balance between protecting new industries and ensuring that they were competitive; to establish a clear strategy and assistance to shift steadily into more technologically advanced areas; and finally to ensure that the correct infrastructure, especially high levels of education, supported these policies. Given these problems, the strength of the core economies and the existing structure of the world economy, it is hardly surprising that only a handful of states were able to make this transformation.

Undoubtedly the most successful economy in the twentieth century was that of Japan. It was the only country in the world to move unambiguously from the semi-periphery to being one of the central core economies, second only to the United States. In the first half of the century, although Japan was industrializing it remained part of the semi-periphery, important regionally but not a major world economy. The first phase of industrialization was under way by the 1880s, but its progress remained limited – in 1900 India exported more manufactured goods than Japan and was not overtaken until the late 1920s. Early Japanese industrialization was dominated by textiles – its largest exports in 1900 were silk and cotton threads – and after gaining control of its domestic market it moved on to dominate the Chinese market; by 1935 it was exporting nearly half of all the world's textiles. In the first third of the century iron and steel production became more important and by the mid-1930s Japan was the third largest shipbuilder in the world. However, industrialization remained limited – until 1930 the majority of the labour force was still employed in agriculture and forestry. Even after recovery from the Second World War Japan showed few signs of developing into a major core economy. In the early 1950s its GNP was at one-fifteenth of the US level and half that of Germany, 40 per cent of the workforce was still employed in agriculture and it was the largest borrower from the World Bank. Most commentators were pessimistic about its future.

In the twenty years up to 1973 Japan achieved the fastest growth experienced by any economy over a substantial period. GDP grew at about 10 per cent a year so that overall it rose more than five-fold. Industrial output grew even faster, at an average of 14 per cent a year. By the late 1960s Japan was the largest shipbuilder in the world, the second largest car manufacturer and the biggest producer of key consumer items such as TVs, radios, cameras and sewing machines. In 1950 it made just 2,600 motorcycles, in 1972 over 3·5 million and rival industries across the world had succumbed to Japanese competition. By 1968 Japan had the second biggest GDP in the non-Communist world and its acceptance as a core state was symbolically ratified when it joined the Organization for Economic Co-operation and Development (OECD) in 1964.

The causes of such unprecedented growth are unclear but probably relate to a combination of factors: the movement of labour from agriculture; rapid adoption of the best available technology; very high investment rates (three times that of the United States); a highly educated workforce; long hours of work and a highly protected domestic market in which manufactured imports were either prohibited or subject to massive tariffs. The phenomenal growth rates of the 1950s and 1960s slowed after 1973, but generally remained in excess of those found elsewhere in the core. The second half of the twentieth century marked a fundamental transformation in Japan's position. In 1948 Japan made 1·6 per cent of the world's industrial output, by the 1990s nearly 15 per cent. Car production was 165,000 vehicles in 1960, but within twenty years it had overtaken the United States as the biggest producer in the world. By the 1990s it was making almost 10 million vehicles a year, half of which were exported. In the last quarter of the century Japan ran the largest trading surplus of any country and was the world's largest creditor nation. Over the course of the century its GDP per head increased nearly fifteen-fold, twice as fast as any other state and more than three times as fast as the United States.

Apart from Japan, the states of the semi-periphery in 1900 fell into two categories – the European settlement colonies of Canada, Australia, New Zealand, Argentina and Uruguay and the states of southern and eastern Europe. The former were relatively wealthy states with economies built on the export of raw materials and agricultural products, mostly to Britain, which also provided most of their investment capital especially for railway construction. In most cases they had only limited industrial sectors: the first steelworks in Australia was opened in 1915 and until the late 1960s nearly three-quarters of Australian exports consisted of wool, meat and minerals. Canada was probably the most advanced industrially because of the adjacent American market and it developed a high standard of living, which in the 1920s was close to American levels. By the mid-century Canada was a significant industrial power. New Zealand, however, remained primarily agricultural and although prosperous found its wealth in relative decline compared with other similar states.

The one clear economic failure in the twentieth century among this group of states was Argentina. In the first decade of the century its GDP per head was as high as that of Italy and twice that of Japan. By the end of the century its GDP per head had only doubled despite relatively low population growth and was about a third of the levels in Italy and Japan. The reasons for this failure were complex. The primary cause was Argentina's comparatively late start in industrialization (a couple of decades later than Canada), which coincided with the collapse of its agricultural export markets in the early 1930s and which limited foreign exchange and investment. This late start was combined with endemic political instability, partly brought on by the economic collapse, chronic inflation and the lack of a major domestic or regional market.

The southern and eastern European semi-periphery was, apart from the Czech lands of the Austro-Hungarian empire, primarily agricultural – even in the 1930s over four-fifths of the population were employed in that sector. There were a few industrial enclaves – the Bilbao region in Spain, the oilfields in Romania – but all these states remained relatively poor in the first half of the century. The available evidence suggests that the income gap between the core and semi-periphery in Europe widened between 1900 and 1950. The situation changed after 1950 when, for the next twenty years, the semi-periphery grew faster than the core. A shift away from agriculture was apparent with the development of new sectors such as tourism and, later, industry. This change was symbolized by the incorporation of Greece, Spain and Portugal into the European Community by the 1980s. By the end of the century the European semi-periphery was significantly wealthier than the great bulk of states in the rest of the world other than those in the core. The division between the northern and southern sides of the Mediterranean had also become much clearer – in 1950 the GDP per head of Egypt and Morocco was about 80 per cent of that in Portugal, by the end of the century it was about 40 per cent.

The most significant state in the European semi-periphery in 1900 was Russia, which, although it was a colonial power itself, demonstrated many of the same features as the economies of Argentina and Australia. It had vast resources but its level of development was still low. Railway construction after the 1870s was important in the first stages of agricultural commercialization and the growth of large cereal exports. New industries such as oil around Baku, metal works in the Ukraine and the shipyards of the Baltics were starting up by 1900, but this development depended on high levels of foreign investment – the oil industry was completely foreign owned, together with nearly all of the mining and half the chemical industries. From 1890 until the First World War industrial output rose at about 6 per cent a year, but the level of industrialization in 1913 was about the same as Britain a century earlier or France in 1860. In the early twentieth century Russia had a fragmented economy typical of the semi-periphery, still overwhelmingly agricultural with a poor infrastructure, limited industrialization and highly dependent on foreign investment.

The 1917 Revolution, the chaos of the civil war and the need for recovery in the first period of Soviet rule under the New Economic Policy (NEP) meant that by the late 1920s output had only just climbed back to 1913 levels. The Soviet government faced an unenviable situation. For political and strategic reasons it wanted to industrialize, but its own policies and the deep suspicions of the capitalist countries meant that it did not have access to foreign investment to finance the industrialization drive. It took a course, unique at that time, of finding the capital needed for investment from its own resources under strict state direction. Since the Soviet Union was an overwhelmingly agricultural society (three-quarters of all workers were peasants) this capital could only come from the farming sector. Intensive industrialization, combined with forcible collectivization, produced an agricultural crisis which resulted in food shortages and mass famine by the early 1930s. However, overall the policy achieved its aims. Investment doubled in the decade after 1928, iron and coal output quadrupled, electricity generation rose seven-fold and machine-tool output seventeen-fold. Even the most conservative western estimates accept that the Soviet economy grew at about 12 per cent a year in the 1930s, producing an overall quadrupling of industrial output. The Soviet government also spent heavily on the social infrastructure, matching industrialization with a mass literacy campaign for adults and a tripling in the school population. However, there were problems. In particular consumer-goods output rose only slowly and private consumption fell substantially (something which was also typical of many capitalist states in the early stages of industrialization).

Once the initial wave of phenomenally fast industrialization was over by the late 1930s problems began to emerge. Strong state direction in a situation where the information available to the government was limited and decision-taking therefore often poor, combined with the growth of state bureaucracies and empire-building, made it very difficult to produce a dynamic, technologically responsive economy. The economy remained good at producing basic industrial goods but relatively poor at making the more sophisticated products typical of the later stages of industrialization. Given its strategic situation, it is hardly surprising that the Soviet economy tended to be autarkic with low levels of foreign trade. After 1950 the growth in industrial output slowed steadily from about 15 per cent a year to less than a quarter of that figure, although that was still as good as that experienced in many of the core states. Overall in the twentieth century the Russian/Soviet economy grew to be the third largest in the world. However, although the growth in basic output was high, the overall level of sophistication in the economy, particularly in terms of technology, meant that it remained well short of the levels achieved by the core economies and Russia was still part of the semi-periphery at the end of the twentieth century. In the course of the century GDP per head increased slightly more than seven-fold, but that was no better than many other countries of the semi-periphery and worse than others such as Portugal.

However, the Soviet model of industrialization was important because it seemed to offer a different path from that found in the capitalist states. The expansion of Soviet control into Eastern Europe after 1945 meant that similar policies were tried out in these countries of the semi-periphery (only Czechoslovakia had made any major steps towards industrialization before 1945). Industrialization produced the same initially high levels of output growth (nearly 6 per cent a year in the 1950s), but like the Soviet Union these economies ran into problems in trying to shift into the consumer goods and high-technology sectors. By the 1980s, however, East Germany and Czechoslovakia had a GDP per head greater than in the USSR. The only outright failure was Romania, where the oil industry was exhausted (mainly through exporting to the Soviet Union) and agriculture still accounted for over half of all output. From the early 1970s Yugoslavia and Hungary in particular tried to move away from the Soviet model towards a more market-oriented approach, with some success in increasing growth. Overall, though, growth in Eastern Europe after 1945 was little different from growth elsewhere in the European semi-periphery in countries such as Spain and Portugal.

Across the globe a few states which were clearly in the periphery in 1900 managed to develop industrial sectors to such an extent that, by the end of the century, they had moved into the semi-periphery of medium-income countries, although they were still a long way behind even the states of eastern and southern Europe. In the Middle East this category included countries such as Turkey and Iran; in Latin America, Brazil and Mexico; in the Far East, South Korea and Taiwan. The routes these states took to reach the semi-periphery were very different, as were the timescales involved.

In 1900 all these states had populations which were almost entirely rural and illiterate. Turkey in 1913, for example, had just 269 factories using machines and they employed only 17,000 people. As late as 1948 the industrial labour force in Iran was 40,000 strong. Turkey was the first country to try to break out of this situation after 1923 as part of the nationalist revival and modernization under Ataturk. A five-year plan, modelled on that in the Soviet Union but without the highly repressive state apparatus to enforce rapid growth, was adopted in 1933. It was based on what was to be a major feature of the Turkish economy for decades – a strong state role in building up the economic infrastructure. However, without the major impetus provided by the exploitation of any major resources, economic growth remained slow and the economy highly autarkic – not until the 1960s did more modern industries such as synthetic fibre production and car assembly develop. By the 1980s industrial output accounted for about a quarter of all output and GDP per head was typical of the poorer countries of the semi-periphery, closer to Peru and Chile than to Czechoslovakia or Argentina.

Iran was far less developed than Turkey until well into the 1950s, despite the bonus of oil revenues and a nationalist government after 1925 with a similar ideology to that of Turkey. In the first half of the century much investment went into the basic infrastructure such as railways to help overcome some of the major geographical obstacles to development. After the restoration of the shah in 1953, about three-quarters of the increasing oil revenue was used to support a state-directed plan for industrialization which, unlike Turkey, utilized a strong private sector. At first efforts were concentrated on light industry and import substitution; only after the late 1960s, when there were about 1·5 million industrial workers, did basic industries such as engineering and electrical equipment develop. Nevertheless, growth rates of more than 11 per cent a year were high – in practice probably higher than the social and political structure could sustain in a highly inegalitarian society. The collapse of the shah's government and the installation of a conservative, religious regime after 1979 did not, however, alter the aim of increasing industrialization. By the end of the century GNP per head in Iran was at about the same level as other countries of the semi-periphery such as Mexico and Malaysia.

In Latin America some states in the semi-periphery were relatively successful economically in the twentieth century, in particular Brazil, Mexico and, to some extent, Venezuela and Chile. In 1900 these states typified the semi-periphery, being dependent on exports of raw materials and agricultural products to the core – oil and minerals in Mexico, Chile and Venezuela, and coffee, sugar, cotton and rubber in Brazil. Until well into the century industrialization in all these states was limited to import substitution industries at a low level of technology. The collapse of export markets in the 1930s during the worldwide depression reduced foreign exchange earnings with which to buy imports and increased the pressure for industrialization. In Brazil industrial production rose by 7 per cent a year in the 1930s, but the steel industry was still based on melting scrap iron. It was not until 1943 that the first integrated steel mill was operational. In Mexico state planning, land reform and nationalization of the oil industry provided the basis for steady industrial growth. In Chile exports fell by a third and imports by a half during the 1930s and industrialization was limited by the size of the shock this caused to the economy.

From the 1940s industrialization in Mexico and Brazil began to take off, although it was not until 1957 that Brazil reached the level achieved by Argentina in 1929. In both countries state direction was important, in Brazil especially under the military government after 1964 when growth rates reached 10 per cent a year. Brazil and Mexico both established vehicle industries in the 1950s and by the late 1980s the Brazilian industry employed 4 million workers and accounted for 7 per cent of the country's GDP, although it was made up almost entirely of subsidiaries of TNCs such as Ford, General Motors and Fiat. Both Brazil and Mexico had substantial domestic markets to support industrialization. This was important because across Latin America manufactured exports were very small, often as low as 1 per cent of production. What could happen if the protected domestic market was removed was illustrated by Chile during the liberal market reforms under General Pinochet after 1973. Tariffs were reduced to a uniform 10 per cent (some had been as high as 700 per cent), with the result that industries such as textiles and footwear collapsed and the manufacturing share of GDP fell by a third in eight years. At the end of the century Mexico and Venezuela were relatively prosperous members of the semi-periphery. Chile's performance over the century was poor given its position in 1900, when it had a GDP per head at the same level as Finland: by the early 1990s it was one-third of Finland's. Brazil, however, did well, particularly in comparison with its neighbour Argentina. At the beginning of the century Brazil's GDP per head was about a third of Argentina's – by the 1990s it was larger.

In the second half of the century four states in Asia – Taiwan, South Korea, Singapore and Hong Kong – industrialized on a substantial scale and moved into the semi-periphery. Subsequent mythology attributed their success to free-market, liberal, low-tariff, private-enterprise economic principles. In practice this was not the case. Hong Kong and Singapore were unique instances of economies built on trade and services from the start. They did not have a massive rural hinterland and so did not have to face the difficult problems involved in the transition from agricultural economies. Both practised free trade because they had no agriculture, the domestic market was so small it was not worth protecting and cheap food imports were required. In manufacturing, economies of scale could only come from exporting. State direction was vital in Singapore but not in Hong Kong. Singapore attached great importance to creating a highly educated workforce and concentrated on information technology industries. By the 1990s it had a GDP per head close to those in western Europe.

Taiwan and South Korea were both authoritarian states determined on industrialization for political reasons and prepared for state intervention on a major scale to direct the process. Both the Taiwanese government and that of South Korea after the military coup of 1961, saw themselves as directing a process of renewal and state growth in much the same way as the Japanese after the Meiji restoration. In Taiwan the state controlled half of all industrial production in the 1950s, as well as all the banks, and it still accounted for a third of total GNP as late as the 1980s. Both states had a range of incentives and subsidies together with a protected home market so as to allow industries to develop. Tariffs in Taiwan were substantial and provided a quarter of all government revenue. Both imports and exports required a licence, but exporters were subsidized by being exempted from paying tariffs on their imports in order to keep costs down. In South Korea the government took tight control over banks in order to provide subsidized help to industry. Controls limited the number of new firms in an industry and there were tax incentives for firms which exported over half their output.

Both Taiwan and South Korea, because they were seen as strategically vital, received massive economic assistance from the United States, especially during the 1950s when the Americans provided over three-quarters of South Korea's foreign exchange and over $1.5 billion for Taiwanese development. In both states major land-reform programmes were the basis for increasing agricultural productivity and providing a workforce for industrialization. Education was also seen as the key to development. In the late 1940s about 40 per cent of the workforce in South Korea was still illiterate and in both states children, on average, spent just over three years in school. By the mid-1980s this figure had risen to over twelve years, near the OECD average and in Taiwan it was higher than West Germany.

The results of this state-directed and assisted industrialization were impressive. Taiwanese growth started in the 1950s, South Korea's a decade later. Industrial output in Taiwan rose 10 per cent a year in the 1950s and 16 per cent a year in the 1960s. In the 1950s almost all of South Korea's exports were primary products and the only substantial industry was textile manufacture based on cheap labour. Both states then underwent an extraordinarily compressed period of development, moving quickly into basic industries such as iron and steel, more sophisticated industries such as chemicals and car assembly and manufacture and finally into high technology electronics. Until the 1960s Taiwan did not have a single steel mill; neither did South Korea until the early 1970s, when the state provided over $3·5 billion to create an industry. By 1986 the Koreans were advising US Steel on how to modernize its plants. South Korea built its first major ship in 1973, yet within a decade the industry had overtaken Japan in output. Both of these examples demonstrate the advantages gained from being able to industrialize using the very latest technology. By the early 1990s South Korea had its own TNCs such as Samsung and Goldstar and had begun exporting cars to western Europe. Overall Taiwan exported almost half of its GDP, South Korea slightly less. GDP per head rose rapidly in the last quarter of the century – in 1975 South Korea was still at the level of Guatemala, by the 1990s it was close to that of Portugal and Greece. The effect of this growth over the century can be seen in the case of Taiwan. In 1900 its GDP per head was only slightly higher than that of Bangladesh (then part of British India), by the end of the century it was over thirteen times higher.

In the last quarter of the century the first signs emerged that other countries in Asia such as Thailand, Malaysia and the Philippines might be moving in the same direction as South Korea and Taiwan. The most important change in this period, though, was the final emergence of China as a major industrial power. Internal disintegration, civil war and the war against Japan all restricted Chinese economic development in the first half of the century. An overwhelmingly agricultural economy did, however, have two major sectors of modern development. The first was in Manchuria, where railway construction – the Chinese Eastern Railway in 1901 and the South Manchurian two years later – turned the area into one comparable to Canada, Australia and Argentina. New agricultural land was opened up and ports were developed for food exports, especially to Japan, as the population grew rapidly through immigration from the rest of China. From the 1920s industry was developed with foreign investment, this time from Japan. By 1940 Manchuria contained about a third of all Chinese industry and the average income was nearly twice that of the rest of China. The second area of growth was in trade through the ports in the south of the country, which produced a limited development of industry, mainly textiles. Although China's industrial output grew substantially after 1914, by the 1930s it still accounted for less than 4 per cent of national income and only employed about 2 million workers. Industry remained small scale and nearly half of it was foreign owned.

By the early 1950s, when the Communist government was in full control of the country, the Chinese economy was still typical of a peripheral state and was probably not even as advanced as Russia's in 1913. A programme of industrialization on the Soviet model was instituted: agriculture was collectivized and emphasis was placed on the development of heavy industry, although there were catastrophic mistakes such as the 'Great Leap Forward' of 1959–60. Overall growth rates comparable to the USSR's in the 1930s were achieved and were sustained over a longer period – industrial output rose at over 10 per cent a year in the thirty years before 1982, doubling China's share of world industrial output. Chinese iron and steel output in the early 1980s was greater than that of Britain and France combined. Investment levels were also the highest in the world. However, the scale of the effort required in China can be judged by the fact that in 1982 only 6 per cent of the population was employed in industry. Although the average number of years children spent in education more than doubled after 1950, at less than six years it was still well below that of most other Asian states. By the early 1980s basic industrialization was complete in China and the party leadership established after the convulsions of the 1965–75 period adopted a series of economic reforms. In many ways they can best be compared with the New Economic Policy adopted by the Soviet Union in the early 1920s but abandoned later in the decade. Under strict political control agrarian reform was instituted, which transformed communes into 'townships' able to sell on the open market. Output rose at 8 per cent a year and the real income of the peasantry doubled in the six years after the reforms were introduced in 1978. This provided a foundation for further industrialization based on the import of foreign technology into four special economic zones in south China and the partial institution of a market. These policy changes provided the impetus for another phase of very rapid growth for the rest of the century, at about 10 per cent a year.

Relative Chinese success under the Communist government after 1949 can be compared with relative failure in India. Together these two countries comprised four out of ten of the world's people and they became either independent or in full control of their own destiny at about the same time. The Indian economy in the first half of the twentieth century suffered almost as badly as the Chinese. In 1890 it had the sixth largest cotton industry in the world, but the British systematically discouraged Indian industry to avoid competition and the proportion of the population in agriculture actually rose by a quarter in the thirty years after 1891. Until 1950 the economy was stagnant, with the amount of food per person in decline and with four out of five children between the ages of six and eleven receiving no education at all. After 1950 growth might at best be described as steady but slow, at worst sluggish. Industrial growth slowed in each successive five-year plan. However, because of the sheer size of the Indian economy, by the 1980s India was the fifteenth biggest industrial power in the world. Until the late 1980s India tried to develop a relatively autarkic economy, but the problem with this strategy was that although the domestic market was large in numbers the very high level of poverty meant that the demand for goods was low. In comparison with China India's performance was poor. Over the last third of the century GDP per head grew in China at four times the rate of India, the mortality rate was a quarter of India's and the illiteracy rate only half as big. Agricultural output in China roughly trebled in the last half of the century, whereas in India, despite the 'green revolution', it only just kept pace with population growth.

The area of the world with the worst economic performance over the century was Africa. Apart from limited industrialization in a few countries – those along the Mediterranean such as Egypt and Algeria, oil-rich Nigeria after 1970 and South Africa, which was, like other European settlement colonies, part of the semi-periphery – the record was one of almost total failure. Throughout the century Africa never produced more than 0·5 per cent of the world's industrial output. In 1900 European control had been established and this was followed by some investment to facilitate the development of the economic activities favoured by the colonial powers – mineral extraction and cash crops for export. Once this had been achieved, usually by building railways from the interior to the coast and constructing ports, investment stopped. The result was that large parts of the local economy remained untouched by any 'development'. Peasants moved between wage-labour and self-sufficiency and no local industrialists and traders emerged. With low commodity prices until 1945 economies stagnated and even the slight recovery after the Second World War had only a limited impact.

On the eve of independence in the late 1950s little had changed and the foundations for future development were poor. Only one in six adults was literate and only a third of children attended any school at all. All but 10 per cent of roads were dirt tracks and half of all the continent's railways were in South Africa. Energy consumption was one-sixtieth of that in the core states. Most assets were owned by foreigners. In the Belgian Congo the 1 per cent of the population who were foreigners owned 95 per cent of the country's capital, 80 per cent of the productive assets and 90 per cent of the private savings – they also accounted for 40 per cent of all consumption. From 1960 to 1975 there was a very slow growth in GDP per head. Then falling commodity prices, rising oil prices, growing debt, rampant corruption by the elite and poor agricultural policies led to economic stagnation and in some cases actual decline. In many countries of sub-Saharan Africa manufacturing made up less than 5 per cent of national wealth and most of the continent seemed to lack nearly all the prerequisites for industrialization. Most states were very small and therefore did not have a domestic market that could be used as a base on which to develop. It was difficult to generate capital given the low incomes, poor agriculture and large external debts. Education levels were very low, the infrastructure was poorly developed and the political elite seemed not only incapable of developing any coherent policy but in many cases they worsened an already difficult situation through corruption and patronage.

What was the overall effect of all these changes? During the twentieth century as a whole, people's average income increased everywhere but at very different rates and from very different starting points. The richest countries in 1900 were still the richest countries in 2000 (though there had been changes within the group) and the poorest were, by and large, still the poorest. Indeed, the disparities in wealth between the core and the periphery grew larger not smaller during the century. In 1900 on average a person living in the core was about three times wealthier than someone in the periphery. By the late 1990s they were about seven times richer. Some of the differences were even greater than the broad figures suggested. By the 1990s income per head in the United States was, on average, eighty times greater than in Zaire. In many countries the situation was deteriorating rapidly. By the mid-1990s, people living in eighty-nine countries in the world were poorer than they were in 1980 and in forty-three countries they were poorer than in 1970 – this was an absolute not relative decline.

The quality of life for people, however, cannot be measured simply by dividing national income by the number of people. This can disguise very stark differences within societies. For example, the infant mortality rate in American cities such as Washington, Baltimore and St Louis in the late twentieth century was worse than in cities in the periphery such as Bangkok, Bogotá and Cairo. Saudi Arabia was technically one of the richest countries in the world, with a GDP per head close to that of Ireland, but half the population was illiterate and life expectancy was lower than in Mauritius. However, social and economic policies could increase the quality of life. Sri Lanka had a GDP per head just one-fifth of that in Malaysia, but it had a similar mortality rate, food intake and number of doctors per head and its literacy rate was substantially better. On the other hand, some countries which experienced rapid growth, for example the Philippines in the 1970s and 1980s, did not reduce the level of poverty. In others, such as Brazil, poverty actually worsened during the period of rapid growth after the mid-1960s.

By the end of the century the disparities in wealth in the world were staggering. The poorest 20 per cent of the world's population (about 1·2 billion people) received little more than 1 per cent of the world's income. They were classified as living in 'extreme poverty' according to the World Health Organization and lacked adequate food, housing and drinking water. A third of the world's children were classified as undernourished and 12 million of them aged under five died every year from poverty-related diseases, mostly from the lack of an oral rehydration therapy costing just thirteen pence. In some countries the number of people living below the official poverty line was enormous: in Guatemala it was nine out of ten of the population, nearly half the people had no access to any form of health care, sanitation or piped water and nearly half the working population had received no formal education.

7 SOCIETIES

FOR INDIVIDUALS life in the twentieth century, as before, revolved around the family, work and a minimal amount of leisure time. Most people were peasants and lived in either China or India. But whether they lived on a *hacienda* in Latin America, a *kolkhoz* or commune in the Soviet Union, or by clearing a small amount of land out of the forest in Africa, their lives were dominated by poverty, insecurity and the difficulty of providing even elementary necessities such as food, housing and clothing. They lived constantly on the margins of existence, where any event – natural disaster, war, illness or unemployment – could be devastating and often fatal. They were illiterate and with so few skills that the avenues of escape from this way of life were very limited.

Although the nature of the societies and the lives people lived in the core and periphery were very different, there were some common threads. In all societies the experiences of men and women were very different. The core states were, throughout the century, urbanized, industrial societies with high and rising levels of consumption and leisure and with sufficient wealth to enable them to provide, by the middle of the century, a basic state welfare system. At the same time they were characterized by high levels of crime and poverty and by major inequalities of wealth and income. The countries of the periphery were, until late in the century, overwhelmingly rural, all but a tiny elite were poor and the state infrastructure was very small. The states of the semi-periphery showed characteristics common to both the core and the periphery. During the century those in Europe became much closer to the core, whilst outside Europe such changes were far less noticeable.

In every society the family was the fundamental unit in which individuals lived their lives, but the experience of family life and the changes in it were very different in the core and periphery. At the

risk of over-simplification it is possible to argue that the family in
the periphery tended to be based more on a highly developed
kinship system, which in some cases meant that the extended family
was a major social force. In China, for example, the extended family
and its complex relationships were very important, which was
reflected in the fact that there were different terms in Chinese for a
paternal and maternal uncle and for first, second and third cousins.
In rural areas an extended family might live together and the
authority of the elder men over the younger and all men over
women would be the central feature. Even in less formally
structured systems without extended families, kinship remained
vital throughout the century in providing help and support to
members. In urban areas, where people were poor and without any
form of state welfare, kinship was a vital network which could
provide jobs, accommodation and support as families moved in
from rural areas. Some features of the family in the core states
illustrated a similar system of supporting networks. In the mid-
1960s a study of Swansea in Wales showed that over 40 per cent of
married women had mothers living in the same district and almost
as many again had mothers living in other parts of the city. Overall
three-quarters of the women saw their mothers at least once a week.
A study of Bethnal Green in east London showed that in the mid-
1950s over half the population had lived all their lives in the borough
and they were part of a dense network of supportive relationships
built up over many years.

In general the family in the core states differed markedly from
that in the rest of the world. By the end of the nineteenth century
what had been until then a traditional family structure was changing
rapidly. The old-style large, inter-generational family which had
been common in most countries other than Britain and the United
States was disappearing. Marriage arranged and determined by
financial and landholding interests was becoming less common at all
levels of society. Families became smaller units of husband, wife and
children. Part of the explanation for this change was increasing
urbanization: as people moved away from rural communities into
more anonymous cities, the family turned in on itself. Individuals
had social contacts through their work and voluntary organizations,
but they were mainly concerned with their immediate family, some
close relatives and a few friends. Gradually the idea of the family as
a loving unit emphasizing domesticity became the norm. Old ways
of dealing with children slowly disappeared. At the turn of the

century in France over 100,000 legitimate children a year were being sent from the towns, primarily Paris, to women in rural areas who specialized in acting as 'wet nurses'. In 1920 such practices still affected nearly one in ten legitimate children. By then, however, the idea that a mother should care for her children was becoming the norm. State institutions also began to take over some of the functions that had traditionally been carried out within the larger family – health care and looking after the aged and mentally ill. The family was now expected to undertake a wider range of functions by providing economic security, a stable environment for children, romance, sexual fulfilment, companionship and emotional satisfaction. Such ideas were epitomized in the middle of the century by the Easter 1954 issue of *McCall's*, the most popular American women's magazine. Ed and Carol Richtscheidt, who lived in suburban New Jersey, were chosen as the ideal family. They were praised because they 'centered their lives almost completely around their children and their home'. They shopped and decorated together and Ed helped out around the home. This, the magazine argued, was a 'new and warmer way of life' in which individuals obtained fulfilment and achievement 'not as women alone or men alone, isolated from one another, but as a family sharing a common experience'.

Although the family remained the fundamental unit of social organization in the core states, to many it seemed to be constantly under threat. In the first decade of the century the American psychologist John B. Watson wrongly predicted, as did many others subsequently, that 'in fifty years there will be no such thing as marriage'. The institution survived, but the reality of marriage was often very different from the ideal. The number of illegitimate births fell steadily from the second half of the nineteenth century until about 1950, but the level of pre-marital intercourse was always high. Births outside marriage fell because of easier access to birth control and the expectation of marriage if pregnancy occurred. In Sweden and Germany in the first two decades of the century over a third of all brides were pregnant and the proportion of pregnant brides doubled in France between 1925 and 1960. Divorce rates were also high in the early twentieth century – a quarter of all marriages in San Francisco in 1916 ended in divorce. Overall the number of divorces in the United States rose fifteen-fold in the fifty years before 1920. States also continued to allow very early marriage. In 1930 a quarter of all American states, together with

France, Japan, Italy and New Zealand, allowed marriage as young as thirteen.

Fundamental changes in family life took place across the core states in the second half of the century. As late as 1960 nearly three-quarters of American households consisted of the idealized nuclear family: the father as breadwinner, the mother as housewife and dependent children. By 1990 this was true for fewer than one in six households. Divorce rates tripled in the United States in the forty years after 1950 so that nearly half of the children born in the 1970s had seen their parents divorce before they were sixteen. The number of illegitimate births began to rise everywhere after 1950, doubling in countries such as Australia and Britain in the next fifteen years. In the United States the rate quadrupled between 1950 and 1990. The combined effect of these two trends was to increase significantly the number of one-parent families – in Britain, for example, from 8 per cent of the total in 1971 to 14 per cent fifteen years later, when one in eight children was affected. The biggest increase was in the number of divorced mothers; only a quarter of the total were mothers who had had children when single. Once the contraceptive pill became widely available in the late 1960s sex before marriage and without marriage became the norm rather than the exception. People spent more of their lives not in marriage – marrying later, having fewer children, divorcing more often and having periods of living on their own in between marriages.

Partly linked to changes in family life was one of the most important social trends in the core states – the slow transformation in the role of women. At the beginning of the century no state in the world recognized the legal equality of men and women and, although in many countries of the core women were given the vote by the late 1920s, this did not bring about equality. Throughout the century core societies remained patriarchal and for decades women were denied access to positions of power and expected to find fulfilment as wives and mothers. This attitude was particularly prevalent in some Catholic countries and was, for example, enshrined in the constitution of Ireland, which was promulgated in 1937. Article 49 stated:

In particular the State recognises that by her life within the home woman gives to the State a support without which the common good cannot be achieved. The State shall, therefore, endeavour to ensure that mothers shall not be obliged by economic necessity to engage in labour to the neglect of their duties in the home.

In the early 1960s Pope John XXIII said that a woman should never forget that 'the end to which the Creator has ordained her whole being is maternity'. Similar attitudes could be found in Nazi Germany, which emphasized women's role in producing large families. The idealization of women's role in the home remained a constant theme – in 1955 the Democratic candidate for President of the United States in both 1952 and 1956, Adlai Stevenson, told women graduating at Smith College that their role in life was to 'influence us, man and boy ... to restore valid, meaningful purpose to life in your home' and to keep their husbands 'truly purposeful'. This was at a time when two-thirds of American women entering college dropped out on marriage or because, as many surveys showed, they feared education might harm their chances of marriage.

Formal legal equality between the sexes was not established in the core states until well into the second half of the century. In France women were first allowed complete control of their wages in 1907, but until 1938 a husband administered his wife's property and his formal permission was required before a wife could either attend university or work. In that year the Code Napoléon, in which the wife was admonished to be 'obedient', was revised but still stated that 'the husband is the head of the family'. In 1962 the Cour de Cassation upheld a husband's right to prohibit his wife from practising a profession and only in the next year was a woman allowed to open a bank account without her husband's permission. Until 1969 the wife of an adulterous husband who was denied a divorce was unable to set up a separate household. Full equality did not come until 1975.

Most countries in the core legalized sexual equality earlier than France: by the end of the 1920s in Scandinavia, most of the United States and Britain; by 1950 in Japan; a decade later in West Germany. Some states took even longer – the late 1980s in Belgium, the Netherlands and Switzerland. One of the key areas of difference between the sexes was divorce. Not until 1923 was the position equalized in Britain. Until then a wife had to demonstrate misconduct over and above adultery to obtain a divorce, a husband only required evidence of adultery. Until 1968 in Italy male infidelity was only grounds for divorce if it was 'open and notorious' and only criminal if a mistress was installed in the marital home. On the other hand any infidelity by a wife was grounds for divorce and also a criminal offence. In the 1960s sixteen states in the United States still defined adultery by a wife as prostitution and therefore a criminal offence. Marital rape was first recognized as an offence in Sweden in 1962 but not until 1991 in Britain. In the last three decades of the century most of the core states finally began, often very cautiously, to grant equality of status to gay men. It was a profound change in the way of life for a significant minority of the population and marked a major alteration in the attitudes of society from the beginning of the century, when homosexuality between men was often treated as criminal and therefore confined to an underground within society.

Outside the core countries progress towards sexual equality was slower or non-existent. In some areas, for example China, there were major changes. Practices such as foot-binding were already dying out by the early twentieth century and after the revolution arranged marriages were prohibited and major emphasis was placed on improving the position of women. By the 1990s most states outside the Muslim world had enacted formal legal equality even though often little altered in practice. Traditional patriarchal attitudes showed little sign of changing in Muslim states and indeed in some cases, such as Iran after 1979 and Afghanistan in 1996, there was a major resurgence. Across the Muslim world most women were not educated, only one in seven was literate and half were married before the age of nineteen, usually in arranged marriages. Islamic law gave the male unilateral power to divorce, to take custody of any children and to confine his wife to the home. If women were allowed in public they usually had to be fully covered. In Saudi Arabia women were not allowed any public life and were not, for example, allowed to drive.

After the family the most important aspect of life for the individual in the twentieth century was work. People spent more time working than any other activity apart from sleeping, and it defined nearly every aspect of their lives from their income to the amount of 'spare' time they had available. For most people work meant long, grinding hours of heavy agricultural labour either on their own land or as a paid labourer for very low wages and usually with no guarantee of any steady employment. However, the most important changes in the nature of work took place in the core states, gradually spread into the partly industrialized countries of the semi-periphery and eventually into parts of the periphery.

By the late nineteenth century the simple capitalism of the early phase of industrialization, typified by the single or family owner and controller of a business, was gradually being replaced by a new structure. As production processes became more complex, mass marketing techniques developed and demands for investment capital became greater, a separation of ownership and management evolved. The owners of companies became shareholders and except in a few cases the holdings of the founding family were dispersed. In their place a new professional group of managers, who held few, if any, shares in the firm, took over the increasingly sophisticated task of co-ordinating the various aspects of the firm's functions – research and development, production, finance, sales, marketing and labour relations. Shareholdings were held by institutions such as banks, pension funds and insurance companies and they chose the top executives who controlled the company. The same capitalist demands as in the early nineteenth century – profit and capital accumulation – were still present but were now more disguised. These changes began first in the United States, then spread to continental Europe in the first decades of the century and much later to Britain, where they were not adopted on a significant scale until the 1930s.

Throughout the twentieth century there was an underlying conflict between management and labour over the control of work in the factory. In the late nineteenth century skilled workers, acting through foremen, were able, to a large extent, to dictate the pace at which they worked and establish a level which they thought was reasonable for the wages they received. From the 1890s the managers of major firms began to assert greater control over the rate at which their workers operated. This was not a simple plot to downgrade the workers but stemmed from market pressures on firms to increase productivity, reduce prices, increase market share and thereby increase profits. To the managers trade unions trying to protect workers, especially skilled workers, were seen as reactionary and out of date, but the managers had little understanding of the effects new production techniques had on individual workers.

One of the first techniques was developed by F. W. Taylor in the United States (hence the term 'Taylorism'). He argued that managements should observe how tasks were done, define jobs very carefully and link pay to performance. This was part of a general move to break jobs down into smaller, simpler units so that workers became 'de-skilled'. Skilled workers needed training and were not subject to the same disciplines as unskilled workers and the unemployed because they could not easily be replaced. The incentive to management was to introduce machines and simplify tasks so that cheaper, unskilled workers could do them. This led to the adoption of various terms, such as 'time and motion' studies and 'scientific' management, and arguments over the 'right to manage' and the demands of workers to retain some control over their labour. Taylor was clear about the underlying purpose of his approach, writing in 1906 that the aim was 'taking the control of the machine-shop out of the hands of the many workmen and placing it completely in the hands of the management'. These ideas were adopted with enthusiasm by a wide variety of people from top executives to Lenin. Workers were asked to accept 'piece rate' pay in which wages were directly linked to the completion of certain tasks. In the Soviet Union these were called 'work norms' and workers were supposed to try enthusiastically to beat the norms so that managers could then raise them for everyone else. The introduction of piece-rate work did not in itself solve every problem because arguments began over the payment for each unit completed. In some countries such as Japan, Taylorism was implemented relatively easily within the prevailing 'paternalistic' framework of strong company control over a workforce. In others, for example the British car industry, such ideas led to decades of labour disputes. In practice 'Taylorism' was never fully implemented, but its aim (of breaking the power of individual workers and trade unions so that workers were paid individually by a supposedly paternalistic but autocratic management) was clear.

Even more significant was the development of new methods of mass production, which could be combined with Taylorism. In the early twentieth century old craft-based methods of production were beginning to be replaced by production lines. This happened first in areas such as meat slaughtering and packing and then in the key twentieth-century industry – vehicle production. It was a technique particularly suited to high-volume production of standardized output, the type of production which dominated the core economies in the first two-thirds of the century. It was first adopted in the Ford motor plants in the United States and this gave rise to the general term 'Fordism' to characterize this method of production.

The system was worked out gradually between 1908 and 1914 by a team of engineers, not by Henry Ford himself. Ford was not an industrial genius, he was lucky in implementing ideas that had been gradually developing elsewhere and which were soon widely adopted in a variety of industries. The idea of a moving assembly line rather than individual production of a vehicle was conceived in July 1908, but it was the opening on New Year's Day 1910 of the new 60-acre Ford plant at Highland Park, Detroit which provided the opportunity for a major change in production techniques. The plant was designed for mass production and by 1914 over 15,000 machines had been installed. The time and motion studies carried out at the old Piquette Avenue plant led to the introduction at Highland Park in 1912 of continuous conveyor belts to bring materials to the main assembly line. Within a year magnetos, motors and transmissions were assembled on moving lines, but the problem was that their output swamped the final assembly operation. This led to the development of a mechanized chassis assembly line, which could produce a finished chassis in less than three hours compared with over twelve hours under the old system. By the end of February 1914 the Highland Park plant was working on an assembly-line production system with the line set on rails at a convenient working height and moving at a steady six feet a minute. Productivity increased enormously: in 1912 a car took 4,664 worker hours to assemble, by the mid-1920s this had fallen to 813 hours.

The effect of this new system on the workers was profound. At one level they benefited – pay was very high at $5 for a relatively short day of eight hours. But the conditions were tough. About two-thirds of the workers were unskilled immigrants from south and east Europe because Ford believed, probably rightly, that only they would stand the conditions (skilled jobs were reserved for Anglo-Saxon workers from the United States, Britain and Germany). Most unskilled workers were under thirty-five and were subjected to monotonous work and stiff discipline. The lunch break was fifteen minutes. Company rules forbade leaning against a machine, sitting down, singing, talking, whistling and smoking. In 1914 Ford introduced a 'Sociological Department' to vet workers: thirty investigators visited homes and gave 'advice' on the family budget, diet, recreation, social outlook and morality. By the 1920s this supervision had become more extreme, the 'Ford Service Department' acted as an internal security unit with spies placed on the workfloor. Trade unions were of course banned and strikes were put down with violence. By the early 1940s Henry Ford was senile and the company was losing over $120 million a year after a long period of gross mismanagement: the best managers had left because of the atmosphere within the company. Other firms also introduced forms of 'welfare' to control their workers: for example, in the 1920s International Harvester began a company pension scheme, but only those who did not join a union or strike qualified to join. Accident benefits were started, but workers were required to waive their legal rights to compensation.

'Fordism' was copied in other industries and especially after 1945 in Europe too. It became the basic method of production in much of the core states' industry. At its height the system can be judged from conditions in a General Motors plant in 1971, which at the time was producing sixty cars an hour. On the line each 'work-station' was no more than eight feet long and here, every minute, a worker in the trim department had to walk about twenty feet to a conveyor belt which brought parts to the line, pick up a front seat weighing thirty pounds, carry it back to his workstation, place the seat on the chassis and put in four bolts, first hand-starting the bolts and then using an air-gun to tighten them. The management decided to speed up the line so that a hundred cars an hour were produced. The number of operations each worker performed was not reduced, however. This now meant that, according to a contemporary account:

> In 36 seconds the worker had to perform at least eight different operations including walking, lifting, hauling, lifting the carpet, bending to fasten the bolts by hand, fastening them by air gun, replacing the carpet and putting a sticker on the hood. Sometimes the bolts fail to fit into the holes; the gun refuses to function; the seats are defective or the threads are bare on the bolt. But the line does not stop.

All of this had to be carried out for eight hours a day, five days a week, often on shift work with night working and with only structured breaks. This was the reality of work for many in the core economies throughout the century. It is perhaps hardly surprising that there were disputes at the workplace.

After the Second World War some firms, especially in tech-nologically new areas, for example IBM and Polaroid, introduced even more complex methods to control their workforce, covering not just production workers but also the white-collar scientists, technicians and managers. Indeed these new techniques often began with white-collar workers and filtered downwards through the company. Polaroid maintained a basic distinction between salaried and hourly paid staff, but each group was drastically fragmented. The hourly paid staff were divided into 18 groups with over 300 job titles in 14 pay grades, each of which had 7 distinct bands with bonuses payable on top. Each job was described in great detail, with a list of duties in addition to general company rules and policy. In these circumstances collective bargaining by the workers, even if the company recognized a union, was almost impossible. Each worker would be assessed separately and what the company judged as 'positive' performance could be rewarded. The company's aim was not to find exceptional performance but to set what it regarded as an acceptable minimum standard as the norm. This was part of a drive to make workers, especially managers, totally dedicated to the aims of the company. Increasingly managers were expected to give up nearly all their lives to the firm, working even longer hours than the production workers and fitting the rest of their lives around the demands of their employers. By the 1960s the average corporate manager in the United States moved home fourteen times in his career because of job changes, with incalculable effects on his family and his children's education.

'Fordism' was, however, far from a universal form of production – it could not be employed in basic industries such as steel-making and oil-refining or in highly complex, low-volume-output industries such as aircraft manufacture. It tended to be inflexible and difficult to adjust to changing demand. In the second half of the century firms began to explore new methods of production which would be more flexible whilst maintaining control of production and the workforce. In the core economies in the 1980s and 1990s another revolution in the organization of work was beginning.

Japanese car firms were some of the first to use so-called 'just-in-time' production methods. Instead of holding large quantities of parts in the main factory, they were delivered as required by a range of sub-contractors. This enabled production lines to switch easily between variants within a single model and placed more of the risk on sub-contractors. Permanent employment was therefore restricted to the smaller workforce at the main factory, with sub-contractors and especially sub-sub-contractors further down the supply chain having to lay off workers at times. These production methods were combined with increasing automation of production lines using industrial robots. Perhaps the most extreme example of this trend occurred in the Victor camcorder plant in Japan, where the use of 64 robots to assemble and check all production resulted in the number of shopfloor workers being reduced from 150 to just 2. In parallel, firms introduced 'team working', which was designed in theory to end the monotony and alienation of the 'Fordist' system by creating small groups of workers who were responsible for a wide range of tasks. In practice this was simply another way of increasing the pressure on workers, which came now from colleagues as well as management. Teams were encouraged to find new ways of working, of speeding up the line and taking up 'slack' in various areas – a concept known as 'management by stress'. The result of all these changes was massive job losses in manufacturing. For example, US Steel employed 120,000 people in 1980 and 20,000 a decade later, yet its output fell only slightly. In the 1980s the General Electric Company reduced its workforce worldwide by over 40 per cent, yet its sales tripled. Overall during the 1980s nearly 2 million jobs were lost in American manufacturing industry.

For most of the twentieth century increasing productivity in industry meant job losses in many sectors (between 1925 and 1980 the number of coal miners in the United States fell by two-thirds but coal output rose by a half), but was compensated for by the growth of new industrial sectors and the shift of employment into service industries. The problem in the last two decades of the century was that the new industrial growth sectors of electronics, computers and telecommunications employed few workers, most of whom were highly skilled technicians and scientists rather than production-line workers. At the same time the service sector also shed large numbers of jobs as computers took over many tasks. In the ten years after 1983 American banks shed 180,000 staff working behind counters (nearly 40 per cent of the total workforce) through use of computers and automated cash machines. In the early 1990s the Swedish ICA food co-operative introduced a new computerized stock-control system, closed a third of its warehouses and made 5,000 staff redundant (a third of its workforce), whilst its revenue increased by 15 per cent. The use of computers also meant that many of the old management layers used to control companies could be eliminated with no loss of performance. In the early 1990s Eastman Kodak reduced its management levels from thirteen to four and the Intel computer chip company from ten to five.

The impact of these changes on workers was harsh. Many lost their jobs or could only find a new one at the cost of a major drop in income. The average weekly wage in the United States fell from $387 in 1979 to $335 a decade later. Shareholders and top management, in particular, reaped the benefits: in 1979 the chief executive of a major US company earned on average twenty-nine times more than an industrial worker, a decade later this had increased to ninety-three times. Most new jobs which were created were part-time as companies moved from the old 'Fordist' concepts of a large permanent workforce to the new concept of a small core of permanent workers and a large number of workers hired and fired as conditions required. For example, at the Nike distribution facility in Memphis 120 permanent staff were paid $13 an hour, while between 60 and 255 temporary staff were paid half that rate for doing the same job but only when the company needed them. By the 1990s temporary jobs made up two-thirds of all the new jobs created in the core states; short-term contract and temporary workers made up a third of the workforce in Spain and the Netherlands. In the service sector the proportion of these workers was even higher – 40 per cent in Britain. In the United States the Manpower agency supplying temporary workers became the largest single employer. Employers demanded more from their workers as their numbers were reduced. At the Hewlett-Packard plant at Grenoble in France the workforce was not only cut, but those remaining had to accept a three-shift system for no extra pay. Although overall the number of hours worked per year fell in the twentieth century, this was largely the result of the introduction of a fairly general eight-hour day, forty-hour week in manufacturing plants in the early part of the century. From the 1960s onwards, across the core, the average hours worked began to increase. By the 1990s the occupant of a higher professional job worked on average a sixty-hour week with only thirty minutes for the 'lunch hour'. In the United States the time worked rose by over 160 hours a year, the equivalent of an extra month, and holiday entitlement fell by over three days a year.

By any proper definition, most work was done unpaid by women in the home, and was often combined with a formal job. Just how demanding household work could be is illustrated by the life of a sixteen-year-old girl in a Senegalese village in the 1980s. She got up at 5 a.m., before it was light, to pound millet for an hour. This was followed by walking to the well for water, making breakfast, going to the village shop, making lunch, taking food to her mother-in-law in the fields, doing the washing for six adults and a child, preparing supper and afterwards pounding millet again before going to bed. In addition, on some days she had to find wood for cooking, which involved a long journey. An older woman who had to undertake these tasks also had to do agricultural work from 7 a.m. to 4 p.m. Throughout Africa in the twentieth century agricultural work was primarily done by women. The trend began in the early colonial period as taxes to be paid in cash were introduced in order to force males to undertake paid employment, leaving women at home. Even when men did do farm work, they usually took the permanent jobs so that women were employed only on a temporary or seasonal basis.

In the core societies the level of women's employment, especially in factories, fell in the late nineteenth century as women were expected to devote themselves to household tasks. In 1911 only one in ten married women in Britain was employed. The 'Fordist' production system was essentially based on males working in factories to support their families. Most women who worked were confined to menial jobs. The largest single category at the beginning of the twentieth century (over four out of ten employed women) was domestic servants. The conditions of employment were highly unequal. Employers were allowed to sack women on marriage and even educated women were only slowly being admitted to the professions: there were just twenty women barristers in Britain in 1902; in Germany the Universities of Heidelberg and Freiberg finally admitted women in 1901; in Sweden, they were barred from practising law until 1933. This pattern changed only slowly. Domestic service declined after 1914 and unmarried women moved into new jobs, such as shop assistants, clerks and telephone operators. The number of women working, especially after marriage, increased steadily, so the percentage of women in the labour force rose from less than 30 per cent to over 40 per cent by the 1990s. By then nearly two-thirds of women worked, with the highest levels in Scandinavia and the lowest in Italy. Often, however, this simply increased the overall amount of work women undertook because it was combined with a disproportionate share of household tasks. Although equal pay for equal work finally became the norm in the last quarter of the century, women remained disproportionately represented in low-paid and temporary jobs and highly under-represented in the professions and senior management. By the 1990s more than six out of ten women who worked were employed in the service sector, where their jobs were predominantly insecure.

In the periphery far fewer women generally undertook paid employment than in the core states. However, apart from in the oil-rich states, where it fell after the early 1970s as wealth increased and older values were reasserted, the level of participation rose, especially in the second half of the century. When women did work they were usually paid less for the same job, on average about three-quarters of the male rate. Industrialization in many states of the periphery in the last quarter of the century was often based on labour-intensive production, using young women for a few years before they married. In some states, such as Hong Kong and Taiwan, over half the industrial labour force was composed of women, whereas in the core throughout the century the proportion nowhere rose above a third. The industries involved varied from country to country and included tobacco processing (India), textiles (south-east Asia), chemicals (Egypt and Kenya) and electronics (Hong Kong, Taiwan and the Philippines). Employment of women at low wages often constituted the foundation of industrial competitiveness for such countries.

There was also a much darker side to work in the twentieth century. Although all but a handful of states in the world had abolished formal slavery by 1900, conditions which were roughly similar could be found across the globe. The colonial powers relied on forced labour on public works and also shipped millions of people around the world as indentured labour. Illegal immigrants had few rights and were badly exploited; even legal foreign workers were treated very badly, for example the Chinese in the South African mines in the first decade of the century and Asian workers in the Gulf states. In agricultural societies poor peasants often incurred debts they could never repay and were forced to labour for their creditors. By the 1990s it was estimated that about 150 million people worldwide were condemned to a life of bonded labour with little or no chance of escape. In the core states child labour had largely been abolished by 1900 and the increasing length of compulsory schooling meant that few children were forced to work. In the periphery child labour was the norm. In rural areas children were expected to help with agricultural work from an early age and for much of the century only a small minority had any chance of more than a few years in school. Although the numbers in school and the number of years spent at school increased, in 1995 the International Labour Organization estimated that in the periphery a fifth of all children had jobs and over 200 million worked in dangerous or unhealthy conditions. Many were sold by their families to raise a small amount of money and then not paid by their employers. In Nepalese carpet factories it was estimated that three-quarters of all the workers were children under fourteen and half the girls were sexually abused.

The nature of work in the core states was fundamental to their social structure in the twentieth century. The system's underlying class basis was still present from the nineteenth century, but it was heavily disguised as economies and societies became more complex. Societies became highly stratified along occupational lines. At the top were the owners or managers of large enterprises and individuals with substantial property or shares (including in some cases the remnants of the old aristocracy). Below them were the higher-grade professional and technical staff and then lower-grade people in the same occupations. Next came the skilled and semi-skilled manual workers, together with clerical and secretarial staff. At the bottom were the unskilled manual workers and those with part-time jobs. (This stratification was made more complex by gender and ethnic differences.) The growth of the service sector and government employment did not change this fundamental structure, since both were modelled on manufacturing industry and had their own very clear hierarchies. Nor did state ownership of industries make a difference since the strict separation of management and workers was maintained.

This status structure was fundamental in determining the very different rewards given to each group. Those in the top group and some in the second group were often able to determine their own, very generous rewards, such as fringe benefits, pensions, performance-related pay and share options, all of which were regarded as essential to motivate them. Others had to bargain for their rewards and their power depended on a number of factors, in particular the indispensability of their skills (hence the desire of management to 'de-skill' jobs) and trade union power. Wage rises at the bottom were rarely enough to reduce the very stark differentials across society. In addition low-paid jobs often involved irregular employment, high health risks, few if any fringe benefits and few opportunities for promotion.

The capitalist core societies had a prevailing ideology that they were 'open', based as they were on 'success' and 'initiative'. Virtues such as 'individualism' and 'self-help' were richly rewarded and anybody with sufficient energy and determination could rise to the top. To some extent shifts in the economy (especially from industry to the service sector which reduced the number of manual jobs) and the general rise in living standards, especially the rapid rise after 1945, gave the impression of general mobility. This belief was reinforced by the fact that most individuals had usually only very limited knowledge of the rest of society. Detailed studies carried out within all the core states showed that in practice social mobility was limited. On the other hand, inheritance of status was very high. Access to elite occupations – the civil service, armed forces, judiciary, politics and professions such as the law and medicine – was very controlled. In Britain a mid-century survey showed that if parental origins played no part in determining life chances then only 3 per cent of the sons of professionals would become professionals too; in fact over 40 per cent did so. In some categories the inherited status level was even higher: the number of senior civil servants with fathers who were also in the same category was seventy-five times greater than pure chance would suggest. On the other hand only 7 per cent of the sons of semi-skilled and unskilled manual workers became professionals. Increasing levels of education were not sufficient to remove these barriers. Certain schools retained a privileged position in training the elite – the fee-paying public schools in Britain, the private schools in the United States such as Groton and Philips Academy and the *grandes écoles* in France. For example, the Ecole Libre des Sciences Politique, founded in 1872, produced from 1900 to 1930 116 out of 120 Conseillers d'Etat, 209 out of 218 Inspecteurs des Finances and 249 out of 284 members of the diplomatic corps. These areas of privilege were reinforced by the position of certain universities such as Oxford and Cambridge in Britain and the Ivy League in the United States. Another major barrier within society until the second half of the century was at the manual/non-manual level. Relatively few people left the unskilled manual-worker group but, on the other hand, there was a gradual tendency, reflecting changing job opportunities, for the sons of skilled workers to move into lower-grade managerial and technical jobs.

Comparative studies of the core countries showed that mobility rates across the manual/non-manual barrier were roughly similar (at about a third leaving the manual-worker category), but that overall Australia was the most open, Britain and the United States were in the middle range and the most closed were Italy, Japan, Spain and Germany. These studies also showed that there was no cycle of deprivation at the very bottom of society. However, there was a very clear cycle of privilege at the top, in which various advantages accumulated and were passed on from generation to generation. Other societies were similarly lacking in social mobility. In the periphery most people found it very difficult to escape from being peasant farmers and workers and, even if they moved to cities, they were restricted to low-paid, poor employment. Although initially the Communist states were relatively open, this changed rapidly with the emergence of a party elite able, like the elites of the capitalist states, to hand on their status to their children.

One of the major characteristics of the twentieth century was the urbanization of the world. In 1900 just 160 million people, one in ten of the world's population, lived in cities. By the end of the century a majority of the world's population was urban – over 3 billion people. There was also a major change in the distribution of the world's urban population. In 1900 two-thirds was in the core states (Britain was the most heavily urbanized – three out of four people lived in cities, with one in five people living in London). Yet by 1975, for the first time, a majority of the world's urban population lived in the peripheral states. The size of cities also increased. At the beginning of the century there were just nine cities in the world with populations of more than 1 million and they were all in the core states. Ninety years later there were thirteen cities with populations of over 10 million and eight of them were in the periphery.

In the nineteenth century the growth of cities in the core states was associated with industrialization. Growth largely came to an end in the early twentieth century, when the urban population stabilized at about three-quarters of the total. This situation lasted until mid-century, when the number of people living in cities began to decline. What changed in the core states was a vast expansion of the area covered by cities as suburbs grew rapidly. This move out from city centres had begun in the mid-nineteenth century as commuter railway lines were built – by 1900 the edge of Boston (Massachusetts) was already ten miles from the city centre. The process continued until the 1930s (especially around cities such as Paris and Tokyo, where new rail networks were constructed), but was then replaced by a new version of the same phenomenon – even larger, sprawling suburbs caused by the widespread use of the car. By the 1980s the urban area of New York covered 2,200 square miles, over five times its extent sixty years earlier, even though the population had only doubled. Elsewhere, too, large urban sprawls emerged. This occurred in Tokyo (which was over fifty miles wide by the second half of the century), the Randstad in the Netherlands (a huge urban area joining Rotterdam, The Hague, Amsterdam and Utrecht, which contained a third of the Dutch population in one-twentieth of the land area) and the massive urban belt stretching from Boston to Washington on the east coast of the United States, where a quarter of all Americans lived on less than 2 per cent of the country's land area. The social and economic costs of moving all these millions of people in and out of the city centres every day by both rail and road was huge. By the second half of the century two-thirds of central Los Angeles was given over to the car in the form of streets, freeways, parking and garages. The huge number of cars meant that massive traffic jams were the norm and there was no improvement in journey times from the horse-drawn era at the beginning of the century. In New York the average speed of traffic was just over eleven miles an hour in 1907, but this had fallen to six miles an hour by the 1980s.

The growth of cities in the periphery was not associated with industrialization; indeed the highest urban growth rates occurred in the poorest, least industrialized states. The rate of growth was on average twice as fast as in the core states during the nineteenth century. In some cases it was even greater. The population of Lagos in Nigeria grew from 126,000 in 1931 to 5 million fifty years later, a thirty-nine-fold increase. Nairobi in Kenya grew faster still from 11,500 in 1906 to 1 million in 1982, an eighty-six-fold increase. This rapid growth was mainly caused by the huge rise in population and large-scale migration from the countryside to the cities. One of the main reasons for urban migration was that, unlike cities in the core in the nineteenth century, many facilities such as health care were far better than in rural areas. Across the periphery by the end of the century three-quarters of the urban population on average had access to some form of water supply, compared with half that number in the countryside, and most had some form of sanitation, compared with fewer than one in six outside the cities. However, conditions in the cities could be harsh in the extreme. Unemployment was usually 20 per cent or more and many of the rest had no regular job but had to scrape a living as best they could. In India in the 1990s 1·5 million people lived on the streets simply because they could not afford housing, even though many had jobs (at the same time nearly 100,000 people slept on the streets of New York every night). Cities in the periphery were generally unable to cope with this rapid growth and most of the new residents had to live in one of the vast illegal squatter areas. They existed everywhere under different names: *barrios* (Latin America), *bidonvilles* (North Africa), *bustees* (India), *kampongs* (Malaya) and *barung-barongs* (Philippines). In Turkey two-thirds of the population of Izmir and Ankara lived in such areas in the 1960s, and in Africa by the 1990s the proportion had reached more than nine out of ten in cities such as Addis Ababa in Ethiopia and Yaounde in Cameroon. People existed in corrugated-iron or cardboard houses with no facilities and tried to make a living on the margins of society.

One of the greatest changes for people in the twentieth century was the growth of education. For the majority in the periphery this meant little more than access to basic primary education, but in the core states it involved much greater opportunities in secondary and university-level education. The most fundamental change was that in 1900 the overwhelming majority of the world's population were illiterate, yet by the 1990s less than a quarter were. By the early twentieth century in the core states the introduction of basic education for all had reduced illiteracy rates to very low levels – 2 per cent in Britain, though that rate was not equalled in the United States until 1952, partly because of the poor standard of education for blacks. In 1900 Japan was already at levels of literacy western Europe had achieved in 1880. Elsewhere in the world the situation was far worse. Even in the European semi-periphery over half the population of Bulgaria, Romania and Yugoslavia were still illiterate in 1920 and the Soviet Union was at the same level of literacy as Spain a century earlier. In the 1930s a massive education drive in the USSR produced one of the most rapid increases in literacy rates achieved anywhere – by 1940 it was at the same level as Britain in 1910. Italy in 1930, however, was still only at the level achieved by Britain in 1870.

By 1950 in parts of the semi-periphery literacy rates were high – in Argentina about 85 per cent (though this was actually falling as relative economic decline set in). In the periphery, in countries such as Mexico, Sri Lanka and the Philippines, about two-thirds of the population were literate. In the rest the situation was much worse – in India, Pakistan, Morocco, Egypt, Iraq, Iran and most of Africa only about one in ten of the population were literate. The second half of the century saw a fundamental transformation. By the end of the century in the Latin American semi-periphery of Uruguay, Chile and Costa Rica literacy rates were almost the same as in Western Europe. In the Middle East countries such as Egypt, Iran and Turkey had reached the levels of literacy found in the core states at the beginning of the century. In Asia, South Korea and China in 1950 were still at the literacy level of Spain in 1820, but major drives, modelled on the experience of the Soviet Union in the 1930s, brought about a rapid improvement to near European levels. However, many areas of the world did not match these achievements. By the 1980s only a third of India's adult population were literate. In six countries, all in Africa, less than a quarter of the population were literate and in the worst, Somalia and Niger, the figure was about one in eight. Even in a relatively prosperous African country such as Nigeria literacy rates were only at the level achieved by Britain in 1820. In nineteen states in the world (seventeen of which were in Africa) the average time spent at school was less than a year. There was also one significant difference in every peripheral state – women were far less likely to be literate than men. Almost half the women in the world were still illiterate at the end of the twentieth century.

If one of the century's achievements was the huge increase in literacy, this was not reflected in a general increase in education levels. Even though education was one of the keys to economic growth, especially in the second half of the century when levels of technological sophistication increased rapidly, most states in the world for most of the century provided very low levels of education. In 1900 the majority of children in the core states spent no more than seven years in full-time education, only about three in a hundred entered secondary education and just one in a hundred went to university. Even a rich country such as Britain spent just over 1 per cent of its GDP on education every year, far less than the average African country was spending by the end of the century. Secondary and higher education were therefore largely restricted to an elite of the children of professional families who could afford to pay for it. Since such education was a prerequisite for entry into the professions, the system reinforced the inequalities within society. In Britain, France and Germany only about one in ten pupils in secondary education came from working-class families and fewer than three in a hundred of the very small number of university graduates came from this section of society.

In the core countries greater access to education did not start until the 1950s. The number of pupils in secondary schools did not reach a quarter of the primary school population until 1946 in Britain and Sweden and 1957 in West Germany. In Britain, universal, free secondary education to the age of fifteen did not begin until the late

1940s and this was not extended to the age of sixteen until the 1970s. The expansion of higher education did not occur until much later in the century. University enrolment did not reach 10 per cent of the numbers in primary schools until 1968 in Sweden and the early 1970s in Britain and West Germany. By the end of the century the number at university had increased remarkably compared with 1900 – in France from 30,000 to nearly 1 million and in Germany from just under 50,000 to well over 1 million. The exception to this general pattern was the United States, where state support for more open access to secondary and eventually higher education was much greater throughout the century.

In many core states education remained elitist throughout the century. In Britain the 1944 Education Act produced a divided system, in which tests at the ages of ten and eleven decided whether pupils were good enough to enter an 'academic' rather than a 'practical' school and this choice effectively determined access to higher education. Some parents could avoid the state system and send their children to fee-paying private schools, which provided privileged access to the university system. Throughout the century most British pupils left school without any formal qualifications not because they lacked ability but because they were not entered for the necessary examinations. The system was therefore structured to ensure that the majority 'failed'. Even when some education was provided for the majority, it had a strongly nationalistic bias and was designed to ensure pupils fitted into the existing social and economic system and did not question accepted values. In every country schools had a strongly nationalistic purpose, from the daily swearing of allegiance to the flag in the United States to more subtle forms. For example, in Britain a *Handbook for Teachers* produced by the government in 1927 suggested that in history lessons pupils should not be 'harassed' by complicated issues. History, it asserted, was 'pre-eminently an instrument of moral training' and in studying the lives of individuals pupils would:

> learn naturally in how many different ways the patriot has helped his [sic] country, and by what sort of actions nations and individuals have earned the gratitude of posterity. Without any laboured exhortation they will feel the splendour of heroism, the worth of unselfishness and loyalty, and the meanness of cruelty and cowardice.

Similarly in 1911 a school textbook of forty important historical personalities contained twenty-four military figures, all of them British.

The expansion of education in the core states was one aspect of a larger transformation – the growth of the state and of its influence over many aspects of human life. Most core countries in 1900 still had very limited state apparatuses which concentrated on foreign policy and defence, as well as playing a minimal role in trade and industrial regulation, the provision of basic education and services such as prisons and a police force. As the core states became wealthier it was possible to provide social services: not just education, but also health care and various forms of support, from unemployment pay and pensions to child allowances and benefits for the disabled. In nearly all cases these services were provided by the state as part of a major redefinition of its functions. For the first time the state gradually took on responsibility for providing a basic level of care for its citizens.

In 1900 the number of people employed by the state in the core countries was beginning to rise rapidly, although generally it was still about 2 or 3 per cent of the labour force and the government only spent about 10 per cent of GDP every year. During the twentieth century this growth in state employment became more rapid. For example, the number employed by the federal government in the United States rose from 372,000 in 1909 to nearly 3 million sixty years later. By the last two decades of the century in the core states governments employed about one in ten workers and spent on average about 45 per cent of GDP every year. The majority of this expenditure was on social programmes. Although some states nationalized key industries, in particular railways and utilities, few moved into manufacturing industry and employment in this sector always remained low – on average less than 5 per cent of total employment and that fell in the last two decades of the twentieth century as most states sold off publicly owned industries.

Outside the core states there were also significant bureaucracies, for example in China, but their function was usually very different from those in the core. They tended to be job-creation areas for the exercise of patronage and influence by politicians and local elites. In the late nineteenth century Greece had, proportionately, seven times as many civil servants as Britain and they comprised a quarter of the non-agricultural labour force. Similarly, in Latin America, countries such as Argentina and Chile had about three times as many state bureaucrats per head of the population as Britain. The same process occurred in Africa after independence. Within two decades the very small administrative elite inherited from the colonial state was transformed, so that almost two-thirds of wage earners were government employees and a half of all government expenditure was on salaries. For example, Tanzania had 65,000 civil servants in 1966 and about 300,000 fifteen years later.

The development of welfare systems within the core states was slow. Until 1914 only a few areas of social need were covered. All of western Europe had some kind of workmen's compensation scheme against accidents. Some countries, such as Britain, France, Sweden, Denmark and Belgium, legislated to force employers to provide payments, while the majority, such as Austria, Germany, Italy and Switzerland, introduced compulsory insurance schemes. Nearly all the core countries had either compulsory state or subsidized private schemes for sickness insurance and about three-quarters provided a very minimal old-age pension. However, less than half had any form of unemployment insurance: only Austria, Germany, Italy and Britain had compulsory state schemes and even these did not cover all workers. In the United States there were virtually no schemes (only a third of the workforce were even covered by minimal industrial accident schemes) and in the late 1920s private charity spending was still six times greater than all public welfare expenditure.

The period between the two World Wars in western Europe saw the gradual extension of existing schemes to cover new risks such as unemployment and occupational diseases and to embrace more workers and other groups such as families and pensioners. By 1939 all of western Europe had schemes of some sort covering the major areas of social and economic risk, with the single exception of Switzerland, which did not provide any old-age pension. Canada introduced major new schemes in the 1930s, as did the United States under the 'New Deal', which in many respects put these two states ahead of countries such as France and Italy, although it was not until the mid-1950s that even half of the over-65s in the United States received any benefits from the 1935 scheme.

Major reforms of the welfare systems in many of the core states only occurred immediately after the Second World War. In Belgium, France, Sweden, Switzerland and Britain this produced almost comprehensive coverage of the population. However, it was not until the late 1960s and early 1970s that fully coherent schemes were established in Italy, Germany, Norway and the Netherlands.

With the exception of Switzerland, which retained subsidized voluntary schemes, all countries moved towards state-run schemes. Canada introduced sickness and health insurance at this time, but there was no major extension in the United States, which remained the only core state not to have national health insurance and family allowances. The expansion of welfare schemes meant that by the early 1970s most core states were spending about a quarter of their GDP on government social schemes, with the overwhelming part going to pensions and health care but only a very small amount on unemployment benefit. After 1973, as the core economies faltered and unemployment rose to post-war highs and stubbornly refused to fall, the established welfare systems began to be placed under strain. This situation was exacerbated by the increasing number of elderly people both drawing pensions and requiring health care. Most states began a process of deconstructing their welfare systems by increasing fees for public services such as medical prescriptions, tightening eligibility for benefits, introducing means-testing for benefits which had previously been universal in scope and abolishing others. Almost the only country to increase its state welfare schemes after the early 1970s was Japan, but it was starting from a much lower base.

On the surface the growth of welfare systems was a process whereby some of the inequalities and injustices produced by the economic system and the types of work people had to undertake were ameliorated and a greater degree of social justice and equality obtained through state action. It might also be seen as part of a process of greater democratization as the adult population of the core states acquired the right to vote and pressurized governments to provide more benefits for the majority. A closer examination would, however, suggest that the types of welfare system introduced, the different benefits and the conditions attached to them served other, more complex, purposes. Welfare provisions were first introduced not by democratic states but by monarchies such as Germany, Denmark and Sweden, where the ruler and the associated elite retained substantial power. These schemes were seen as vital to retain the loyalty of the growing working class produced by industrialization and increase the stability of the existing social and political system. In states still dominated by landed interests it was possible, either through taxation or by making employers pay, to shift the cost of such schemes on to the urban middle class. However, even in semi-democratic countries such as Britain before

1918, similar motives were important. Political and social elites saw welfare benefits as a way of giving the politically excluded classes at least a minimum stake in the existing society and diminishing any revolutionary enthusiasm they might have.

In welfare systems the way benefits were funded (by taxation, contribution or subsidized private insurance) and the way they were paid (universally or means-tested) influenced not just the level of benefits but also their social impact. Contribution and insurance-based schemes favoured those in regular work, means-testing reinforced social divisions between rich and poor and universal benefits were rarely high enough to have a major impact because they were so costly. Throughout the century the widespread view in the core states, especially among elites, was that the poor tended to be 'undeserving', so the benefits paid to them needed to be subjected to strict tests and not large enough to remove the 'incentive' to work. Although, for example, the strict discipline of the workhouse in Britain might be replaced by social assistance schemes, the deterrent and reformatory aim of benefits remained. In 1909 the Royal Commission on the Poor Law concluded that 'the causes of distress are not only economic and industrial: in their origin and character they are largely moral'. When unemployment benefit was first paid on a non-contributory basis in the early 1920s, three very strict tests were introduced: the subjective requirement to be 'genuinely seeking work' was applied to men; to be 'available for work' was taken as automatically excluding most women since they were housewives; and means-testing was applied to whole families not just to individuals so that many of the unemployed received no assistance. The state was therefore acting in much the same way as private charities in the nineteenth century by applying essentially moral and disciplinary tests to benefits. In the early 1940s, when Sir William Beveridge was writing the report which formed the basis for the post-war reform of the benefits system, he insisted on a number of similar points. First, benefits needed to be set at a level which did not remove the 'disciplinary' effect of the incentive to work: 'the gap between income during earning and during interruption of earning should be as large as possible for every man.' (It was typical of the period that women should be excluded from consideration since the report believed that their place was in the home.) Access to benefits should be 'subject to any condition as to behaviour which may hasten restoration of earning power', and in the last resort 'a limited class of men who through weakness or badness of character fail to comply . . . must be subject to penal treatment'.

The British benefit system was similar to those in Canada and Australia and to a large extent in the United States. Most benefits were strongly means-tested (with the social stigma this implied) and set at a low level to encourage recipients to take poorly paid jobs. Such a system therefore only tended to strengthen the power of the market over individuals. Universal benefits, which had no social stigma, such as child benefit and old age pensions were set at a low level so that they were only of importance to the poorer groups in society. This tended to decrease middle-class interest in, and support for, state welfare because they were able to buy private benefits or obtain fringe benefits through their employment and therefore largely exclude themselves from reliance on the state system. Other systems, for example in France, Austria, Germany and Italy, were less concerned about maintaining the discipline of the market and more influenced by conservative attitudes, especially those of the churches with their emphasis on the family and childcare and the exclusion of non-working wives from the system. These states produced highly conservative schemes based on status, with different programmes for different occupations (the best benefits usually went to civil servants). Since many benefits were based on long periods of contribution the schemes tended to exclude the poorest, who suffered from numerous periods of unemployment, and their redistributive element was minimal. Only in the Scandinavian states were much larger welfare systems developed that incorporated the middle class. Standards of benefit were high and universal, so there was little incentive to the middle class to move outside the state system. Although levels of taxation were necessarily high to support high levels of benefit, the system retained the support of the middle class. This was not the case elsewhere in the last quarter of the century. In countries such as Britain and the United States the middle class began to favour reducing taxation and shifting towards private provision, especially if the state was prepared to introduce tax incentives for doing so. The state system therefore became even less attractive and the social stigma attached to state benefits increased.

Outside the core states welfare systems were generally much less developed. Only a few oil-rich states such as Brunei, with a high revenue and a small population, could afford to provide free schools, hospitals and even housing. Some states in the semi-periphery such as Chile and Argentina spent almost as much of their national budgets on welfare as the core states, but in others such as Colombia only a minority of people were covered – in Bogotá in 1980 only a third of workers were covered by unemployment insurance. Some states such as Malaysia had no state spending on welfare as a matter of principle. In others spending was so low as to have no measurable impact. In fourteen states in Africa in 1990 welfare spending was less than 3 per cent of the national budget (in most core states it was still about half the total).

The impact of welfare systems on the distribution of wealth and income within societies was very limited in the twentieth century. The measurement of wealth is an extremely difficult task and few statistics exist covering the whole of the century, Britain and the United States apart. In 1900 the United States was probably the most egalitarian of the core states – the top 1 per cent of the population owned about a third of all assets, whereas in Britain they owned two-thirds. In general in the course of the century the ownership of assets became less direct (from the single proprietor of a business to shareholdings for example), the middle class gained new assets, in particular houses (though these were not readily marketable) and the rich were able to maintain and pass on their capital. In Britain there was a very slight equalization of wealth, but it was nearly all within the wealthiest groups – from the top 1 per cent to the top 5 per cent. By the end of the century Britain was probably the least egalitarian of the core states – the bottom half of the population owned less than 7 per cent of all the wealth. The United States became more egalitarian until about the early 1960s, but then became less equal so that by the 1990s the top 1 per cent of the population owned 40 per cent of the country's assets, a higher proportion than in 1900. Outside the core the sporadic information available suggests that the ownership of wealth was far less equal, especially in areas such as Latin America, where landholdings were concentrated in a few hands.

Income was more evenly distributed than wealth but there were, throughout the century, massive inequalities within societies. In general the core states had a more even distribution of income than those elsewhere, but nowhere did the substantial economic growth which characterized the century lead, in itself, to greater equality. At the start of the century in the core states the distribution of income was largely determined by the relationship between wages and the income derived from assets. However, the growth of direct and indirect taxation, the provision of public services and transfer payments, in the form of benefits, significantly complicated the situation and did, to varying degrees, affect the distribution of income. For example, in 1900 on average only about one in ten of the population paid income taxes in western Europe. Between the two World Wars the proportion rose to slightly less than half and by the 1960s to about four out of five people.

The result of introducing progressive income taxes and state benefits was that between 1900 and about 1960 there was a general increase in equality. In both Britain and Denmark the top 10 per cent took about 45 per cent of all income in 1900, but this share had fallen to about 25 per cent by 1970. The only exception to this trend was the United States, where income inequality increased until about 1930. However, this general reduction in the share taken by the richest groups resulted mainly in a redistribution to upper middle levels. Across the core states there was very little change in the share of income taken by the bottom 60 per cent – fairly consistently they received only about a third of total incomes. The trend towards greater equality of income slowed in mid-century and by the last third of the century had gone into reverse across the core states. The restrictions imposed on state benefits, combined with the collapse in demand for unskilled labour, the huge increase in the number of part-time jobs, massive increases in top professional salaries and the sale of state-owned industries which increased income from asset holding, helped produce greater income inequality. The share of total income taken by top groups rose and those at the bottom saw their share fall. By 1995 in Britain, for example, the bottom half of the population received a share of total income lower than they had in 1945. In general the United States and Switzerland were the least egalitarian states and the Scandinavian countries, which largely maintained their state welfare programmes, were the most equal. By the 1990s in the United States the bottom fifth of the population received less than 6 per cent of all incomes, whereas in Finland they received nearly twice that. The degree of inequality within societies also meant that comparisons of average incomes between countries could lead to seriously misleading results. In the mid-1990s the average income in Britain was just over £11,000, significantly above that of Hungary. However, the bottom 20 per cent in Britain earned £2,500, the same as the bottom 20 per cent in Hungary.

Outside the core states comparative income figures are far from reliable and are also difficult to interpret. However, it seems clear that despite almost complete state ownership of assets and control over incomes the Communist states were not particularly successful at creating income equality except in China. In the 1960s and 1970s the Scandinavian states had greater income equality than the Communist states of Eastern Europe. In most countries of the periphery there were huge differences in income between the elite and the mass of the population. However, there were significant differences. For example, income equality in Argentina was greater than in Mexico and Brazil, where economic growth produced growing inequality. In Brazil by the last third of the century the top 1 per cent of the population had a greater share of the national income than the bottom 50 per cent. Overall between 1960 and 1990 the bottom half of Brazilian society saw its share of national income fall from about 18 per cent to 10 per cent. Only a few states, such as Hong Kong, South Korea and Taiwan, managed to produce high growth and a lessening of income differentials.

Because of this major income inequality, poverty remained an enduring feature in all societies. However, poverty is a difficult concept to define. At one level it was the inability to buy even a minimum diet for a family. At the next it could be the inability to afford more than basic subsistence – food, clothing, housing, heating and a few household utensils. At a higher level poverty, in the form of relative deprivation, meant an income below the level at which it was possible to participate fully in society. In the core states most people were always able to afford a minimum diet and only in times of severe depression such as the 1930s did this form of poverty become common. In 1934 over a hundred people starved to death on the streets of New York, in St Louis people were digging through rubbish dumps for food and in Oakland (California) families were living in sewer pipes. In the Pennslyvanian coal-mining areas three or four families were living together in a one-room shack, trying to survive on wild weeds. In South Africa at this time over 300,000 whites (one in six of the total) were dependent on charity for survival. In the periphery such conditions were common through-out the century, not just in times of economic depression or famine. A study carried out in the mid-1970s showed that three-quarters of the rural population in Pakistan had incomes below minimum subsistence levels. In the late 1980s nearly nine out of ten people living in Bangladesh (about 100 million people) were estimated to live in absolute poverty. Overall in the world by the 1990s about a quarter of the population (1·5 billion people) nearly all of them in the periphery, lived in so acute a state of poverty that they were unable to afford a subsistence diet for much of their lives. If those who lived on the margin of subsistence were included the total would rise to 2 billion people.

The basic subsistence definition of poverty was used by Seebohm Rowntree in his classic study of poverty in York in 1899. Even this more restrictive definition showed that in one of the wealthiest core states a third of the population lived in such conditions. This had fallen to about one in five of the population when the study was repeated in 1936 (though similar studies suggested that nearly half the American population might have been in such circumstances during the depression of the 1930s). By 1950 the number living in York at the subsistence level had fallen to below 2 per cent of the total population and it was widely believed that, with the arrival of state welfare programmes, poverty had been eradicated in the core states. In the 1960s, however, poverty was 'rediscovered': in Britain it was found that about one in eleven of the population was living below the minimum state benefit level, mainly because of low wages. In the second half of the century most core states defined poverty as having to live on an income of less than half the national average. On this definition a comparative survey carried out in the 1980s suggested that it affected about one in twelve of the population in Britain, slightly less in Germany and only one in twenty in Sweden. The United States had a higher level of poverty than any other core country – it affected about one in six of the population. The people who tended to live in poverty were usually the elderly, single mothers and those in work (and therefore disqualified from state welfare benefits) but on very low incomes. However, there were significant differences between countries. In Sweden almost none of the elderly were poor because of the high level of state pensions. In the United States only about a quarter of the elderly were poor, again because social security payments were high. In Britain on the other hand about half of elderly families lived in poverty because of the low level of the state pension, which was reduced further in the early 1980s when it was no longer linked to the increase in average earnings.

Statistics for poverty in the Communist countries were highly unreliable partly because the official definition set very low levels of income. However, it is clear that these states did not eliminate poverty and rates remained comparable with those in the core states – about one in twelve of the population in Czechoslovakia, one in six in Hungary and the USSR and as high as one in four in Poland. By the 1990s about 100 million people in the former Communist states were living in poverty. This compared with a figure of 44 million in the European Union (about 15 per cent of the population) and about 50 million in the United States. In the last two areas the number of people affected by poverty was rising not falling at the end of the twentieth century. The scale of poverty in the core states meant that in many cases the poor had incomes little different from the average in the periphery. Over 50 million people living in the United States in the mid-1990s had an income the same as the world average and lower than a large proportion of the population of states such as Sri Lanka, Morocco and Egypt.

Despite the problem of endemic poverty, people living in the core countries (a small minority of the world's population) enjoyed a substantial rise in living standards over the century and took part in a huge consumption boom. In the early decades of the century, as the industrialized societies raised incomes and produced enough goods to satisfy all basic wants, considerable concern was expressed among the elite about the future. Once workers were able to buy all necessities would they still be willing to work long hours in factories, to play their vital role in 'Fordist' production methods? Would work still exercise what the elite saw as its necessary disciplining force over the masses? Might they not choose to reduce hours of work and enjoy more leisure instead? These concerns were articulated by John Edgerton, the President of the National Association of Manufacturers in the United States, in 1926:

> it is time for America to awake from its dream that an eternal holiday is a natural fruit of material prosperity . . . I am for everything that will make work happier but against everything that will further subordinate its importance . . . the emphasis should be put on work – more work and better work, instead of upon leisure.

In practice these fears went unrealized. Once workers had achieved the eight-hour day and forty-hour week as normal, they were content to go on working (often including substantial overtime) in order to pay for greater consumption. In the depression of the 1930s and again in the 1970s and 1990s any attempt to reduce working hours so as to reduce unemployment was generally rejected.

The major change came in the amount of paid holidays. At the beginning of the century they were the exception rather than the rule and were normally confined to salaried white-collar staff. By 1930 only one in ten American wage-earners had paid holidays but only one in ten salaried staff did not. In Britain only about 2 million workers had paid holidays. In France a two-week paid holiday was first introduced under the Popular Front government in 1936 and was gradually extended to three weeks (1956), four weeks (1962) and to five weeks in 1982. In the United States there was little improvement and in Japan holidays remained frowned upon and were usually restricted to a week at most. The consequence was that the continued emphasis on work meant that incomes grew steadily enough to provide the motor for the continued expansion of the industrial economies and the demand for an ever-increasing range of goods. Once basic needs were generally met, companies needed to create markets for their new products if they were to continue to expand and increase profits. New forms of credit and deferred payment, which became widespread in the United States in the 1920s, linked to a massive boom in advertising, helped to feed competitive pressures for positional goods (expensive holidays, cars and new consumer products) to demonstrate superiority over other members of society. All these trends meant there was little danger that the expansion of the industrial economies would run out of steam.

Throughout the twentieth century the United States was the wealthiest country in the world with the highest levels of consumption. Until late in the century (when Japan in particular developed a high-technology electronics industry) most new products first found a mass market here and only later elsewhere. This was the case for the car, which was largely invented in Europe, but first produced and owned on a major scale in the United States. As early as 1905 the United States had more cars on the road than Britain, France and Germany combined. By the end of the 1920s the USA had one car for every five people, a level not reached by Britain until 1966 and the Netherlands until 1970. In 1927, when production of the 'T' Model Ford ceased, replacement demand exceeded new owners for the first time. Banks began giving loans for car purchase in 1911, Ford began their own instalment buying plan in 1915 and by 1926 three-quarters of all cars in the United States were bought on credit.

Although car ownership grew everywhere, levels of ownership were very different worldwide by the end of the century. The United States had over 500 per 1,000 of the population, Germany just over 400, Qatar 250 (twice the level of Greece), Russia 40 and China had one car for every 3,000 people. Hundreds of millions of people benefited from the convenience and freedom of car ownership, but there were also numerous drawbacks, not just in terms of pollution. By 1916 the first public complaints about the difficulty of parking in American cities were being made and by the mid-1920s cars were killing over 23,000 Americans a year (including 10,000 children) and injuring another 700,000. By the late 1960s these figures had risen to 55,000 killed and over 4 million injured every year. The worst accident rates were, however, in the periphery. In the mid-1990s 500,000 cars in New Delhi were killing more people than 21 million vehicles in the whole of Britain. Overall by the end of the century with almost 600 million vehicles on the world's roads nearly 900,000 people a year were being killed by them (a third were children).

Greater wealth enabled families in the core states to purchase a large range of consumer items – refrigerators, washing machines, vacuum cleaners, radios, televisions and telephones. Americans were able to buy many of these products in the 1920s but it was not until the 1950s that western Europe moved into this phase of mass consumption, followed a decade later by Japan. Radios were the big consumer item of the inter-war period. Most countries only began broadcasts in the early 1920s, yet by 1925 there were over a million families with radio sets in Britain and by 1940 nearly 9 million. Very limited television broadcasts began in the mid-1930s (the first was in Germany in March 1935), but it was not until the 1950s that major expansion took place. In 1950 Britain had 340,000 households with television sets (the highest in western Europe), by 1960 the figure was 10 million and by 1990 nearly 20 million. Outside the core states these consumer items were much rarer and in many cases non-existent. By the end of the century there were over 600 million telephones in the world, but three-quarters of them were in just nine countries.

Higher earnings and more leisure time meant that the majority of the population in the core states was able to participate in a number of new activities. The first decade of the century was marked by a huge boom in the new medium of cinema. There were two cinemas in Germany in 1900 and 2,500 by 1914. In Britain the weekly audience was about 8 million by the outbreak of the First World War. The addition of sound in the late 1920s and the production of newsreels made the 1930s the boom period for cinema. In Britain by the end of the decade the weekly audience was about 20 million (nearly half the total population) and there were over 5,000 cinemas in the country. After 1950 this predominance gradually faded to be replaced by television, which rapidly became the chief leisure activity of most of the population and took up on average about twenty-eight hours a week across the core states – indeed children in the United States spent as much time watching television as they did at school.

Paid holidays and easy transportation meant that many people in the core states could go away on holidays and this led to the development of a new industry – tourism. At the beginning of the century tourism was still largely restricted to the elite, especially those who could afford foreign travel or cars – in France the Michelin guide to hotels was first published in 1900; a decade later the Automobile Association published a similar guide to Britain. In the United States people began to take holidays in their cars – there were over 5,000 'motor camps' across the country by the mid-1920s – but in Europe holidays were still largely taken by train. In Britain the Youth Hostel Association was founded in 1929 to provide basic accommodation for walkers and cyclists and the Worker's Travel Association (founded in 1921) organized inexpensive foreign travel. By the late 1930s there were over 200 holiday camps for cheap domestic holidays and a major seaside resort like Blackpool was receiving over 7 million tourists a year. Rising living standards in the 1950s saw a boom first in domestic holidays and then, with the development of cheap air travel, of overseas holidays. In total the amount of international air travel grew seventy-fold between 1950 and the early 1990s and the level of overseas tourism grew at nearly 10 per cent a year.

By the mid-1990s over 500 million people a year were taking holidays abroad and the tourist industry was worth about $3·4 trillion a year (equivalent to the GDP of Japan). Four out of five tourists came from the core states and most travelled within Europe and the Mediterranean areas. Only from the 1980s, with falling air travel costs and growing wealth, did inter-continental tourism develop as people from Europe went on holiday to Africa, the Caribbean and the Far East. Some states came to rely on tourism as a major source of revenue. It was vital in the development of Spain and Portugal in the 1950s and 1960s and Greece in the 1970s and 1980s. By the 1990s two-thirds of Egypt's foreign exchange earnings came from tourism. In some states, such as the Maldives, the economy was dominated by tourism, which was by far the biggest industry.

Greater leisure, wealth and easier transportation also led to the development of sport as both a spectator and participatory activity. In the late nineteenth century Britain, which was the wealthiest country in the world, first developed professional sport, particularly football. The first professional league in the world was formed in 1885, based primarily on clubs from the industrial working-class areas. By 1905–6 the seasonal attendance at Football League matches was over 6 million with an average of 300,000 every week. Three years earlier 40,000 people watched Yorkshire play Australia at cricket. In the United States similar crowds watched baseball. Participation was also high – at the beginning of the century about 300,000 people a week played football, there were over 20,000 registered anglers in Sheffield alone and thousands also cycled regularly. By 1914 the daily sports newspaper *L'Equipe* was selling 40 million copies a year in France and at times over 500,000 copies a day during the Tour de France cycle race. However, sport tended to follow and reinforce existing social divisions. For the most part it remained divided along class lines through the distinction between amateurs and professionals (which split rugby but not cricket and football) and through who played which sports: rugby remained in England (though not Wales) primarily an upper-class activity, tennis and golf clubs catered mainly for the middle classes and some sports such as polo were always highly exclusive. Horse racing remained a sport for the wealthy, except for the spectators and those who gambled on the outcome, whereas greyhound racing was for the working class. On the other hand snooker, which began as a game played by Indian army officers, became a largely working-class game.

Many in the elite were worried by this proliferation of activity by the masses and sought to channel it into what they regarded as suitable ends. On the continent of Europe in the early twentieth century gymnastics was promoted by the churches and conservative and military groups as a way of 'improving' the workers, creating physically fit men for the army and achieving many of the aims of the eugenics movement. In Britain sport had long been seen as a way of inculcating suitable values and not only in the ruling elite. In 1893 Edward Lyttelton (later headmaster of Eton, the most exclusive school in the country) advocated sport because:

A boy is disciplined in two ways: by being forced to put the welfare of the common cause before selfish interests, to obey implicitly the word of command . . . and, secondly . . . he is disciplined by being raised to a post of command where he feels the gravity of the responsible office.

Similar values were seen as vital in Vichy France in the early 1940s, where the new conservative education syllabus enforced nine hours of sport and physical education a week. Jean Borotra, a former Wimbledon tennis champion, wrote in a Vichy pamphlet, 'in sport you are preparing your apprenticeship for full social life . . . If you are obedient and respect the rules of the game on the pitch, then you will behave similarly when you are not at play.'

Communist governments also saw benefits to society in the 'discipline' of sport. In October 1920 the Third All-Russia Congress of the Russian Young Communist League stated:

The physical culture of the younger generation is an essential element in the overall system of communist upbringing of young people, aimed at creating harmoniously developed human beings, creative citizens of communist society. Today, physical culture also has direct practical aims: (1) preparing young people for work; and (2) preparing them for military defence of Soviet power.

In the 1930s the Soviet state adopted a fitness and gymnastics programme entitled 'Prepared for Work and Defence'. Similar aims were adopted in eastern Europe and China after the late 1940s.

Sport also had a strongly nationalistic basis. The development of international matches, first in football (originally 'internationals' were between the nations of Britain – the first not involving a British side was in 1902 between Austria and Hungary), then cricket (within the British empire), followed by the revival of the Olympics in 1896, created a focus around which national sentiment could rally. The adoption of certain sports also had political overtones. The revival, and in some cases invention, of Gaelic games in Ireland from the 1890s was a major symbol of the growing revolt against British rule. On the other hand cricket was seen as playing an important role in holding together the disparate British empire. In 1919 the Tour de France was deliberately sent through the battlefields of the war and into Alsace–Lorraine as a symbol of French revival and victory. After 1945 the Communist states saw sport as a way of establishing their identity (especially in East Germany) and marking their status in the world. Individual athletes were identified at a young age and sent through a series of sports schools to develop their talent, where they were subjected to large-scale drug taking to enhance performance. Such efforts were successful. In 1952 Communist states took a third of the medals at the Helsinki Olympics. In 1988 at Seoul they took two-thirds. In 1956 East Germany was ranked fifteenth in the medal table, by 1988 they had overtaken the United States. Cuba rose from fifty-fourth in 1960 to fourth twenty years later.

Improving global transportation networks were essential for the development of international sport. By the 1920s inter-continental competition began on a modest scale. However, it was not until the development of international air travel after 1950 that large-scale competition was possible. The first football World Cup was held in 1930 in Uruguay, but only thirteen countries took part, just four of which were from Europe. By 1998 over 180 countries entered, a two-year qualifying competition was necessary and the number of countries in the final stages had expanded to 32, with the tournament taking in teams from across the globe rather than the Europe-Latin America contests that dominated the competition until 1970. A cricket World Cup started in 1975 and one in rugby in 1987. Baseball had a 'World Series' from 1903, but since only American teams took part it was hardly an international tournament and even after the game took off in Japan and Cuba the tournament was confined to American teams.

As professional sport developed, its sources of finance became increasingly important. In most cases revenue from paying spectators did not cover expenses. In the United States sport was commercialized from the beginning, with businessmen owning the major baseball teams and selling the franchises to run a team. Cycling was also a professional, team-sponsored sport almost from the beginning. In Britain football clubs were usually owned by local businessmen who were prepared to invest money in return for the prestige associated with the club. On the continent of Europe many teams were essentially company clubs – PSV Eindhoven (Philips), Bayer Leverkusen (Bayer), Juventus (Fiat) – and this was also the case in Japan when professional football was established in the 1980s. In Communist countries footballers were often technically 'amateurs', but teams were run by the army – Honved (Hungary), Steaua Bucharest (Romania) and CSKA Sofia (Bulgaria) – or by the security police – Moscow Dynamo, Dinamo Bucharest and

Dynamo Berlin. With the development of television, commercial sponsorship of events, especially by tobacco companies, became attractive because of the free advertising involved. Eventually television fees, particularly after the development of satellite sports channels, became a major source of revenue for some sports, such as football. By the mid-1990s Spanish television was showing 788 football matches a year, 512 of them live. The demands of television also affected sports scheduling. At the Wimbledon tennis tournament the prestigious men's singles final was originally played on a Friday afternoon when the television audience was minimal and only those able to buy a ticket and take time off from work could attend. Under pressure from television it was shifted first to Saturday afternoon and then Sunday afternoon. In the football World Cup the quarter-finals and semi-finals were originally played simultaneously to suit the paying spectators, until the development of satellite communications and a worldwide television audience of billions. By 1982 matches were rarely played at the same time and in both the 1986 and 1994 tournaments in Mexico and the United States matches were scheduled in the midday heat to meet the needs of the European television audience.

Although, at least in the core states, the twentieth century was marked by growing wealth and greater leisure opportunities there was also a darker side – the problem of crime in society. However, the analysis of crime in the twentieth century is complex and difficult for two main reasons. First, definitions of crime changed during the century. Prohibition in the United States between 1920 and 1933 created a whole new series of offences. Abortion was a crime in some states but not in others. Large-scale car ownership also created a vast new range of crimes, from driving offences (dangerous driving and later drink-driving) to theft of cars and speeding and parking offences. (By the 1980s over 1 million offences a year in England and Wales were related to motor vehicles, crimes that could not have been committed earlier in the century.) Until 1919 in Britain and 1914 in the United States the possession and sale of heroin was not a criminal offence (indeed until the 1960s heroin was prescribed to addicts by doctors in Britain). The use of marijuana was not illegal in Nepal and coca was widely available in South America. New crimes also emerged with the development of financial markets and the greater regulation of business behaviour. The second major problem involved crime statistics, which are notoriously unreliable and very difficult to compare between countries (those published by the Soviet Union before 1988, for example, are useless because they were deliberately distorted for political reasons). Most crime (perhaps as much as three-quarters) was never reported and what was recorded was usually intended for other purposes, in particular monitoring police efficiency. Changing attitudes also resulted in changed reporting levels. More sympathetic approaches by the police towards the victims of rape certainly increased the number of reported offences in the late twentieth century. Similarly, decreasing tolerance of child sexual abuse and violence within marriage increased reporting rates.

Some general trends can, however, be established within the core states, where most of the reliable statistics were gathered. The level of crime seems to have declined in the first half of the century: by 1930 it was probably at about an eighth of its level a century earlier. Crime rates rose everywhere after 1950, except in Japan, but not back to nineteenth-century levels. By the late twentieth century car crime was the most prevalent offence in the core societies, followed by theft from homes and fraud. Serious crimes – homicide and armed robbery – were generally very rare and there was no major increase in homicide during the century as a whole. Crime rates were much higher in urban areas and overwhelmingly crimes were committed by males – about four-fifths of youth crime in the United States and Britain in the late twentieth century. All surveys showed that fear of crime was much greater than its actual occurrence. Indeed fear of particular groups – such as the 'dangerous classes' of the late nineteenth century, vagrants, delinquents, male youths in various guises ('Teddy Boys', *blousons noirs*, punks, muggers, 'football hooligans', gangs) – was a constant theme.

Despite the fallibility of the available statistics, it is possible to make a number of comparisons of crime in the core states. The most crime-ridden country throughout the century was the United States. On average the homicide rate was seven times that of west European states. Indeed, in the mid-1980s, the homicide rate in an American city such as St Louis was nineteen times that in Bombay and New Delhi, and the number of criminal offences committed in Boston was over forty times greater than in Rio de Janeiro. One of the reasons for the high homicide rate in the United States was the easy availability of guns. In the twenty years after 1963 440,000 people were killed, 1,700,000 injured and 2,700,000 robbed by people carrying guns. It was estimated in the 1980s that 270,000 children carried guns to school in the United States and over 3 million crimes a year were committed in schools. The New York school system had a security force of 2,400 officers, which made it the eleventh biggest in the country. In the 1980s over 18 million homes in the United States were robbed and nearly half of the population was the victim of some sort of crime in any one year. This was far higher than rates in western Europe and twice that of Surabaya in Indonesia, where a detailed comparative study of crime was carried out as part of a United Nations programme.

Significant, but largely unexplained, differences also existed between other core states. Crimes of violence were very low in Britain, about a third of the rate in Australia. In West Germany in 1988 just over one in ten people were the victims of car crime, but this was higher than in the United States and twice the rate experienced in Switzerland and Finland. The problem of how to deal with crime remained intractable throughout the century. The highest number of police per head of the population in the late twentieth century was in West Germany, but this did not produce a lower crime rate. Neither did the use of private security firms in the United States, where they spent twice as much as the whole state system and employed more than twice as many people. The development of closed-circuit television cameras and video recorders in public places helped to reduce some crimes, but in many areas of the core countries by the end of the century the rich were retreating into private security enclaves away from the crime-ridden cities.

In terms of punishing crime the general trend over the century was to abolish capital punishment for murder. Italy did so in 1890, as did most of the Scandinavian states by 1950, followed by Britain in 1965 and 58 more countries by the 1990s. The United States followed this general trend and between 1968 and 1977 no executions were carried out. Then a number of state governments began to reintroduce the death penalty, against the general trend among the core countries, so that by the mid-1990s about 50 people a year were being executed in the United States. The death penalty was also still used in 78 other countries outside the core states. Saudi Arabia even used public beheading for a variety of crimes: murder, possession of alcohol, drug offences, adultery and rape (about two-thirds of those executed were foreigners). Imprisonment was an equally problematic solution to dealing with crime. Britain had proportionately the highest prison population in Europe (except Turkey), but crime levels the same as in the Netherlands which only imprisoned a third as many people. For the first eight decades of the century the prison population in the United States was stable. Yet by the end of the century numbers had trebled in an attempt to combat crime. By 1989 the USA imprisoned a higher proportion of its population than the Soviet Union, seven times as many as western Europe and as many people were in jail in just one state, Texas, as in the whole of the United States in 1948. In many cities one in three of all black males aged between eighteen and thirty-four were either in prison, on parole or on probation.

The twentieth century was also marked by the rise of organized crime in a number of areas – American inner cities, the Mafia of Sicily and southern Italy, the Triads of Chinese society (particularly outside China after 1949) and the extensive criminal organizations in the Soviet Union. By the latter part of the century organized crime was following many of the trends found more generally in societies and economies, in particular the shift into business and international finance (disguised as legitimate companies) and globalization, with the development of links between different groups especially through involvement in drugs. Crime organization also came to dominate politics in a number of areas. For example, the Mafia and similar organizations in many American cities were powerful because of their close links with politicians and use of widespread corruption. In the south of Italy the situation was far worse. Until the 1950s the Mafia was part of a traditional cultural system based on honour and violence, and politicians and the state authorities co-operated with these groups in order to maintain order locally. In 1943–5, during the occupation of Italy, the Allies appointed many Mafiosi mayors in Sicily and Calabria and the economic expansion in the region after 1950 shifted the focus of the Mafia into commercial activities, where they took control over a large proportion of the public contracts in the area. Links between the Mafia, the political parties, in particular the Christian Democrats, and the judiciary remained close. In 1955 Giuseppe Guido Lo Schiavo, a member of the Supreme Court of Appeal, wrote: 'The mafia has always had respect for the magistracy and for Justice . . . in the pursuit of bandits and outlaws it has openly sided with the forces of law and order,' and added about the new head of the Mafia: 'May his labours increase the respect in which the laws of the State are held, and may they be for the social betterment of all.' In Colombia crime syndicates also moved into legitimate business, owning radio and television stations, film companies, football teams and even a zoo. After the collapse of the Soviet Union and the Communist regimes of eastern Europe crime organizations, which had always been widespread, came to dominate whole areas of business and politics.

Certain drugs had to be made illegal before a criminal international trade in them developed. In 1900 the core states not only tolerated drug use domestically but many still actively promoted it internationally. Opium had been immensely popular in the nineteenth century as a pain reliever (consumption rose seven-fold in Britain in the last half of the century) and in 1898 the Bayer chemical company in Germany first marketed diacetylmorphine as a non-addictive panacea for adults and infants under the trade name heroin. It was approved for use by the American Medical Association in 1906. Cocaine had been manufactured since the 1850s (Sigmund Freud took it and argued it was non-addictive) and it was widely used, in Coca-Cola until 1903, and the Parke-Davies pharmaceutical company of Detroit manufactured coca cordials, cocaine cigarettes, ointments and sprays. Internationally the British in the 1840s had forced China to open up trade in opium grown in India, which was a vital source of Indian government revenue. The result was that by 1900 there were over 13 million opium addicts in China. The British government did not formally abandon its advocacy of the drugs trade until 1907. In 1899 the new French governor of Indo-China, Paul Doumer, reorganized the opium industry in the country, built a modern refinery in Saigon and within four years taxes from the trade made up a third of the government's revenue. By 1940 over 100,000 Indo-Chinese people were addicts.

From the first decade of the century onwards the governments of the core states began to prevent drugs such as cocaine and heroin being freely available domestically. International control came with the 1925 Geneva Convention, although some states refused to accept regulation. Iran increased production and by the mid-1930s was supplying nearly half the world's trade, from which it obtained about a sixth of its exports earnings. (By 1949 about one in ten of the Iranian population were addicts.) There were still large numbers of drug addicts – 200,000 in the United States in the mid-1920s – and to supply them an illegal, criminal trade developed, centred on Marseilles. Controls over shipping in the Second World War reduced the trade drastically and the number of addicts in the United States fell to about 20,000. However, after 1945 a number of decisions helped to recreate the trade. The United States backed the Corsican criminal syndicates in Marseilles as a way of keeping the port out of Communist control; it also supported the Chinese nationalists in northern Thailand and the Shan states of Burma after their defeat in the civil war with the Communists. Some heroin was grown in Turkey, Pakistan and India, but the new centre of world production was the 'Golden Triangle' in south-east Asia, which supplied about three-quarters of the illegal trade. Peasants in the area grew poppies because as a cash crop they were the easiest and most lucrative way of earning a living. By the 1960s there were over 50,000 addicts in the United States. Although production in Turkey and the trade through Marseilles was stopped under American pressure in the 1960s, new sources of supply and routes to markets soon emerged, centred on Hong Kong, which by 1970 had the highest proportion of drug addicts of any country in the world. In the American forces fighting the Vietnam War heroin addiction rates reached one in five in some units. The illegal trade involved a vast range of people – in 1971 Prince Sopsaisana, the Laotian ambassador to France, was caught smuggling sixty kilos of heroin worth $13·5 million through Paris airport. In the late 1980s much of the international trade was supplied through corrupt members of the Burmese military government.

The trade in cocaine, which only emerged in the last quarter of the century, was centred on Latin America and was under the control of Colombian crime organizations based in two cities – Medellin and Cali. Most of the crop was grown in Bolivia and Peru where, as in south-east Asia, the peasant farmers had little alternative and found it was by far the most profitable crop. In Bolivia about a fifth of all workers were engaged in the trade and it was worth more than all of Bolivia's legal exports. By the mid-1980s about 6 million people in the United States were using cocaine in some form. By the 1990s the trade had expanded into Europe via Brazil and Nigeria, involving criminal groups in Russia and eastern Europe.

By the late 1990s the United Nations estimated that the world's drug trade was worth about £250 billion a year – more than the international trade in iron and steel and motor vehicles. It was equivalent to about 8 per cent of all world trade. In the ten years after 1985 world production of coca leaf doubled, while opium production more than tripled. Street prices fell in the period, suggesting that drugs traffickers were generally able to avoid detection. The report estimated that across the world about 8 million people took heroin, 13 million took cocaine and 30 million used amphetamine-type drugs. About 140 million people used cannabis. This figure was, however, dwarfed by 230 million people who were prescribed legal sedatives and the even greater number who smoked.

Part Three

INTERNATIONAL HISTORY

8 EMPIRES

THE FIRST half of the twentieth century was an age of empires, in which about half the world's population (700 million people) was subject to alien rule, mainly by the core states of western Europe and the United States, but also by Japan, China and Ethiopia. During this period the emphasis was on the consolidation of empire and there were few signs that after 1945 these empires would collapse rapidly – the colonial rulers assumed their control would last for centuries.

There were two worldwide empires in 1900 – the British and the French. By far the largest was the British, which controlled almost 350 million people. Most important were the white-settled and self-governing colonies of Canada, Australia (newly created as a single entity), New Zealand and South Africa (where the British were in the process of finally defeating the Boers and annexing the Transvaal and Orange Free State). India was regarded as the 'Jewel in the Crown' and was governed by a mixture of direct British rule and indirect rule through the 562 'native states'. The possession of India led the British to try to control bases in the area and on the route to India, especially in the Middle East. Elsewhere the West Indian colonies were in severe economic and social decline and there was little sign of any major progress in the African colonies. In the Far East were the highly valuable trading colonies of Hong Kong, Singapore and Malaya.

The French empire consisted of about 56 million people. The old West Indian colonies (Guadeloupe and Martinique) and the old fishing bases (St Pierre and Miquelon) were in decline. Central to the empire was the large bloc of colonies in West and Equatorial Africa and, in North Africa, Algeria with its considerable French settlement, and the protectorates of Morocco and Tunisia. In addition, the French controlled a small empire in East Africa (Somaliland and Madagascar), a major colony in Indo-China and small islands in the Pacific.

The third largest European overseas empire with 35 million people was that of the Dutch. The Dutch East Indies dominated the empire – elsewhere there were only the poor sugar colony of Surinam and a few islands in the Caribbean. The Dutch empire did not expand in the nineteenth or twentieth centuries. In theory, Portugal had the oldest empire, although most of it had actually been acquired after 1884. After the loss of Brazil in 1822, Portugal controlled only the islands of São Tomé and Principe, the ports of Benguela and Luanda in Angola, the coastal area of Mozambique and three small territories – Goa, Damao and Diu. The partition of Africa and rivalries between the other European powers in the 1880s led to Portugal gaining Angola and Mozambique, although most of these territories, comprising about 10 million people, remained unexplored and uncontrolled in 1900. Portugal's neighbour, Spain, had just lost nearly all of its empire – Cuba, the Philippines and the Pacific islands and controlled only Rio Oro and a few other insignificant parts of Africa (fewer than 1 million people). The German empire (15 million people) was created after the mid-1880s, but its territories – Tanganyika, South-West Africa, Cameroon and Togoland in Africa and some island possessions in the Pacific – were of little value. The Danish empire was even smaller in population than that of Spain and concentrated in the Atlantic – Iceland, Greenland and the Faeroes – but also included part of the Virgin Islands in the Caribbean.

The empire expanding most rapidly at the end of the nineteenth century was that of the United States, with over 10 million people. Until 1898 all the territory acquired by the United States had (bar the naval base on Midway Island) been on the continent of North America and its inhabitants had been promised citizenship and eventual incorporation into the United States. That changed after the 'splendid little war' against Spain in 1898, when it acquired an empire for a toll of just 385 dead. Cuba was allowed its independence, although under strict American supervision. Puerto Rico, Guam and the Philippines were taken from Spain with no promise of future statehood. Hawaii was annexed and incorporated, partly to stop any Japanese takeover. At the same time Wake Island was annexed and partial control over Samoa established. In 1903 the USA took control of the Panama Canal Zone and in 1917 bought the Virgin Islands from Denmark for $25 million.

There were four non-European empires in 1900. In the Middle

East the remains of the old Ottoman empire included about 15 million people in the area of modern Iraq, Syria, Lebanon, Jordan, Saudi Arabia and Israel. China controlled about 17 million people, mainly in Tibet. The Japanese was the most rapidly expanding empire, partly as a response to the late nineteenth-century expansion of European empires in east Asia. It was a regional empire based on local military supremacy and consisted of about 16 million people primarily in Taiwan and Korea, although European pressure stopped Japan from establishing any major colonies on the mainland of China even after its victory in the war of 1894–5. Probably the least-known empire was the Ethiopian, which tripled in size from 1880 to 1900 to take control of Tigre, parts of Somalia, the Ogaden and Eritrea.

The final division of the world between the core countries in the last two decades of the nineteenth century, in particular the 'scramble for Africa', was not a rational or carefully planned operation. It was to a large extent defensive, stemming from a desire to formalize control over existing areas of influence (which had until then usually been kept on an extremely limited basis such as a naval base or trading fort) and deny them to the other major powers. The result, especially in Africa, was an extension of control over areas of dubious economic benefit, which could probably have been exploited without formal political control and which were not suitable for European settlement. By 1900 most of Africa, south-east Asia and the Pacific was divided up into colonies, protectorates and spheres of influence. However, in many areas this division existed only on paper and effective control still had to be asserted through military conquest and 'punitive' expeditions. Between 1871 and the outbreak of the First World War the only French, British, German and Portuguese military activity was in colonial wars. In 1900 the British had just concluded the first phase of the largest colonial war – the conquest of the Transvaal and Orange Free State – which had taken nearly all the military resources of the British empire. In the same year the last major revolt in Asante (West Africa) was put down, but only three years earlier the British had been forced to give up most of the interior of Somalia and confine their influence to the coastal strip. The French were still trying to complete their conquest of Morocco – not until 1911 were the eastern and Atlantic areas controlled – and a three-year campaign followed, involving over 70,000 troops to conquer Fez and the Atlas mountains. In 1909 the Spanish were defeated when they tried to extend their control out of the coastal enclaves of Ceuta and Melitta in Morocco. In 1911–12 Italy fought a major war with the Ottoman empire to gain Libya, which was successful in theory, but by 1914 the Italians actually controlled little more than the coastal fringe.

In these various campaigns the small, professional, imperial armies conducted operations, especially against the local population, with a degree of barbarity not found in wars between the core states. The imperial forces had technological superiority which could be used in open battle: at the 'battle' of Omdurman in the Sudan in 1896 11,000 Africans were killed but only 140 British. However, this superiority was often of little use in less conventional warfare. In many colonies in the early twentieth century there was almost constant low-level warfare. In 1906 the Colonial Office in London had to ban expeditions to northern Nigeria to subdue the Tivs because of the brutality involved. In Kenya war lasted from 1893 to 1911 – about six British soldiers were killed but about 4,500 Africans – the local people also lost 150,000 cattle, which were 'confiscated' and given to the new white settlers. For eight years after 1896 the Dutch fought a bitter 'pacification campaign' (a favourite European term) to control the sultanate of Achin in Sumatra. Similar campaigns lasted in French Equatorial Africa from 1897 to 1920 as taxation was imposed and French forces looted what was not provided 'voluntarily'. The Germans conducted a war of extermination against the Herrero and Nama in South-West Africa with catastrophic results. About 10,000 died during the Japanese conquest of the interior of Taiwan. Warfare was continual in Portuguese Angola and Mozambique and by 1910 the Portuguese still controlled less than a tenth of these colonies and were also mounting a major war of conquest in East Timor. Although the Americans formally gained the Philippines from Spain in 1898, they then fought a brutal three-year war against the nationalists, who had declared independence. Over 120,000 American troops were involved, of whom 4,200 were killed, although this figure should be compared with the 200,000 Filipinos who died, of whom over four-fifths were civilians. The type of warfare involved was described by a soldier from New York writing home to his parents:

> Last night one of our boys was found shot and his stomach cut open. Immediate orders were received . . . to burn the town and kill every native in sight . . . About 1,000 men, women and children were reported

killed . . . I am in my glory when I can sight my gun on some dark skin and pull the trigger.

Like the British in South Africa, the Americans used concentration camps to incarcerate civilians in dreadful conditions. In the early 1890s the British developed the expanding 'dum-dum' bullet, which had become standard issue in colonial campaigns by the early twentieth century. In 1899 The Hague Conference banned its use among 'civilized' nations, but the British successfully objected to a total ban because it 'would favour the interests of savage nations and be against those of the more civilised'. The first use of aircraft to bomb civilians took place on 30 October 1911 when Italian planes dropped grenades on a Libyan town.

The defeat of Germany and the Ottoman empire in 1918 brought about the first major redivision of colonies for a century. After long and vicious arguments between the British and French the Ottoman empire was partitioned, with the French gaining control of Syria and Lebanon and the British Palestine, Transjordan and Iraq. The German empire was taken away on the dubious basis that there had been 'dereliction in the sphere of colonial civilization'. Part of the indictment was that the Germans had undertaken twenty-nine punitive expeditions in the Cameroon between 1891 and 1903, even though the British privately admitted to over forty similar expeditions in an even shorter period in northern Nigeria. Togoland and the Cameroon were divided up by the French and the British (the former gained most), Tanganyika went mainly to Britain, with a small part to Portugal, and Rwanda and Urundi went to Belgium. Most of Germany's Pacific colonies went to Japan and new mini-empires were created by Australia, New Zealand and South Africa, with the last gaining German South-West Africa. Even after 1918 the core powers made further adjustments to their empires, without, of course, consulting the local inhabitants. Between 1919 and 1935 the Italian colony of Libya was given parts of Egypt, Sudan, Algeria and French West Africa. Italian Somaliland also took in part of north-east Kenya. In 1945 the United States took over the Japanese-controlled islands of the Pacific. The last major reallocation of territory took place in 1952 when the United Nations awarded Eritrea to Abyssinia. After full incorporation into Abyssinia in 1962 a thirty-year war followed.

Even after 1918 warfare in the colonies continued as the imperial powers tried to gain and maintain control. Both Spain and France fought until the mid-1930s to establish their rule over the interior of Morocco. The French also had to put down rebellions in Lebanon and Indo-China in the mid-1920s. The last British cavalry charge took place in Afghanistan in 1919, but at the same time new technologies were being adopted – armoured cars were used, aircraft bombed civilians to gain control of Somaliland and keep control of Iraq, and poison gas was also used. The last major war of colonial conquest took place in 1935–6 with the Italian attack on Abyssinia, where gas was also used. Even after 1945 there were still colonial expansion and warfare to impose control – the Chinese in Tibet after 1950 and the Indonesians' attack on the former Portuguese colony of East Timor in 1975.

Once the imperial powers had established control over their colonies, they had to decide how to govern them. The two extreme solutions were self-government and incorporation into the imperial state. Self-government was reserved solely for the white settlement colonies of the British empire – Canada, Australia, New Zealand, South Africa and Southern Rhodesia after 1923. With the 1926 Balfour Declaration and the 1931 Statute of Westminster formal British control over internal matters was ended and gradually local power over foreign policy and defence was extended. Incorporation into the imperial state was applied in a number of cases, but did not usually bring with it the same political rights as the citizens of the imperial power enjoyed. Algeria was incorporated into France (Morocco and Tunisia were not), but the Muslim community was restricted to some control over municipal affairs and only the French settlers could vote for representatives in the French Assembly. After the Second World War the French extended this status to their colonies in the Caribbean together with Réunion and New Caledonia. In the French empire the local population could in theory become French citizens, but by 1938 in French Equatorial Africa just 5,000 out of a total population of 3,400,000 had been given this privilege. The Americans allowed Hawaii to become a state of the union in 1959, but retained Puerto Rico effectively as a colony. In 1951 Portugal dropped the term colony and Portuguese Guinea, Angola and Mozambique became provinces of Portugal. Only the British rejected this option, apart from Ireland before 1922 and a proposal, rapidly abandoned, to incorporate Malta in the 1950s.

Some parts of empires remained as protectorates under local rulers and were never formally brought within the imperial structure. This solution was common in the British empire in areas such as Malaya, Borneo, Tonga, the emirates of the Gulf, Egypt and in the even more complex case of Sudan, which was ruled jointly by Britain and Egypt. The French adopted the same solution in Morocco and Tunisia and nominally in Laos and Cambodia. (The United States had, in effect, a similar relationship with many states in Central America and the Caribbean in the first four decades of the century, in particular Haiti and the Dominican Republic, where they were able to manipulate local rulers.) India was governed under an even more complex regime of directly controlled British territory and indirect rule through the 562 states under native rulers, some of which (for example, Hyderabad with its population of over 12 million), were substantial, while others controlled only a few acres of land. The native princes were under British 'paramountcy' – in particular, the British controlled foreign relations – but they retained autonomy in fiscal, legal and administrative matters, always subject to the 'advice' of a British resident.

With the division of the German and Turkish empires in 1918 a new type of colony emerged – a mandate or trust under League of Nations, later the United Nations Trusteeship Council, supervision. Mandates were divided into three types, the most limited of which covered Palestine, Iraq, Jordan and Syria, which were judged to be sufficiently advanced to allow independence fairly rapidly. The second category covered Tanganyika, Togoland, Cameroon and Rwanda which, in effect, became colonies, although they could not be merged with other colonies and they had to be open to free trade. On the other hand, South-West Africa and the German Pacific colonies were deemed to be so backward that they could become 'integral portions' of the colonial power's territory. In practice these international controls had little impact – they may have stopped Tanganyika being incorporated into the rest of British East Africa but they did not prevent the integration of the British Cameroons into Nigeria. The League of Nations Mandates Commission was largely inactive. It was composed of former colonial officials who refused to visit any of the territories they nominally supervised, relying instead on written reports. A few territories were ruled as personal possessions, for example the Congo, until 1908, by Leopold II of Belgium. Others were run by trading companies until well into the twentieth century – Rhodesia (1923), North Borneo (1942) and large parts of Mozambique (1942).

The most common form of colonial government was direct

authoritarian rule by officials of the imperial power. The problem faced by all the colonial states was that they were both powerful and weak at the same time. They were powerful because ultimately they could mobilize overwhelming military strength, but they were weak because normally in any colony they only had limited military force available and a thinly dispersed administration. In Nigeria in the early twentieth century the British had 4,000 soldiers and a police force of 4,000, but in these units all but 75 officers were African. In Northern Rhodesia (an area as big as Britain, Germany, Denmark, Switzerland and the Benelux countries combined) the British relied on just one badly equipped battalion of 750 Africans under 19 British officers and 8 NCOs. In 1914 French forces in West Africa (which had a population of 16 million people scattered over an area fourteen times the size of France) consisted of 2,700 French officers with 230 African interpreters, 6,000 armed African *gardes civils*, 14,000 African troops and one all-French battalion. European administration was equally thin on the ground. In India in the 1920s there were no more than a thousand British civil servants to govern the country. In practice therefore people rarely saw a representative of the imperial power: in 1909 the British had five District Officers to govern half a million people in the Ashanti region of the Gold Coast, and in the 1920s the French had 5,000 administrators for the 30 million people of Indo-China. In 1914 there were just ninety-six Europeans (including missionaries) living in Rwanda.

Except in the areas of white settlement such as Algeria, Southern Rhodesia and Kenya, the colonial power had to rely on a number of collaborators in order to impose any sort of rule. As Lord Lugard, one of the pillars of the British colonial establishment put it in 1904: 'we need a class who in a crisis can be relied on to stand by us, and whose interests are wholly identified with ours.' The British developed a 'philosophy' called 'indirect rule', which was meant to provide a justification for colonialism by, in theory, allowing the 'natives' to rule themselves in many areas. In some places such as Fiji, Tonga and Buganda in Uganda, where strong local rulers had been incorporated into the imperial structure, this was possible. One of the most developed examples of this process was northern Nigeria, where the Fulani governments of the urban-centred Hausa states, with their established bureaucracies, law courts, fiscal and legal records and educated, literate elite, were assimilated into the imperial structure. Elsewhere the theory proved more problematic. The British were often reduced to appointing important locals as paid 'chiefs' to rule over artificially created 'tribes', as for example in Northern Rhodesia and elsewhere across much of East Africa in the 1930s. The Belgians adopted similar methods in the Congo, creating 6,000 'chiefs' in 1917 but then reducing their number to just over 1,000 by 1938. The French were more reluctant, trying as far as possible to maintain direct rule, although they developed a sophisticated 'divide and rule' policy in the Lebanon and Syria, which relied on the Christian Maronites but also encouraged minorities such as the Druze and the Alawis as alternative centres of power.

Imperial administration was often a shambles. The British had a Colonial Office but until 1930 no single colonial civil service, India was run by the India Office, Egypt, Iraq and parts of the Gulf by the Foreign Office and the white dominions had a separate Dominions Office after 1930. The French had a Colonial Office after 1894, but Algeria was treated as fully assimilated and Tunisia, Morocco and the post-1918 mandates were run by the Foreign Office. In Japan the military ruled Korea but the civilians ran Taiwan. In Germany there was an efficient Colonial Office but the navy ran the concession in China. In Portugal until 1911 the empire was run from the navy ministry. The United States, for ideological reasons, tried to pretend that it did not have an empire and therefore did not have a Colonial Office. Responsibility for the various colonies and dependencies was spread around existing departments – Interior (which had a Division of Territories and Island Possessions after 1934), War (the euphemistically named Bureau of Insular Affairs) and the State Department. Guam, Samoa and the Virgin Islands were run by the navy after 1931, as was Micronesia when it was taken from Japan in 1945.

One of the major impacts of colonialism was on the imperial powers themselves. Rule over other parts of the world for the benefit of the home country fitted easily into the prevailing intellectual atmosphere and unwritten assumptions of the European states and the United States, dominated as they were by racism, social Darwinism and the unquestioned view that they represented progress and therefore had the right to rule other people. The inherent contradiction within this view of imperialism was well expressed by Lord Lugard when he wrote that in Africa Britain was 'bringing to the dark places of the earth, the abode of barbarism and cruelty, the torch of culture and progress, while ministering to the material needs of our own civilizations'. It was always possible to provide justifications for imperial rule as, for example, President

McKinley did with his defence of the acquisition of the Philippines: 'we could not leave them to themselves – they were unfit for self-government and would soon have anarchy and misrule over there worse than Spain's was [sic]'. He asked rhetorically, 'Did we need their consent to perform a great act of humanity?' The idea that the 'natives' could decide major issues for themselves was rejected as clearly inappropriate. William Howard Taft, the first civilian governor of the Philippines and later US President explained:

> it is absolutely necessary, in order that the people be taught self-government, that a firm, stable government under American guidance and control . . . should be established. Nothing but such a government can educate the people into a knowledge of what self-government is.

Similar views were also apparent on the left of politics. The British Labour Party programme of 1918 rejected 'the Imperialism that seeks to dominate other races' but accepted 'the moral claims upon us by the non-adult races'. The idea that the natives were children who needed to be taken under the benevolent and protective wings of the white man was widespread. During his journey through East Africa in 1907, Winston Churchill wrote of the Kikuyu of Kenya as 'these light-hearted, tractable, if brutish children'. Taft spoke of 'our little brown brothers' and Albert Schweitzer, working in his African leper colony, admonished 'his' Africans: 'I am your brother, but your elder brother.'

A number of organizations, official, semi-official and independent, grew up to promote imperial values and interests. These included the Colonial Society in Germany and the Kokuryukai (Black Dragon Society) in Japan, which saw 'the mission of imperial Japan' as being to 'check the expansion of the western powers', fight Russia and establish a continental empire in Manchuria, Mongolia and Siberia. In France there were the Naval and Colonial League, the General Colonial Agency, founded in 1919 to promote trade, and the Federation of Colonial Youth, which sponsored an annual 'colonial week' which was introduced into the school curriculum in the 1920s. One of the most extensive networks of imperial propaganda was found in Britain. Many in the elite thought that the empire was a way of inculcating the 'correct' values into people, especially children, through an emphasis on power, authority, responsibility, militarism and preparedness as part of a general quest to improve 'national efficiency'. There were a few government organizations such as the Imperial Institute, the Empire Marketing Board (trade marks were introduced in 1926 to distinguish 'empire' from 'foreign' goods), the Royal Colonial Institute and the Colonial and Empire Film Unit. Most of the activity, however, came from private organizations such as the Primrose League, Victoria League, League of the Empire, British Empire Union, United Empire Trade League, Women's Guild of Empire and the Imperial South Africa Association. Empire Day (24 May) was first celebrated in 1916 under its motto of 'One King, One Flag, One Fleet, One Empire'. It was founded by Lord Meath with the aim of inculcating the Japanese spirit of *bushido* into the British, emphasizing loyalty, patriotism, sacrifice and duty. In 1932 the BBC began an empire radio service, and in the same year a new 'tradition' was founded – the monarch's radio broadcast to the empire.

Equally important were the great exhibitions which were designed to spread the imperial idea. The French held colonial exhibitions at Marseilles in 1906 and 1922, and in 1931 the Bois de Vincennes in Paris was host to the International Colonial Exposition, with pavilions from Britain, Belgium, Portugal, Italy, Japan and, interestingly, the United States. These and other similar exhibitions had a number of clear messages. In 1909 the Anglo-French event at the White City in London had a model of a supposed village from Dahomey with what were described as its 'bloodthirsty potentates' and 'women warriors'. The programme pointed out:

> Order and decency, trade and civilization have taken the place of rule by fear of the sword. France has placed its hand on the blackest spot in West Africa, and wiped out some of the red stain that made Dahomey a by-word in the world. Today Dahomey is a self-governing [sic] colony of France, with a revenue which exceeds its expenditure . . . the days of savagery are passing away.

One of the largest events of this type was the British Empire Exhibition at Wembley in 1924–5. The official programme described it as 'a Family Party of the British Empire . . . an Empire with a hundred languages and races had one soul and mind'. The message was that the empire stood for 'justice, progress and liberty'. The aim of the 'Pageant of Empire' was to give the British people 'a fuller knowledge of our Imperial inheritance and its wonderful development by the peoples under our flag'. The peoples of the empire were noticeable mainly by their absence. All the 'Commissioners' from the dominions and colonies who organized the exhibits were British and when the Prince of Wales suggested that natives should take part in some of the pageants the Colonial Office was worried by a possible increase in 'half-breed births' and a 'marked demoralization' of the natives on their return. The idea was therefore dropped and British people played the part of the colonials. Although 8 million people visited the exhibition, this was partly because of the vast amusement park which had been added to tempt potential visitors. Overall the exhibition lost about £1·5 million and had to be extended into a second year in an unavailing attempt to recover its costs.

Education also played a major role in spreading the idea of empire. By 1940 Britain had eight professors of imperial history and there were numerous imperial education conferences. The message in school textbooks was clear. *The British Empire* written by J. M. D. Meiklejohn and published in 1907 stated, 'We have succeeded by moral influence alone in establishing the Pax Britannica', and that in their colonies Europeans were 'spreading a hard-won civilization'. Popular education had titles such as *The Wonder Book of the Empire* and *The Empire Annual for Girls*. At a more popular level the craze for collecting cigarette cards meant that every manufacturer produced numerous imperial sets, including ones on the armed forces, colonial troops, Indian regiments, empire flags and coats of arms, the dominions, 'Builders of Empire', empire scenes, peoples of the empire, industries of the empire, governors-general of India, empire air routes and 'Picturesque People of the Empire'.

Life in the empire was very different from the mythology created by imperial propaganda. The imperial power's impact on a local society centred on two key areas – labour and land – which were central to economic exploitation. The situation varied in each colony because of the varying balances between the two factors. In a minority of cases the local population was willing to grow crops for export on its own land, partly because of the cash incentive provided through the market and partly because the colonial authorities used taxes to increase the incentives. This situation applied in the Dutch East Indies and elsewhere in south-east Asia, where local peasants grew sugar, cotton, tobacco, spices and rubber. It also applied to a limited extent in West Africa, where peasants produced palm oil and groundnuts for export. However, attempts to force peasants to cultivate particular crops usually failed. In East Africa in 1903 the

German authorities imposed cotton cultivation but on highly disadvantageous terms – the local peasants received only a third of the sale price, with the rest being split between the German agent and the government. Within two years of the scheme's start there was a major rebellion in which about 75,000 Africans died. The Portuguese also imposed cotton cultivation on Angola in the 1920s and rice on Mozambique after 1941. The problem for the over 100,000 peasants involved was that if the crop failed they had no money and no means of subsistence. Thousands of peasants fled into neighbouring colonies to avoid the system, and the problems it caused were a major factor behind the nationalist revolts that began in the early 1960s.

If the local peasants would not grow the crops the colonial authorities wanted, then an alternative was to move in white settlers. In Canada and Australia the indigenous population could easily be cleared and the climate made the country suitable for European settlement. The Maoris in New Zealand resisted the European incursion more strongly, but the British obtained most of the land they wanted. Elsewhere the situation was more difficult, especially in Africa, where only a few areas were suitable for European settlement. In Togo there were just 345 German settlers in 1912 and a decade later Europeans owned just over 1 per cent of the land in the Gold Coast. It was often very difficult to attract settlers. In the first four decades of the century over 1 million Portuguese emigrated to the United States, Brazil and Argentina, but only 35,000 went to Angola and only a tenth of those took up agriculture. Under Mussolini Italy attempted to create a new settlement colony in Libya. In November 1938 1,800 families left Genoa and Naples for specially built villages created by removing the local population. The land was poor and largely unsuitable for agriculture and the scheme was a failure. However, in the parts of Africa that were suitable for European settlement the takeover of Africans' land was on a massive scale. In South Africa, by the early 1930s, 6 million Africans were confined to the 'native reserves', which comprised 34,000 square miles of the worst land. Less than 2 million whites were allocated 440,000 square miles, much of which was never cultivated. The same pattern was imposed in Southern Rhodesia. In Kenya a few thousand whites were allocated the prime land of the so-called 'White Highlands'. The Africans, who made up over 90 per cent of the population, were left with less than half the land in the country. In other colonies vast tracts of land were granted to companies as concessions. Nearly three-quarters of the French Congo was given to forty companies. The British company Lever Brothers was given 350,000 hectares of the Belgian Congo, but only cultivated a sixth of its concession. Overall, across the continent, millions of people were uprooted from their native villages and forced to move, usually on to overcrowded marginal land.

The colonial authorities also needed labour, not just to help cultivate European-owned land but also for public works. Slavery was ruled out in the twentieth century except in the Portuguese colonies. It was not formally abolished there until 1913 following a revolution which ended the monarchy and under pressure from an international boycott of Portuguese goods. At the time of abolition there were probably about 40,000 slaves on plantations on São Tomé and Principe and roughly half that number in Angola, where a slave could still be bought for about £30. In addition about 100,000 people had been forcibly sent to São Tomé to work on the cocoa plantations. Although they were paid a nominal wage, they were effectively slaves. In French colonies, and Portuguese after 1913, forced labour was the norm, either for the state or for contractors approved by the state. In the Portuguese colonies this amounted to about four months a year and between 1922 and 1934 the French used over 120,000 forced labourers to build a railway in Equatorial Africa. The French did not commute the forced labour requirement to a money payment until 1937 and the Portuguese refused to ratify the International Labour Organization's Forced Labour Convention of 1930 until 1956. In the Belgian Congo after 1908 forced labour was used not just for public works but also to cultivate specified crops on communal lands. Apart from forced labour, the Africans were also made to take up paid work for the whites and leave subsistence agriculture through the imposition by nearly all colonial governments of either a poll tax or a hut tax, both of which had to be paid in cash. As Pierre Ryckmans, the governor of the Belgian Congo, put it in 1934: 'What we must overcome in order to lead the Black to work is not so much his laziness as his distaste for *our* work, his indifference to *our* wage system.' Most of the wages paid, except in the mines, were low and the consequence of forcing the men out into work was that the women who stayed at home were responsible for subsistence agriculture. In the mines, although the wages were relatively high (but far below European levels), the migrant workers were kept in poor conditions in squalid barracks under strict disciplinary regimes.

One of the fundamental questions raised by colonialism was the extent to which the imperial powers exploited the territories under their control. Colonies were normally expected to be self-financing and through taxation pay for all their services, including defence. Normally they did not make a direct contribution to the imperial power. The exception was the Congo when it was a personal possession of the Belgian monarch, Leopold II. By 1901 the annual profit extracted from the Congo was a minimum of 18 million francs a year, which Leopold used to build the Arcade du Cinquantainaire in Brussels and the Tervuren Museum and to enlarge Laeken Castle. After 1901 this system was institutionalized in the Fondation de la Couronne, which was granted 10 per cent of the Congo (equivalent to half of France) and the revenue which it generated was spent in Belgium. This was what Leopold called 'legitimate compensation' for his efforts and a 'just share in the embellishment' of his other territory, Belgium. The situation was so corrupt and the conditions in the Congo so appalling that about half the population died in twenty years. The situation was exposed through the efforts of Sir Roger Casement (who was executed by the British as a traitor in the First World War for his support of an independent Ireland) and the Belgian state took over the territory from the king in 1908.

In most states exploitation was achieved in a less direct manner through trade and currency manipulation. The French imposed the metropolitan franc throughout their empire (except in Indo-China), which meant that the local currency was tied to domestic French economic policy. The British created regional currencies, managed from London and convertible only into sterling. Colonial governments were also forced to keep huge currency balances in London, which were deflationary for the colonial economy but beneficial to the British. Trade with the colonies was usually dominated by metropolitan firms through institutional and political links even where, as in the British empire before 1932, there was nominal free trade. However, the scale of this trade should not be exaggerated – in 1914 total German trade with its empire was worth less than that with neighbouring Luxemburg. Once ports and a few railways had been built to bring products down to the coast the imperial authorities lost interest in any major 'development' of the colonial economies, which they left to stagnate. The British first established a Colonial Development Fund in 1929, but it was limited to no more than £1 million a year and most of that went in subsidies to British exporters. The French drew up a similar plan two years later, but half of the money allocated remained unspent. Even basic planning often failed. In the 1920s the roads and railways built in both Algeria and Morocco stopped a few hundred metres short of the border on both sides because the colonial authorities could not agree on how to finance any links.

In general the development of industry was not encouraged. Although labour was cheap it was largely untrained and with poor, impoverished local markets it was usually easier to import goods, particularly when the absence of tariffs meant there was no protection for local industry. In some cases there was an active policy of de-industrialization. After 1890 the British discouraged the Indian cotton industry, and the Portuguese did the same in southern Angola by putting a duty on imported cotton thread in 1892. Within six years over 90 per cent of requirements were imported from Portugal and until the 1940s the Portuguese did not allow any industrial development in their colonies. One major area of investment was mining, which took up two-thirds of all the capital investment in Africa before 1935. Two-thirds of the continent's railways were also in the mining countries of South Africa, the Rhodesias and the Belgian Congo. By 1935 minerals accounted for over half the continent's exports and in some cases such as Northern Rhodesia they were all but 4 per cent of the total.

Little attempt was made to educate the local population. In 1921 out of a population of nearly 3 million in French Equatorial Africa only 4,000 children attended primary school, and even by the late 1930s less than 2 per cent of the children in Upper Volta were being given the most basic education. At a higher level the British established a Royal Indian Engineering College. Although it was paid for by the Indian government, it was located in Britain and students had to be 'British subjects of European race' except for a maximum of two 'natives of India' who could be admitted only if there were vacancies. Indians therefore tended to go to the much less prestigious Jamshedpur Technical Institute set up in 1921, which slowly produced a small number of technically trained people to work in Indian industry. A few 'natives' were allowed into the lower levels of the civil service but, although the civil service in Ceylon, for example, was theoretically open to all, an entrance examination was not held in the country until 1924.

The reality of colonialism can be judged by its impact in three cases – the French colony of Guinea, the British colony of Kenya and the Pacific territories of Ocean Island and Nauru. Guinea had long been a trading area for the French; by 1890 the coastal strip had been brought under French control and a decade later this was extended into the hinterland. Until 1920 the main economic activity was gathering rubber from the trees that grew wild in the area. The French built the port of Conakry and a railway to Kankan in the heart of the rubber-producing area, but undertook no further infrastructure projects. They imposed a poll tax on all Africans over the age of eight, which provided 90 per cent of state revenue. Most people had no money to pay the tax and French companies would only pay them a derisory amount for collecting rubber to prevent costs rising to uneconomic levels. The industry collapsed by 1920 under competition from British production in Malaya. The colonial authorities tried to shift the economy to producing bananas and coffee for export, but neither was very successful. The main requirement was cheap labour and 2,700,000 man-days a year of forced labour were extracted by 1935. As well as financing the colony through the poll tax and forced labour, the Africans were also subject to conscription. The handful of white settlers paid no direct taxes and the trading companies no taxes at all. By 1902 it was known that the country contained large amounts of bauxite and iron ore, but these deposits were not exploited until 1948 because the French had adequate supplies from elsewhere. The French built one hospital in Conakry in 1902, mainly for the settler community. A second hospital in the colony was not built until 1955.

Kenya was taken over by the British in 1895 and the economy was transformed by 1914. It was decided that the Africans were too lazy to develop the colony and an initial decision to bring in Indian labour was defeated by opposition on racial grounds from the 500 or so Europeans who lived in the territory. In 1905 the British decided to open areas to European settlement especially in the Highlands, which had the most fertile soil and access to the sole railway in the colony. Land was forcibly taken from the Africans and their cattle were sold if they objected. By 1910 about 600,000 acres a year were going to the Europeans, who rented farms on 999-year leases from the government at £10 a year for a 5,000-acre holding. By 1930 2,000 white settlers owned over 5 million acres of Kenya, all formerly held by the Africans, although they cultivated less than an eighth of their holdings. The crops they cultivated were chosen by the government for broad imperial reasons and shifted from maize to sisal and eventually to coffee, to reduce Britain's dependence on imported coffee from Brazil. The colonial government's main role was to provide a controlled African wage labour force to work on the European farms. The Africans were moved from their ancestral lands to overcrowded 'reserves' (overall the population fell from 4 million in 1902 to 2·5 million twenty years later). A hut tax was imposed in 1897, but when more Africans started living in each hut this was shifted to a poll tax. Forced labour of up to sixty days a year was also imposed in 1910. An import tax was instituted, but only on agricultural implements used by the local population – those for the European settlers were duty free. By 1920 the European settlers felt that African labour was still in short supply and so the poll tax was tripled to force more people to work. The burden of financing the government was imposed on the Africans: in the 1920s the white settlers paid £7,500 a year in direct taxes and the African population £558,000.

Ocean Island and Nauru in the Pacific were tiny islands with a Polynesian population of about 3,500 at the beginning of the twentieth century. Ocean Island was bought by the British in 1901 for £50 from a man posing as a local chief. Nauru was a German colony until its conquest and annexation by Australia after 1914. The attraction of the islands was that they were composed of solid phosphate and could therefore provide cheap fertilizer. Mining started in the first decade of the century, using imported Chinese labour and Fijian police to keep order. By 1911 the British Phosphate Company was paying the Ocean islanders £250 a year, but making profits of over £20 million with dividends of up to 50 per cent for shareholders. Under pressure from the government the company agreed to pay the islanders a levy of sixpence a ton on the phosphate. However, the British government had deeper motives than philanthropy towards the islanders. They incorporated Ocean Island into the Gilbert and Ellice Islands and used the levy money, which they held in trust for the islanders whom they regarded as too primitive to spend it wisely, to pay the administrative costs of the Gilbert and Ellice colony. In 1919 the British bought out the company on generous terms and set up a joint commission with Australia and New Zealand to provide cut-price phosphate fertilizer at below world prices. In 1927 the British gave themselves the power to acquire forcibly any land the locals refused to sell. By the 1930s about 1 million tons of phosphates were being mined every year as all the vegetation and the top fifty feet of land on the islands were stripped away.

During the Second World War the British evacuated the whites and labourers on the islands, but left the locals to face Japanese occupation. The Japanese took them to the Caroline Islands and in 1945 the British refused to let the troublesome natives back to Ocean Island, sending them instead to Rambi in Fiji. This new home was 'bought' by the British on behalf of the islanders using some of the levy money, which was paid to the colonial government in Fiji. With the islanders removed, more labourers were moved in and deep mining started. On Nauru, which was under the supervision of the United Nations (as an ex-Germany colony and League of Nations mandate), the islanders had to be allowed home. By the mid-1960s about 3 million tons of phosphates were being removed from the two islands every year and sold cheaply to Australia and New Zealand. Under pressure from the United Nations, Australia granted Nauru independence in 1968. Then the newly independent government was able to negotiate substantial royalties, which provided a base to sustain the islanders when the phosphates ran out in the mid-1990s and they were left with no other resources on which to live. The Ocean Islanders were not so lucky. By 1980 all the phosphates were exhausted and the islanders were left on Rambi in Fiji with no income. They brought a legal action against the British government for compensation, but the British court ruled that the island had been legally acquired for £50 in 1901 and that the actions taken by the British government had been in the best interests of the islanders. They were awarded £500,000 as compensation but all of that was needed to pay their legal costs. They were left penniless and living in exile with their homeland ruined and uninhabitable.

Daily life in the colonies demonstrated the almost total gulf between the ruling white elite and the local people. The Europeans tried to restrict their contacts with the indigenous population as much as possible and confine it mainly to the mass of servants they employed. Separate living areas and social facilities for the rulers in civil and military quarters well away from the native city were the norm. The colonial rulers were provided with modern water supplies and sanitation and their fear of disease was a common argument for removing the local people. In 1910 the German administration in Cameroon came up with a plan to relocate the entire African population of Douala inland, leaving the harbour area for the 400 whites in the colony with a 1-kilometre wide uninhabited zone to keep out the natives. In Senegal the lieutenant-governor devised a similar relocation policy for Dakar, declaring, 'It was necessary to create near Dakar a large segregation camp to which we could send, after isolation and disinfection, the native population.' In 1921 the British introduced strict residential segregation between Europeans, Indians and Africans in Kenya on public health grounds.

In general, most whites lived in small, isolated communities with minute status differences and strong codes of conduct, while maintaining social rituals that were often long out of date in the home country. Life centred around the club, membership of which was virtually obligatory, where few if any natives were allowed and where people gathered for drinks and gossip on the veranda waited on by an army of servants. There were, however, some differences in relations with the locals. In 1902 the French Colonial Office recommended 'a temporary union with a well-chosen native woman', whereas the British seven years later issued instructions that having a native mistress was an 'injurious and dangerous evil' which would involve severe disciplinary measures because a European would thereby 'lower himself in the eyes of the native'. In practice such behaviour had been usual in the nineteenth century and was to remain common in the twentieth. The 1909 British instructions had followed an investigation in Kenya, where it became clear that nearly every British administrator had a native mistress. Twenty years later complaints were still being made about the situation. In the late 1920s the governor of the Gold Coast made it clear that he expected senior officials to set an example but juniors should only be careful and not cause a public scandal.

By the 1930s colonial rule seemed to be well established across the world. Nearly half the world's people were ruled by foreigners and the initial period of conquest and 'pacification' had given way to one of consolidation and administration. All the colonial authorities believed they were in for the long haul. No non-white colony had been given independence. Elsewhere India had been granted some very limited self-government with the possibility of dominion status at an unspecified date in the future and the Philippines had been promised independence, to take effect in 1944. In 1929 the British Colonial Office decided that self-government for black Africa could be deferred until 'the next century and possibly the next'. Ten years later during a conference on West Africa a senior Colonial Office official commented, 'Well, at any rate in Africa we can be sure that we have unlimited time in which to work.' Three years earlier the governor-general of the Dutch East Indies remarked, 'We have ruled here for three hundred years with the whip and the club and we shall be doing it in another three hundred years.'

The Second World War produced a major challenge to the colonial empires in the Far East with the breakdown of colonial rule under Japanese conquest. The Atlantic Charter (effectively a declaration of war aims by the Allies) contained in Article Three a passage about 'the right of all peoples to choose the form of government under which they live'. The British decided that this could not possibly apply to the European empires and in May 1943 a cabinet committee decided, repeating a statement made in the House of Commons in 1939, that

> Many parts of the Colonial Empire are still so little removed from their primitive state that it must be a matter of many generations before they are ready for anything like full self-government. There are other parts inhabited by people of two or more different races, and it is impossible to say how long it will take to weld together these so-called plural communities into an entity capable of exercising self-government.

In January 1944 when the Free French held a conference in Brazzaville on the future of the French empire after the war they agreed that possession of colonies was one of the French claims to greatness and that there should be, as General de Gaulle put it 'unity of nation and the Empire'. The conference concluded:

> The goals of the task of civilization accomplished by France in her colonies rule out any idea of automony, any possibility of evolution outside the French bloc of the empire; the eventual creation, even in the distant future, of self-government for the colonies is to be set aside.

Similarly, after the war the British Labour government saw the development of the empire as a way of increasing Britain's wealth and status. In October 1948 the Foreign Secretary, Ernest Bevin, wrote to Hugh Dalton, the Chancellor of the Exchequer, that 'if only we pushed on and developed Africa, we could have the United States dependent on us, and eating out of our hand, in four or five years . . . The United States is very barren of essential minerals, and in Africa we have them all.' Hugh Dalton wrote privately, in a vein which was common to many Europeans and which typified some of the ambivalent attitudes to empire, of the 'pullulating, poverty-stricken, diseased nigger communities, for whom one can do nothing in the short run and who, the more one tries to help them, are querulous and ungrateful'.

9   FREEDOM

DESPITE THE belief expressed during the Second World War by the colonial powers that the subject peoples of the empires were totally unsuited to self-government, within twenty years the colonial empires had effectively ceased to exist. Why did this happen? Harold Macmillan, the prime minister who presided over the rapid end of the British empire, wrote in his memoirs that the British people:

> had not lost the will or even the power to rule. But they did not conceive of themselves as having the right to govern in perpetuity. It was rather a duty to spread to other nations those advantages which through the course of centuries they had won for themselves.

This attempt to describe a complex process as an act of magnanimity by states who had only ever had in their hearts the best interests of the people they ruled does not bear even the most cursory scrutiny. The process was less one of magnanimity, still less one where large-scale revolt against foreign rule was the norm; it was more a matter of redefining the links between the core and the periphery. The core states found they were able to retain their influence over the periphery by methods other than direct political control, which had lost much of its utility in the changed circumstances after the Second World War.

The end of the colonial empires was part of the wider process of declining European influence in the world in the twentieth century. Early signs of this changing balance were visible in the first thirty years or so of the century in three states – Turkey, Iran and China. In 1900 all these states had seemed likely to fall under European political control. However, they were gradually able to ensure their formal independence, limit foreign influence and begin the long process of building new economies and societies. For more than two centuries the Ottoman empire had been the 'sick man of Europe'. Yet in the early twentieth century it was, after Japan, the second state to begin a process of 'modernization' without direct Western intervention. The Young Turk movement was founded in 1889 by an Albanian, Ibrahim Temo. In 1908, acting through the Committee of Union and Progress, the Young Turks staged a military coup and forced the sultan to restore the relatively liberal 1876 constitution. Elections were held in late 1908 under the control of local elites, but the power of the committee depended on the army, especially the Third Army under Enver Pasha and Mustafa Kemal. Defeat in the Balkan wars and then entry into the First World War on the side of the Central Powers limited the reforms, but the basis had been laid for Mustafa Kemal, when he took power in 1923, to begin the process of 'Westernization' and modernization within the new state of Turkey.

Under the weak Qajar dynasty (a minority Turkman tribe which had ruled since 1796), Iran seemed on the point of being divided between the British and the Russians in the early twentieth century. An elitist revolution which created the first national assembly (the Majlis) in 1906 was countered a year later by an Anglo-Russian agreement which created 'spheres of influence', with the British predominant in the south where the oilfields were located. After the 1917 Revolution in Russia the British took effective control of most of the country and, although their troops were withdrawn in 1921, they continued to dominate Iranian finances. In 1926 a new ruler, Reza Khan, seized power and founded his own dynasty. Nominally a nationalist whose aims were similar to the Turkish nationalists', he found it difficult to make any significant steps towards modernization. His attempt to end the British oil concession in 1933 only led to the imposition of a worse deal for the Iranians. However, Iran survived as an independent state and remained so despite occupation by British and Soviet forces in 1941 and the imposition of Reza Khan's son as the new Shah.

The Boxer revolt in China in 1900 had already demonstrated the strength of Chinese nationalism. Imposition of harsh terms by the western powers after the occupation of Peking only increased such feelings. After 1900 the imperial government began its own programme of change, designed to strengthen the state, which it hoped would be along the lines of the successful Japanese reform after the Meiji restoration. The education system was remoulded along Japanese lines and over 100,000 modern schools were opened by 1909. The old imperial army was disbanded and new units were formed, organized along western lines. New ministries of trade, police, education, war and foreign affairs were established. The first cautious steps were taken towards a parliamentary system with the establishment of provincial assemblies in 1909 (on a very restricted franchise) and a national consultative assembly (but not a parliament) the next year. Although these essentially conservative reforms were not sufficient to win over the more revolutionary groups, they went too far for the ultra-conservative groups in the imperial court and government where the child emperor Pu-yi was under the control of a reactionary regent.

Growing Chinese nationalism expressed itself in both anti-Manchu-dynasty and anti-foreign sentiments through the creation of numerous secret societies. Many of the revolutionary leaders such as Sun Yat-sen were in exile and therefore not influential. However, the United League, formed in 1905 by a fusion of the Revive China Society, the China Revival Society and the Restoration Society, did accept Sun Yat-sen's three principles of nationalism, democracy and socialism. In practice these principles were limited to being opposed to the Manchu dynasty, advocating a representative government with separation of powers and a land tax. Overall, there was a highly optimistic belief that this limited programme would bring about 'progress', but it ignored the three major problems facing China – peasant discontent (there were over 280 peasant risings in 1910 alone), hostility to existing political and social structures and huge external pressures.

The spark that brought down the imperial government was, surprisingly, the decision to nationalize the railways in May 1911. This alienated the local gentry who owned the railways. Financing the programme with a £6 million foreign loan alienated the nationalists. During the second half of 1911 three disparate movements came together: the gentry in the 'Railway Protection League', peasant uprisings and army mutinies. In November the Manchu dynasty was removed and once the revolutionaries had accepted all treaties and loans made by the imperial government, the Western powers reluctantly allowed them to take power. Sun Yat-sen was in Denver when the revolt began, but he quickly returned and was elected president of the new republic on 1 January 1912, which became Year 1 of the new calendar.

The main problem facing the new government, given its dreadful inheritance, was whether it could organize and unify China and begin the process of renewal. The high level of foreign influence was combined with difficulty in raising new loans from the west. Even when loans were obtained, more Chinese assets had to be handed over as collateral. Sun Yat-sen proved incapable of strong leadership and resigned within six weeks, to be replaced by a very weak parliamentary system (in which most MPs belonged to more than one party). This was itself replaced in late 1913 by a military dictatorship under Yuan Shi-kai, who was supported by the consortium of foreign banks which provided the loans necessary for the administration to function. Britain and Russia refused to recognize the new government until it had, in its turn, recognized the autonomy of Tibet and Outer Mongolia. On the outbreak of the First World War Japan invaded and took over the German concessions in China. In January 1915 it presented the 'Twenty-One Demands' which would have turned China into a Japanese dependency with Japanese 'advisers' in all the key posts and with only Japan allowed to supply China with arms. The Chinese government accepted despite popular opposition, but the demands were opposed by the western powers, especially the United States, whose own interests would be affected. Between 1916 and 1919 a central state in China existed in name only after the death of Yuan Shi-kai and the emergence of regional military rulers.

A major turning point came on 4 May 1919 when news of the Treaty of Versailles reached China. Although China had declared war on Germany in August 1917 and sent over 200,000 coolies to Europe to assist the Allies, the treaty confirmed that the German concessions would not be restored to China, but instead they would be given to Japan. Student demonstrations and strikes by workers across the country were a massive patriotic protest against both the government, which was prepared to accept the western demands, and the Japanese. It was a spontaneous series of protests led by a new generation of leaders (many of the key figures in the Communist Party such as Mao Tse-tung and Chou En-lai began their political careers in this way) and another example of the strong current of Chinese nationalism. China, despite the 1911 Revolution, had been unable to produce the strong reforming government found in Turkey, but it had survived as a political entity less through its own strength than because of the divisions among the western powers, who could only agree that a weak Chinese government was better than a rival power taking control of the country.

The Fourth of May movement was only one aspect of growing

anti-western sentiment in the periphery, a belief that indigenous cultures and values were important and that national reassertion against the imperial powers could, and should, be undertaken. In 1921 in his novel *Batouala* the West Indian writer René Maran wrote of 'Civilization – the Europeans' pride and their charnel house of innocents', a view also expressed by the Indian poet Rabindranath Tagore in his accusation, 'You build your kingdom on corpses.' In February 1927 the first meeting of the International Congress of the League against Imperialism and Colonial Oppression in Brussels declared:

> The development of the African people was abruptly cut short and their civilization was most completely destroyed. These nations were later declared pagan and savage, an inferior race, destined by the Christian God to be slaves to superior Europeans.

Five years later Emile Faure, writing in *Race nègre* argued:

> Because for centuries a few vicious rakes and whores succeeded in having palaces built for themselves at Versailles, and temples elsewhere, they're called 'civilised' . . . Peasant people, unambitious and hard-working, who till the land, tend their herds and venerate their ancestors, are despoiled and decimated by nations as industrious as they are inhuman.

Political movements were beginning to emerge across the periphery dedicated to achieving independence. One of the first was the Indian National Congress founded in 1885, which by 1906 had adopted the aim of *swaraj* or 'home rule'. In neighbouring Burma and Ceylon there were also nationalist movements, in the former under the guidance of U Ottoma, leader of the General Council of Buddhist Associations. In the 1900s a nationalist movement, Sarekat Islam, was founded in the Dutch East Indies. In 1919 a delegation seeking independence for the Philippines was sent to the United States.

In general the imperial governments were able to keep these movements under control until the outbreak of the Second World War. The only exceptions were in Egypt and India, where the British faced major problems. Britain formally declared Egypt a protectorate in 1914 although they had occupied the country since 1882, ruling through a weak king. Nationalist agitation increased in 1919 when the British initially refused to allow Egypt its own representation at the Versailles conference. In order to contain nationalism and retain effective control, the British recognized Egypt as formally independent in 1922, but subject to conditions giving the British all the essential powers over military and foreign policy that they thought they needed. The main nationalist party – the Wafd – was a party of conservative, elite landowners unwilling to risk any widespread nationalist agitation that might undermine their social position. In 1936 after the first moderately free elections the Wafd formed a government and the British negotiated a new treaty. This restricted British troops to a zone along the Suez Canal in peacetime, agreed a final withdrawal in 1956, but allowed the British to re-occupy the country in the event of war. The British retained effective control and found nominal Egyptian independence no hindrance to their military operations during the Second World War.

The situation in India was much more complex. At one level (and in conformity with Harold Macmillan's argument) it might seem that the British made a series of reforms and declarations, in 1908, 1917, 1919, 1929 and 1935, which were all designed to move India progressively along the road to independence as Indian capability for self-government increased steadily. In practice the situation was much more complex. The British needed to find a group of collaborators to help run India. The princes provided this in their states, but in British India a different solution was required. A permanent British policy was to divide India into as many different communities and political units as possible so as to make it more difficult for a single movement dedicated to removing the British to emerge. When the Congress Party became stronger after 1919, the British tried to limit its influence as far as possible.

In 1908 the Morley–Minto reforms set up local councils in British India, elected on very restricted franchises to provide both a group of Indians prepared to work with the British and a vast patchwork of centres of power. In 1917 the British committed themselves to the 'progressive realization of responsible government', but the phrase was so ambiguous it could mean almost anything. In 1919 the Government of India Act (the so-called Montagu–Chelmsford reforms) continued the process started in 1908, of decentralizing power and widening the group of local collaborators with the British. Eight uniform provinces were created in British India with limited local administration of those policies which were unimportant to the British – health, education, public works, agriculture and industry – with all other powers being retained by the governor. In New Delhi a powerless parliament was created with a majority of elected members (fewer than 7 million people were allowed to vote). The viceroy retained control of finance and could promulgate legislation regardless of the wishes of the legislature. Congress refused to co-operate with the reforms and a campaign of nonco-operation and civil disobedience under Gandhi was suppressed by the British. Between 1920 and 1939 the British were able to keep control of Indian resistance and the various campaigns run by Gandhi. These campaigns were acceptable to the socially conservative groups which supported Congress in that they were strongly anti-British and helped to divert any enthusiasm the peasants might have for land reform or economic change.

In 1929 the British committed themselves to eventual dominion status for India, but the timescale remained carefully undefined, as did the internal governmental arrangements. The British were still determined to avoid the emergence of a united India under Congress control and the Government of India Act 1935 was designed to ensure that the British aims were achieved. Control of the provinces' mundane affairs no longer seemed very important for the British and they did not recruit civil servants for this role after 1924. Under the 1935 scheme each province in British India was to have an autonomous Indian government, although the British governor retained the right to declare a state of emergency and rule by decree. The electorate was small (about 10 per cent of the adult population) and the distribution of seats far from democratic – in Bengal, for example, a few thousand Europeans controlled twenty-five seats and 17 million non-Muslim Indians controlled fifty seats. These separate racial and religious electorates (a separate Muslim electorate had been conceded as early as 1906) were part of the aim of fragmenting India as much as possible. New provinces such as Sind and North-West Frontier were created to provide areas with a Muslim majority. The viceroy in Delhi retained full control of all imperial matters, but his Executive Council was carefully constructed to reflect the divisions the British wished to emphasize in India. It was composed of representatives not just from the major communities but also from both artificial and minute social categories – caste Hindu, Muslim, scheduled castes, Sikhs, Europeans, Christians, Parsees, landlords and businessmen. The 562 princely states were excluded from all these arrangements. A federation comprising all of India (Burma became a separate colony)

– the eleven provinces, the small group of territories controlled directly by Delhi and the princely states – was in theory possible but in practice highly unlikely because the princes had a veto. The Congress leadership wanted to refuse to co-operate with such a deliberately divisive scheme, but local Congress politicians, attracted by the possibility of power in the provinces, forced them to change their minds. The British were pleased that Congress had been forced to collaborate with a scheme which ensured they could never control a unified India, but worried that Congress controlled all the provinces except Punjab and Bengal when the new system began operating in 1937. However, the new arrangements only survived for two years before they collapsed at the outbreak of the Second World War. In September 1939 the Viceroy declared war without consulting any Indian politicians. This gave Congress the excuse it needed to withdraw from the British system by resigning from all its provincial governments, leaving the governors to declare a state of emergency and rule by decree. Congress could return to the more congenial politics of opposing British rule.

The crisis of imperial rule in the Far East came in 1940–2. In the summer of 1940 the French and Dutch colonies were left highly vulnerable following defeat by Germany in Europe and Japan took over the northern part of Indo-China. The most decisive event came with the Japanese attack in December 1941, which led to their occupation of the Philippines, Hong Kong, Malaya, Singapore, the Dutch East Indies, Indo-China and Burma. The carefully maintained façade of western superiority, which was so vital for colonial governments because of their military and administrative weakness, was destroyed in a few months by an oriental power. It was a blow to their prestige from which the imperial powers were never to recover. In the major colonies – India, Burma, Ceylon, Indo-China, the Dutch East Indies and the Philippines – it proved impossible to restore effective imperial rule after 1945.

In 1942, with Japanese troops on the borders of India, the British tried to come to terms with Congress. The negotiations failed because many in the British government, especially Churchill, did not want the talks to succeed and Congress was reluctant to take over responsibility in the middle of a disastrous war. Congress then shifted to a policy of 'Quit India' and civil disobedience. The British were able to use force to keep control and arrested the leaders of Congress. However, by 1943 over a hundred battalions were being used on internal security duties rather than fighting the Japanese.

The British believed they could continue to control events and keep Congress from power at a national level. For many it was still a racial problem. Leo Amery, the Secretary of State for India during the war, wrote to the viceroy:

> If India is to be really capable of holding its own in future without direct British control from outside I am not sure that it will not need an increasing infusion of stronger Nordic blood, whether by settlement or intermarriage or otherwise. Possibly it has been a real mistake of ours in the past not to encourage Indian princes to marry English wives . . . and so breed a more virile type of native ruler.

In other colonies, in particular, Burma, the Philippines and the Dutch East Indies, local nationalist politicians were happy to work with the Japanese and they gradually established positions from which it would be difficult to dislodge them when the colonial powers took back control at the end of the war. This problem was made worse by the fact that no colony was fully reoccupied before the Japanese surrender in August 1945 and the resulting hiatus in power before colonial rule could be re-established further strengthened the position of the nationalists.

Ten years after the war imperial rule in the Far East was essentially over; only a few relatively unimportant colonies were not either independent or clearly on the road to independence. In the Philippines the United States transferred power to the local oligarchy, which had long dominated the economy and society, and in return a compliant government granted the Americans the extensive military facilities which were all that they really wanted. The British had much greater difficulty in finding any basis on which they could hand over power in India without massive loss of face. During the war the Muslim League, which demanded a separate Muslim state of Pakistan, continued to co-operate with the British and was in a strong position by 1945. Congress was deeply opposed to a partition of India and also continued to oppose the British insistence on a weak central government based on a federation including the princely states. The British tried, in a number of different negotiating rounds, to reach a settlement, but by early 1947 it was clear that their rule was beginning to break down. The only option left was to announce a date for withdrawal (August 1947) and negotiate the best deal possible. In the end the solution was one which none of the parties wanted and one that met none of the British aims. The Muslims gained an independent Pakistan, but it was weak and geographically divided and hundreds of thousands of Muslims died in the communal riots that followed the partition of Bengal and the Punjab. Congress took power over a unified but shrunken India. The British had to accept the domination of Congress, the princes were left in the lurch to get the best deal they could from Congress and the Sikhs, the supposedly loyal warrior group, were left without their own province or separate state. Most importantly, from Britain's point of view, India refused to play the role allocated to it by the British of being a bulwark of British power and defence policy in south-east Asia.

In Burma all attempts to slow down progress towards independence failed and the British were forced to deal with the man who had co-operated with the Japanese, Aung San, in order to maintain some vestiges of control. The Burmese nationalists insisted on becoming a republic on independence and rejected any defence arrangements with Britain. In the end the British had no power to impose a different solution and Burma became independent in January 1948. The only area where the British faced few problems was in Ceylon, where they were able to hand power over to conservative Sinhalese landowners and obtain the military bases they regarded as essential. In Indonesia the Dutch attempted to restore colonial rule in the last months of 1945, even though the nationalists under Sukarno had already declared independence in the immediate aftermath of the Japanese surrender. There was bitter fighting as the Dutch tried to gain control of Java, while they also tried to impose a federation in which the outlying islands, still under Dutch influence, would provide a counterbalance to nationalist-controlled Java. Once Sukarno had suppressed the Communists the Americans pressurized the Dutch into a settlement and in August 1949 a solution which sketched the outlines of a Dutch-Indonesian union provided enough of a fig-leaf for the Dutch to withdraw, leaving behind a unified Indonesia.

The colonies which provided the greatest problems in the decade after the end of the war were in Indo-China. In the months of chaos following the Japanese surrender the Vietminh nationalists under the Communist Ho Chi Minh (who had been backed by the Americans during the war) were able to gain control in the north around Hanoi. The French, with British assistance, controlled the south, in particular Saigon. During 1946 the French tried to negotiate a new form of colonialism based on a federated Indo-

China consisting of a French-controlled southern Vietnam, monarchical Laos and Cambodia and Vietminh control of the north. At the end of the year the French decided to pressurize the Vietminh into a quick agreement by bombarding Haiphong. They occupied Hanoi in February 1947. The result was a growing guerrilla war and Vietminh control of much of the north. By emphasizing the anti-Communist rather than the colonial nature of the war, the French gained increasing American support. However, they were unable to control the guerrillas and by 1954 they were also facing regular units of the Vietminh army. An attempt to fight a large conventional battle at Dien Bien Phu was a disaster and led to the surrender of the French army in early May 1954. At this stage the great powers intervened to divide Indo-China at the July 1954 Geneva conference. Laos and Cambodia became independent and Vietnam was split along the old wartime boundary of allied spheres of interest – the seventeenth parallel. Both sides promised to hold 'free elections' in 1956 to produce a unified Vietnam, but nobody really believed this was likely. The United States took over the French role of trying to build a coalition in South Vietnam that could govern the country whilst the north was controlled by the Communist Vietminh, who never accepted the division of their country.

Although in the immediate post-war period nearly all the colonial empires in the Far East collapsed, this was not seen by the imperial powers as signalling the end of empire worldwide. The British and French, in particular, regarded possession of empire as a way of maintaining their role in world politics and asserting their claim to be substantial powers in an age dominated by the United States and the Soviet Union. They began, almost for the first time, programmes of economic development within their empires, especially in Africa. The British aimed to extract cheap minerals and food from within a monetary area they controlled at a time when they were very short of dollars. The French started constructing mines and deep-water ports, as, to a more limited extent, did the Belgians in the Congo.

Britain was determined to hold on to its empire by force if necessary and to create new structures to maintain imperial control. In Malaya, after the failure of the scheme to produce a unified colony out of the old federation, the British found themselves by the late 1940s involved in a war against the Chinese community and the Communists. The British allied with the Malays against the Chinese and Indian communities in a vicious guerrilla war involving the forced resettlement of almost a quarter of the Chinese people in

Malaya. Britain fought in Malaya because it provided tin and rubber which could be sold to the United States for dollars and to retain Singapore as a military base. By early 1954 the British had secured control of most of the colony in collaboration with the Malays, who were happy to see the Chinese community kept in a subordinate position. In Africa the British were also trying to create a new dominion – the Central African Federation – from the colonies of Nyasaland and Northern and Southern Rhodesia. The aim was to prepare the federation, which would be run by the local white settlers, for independence by the early 1960s.

In 1954 the British government carried out a review of the future of its empire. The cabinet greatly resented the fact that since 1947 a number of non-white countries had achieved independence and entered the Commonwealth:

> The admission of three Asiatic countries to Commonwealth membership had altered the character of the Commonwealth . . . [and it] would be further diluted if full membership had to be conceded to the Gold Coast and other countries . . . It was unfortunate that the policy of assisting dependent peoples to attain self-government had been carried forward so fast and so far.

The review concluded that colonies such as Cyprus, Malta, Aden and Somaliland were never to be granted independence; they were too important as military bases on which Britain's continuation as a world power depended. By the mid-1970s it was thought that only a handful of colonies would be independent states: the white-run Central African Federation, Malaya, a federation of the West Indian islands and Nigeria and the Gold Coast in Africa. The French too felt that despite events in Indo-China they would be able to hold on to the rest of their empire. As René Pléven, colonial minister, put it: 'The African peoples want no other liberty than that of France.' Similarly, the Belgian and Portuguese governments were still determined to maintain their empires.

During the mid-1950s both the French and the British began new and difficult military campaigns to hold on to parts of their empires. On 1 November 1954 a revolt by the National Liberation Front (FLN) in Algeria signalled the start of what was to become the most vicious of all the wars for colonial independence. The French government under strong pressure from the determined and powerful settler lobby (the *pieds noirs*) fought hard to defeat the nationalists. Within a year nearly half a million troops were in the colony. In early 1957 the tough parachute troops under General Jacques Massu were let loose on the capital, Algiers, in a brutal campaign of reprisals, killings and torture, strongly supported by the French public and the *pieds noirs*. By the end of the year the French had regained control of the city. The war brought about the fall of the Fourth Republic in 1958, when the government appeared to be willing to negotiate with the FLN. This led to a general strike in Algiers by the *pieds noirs*, an army takeover in Corsica and the threat of a coup in France itself. General de Gaulle took power, established the Fifth Republic and backed continuing French rule over Algeria.

In the summer of 1954 the British stated publicly that Cyprus could never become independent. Their reasons were essentially strategic – after finally agreeing to leave the Canal Zone in Egypt they did not, for reasons of prestige, want to make another withdrawal and they intended that Cyprus should become their major base in the Middle East. This meant opposing the demands of the Greek community on the island under the leadership of Archbishop Makarios for union with Greece, something which was anathema to the minority Turkish population. Guerrilla war began in April 1955 and a year later Makarios was arrested and exiled in the Seychelles.

However, as these new military campaigns to sustain empires were being launched, a reappraisal of imperial policy began, which led to the almost total end of empire within a decade. This was the result of a number of factors. The humiliation of the failed Anglo-French invasion of Egypt in the Suez crisis of 1956 demonstrated that neither was a world power capable of acting on its own. This, combined with the emergence of the European Economic Community with the signing of the Treaty of Rome in 1957, produced a policy reappraisal, particularly in France after de Gaulle's accession to power. French interests seemed to be at stake in Europe, especially in controlling the rising economic power of West Germany. (The British arrived at the opposite conclusion and tried to draw closer to the United States.) Within the colonies it was also becoming clear that, following decades of neglect, economic development would be very expensive and it was unlikely that the colonial power would see much benefit from the huge investment required. The strategic situation had also changed. The great imperial expansion of the late nineteenth century had, to a large extent, resulted from competitive pressures within Europe – the need to deny territories to rival powers. After 1945 that was no longer the case. There was no competition for colonial possessions and any that became independent would not be taken over by rivals. There was the possibility of an expansion of Communist influence, but countering that threat could be left to the Americans with their larger resources. In this situation the economic rationale for colonial possessions could be reassessed. The imperial powers had always been concerned about their access to certain raw materials, but it was possible to obtain this without formal political control. The core powers and transnational corporations dominated the world economy and they were powerful enough to ensure that any newly independent powers had little choice but to allow continued access to the resources they controlled. The imperial powers always relied on the collaboration of certain groups within their colonies; independence would therefore mean little more than handing over formal political power to these groups while leaving the core powers with access to the resources they required. In this situation the task facing the imperial powers was to select which groups would be allowed to take power in the newly independent states. Once this process started, with one state moving down the road of decolonization, it was more difficult for others to resist and so the process snowballed.

The first signs of this new approach can be traced back to the immediate post-war period in the relatively stable and prosperous Gold Coast colony. In 1946, as part of the policy of economic development, the British decided they needed a new group of collaborators to support the changes. The old system of 'indirect rule' was abandoned. Provincial legislatures, dominated by conservatives, were established. They elected members to the central Legislative Council, which had a majority of Africans rather than British officials, although the governor retained his absolute veto. This scheme might have produced a new and larger collaborating group than the rural chiefs who dominated under 'indirect rule', but new leaders, in particular Kwame Nkrumah and his Convention People's Party were able to gain the support of the urban Africans. In February 1948 riots in the capital Accra led to a breakdown in security and the arrest of Nkrumah and other nationalist leaders. The 1951 elections, which the British expected the conservative groups to win, instead saw the victory of Nkrumah and the CPP, even though their support came mainly from the coastal and urban elite. The British had to release Nkrumah from jail and work with him. He was happy to do this on condition that the CPP dominated and the rural groups were excluded. Over the next six years more functions were gradually transferred to the African government, as both the British and Nkrumah wanted the transition of power to be smooth. On 6 March 1957 the Gold Coast became the first black African country to become independent and changed its name to Ghana. The transition was relatively straightforward: an African group had emerged to take power, the country was of no strategic importance to Britain, there were no white settlers to complicate the process and the British would, after independence, still be able to obtain what they required.

The political changes in the Gold Coast had an impact on neighbouring French West Africa. Here, after 1945, the French had been able to strike up an alliance with local political groups and politicians who were interested in bargaining with the French over patronage and positions in the bureaucracy. Men like Félix Hophouët-Boigny in the Ivory Coast did not represent mass political movements and were no more than educated, elite politicians interested in local power. In 1956 the French offered them a deal similar to that in the Gold Coast in the late 1940s – responsibility for local affairs within the French empire – as a way of heading off more radical demands and more radical politicians. In 1958 de Gaulle, seeking to dominate a French community in West Africa, offered a referendum. The choice was between immediate independence with no French help or membership of a federation with French aid and control over foreign and defence policy, ultimately the subjects that always interested the imperial powers. The voting was rigged and all the French colonies except Guinea under Sékou Touré voted in favour of federation. Sékou Touré saw himself as another Nkrumah gaining the prestige associated with independence, but the French cut off all aid in retaliation. In practice the French could not keep control of developments. The federation of the remaining French colonies broke up in 1958 under pressure from Houphouët-Boigny and two years later all the French colonies in West and Equatorial Africa became independent, partly because they did not wish to be seen as lagging behind the ex-British colonies of Ghana and Nigeria (which became independent in 1960). Nevertheless the French retained a huge degree of influence over their ex-colonies.

General de Gaulle faced a far more difficult situation in Algeria, where he had to manoeuvre between the nationalists, the settlers, their terrorist group the OAS, and the army, some elements of which were prepared to support the settlers. On taking power in 1958 he seemed to symbolize the movement to keep Algeria French, but almost immediately he began to search for new solutions. In September 1959 he suggested three options, none of which was the status quo or independence. Algeria could secede from France without the Sahara, which with its extensive oil and natural gas reserves was also where the French conducted their nuclear tests. Algeria could be fully assimilated into France, although de Gaulle did not favour this option because he thought too many Muslims and 'foreigners' would move across the Mediterranean. Finally, there was the option de Gaulle himself favoured, under which Algeria would have limited self-determination but France would control foreign affairs, defence and the economy. None of these options was acceptable. The war against the nationalists continued. The settlers barricaded part of Algiers in January 1960, but received no backing from the army, and in April 1961 an attempted army coup failed, as did a number of attempts by the OAS to kill de Gaulle. Eventually de Gaulle agreed to negotiate with the Algerian nationalists at the Evian conference, which lasted for nearly a year before agreement was reached in March 1962. The French gained hardly any of their objectives. In particular they lost control of the Sahara and hundreds of thousands of settlers left for France. The most bitter of all the colonial struggles ended after eight years of conflict with complete victory for the Algerian nationalists.

French policy, especially in West and Equatorial Africa, increased pressure on other imperial powers to follow suit. The Belgian Congo controlled a vast range of important minerals and was a stable colony. For fifty years the Belgian government had made no attempt to promote local groups, other than a few chiefs with whom they might collaborate. Then suddenly in January 1959 they announced that they intended to move towards independence. As late as October 1959 the earliest date envisaged was 1964. In mid-December the Belgians decided on independence within a year and a conference with local leaders in January 1960 agreed on independence within six months. Not surprisingly, there was a political vacuum in the country as a few leaders scrambled to create organizations which might be able to govern the country and, more important, secure them power. Politics fragmented along ethnic lines. The rapid withdrawal of Belgian rule led to chaos and anarchy within weeks. The army mutinied against its European officers in order to gain the pay and status it saw as one of the benefits of independence. The premier, Patrice Lumumba, was murdered and the mineral-rich province of Katanga seceded under the leadership of Moishe Tshombe, who had the backing of the Belgian settlers and the corporations controlling the mining operations. It was another four years before an elite group subservient to western industrial interests gained power across the whole of the country.

Events in the Congo only increased the pressure on the remaining colonial powers, especially the British, to withdraw before they too were caught up in similar disasters. The British had, in the late 1950s, given independence to Malaya once the local elite agreed to the continuation of the military base in Singapore and to remain in the sterling area so that the British could still benefit from the sale of tin and rubber on the world market. They also agreed to grant independence to the West Indian islands, as they were of no strategic value (they had long been within the American sphere of influence) and little economic benefit. The British felt that they wanted to keep pace with the French and ensure that there were a number of English-speaking African states to balance the Francophone bloc. However, Britain had no plans to end its empire in East Africa, where they faced problems with the small group of white settlers. In January 1959 a conference of governors, Colonial Office officials and ministers suggested independence could not be achieved before the mid-1970s at the earliest. In April that year the colonial secretary told parliament that he could not foresee a date when Kenya could be independent. At the same time it was still intended that the Central African Federation should become independent under local white settler rule. Such political developments as did take place were designed to uphold the position of the tiny number of white settlers. The 'Mau-Mau' revolt among the Kikuyu in Kenya was brutally suppressed and across East Africa the aim was to develop so-called 'multi-racial politics', which were, in practice, no more than a fig-leaf for white 'leadership'. By the late 1950s the Africans were allowed the same number of seats as the whites in the Legislative Councils of both Kenya and Tanganyika, but this was at a time when in the latter colony there was one white for every four Asians and 430 Africans.

The events of 1960, with the mass of French colonies becoming independent and the disaster in the Belgian Congo, concentrated the minds of policy-makers in London. The British, having neither the military capability nor any over-riding economic reason to take on massive internal security problems across Africa, decided on a new, more ruthless policy. Colonies would be forced to become independent and the white settlers would be abandoned. Within four years all the colonies in East Africa were independent and the Central African Federation was dissolved, with Northern Rhodesia and Nyasaland becoming independent but not the white-settler-run Southern Rhodesia. As late as December 1959 the British refused to even consider universal suffrage and responsible government for local affairs in Uganda, yet in less than three years the colony was independent. Tanganyika became independent in 1961, Kenya and Zanzibar in 1963, Nyasaland (as Malawi) and Northern Rhodesia (as Zambia) in 1964. Other smaller colonies were pushed along the same road. Malta, which had seemed so important for strategic reasons, was given independence in return for the right to use the naval base and other facilities for ten years. Cyprus became independent, but Britain retained two substantial areas on the island as its own sovereign territory to provide military bases. Less strategically important colonies followed: Gambia and the Maldives in 1965; Botswana, Lesotho, Barbados and Guyana the next year; Mauritius and Swaziland in 1968; and Fiji and Tonga in 1970. The fastest scuttle of all came not in the Belgian Congo but in British Somaliland. As late as February 1960 the colony still did not even have an elected majority in the governor's Legislative Council. At this stage a handful of local politicians demanded unification with Italian Somaliland, which was due to become independent in mid-1960. In May 1960 the independence conference in London agreed to grant self-government on 26 June and after five days of self-government a united, independent Somalia came into existence. The British had moved from colonial autocracy to independence in the space of just four and a half months.

Elsewhere Spain divested itself of its small empire relatively painlessly. It withdrew from its protectorates in Morocco when the French granted independence in 1956, Ifni was given back in 1969, but the coastal towns of Ceuta and Melilla were retained. The island of Fernando Po and the coastal area of Rio Muni were united to form Equatorial Guinea, which became independent at the end of 1968. The major problem was the mineral-rich but largely un-inhabited Spanish Sahara. This was eventually split between Morocco and Mauritania in 1976, although Algeria sponsored the Polisario Front which claimed independence for the territory.

The one European power not to follow the general trend of decolonization was Portugal. At the very time that the British, French and Belgian empires in Africa were disintegrating, the Portuguese were making a major effort to retain and develop their empire, despite the loss of a few small enclaves such as Goa to India and Ajuda to Dahomey. After 1960 over 350,000 new white settlers moved to Angola, but many of the old abuses, in particular extensive forced labour, remained. The problem the Portuguese faced was a growing revolt against their rule from Guinea and the Cape Verde islands to Angola and Mozambique. The successful containment of these revolts until the mid-1970s was a major burden – one in four adult Portuguese males was serving in the armed forces. However, the empire was maintained until a military coup in Lisbon in April 1974 unseated the right-wing dictatorship. The military situation in Guinea was so bad that independence was granted immediately and in Mozambique it was possible to negotiate a deal with the FRELIMO rebels under Samora Machel. Angola posed more difficult problems because of the number of Portuguese settlers, the mineral resources of the colony, the divisions along ideological grounds between the nationalist forces and external intervention, in particular from the United States. An attempted settlement collapsed and the newly independent country plunged into a long and bitter civil war. In the Far East, Indonesia invaded East Timor in the 1970s and imposed its rule in what was the last war of colonial conquest in the twentieth century.

After the wave of decolonization in the 1960s Britain was left with one major problem – Southern Rhodesia, which had been a self-governing colony since 1923. The white minority was well entrenched and the constitution had changed so that it was almost impossible for the African majority to take power within any conceivable timescale. When the Central African Federation was wound up, Britain refused to grant independence to the white government in Southern Rhodesia without a guarantee, however convoluted, of eventual majority rule – given the international climate of the 1960s any other policy would have been impossible to justify. Eventually in November 1965 the white government declared unilateral independence. The white settlers were viewed sympathetically by considerable sections of both the population and Conservative politicians in Britain, and the government decided against using military force to remove the rebel government. In these circumstances, and with only limited and poorly enforced sanctions in place, a stalemate ensued. Attempts to reach a negotiated settlement in December 1966, October 1968 and late 1971 failed even though the British government was not insisting on more than very weak guarantees about majority rule at some point in the future. The Southern Rhodesian government believed that, with the support of the South African government, they would survive and until 1974 they were able to contain the ethnically divided nationalist politicians and the relatively weak guerrilla forces. The situation changed radically with the collapse of the Portuguese empire and the decision by the new government in Mozambique to give major support to the guerrillas. The South African government also decided that, in the last resort, it was not prepared to engage in a major war to prolong white rule in Southern Rhodesia. By early 1978 the white government had been forced to negotiate an 'internal settlement' with moderate nationalists which excluded the guerrillas and which left the whites effectively still running the country. The British government was tempted to accept this deal, but pressure from the Commonwealth at the Lusaka conference in August 1979 produced a new settlement. The white government finally gave up power and a British governor took over as ruler. Elections were held in March 1980 and, much to the annoyance of the British, were won by the leader of the guerrillas, Robert Mugabe and his ZANU Party, which took power on independence. The only consolation for the British was that a long-running problem had finally ended.

By the mid-1960s all but a handful of the European colonies had become independent. However, their inheritance from the imperial powers was dire. When it became independent, the Belgian Congo had just sixteen African university graduates in the whole country and not one lawyer, engineer or doctor. In the top three grades of the administration there were 4,500 Europeans and six Africans. The main reason for this appalling situation was that the Belgians had not provided secondary education for the local population. Although the Belgian Congo was perhaps an extreme example, in most colonies little had been done to prepare for independence. During the decades of colonial rule little money or effort had been invested in developing the economic and social infrastructure necessary for self-government or in providing a stable political base. Everywhere only a weak administrative infrastructure was left behind. The rush to independence only exacerbated an already poor situation.

In Asia, where societies had long been more developed than in

Africa, most ex-colonies finished up as authoritarian one-party states. Only India managed to keep the structure of democracy at a national level. In Africa the situation was much worse. Apart from huge inherited economic and social problems, the boundaries left by European colonialism were artificial, reflecting deals between the European powers rather than ethnic realities on the ground. During the colonial period the imperial powers had often created artificial chiefs and tribes for their own purposes. This meant that most of the new states were neither nations nor effective states. In addition many countries were so small as to be hardly viable. By 1980 twenty-two out of the forty-nine independent states had populations of fewer than 5 million and nine had fewer than 1 million people. The deals made at independence and the constitutions imposed were usually the result of an agreement between the imperial power and whichever group it judged was most likely to take over the colony smoothly. Little thought was given to the place of minorities or the general acceptability of the new arrangements. As a result factional groups came to dominate the new states: rich landlords in the Ivory Coast, the Mossi in Burkina Faso, the Shona majority in Zimbabwe and not the previously dominant Ndebele, the 'protectorate peoples' in Sierra Leone rather than the creole descendants of the freed slaves, the Malinke in Guinea. In many states the divisions were fundamental – in Togo, Ivory Coast, Kenya, Tanzania, Liberia, Zaire and Uganda no single ethnic group made up more than a quarter of the population. In Dahomey there was a three-way split between the Abomey-Fou, Nagot-Yoruba and the Maga. In the immediate post-independence period presidents from each of the groups tried to dominate the other two and failed and each tried an alliance of two against the third and failed. Between 1970 and 1972 there was a bizarre three-man presidency. The army coup in 1972 not surprisingly also failed to resolve the ethnic conflict. In some states, such as Tanzania under President Nyerere and neighbouring Kenya under President Moi, the solution was rule by a member of a small minority group who was forced to balance between the major groupings.

In some African states such as Ghana under Nkrumah and Ivory Coast under Houphouët-Boigny, there was one-party, authoritarian rule from the start. By the early 1960s a similar situation prevailed in Senegal, Guinea, Mali, Niger, Benin, Togo and Mauritania. Nearly everywhere the constitutions imposed at independence disintegrated and were ignored. In many states effective power rapidly devolved to the army and military coups became commonplace. Once the legitimacy of the initial post-independence ruler was destroyed there was little legitimacy for any successor; anybody who could find the resources for a successful coup could take power and claim the right to rule. Politics disintegrated into clientèlism, corruption and ethnic (real or imagined) conflict. In some states, such as Sudan, Zaire and Nigeria, civil war broke out over the secession of one area of the country, but in general the colonial boundaries were maintained because all states had a vested interest in not disturbing the existing arrangements however artificial they might be. Inter-state conflict was generally limited and violence was concentrated within the state. By the 1990s some states such as Somalia, Liberia and Sierra Leone had disintegrated into anarchy as economic decline, political factionalism and recurrent coups took their toll.

By the end of the twentieth century the colonial empires that had dominated the world in 1900 had almost ceased to exist. In 1997 Britain returned Hong Kong to China followed by the last Portuguese colony, Macao in 1999. This ended European rule in Asia. It was symbolic of a general trend throughout the century – the renaissance of Asia. Of the British empire only a few territories remained. They included those such as Pitcairn Island (population 50) and Tristan da Cunha (population 300) which could not become independent because they were too small. Others were military bases leased to the Americans, such as Ascension Island and the British Indian Ocean Territories (Diego Garcia), from which the population was forcibly removed in the late 1960s. In Gibraltar and the Falkland Islands the British allowed the local white population to exercise a veto over incorporation into Spain and Argentina. The Dutch still controlled Surinam and the French retained a small empire once New Caledonia and Tahiti in the Pacific were incorporated into France. The ultimate irony was that the supposedly anti-imperial power which believed that it did not possess an empire, the United States, was the largest imperial power at the end of the twentieth century. In total it controlled nearly 4 million people including Puerto Rico and the Virgin Islands in the Caribbean together with the Pacific islands of the Marshalls, Samoa and the Marianas. Most of the Pacific islands were used for military purposes, including nuclear testing. However, even on a generous estimate the colonial empires in 1999 contained no more than 5 million people (less than 1 per cent of the world total) compared

with about 750 million (a third of the world's people) only sixty years earlier. The end of empire appeared to be a fundamental transformation in the structure of the world. In practice the relations between the core states and the periphery continued in much the same way as before. Given the economic and political power of the core, such an outcome was not surprising.

10 NATIONS

THE END of the colonial empires was only one aspect of one of the most important trends of the twentieth century – the huge increase in the number of states in the world. For much of the century it is difficult to determine their exact number – for example, were the British dominions really independent states? Was Tibet part of China? Were Andorra and San Marino really states? Allowing for these uncertainties, there were about forty-five independent states in 1900, nearly half of them in Latin America. By 1945 the number had increased to just over sixty, but the newly independent states in Asia and Africa doubled that number over the next quarter of a century. By the 1990s the total had risen to over 190, about four times the number a century earlier. The ex-colonial states, particularly those in Africa and the Middle East, were the most artificial creations, many of them stemming from lines drawn on a map somewhere in Europe in the late nineteenth century or at the end of the First World War. They cut across tribal and ethnic boundaries with little regard for the peoples involved. However, the new states which emerged in Europe claimed to be not just states but nations. They were seen as the embodiment of a particular people, their history, their language, their religion and their culture, all of which were different from those of any other group. In this form nationalism was one of the great twentieth-century forces.

Nationalism was a highly ambiguous concept. On the one hand, it was about the process of nation building. This aspect was particularly important for states like Turkey, Egypt, China and Iran, which were trying to establish themselves as independent entities against strong outside pressure and begin the long process of 'modernization' and the creation of an industrial economy. In some cases, such as the United States and Australia, nationalism was derived from the existence of a state and its requirement to mould its citizens, many of whom were immigrants, into a common identity.

On the other hand, nationalism was also about the resistance of groups, usually on the geographical periphery of existing states, to this very process of national integration. It was also about resistance to the forces which stemmed from the development of the world economy and a growing, homogenized world culture.

The fundamental question raised by nationalism was what exactly constituted a nation and, therefore, which groups could make a legitimate claim to separate nationhood. Only in a few cases, such as the Jews, Kurds and Tamils, was it asserted that national identity could only be inherited. In many respects, therefore, nations were 'imagined' or 'invented' communities, although extremely powerful ones because the national mythology took on a life and meaning of its own. In practice nations were deeply divided politically, economically and socially: take, for example, the huge differences in almost every aspect of life between the industrial, urbanized valleys and lowlands of Scotland and Wales and the rural areas of these nations. Centrally important was a belief that a separate national identity often came through asserting that identity against the beliefs of different groups. The clash of these rival, intolerant, irreconcilable nationalisms caused many of the problems of the twentieth century. Many of these clashes took place in Europe, especially in the central and eastern parts of the continent.

The assertion of a 'national identity' was often based on factors which in practice turned out to be either ambiguous or false. Nations believed that they belonged in a defined territorial space, which had what were believed to be unique attributes and special sacred, religious and national sites. In practice this territorial dimension was problematic; for example, none of the various Polish states of the last millennium have occupied the same area in eastern Europe. People were believed to be organically part of a national community by common descent and shared language, history, religion and culture, but in many cases these were the creations of intellectuals in the eighteenth and nineteenth centuries. For example, the first attempt to create a Slovak language in the 1790s failed, but the second in the 1840s succeeded. Modern Hebrew, the language of Zionism and of Israel, was an artificial construct. Others were merely regional languages writ large: the literary Ukrainian of the nineteenth century was no more than the dialect of the south-east Ukraine, and likewise west Bulgarian became literary Bulgarian. In the twentieth century the Italian language was still being created from a multitude of local and regional languages, mainly through the power of the national media.

Religion was also a vital force in nationalism. It was almost the sole basis of Pakistan's claim to be a separate nation. It was central to defining the separate nationalisms of the Serbs and Croats and it was also a focus for nationalism in Ireland and Poland (through symbols such as the Black Madonna of Czestochowa). Some nations even saw themselves as embodying a divine mission. This was true not just of Zionism in Palestine but also of Afrikaner nationalism in South Africa. Dr Malan, the first National Party prime minister in 1948, said, 'Afrikanerdom is not the work of man but the creation of God . . . Our history is the highest work of art of the Architect of the centuries.' On the other hand, many nations existed by embracing a multitude of religious beliefs. Given the artificiality of many nationalisms, it is possible in some cases to trace the exact process of the emergence of a national identity. For example, although the Basque language is unique in Europe since it bears no relation to any Indo-European language, the idea of the Basques as a separate nation was invented by Sabino Arana in the late nineteenth century. He named the Basque country Euskadi, he designed the national flag and he created an ideology of racial purity and Basque superiority to justify independence.

In practice it proved almost impossible to construct states that did meet the ideal of a 'nation-state'. In only a handful of states in the world, such as Denmark and Iceland, did the boundaries of state and nation coincide with the population sharing a single culture. Everywhere else the mixture of peoples, cultures, religions and languages meant that states had minorities who did not share in the dominant nationalism of the state. The problem posed by nationalism in the twentieth century was: when did the claims of small groups to a separate identity and their own state cease to be legitimate? In practice no line could be drawn and once one nationalism had been asserted other groups could reasonably claim similar rights. States survived for as long as they were able to contain these claims by a variety of policies, including repression, regional government, rights for minority languages and special economic privileges.

In the nineteenth century nationalism was usually seen as a 'progressive' force in the building of the modern state. In much of western Europe the long process of nation building seemed to be reaching a conclusion. States such as Britain, France, the Netherlands, Sweden, Portugal and Spain had been established for centuries and they appeared to be identifiable national units. In practice many of them were highly diverse, with separate languages and cultures contained within an overall identity. In some cases nation building was still under way. In France in 1871 about three-quarters of the population of Languedoc were still monolingual in Occitan rather than French and surveys showed that most schoolchildren did not identify themselves as being 'French'. In the last quarter of the century the French government undertook major campaigns in the schools to create 'Frenchmen' out of the existing diversity, with emphasis on 'the one and indivisible republic'. In Britain there was a similarly strong campaign against the Welsh language. The new 'nations' of Italy and Germany were largely created by a single state (Piedmont and Prussia respectively) and were in many respects deeply ambiguous. Even after the establishment of Italy, immense regional and cultural differences persisted to the end of the twentieth century. The creation of Germany in 1871 meant the exclusion of other German-language speakers in Austria and major cultural and religious differences, in particular between Bavaria and the rest of Germany. Nineteenth-century nationalism also had a darker side. The creation of the 'nation-state' was often the result of a vast effort by politicians, civil servants and the elite through the use of the national flag, the national anthem, rhetoric, instruction in schools and publicity for sporting success, to integrate the population into the state. In these circumstances it was very easy to place the rights of the state and the nation above those of the individual. In the last resort it was asserted that the state had the right to mobilize every citizen and call on them to die for the nation.

In practice at the beginning of the twentieth century nationalism was moving away from liberalism towards a deep conservatism. Increasingly it was opposed to many of the forces which had shaped the nineteenth century in the core states – industrialization, urbanization, the growth of the working class and the resulting social and economic conflicts within the nation. Nationalism came to be characterized by rejection of the modern world, belief in an illusory past and a desire for a utopian future of unity, stability and order in a nation without class and other conflicts. In this process religion was an important motivating factor, especially conservative Catholicism in areas such as Ireland and Brittany and Non-conformity in rural Wales.

In the late nineteenth century across western Europe an upsurge of nationalism challenged existing states. Sweden allowed Norway to secede and form a separate state in 1905. In Spain and particularly Britain it produced conflict, violence and secession. The British faced the most acute problem in Ireland, which was an ancient political entity with a clear sense of national identity, although much of it was formed in reaction to British colonialism. The Act of Union between the two countries in 1800 solved few problems. Ireland was treated as a separate political unit and governed under a semi-colonial regime in Dublin. This involved appointing British officials rather than local landowners as magistrates and establishing a unified police force with special 'Coercion Acts' to maintain security. All these measures were regarded as unacceptable in the rest of Britain. Demands for Home Rule in the 1840s and 1860s were suppressed, but by 1880 British political parties had largely lost their base in Ireland. In their place there was an Irish party which, if it was not capable of securing self-government, was capable of disrupting British politics. Attempts by Liberal governments to give Ireland Home Rule in 1886 and 1893 (as a way of removing the Irish from British politics) failed. At the same time a new form of Irish nationalism began to emerge. It was based less on an appeal to universal rights and social justice than on the assertion of historic wrongs by the British. It was about the purification of a Catholic, conservative and rural nation from the corrupting influence of the modern world personified by Britain. A cultural mythology was created through two groups. The Gaelic Athletic Association was formed in 1884 for the revival (and in some cases invention) of ancient Gaelic sports such as hurling. The Gaelic League was set up in 1893 to promote Gaelic, even though it was spoken by fewer than one in six of the population.

Irish nationalism came up against another political force – Ulster Unionism. On any normal definition of the term, Ulster Unionists constituted a 'nation': they had a common identity stemming from their settlement in Ireland, a strong sense of the past, a defined territory and a distinctive Nonconformist religion. From the 1880s, however, they defined themselves not as a nation but as Irish people loyal to Britain and therefore to be excluded from any broader Irish nation. Politics in Ulster came to be organized on a local and religious basis rather than in the way found in the rest of Britain. In the first decade of the twentieth century the Labour Party did not organize in Ulster. In fact there was no unified working class in the province on which it could base itself: in 1912 the Protestant workers expelled the Catholics from the shipyards. The problem was that Ireland was a plural society, but Irish nationalism could not recognize this and instead defined itself in two mutually exclusive ways.

The complexities of these different demands combined with political differences over the issue in the rest of Britain produced an insoluble problem. The attempt to implement Home Rule for the whole of Ireland brought Britain to the verge of civil war by 1914. The opposition Conservative Party backed armed resistance by the Ulster Unionists to any attempt to incorporate them in a unified Ireland and the Irish nationalists also began to arm themselves. Parts of the army mutinied rather than coerce Ulster into a united Ireland. The situation was shelved temporarily at the outbreak of war in August 1914 and it was agreed to postpone any conclusion until the conflict was over. However, the balance of forces within Irish nationalism was beginning to change. The Irish parliamentary party had shown itself unable to produce self-government by operating within the British political system. It lost its predominance to the more radical Sinn Fein, whose MPs refused to attend parliament in London because this would imply recognition of the legitimacy of British rule. A group dedicated to force, the Irish Republican Brotherhood, launched an uprising in Dublin during Easter 1916, but it was a failure and those involved were jeered in the streets after they surrendered. The British decision to execute nearly all the leaders was a huge and costly mistake which served to create a pantheon of heroes and a new chapter in the nationalist mythology.

The election held immediately after the German surrender in 1918 transformed the situation – Sinn Fein swept the board in most of the country and the moderates were defeated. This was followed by an increasing cycle of violence and terrorism from the Irish Republican Army and increasing repression and widespread reprisals by the British. The British attempt to suppress Irish nationalism was doomed to failure: even had they been militarily successful, which was extremely unlikely, they would have been unable to construct a viable political settlement. Eventually in 1922 the British recognized this and the Irish nationalists accepted they would not gain all that they wanted. The fiction of British unity was maintained through all of Ireland being nominally under the British monarchy. Ulster was given its own separate government in what was presented as a temporary solution, although in practice both sides recognized that it was permanent. The nationalists were given effective control over the majority of the country. The deal suited the British as it removed the Irish from British politics (apart from a minimal number of representatives from Ulster). However, it split Irish nationalism and produced a civil war over whether to fight on to secure a fully independent republic rather than the 1922 compromise. The Catholics of Ulster were left to their fate under a narrow, sectarian Protestant, Unionist government.

In the late 1940s Ireland became a fully independent republic rather than a British dominion, but it remained a poor country on the fringes of Europe, inextricably linked to the dominant British economy. In many ways the politicians and most of the people of the south of Ireland were easily reconciled to the creation of a conservative, rural, Catholic state which, although it formally claimed jurisdiction over the whole of the island, was quite happy not to have to govern the industrialized, Protestant enclave of Ulster. The 1922 solution lasted until the late 1960s, when the separate Ulster state collapsed because of its massive discrimination against the minority Catholic population and Britain resumed direct rule. This did not end the fundamental split within Ireland nor, by the end of the century, did there seem any realistic prospect of resolving the deep and fundamental contradictions within Irish nationalism.

The problems caused by nationalism in Spain were in some respects more complex, but at the same time less intractable, than those in Ireland. By the early twentieth century the long-established Spanish state was weak, held together by a network of local politicians supporting national political factions, but with growing movements in the peripheral territories which seemed to threaten major fragmentation. It was unclear on what basis unity could be maintained. The existing conservative, military, clerical regime seemed to have failed after the catastrophic loss of empire following defeat in the war with the United States in 1898. The alternatives were highly problematic. A modernizing, centralizing radical solution would be unable to accommodate demands for regional autonomy. On the other hand, a general federal solution would not meet the demands of some regions while it would go too far for others. In the south of the country Andalucia and Extremadura were poor, backward regions dominated by peasant agriculture, with little to gain from autonomy or separation. In Galicia, despite a separate language and a cultural revival in the late nineteenth century, regionalism was kept in check by a strong network of politicians tied to Madrid. In the Basque country rapid industrialization, especially around Bilbao, tied the area into the Spanish economy and political system and ensured that the nationalist PNV Party, which drew its strength from the most conservative, racially exclusive, Catholic and anti-socialist elements in Basque society rarely got more than a third of the vote.

The major problem for the Spanish state was in Catalonia. Catalanism began in the mid-nineteenth century as an elite, conservative, cultural-linguistic movement, initially obsessed by poetry, which did not produce its first newspaper until 1880 or a standardized Catalan language until the early twentieth century. Growing industrialization, and lack of support for it in Madrid, led to the formation in 1892 of the Lliga Catalana to promote the Catalan language and campaign for self-government. In 1907 the Lliga won nearly all the Catalan seats in parliament and inaugurated a phenomenon that persisted for the rest of the century – separate Catalan political parties.

However, the Lliga was also very conservative and religious and it needed the support of the government in Madrid to repress the increasingly radical and anarchist workers' movement. The Lliga backed the authoritarian coup by Primo de Rivera in 1923, but then found that the new government wanted to suppress regionalism. The result was that the Lliga was discredited by its support for de Rivera and was replaced by the more left-wing Esquera Republicana de Catalunya (ERC), which dominated Catalan politics until the civil war. The new republic proclaimed in 1931 faced major problems in dealing with regional demands when it drew up the new constitution. Catalonia insisted upon sovereignty within a non-existent Iberian confederation. The Basques wanted autonomy but on a conservative-clerical basis with their own separate links with the Vatican. This caused the neighbouring region of Navarre to become strongly centralist in order to assert its own separate identity. A separate Catalan political and administrative system was approved in 1932, but autonomy was not conceded to Galicia and the Basques until just before the outbreak of civil war in 1936. By then the state appeared to be disintegrating, with regionalist demands also coming from Andalucia, Aragon, Mallorca, Valencia and the Asturias. The victory of the conservative, clerical and military forces under General Franco in the civil war temporarily resolved the problem by imposing a unitary state that would not tolerate regional and national demands.

Across central and eastern Europe the huge problems caused by rival nationalisms, which were to dominate the history of the twentieth century, were already apparent in 1900. Repeated waves of invaders and colonization over the previous millennium, combined with different religious histories, had produced a highly complex situation. Rival claims to distinctiveness and territory were based on highly partial historical assertions amongst groups divided by language and religion and who, in themselves, often represented a dubious ethnic identity. This patchwork of nationalisms was – apart from the Balkan states which had recently emerged from the disintegrating Ottoman empire – under the control of the Austro-Hungarian and Russian empires. Many of the problems these two empires faced were similar, but the solutions they adopted were not, nor was the outcome in the turmoil of the years between 1917 and 1922.

Austria–Hungary was a relic of Europe's past. It was a dynastic power – merely a collection of territories over which the Habsburgs ruled. The crucial change in the nature of the empire came in 1866–7 following defeat by Prussia, the emergence of a 'little German' national solution and the acceptance of Hungarian claims to equality of status. Italian and German unification pushed the empire's centre of gravity further south and east, a trend increased by the incorporation of Bosnia-Herzegovina in 1878. The most significant factor within the empire was that there was no dominant majority or even minority. Although all the surveys were rigged, it is clear from the 1910 census that the Germans, the largest group in the empire, made up less than a quarter of the population and their pre-dominance was restricted by the need to share power with the Hungarians, who were about a fifth of the population. Apart from the Czechs, who made up about an eighth of the people of the empire, no other national group made up even a tenth of the total. To some extent this made the empire easier to rule because every group was a minority. However, in practice there were huge tensions between the different nationalities: a fully federal structure was not possible because the dual German and Hungarian basis of the empire, agreed in 1867, had to be maintained.

In 1866–7 the Czechs missed their opportunity to establish a separate status like the Hungarians, but the cultural renaissance of the nineteenth century was as important in defining Czech identity as was the claim of the nationalists to all the old 'Crown Lands' of Bohemia, which went far beyond any ethnically Czech areas. However, Bohemia was still dominated by the German-speaking population. The Habsburg authorities encouraged the claims of the Slovaks (still a relatively artificial group) against both the Czechs and the Hungarians. Further east in Galicia, the part of Poland occupied by Austria–Hungary, the population, led by the gentry, were loyal to the empire. This was mainly in order to maintain their position when the imperial authorities subtly favoured the minority Ruthene (Ukrainian) population as a way of both keeping the Poles under control and discouraging any Russian appeal to the Ukrainians.

In the south of the empire the Slovenes were given a degree of autonomy partly because they hated the orthodox Serbs and opposed any demands for an expanded state based around an independent Serbia. The Serbs were, in the main, supported by the Hungarians because of their joint opposition to the Croats. In many respects the Austrian part of the empire was more tolerant than the Hungarian-ruled areas, where the Magyars were free to indulge their prejudices. In the gerrymandered Hungarian parliament the Magyars had 405 seats, the minorities a total of eight, and the Germans, Croats, Serbs and Ruthenes had none at all. Although the Hungarians were less than half the population in their part of the empire, nine-tenths of the teachers and civil servants were Hungarian. In general, though, the Habsburgs were able to keep the Hungarians under control. In 1905–6, when pressure was growing for full Hungarian independence, the imperial authorities supported a proposal to introduce manhood suffrage which quickly brought the ruling Hungarian aristocracy back into line.

In the last resort the Austro-Hungarian state worked. Although the mobilization orders in 1914 had to be issued in fifteen languages, all the minorities fought for the empire until 1918. The empire did not collapse because of its nationality problems but because it lost the war. In April 1918 the Rome 'Congress of Oppressed Peoples' (an unrepresentative collection of politicians and groups from across eastern Europe) made a major impact on Allied opinion at a time when they had already agreed to divide up the Ottoman empire and when drastic punishment for the Central Powers was a highly popular war aim. In November 1918 the Habsburg empire disintegrated in defeat and numerous groups tried to seize power and land.

The Allied leaders gathered at the Versailles peace conference had minimal control over events, little information about the complexity of the ethnic map of eastern Europe and were subject to extensive lobbying from vested interests. Allied rhetoric about self-determination and the idealism of President Wilson proved difficult to apply in practice and often conflicted with Allied strategic and political requirements, especially the need to reward the minor Allied states. The idea of creating ethnic nation-states in eastern Europe came up against the realities of the ethnic map and the strategic requirement to contain both Germany and a newly revolutionary Russia. If every nationality was allowed to exercise a 'right' to self-determination then there would be chaos, with a patchwork of politically and economically unviable mini-states. The problem with the 'solution' adopted in the Versailles settlement was that in the last resort it was a victor's peace. Instead of a mass of nation-states, a series of 'mini-empires' was created, in which previously important minorities became dominant nationalities and other states such as Poland and Romania were either created or expanded. The frontiers established were to a large extent arbitrary and little account was taken of local opinion, except in a few instances when plebiscites were held. However, the holding of these votes in places such as Upper Silesia merely reinforced separatism by assuming that communities would vote along ethnic lines.

The creation of Czechoslovakia was never put to a vote. The idea of such a state came from pressure on the Allies by Czech exiles, in particular Tomáš Masaryk and Eduard Beneš, and by deals between them and an unrepresentative group of Slovak exiles in the United States on the nature of a federal state. There were major economic and social differences between the industrialized Czech area of Moravia and Bohemia and rural Slovakia. The decision by the Allies to include the Sudetenland with its majority German population, to give the new state defensible frontiers, only increased the minority problem. In 1920 Beneš promised to make Czechoslovakia 'a kind of Switzerland', but that undertaking was broken comprehensively in what became in effect a Czech empire. In the new state Czechs were a minority in the country they ruled, with over 3 million Germans, almost the same number of Slovaks and just under a million Magyars along the southern border of Slovakia.

Even more problematic was the new state of Yugoslavia, which contained numerous nationalities, several religions, eight different legal systems and two alphabets for the basic language. The proposal for the new state was put forward by Franco Supilo and Ante Trumbic during their exile in London in the war, but it had even less legitimacy than the Czechoslovak idea. In December 1918 the Allies recognized a 'Kingdom of the Serbs, Croats and Slovenes' embracing pre-war Serbia and Montenegro and a large group of territories taken from the Austro-Hungarian empire. All the frontiers lacked legitimacy, but they were seen as a reward to Serbia for its efforts in the war when it had lost over a million people (a quarter of the population). The inclusion of the Istria area with its Slovene population, including Trieste and Fiume (which had been promised to Italy in 1915 as a reward for joining the war) alienated the Italians. The frontier with Hungary was a major problem because of the Magyar minority in Banat and the Hungarian claim to Vojvodina. The Albanians complained about the large number of Albanians living around Kosovo who were included in the new state (nearly as many Albanians lived outside Albania as in it). The incorporation of Macedonia alienated both Greece and Bulgaria, which had rival claims. Only on the frontier with Austria was there reasonable stability after the Klagenfurt plebiscite in 1922. Yugoslavia became effectively a Serb empire with the continuation of the old Serbian monarchy, the retention of Belgrade as the capital, the invention of a fake Serbo-Croat identity and the inclusion in the constitution of a national celebration of the Serb holiday of Vidovan. The Croats were the biggest minority, but their advocacy of a federal constitution was rejected and when their leader, Stjepan Radic, was shot in parliament in 1928 a new monarchical, authoritarian constitution was imposed.

Although the creation of Poland involved minority problems (about a third of the population was non-Polish) the major issue was the new state's frontiers. The creation of a corridor to the sea at Danzig split Germany into two parts. In the east the Poles established their control over territory 200 miles beyond the border agreed by the Allies (the so-called Curzon line) and took over the Lithuanian city of Vilnius. The population of this area was never reconciled to Polish rule: in 1924 Belorussian schools, societies and newspapers were closed; in 1930 a 'pacification' campaign was conducted by the Polish cavalry; and in the late 1930s the Poles set up a special concentration camp at Bereza Kartuska for the nationalists in the minority population.

In the Balkans the rewards went to Romania for joining the Allies in 1916. It took over Transylvania and Bukovina from Hungary and Bessarabia from Russia (it also ruled southern Dobruja with its ethnically Bulgarian population, which it had taken after the Second Balkan War in 1913). The result was that about a third of the population of the expanded Romania were minorities and only the borders with Czechoslovakia and Poland were uncontentious.

Two states were clear losers from this settlement. Bulgaria failed to gain Macedonia and also saw Thrace go to Greece, thereby denying it access to the Aegean. It was, however, relatively homogeneous, only about one in six of the population were minorities. The biggest loser of all was Hungary. It lost a third of its pre-war territory in the peace settlement and a third of the Magyar population now lived outside of the country. Both Bulgaria and Hungary became strongly revisionist states which did not accept the Versailles settlement.

Only a few population transfers took place after the war. They were mainly confined to the Greek population of Bulgaria (about 46,000 people) and of Turkey – about 1 million people were 'transferred' (although this was largely a cover for expulsion by the Turks). The result was almost to bankrupt Greece: by the mid-1920s it had to support about 1·4 million refugees in a total population of 5 million. The League of Nations set up a Minorities Commission in 1920, but this was criticized on a number of grounds. Its very existence seemed to confirm the status of minorities who were not part of the dominant culture of a state and therefore needed protection. Second, it only applied to the states established at Versailles not all European states, such as those in western Europe which also had minority populations. Third, the minorities complained because it did not in practice protect them. In 1934 Poland repudiated all of its obligations to the Commission and when the League made no response the system effectively came to an end.

The Versailles settlement was destroyed between 1938 and 1941. In September 1938 Czechoslovakia lost the Sudetenland to Germany, Teschen to Poland and the border areas of Slovakia to Hungary. Less than six months later Czechoslovakia itself ceased to exist – Slovakia became nominally independent, Ruthenia went to Hungary and the Czech lands were taken over by Germany. In September 1939 Poland was once again partitioned by Germany and the Soviet Union, and Vilnius was returned to Lithuania as envisaged at Versailles. In the summer of 1940 Romania was peacefully partitioned. Bessarabia went to the Soviet Union, southern Dobruja to Bulgaria and northern Transylvania to Hungary. In the spring of 1941, after the German attack on Yugoslavia, the last of the states created at Versailles disappeared. Hungary gained Vojvodina, Bulgaria (still neutral) Macedonia, Italy the Dalmatian coastline, Germany Slovenia and a nominally independent Croatia controlled

Bosnia-Herzegovina. Yugoslavia disintegrated into civil war with large-scale ethnic violence between the Serbs and Croats. The victory of the Allies in 1945 restored some but not all of the Versailles settlement. Romania did not regain Bessarabia and the southern Dobruja and took control of only part of northern Transylvania. Bulgaria and Hungary were larger than in 1919 but far short of their gains in 1938–41. Yugoslavia was reconstituted, as was Czechoslovakia minus part of Ruthenia, which went to the Soviet Union. Poland was shifted hundreds of miles to the west, losing most of its eastern territories to the Soviet Union but gaining East Prussia and Silesia up to the line of the Oder and Neisse Rivers. The only way this settlement could be justified was through the mass expulsion of 12 million Germans from territories that had been ethnically German for centuries. About 2 million died in this often brutal process.

The other great European empire of the early twentieth century, that of Russia, was very different from that of the Habsburgs. Article One of the Basic Law of Imperial Russia in 1906 stated that 'the Russian state is unified and indivisible'. The Russians, although a minority within the empire, were twice as dominant as the German speakers in the Austro-Hungarian empire and close to being a majority. In addition a large proportion of the minorities, such as the Ukrainians and Belorussians, were Slav and therefore, to some extent, were regarded as being close to the Russians. Nationalism was only strongly developed in two areas of Russia before 1914 – Finland and Poland. The former had been incorporated into Russia in 1809 as a Grand Duchy, but it retained its own army, legal system, currency, taxation, religion (Lutheran) and frontier tariff against Russia. Language was not a major issue until the late nineteenth century (the elite spoke Swedish). However, a major 'Russification' campaign in the 1890s ended the separate postal system and military units, and declared Russian to be an official language. During the 1905 Revolution the Finns were able to regain their autonomy and largely maintained it until the outbreak of war in 1914. The Poles were not granted such a privileged position and revolts in 1830 and 1863 were suppressed. Nevertheless Polish national feeling remained strong and was manifested in particular by opposition to other minorities, especially the Belorussians and Ukrainians.

Elsewhere in Russia nationalism was only weakly developed. Belorussia (which had never been an independent state) was under pressure from Russia throughout the nineteenth century. Its name was changed to West Russia, in 1839 its language was prohibited as a Polish dialect and the Uniate church was incorporated into the Orthodox. The Russians could play on Belorussian hatred for the Poles (they took no part in the 1830 and 1863 revolts) and the ban on the language was lifted in 1906. However, there was no literary tradition, no grammar of the language until 1918 and even in the capital Minsk fewer than one in ten of the population spoke Belorussian (over half spoke Yiddish). In an overwhelmingly peasant country with a wide variety of dialects, there was little national consciousness. In the neighbouring Ukraine, there was little more than the idea of a nation which had been cultivated by a few academics interested in literary and historical traditions. Ukrainian nationalism was only important in Galicia, where it was cultivated by Austria–Hungary as a way of weakening Russia. Lithuania had once been a major state, but in the capital Vilnius in 1900, 40 per cent of the population spoke Yiddish and 30 per cent Polish. Not until the 1870s had a separate Lithuanian culture emerged out of Polish and even then there were three separate languages. Eventually Jonas Jablonskis established his own dialect (West High Lithuanian) as the modern standard. Neighbouring Estonia and Latvia had never been independent states. Much Latvian nationalism developed outside the country in the late nineteenth century and Estonian nationalism was largely a reaction against the domination of the German population: in 1900 the capital Tallinn was essentially a German town.

In the chaos of the 1917 Revolution independence movements, often under German tutelage, emerged across western Russia and were for short periods able to take control. In March 1917 a Ukrainian National Congress demanded far-reaching autonomy and in Belorussia a Council (Rada) made similar demands. In November the Ukraine declared itself independent. A month later the new Bolshevik government recognized Finland as an independent country. The German advance in early 1918, civil war and confused fighting eventually led to the independence of Latvia, Estonia and Lithuania, but elsewhere rule from Moscow was re-established. In the Caucasus independence was briefly asserted in Azerbaijan and Georgia, but by 1920 Moscow was back in control.

The new Bolshevik government faced a number of ideological contradictions and practical problems once it had, by the early 1920s, established control over the old Russian empire shorn only of some parts in the west. According to Karl Marx, 'national differences and antagonisms between peoples are vanishing gradually from day to day . . . the supremacy of the proletariat will cause them to vanish still further'. During the Revolution the Bolsheviks argued that the tsarist 'peoples' prison' was ended, national oppression abolished and all nations were declared equal. In the period between 1917 and 1922 the Bolsheviks adopted the rhetoric of self-determination, liberation, independence and anti-imperialism, as when Lenin spoke of 'the full right of separation from Russia of all nations and nationalities oppressed by tsarism'. At the same time the aim of the government was to create the largest possible state under Bolshevik control. In only a few cases was independence recognized. Elsewhere the government in Moscow encouraged local Bolsheviks to seize power or intervened to ensure their success as in the Ukraine and Belorussia. Then the new rulers 'freely' chose to join the new Bolshevik state. At the Third Congress of Soviets in January 1918 the Bolsheviks proposed as the basis for the new state 'the free union of free nations, as a federation of Soviet national republics' and the first constitution, promulgated six months later, meant that Soviet Russia became the first state to have the nation as the organizing principle of its federal structure.

Throughout its history the Soviet Union had to reconcile two conflicting principles. On the one hand, the federation was made up of separate national units: union republics, autonomous republics, autonomous regions and national territories. In theory, the union republics, of which there were four under the 1924 constitution but eleven in 1936, had the right of secession (which was only given to republics on the borders of the Soviet Union). All of these units were taken as representing separate nations and they were therefore bound to act as a focus for national feeling. On the other hand, these nations chose not to exercise the right of secession because as 'workers' republics' they were naturally better off within the Soviet Union. In practice there was conflict between the assertion of national status and identity and the pressure from a greater Russian nationalism (as in the tsarist period) which was now identified with the interests of the Soviet Union as a whole. Between the early 1920s and the collapse of the Soviet Union in the late 1980s the balance between the two forces varied, but in general Russian nationalism was predominant.

For much of the 1920s, in the first flush of enthusiasm and idealism after the Revolution, there was a relatively liberal policy towards the nationalities of the Soviet Union. Written languages were produced for forty-eight nations, some such as Turkmen and Kirgiz for the first time. Elsewhere there was a strong development of Ukrainian and Belorussian, although this was partly in response to forced Polonization further west. The Latin alphabet (not Cyrillic) was adopted to replace Arabic script in the Muslim republics for over seventy languages. As late as 1933 a quarter of all the books published in the Soviet Union were in non-Russian languages. In the 1920s some groups such as Jews, Armenians and Ukrainians had special privileges and were granted the right to their own schools and even soviets within the republics of other nationalities. There was also a strong programme of *korenizatsiia* or 'nativization' – a drive to increase local membership of republic Communist Parties. At the same time the republics were encouraged to develop their own infrastructures, with national operas, academies of science and film studios. However, even in the early years of the Soviet Union there were strict limits on national self-assertion. About three-quarters of the Bolshevik Party were Russians and all the key elements of the state, such as the Red Army, were kept as national not republic institutions. There was also massive discrimination against non-Russian nationalities. At the giant Magnitogorsk steelworks a third of the workers were non-Russians, but they received no bonuses, no working clothes and there were no schools for their children. In the oilfields and sulphur mines at Shar-Su in Uzbekistan three-quarters of the workers were Uzbeks, but only one of the fifty managers spoke the language and the goods in the factory stores were sold to Russians first.

By the late 1920s, as Stalin, a Georgian who had never favoured allowing national identities to assert themselves, became more powerful, the emphasis of policy changed. There was increasing repression of those suspected of 'local nationalism' and after 1930 criticisms of 'great Russian chauvinism' were dropped. The first clampdown on Communist Parties in the republics started in the Ukraine and in 1933 the entire leadership in Tadzhikistan was replaced and three-quarters of the membership expelled. From 1934 the school history curriculum was changed, the emphasis being placed not on the Marxist development of classes but on states and nations. The past of the non-Russian peoples was now seen only as a precursor of integration into the Russian empire and then the Soviet Union. In 1927 the Soviet encyclopaedia described patriotism as 'an extremely reactionary ideology whose task is to justify imperialist robbery and to lull the proletariat's class consciousness to sleep'. Eight years later *Pravda* said that Soviet patriotism was 'the burning sensation of boundless love, unreserved devotion towards the homeland, deep responsibility for its fate and defence – it bubbles from the depths of our people like a mighty spring'. However, not only patriotism was emphasized – the role of the Russians within the Soviet Union became important. In January 1937 *Pravda* described 'the great Russian people', who were 'first among equals' and whom 'all the Union's peoples' treat with a 'holy feeling of friendship, love and gratitude'. This was combined with the 'Russian people's help' for the Soviet Union's 'underdeveloped nations in building socialism'. From March 1938 compulsory Russian classes were introduced in all schools, the Red Army used only Russian and at all universities (except those in the Caucasian republics) Russian became the medium of teaching. The Latin script in the Muslim republics was abolished and replaced by Cyrillic. This was used in other areas, for example in Bessarabia after it was taken over from Romania in 1940, deliberately to differentiate the people of the Soviet Union from their neighbours.

The Second World War, or the Great Patriotic War as it was called in the Soviet Union, saw an even greater emphasis on Russian nationalism and heroes from the Russian past such as Alexander Nevsky, Peter the Great and General Kutuzov. After 1945 there were strong attacks on all forms of 'bourgeois nationalism' and at the same time everything Russian was idolized. In 1950 *Literaturnaia gazeta* claimed, 'Russian literature and Russian art have won first rank in the world ... Russian opera is the world's best opera', and went on to say the peoples of the Soviet Union see 'the Russian people as their paragon'. The new territories taken over in the west were integrated through the immigration of hundreds of thousands of ethnic Russians (similar policies had been adopted in central Asia since the 1920s) and by ensuring that ethnic Russians controlled the administration and local Communist Parties. By 1949 two-thirds of the membership of the Lithuanian Communist Party were Russians.

By the middle of the twentieth century nationalism, in the form of separatist demands, appeared to be a dying force across Europe. The Soviet Union appeared to have integrated its various nationalities. In eastern Europe, the new Communist governments suppressed any nationalist separatism and ignored potential national conflicts. Everywhere national demands were hardly on the political agenda. In western Europe, increasing prosperity in every country combined with strong regional policies seemed to be reducing demands for regional autonomy to insignificance. The relatively sudden re-emergence of regional and national demands for autonomy and independence after 1960 in the 'nation-states' of western Europe was therefore surprising. The phenomenon was found in Scotland, Wales, Corsica, Brittany, the Languedoc, Catalonia, Galicia, the Basque country and in Belgium, Italy and Switzerland. (A similar resurgence was found in the French-speaking province of Quebec in Canada.) The movements making demands were typified less by the reaction against modernity that was so evident in the national movements of the early twentieth century than by the reassertion of what were seen as old identities and separate traditions. Most of these claims failed to attract major support and much of the support that was given expressed growing dissatisfaction with the existing political parties rather than positive support for the alternative. Only in a few cases was there a small fringe of violent nationalists: in the Basque country, Corsica, the Jura and Wales. The regional movements faced the problem that the more they emphasized differences between their region and the rest of the state, the more they had to argue for an identity of interests within the region even though in every case there were in fact major social and economic differences. In these circumstances the movements could easily slip into a generally conservative, anti-centralist populism. In some cases, for example Wales and Languedoc, the emphasis on the revival of a minority language divided rather than united the population. Nevertheless, despite their limited effectiveness, these movements posed awkward questions for existing political parties and administrative structures. This was particularly the case if the major political parties drew substantial support from the area demanding autonomy, for example the Labour Party in Scotland and Wales, and therefore could not afford to grant full political autonomy.

In practice the states of western Europe (and Canada too) proved remarkably resilient in the face of this challenge. In the main the movements were contained in the decades after 1960, usually with only a few, if any, changes in the constitutional arrangements of the states involved. Only rarely did any of the movements gain more than about a quarter of the vote, usually much less. In these circumstances it was possible for central government to buy off the movement by conceding, depending on the circumstances, greater autonomy, equality for minority languages and more economic aid.

These policies did not solve any of the underlying problems, but they meant that support for separatism remained limited. (In Quebec, although the separatist party twice won elections, the electorate twice rejected independence in a referendum.)

Only in a few cases were there major problems. In Spain the Franco government was highly centralist and in the first decades of its rule it was a crime to speak Catalan or Basque in public. A more tolerant policy in the 1960s led to a cultural revival, particularly in Catalonia, but also to a more violent Basque nationalist movement under the control of ETA, the terrorist organization, which was capable of killing the highly centralist Spanish Prime Minister, Carrero Blanco. With the transition to democracy in the late 1970s, much of the debate on the new constitution turned on the degree of autonomy to be granted – apart from a few extremists there was no desire for independence. In the end autonomy was effectively restricted to three regions – Catalonia, Galicia and the Basque country – elsewhere the procedure necessary to implement any changes was highly complex and specifically designed to stop the federalization of the Spanish state.

Major problems were also experienced in Belgium, which had always been split between the majority Flemings and the French-speaking Walloons. However, from the foundation of the state in 1830 French had been the official language. Not until 1914 was Flemish taught in primary schools and it was 1932 before each community was allowed to be taught in its own language. By the 1960s the language question was threatening to split the state and every major political party was divided on the issue. Eventually in 1977 agreement was reached on the creation of a new state structure with three autonomous regions (Flanders, Wallonia and Brussels) and a federal government dealing only with defence, foreign affairs, finance and justice. All the major political parties split into separate Flemish and Walloon parties. Nevertheless, the settlement was sufficient to sustain Belgium as a state.

After the death of Stalin in 1953 there was a slight decline in 'Great Russian chauvinism' within the Soviet Union, but the prevailing ideology remained strongly assimilationist. A leading role was allocated to the Russians, who continued to dominate the upper echelons of the Communist Party. The official doctrine remained that a new 'Soviet' people would be created through a merger of the nations within the Soviet Union. However, the formal federal structure and the existence of republics organized on 'national' lines meant that national questions could not be ignored; beneath the façade of assimilation, economic and social inequalities between the republics remained substantial. Income per head in the Baltic states was the highest in the Soviet Union (about a quarter higher than the average) whereas in the central Asian republics it was about two-thirds of the average. In practice there was little assimilation – by the late 1970s fewer than one in six Soviet families was ethnically mixed. The population of the Muslim republics of central Asia was also rising far more rapidly than in other regions – by the mid-1980s they were providing over a quarter of all recruits into the Red Army.

The most important development was the emergence of local and national elites, which controlled local politics and the economy through a network of patronage and corruption. These leaders were prepared to tolerate, or in some cases encourage, the development of national cultures and they acted as a focus for developing national identities. This phenomenon was first seen in the Ukraine after 1963 under the party leader Petro Shelest, who promoted 'controlled Ukrainian autonomism' and the revival of the national culture and language. He was removed by the central party authorities in 1972 and the local party was purged of 'nationalist elements'. Elsewhere long-serving local leaders such as Vasilii Mzhavanadze (Georgia, 1953–72), Anton Kochinian (Armenia, 1952–74), Sharaf Rashidov (Uzbekistan, 1959–83), Jabar Rasulov (Tajikistan, 1961–82) and I. G. Kebin (Estonia, 1950–78) dominated politics and built their networks of power. Attempts to contain nationalist manifestations usually ended in failure. In Armenia in April 1965 there were un-official demonstrations on the fiftieth anniversary of the massacres by the Turks, which forced the authorities to allow a monument to be built and to tolerate an annual ceremony. In Georgia the central party authorities appointed Eduard Shevardnadze as party boss in 1972 with instructions to reduce nationalist manifestations. In 1977 there were riots against plans to end the official status of the Georgian language. The plans were abandoned as were similar proposals in Armenia and Azerbaijan.

Nationalism was, however, contained until the mid-1980s when the new party leader Mikhail Gorbachev began his twin reform policies of *perestroika* (restructuring) and *glasnost* (openness). These reforms gave expression to a growing wave of nationalism that was eventually to cause the collapse of the Soviet Union. This largely peaceful disintegration was unprecedented and demonstrated the immense power of nationalism at the end of the twentieth century.

Gorbachev did not, of course, intend the eventual outcome of his policies. In 1987, in a speech on the seventieth anniversary of the revolution, he repeated the standard Soviet claim that the nationalities' question had been resolved and that the people of the Soviet Union were filled with respect and gratitude to the great Russian people for their 'selflessness' and 'invaluable contribution' to the creation of the Soviet Union. By the time of that speech the first signs of growing nationalism were already apparent. In December 1986 there were riots in Alma-Ata over the replacement of Dinmukhammed Kunaev as the Kazakhstan party boss by a Russian, Gennadi Kolbin. In the summer of 1987 there were demonstrations across the Baltic states on the anniversary of the German-Soviet pact of 1939, which had led to their take-over by the Soviet Union. Language issues grew in importance. In Estonia there were demands for the sole use of the local language and in Moldova (the old Bessarabia) pressure for recognition of the local dialect and the use of the Latin not Cyrillic alphabet. These demands were directed against the large Russian minorities in the republics. A darker side to the growing nationalism was also quickly apparent. It followed the insistence of Armenia, in defiance of the policies of the government and the Politburo of the Communist Party, that Nagorno-Karabakh, an Armenian enclave in the neighbouring republic of Azerbaijan, should be incorporated into Armenia. Ethnic violence followed and Moscow could find no way to resolve the conflicting claims of the two republics: even a period of direct rule from Moscow was a failure. By late 1988 hundreds of thousands of refugees were moving in both directions to escape the violence as nationalist movements effectively took control of the two republics.

The beginnings of constitutional reform and multi-candidate elections in 1988–9 only compounded these nationality problems especially when the government, worried by the reaction to the army killing of demonstrators in Tbilisi in April 1989, proved unwilling to use force to suppress nationalist demands. Popular fronts were formed in the Baltic states as local Communist leaders tried to keep control of growing nationalist demands. In late 1988 Lithuanians were allowed to display the old national flag and in Estonia the Supreme Soviet argued that federal law did not automatically apply in the republic, a challenge the Moscow government chose to ignore. Constitutional changes were adopted in November 1989, which allowed the Baltic republics and then all republics, to adopt a form of 'home rule'. This gave them power over social and economic questions and left Moscow in charge of inter-republic trade, army bases and important parts of the national infra-structure such as the oil and gas pipelines. These measures came too late: on 16 November 1988 Estonia declared itself to be a sovereign republic. Most other republics followed suit and in March 1990 Lithuania declared itself independent. The Moscow government was unable and unwilling to take decisive action. The proposals adopted in April 1990 for legal secession from the Soviet Union – a two-thirds majority in a referendum and two referenda for minorities five years apart in order to protect the position of the Russians – proved to be irrelevant as events on the ground moved beyond Moscow's control.

By the middle of 1990 the Soviet Union was beginning to disintegrate. The central government in Moscow could not enforce its decrees and laws in the republics and was even losing control over the Russian republic. A new federation not 'union' was proposed in the spring of 1991, under which the republics would have con-siderable autonomy but federal law would remain supreme; there would be a single currency and responsibility for security and foreign policy would remain in Moscow. Over three-quarters of those voting in the March 1991 referendum approved the proposals, but the limitations on Moscow's power were made starkly apparent by the fact that the Baltic states and Armenia, Georgia and Moldova refused to participate. The drafting of the new federal treaty, which was completed by August 1991, was based on the tacit assumption that these six republics would in practice secede. The day before the treaty was due to be signed an attempted coup by conservative groups in the Communist Party and armed forces, which rapidly collapsed, produced a new political environment. Now the proposals were for a union of sovereign republics which would have the right to suspend federal legislation if it contradicted their own constitution. This was a very different balance of power, but was itself quickly shown to be irrelevant as republics simply asserted their independence. In early September the independence of the Baltic states was recognized and that of Georgia, Armenia and Moldova accepted but not recognized. By the last months of 1991 even the Slav republics were insisting on independence. In early December Russia, Ukraine and Belorussia formed a Common-wealth of Independent States and declared that the Soviet Union 'as a subject of international law and geopolitical reality' had ceased to exist. The Muslim republics joined the new grouping, but the CIS had no effective central authority and was no more than an association of sovereign states. On 25 December 1991 Gorbachev resigned as president of the Soviet Union – a state that no longer existed beyond the confines of his office in Moscow.

The late 1980s and early 1990s also saw the disintegration of two of the states created at Versailles in 1918 – Czechoslovakia and Yugoslavia. The first was a peaceful process; the second was extremely violent, far more so than the disintegration of the Soviet Union. The underlying tensions between Czechs and Slovaks survived the imposition of Communist rule in the late 1940s, resurfaced briefly in the 'Prague Spring' of 1968 under the Slovak, Alexander Dubček, but were contained until the collapse of the Communist regime in 1989. A Slovak nationalist party emerged almost immediately, but it had little support and only grew in strength because the Czech elite under Vaclav Havel paid little attention to the Slovak problem, although the name of the state was changed to the 'Czech and Slovak Federative Republic' or Czecho-Slovakia for short, as had originally been intended in 1918. Negotiations on a new constitution started in February 1991, but they were a dialogue of the deaf. The Slovaks wanted a con-federation of two independent states, but with a common currency and joint responsibility for defence and some aspects of foreign policy. The Czechs wanted to maintain the federation, and were suspicious that the Slovaks wanted effective independence but Czech help in sustaining a welfare state and their poorer, rural economy. The negotiations were deadlocked and in the June 1992 elections hardline parties won majorities in both the Czech areas and Slovakia. With neither willing to compromise, they eventually agreed to split and on 1 January 1993 the two new states of the Czech Republic and Slovakia came into existence.

The establishment after 1945 of Communist rule in Yugoslavia under the partisan leader, Tito, seemed to signify a new era in the deeply divided state. Unity was helped by carefully cultivated myths about Tito and the wartime resistance and by the need to defend the newly created socialism, federalism and non-alignment after Tito's break with Stalin and the rest of the Soviet bloc in the late 1940s. In 1962 Tito declared that the national problems in Yugoslavia had been solved. In practice Tito, a Croat-Slovene, had deliberately reduced the power of the Serbs. The creation of a separate Montenegro could be accepted by the Serbs because of its past independent history and the fact that it was a Serb state. The creation of a separate republic of Macedonia was a deliberate insult, since the Serbs regarded it as theirs; they also disliked the establishment of Kosovo and Vojvodina as autonomous provinces and even more the provisions of the 1974 constitution, which gave the Albanian majority in Kosovo a veto at federal level. The acceptance by Tito of a separate Muslim nationality in Bosnia-Herzegovina was another potential problem. However, the Serbs retained a major role in the state: they dominated the armed forces and the capital was still at Belgrade in Serbia.

Despite some demonstrations and crises in Kosovo and Croatia in the late 1960s, Tito was able to control the situation because of his strong personal rule. After his death in May 1980 the constitution he had forced through in the late 1970s came into effect. The provision that the posts of president and party leader should rotate every year on a national basis only legitimized divisions and proved to be unworkable. The reassertion of the latent divisions within Yugoslavia, when combined with economic decline and the emergence of a multi-party system, was a potent cocktail that destroyed the fragile Yugoslav state. The first problem was the revival of a strong Serb nationalism under Slobodan Milosevic, who took power in Serbia in 1987 and who regarded himself as the protector of Serbs throughout the federation. Yugoslavia broke up rapidly at the end of the 1980s, starting with the relatively prosperous area of Slovenia. An assembly in the capital Ljubljana declared Slovenian sovereignty in 1989 and at the end of 1990 a referendum voted in favour of independence. In June 1991 Slovenia claimed complete independence and despite some military skirmishes there was no real fighting. In the end Slovenia could be allowed to leave the federation because it was ethnically homogeneous, on the border, not central to the main issues in Yugoslavia and had always been closer to Austria than the rest of the country.

The central problem was the Serb-Croat antagonism, which came to the forefront under the new leadership of Franjo Tudjman in Croatia. The Croats opposed demands for a Greater Serbia and a Serb veto over any break-up of Yugoslavia. The Croat constitution of 1990 contained no minority rights for the roughly half-million Serbs in the country and this led to the declaration of the 'autonomous region of Krajina' in ten areas of Croatia where the Serbs were a majority. This was intended to form part of new West Serbia. The Serbs eventually accepted an independent Croatia (short of all-out war they had little alternative), but kept control of

'Krajina' until 1995. The Serb-Croat antagonism was mainly restricted to a series of conflicts over ethnically confused border areas. In the south the nationalists in Macedonia won power in the 1990 elections and were eventually able to obtain independence after complex negotiations involving other states with traditional claims over the area, such as Bulgaria and Greece. The Serbs took total control of their own areas by ending the autonomy of Kosovo and Vojvodina. The major problem posed by the disintegration of Yugoslavia was the future of Bosnia-Herzegovina. It had a highly complex ethnic map and a population in which the Muslims were the largest group but not a majority, the Serbs were a third of the population and the Croats a fifth. The Muslims under Alija Izetbegovic won power in the November 1990 elections, but both the Serbs and Croats had claims to parts of Bosnia (though these often overlapped). In practice a federal Yugoslavia was the only institution that could make sense of a highly divided Bosnia. Once that had collapsed the different communities were bound to feel isolated and turn to their outside supporters. International recognition of Bosnia as an independent state in April 1992 only worsened the situation. Serbia invaded, nominally to keep Bosnia in a non-existent 'Yugoslavia', but in practice to establish its own claims. Shifting alliances between the three communities, weak outside intervention and vicious 'ethnic cleansing' to establish ethnically pure areas lasted until 1996, when a limited and fragile settlement was achieved. After six years of intermittent but occasionally extremely nasty civil war Yugoslavia had effectively ceased to exist and been replaced by states with fairly strong ethnic identities. It was yet another demonstration of the power of nationalism in the late twentieth century.

The national demand which created the greatest problem was Zionism, which made the most extreme claims of any nationalism. It emerged in the 1890s primarily under the influence of Theodor Herzl, who published *Der Judenstaat* in 1896 and chaired the first Zionist Congress in Basle in August 1897. Herzl was himself an example of an assimilated Jew – he was editor of the *Neue Freie Presse* in Vienna and in 1893 had openly advocated a mass conversion to Catholicism. However, he now argued that assimilation was not working and that anti-Semitism would grow. He therefore proposed the 'restoration' of the Jewish state of Palestine, even though there had been no Jewish state there for nearly 2,000 years. Zionism chose as a language a modern Hebrew which nobody actually spoke. It deliberately rejected Yiddish, which was spoken by nearly all Ashkenazic Jews in Eastern Europe and which was a major literary language. Even more important was the Zionist attitude to the existing inhabitants of Palestine. At the end of the nineteenth century, out of a total population of over 300,000 fewer than 24,000 were Jews, yet this was to be the site of the new Jewish state. Zionism was therefore in many respects a form of European colonialism. It was also typical of its period in its attitude to the Arab population and in refusing to recognize that they had any rights. The supposed historic claims of the Jews were to override all other rights. In 1895 Herzl wrote in his diary:

> We shall have to spirit the penniless population across the border by procuring employment for it in the transit countries, while denying it any employment in our own country. Both the process of expropriation and the removal of the poor must be carried out discreetly and circumspectly.

A few Jews had been encouraged to settle in Palestine under private schemes, but by 1907 the Jewish National Fund was operating in Palestine. It raised money among European Jews and used its assets to buy land. However, this was a one-way process – once land became Jewish owned it was inalienable in perpetuity.

Jewish emigration into Palestine remained low and half of those who moved there before 1914 left again. The situation was transformed by the First World War, Allied requirements in that war and the competing claims of Britain and France to the territories of the Ottoman empire. In a series of meetings with Jewish leaders from February 1917 the British drafted what became the Balfour Declaration, which was designed to appeal to Jewish opinion and impress the Americans with its idealism. It was a document typical of European attitudes to the rest of the world – a promise made by Britain about a territory it did not control to an outside group, without any consideration of the wishes of the existing population. Although the British rejected some of the claims of the Jewish leaders, they said that they would 'favour the establishment in Palestine of a national home for the Jewish people'. Exactly what this meant was deliberately left unclear. Although it was stated that nothing would be done that would prejudice the civil and religious rights of the existing population, that promise carefully excluded their political rights. In practice the Allies did not believe the

Palestinians had any political rights. Winston Churchill, a strong supporter of Zionism, compared them to the Aborigines and native Americans, and in 1919 Balfour told the British cabinet:

> in Palestine we do not propose even to go through the form of consulting the wishes of the present inhabitants of the country . . . The four great powers are committed to Zionism . . . [it is] of far profounder import than the desire and prejudices of the 700,000 Arabs.

From the beginning of the British mandate over Palestine the Jews were treated as a privileged group, even though by then they made up only a tenth of the total population. Any form of self-government was denied because the Arab majority would ban Jewish immigration. In 1919 the British accepted Hebrew as one of the three official languages despite the fact that fewer than 20,000 people spoke it. After riots in 1921 Jewish immigration was restricted, but the level set was above that which the Zionists could fill. Nevertheless by 1936 the Jewish population in Palestine had risen to about 400,000 (a third of the total). The problem for the British administration was that Zionist nationalism was, not surprisingly, coming into conflict with a developing Palestinian nationalism as the majority Arab population saw their land and country being taken over by outsiders. Capital raised in Europe and the United States enabled the Zionists to buy up land which was sold by largely absentee Arab landlords. Jewish land was inalienable and the discriminatory policies of the Histradut (Hebrew Workers' Union), under which non-Jews could not be hired to work on Jewish land, only worsened the situation. In May 1939 the British decided on a policy of partitioning Palestine into an Arab and a Jewish state with a strict limitation on Jewish immigration. It was accepted by neither side and was only partially implemented before it was overtaken by events in the Second World War.

The Arab states finally accepted the British partition plan in 1944, but by then it was too late. The Zionists were planning on the immigration of about 3 million Jews within two years of the end of the war. As the scale of the German killing of European Jews became clear, few states felt that they could object on moral grounds to these plans, even though the people who would suffer would be the Palestinians. When the British showed few signs of meeting Jewish demands, the Zionists turned to terrorism. Groups such as Hagana, Irgun and Lehi undertook various acts from killing the British High

Commissioner, Lord Moyne, to blowing up the King David Hotel in Jerusalem, where over a hundred British soldiers died. The British, unable to find a solution, gave up their mandate and left the United Nations to sort out the mess. A partition plan was overtaken by events on the ground as the state of Israel declared its independence and fought to establish its own borders in May 1948.

However, even at this date the Jews were still only a third of the population of Palestine. The Zionists realized that on this basis they could not establish a Jewish state. As early as December 1940 Joseph Weitz, the director of the Jewish National Land Fund, wrote in his diary:

> It must be clear that there is no room for both peoples in this country . . . there is no way besides transferring the Arabs from here to the neighbouring countries, to transfer them all . . . we must not leave a single village, not a single tribe.

During 1948 nearly 800,000 Arabs were expelled from Israel, some 'encouraged' by the massacre in April 1948 of over 250 Arab villagers at Deir Yassin by Irgun terrorists under Menachem Begin (later prime minister of Israel). The refugees, numbering over 2 million by the 1970s, had all their land confiscated and handed over to Jewish settlers and their villages were obliterated by new Jewish settlements. Israel did not accept that the territories to which it was restricted in 1948 formed the ultimate borders of the Jewish state, even though they were already far greater than those allocated in the UN partition plan. After the 1967 war it took over the west bank of the Jordan, Jerusalem and the Golan Heights and began a massive settlement programme. In the 1970s it took effective control of southern Lebanon up to the Littani River, an area which the Zionists had always claimed for themselves. The attempt to build a Jewish state through intransigent Zionist nationalism, with its total disregard for the rights of the Palestinians, was to create an appalling problem throughout the second half of the century.

Although the twentieth century was characterized by growing nationalism, there were some major and deeply rooted nationalisms which were unsuccessful in achieving states of their own. In the Middle East there were two failed nationalisms. Armenian and Kurdish nationalism had far greater historical justification than the Zionist demands, but the Allies chose to ignore them at the end of the First World War. The Armenians, as Christians, had been persecuted by the Turks in the Ottoman empire for decades and in 1915 were subject to the first of the century's genocides. Despite these events and the setting up of an Armenian republic around Erevan in May 1918 by the Dashnaks (the Armenian Revolutionary Federation), the Allies gave them little support. In August 1920 at the Treaty of Sèvres an independent Armenia was supposed to be established, but the Allies took no action when the Turkish nationalists under Mustafa Kemal destroyed the fledgling republic. The Armenians were left with no more than a separate republic within the Soviet Union as a focus for their nationalism. A separate state was finally established in 1991 as the Soviet Union collapsed, although it covered little of the historic area of the Armenian homeland.

At the Treaty of Sèvres the Allies also undertook to establish an independent Kurdistan, but by 1923 most Kurdish territory had been incorporated into the new state of Iraq. There were numerous and widespread revolts aimed at establishing a Kurdish state, but they were suppressed by the British authorities in Iraq and by the Turks on three occasions between 1925 and 1937. The Kurds were a relatively homogeneous community, living in an area controlled by Iran, Iraq, Turkey, Syria and the Soviet Union. They were the fourth largest national group in the Middle East and, at the end of the twentieth century, the largest national group in the world without their own state. They met all the criteria for the definition of a nation, with a separate language, culture and myths, although they were badly divided by the mountainous terrain which they occupied. A national movement emerged in the late nineteenth century with the publication of the first newspaper *Kurdistan* in 1897, at first in Cairo but eventually in the unlikely location of Folkestone.

The problem for the Kurds was that, in the last resort, the states in which they lived were prepared to combine together to suppress Kurdish nationalism. This was first apparent in the Treaty of Saadabad in 1937 between Turkey, Iraq and Iran. Only occasionally was one state prepared, for a short period, to support Kurdish revolts as part of a wider strategic campaign against a rival. This occurred with the Soviet Union's support for the 'Democratic Party of Kurdistan' and a Kurdish republic during their occupation of northern Iran in 1945–6 and with Iran's support for the Kurds against Iraq in the early 1970s. Even during and after the Gulf War of 1991, the Allies gave only limited support for the Kurdish rising

against Iraq and they would not countenance any claim to a separate
state because, as throughout the century, recognition of such a claim
would be too destabilizing for the other states in the area. The Kurds
were left to fight a low-level guerrilla war, particularly against
Turkey. At the same time they were badly divided into rival
factions, each seeking outside support from rival powers.

The Himalayan country of Tibet was recognized as independent
by Britain and China in the early twentieth century. Its distinctiveness as a nation was clear, based on its own language, culture and
highly developed types of Buddhism, all of which had evolved over
the previous millennium. It was ruled by the leader of one of the
Buddhist traditions, the Dalai Lama, and it was utterly distinct from
Chinese civilization and culture. Its independence as a nation was
maintained until the Chinese invasion in 1950. The Chinese justified
their invasion on the basis of dubious claims to ultimate sovereignty
in the imperial period. The Dalai Lama fled into exile in 1957,
followed by tens of thousands of refugees. The Chinese Communists deliberately set out to destroy as much of Tibetan culture as
possible. The numerous monasteries were vandalized and most of
the monks sent to forced labour camps. The Tibetan social system
was uprooted and any expression of Tibetan culture and religion
was ruthlessly suppressed. Waves of Chinese immigrants were
moved in so as to turn the Tibetans into a minority in their own
country. Parts of the country were used to test nuclear weapons.
The major powers, in particular Britain and the United States, took
no effective action – they were too concerned about their own
relations with China.

The demand for separate status and independence for the 'nation'
was one of the dominant forces of the twentieth century, destroying
many states and altering the constitutional structure of others. Many
demanded national status, but many did not succeed. The expression
of these national demands often involved violence, long conflicts,
bitter divisions between people, huge numbers of deaths and the
uprooting of millions of people to meet the desire for an ethnically
and culturally pure nation. In practice none of the new 'nation-
states' achieved the purity they sought. All were left with minorities
of varying sizes who did not share in the majority culture and were
excluded and alienated from the state within which they lived. Once
national demands had been made and vaguely justified, the process
could be extended to other groups almost *ad infinitum*. The
achievement of a recognized separate 'nationhood' depended less on

the validity of the claim (however that could be judged) and more on circumstances and events beyond the control of most states.

In the twentieth century there was only one exception to the prevailing trend – Switzerland. A country with four languages in sharply delineated geographical areas, two religions and a history of deep divisions between the different groups, including the Sonderbund civil war of 1847, ought, by most criteria, to have disintegrated in the twentieth century. Yet apart from a separatist movement in the Jura in the early 1970s, which was appeased with the creation of a separate canton in 1979, the state was remarkably stable. This was achieved through a number of processes. The language division remained almost unaltered throughout the century (about three-quarters speaking German or dialect versions of it such as Schwyzertutsch, a fifth French, 4 per cent Italian and 1 per cent Romansch). The religious divide between Catholic and Protestant cut across the language divide, with only the small Italian group being overwhelmingly Catholic. (The German- and French-speaking communities were almost equally divided between the two religions.) Individual cantons tended to be composed overwhelmingly of a single religion for historical reasons.

Overlying all these divisions was a very strong sense of Swiss identity through an emphasis on national history and universal service in a citizen army. The sense of Swiss exceptionalism was increased by successful neutrality in two World Wars. Internally the overriding Swiss identity emphasized diversity and equality, for example all languages were given equal status. The political system followed this pattern, in that no political party ever represented just one region or language. In 1919 proportional representation was adopted and this was later extended to the federal executive with its fixed representation between parties. This emphasis on a deeply consensual political system with extensive use of referendums produced a highly conservative society and a static political system as the only way in which all groups could be reconciled. The survival of Switzerland owed much to the creation of a strong Swiss identity (which its citizens could adopt in the face of the outside world), with that identity based on an equally strong acceptance of diversity within the state. The maintenance of that unusual mixture was to make Switzerland the exception rather than the rule in the twentieth century.

THROUGHOUT THE twentieth century the distribution of military
and strategic power between the increasing number of states of the
world was as uneven as the disparities of wealth and economic
power. A handful of states dominated the world power structure.
Many, especially the smaller states and those which gained
independence in the middle of the century, had little or no influence
at all. The relative strengths of the major states reflected the complex
and changing balances between a number of factors: population; the
size and rate of growth of the economy; financial resources; the
impact of technological changes; the amount of national wealth
governments were prepared to devote to military expenditure; the
extent of the territory to be defended; the threats they believed they
faced and their ability to secure powerful allies. There was no simple
relationship between economic and military strength. The
economically weaker powers of the semi-periphery (such as Japan
between 1930 and 1945 and the Soviet Union for most of its history)
could decide to channel more of their resources into building up and
maintaining their military strength. On the other hand,
economically strong powers (such as the United States until 1938)
might, because they faced few direct threats to their security,
maintain only very small armed forces.

The distribution of power was affected by four overlapping
trends during the century. First was the decline in European
predominance. In 1900 the European states dominated the world
power structure and the rivalries between them influenced events
across the globe. The major problem was Germany's status. Would
the demands of a wealthy and powerful Germany to a rough
equality of status with the existing powers either be accepted by
them or be forced on them through German military victory? After
the early 1940s the European states were no longer predominant.
The formal loss of empire by countries such as Britain and France

was no more than a confirmation of their decline in status and
power, the first signs of which had been apparent some decades
earlier. Second, in parallel with this decline, came the rise of the two
continental powers – the United States and the Soviet Union.
Although the United States played a vital role in rescuing the Allies
during the First World War, after 1920 it retreated back into
isolation. The Soviet Union was, from its beginning, shunned by the
major powers on ideological grounds. This situation was altered by
the events of 1939–41 and the rise of these two powers was
effectively formalized in 1943 at the meeting of the Allied leaders in
Teheran.

The third trend was the emergence of an increasingly complex
power structure in the second half of the century. This resulted
partly from the decolonization of the European empires and the
emergence of local security and power structures in different parts
of the world; but it also reflected the increasingly diverse and
intangible nature of power itself. Power was no longer simple
military strength because many of the weapons, in particular
massive nuclear arsenals, were effectively unusable. In these circumstances economic and financial strength and their protection became
increasingly important. By the end of the century, following the
collapse of the Soviet Union, the United States was the world's
predominant military power, but economic power was much more
diffuse within the core states. The emergence of completely new
threats to the security of states, with conflicts, actual and potential,
over resources such as water and developing worldwide environmental problems, such as the destruction of the ozone layer and
global warming, posed new non-military threats. In addition to
these three trends there was a fourth, of even greater long-term
historical significance. This involved the slow decline of the
'Atlantic world' of western Europe and North America, which had
dominated the globe for centuries and the increasing importance of
the Asian powers, in particular Japan and, after 1949, a reunified and
revitalized China.

Although in 1900 the states of western Europe dominated the
world power structure through their control of vast colonial
empires and their predominant economic power, it was apparent to
even moderately astute observers that this position was unlikely to
be maintained throughout the new century. The main threat did not
come from any prospect of revolt in Asia and Africa. Rather it came
from the sheer physical size and economic potential of the United

States and Russia, which meant that they had the capability to be military and economic powers on a scale far beyond that of any state in western Europe. The population of the United States in 1900 at over 74 million was already nearly twice that of Britain, and the Russian population was nearly double that of the United States. The United States was already the largest industrial power in the world with its self-contained internal market and resources. In parallel with its industrial growth, the United States expanded its navy massively. In the 1880s it was still smaller than that of Chile, but a six-fold increase, which meant that by 1904 the Americans were building fourteen battleships and thirteen cruisers simultaneously, turned it into the third largest in the world. However, facing no threat of invasion, the army was neglected and remained smaller than those of Serbia and Bulgaria. Nevertheless the United States in 1900 was, like the rest of the core states, an expansionist power. For much of the first decade of the century the United States played a moderately important part in international affairs, but then returned to its traditional posture of disinterest except when it thought its economic interests were at stake, as for example in China. Russia, unlike the United States, was still an agricultural state of the semi-periphery, dependent on overseas investment for its growing industrial sector. It was economically weak but militarily powerful. Although it was the fourth largest industrial power in the world, this was based on its size; its per capita level of industrialization was only one-sixth that of Britain. Because of its huge population Russia could maintain armed forces of nearly 1·2 million men (more than twice those of Germany), but the infrastructure to support them in terms of munitions output and railways was limited.

If there was a single 'world power' in 1900 then the British had the best claim to that position. They were the first state to industrialize on a major scale, but the peak of their power was over by the 1870s as other states, in particular the United States and then Germany, overtook them. Britain's share of the world's manufacturing output fell by nearly half between 1880 and 1913. The expansion of the empire in the late nineteenth century, in order to control about a quarter of the world's population was, in many respects, a sign of weakness. A determination to deny control of various areas to rival powers increased liabilities rather than strength. The Boer War at the turn of the century also demonstrated to the British the dangers stemming from their lack of allies. Britain's strategic problem was that as a status quo power it could not benefit from any likely redistribution of power in the world. The main aim of British policy-makers was therefore to try and preserve Britain's position for as long as possible in the face of a series of economic, military and strategic developments that threatened to undermine it. As the predominant naval power, Britain was adversely affected both by the increasing importance of railways, which enabled the continental powers to move troops more quickly by land than the British could by sea, and by the rise of powers outside of Europe. The most important of these was the United States. By the 1890s the British privately admitted that they could not fight a successful war against the Americans, and that they would have to concede to them effective supremacy in the western hemisphere by allowing them to build the Panama Canal on their terms rather than on those agreed between the two countries in the mid-nineteenth century. The rise of even relatively small navies in South America, particularly those of Chile, Brazil and Argentina, meant that the British could no longer sustain naval supremacy in this area as they had earlier in the nineteenth century. At the same time Japan's rise to the status of an important regional power posed additional problems. The European powers had very long lines of communications either by sea or along the single-track Trans-Siberian railway. The British felt particularly vulnerable with their Far Eastern empire, in particular the trading colonies of Hong Kong and Singapore and the white dominions of Australia and New Zealand. All of them were vulnerable to a Japanese attack. Britain therefore sought an alliance with Japan in 1902. For the next twenty years the alliance was to be a cornerstone of British policy, since it provided a security guarantee for these vulnerable possessions.

The alliance also helped in dealing with the central British strategic problem – the defence of India. Britain's naval supremacy was of little help in this area and even recruitment of an Indian army to the maximum the British thought safe, in the light of its potential for revolt, could not provide sufficient forces to repel a Russian attack from the north. Although the logistical problems involved in such an attack were immense, they were slightly eased in the late nineteenth century by the construction of railways in central Asia. The possibility of attack was remote, but the British felt that they could not discount it. The alliance with Japan provided some support against Russia, but the British felt that they also needed to come to an agreement with Russia. This in turn meant that they first needed to come to a settlement with Russia's ally, France, with whom they had a series of colonial disputes. The agreement reached with France in 1904 resolved the immediate problems and led to an agreement with Russia in 1907, which effectively removed any major worries about the security of India.

In the first decade of the century, the British reduced the threats to their worldwide empire by accepting American supremacy in the west, allying with Japan in the east and coming to agreements with the two European powers that posed the most direct threat to their empire – France and Russia. However, this strategy involved a major cost: it forced the British to take sides implicitly in the alliance system that had divided Europe since the early 1890s. The European rivalries stemmed from the Franco-Prussian War of 1870–1. Prussian victory and the annexation of Alsace–Lorraine permanently alienated France. The subsequent creation of a unified Germany fundamentally altered the power structure in Europe, especially since it was followed by rapid industrialization. Until the 1890s Bismarck was reasonably successful in postponing the inevitable impact of this increase in German power and the challenge it posed to the status quo. The German alliance with the relatively weak Austro-Hungarian empire was probably a mistake, which was made worse by the Franco-Russian alliance of 1894, which effectively split Europe into two structures – the Dual Alliance of France and Russia and the Triple Alliance of Germany, Austria–Hungary and Italy. To some extent, Russian manpower compensated for French weakness, but French industrial output was less than half that of Germany and with a smaller and slowly growing population it was extremely difficult for France to sustain an army capable of matching Germany's. The only consolation for the French was that, following agreements with Italy and Britain, Germany was the only likely enemy.

In the Triple Alliance Germany could only rely on Austria–Hungary, which was industrializing rapidly but was weak militarily. In the Mediterranean its navy was smaller than Italy's, let alone France's, and spending on the army was at about a third of the level in Germany and Russia. In many respects Austria–Hungary was a liability rather than an asset to Germany. Italy was still only a semi-industrialized society which was militarily weak, as was demonstrated by its defeat by Abyssinia at the Battle of Adowa in 1896. Italy's position in the alliance was anomalous, given its disputes with Austria–Hungary over territory in the Alps and Dalmatia, its long coastline, French naval supremacy and its dependence on Britain for over four-fifths of its coal. By the first decade of the twentieth century most strategists and diplomats did not expect Italy to join its nominal allies in any European war.

The fundamental problem facing the core powers in Europe, divided as they were by rival alliances, was how to incorporate an increasingly powerful Germany into an imperial and European system which largely reflected the interests and power of the other European states. German unification and industrialization came late in European terms and by the end of the 1880s, when the Germans asserted their claim to an imperial status equal to that of other states, there were few parts of the world left to be taken over and the German empire therefore remained small. Germany was a highly successful industrial power (by 1913 its steel output was equal to those of Britain, France and Russia combined), but it felt, with some justification, that its status was inferior to that of the established powers. German rhetoric and attitudes, based as they were on the common early twentieth-century mixture of social Darwinism, racism, militarism and imperialism, were no different from those of the other powers. The problem was that an increase in German power destabilized the existing power structure because it was concentrated in Europe and therefore threatened the status quo, which benefited the other powers.

Although in retrospect Germany was portrayed as uniquely militaristic, in fact this was not the case. The navy was expanded after 1898 (posing what the British could only regard as a direct threat to their interests), but it was still less than half the size of the Royal Navy by 1914. Until 1912 the size of the German army was deliberately limited in order to maintain the aristocratic pre-dominance of the officer corps, and only just over half of the eligible population of young males were conscripted, compared with nearly nine out of ten in France, where the population was much smaller. The major expansion of the German armed forces after 1912 still left them smaller than those of France in 1914 and far below those of Russia. Between 1890 and 1914 Germany spent on average just over 3 per cent of its GDP on defence, but nearly twice as much on social welfare programmes. Everywhere among the core powers military expenditure rose in the early twentieth century, but on average Germany spent less than Britain and the power which expanded its military spending the most was the United States, which faced no direct enemy.

In the period immediately before 1914 it is too simplistic to see

Europe as divided into two heavily armed camps engaged in a major arms race and waiting for war to break out. There were rivalries, but the major diplomatic crises – Morocco in 1905–6 and 1911 and the Austro-Hungarian annexation of Bosnia-Herzegovina in 1907 – were successfully resolved. Spending on armaments was at a level which was to become the norm for the rest of the century in times of peace, about 2 or 3 per cent of national income. There were, however, some indications that after 1912 the major powers were increasingly prepared to consider a war, which they expected to be relatively short, as a possible solution to the problems they faced. In particular the German government, seeing itself as encircled by France and Russia, felt that the strategic balance was becoming increasingly unfavourable. Facing a probable two-front war, they believed that the construction of new railways by the Russians would significantly speed up their mobilization schedule and ruin German war plans by making it impossible for them to defeat France quickly before facing the Russians. Growing Social Democratic strength in Germany also convinced many in the elite that war might be the only way to maintain the existing social and political order, by creating an atmosphere in which the working class would rally to support the nation.

During the diplomatic crisis in July 1914 following the assassination of the heir to the Austro-Hungarian throne by Serb nationalists, the German government encouraged the government in Vienna to make extreme demands and showed little concern about the risk of a general European war. If the primary responsibility for the outbreak of the First World War rests with the German and Austro-Hungarian governments, it is also true that neither the Russian nor the French governments showed much desire to avoid war. The British were left in a quandary. A German victory would leave them dangerously isolated, but on the other hand if France and Russia defeated Germany while the British remained neutral, they would have alienated the two powers which posed the greatest threat to their empire. The German invasion of neutral Belgium provided a suitable justification for entry into the war. The war was not the short conflict most strategists had expected. It developed into one in which the increasing mobilization of peoples and economies placed huge strains on the states involved. By early 1917 Russia was about to collapse, the French army was on the verge of disintegration and the British, who were financing purchases by their allies in the United States as well as their own, were on the edge of bankruptcy. US entry into the war in April 1917 enabled the British and French to keep fighting, but revolution in Russia and its exit from the war in early 1918 gave the Germans a last chance of victory in the west which they nearly took. Eventually the collapse of Austria–Hungary, the effects of the long Allied blockade and failure to defeat the Allies on the western front led the Germans to seek an armistice in November 1918. Revolution in Russia, the disintegration of the Habsburg and Ottoman empires and chaos across central and eastern Europe left the Allied leaders with a huge task at the peace conference.

The outcome of the First World War and the settlement reached at Versailles in 1919 created many of the unusual features in the world power structure which dominated the inter-war period and which produced major instabilities. The Russian Revolution and the eventual triumph of the Bolsheviks in the civil war led to the exclusion of the Soviet Union from world affairs. The Versailles settlement, in particular the 'war guilt' clause and the level of reparations (although they were never enforced), were sufficient to alienate the Germans yet not sufficiently draconian to permanently weaken German power. Germany was left almost intact within its pre-1914 boundaries and once its economy had recovered from the war the old question of how to accommodate an economically powerful and united Germany in the centre of Europe was bound to re-emerge. The balance of forces facing Germany after 1919 was also very different from that in 1914. It no longer faced a strong Russia but only a series of weak states across central and eastern Europe, each of them internally divided over nationality questions. The United States, whose economic and potential military strength had been so vital to the eventual Allied success, withdrew from European political affairs after its failure to ratify the Versailles Treaty.

The structure of world power after 1919 was therefore highly anomalous, with the two strongest powers (the United States and the Soviet Union) standing aside. This meant that the responsibility for maintaining the post-war settlement fell on France and Britain. Both were gravely weakened by the war. French losses in the war (1·5 million dead and 1 million wounded – a quarter of all males under thirty) left it potentially vulnerable because the German population was still a third bigger. Also it had only very weak allies to the east of Germany. Britain was left with even greater problems, despite the expansion of the empire in the Middle East, which brought it to its greatest-ever extent. The British had both huge debts to the Americans and a national debt which had risen eleven-fold during the war. In 1919 the government decided that they could not afford to compete with the United States in a naval race and therefore conceded supremacy to the much larger power. Three years later an even more fundamental decision was taken, which determined British strategy for the next two decades. At the Washington naval conference the Americans proposed an agreement on naval parity between Britain and the United States, with Japan having a navy three-fifths the size of those of the two major powers. Although the agreement gave Britain and the United States overall superiority, it allowed Japan local dominance in the Pacific. The problem for the British was that the Americans insisted that they end the twenty-year-old alliance with Japan. The British, realizing that ultimately the United States was more important than Japan and needing a limitation on armaments for financial reasons, felt that they had little choice but to agree. The 1922 agreement left Britain with a major strategic problem. In the past Japan had, in effect, protected the Far Eastern empire and the white dominions of Australia and New Zealand. Now Japan had to be treated as potentially hostile and plans were drawn up so that, in a crisis, most of the Royal Navy could be sent to a new base to be constructed at Singapore. However, it was far from clear that Britain would be able to send nearly the whole of its fleet to the far side of the globe, particularly if it faced the possibility of a simultaneous crisis in Europe.

Until the early 1930s these strategic problems remained latent. Then, following the Japanese invasion of Manchuria and Adolf Hitler's accession to power in Germany, the British began to face an insoluble problem. They were, as in the past, a status quo power trying to protect an empire which covered a quarter of the globe against the shifting balances of the world power structure. At the same time they accounted for less than 10 per cent of the world's industrial output and were gravely weakened by debt and the economic depression. Potentially they faced two strong enemies – Germany and Japan – in different parts of the world without the resources to meet more than one adequately. The United States was isolationist and France still weak. The British considered trying to make a deal with Japan, but decided that the likely price (Japanese predominance in China) would only alienate the Americans and this they could not afford. In the circumstances they could do little else than to begin rearmament (directed primarily against Germany), try to postpone any conflict for as long as possible and hope to find a diplomatic solution. The situation was then made far worse by the alienation of Italy over its conquest of Abyssinia and its move towards a German alliance. The British now had to plan for another potentially hostile power, this time in the Mediterranean across the lines of communication between Europe and the Far East.

In the end the British found that no diplomatic agreement which preserved Britain's position and status could be made with the expansionist powers of Germany, Japan and Italy. Hitler was able to exploit the undeniable grievances of Germany over the Versailles settlement to redraw the boundaries of Europe – sending forces into the demilitarized Rhineland zone in early 1936, annexing Austria in early 1938 and taking over the Sudetenland at the Munich conference at the end of September 1938. British rearmament at sea and particulary in the air was proving expensive. In the winter of 1938–9 the French demanded that Britain equip a continental-scale army as they had done in the First World War, threatening that otherwise they might seek a separate deal with Germany. Britain now faced the first stages of the crisis that was to mark its end as a world power. The British were unable to raise any loans in the United States, as they had done in the First World War, because of their outstanding debts, yet official, and highly secret, estimates showed that their gold and foreign currency reserves were only sufficient to finance a major war for, at most, three years. Military advice suggested that it would take at least that amount of time for Britain and France to defeat Germany. Continuing rearmament without war would use up these limited financial reserves, leaving Britain even weaker when war did come. By early 1939 the British realized that they were in an impossible situation. As a status quo power they could only lose from another war. Either they would be defeated or, in trying to ensure victory, they would become dependent on the United States and possibly the Soviet Union too. Their one slim hope of remaining a major power was to win a limited, fairly quick war against Germany while Italy and Japan remained neutral.

Hitler's determination to solve every problem through the use of force gave the British their slim chance. Hitler was determined to enforce his demands for a return of the 'corridor' of territory to Danzig, which had been given to Poland in 1919 to ensure that the country had a major port. In late August 1939 he achieved the limited war he wanted by agreeing with the Soviet Union on the division of Poland and the rest of eastern Europe into spheres of interest. Britain and France eventually decided to fight over the issue. Any chance Britain and France had of defeating Germany on their own disappeared with the stunning German military conquests in the early summer of 1940. After the conquest of Norway and Denmark, German forces rapidly defeated the Netherlands, Belgium and France and established domination over western, central and south-eastern Europe. The French were forced to accept an armistice, but the British were able to fight on even after Italy entered the war. However, it was clear that they could not win without massive external help. By the end of 1940 their financial resources were exhausted and they were only rescued from a compromise peace with Germany and Italy because the United States provided free financial help, raw materials and military supplies. In the summer of 1941, after half-hearted attempts to agree on division of the world had failed, Hitler turned on his long-term ideological enemy, the Soviet Union. In the Far East Japan took advantage of the collapse of European power to extend its influence. However, it did not engage in open aggression at what would have been the most favourable time – the summer and autumn of 1940 – when the European empires were defenceless and the United States was unwilling to help. By the time the Japanese had decided on a policy of aggression to secure their long-term aim of regional predominance it was too late and the United States was prepared not only to block these demands but also to insist on Japan conforming with American security interests in the Pacific.

The Second World War really began in December 1941, following the Japanese attack on the United States and European possessions in south-east Asia and the German and Italian declarations of war on the United States. However, the new structure of power in the world only emerged in 1943 once it was clear, after the Soviet victory at the battle of Stalingrad and Anglo-American success in North Africa, that the Allies would win the war within a relatively short period. In 1943 military planners in the United States began to consider what would be the main features of the post-war world. They concluded:

> The successful termination of the war against our present enemies will find a world profoundly changed in respect of relative national military strengths . . . After the defeat of Japan the United States and the Soviet

Union will be the only powers of the first magnitude. This is due in each case to a combination of geographical position and extent, and vast munitioning potential.

Although this assessment overstated the strength of the Soviet economy, it was clear that the transformation of the world power structure that many had anticipated at the beginning of the century had finally arrived.

The Soviet Union had always been a major military power (it was the country which had spent the largest proportion of its national income on defence in the 1930s), but the most significant change occurred in the United States. In the late 1930s the United States was, despite its huge economic potential (it was producing 30 per cent more steel than Germany even though two-thirds of its steel plants were idle in the depression), a sleeping giant in military terms. It spent about 1 per cent of its national wealth on defence and, although it had a strong navy, its army was minute and ill-equipped and its air force largely obsolete. That situation was transformed by rapid rearmament between 1939 and 1941 (defence spending increased to 11 per cent of national wealth) and by a massive mobilization of resources during the war. In 1939 the United States built 2,100 military aircraft; in 1944 the figure was 96,300. At the same time it equipped a major army to fight in both the Pacific and Europe, built ten battleships, eighteen fleet carriers and over a thousand cruisers, destroyers and escorts. In addition it supplied much of the equipment used by its Allies, in particular Britain. By 1944 it was producing 40 per cent of all the armaments made in the world and 60 per cent of Allied output.

By the end of the war the United States was the only global military power. In 1945 it deployed 1,200 warships and 3,000 heavy bombers; it had sixty-nine divisions in Europe and twenty-six in the Pacific, and was the only state to possess the atomic bomb. It was also the predominant economic power in the world – it produced half the world's industrial output and held two-thirds of the world's gold. At the same time Germany, Italy and Japan lay in varying degrees of ruin and France was eclipsed as a power following defeat and occupation. Although Britain emerged victorious, its position was weak, especially economically, where it was dependent on American help for post-war recovery. It was nominally a world power, but in practice its position was precarious. The Soviet Union lay devastated by the most brutal war in modern history. The true scale of the Soviet losses in the war only became apparent in the early 1990s. In total it lost about 13 million military personnel but probably 35 million civilians were killed – equivalent to about a quarter of the pre-war population. Nearly all the death and destruction were concentrated in the western Soviet Union, especially in the republics of Ukraine and Belorussia, where whole regions were devastated and depopulated. Overall the Soviet Union lost a third of its capital assets and the total cost was equivalent to ten years of its pre-war economic output.

In 1945 the United States, as the predominant economic and military power, inevitably asserted its influence in a world structured very differently from the previous era. No longer would disputes and rivalries between the European powers determine world politics and strategy. The United States would now ensure that its interests and demands predominated. In October 1944 President Roosevelt reminded Churchill, during Churchill's visit to Moscow to negotiate with Stalin over the future of Europe, 'in this global war there is literally no question, political or military, in which the United States is not interested'. At the same time, the United States was itself transformed by the war – it was no longer a demilitarized state. What later became known as 'the military-industrial complex' was created by the war and survived into peace, as the United States continued to maintain and deploy forces on an unprecedented scale. A 'national security' state emerged, in which new institutions such as the Central Intelligence Agency and a more powerful military produced a new emphasis in decision-taking. By 1949 the United States was spending nearly $15 billion a year on defence and had about 1·5 million people in the armed forces.

The Soviet Union spent about the same amount but, like Russia earlier in the century, had armed forces of over 4 million (about a third of the level at the end of the war). In global terms, however, the Soviet Union was weak. It was a land-based power and unable to deploy forces far beyond its borders. Its main aim was the stabilization of those borders on favourable terms by ensuring that there were compliant regimes in eastern Europe and that Germany remained extremely weak and under control. Both requirements were easily explained by what had happened to the Soviet Union during the war. Its view of the outside world was suspicious, formed as it was by its ideological isolation and the experience of outside intervention during the civil war. Like Germany before 1914 it was easy for Soviet leaders to see themselves as 'encircled' by hostile states. The Soviet Union maintained its armed forces to protect itself and the territorial and political gains it had made during the war. Its foreign policy, despite its rhetoric, was in practice cautious, though it was often carried out in a crude and clumsy manner.

Before their wartime negotiations as allies the United States and the Soviet Union had had very little contact with each other. Relations remained difficult after the war. The United States had its own clear view about its role in the world. In public it emphasized the liberal, Wilsonian idea that it was the American mission to change the rest of the world, 'make it safe for democracy' and remould it in the American image. There was also no doubt about the American detestation of Communism, which arose partly from its own domestic politics with its strongly anti-Communist tradition and the continual search for 'un-American activities'. In the immediate post-war period, reflecting both this tradition and its military and economic power, the US government saw itself as the leader of the world and allocated the Soviet Union a subordinate role, which it believed could be enforced through appropriate pressure. When the Soviets refused to accept that role and asserted their own national interests, disagreements were bound to arise. Very quickly a 'ratchet effect' operated – failure to agree or the expression of different perceptions of a problem simply 'proved' Soviet intransigence, increased American hostility and made future agreement even more difficult. The United States rapidly came to see the Soviet Union as an inherently aggressive, ideologically committed power with whom it was impossible to reach any agreement. In these circumstances the only policy was 'containment' – opposing the Soviet Union on every possible occasion, ensuring that it achieved no gains and surrounding it with a cordon of military power.

Given the structure of world power immediately after 1945, the policy of 'containment' could more accurately be described as one of a massive expansion of American power. This included not just acting against the Soviet Union but also replacing British and French power, particularly in the Far East and the Middle East. In private the US administration recognized its national interest in such a policy. In February 1948 the Policy Planning Staff of the State Department wrote a shrewd assessment of American interests and requirements:

We have about 50% of the world's wealth but only 6.3% of its population . . . Our real task in the coming period is to devise a pattern of relationships which will permit us to maintain this position of disparity without positive detriment to our national security . . . We should cease to talk about vague and . . . unreal objectives such as human rights, the raising of living standards, and democratization . . . We should concentrate our policy on seeing to it that [important] areas remain in hands which we can control or rely on.

In practice the United States continued to talk about 'vague and unreal objectives', but its underlying aims remained the same. A few years later President Eisenhower told Earl Schaefer, head of the Boeing aircraft company, that American foreign policy should be based on 'the need for the U.S. to obtain certain raw materials to sustain its economy and when possible to preserve profitable markets for our surpluses'.

The United States began to build a series of new alliances across the globe and to deploy military forces to defend its interests. In 1947 the Truman doctrine provided immediate economic and military resources for Greece and Turkey, replacing a long tradition of British influence. Two years later the creation of NATO established an American-led alliance, which rapidly embraced the entire area from the North Cape in Norway to Turkey's Asian borders. The Rio pact confirmed American supremacy in the entire western hemisphere. In 1950 the ANZUS treaty made clear American domination of the south-west Pacific and the reliance by Australia and New Zealand on American not British support. In the early 1950s bilateral treaties gave the Americans military facilities in Japan, South Korea, Taiwan, the Philippines and Spain. In 1954 the creation of SEATO brought in Pakistan and Thailand, and after the French withdrawal the United States dominated South Vietnam too. The CENTO alliance included Turkey, Iraq, Iran and Pakistan. Elsewhere in the Middle East British and French influence declined drastically, especially after the Suez crisis. They were replaced by the Americans, who made special agreements with Israel, Saudi Arabia and Jordan. In 1957 the Eisenhower doctrine extended aid and the prospect of military intervention to all Arab states. By the early 1960s the United States had over 1 million servicemen deployed overseas in over 30 countries. It was part of 4 regional defence arrangements, it had 'mutual defence' treaties with 42 countries and it gave military aid to over 100 states. In 1965 the Secretary of State, Dean Rusk, repeated Roosevelt's wartime caution to Churchill in a slightly different formulation, when he publicly stated the aims of

American policy: 'This has become a very small planet. We have to be concerned with all of it – with all of its land, waters, atmosphere and with surrounding space.' This was an unprecedented assertion of global power and the USA's right to interfere in any part of the world.

The Soviet Union, on the other hand, pursued a much more limited policy. It concentrated on trying to maintain control of its sphere of influence in eastern Europe. It intervened to support the Communist governments of Hungary and Czechoslovakia in 1956 and 1968. Even here, though, it had to contend with Tito's government in Yugoslavia, which rapidly asserted its independence from Soviet influence, and also with the infinitely less influential but equally independent Albanian government. From the early 1960s the Soviets also had to take account of the growing rift with China, which rapidly developed into a series of border clashes. In 1967 the Soviets maintained 15 divisions along the Chinese border; by 1972 this figure had risen to 44 (compared with 31 in eastern Europe). Not surprisingly the Soviet Union saw itself as 'encircled' by hostile powers and its strategic situation was indeed remarkably similar to that of Germany before 1914. Not until the late 1950s did the Soviets begin even a limited extension of influence, through arms supplies and some economic help to a handful of states such as Egypt and India, and later to Cuba following the 1959 revolution. In many areas its influence was minimal and even where it was successful it was rarely able to sustain its position for very long against American pressure. For example, President Sadat of Egypt expelled over 20,000 Soviet 'advisers' in 1972 and one of the few Soviet bases apart from those in its European satellites, Mogadishu in Somalia, was lost in 1977. The Soviet Union used force outside its sphere of influence in eastern Europe just once, in Afghanistan in 1979. In comparison, the United States either engaged in war or other military operations, deployed troops and went on nuclear alert on nearly 300 occasions in the forty-five years after the end of the Second World War.

Despite the disparity in both political influence and willingness to use military force, the United States and the Soviet Union remained the two major powers in the world in terms of military strength, with capabilities far beyond those of any other state. By the 1970s American and Soviet military expenditure was about ten times that of the next major powers, Britain, France and West Germany. The United States had about 2 million men in the armed forces, the Soviet Union about 3 million. The Soviet Union was still, like

Russia, primarily a land power with a large army. Although it developed an ocean-going navy from the mid-1960s, it remained limited in size and capability. At this time the largest navy in the world (over seven times the size of Britain's) was the US navy and the second largest was the American reserve fleet. The Soviet Union had the largest air force in the world, but the second and third largest were the US Army Air Force and the US Navy Air Force. The United States continued to base its military plans on being able to fight two major wars simultaneously – one in Europe, one in Asia and a slightly more limited war elsewhere, probably in the Middle East. The greatest difference between these two states and the other powers, was, however, in nuclear weapons and delivery systems, which became the symbol of great power status. The United States and the Soviet Union were the only powers to deploy inter-continental ballistic missiles (over 1,000 each) and both also had about 700 submarine-launched missiles by the early 1970s. Britain and France, the other significant nuclear powers, could deploy at most about thirty missiles and the British were dependent on the Americans for the supply of all the key parts of their system apart from the nuclear warheads.

Although at the time, particularly in the United States, it was argued that the period between the end of the Second World War and the collapse of the Soviet Union in 1989 constituted a 'Cold War' which divided the world into two hostile camps, this analysis is too simplistic. Much of the emphasis in forcing world politics into this framework can be seen as an American attempt to justify the expansion and maintenance of their own power (often at the expense of their allies). In practice the power structure in the world was always more complex. The period between 1945 and 1990 can best be analysed in terms of the evolution of an increasingly complex and diverse power structure in the world, in which the struggle between the United States and the Soviet Union was merely a part, and a decreasingly important one, of the overall pattern. The second half of the twentieth century was characterized by a number of increasingly important trends: the reassertion of diversity within the core states; the emergence of new states, many of which tried to stand aside from the 'Cold War'; the growth of different security complexes around the world; and the increasing importance of economic power (for example, oil supplies). At the same time the concept of power became more fluid, with a shift from military to economic power and rising trade and financial rivalries between the core states. From a longer-term historical perspective the expansion of American power can be seen as a last attempt to maintain the influence of the 'Atlantic world', which had dominated the globe for the previous five centuries. Although in many areas the United States was able to replace Britain, France and the Netherlands, nowhere was it able to extend 'Atlantic' influence beyond the areas dominated by Europe in 1920. From the 1950s onwards, more and more areas of the world were able to detach themselves from this political sphere of influence and begin to assert some independence – China, North Vietnam, Burma, India and the states in the Middle East. Many of the military interventions by the United States were, in practice, far more about maintaining 'western' and 'Atlantic' influence than countering 'Communism'.

Although the states of western Europe were, in the immediate post-war period, highly dependent on the United States for their economic recovery, they were determined not to become overly subordinate to American economic interests. Initially the British and French believed that their colonial empires might be the route towards economic independence, but increasingly the favoured solution was some form of European economic integration. The Coal and Steel Community of the early 1950s led to the creation of the European Economic Community in 1957, although the British chose to stand aside and create a looser grouping, the European Free Trade Area. Throughout the decade after the war the European countries operated their own payments union as a way of reducing the power of the then dominant dollar over finance and trade. In strategic terms the British and French tried, as far as possible, to follow their own agendas outside Europe. It was not until their failure at Suez in 1956, when they deliberately excluded the Americans from the operation, that the limitations on their power were starkly revealed. The British drew the lesson that they should become more subordinate to the United States, whereas the French, especially after de Gaulle took power in 1958, chose to emphasize their independence, even though this was largely rhetorical. The Franco-German entente of 1963 was followed by the French expulsion of American and NATO forces in 1966. Then West Germany, in particular under Chancellor Willy Brandt, adopted a new policy of so-called *Ostpolitik* – an opening towards, and reconciliation with, the states of eastern Europe. This was based on acceptance of the 1945 boundaries and mutual recognition, especially between the two German states. This new settlement was more widely accepted with the Helsinki agreements in 1975 and the setting up of the first European-wide security and human rights agreements, though they were limited in scope.

In the Far East the rapid economic growth of Japan after 1955 produced a new locus of economic power within the core, which carried profound implications for the economies of the other core states, including the United States. It was part of a general trend towards the increasing importance of the Pacific area, compared with Europe, and a more equal sharing of economic power between the core powers. By 1980 the share of world output controlled by the United States and the European Community was roughly the same, at about a fifth each. Japan on its own accounted for about half this figure, but the Pacific area as a whole was about the same size as the other two major regions. The United States was shifting in focus away from the Atlantic towards the Pacific as the balance of its population moved westwards and California became the most populous state in the union. In 1960 US trade with the Pacific area was about half that with western Europe, by the early 1980s it was significantly larger.

From 1947, as the European empires began to disintegrate, nearly a hundred new states emerged. Although the United States tried to force both the anti-colonial struggles and the chaos that often followed independence on to the Procrustean bed of the 'Cold War', in reality the situation was far more complex. These conflicts were never about a simple contest between 'Communism' and 'freedom'. Some states, such as India and Indonesia, tried to maintain a degree of 'neutrality' between the United States and the Soviet Union from the moment of their independence. In 1955 the first summit of non-aligned nations, including Yugoslavia, India and Egypt, was held in Bandung. In Africa newly independent states such as Ghana and later Tanzania tried, not very successfully, to develop their own approaches to international politics. However, the huge increase in the number of states did make world politics much more complex. The ex-colonial states in Asia and Africa soon became a majority in the UN General Assembly and by 1964 had formed the so-called 'Group of 77' to try to co-ordinate their activities and lobbying. The core states of the United States, Britain and France, together with the Soviet Union were able to retain control of the United Nations through their vetos in the Security Council. All the core states had to take account of the questions raised by these new states, especially the problems of 'development' and the relationship between what became known as the 'North' and the 'South' rather than the 'Cold War' division of 'East' and 'West', even if in practice little was done to solve these structural economic problems.

The increasing number of independent states in the world also led to a rise in the number of so-called 'security complexes', regional security regimes with their own dominant and subordinate powers and their own conflicts. Until the early 1940s there were only two security complexes in the world – Europe and the Far East. Of the two, Europe was overwhelmingly the most important because it dictated so much of what went on elsewhere in the world. It could even affect the security of states such as the United States, as they discovered in 1917 and again in 1940. The Far East complex was made up of a strong regional power, Japan, the European colonial powers, a weak power, China, and the latent power of the United States. In general the United States was prepared to intervene more forcibly in the Far East than in Europe. It was not until the Japanese attacks of December 1941 that these two security complexes were brought together in the first truly worldwide conflict.

After the end of the Second World War new security complexes emerged very rapidly. The first was in south Asia after 1947. It was dominated by India and the Indo-Pakistani conflict, with a number of small states such as Nepal, Sri Lanka, Bhutan and later the Maldives and Bangladesh playing a subordinate role. At the same time, another complex emerged in the Middle East centred around the newly independent state of Israel and the opposition to it of the Arab states, in particular Egypt, Jordan, Syria and Saudi Arabia. In the Gulf area a complex involving Iran, Iraq and Saudi Arabia and later the smaller states such as Bahrein, Kuwait and the Emirates developed. In the Horn of Africa by the early 1960s there was a security complex consisting of Ethiopia, Sudan and Somalia. In the Maghreb a smaller unit involved Algeria, Morocco, Tunisia, Libya and also Chad and Mauritania. Elsewhere in Africa most states turned inwards and external conflict was rare. However, in southern Africa international politics were dominated by the massive power of South Africa and the determination of its white minority government to maintain itself in power and, to a more limited extent, by the attempt of Rhodesia's similar government to do the same. The most peaceful area in the world was South America. There were only very limited conflicts, restricted to the border disputes between Ecuador and Peru and between Chile and Argentina. In all of these areas, although the 'Cold War' had an impact, the struggle between the

United States and the Soviet Union did not dictate the shape and outcome of the particular conflicts and power struggles involved.

The collapse of the Soviet Union and the end of the 'Cold War' in the late 1980s only increased the differences between the various security complexes and made it impossible to define any overarching conflict which would unite them all. The greatest impact of these changes was obviously in Europe. Between 1945 and 1989 a relatively rigid structure had remained in place with a clear distinction between east and west and with only a few neutrals (Sweden, Finland, Switzerland and Austria) able to step aside from the rival blocs whilst sympathizing with the West. The events of 1989–91 radically altered the security situation in Europe.

After the collapse of the Soviet Union three different but linked factors tended to revive older questions that had been submerged in the wider rivalry of the 'Cold War'. First, Russia was left weaker and with its borders further to the east than they had been for the previous two centuries. Second, the reunification of Germany and the end of the remnants of Allied occupation, produced once again the strongest state in Europe in the centre of the continent. It left many other powers, as in the past, wondering how to contain German power. Although Germany was tied to the European Union, it was also bound to look eastwards. Deeper questions still remained about the disparity between German economic, political and military power, whether it should have a seat on the UN Security Council and its possible possession of nuclear weapons. The acceptance by Germany of the Oder–Neisse line (agreed by the Allies in 1945) as its eastern boundary was only a minimal reassurance. The third factor was the re-emergence of independent states in central and eastern Europe, not just those created at Versailles, but others, like Ukraine and Belorussia which had only briefly been independent and some such as Moldova which had never been independent. In some places the map of eastern Europe looked more as it had done after the Treaty of Brest-Litovsk in early 1918, when Germany had imposed its war aims on a defeated Russia. Many of the nationality problems which had plagued eastern Europe remained unresolved apart from the expulsion of the German minorities in 1944–6. Czechoslovakia divided peacefully, but Yugoslavia suffered a bitter ethnic civil war which the states of western Europe were unable or unwilling to stop.

The old dichotomy between the relative stability of western Europe and instability in the east returned. Only a few weak structures such as the Organization for Security and Co-operation in Europe, which had been set up at Helsinki in 1975, embraced the whole of Europe. In the west the European Union and the Western European Union were important, but the role of NATO (a product of the 'Cold War') was more problematic. The agreement between Russia and NATO in 1997 marked the final end of the 'Cold War', but the eventual incorporation of some of the states of eastern Europe into NATO raised fundamental problems for Russian security that remained unresolved. It was unclear whether the exclusion of Russia from central and eastern Europe was sustainable in the long term and whether the fragile states in the region could survive. The wisdom of extending NATO into such an unstable region was widely questioned. A whole range of new problems, many bearing an uncanny resemblance to past problems, emerged, which suggested that the 'Cold War' was no more than a passing phenomenon in the longer-term European security and power structure.

In parallel with the emergence of different security complexes around the globe, there was growing economic differentiation and conflict within the core states. Military power declined in importance and economic and financial power became a major determinant of the security of states. During the 'Cold War' both the United States and the Soviet Union found that the possession of nuclear weapons restricted their ability to use military force except in a number of limited circumstances. The risk of any conflict escalating to the possible use of nuclear weapons meant that military power was often of questionable value. At the same time other forms of power became increasingly important. Throughout the century the core powers were able to keep control of the one resource vital to their economies – oil. This was relatively easy in the first half of the century with British domination of the Gulf region. The United States was effectively self-sufficient in oil and able to import any extra it needed from Venezuela and Mexico, which it dominated even though it had to tolerate Mexican nationalization of the industry in the 1930s. However, the British and the Americans were rivals for the control of Middle East oil. Over time the British had gradually to concede predominance to their rival: first by including them in the 'Red Line' agreement in the 1920s; then by accepting their effective control of the Saudi Arabian reserves during the late 1930s and the Second World War; and then in Iran in the mid-1950s after both powers had organized a coup to restore the shah to power. The shift of the United States from being a net exporter of oil to being a net importer after 1948 (by 1960 it accounted for a fifth of all the world's oil imports) only increased American determination to control the region. Although complicated by US support for Israel and claims that they were only acting to 'contain' the Soviet Union, the Americans were able to maintain control over this vital resource. Even the increase in the power of the OPEC states after 1973–4 was relatively short-lived and they were generally content to accept a higher price for their oil rather than use it as a strategic weapon. More radical states such as Libya, which advocated this course, remained relatively powerless. The Soviet Union, self-sufficient in oil, was able to ignore these problems. The importance of these concerns to the United States together with the other core states (and the irrelevance of the 'Cold War' to these concerns) was demonstrated in 1990–1. Following the Iraqi invasion of Kuwait, the United States, under the guise of a UN force, mounted a major military response to restore the status quo, support the conservative Arab states and demonstrate a willingness to use force to secure the supply of oil.

The core states were able to secure control of the resources they needed and were able to reject demands from the Group of 77 for a New International Economic Order which would provide greater benefits to the states of the periphery. However, they found that their economic independence was being undermined by a variety of processes. Economic competition between the core states, even in circumstances where trade was becoming increasingly regionalized, devastated some industries. For example, the European ship-building, motor-cycle and television industries collapsed under Japanese competition. By the 1980s the United States found that its superiority in the production of sophisticated armaments did not protect it from the devastating consequences of Japanese competition in the car and consumer electronics industries. At the same time the ability of states to maintain a national economic policy which ran counter to the beliefs and demands of the international financial community became increasingly questionable. The British Labour government found as early as 1931 that it had to bow to the demands of the international bankers to cut social spending in an unavailing attempt to preserve the value of the pound. By the 1960s, as international financial flows increased dramatically, these problems became even greater. The rise of the Eurodollar market and foreign exchange transactions, which in total were far beyond the reserves held by a single state or even all the major core states together, meant that even these states were losing control over their own economic security. In the early 1980s the French government found that it could not conduct an expansionist economic policy against the beliefs of international financiers and in the early 1990s the attempt to create European monetary union collapsed under market pressures.

In the 1990s the United States was by far the most powerful state in military terms. It was the only state to deploy certain types of weapon and its technological resources were unmatched. By the end of the century its military expenditure was greater than that of Russia, Britain, France and Germany combined and its relatively small Marine Corps was bigger than the entire British army. However, this military power was of limited use. The economic rivals of the United States, in particular the European Union and Japan, created a different nexus of economic power. In addition, all the core states had to deal with the fact that much of their economic policy was determined by forces outside their control. Across the globe increasingly independent security complexes meant that a vast number of diverse security problems existed which were immune to any simple overarching solution. The distribution of military, economic and financial power in the world by the end of the twentieth century and the conflicts, actual and latent, which it created were of unprecedented complexity.

12 CONFLICT

THE TWENTIETH century was characterized by an unprecedented level of war and civil conflict. The exact casualty figures will never be known, but the best estimate suggests that at least 150 million people died in the century's conflicts. About 100 million died in the two World Wars and probably three-quarters of all the deaths were among civilians. The level of conflict was not steady throughout the century: the greatest number of wars and civil wars occurred after 1945, whereas before 1914 and during the inter-war years the world was relatively peaceful. Neither was the level of conflict spread evenly across the globe. Some areas, for example South America and Europe after 1945, were almost entirely free of international conflict. Most civil wars also took place outside Europe, although the continent did witness three of the most bloody – Russia (1918–22), Spain (1936–9) and Yugoslavia (early 1990s). The majority of conflicts took place in the periphery and semi-periphery. In the first decades of the century the imperial powers were still fighting to establish colonial rule and after 1945 numerous wars of independence took place. After independence there were widespread international and civil conflicts. In particular there was a succession of wars in the Middle East between Israel and the Arab states, between Iraq and Iran and between Iraq and Kuwait and on the Indian subcontinent between India and Pakistan.

The nature of warfare altered dramatically in the course of the century, largely as a result of technological changes. During the late nineteenth century industrialization, in particular the development of railways which were able to move large numbers of troops very rapidly, meant that mass armies could be conscripted, mobilized and deployed. The available armaments, especially rifles, machine-guns and their ammunition, could be mass produced easily and quickly and therefore these large armies could be sustained in the field. (By 1918 the German army was using 300 million rounds of infantry ammunition every month.) Wars with mass armies of several million soldiers necessitated a war economy, greater state direction, mobilization of the 'home front' and a near total national effort to secure victory. Inevitably victory became more difficult to achieve and war aims expanded in order to recognize the vast effort and casualties involved in this type of war. These trends reached their apogee in 1943, when the Allies called for the 'unconditional surrender' of Germany and Japan in order to secure total victory. After 1945 this type of mass warfare became less important (although it was still found in the Iran–Iraq war of the 1980s). The decline in mass warfare was primarily the result of changing technology, in particular the development of jet aircraft, missiles and the increasing use of highly sophisticated electronics. These weapons could not be mass produced – they were too expensive and took too long to manufacture. Huge armies could not be maintained with these weapons and even smaller elite armies could not fight long wars with them unless they received supplies from other states. The increasing complexity of weapons meant that after 1945 guerrilla warfare became an attractive option, particularly in wars of independence. In these conflicts a large force equipped with low-technology weapons such as rifles and machine-guns could fight in a way that largely neutralized the effectiveness of the expensive, sophisticated weapons.

The increasing involvement of civilians in the war economies which supported the earlier mass warfare reflected another major change in the nature of war. Civilians had always been targets in the zone of military operations, but during the twentieth century they became targets everywhere. From the outbreak of war in 1914 the British blockade of Germany was deliberately targeted at civilians and designed to break their morale through starvation. The Germans responded by using submarines to sink unarmed merchant ships without warning. The bombing of cities by airships and airplanes began in colonial wars, but was first used in Europe by the French against German cities in December 1914. The scale of these operations expanded steadily during the First World War, involving extensive campaigns by Germany against British cities and by the Allies on Germany. By the end of the war both sides had developed long-range four-engined heavy bombers specifically designed to bomb cities and kill civilians.

After 1918 most major powers concentrated on developing the tactical use of air power on the battlefield. However, Britain and the

United States regarded air power as a strategic weapon to be used against the enemy homeland to destroy industries, houses and people. They used it for this purpose in the Second World War on a large scale, although this was partly because technological limitations made it very difficult, especially at night, to target anything much smaller than a city. Massive raids on cities like Hamburg and Dresden killed between 50,000 and 70,000 people in a single night and in Tokyo in early 1945 the Americans killed over 100,000 people in one raid. The targeting of civilians reached its height when atomic bombs were dropped on Hiroshima and Nagasaki in August 1945. Thereafter the strategies of both the Soviet Union and the United States were based on their ability to kill tens of millions of people in a single nuclear strike. After 1945 civilians also suffered in the numerous wars of independence and in guerrilla wars. Casualties were high simply because it was often almost impossible to distinguish combatants from non-combatants and because reprisals against civilians were an accepted way of conducting such conflicts.

The major waves of change in military technology during the twentieth century came not during the two World Wars but in the periods of 'peace' before 1914, in the 1930s and after 1945. In the decade or so before the First World War a number of new technologies emerged. The development of the internal combustion engine led most armies to adopt motorized supply columns between railheads and the front-line troops – in 1914 the British were using 1,200 lorries, a figure which had risen to 121,000 by November 1918. During the battles at Verdun the French forces were supplied along a single road, the Voie Sacrée, with a vehicle passing, on average, every fourteen seconds. The development of the tank during the first years of the war was not a major technological step, it involved no more than bringing together the existing technologies of the internal combustion engine, armour plate and the caterpillar track. Parallel with this development was the decline in use of cavalry. This was already apparent by the end of the nineteenth century and was confirmed during the First World War despite some cavalry actions on the eastern front. The last major use of cavalry came in the Russian civil war and the Russo-Polish War of 1920, although the final, disastrous cavalry charge was by the Italians at Keren in Eritrea in 1941. In two areas, however, horses remained vital: the distribution of supplies and providing mobility for troops away from railway lines. In the Second World War the German army used 2·7 million horses, twice as many as in the 1914–18 conflict.

A major new area of warfare in the early twentieth century was in the air. Although the first Zeppelin airship flew in 1900, Germany only had eight machines operational in 1914 and had little idea how to use such relatively clumsy weapons. The picture was very different with aircraft, where there were rapid military developments after the first flight took place in December 1903. All the powers realized the utility of aircraft in reconnaissance and in 1912 the British set up a Royal Flying Corps in the army and a separate organization in the Royal Navy. By 1914 Britain, France and Germany each had several hundred aircraft operational, although they were still far from clear exactly how they would be used.

At sea the beginning of the twentieth century saw the first submarines coming into service, initially in the United States, Italy and Russia. Germany did not begin constructing submarines until 1906, by which time the French had over eighty-five boats operational. The development of the diesel engine, first adopted by the British in 1908, changed their role from defensive to offensive weapons as their operational range increased to about 5,000 miles. Torpedoes using gyroscopes for relatively accurate target finding were also developed. How to use the submarine was a major problem facing all navies in 1914. On the surface there were major improvements in technology with the adoption of the all-big-gun battleship with heavy armour, using special steels, oil-fired turbine engines and mechanical computers for range-finding and gun-laying. The range of guns was now so great that opposing fleets could engage when only just in sight of each other.

Equally important was the development of communications, which affected all areas of warfare. Telephone networks were available by the end of the nineteenth century. In 1897 Marconi took out a patent for radio and in 1901 he transmitted signals across the Atlantic. By 1914 the Royal Navy had equipped 435 ships with radio and built thirty shore stations to communicate with them. However, radio signals gave opponents a chance to monitor signals and even if the messages could not be decoded the transmissions could be used for direction finding.

The outbreak of war in August 1914 demonstrated the power of the modern state to mobilize mass armies and transport them to the front by rail in a highly complex operation. In two weeks the French mobilized 3.7 million men and moved them on over 7,000 special trains to their eastern frontier with Germany. Other states were doing the same. The war in the west was characterized at first by fairly rapid movement. However, within five weeks, after the German defeat on the Marne, the armies were manoeuvring around each other towards the Channel coast. By the autumn a line stretching from the Swiss frontier to the Belgian coast had stabilized and highly complex trench systems and static warfare became the norm. Only in the east, where the front was over 750 miles long, did relatively fluid warfare prevail, although the huge distances involved meant that truly decisive engagements were rare. On the western front the defence held the upper hand through the combination of trenches, barbed wire and machine-guns. These made any substantial breakthrough almost impossible and it was difficult to co-ordinate attacks because telephone cables were easily broken and no portable radios had been developed. The war was dominated by large-scale artillery bombardments, which caused the majority of casualties but were unable to break down defences.

Developments in technology were unable to end the deadlock. At sea the British navy was able to maintain supremacy despite a tactical defeat in its only major clash with the German fleet at Jutland in 1916. The main German effort came in the use of submarines. By early 1917, with over 100 boats available, the Germans sank nearly 3 million tons of shipping in three months, almost breaking the supply lines to Britain. The introduction of convoys in April slowly stemmed the losses. On land there were two new weapons – chemical warfare and tanks – and neither was decisive. The Germans first used chlorine gas against the Russians at the end of January 1915, but it was ineffective because of the cold. It was first used on the western front in late April near Ypres. After an initial shock its impact was limited. The first gas masks were available by July 1915 and a box respirator by 1916. New gases were used (phosgene in December 1915, mustard in 1917 and sixty-three different types by 1918), but none had a major impact, despite the fact that on occasions over 40,000 gas shells were fired in a single night before an attack. The first tanks were available for operations in September 1916, but they were trench-warfare machines designed to break wire and cross trenches. Given the level of development of the internal combustion engine, they were bound to be slow (in theory four miles an hour, but on the battlefield less than a mile an hour) and their reliability was poor: in July 1918 during a French counter-attack along the Marne nearly 350 tanks were used, but within three days only a tenth of them were still operational.

Aircraft were also problematic weapons. During the early years of the war ideas about what aircraft could actually achieve developed rapidly. At first crews fought with revolvers, rifles and steel arrows and supremacy fluctuated from side to side according to designs and technological improvements. The Germans did well in 1915 when they adopted a mechanism designed by the Dutchman Anthony Fokker to allow guns to fire forward through the propellors, but it was soon copied by the Allies. Widespread bombing of civilians began in January 1915 with Zeppelin raids on Britain, but search-lights, balloons and night fighters were soon developed in defence. The use of bombers later in the war did not fundamentally change the balance. The raids were not decisive, despite some impact on morale, because the bomb-loads that could be carried were small.

The war was prolonged by the rough balance between the two sides and the nature of coalition warfare. The British were able to provide vital financial support to their Allies until April 1917, when the United States took over the role. British support also helped to keep the French fighting through the disastrous winter and spring of 1916–17 and both Britain and France kept Italy in the war after the defeat at Caporetto. Austria–Hungary probably would not have survived the 1914 failures in Galicia and Serbia and the heavy losses of 1916 without German support. The Allies' major problem was supplying aid to Russia, especially once Turkey joined the war, since there was no direct route for supplies. By the end of 1916, after losses of 3·6 million dead, wounded and sick and 2·1 million prisoners, the Russian war effort collapsed into revolution. Both sides mobilized their economies for war production: British aircraft output rose from 200 a year in 1914 to 32,000 by 1918 and machine-gun production rose from 300 to 120,000 in the same period. However, the rough economic parity between the two alliances meant that neither side could out-produce the other. By early 1917 the Allies seemed on the verge of losing the war – Russia was in the throes of revolution, the French army was racked by large-scale mutinies and Britain was on the verge of bankruptcy and starvation. Intervention by the United States provided enough support and hope of final victory to keep them fighting. In the event the American military contribution was very limited – when American forces went into action for the first time in early September 1918 at St Mihiel they used over 3,000 guns but not one was American and nearly all of the 1,400 aircraft and 260 tanks involved were French. Despite victory in the east in early 1918 the Central Powers disintegrated suddenly in the autumn, even though the western front was still far from the German border. The end of the war followed an Allied attack through the Balkans, clear signs of eventual failure in the west and political collapse in Vienna and Berlin.

The losses in the war were the heaviest then known. In total over 8 million servicemen were killed (nearly two-thirds on the Allied side because of heavy Russian losses and because in the west Germany stayed on the defensive apart from the Verdun attack) and 21 million were wounded. By far the greatest losses were borne by France. They mobilized nearly 8 million men and more than six out of ten were either killed or wounded. The British mobilized the smallest percentage of their male population of any of the major combatants and bore the lowest percentage of losses. Even greater than the total military losses were the roughly 10 million civilian deaths, principally from starvation and disease.

The next burst of technological development came in the 1930s and this largely determined the weapons that would be used in the Second World War. The most fundamental changes came in air warfare. In the early 1930s fighters were still very like their pre-decessors in 1918 – lightly armed, fabric-covered biplanes capable of about 200 m.p.h. By the late 1930s they had been replaced by aluminium monoplanes with multiple machine-guns or cannons, cockpit armour, self-sealing fuel tanks, and very powerful engines capable of top speeds approaching 400 m.p.h. Two-engine short-range medium bombers were standard by the late 1930s, but already Britain and the United States were developing four-engine machines designed to carry a much heavier bomb load over a range of about 2,000 miles. At the beginning of the 1930s it was universally assumed that no effective defence could be mounted against bombers because no adequate warning of an attack was possible. The problem was solved in the mid-1930s by Britain and Germany through the development of radar (the use of radio waves to locate attacking aircraft). Once radar stations were linked to ground-control centres and these by radio to aircraft, it was possible to guide the fighters on to the attacking bombers. On the ground more efficient engines meant that tanks could become heavier and carry more armour and bigger guns. The light tanks with machine-guns which characterized the early 1930s were replaced by heavy tanks with 75mm guns. At sea the battleship was gradually giving way to the aircraft carrier as the main capital ship and the introduction of sonar (location by sound) gave a minimal capability to detect submerged submarines.

During the 1939–45 war most effort was devoted to improving

output by simplifying designs, improving production methods and increasing the performance of existing equipment; for example, the Spitfire went through twenty-four different marks and its speed rose from 355 m.p.h. to 450 m.p.h. The Soviet Union concentrated on building just six basic aircraft – two fighters, one fighter-bomber, one medium bomber and two trainers. The main Soviet tank, the T-34, remained largely unchanged apart from the introduction of a high-performance 85mm gun. In general, firepower was increased by more effective explosives, armour-piercing ammunition and proximity fuses. In 1940 the Luftwaffe was dropping bombs weighing only a few hundred pounds on Britain, but by the end of the war Allied bombs weighing 12,000 pounds and even a few of 22,000 pounds were operational. Until 1944 nearly all the equipment used in the Second World War was based on designs either in production or development before the outbreak of the war. Only in the last year or so of the war did the new technologies – jet aircraft, pilotless bombs, long-range rockets and the atomic bomb – become operational. Their impact on the outcome was therefore limited.

As in the First World War all the combatants mobilized their economies and societies, although because of the limited nature of the war until 1941–2 this did not occur everywhere in the early stages. A careful balance had to be struck between the size of the armed forces that could be maintained and the ability of the economy to support them with armaments. Even so the front-line armies needed a huge level of support – in 1945 there were 11 million men in the US army, but only 2 million were in the ninety combat divisions and just 700,000 in the infantry, which, as in the past, bore the brunt of the fighting and casualties. The United States and the Soviet Union provided the chief economic strength of the Allies, but the Soviet Union bore the brunt of the war effort: it lost control of 40 per cent of its population and an even higher proportion of its productive resources and arms industry when Germany conquered the western Soviet Union in 1941. This burden was increased by the mobilization of 12 million people to replace early losses. Only by an unparalleled national effort was it able to stay in the war. Germany was not fully mobilized before the spring of 1943 and although output increased phenomenally it could not match Allied production. A major determining factor in Allied victory was the simple fact that they could out-produce Germany, Japan and Italy (indeed the last two were only semi-industrial countries and unable to compete with the power of the major economies). In total the

Allies produced more than four times as many tanks and artillery pieces as the Axis, nine times as many mortars, seven times as many machine-guns and three times as many combat aircraft.

However, this economic and military power had to be used effectively. Until late 1942 the strategic initiative was held by the Axis, and Germany in particular was able to fight limited campaigns which enabled it to conquer almost all of western Europe and dominate the rest of the continent. The British were able to survive a limited aerial attack in the summer of 1940, but were unable to devise any strategy that seemed likely to produce victory without outside help. In just over a year of war they were in a worse situation than they had been in 1917, when they had been rescued by the United States. They were only able to stay in the war after 1940 because of total American financial and economic help, even though the United States was still neutral. The German attack on the Soviet Union in June 1941 provided a breathing space for the British. Although Hitler, the British and the Americans expected this to be another attack on a weak state which would collapse in a matter of weeks, it turned out to be the turning point of the war as relatively weak German forces were unable to secure a decisive victory. The entry of Italy into the war in 1940 was not crucial, though it caused some problems for the British. However, the Japanese attack in December 1941 finally brought about a global war. Once that initial attack had been contained and the Germans defeated at Stalingrad and in North Africa, the balance of the war shifted rapidly in favour of the Allies. There was little co-ordination of strategy between the British and the Americans on the one hand and the Soviet Union on the other. There were also a number of strategic mistakes by the two western powers with too great a shift of resources to the Mediterranean and Pacific battles, which delayed a cross-Channel invasion by a year, but in the end greater economic and military power inevitably predominated.

The Second World War was retrospectively portrayed as very different from the battles of 1914–18, with static trench warfare being replaced by fast-moving tank battles. In fact very little changed. Mobile campaigns such as those in France in 1940, the Soviet Union in 1941 and 1944 and north-west Europe for a few weeks in the summer of 1944 were the exception not the rule. Much of the warfare, especially in Italy and the Pacific but also at Stalingrad, for example, consisted of slow-moving infantry battles where tanks were of little importance. Tanks remained highly unreliable: in 1940 mechanical breakdowns made up three-quarters of all British tank casualties. The main weapon, apart from the infantry, was still artillery – in 1944–5 in north-west Europe the Allies fired over 48 million rounds at about the same rate as in 1914–18. Combat casualties were as high as in the First World War and in some cases, particularly on the eastern front, far worse. German submarine crews had a death rate of over 60 per cent and British Bomber Command had a death toll only slightly lower. In the first battles of 1941 the Soviet Union was losing about half its front-line strength of aircraft and tanks every month and even during the rout of the German army in the summer of 1944 it still lost 2,000 tanks and 3,000 aircraft a month.

Overall the death toll in the most terrible war in human history was about four times that of the First World War. In total about 85 million people died, of whom three-quarters were Soviet citizens. Between 1941 and the summer of 1944 the Soviet Union never faced less than 90 per cent of Germany's combat forces and in total they lost about 20 million servicemen. They lost nearly 6 million as prisoners to the Germans (equivalent to the total American army deployed overseas), and of this total over 3 million died (equivalent to the entire British army). (The United States lost 320,000 servicemen killed in the whole of the war.) Of the over 13 million German casualties and prisoners in the war, 10 million were lost on the eastern front. Soviet civilian casualties were on an even higher scale as a result of deliberate German killings, deportations, slave labour and 'reprisals'. During the 900-day siege of Leningrad about 1·3 million people died, more than the military and civilian casualties in Britain and the United States combined for the whole of the war. During the worst winter of 1941–2 about 100,000 people died in Leningrad every month, which was twice the total British civilian casualties for the whole of the war. In 1943 over 3 million people died of starvation in Bengal as food supplies collapsed in the chaos caused by the war and because of the refusal of the British authorities to organize a relief programme. In total the Germans dropped 74,000 tons of bombs on Britain, killing 51,000 people. The Allies dropped nearly 2 million tons of bombs, killing 600,000 German civilians, 62,000 Italians and more than 900,000 Japanese. During the war and its immediate aftermath 25 million civilians became refugees and another 23 million were forcibly resettled or deported. By 1945 about 60 million people were homeless, two-thirds of them in China.

After the Second World War the pace of technological change increased, particularly as electronics and computers were developed, although the types of weapons used hardly changed at all. In the air the United States replaced the B-29, operational at the end of the war, which had a range of less than 2,000 miles with the B-52, which was capable of carrying nuclear weapons over an 8,000 mile intercontinental range. Until the Korean War jet aircraft were still armed with cannon and machine-guns. Although their speed increased, once it reached about 1,500 m.p.h. there was no gain in going faster and improvements concentrated on greater manoeuvrability. At the end of the Second World War the first primitive guided weapons were used and these were developed rapidly. The first, based on heat-seeking techniques, later the more technically difficult forward firing, were used for air-to-air combat and later for air defence, fired from ships and land sites. By the 1960s missiles were being used on the battlefield to attack tanks. Based on German V-2 rocket technology, both the United States and the Soviet Union were able to develop intermediate-range, and then by the 1960s intercontinental-range, missiles to carry nuclear warheads. By the 1980s long-range, very accurate cruise missiles, developed from German V-1 technology, were operational. Radars were developed for every environment, but, as in the Second World War, countermeasures were developed in parallel. The first primitive electro-mechanical computers were used for code-breaking in the Second World War. In 1946 all-electronic machines were operational, but not until the 1960s did they have a major military impact in command and control, communications and data processing. In the 1960s aircraft were still being used for reconnaissance, often at very high altitudes, but they were being partially replaced by satellites for intelligence gathering, communications and location. At sea submarines were nuclear powered from the late 1950s.

Despite these changes the conservatism of the armed forces everywhere ensured that much remained the same. Surface ships survived, submarines still fired torpedoes and relied on quietness to avoid sonar detection. Aircraft performed the same roles despite the advent of missiles, and the impact of the helicopter remained limited. On land the tanks of the 1990s, despite having gas-turbine engines in some cases, stabilized turrets, laser range finders and complex fire-control systems, were still recognizably the same as models from the 1940s. Artillery fired over longer ranges and much of it was self-propelled, but otherwise little altered. The infantry still carried rifles, machine-guns, mortars and small anti-tank weapons. What did change was the rapid increase in the real cost of each item of military equipment. Before the First World War the most advanced battleship cost about £2·5 million, equivalent to about £45 million at 1990 prices. Yet in 1990 even a small frigate cost over £200 million. After 1945 the greater use of electronics increased costs very rapidly. Between 1955 and 1990 the real cost increase in the airframe of a military aircraft was five-fold, for the engine it was twenty-fold and for the electronics and radar it was forty-fold. The result was that as costs rose the number that could be afforded fell. In the late 1930s the United States could order thousands of the new B-17 bomber. By the 1980s, when even a single B-1 bomber cost over £2 billion, only a handful could be ordered. For some states increasing costs meant that they could not afford certain types of weapons at all. The British attempted to build an intermediate-range rocket (Blue Streak) in the late 1950s, but eventually had to abandon it and rely on American missiles. No attempt was ever made by the British to build intercontinental missiles, satellites, submarine-launched strategic missiles and 'stealth' bombers and in 1966 even an attempt to build a major aircraft carrier was abandoned as too expensive.

New technology posed fundamental and unprecedented problems in one area – nuclear weapons. Given their destructive power, could they simply be regarded as just another weapon to be used whenever the circumstances seemed propitious? In 1945 they had been used against Japanese cities and civilians simply as more powerful bombs, but how should they be used in future? In the early 1950s the United States, which had overwhelming nuclear superiority, considered plans to use nuclear weapons in the Korean War but drew back. In 1953 there was a major debate in the newly elected Eisenhower administration. The minutes of the National Security Council in February 1953 record that Eisenhower and the Secretary of State, Dulles, were concerned about the 'Soviet success to date in setting atomic weapons apart from all other weapons as being in a special category', which Dulles described as being a 'false distinction'. At the end of March Eisenhower and Dulles agreed 'that somehow or other the tabu which surrounds the use of atomic weapons would have to be destroyed'. At the beginning of May Eisenhower told the NSC 'we have got to consider the atomic bomb as simply another weapon in our arsenal'. In April 1954 the United States offered to drop two atomic bombs at Dien Bien Phu in an attempt to rescue French troops from the Vietminh forces surrounding them. Both Britain and France rejected the offer.

One of the major problems facing the United States was that although it had a complete monopoly on nuclear weapons until the first test by the Soviet Union in 1949 (and an effective one for some years thereafter), it had only a limited stock of weapons, about 130 in 1949. These it was estimated would not be sufficient to stop a Soviet conventional offensive, even though about 10 million casualties might be caused. The development of the hydrogen bomb, which was vastly more destructive, was seen as a possible solution. Although the H-bomb was first tested in October 1952, a weapon which could be dropped from an aircraft was not tested until 1956 and it was the late 1950s before it was deployed in quantity. By 1953–4 the US government believed that it might have accumulated a large enough stockpile of the less powerful atomic weapons (about 1,750) to consider the possibility of destroying the Soviet Union. The 1954 Basic War Plan envisaged an attack by 735 bombers, which would mean 'virtually all of Russia would be nothing but a smoking, radiating ruin at the end of two hours'. In September 1953 Eisenhower told Dulles, 'We should be forced to consider whether or not our duty to future generations did not require us to *initiate* war at the most propitious moment.'

The problem for the United States was that its intelligence estimates showed that the Soviet Union probably held a stockpile of about 200 A-bombs. Even with its limited delivery capability it was possible that as many as 30 million Americans might be killed in a retaliatory strike. The United States was in effect deterred from initiating war. As Soviet capabilities increased, at first with long-range bombers and then with missiles, a theory of deterrence developed which became increasingly intellectually complex and tortuous. In practice both major nuclear states developed weapons systems with little idea of their theoretical deterrence function. The number of nuclear weapons increased rapidly for two reasons. First, inter-service rivalry ensured that each of the three American services deployed nuclear weapons as soon as it was technically feasible. Only when the US navy began deploying missiles capable of being fired from submerged submarines, did the concept of 'second strike' capability, which was thought to be stabilizing, enter into the doctrine of deterrence. Second, hopelessly inaccurate intelligence forecasts and a determination by the United States to maintain what it saw as its 'lead', ensured that more and more systems were developed and weapons deployed. In 1955 the American military forecast that the Soviet Union would have over 700 long-range bombers by 1960. The so-called 'bomber gap' led to the United States air force deploying 538 B-52s, 67 active and 55 reserve interceptor squadrons and 7 batteries of nuclear-armed air-defence missiles. In 1961 the Soviets had just 190 long-range bombers and the total never rose above 210. A similar panic was repeated in 1959–60 with the so-called 'missile gap'. By 1964 the Soviets, it was claimed, would deploy 2,000 intercontinental missiles compared with 130 for the United States. A massive programme was started which led to the United States deploying 830 missiles by 1964, while the Soviet Union had a total of less than 200. From the mid-1960s missile numbers continued to increase and new technologies such as multiple warheads and multiple independently targeted warheads were introduced, but neither side could establish any significant strategic advantage. By the 1980s the United States had over 30,000 nuclear warheads, but most had no real military function because the use of even a small proportion of them would be sufficient to destroy the Soviet Union and kill several tens of millions of people immediately.

Long before the Soviet Union had the capability to attack the United States on a considerable scale and had achieved 'nuclear parity', both powers found that nuclear weapons were unusable. Their military and diplomatic actions in any crisis would therefore have to ensure that the risk of use was minimized. In practice, the conflicts between them were limited and mainly rhetorical. There were no direct territorial disputes between the two states, nor were they in geographical proximity, apart from the Bering Straits. The status quo was also acceptable to both sides. Even in the mid-1950s, before ideas of deterrence had been elaborated, both powers had worked out an effective modus vivendi. Each recognized the other's sphere of influence, particularly in Europe. In 1953 the United States did not intervene when the Soviets suppressed workers' demonstrations in East Berlin, nor did it do so during the USSR's more violent repression of the widespread revolt in Hungary in 1956. There were only a few direct confrontations (Berlin in 1960–1 and Cuba in 1962), but these were contained and resolved. Nuclear weapons probably played only a limited role in avoiding conflict from which neither side could gain. Even without nuclear weapons, neither side could have won a war in any meaningful sense, given the geographical size and economic power of the two states.

Both the United States and the Soviet Union and, to a lesser extent states such as Britain and France, found that the 'Cold War' led to a state of almost constant military preparedness and higher levels of spending on defence than had been typical in peace before 1939. Each state became semi-mobilized, retaining some of the features of a wartime economy, in particular the strong linkage between the military, who became more important in national decision-taking, and those sectors of industry which supplied the armed forces. Both industry and the military had a strong vested interest in retaining high levels of defence expenditure. Firms became dependent on defence contracts (by the mid-1980s General Dynamics in the United States was selling nearly 90 per cent of its output to the military), and the military became dependent on these firms to manufacture the equipment they judged to be necessary. As costs rose and the number of weapons that could be afforded fell, often only one firm was left in each industrial sector to supply the military. The scope for corruption and misallocation of resources was immense.

All of these states saw the emergence of what President Eisenhower dubbed 'the military-industrial complex'. Many of the weapon systems which were developed and manufactured had less to do with military requirements than the needs of the firms involved. Equipment became more complex and difficult to maintain not just because of technological change but because it was in this area that firms could make substantial profits through the supply of spares. By 1980 two-thirds of the F-111D bombers in the US air force were grounded at any one time and they required ninety-eight hours of maintenance after every flight. The new Abrams tank failed on average every 100 miles. In the Soviet Union the same relationships were apparent within different parts of the state sector. A powerful grouping was created out of the armed forces, research and development institutes, the ministries responsible for heavy and defence industries and conservative groups within the Communist Party. Although Soviet defence expenditure and equipment development was reactive to American policy, the defence grouping kept military expenditure high. In the United States, Britain and France, firms in the defence sector employed large numbers of ex-military officers in order to maintain their contacts in the defence establishments. In every state the military-industrial complex took a disproportionate share of scientific expertise and investment. In the United States by the 1960s over half of all scientists and engineers worked in this area and by the 1980s the sector accounted for nearly half of all the nation's capital investment.

Although the stand-off between the superpowers produced two heavily armed states, there was stability in the one area where the two sides directly confronted each other – Europe. Until the collapse of Communism, Europe was generally peaceful, with just three conflicts. The most important was the Greek civil war from 1945 to 1949, in which about 160,000 people died, followed by the Soviet interventions in Hungary (1956) and Czechoslovakia (1968) in which at most 10,000 died, nearly all of them in Hungary. Outside this zone of stability, and the generally peaceful South America, the world after 1945 was racked by almost continuous conflict. The result was that nearly 30 million people were killed, 24 million were refugees within their own country and another 18 million were refugees abroad. Four out of five of all the casualties were civilians; most of them were in Asia, in particular during the thirty-year conflict to secure an independent and united Vietnam, together with the three Indo-Pakistan wars, the Korean War and the major revolts in Kashmir and East Timor. The other major zone of conflict was the Middle East. There were six Arab-Israeli wars (1948–9, 1956, 1967, 1969–70, 1973, 1982), together with almost continuous low-level conflict involving the Palestinians. In addition there were the Gulf War of 1991 and the conflict between Iran and Iraq, which lasted for most of the 1980s. In Africa many of the problems were internal, but there were conflicts between Libya and Chad and Tanzanian intervention in Uganda. In addition there was widespread fighting for decades against Portuguese rule in Angola and Mozambique, which after the mid-1970s involved other powers too, especially South Africa. Apart from a few border disputes, the only major conflict in South America was between Britain and Argentina in 1982 over the Falklands/Malvinas. In Central America there were many internal conflicts with interventions by the United States on numerous occasions including Guatemala (1954), Cuba (the 1960s), Nicaragua, El Salvador, Grenada and Panama (the 1980s) and Haiti (the 1990s).

Some of these wars, in particular Korea, Iran–Iraq, the Gulf and the Arab-Israeli conflicts involved relatively sophisticated weapons, often bought from the United States, the Soviet Union, Britain or France. However, many were guerrilla wars. This was particularly the case in the wars of independence, which showed that small, lightly armed forces supported by the local population were very difficult to defeat with conventional armies. There was nothing new in this strategy when it was adopted after 1945: it had been used at the beginning of the century by Filipino forces opposing conquest by the United States, and by the Boers after the defeat of their conventional forces by the British in 1900. It was also used in numerous colonial conflicts in the first two decades of the century – in Morocco against both the French and Spanish, in Somaliland against the British and Italians and in Iraq against British forces after 1919. It was used more rarely in general conflicts, its main successes being in Yugoslavia and the western Soviet Union during the Second World War. Without the support of the majority population, as for example in Malaya in the late 1940s and early 1950s, such a strategy was far less successful. Also, as Mao Tse-tung recognized in the 1930s, guerrilla warfare was rarely successful on its own. Ultimate victory, as in the Chinese civil war, usually depended on the mobilization of conventional forces.

The use of a combined guerrilla and conventional war strategy reached its height in Vietnam between 1945 and 1975 under the guidance of Vo Nguyen Giap who directed the nationalist and communist Vietminh forces. It was based on three phases: first, resistance and defence of guerrilla-controlled areas; second, active resistance with guerrilla attacks and propaganda, before the third phase of conventional operations. By 1949, with some Chinese support, the Vietminh forces were able to gain control of the north of Vietnam around Hanoi and begin guerrilla warfare in the south. After 1950 conventional warfare against French forces began. By 1953 the French had over 500,000 troops in Vietnam, but most were tied up in static duties, only 90,000 were available for combat and the French controlled few of the villages, especially in the north. The surrender of 17,000 French troops at the major battle of Dien Bien Phu in 1954 marked the end of French colonial rule. The division of the country at the Geneva conference of 1954 and the establishment of a corrupt regime in the south under American patronage only led to further conflict once the nationalist forces had regrouped.

By 1963 the National Liberation Front (effectively run by the Communists) controlled about 40 per cent of the south, including much of the agriculturally rich Mekong delta. The United States found it impossible to construct a viable regime in South Vietnam, despite backing a coup in 1963 to replace Ngo Dinh Diem, the leader since 1955. The Americans had little idea how to fight a war against the guerrillas and they also had to cope with the large-scale incompetence of the South Vietnamese army. Most of the support for the nationalists in the south was indigenous and by early 1965 the American government believed the south would collapse without further support. Between 1965 and early 1968 the United States steadily escalated its commitment to about 500,000 troops. It fought four different wars: a quasi-conventional war along the border with North Vietnam; a war at sea; a growing bombing campaign against the north; and a guerrilla war in the south, which was the most problematic. After the United States began deploying troops, the guerrillas were reinforced by troops from the north. Like the French, the Americans were only able to deploy a small proportion of their forces for combat (the rest were in support units). The use of 'search and destroy' operations, a 'body-count' to measure the number of 'guerrilla' deaths and 'pacification' campaigns destroyed both the social fabric of the country and what little support there was among the population for the government of South Vietnam. Highly sophisticated weapons proved to be of little use and by late 1967, although the Americans had avoided an immediate defeat in the south, they were as far as ever from any 'victory' – even if it was possible to define what that meant. The war was also causing severe problems within the United States. Although the 'Tet' offensive of early 1968 was defeated militarily, the American government finally decided it could not increase troop levels further, especially when there was no guarantee of ultimate success. Instead it began the long process of scaling down its support for the south and extricating itself from the mess it had created. Within two years of the final American withdrawal in 1973 the Saigon government was defeated and Vietnam reunified. The war demonstrated to both the French and the Americans the immense difficulties involved in defeating guerrilla forces as long as they had the support of a large part of the population. Crude military campaigns against the guerrillas usually achieved little except the alienation of the local population.

Guerrilla warfare was at its peak during the 1940–70 period. In the last quarter of the century, once the ex-colonial states had gained independence, it was far less important. In this period it was mainly used in Afghanistan in the 1980s and in Sri Lanka by the Tamils, who were seeking a separate state in the north of the island. To some extent it was replaced by a lower level of conflict – terrorism. Like other forms of warfare, terrorism was not new and was influenced by developments in technology. At first almost the only weapons available were dynamite (of which vast quantities were needed to have any effect) and pistols. The first letter bomb was used before the First World War by Romanian terrorists against a Hungarian church leader in Transylvania. By 1918 the Irish Republican Army had moved on to using sub-machine-guns against the British. So-called 'plastic' explosives were first used by British agents to kill Reinhard Heydrich, the German governor in Bohemia, in 1942, but after the war they became widely available and were combined with increasingly sophisticated detonators. From the late 1960s terrorist groups, particularly the Palestinians, used the hi-jacking of aircraft as a weapon, together with hostage-taking. Security measures quickly brought this type of action under control and terrorist groups turned to using massive car and lorry bombs, often involving suicide bombers. The main problem such groups faced was not obtaining weapons, which was usually fairly easy, but finding sources of finance.

Terrorism was adopted as a strategy by a wide variety of groups across the world – socialist revolutionaries and anti-Semitic fanatics in Russia before 1914, Armenians, Macedonians, the Irish, Zionists, Palestinians, revolutionary groups in South America in the 1960s and 1970s and during many struggles for independence, in particular in Cyprus, Algeria and Aden. The violence was rarely indiscriminate and publicity was as important as the action itself. Often terrorism was undertaken with the deliberate intention of forcing authorities to increase repression, thereby alienating the population or provoking outside intervention. In the second half of the century over fifty prime ministers and heads of state were assassinated, but this was nothing new. King Alexander of Yugoslavia was assassinated in 1934 and the killing of Archduke Ferdinand by Serbian terrorists at Sarajevo in June 1914 led to the First World War. Most leaders, for example President McKinley, Mahatma Gandhi and Olaf Palme, were killed by isolated fanatics or the mentally unstable rather than by organized groups. Often such acts had very little impact, for example the deaths of Indira Gandhi and Anwar Sadat brought no fundamental changes. State support for terrorism in the latter part of the century was also nothing new: Serbia backed the group which killed Archduke Ferdinand; Bulgaria supported Macedonian terrorists; both Iraq and Iran backed the Kurds at different times, as did the Greeks in the 1990s. Palestinian groups had substantial financial and material support from some Arab states. By the end of the century the only new threat seemed to come from quasi-religious groups such as the Aum Shinrikyo sect which launched a nerve-gas attack on the Tokyo underground in 1995, killing twelve people.

Throughout the twentieth century attempts were made to limit the impact of warfare on both military and civilians and to prohibit certain types of warfare altogether. In practice these attempts had only a limited impact and states adopted and used whatever technology was available. For example, the rules of war at sea before 1914 assumed that a warship would capture an enemy merchant ship and take it to a port as a prize. However, a submarine could only sink an enemy ship, probably with all hands on board. The submarine was potentially a major threat to British trade in any war, but most of the strategic planners in Britain did not believe that any state would carry out what Admiral Fisher called 'an altogether barbarous method of warfare'. In practice both sides in both World Wars adopted this method of war. An attempt to codify the so-called 'laws' of war was made at the two Hague Peace conferences of 1899 and 1907 (the third, scheduled for 1914, never met). These provided little protection for civilians and although they prohibited certain types of warfare – dropping bombs from balloons and the use of 'asphyxiating gases' – they were ignored. After the First World War a further attempt was made to regulate some aspects of war. The 1925 Geneva Protocol prohibited the use of gas and bacteriological warfare (the former had been common not just in the First World War but also in Britain's colonial wars). Gas was subsequently used in some conflicts, for example by Italy in Abyssinia in 1935–6 and in the Iran–Iraq war in the 1980s, but generally the prohibition held. This was probably less because of the Protocol itself than from fear of retaliation and because bacteriological warfare was of dubious utility. The 1929 Geneva Protocol set out a series of rules governing the treatment of prisoners-of-war and in general both sides in the Second World War followed the agreement. The main exception was on the eastern front. The Soviet Union did not sign the Protocol and the treatment of prisoners by both sides was barbaric.

After the Second World War further agreements were made to deal with many of the activities that had taken place in that conflict. In 1948 a Genocide Convention was agreed and in 1949 the existing Geneva Conventions were expanded to deal not just with prisoners-of-war (where the 1929 provisions were made more detailed), but also civilians (where collective punishment, reprisals and hostage-taking were specifically prohibited), together with providing protection for the sick, wounded and the shipwrecked. In 1954 The

Hague Convention set out rules for the protection of cultural property. By the middle of the century certain general principles were accepted: the treatment of prisoners-of-war was regulated; military occupation could only be temporary and involved duties as well as rights; some places such as hospitals and hospital ships were not regarded as legitimate targets; torture and genocide were not justified by war; and non-combatants were to be spared as far as possible. In practice these agreements were not always applied in conflicts, but they provided some restraint on the most barbaric forms of warfare. Extension of these agreements in the latter half of the century was limited. In 1972 the development and production of biological weapons was prohibited, as it was for chemical weapons by the late 1990s. The 1977 Geneva Protocols, designed to apply to 'wars of liberation' and give rights to some guerrilla groups, produced a highly politicized debate and were rejected in the end by the major states including both the United States and the Soviet Union. The attempts to regulate certain conventional weapons in 1981 and the use of mines in 1996 were largely unproductive. The greatest gap of all was on nuclear weapons where, apart from an atmospheric test ban in 1963 and a total test ban in the mid-1990s no agreements were reached apart from a reduction in numbers. Any use of nuclear weapons would have breached all the Geneva Protocols and probably that on genocide too, but none of the states which possessed such weapons was prepared to agree any restrictions on the potential uses of what they regarded as the ultimate weapon.

The two most important developments in the attempt to resolve international disputes and conflicts were the establishment of the League of Nations after the First World War and its successor the United Nations in 1945. Before 1914 a number of mechanisms to reduce international conflict were in use. There were international conferences on specific disputes, for example at Algeciras on Morocco in 1906; adjudication was often undertaken (in 1902 Britain did so over a boundary dispute between Argentina and Chile); and a 'Court of Arbitration' was established at The Hague in 1899. However, many, not just President Wilson, felt that the outbreak of the First World War marked the breakdown of the old international system and argued for a new start. After much discussion, both public and private, a League of Nations was established as part of the Versailles Treaty and the court in The Hague became the permanent International Court of Justice.

Originally the League consisted of forty-four states, but most of the ex-enemy states including Germany had been accepted by the mid-1920s. However, the United States refused to join and the Soviet Union was only intermittently a member. The League was made up of an Assembly of all members and a Council, of which the main Allies (and Germany after 1926) were permanent members and there were also four rotating members. The permanent secretariat, under its British head, the diplomat Sir James Drummond, was conservative and took few initiatives. In practice the League was no more than a framework for co-operation between states and inter-state relations remained largely unaltered, subject to a few marginal adjustments to adapt to the new framework.

Under Article 10 all members of the League undertook 'to respect and preserve, as against external aggression, the territorial integrity and existing political independence' of all other members. In practice states were unwilling to accept such a wide-ranging and open-ended commitment. The League tried instead to operate in two major ways and in both it was relatively ineffective. On disarmament the major conference envisaged when the League was founded did not take place until 1932 and was quickly overtaken by events following Hitler's accession to power. In any case some of the most important measures, such as the Washington and London naval limitation conferences of 1922 and 1930, took place outside the League. Second, the League tried to settle disputes through arbitration, judicial settlement or an inquiry by the Council. There were highly complex rules about the submission of disputes, the procedures for resolving them and, in the last resort, the imposition of economic sanctions on errant states. Although there was no formal great power veto, the League worked on the principle of unanimity. It also operated on the basis that international problems were created by 'disputes' which needed to be resolved, and this produced a tendency towards a legalistic view of its work. In its early years the League managed to settle a few disputes such as those over the status of the Åland Islands between Sweden and Finland, the border between Germany and Poland in upper Silesia, the Corfu incident between Greece and Italy in 1923, and some minor border fighting between Bulgaria and Greece in 1925. However, when faced with major problems – the first being the Japanese takeover of Manchuria in 1931 – it was unable to find any solution or take effective action. Again in 1935, although a few sanctions were imposed on Italy for attacking Abyssinia, the aggression was not halted. After this failure, the League was largely irrelevant to the acute international problems of the late 1930s. Many states left, especially those from Latin America and almost the last action the League took was to expel the Soviet Union in the autumn of 1939 following its attack on Finland. It was an inconsequential gesture.

In the last two years of the Second World War the Allied powers turned their attention to an organization to replace the League. Their proposals were to shape the United Nations when it was established in 1945 at the San Francisco conference. The general structure of the UN followed that of the League, but the important difference was that the major powers (the United States, the Soviet Union, Britain, France and China) gave themselves the right of veto in the Security Council over any action the UN might take. Although the role of the secretary-general was slightly increased, the main powers ensured that they dominated the organization – the Assembly, which took most decisions by majority vote, was left relatively powerless. Both the United States and the Soviet Union also continued to refuse to accept the compulsory jurisdiction of the International Court of Justice. In some respects the UN did mark an advance over the League – all members were pledged to support the use of sanctions or force if they were agreed by the Security Council; the procedures for dealing with disputes were far less legalistic; the UN Charter also contained some limitations on the ability of states to use force. The UN had an expanded role in other areas. The League had been largely restricted to supporting the International Labour Organization. At the United Nations a Trusteeship Council was set up to oversee the activities of the imperial powers in some of their colonies, and an Economic and Social Council was also established, followed by organizations for refugees, children, cultural and educational matters and later development and trade and the environment.

In practice the UN was riven by disputes, largely those generated by the ideological war between the United States and the Soviet Union. Both superpowers were prepared to use their veto to protect what they saw as important national interests, even when they were not party to a dispute or even directly involved in a problem. The idea of establishing a permanent military force at the disposal of the UN never got off the ground and military units were only provided when states made specific decisions. In its first years the activities of the UN were dominated by the United States and its allies. They effectively controlled all the institutions, including the General

Assembly, since the Latin American states usually sided with the United States and there were only a few African and Asian states to take a more independent line. The United States used its veto to achieve its aims, as in its refusal to admit the Communist government of China to the UN (and therefore the Security Council veto). It preferred to continue with the pretence that the nationalist government on Taiwan was the representative of China. Inevitably the Soviet Union also fell back on use of its veto. It realized that this, rather than a boycott, was the safest procedure when in 1950 a UN force to intervene in the Korean War was agreed in its absence. Nevertheless the UN did change the nature of international relations and the ability of states to use force whenever they chose, as the British and French found out in 1956 when they invaded Egypt.

The nature of the UN began to change in the late 1950s and early 1960s as the newly independent states of Asia and Africa became members. Very quickly they became a majority in the General Assembly and the United States found that these members were able to use it to further their interests. This shift in membership produced some changes in policy and growing American disillusionment with the UN once they could no longer control it. In the end, however, through the Security Council the major powers were able to ensure that policies which they did not approve were not agreed. The one area of UN activity which did unexpectedly develop, since it was not envisaged in the original Charter, was peace-keeping. This was first used in the Suez crisis of 1956 and later extended into other areas of conflict, such as Cyprus in the early 1960s and the Middle East. In some cases these forces were able to ensure at least a temporary cessation of hostilities, but they were often ignored, for example in Cyprus in 1974 during the Turkish invasion of the north of the island and in Lebanon in 1982 during the Israeli invasion. The UN became increasingly marginal in the resolution of international problems in the 1970s and 1980s, but did some important work in other areas. The end of the 'Cold War' seemed to presage a new age for the UN, but in practice its role remained limited. Even during the Gulf conflict in 1990–1 it acted as little more than a convenient cover for the objectives of the United States. The UN, like its predecessor the League, was a forum within which some aspects of international diplomacy could take place, but it made little difference to the underlying realities of world politics and conflict.

Part Four

DOMESTIC HISTORY

13 TRADITION

AT THE beginning of the twentieth century the states of Europe were under strain from a multitude of forces, especially continuing industrialization and urbanization and the economic and social changes that came in their wake. None of the states was fully democratic and old elites, mainly deriving their power from landed wealth, still dominated as they had done for centuries. However, they saw their position as being under threat from a variety of forces, such as demands for greater democratization and some measure of social and economic equality. Everywhere the existing structures were able to survive until the First World War and the collapse of the Russian, German and Austro-Hungarian empires in 1917–18. The problem after the war was whether the conservative forces in society could find a way of reconciling themselves to the new democracies which had emerged in 1918. In most states they did not and conservative, traditional groups drifted towards authoritarian solutions to cope with what they saw as threats to the existing order. It was only after 1945, with the effective demise of fascism and Nazism, that new conservative groupings emerged which were fully reconciled to a liberal democratic system and prepared to work within it. In practice they turned out to be remarkably powerful and often dominated politics.

In the period before the First World War, despite large differences between European countries, they had many common features. In all of them the ownership of land was still a major source of wealth and privilege. In Britain about 7,000 people owned over four-fifths of all the private land in the country and they could also rely on the income from rents on town properties and mineral royalties. In Austria twenty-five aristocratic families owned over 250,000 acres each and in Russia about 50,000 nobles owned half of all the land in European Russia. Such groups still dominated politics and had effective control of the armed forces and diplomatic corps.

Aristocratic groups were able to absorb new social elements, who derived their initial wealth from industry and trade, because status was still derived from the possession of land and it remained the prime requirement for social advance. The aristocracy was carefully graded by title, and honours systems effectively vetted candidates for incorporation. In Britain ennoblement of businessmen usually only followed the purchase of a landed estate and evidence that a candidate had sufficient wealth to sustain any new status. The award of knighthoods was largely confined to public life and the professions. Most of the elite were educated in exclusive 'public' schools and at either Oxford or Cambridge Universities, which almost guaranteed access to status occupations and elite positions. Even in republican France titles still existed and the aristocracy dominated the social world.

France was in fact one of the few non-monarchical states in Europe in the early twentieth century, the other was Switzerland and they were joined by Portugal after the revolution in 1910. In Italy and Britain the power of the monarch was circumscribed though still important – it was, after all, the king who removed Mussolini from power in 1943. Elsewhere, particularly in Germany, Austria–Hungary and Russia the monarch remained central to the political system. Everywhere the nobility and landowners were closely associated with the monarch and were important politically through their domination of the upper houses of the national parliaments. Apart from a few senior judges and bishops, Britain had an entirely hereditary upper house, which until 1911 had a complete veto over legislation which it often used in a highly partisan manner. Even after reforms in 1911 and 1949 and the introduction in 1957 of life peers chosen by the government, the House of Lords was still able to delay and modify legislation. Prussia also had a house of peers, which was made up of royal princes and life members from high state offices, the remainder being nominated by corporate bodies, landowners, universities and cities. The upper houses in Austria, Hungary and Italy were similar.

The monarchical nature of Europe before the First World War was demonstrated at the state funeral of Edward VII in London in May 1910. In the procession through London to Paddington station for the journey to St George's Chapel at Windsor, where the private burial took place, the coffin was placed on a gun-carriage and followed by the monarchs on horseback in strict order of kinship. In the first file were Edward's son, the new King George V, his brother the Duke of Connaught, and his nephew Kaiser Wilhelm II. They were followed by Kings Haakon (Norway), George (Greece), Alfonso (Spain), Ferdinand (Bulgaria), Frederick (Denmark), Manuel (Portugal) and Albert (Belgium). Czar Nicholas II of Russia was represented by his brother Grand Duke Michael, the Emperor Franz Josef of Austria-Hungary by his heir-apparent Archduke Franz Ferdinand and Victor Emmanuel III of Italy by his cousin the Duke of Aosta. Also in attendance were princely and ducal representatives of the Netherlands, Sweden, Romania, Montenegro, Serbia, and three non-European states – Turkey, Egypt and Japan. By the end of the century, of these twenty states less than half were still monarchies and none of these rulers had more than symbolic or very limited powers.

Britain was not alone in staging such elaborate rituals. Equally grandiose were the celebrations for the silver jubilee of the accession of Kaiser Wilhelm II in June 1913, the sixtieth anniversary of Emperor Franz Josef's accession in December 1908, the celebrations in Moscow of 300 years of Romanov rule in February 1913 and the fiftieth anniversary of the unification of Italy in June 1911. Much of this ceremonial was competitive, particularly between Britain and Germany. New 'traditions' were invented as the role of the monarch changed from being the head of aristocratic 'society' to being a symbolic embodiment of the nation. From the late nineteenth century, partly to compensate for Britain's loss of real power, new rituals emphasizing glory and continuity were developed. Edward VII was the first monarch to be crowned, in an imperial pageant at Westminster Abbey, as emperor of India and ruler 'of the British Dominions beyond the seas'. The state opening of parliament, which under Queen Victoria was conspicuous mainly by its absence, was built into a major state occasion by Edward VII. New honours were invented, such as the Royal Victorian Order, the various Indian orders, the Order of Merit and the Companionship of Honour. After 1918 ceremonial was less competitive and monarchs combined state occasions with an outward show of middle-class respectability in their private lives. However, new traditions were still invented such as Trooping the Colour, the Christmas broadcast to the empire, the Armistice Day ceremonial, and royal weddings were moved from the privacy of Windsor to the public domain in Westminster Abbey and St Paul's Cathedral.

Other states developed their own traditions. In France the celebration of Bastille Day began in 1880 and other important symbols were the tricolour, the republican motto of Liberty, Equality and Fraternity, the singing of the Marseillaise and the invention of the symbolic Marianne. Germany, as a very new state, had problems in devising symbols which were not specific to Prussia. Much was built around memorials to Wilhelm I and Bismarck, celebrations of the Battle of Leipzig, especially on the centenary in 1913 and the construction of the Siegesalle in Berlin between 1896 and 1901. Even in the United States there were similar movements, partly as a way of integrating the great wave of immigrants, seen in the cult of the Founding Fathers, the rituals of the Fourth of July and the more Protestant and English-speaking celebration of Thanksgiving Day, together with the swearing of allegiance to the flag every day at school – a movement which grew rapidly in the late nineteenth century. Also important was the construction of ceremonial cities. Paris already had the Champs Elysées, but in London in the early twentieth century a new ceremonial way was built through the widening of The Mall, the construction of Admiralty Arch, the refronting of Buckingham Palace and the placing of the Victoria Monument at the end of The Mall in front of the Palace. Berlin had its ceremonial way and in Washington the Lincoln Memorial was completed, together with Arlington Bridge and offices along Constitution Avenue.

One of the most potent manipulations of symbols and tradition took place on 21 March 1933 in the Garrison Church at Potsdam, near Berlin. The wreath-laying ceremony was formally to mark the opening of the new Nazi-dominated Reichstag, but was in practice a dedication of the new regime in front of the tomb of Frederick the Great – a symbolic representation of a renascent Germany linked to the traditions of the past. The new Chancellor Adolf Hitler was present with the President, Field-Marshal Paul von Hindenburg, who symbolized the conservative Prussian tradition. Also present were four of the six sons of Kaiser Wilhelm II and a chair was left vacant for the ex-Kaiser, who was in exile in the Netherlands. A guard of honour was drawn from the army, two Nazi organizations (the SA and SS) and the right-wing paramilitary group, the Stalhelm, of which Hindenburg was the honorary president. Hitler spoke of 'the marriage between the symbols of past greatness and the vigour of youth' and bowed to Hindenburg. The new regime was identified with the Prussian and German past.

Another state which was, in the early twentieth century, under-going the process of industrialization while trying to retain what were regarded as ancient traditions was Japan. In the late nineteenth century Japan was facing the aggressive expansion of the western powers and attempting to 'modernize' at the same time. What took place was not a Japanese 'adoption' of western attitudes and policies, but a use of these policies to achieve the aims of the conservative Japanese elite and avoid any major transformation of national values. Thus capitalism was justified not on the grounds of wealth creation and economic and social progress but as being in the national interest. After a brief flirtation with all things foreign, the Japanese elite, especially after the victories over China in 1895 and Russia a decade later, placed growing emphasis on the preservation of traditional values, but also on the darker side of western values such as social disruption, urban growth and pollution. This was based on the *nihonjinron* school of literature, which emphasized the uniqueness of Japanese life over thousands of years. It assumed that the Japanese were culturally and socially homogeneous, consciously nationalistic and radically (and racially) different from all other peoples. School textbooks and the curriculum were rewritten, youth groups were mobilized and a host of Japanese intellectuals emphasized the Japanese past and its distinctive tradition. Typical was Kawakami Hajime, who in 1911 set out what was to become a common element in the Japanese tradition. He argued that in Japan an individual's value consisted only in his being an instrument of national growth and that western individualism was not in the Japanese tradition. Instead, he argued, this emphasized the 'family-state' (*kokkashugi*) and the absolute identity between the individual's 'private' interest and the wider 'national' interest.

There was therefore in Japan a unity of individual, nation and emperor. Increasingly, if a western model was to be adopted, it would be that of German authoritarian modernization after 1870, in which the elite dictated the national goals and the good of the community overrode any individual desires. As in the west, the Japanese elite 'invented' traditions to support these aims. Shinto, the imperial cult, was regarded as primitive and discredited in the mid-nineteenth century, when most of the Japanese population were Buddhists. It was revived to encourage 'traditional piety' and reverence for the emperor, although in practice the emperor had been ignored for centuries and Buddhism remained the main 'personal' religion. Similarly the code of the *samurai* (warrior caste) was hailed as an ancient value system integral to Japanese culture, although the key concept of *bushido* was unknown as a word until the twentieth century.

Across the core states (and Japan) politics in the early twentieth century was dominated by essentially conservative groups, even though their exact title varied from country to country. In many cases, such as Germany and Sweden, there were stark divisions between the monarch, the landed aristocracy and the elite on the one hand and those such as the Social Democratic Party in Germany, which demanded a more democratic political system and major social changes. In Britain the Conservative Party was prepared to use its majority in the hereditary House of Lords to defeat the Liberal government, even when it had passed its proposals for Home Rule for Ireland through the elected House of Commons in 1892. When a Liberal government was elected with a huge majority in 1906 the Conservatives similarly refused to accept many pieces of legislation with which they disagreed, leading to their unprecedented rejection of the Budget in 1909. The outcome was a constitutional crisis, finally resolved in 1911, after two more elections, by a removal of the absolute veto of the House of Lords. The attempt to pass Home Rule legislation in this new situation was followed by the Conservatives openly advocating defiance through revolt and resistance in Ulster and a political crisis only temporarily resolved by the outbreak of war in August 1914. In Switzerland, although 'conservative' disappeared as a political label in the late nineteenth century, politics remained deeply conservative and traditionalist, reflecting the nature of Swiss society. Similarly in the Netherlands no party called either itself or its programme 'conservative' because such phraseology was deeply unpopular in the Dutch political tradition. Nevertheless there was a strong, mainly religious, conservative bloc which dominated politics. In Italy the so-called 'liberals' were, in reality, conservatives. In 1897 one of their leaders, Sidney Sonnino, called for a return to the old 1848 Piedmont constitution with the powers of parliament curbed, more power for the king and a restriction on those able to vote. Such calls were rejected and power remained in the hands of the more pragmatic though still conservative Liberals grouped around Giovanni Giolitti.

In Japan the oligarchs who ran the political system after the Meiji restoration of 1868 were losing power by the early 1890s. Although this trend was symbolized by the creation of a 'representative' Diet in 1890, conservative politicians remained in control. The animating philosophy of all governments was that of *keisei saimin* – the elite, dedicated to conserving morality and order, should govern the people, who wanted only selfish ends not the 'public good'. There was, as in Germany, no link between the majority in the Diet and the government. As Prime Minister Kuroda told local governors, 'The government must always take a fixed course. It must stand above and outside political parties.' Two political parties did emerge – Seiyukai in 1900 and Doshikai in 1913 – but they were closer in policy and general outlook than those in any of the other 'democratic' systems in the world. There was a consensus about generally conservative aims, the preservation of the status quo at home and Japan's development as an economic and world power.

After the First World War and the collapse of the old regimes in Russia, Germany and Austria-Hungary, there were two key questions for conservatives and members of the traditional elites across western Europe. First, were they prepared to work within the framework of the liberal democracies which had emerged everywhere in the aftermath of the war? Second, how would they react to what they saw as threats to their position, property and status from increasing taxation and an ill-defined 'socialism'? In many cases the old nineteenth-century liberal parties either split or went into decline as many of their supporters moved towards more conservative parties. This was particularly apparent in Britain. The Liberal Party, which won a landslide victory in 1906, remained in power until 1915. It was still intellectually vibrant, but split in 1916 when Lloyd George replaced Asquith as prime minister. It never recovered its position: between 1918 and 1924 there was a major realignment in British politics which produced a structure that was to endure with little major change until the end of the century. A straightforward division between the Conservatives and Labour came to dominate politics, leaving only a small Liberal Party which was permanently excluded from power. The Conservatives became one of the most successful of all political parties, being in government for all but nineteen years during the period 1918–97. Much of the emphasis in the party, especially until the 1980s, was simply about being in power. It was based on a generally conservative financial, economic and social policy only slightly modified by the occasional electoral defeat and grudging acceptance (until the 1980s) of the social and economic changes introduced by the Labour government of 1945–51.

The shift of the liberals to the right was also clear in Sweden.

Following a number of short-lived socialist governments after 1917, the social democrats were excluded from power between 1926 and 1932 even though they were the largest party. In the Netherlands the growing alliance between the Catholic and Calvinist parties over issues such as education and the lack of state funds for religious schools led to a de facto conservative bloc after 1918. The two confessional parties, together with the more right-wing liberals, came to dominate inter-war politics. In Switzerland after 1919 politics was dominated by an anti-socialist bloc of conservative parties (the Radicals, the Catholic conservatives and the Peasants Party). In Ireland both the major parties were socially and economically conservative in a largely rural, Catholic country and were divided only by their different views on the relationship with Britain after independence. Finland too was governed by a conservative, nationalist bloc. In Germany the short-lived Weimar Republic was, after an initial burst of enthusiasm for the Social Democrats, dominated by the conservative Catholic Zentrum and other parties of the centre-right. In France the socialists were largely excluded from power in a complex party system until the short-lived Popular Front government of 1936.

In many countries, however, the conservative acceptance of liberal democracy was limited and easily shifted into acceptance of authoritarian solutions in crisis situations. Such changes occurred in Italy and Spain in the early 1920s, Germany and Austria in the late 1920s and Japan, always authoritarian, became even more so from the early 1930s. Many of these attitudes became increasingly prevalent under the pressure of war and foreign occupation. For example, the Vichy government in France, the Tiso government in Slovakia and the Nederlands Unie movement in the Second World War were all based on a rejection of liberal democratic values. It was not until the defeat of Germany and Italy in 1945 that conservative groups across western Europe finally came to accept a liberal-democratic system. They did so in conditions that were highly favourable to them. The presence of American troops, a strong anti-Communist, free-market consensus, very moderate socialist parties prepared to work within that consensus and a long period of economic growth, all contributed to a new stability in politics.

In western Europe the most remarkable post-war development was the emergence of strong Christian Democratic parties, which came to dominate post-war politics. Before 1945 Catholic parties, such as the German Zentrum and those in Belgium and the

Netherlands, tended to be strongly confessional and defend particular religious interests. In Italy, although the absolute ban on Catholic participation in politics following the papal decree *Non Expedit* of 1874 was lifted in 1904, there were only a few Catholic deputies until the formation of the Partito Popolare Italiano in 1919, which won about a fifth of the votes. It effectively destroyed the old liberals, but split over participation in Mussolini's first government. The emergence of strong Christian Democratic parties after 1945 was partly the result of a change in attitudes by the Catholic Church. In the early twentieth century the Church was not only anti-socialist, but it also strongly rejected liberalism, pluralism and individualism. It favoured corporatist values and therefore strongly supported both the Vichy and the Tiso governments in the Second World War (Tiso was a Catholic priest) and tended to be introverted and exclusive, drawing little support from other groups.

After 1945 the Church remained strongly anti-Communist (which tended to obscure its still latent anti-liberalism), but was prepared to embrace democracy as a way of protecting the Church in a new environment and because many Catholics felt that an exclusively Catholic movement was not the way to proceed. These developments made possible a wider appeal and collaboration with other parties and churches. This was a major break with the past on the right of politics and the new party names were intended to be symbolic of this new departure. However, the central political fact was that with the disintegration (and to some extent discrediting) of the authoritarian, monarchical right and many of the pre-war parties, there was a clear space in the political spectrum to be filled by generally conservative parties. These favourable trends were aided by the enfranchisement of women, who tended to vote much more strongly for the Christian Democratic parties. It was not, however, easy to place the Christian Democratic parties on a simple left–right spectrum. They had a clear tendency to be collectivist on social and economic policy, putting them nearer to the Social Democratic parties and to the left of liberalism (hence their refusal to allow the British Conservatives to join their group in the European Parliament after 1973). However, in areas such as education, defence and foreign policy they were strongly on the right of politics. They supported the United States and opposed Communism, both internationally and domestically. (In France and Italy the strong Communist Parties were permanently excluded from power from the late 1940s.) The Christian Democrats were also traditionalist, not in the monarchical, authoritarian sense of the pre-war right, but in supporting social responsibility, solidarity and the family.

The strength of the new parties was apparent in the very first post-war elections. In Italy they gained almost half the vote, they also took power in West Germany and even in France the MRP under Georges Bidault gained a quarter of the vote. Very rapidly in Italy and Germany the Christian Democrats came to dominate politics. In Italy they remained the largest party and were in power continuously in a multitude of shifting coalitions until the political crisis of the late 1980s and early 1990s. They provided every prime minister until the early 1980s. In Germany the Christian Democrats, in alliance with the more conservative Christian Social Union of Bavaria, were in power for twenty years after 1949 and remained the largest party in the Bundestag except for a brief period in the mid-1970s. In Belgium the Social Christians were the largest party and in Luxemburg they were continuously in power from 1919 to 1974. Only in France were they under pressure from the right – the Gaullists – and saw their vote decline rapidly by the late 1950s. However, the Fourth Republic was governed by generally conservative groupings and after 1958, under General de Gaulle and then Georges Pompidou, the right dominated the Fifth Republic. Authoritarian trends were still apparent particularly in some politicians, like Franz-Josef Strauss the leader of the CSU in Bavaria and General de Gaulle in France. The same was true of some voters – as late as 1959 nearly half of the respondents in an opinion poll in West Germany thought the country had been best off under the Third Reich. However, all these groups accepted the broadly conservative consensus which prevailed across western Europe after 1945.

In the other major countries of the core politics was not based on even a weak confessional structure, but similarly conservative groups still dominated after the Second World War. In the United States both major parties accepted a broadly conservative view of American society and both were closely attuned to business interests. The brief period of reform under Roosevelt's New Deal was over by the late 1930s as American politics moved further to the right, a trend clearly confirmed in the 1944 and 1946 elections. The minimum gains made by the trade union movement in the 1930s were eroded by the Taft–Hartley Act of 1947 and a virulent anti-Communism came to dominate politics. The election in 1952 of the military leader from the Second World War, General Eisenhower, completed the move to the right and the establishment of a deeply conservative consensus on social and economic policy. In Britain the major reforms of the post-war Labour government were reluctantly accepted by the Conservatives, who were in power for thirteen years after 1951. However, they were determined to restore as much as possible of free market, liberal capitalism and they were cautious on social issues. They tried to avoid confronting the trade unions, but remained latently hostile. In Japan constitutional reforms during the American occupation removed many of the old centres of independent power and the government became reliant on a majority in the Diet. However, in terms of the generally accepted assumptions about Japan's position in the world and the uniqueness of its culture little had changed from the beliefs current at the beginning of the century. In 1955 the fragmented conservative parties came together to form the Liberal Democratic Party, which was to remain in power for more than thirty years. The Socialist Party split in 1960, a revised treaty with the United States in the same year removed the worst of the inequalities from the peace settlement and politics settled down to being little more than fighting between the various highly organized factions within the Liberal Democrats.

In all the core countries the underlying factor which helped to produce stability in politics and acceptance of a generally conservative consensus after 1945 was the long post-war boom, which lasted until 1973. During a period of steady growth, low unemployment and low inflation it was relatively easy for governments to deal with any social discontents by spending more money. Most people were satisfied with the huge growth in consumer spending, which brought levels of consumption that were unprecedented, particularly in comparison with the depressed pre-war years. In these circumstances there was little demand for any alternative.

In the 1960s, across the core states, there was a trend towards slightly more reformist solutions. In Italy in 1963 one of the Socialist parties was brought into government for the first time since 1947. In Britain Labour was in power from 1964 to 1970, and in Germany there was a 'grand coalition' between the Christian Democrats and the Social Democrats between 1966 and 1969 before the SDP gained power for the first time since the 1920s. In the United States the Democrats won the 1960 presidential election and stayed in power until 1968. They inaugurated a moderate reform policy at home, where the major problem was how to deal with the demands of the black minority for full civil rights. The 'Great Society' programme under President Johnson after 1964 was, however, rapidly overtaken by a continuing strong anti-Communist foreign and defence policy leading to the disaster of the Vietnam War. However, in none of these countries was there any major departure from the prevailing post-war consensus about social and economic policy and these governments were content to proceed along well-trodden paths.

From the early 1970s all the governments of the core states had to deal with the problems caused by the end of the post-war boom, inflation brought on by the rise in oil prices and the much more difficult economic conditions of the last quarter of the century. Faced with high unemployment and persistently high levels of inflation, governments found it difficult to maintain the levels of public expenditure that had been considered normal during the long post-war boom, especially when reductions in taxation were regarded as a high priority. The political consensus in the core states moved further to the right and in favour of a restoration of many of the policies current before the Second World War – orthodox finance, low taxes and lower state provision of services, with priority being given to low inflation over reducing unemployment. This was combined with a revitalized belief in the efficacy of markets to solve problems, which in turn led to a range of measures to deregulate capitalism and privatize state-owned industries. The trend was first apparent in Britain after the Conservatives returned to power in 1979 and was followed almost immediately in the United States under President Reagan after 1980, in the most right-wing government since the 1920s. In Germany the Christian Democrats regained power in 1983. The socialist parties found that they too had to adapt to this new consensus. This was painfully demonstrated by President Mitterrand's government in France in 1981 when, within two years of taking office, they had to abandon attempts to adopt a more interventionist economic policy and accept the prevailing orthodoxy.

By the 1990s a very conservative view of the social and political role of the state was deeply entrenched across the core countries. It reflected what were seen as the realities of an increasingly global capitalism with its large financial flows across national borders. These lessened still further the state's ability to undertake policies which ran counter to the general consensus. Within the core states social changes, partly brought on by the quarter-century long boom before the early 1970s, created a new political environment. The majority of the population now owned their own homes (or, as in Britain after 1980, had state housing sold to them at huge discounts), were affluent and paid a significant proportion of their income in taxes. Once the cost of maintaining the welfare state in difficult economic circumstances became apparent, it was possible for conservative political parties to construct a majority around a new consensus. It was based on those groups who would benefit from lower taxes even if this involved a reduction in public services. The cost of these policies was borne by the low paid, the unskilled and the unemployed, especially the long-term unemployed.

In the core states traditional, conservative values remained powerful throughout the century reflecting the fact that old elites survived and indeed prospered even though some adaptation and incorporation of new elements were a key part of this process. The societies of the core countries evolved and changed over the century, everybody became wealthier, but the basic social structure remained little altered. In part this was the result of the broadly conservative parties' success in limiting change and stressing traditional values and goals. They were able to articulate the demands of what were in the main conservative populations, content, except in very exceptional circumstances, to accept the existing values of their society.

Outside the core the idea of tradition was much more problematic. In many cases it was swept away in war, civil war and revolution although new regimes often tried to create their own traditions. In many areas, for example Latin America, the traditional society and the politics associated with it was so dominated by the elite and worked so much to their advantage that they had little support from other groups in society. These societies were highly divided and the peasant communities usually had little involvement in the traditions of the elites and instead continued with their own traditions which were deeply embedded in their own histories and cultures. In the colonial empires traditions had to be 'invented' as part of incorporation into empire. It was a way of asserting European superiority and creating a set of institutions to encourage some of the local population to undertake the role of 'collaborators' and work for the new regimes. In India, for example, the British were keen to emphasize the ceremonial aspects of their rule as a way of demonstrating their power over the large number of local princes. In 1877 Queen Victoria was declared empress of India at an assembly of local rulers and princes, a ceremony which was repeated in 1903 when the Viceroy, Lord Curzon, declared Edward VII the emperor of India. The ceremonial was even more elaborate eight years later when George V crowned himself emperor at a massive imperial 'durbar' at Delhi. In Africa both the British and the Germans stressed the role of the monarch as a fatherly, god-like person in charge of the destinies of the children over whom he ruled. (Such attitudes were much more difficult for the republican French and Portuguese to adopt.) New traditions were invented, especially for the British Silver Jubilee of 1935 and the Coronation of 1937, although it is doubtful whether they made much impression on the local populations. Regiments such as the King's African Rifles and even 'public' schools such as King's College, Budo tried to create institutions and ideas that would incorporate an elite of the colonial population into European values. The European emphasis on 'indirect' rule involved the creation of traditions and identities called tribes with little relation to the African past. They had much more to do with the convenience of the colonial authorities and the advantages to be gained by the few Africans who became 'chiefs'. The result of these policies was that after independence there were few authentic traditions and institutions to bind together the new states.

By the 1990s there were still twelve states in the world where old-fashioned monarchies and traditional regimes survived with almost no power-sharing outside the royal family. Most were in the Middle East (Morocco, Jordan, Saudi Arabia, Oman, Kuwait, Qatar, Bahrein and the sheikhdoms of the United Arab Emirates) together with Swaziland in southern Africa, Bhutan, Brunei and Nepal in Asia. Of these states three-quarters had populations of under 3 million. Nepal was also moving towards a more open system, after a period of monarchical rule following the bloodless coup which ousted the aristocratic Ranas as the hereditary prime ministers in the early 1950s. The most extreme examples of personal rule and the lack of any distinction between the ruling family and the state were found in the oil-exporting countries of the Middle East. In the Gulf Emirates the ruling sheikh owned all the land and was able to distribute it as he thought fit. Theoretically all the oil revenues went to the sheikh. In practice they were paid to the state treasury and the ruling family took a percentage for their personal use, the exact amount individuals received depending on their position within that ruling family. In addition the state budget paid for the palaces, servants, aircraft and similar expenditure by the royal family. The exact percentage taken for personal use varied from about 10 per cent of all revenues in Abu Dhabi to 25 per cent in Qatar. In Qatar, when Sheikh Khalifa was deposed by his son in a bloodless coup in 1995, he was given a $5 billion pension fund, despite the fact that between 1981 and the coup he had removed about $1.5 billion a year (over half the state's GDP) to his private bank accounts in Switzerland. When questions were asked, the old Sheikh remarked, 'One cannot steal one's own money.'

Although the oil states had deeply traditional structures they were often relatively new inventions. This was particularly the case with Saudi Arabia, where even the name of the state was not invented until 1932. It was created by Ibn Saud, a member of the deeply puritanical minority Wahhabi sect and a local chieftain, through a series of wars between 1902 and 1925. He was strongly supported by the British, who provided him with an annual grant equivalent to over two-thirds of the total income of the new state. During the 1930s and 1940s the British were replaced by the United States as his main external protector and American companies in the Aramco consortium obtained the main oil concessions. Most of the money from oil revenues went to the royal family. In 1946 the state spent $150,000 on schools, but $30 million on a palace for one of the royal princes and $2 million on a royal garage even though the cars were thrown away when they ran out of petrol. One in ten doctors in the country were the king's personal physicians. In the early 1950s the wealth from oil rose rapidly. By 1955 the state's income was $2 million a day compared with $1,500 a day twenty years earlier. By the early 1970s, following the oil price rise and the renegotiation of the oil concessions, the revenues were astronomical, but the government of the country was still treated as personal to the vast royal family.

By the late 1980s the personal wealth of King Fahd was estimated at about $30 billion excluding the palaces in Saudi Arabia (worth about $11 billion) and those in Marbella, Paris, Geneva and near London, together with the Boeing 747, equipped with a sauna, and his $50 million yacht. All the members of the royal family (several hundred people), together with their wives and children, were paid salaries by the state, which amounted, even at the lowest level, to a minimum of $300,000 a month, with larger amounts going to more senior members. Four-fifths of all the land in the country was owned by the royal family; they held the key posts throughout the government and chaired the boards of over 500 corporations. In 1992 one prince, Walid bin Tallal, acting as an agent for Diners Club, gave out credit cards to members of the family, who then ran up bills totalling $30 million. They refused to pay them because they thought the cards were gifts. Because the contract was under Saudi law the company did not bother to sue, but instead withdrew from the country. Huge 'commissions' were paid to members of the family on all major contracts, especially on arms deals, and their support was necessary before any contract could be agreed. Oil was often sold privately by the family not the state. In the early 1980s Princess Hia (a full sister of King Fahd) was short of money and was given one million barrels of oil (worth about $30 million) by the state petrol company to sell on her own behalf. In 1981 Prince Muhammed bin Fahd was selling oil to a nominally Japanese company, which he in fact owned, and profiting to the extent of $1 million a month. Saudi Arabia was an extreme example of the adaptation of a traditional political structure to the unparalleled wealth available in an oil-exporting state in the late twentieth century. The governments of the core states accepted these conditions because of their interest in preserving the flow of oil, exploiting the vast reserves within the kingdom and obtaining lucrative arms sales contracts.

14 FASCISM

IMMEDIATELY AFTER the First World War, the emergence of a mass electorate, economic instability, military defeat (or denial of what were seen as the legitimate spoils of victory) and the threat to the existing social and economic order from the Communist victory in Russia posed major problems across Europe. In some countries, such as Britain and France, the existing political, social and economic relations seemed to be broadly confirmed by victory. In other countries, elites rejected liberal democracy and drifted towards authoritarian solutions as a way of protecting their position. Elsewhere, at first in Italy, then in Germany and later in central and eastern Europe new political movements emerged which capitalized on many of the discontents apparent after 1918. Despite the very real differences between the various movements, especially between those in Italy and Germany, they were broadly described as fascist. Although limited in scope, they came to dominate much of European politics between the two World Wars.

Fascism was the only major ideological innovation to emerge in the twentieth century. Fascist parties were not found before 1914 and the lateness of their arrival partly explains why so many of their ideas were defined in terms of opposing existing movements and ideologies. Fascism was anti-liberal, anti-democratic, anti-Communist and in many respects anti-conservative. It advocated a new, national, organic, authoritarian state, a rebirth or 'cleansing' of the nation and broadly corporatist economic solutions which adopted some of the ideas of socialism. Its style and method of organization were also part of its appeal. It stressed symbolism in mass meetings and emphasized the romantic and mystical aspects of history and culture. The aim was mass mobilization of society and the creation of a party militia stressing youth and masculinity. These elements were all combined under authoritarian, charismatic leadership.

The emergence of fascism took most contemporaries by surprise. Those brought up in the optimistic culture in the late nineteenth century with its emphasis on progress and perfectibility (including Marxists) believed that the western intellectual and political tradition was built upon reason. Liberal democracy and Marxism both shared a common belief in the ability of human societies to purposively construct institutions and a better future. From this point of view fascism seemed to be a radical break with the past, a rejection of the inherited values that had dominated Europe for centuries. Fascism could therefore be blamed on a few 'rogue' thinkers, such as Count Gobineau, Friedrich Nietzsche and Houston Stewart Chamberlain, and the impact of a few mentally unstable leaders, such as Mussolini and Hitler, who were able to appeal to the discontented. Although this left open the question of why people should want to follow such psychopathic leaders, fascism could be dismissed as untypical. Liberal democracy and Marxism remained the true European traditions.

However, fascism was deeply rooted in the European tradition. Much of the liberal democratic tradition, especially in the revolutionary form found, for example, in France in the early nineteenth century with its emphasis on the mobilization of the masses, could, when combined with strong nationalism, be highly destabilizing. Many of the other constituents of fascism formed part of European mainstream thinking in the early twentieth century. These elements included social Darwinism, which emphasized struggle and the 'survival of the fittest', eugenics with its aim of creating a better stock of people in the nation, the growing importance of military values, the belief that war was a positive force, revolutionary socialist ideas and also anti-Semitism. After 1918 many argued, with some plausibility, that a major task in politics was to combine the two forces that seemed to be 'the wave of the future' – socialism and nationalism. Many of fascism's leaders came from the left of politics either as Communists (Doriot) or as socialists (Mussolini, Déat and Mosley). Although the Nazis under Hitler eventually dropped their earlier socialist ideas, this aspect of fascism remained important for many followers. It appealed to people who felt marginalized and powerless in the face of the impersonal economic forces, especially inflation and unemployment, which were increasingly dominating the core states. Many felt that by organizing themselves they might be able to resist the power of 'big business'. Unlike other authoritarian systems fascism tended to break from existing elites (initially they had little support in the military) and bring forward a new generation of leaders. The most socially marginal of all were the Nazis. In 1928 none of the leadership was in the German *Who's Who* (which had over 15,000 entries) and they were untypical of normal political elites – they were poorly educated and contained few lawyers and teachers.

In practice fascism had a limited impact. Established liberal democratic regimes such as those in Britain, France, Scandinavia and the Benelux countries did not break down. Existing authoritarian regimes or those where the military kept control (for example, Spain under Franco) rarely allowed the level of mobilization and challenge to the system that was necessary for fascism to succeed. Fascism only gained power in two countries, Italy and Germany, apart from those in which small, uninfluential groups collaborated with an occupying power in the Second World War. Both the Italian and German parliamentary systems were under strain. In the former the transformation to a full liberal democracy was still incomplete after 1918 and there was widespread discontent over the failure to make any major gains from the decision to join the Allies in 1915. In the latter the Weimar Republic lacked a firm base in society and the trauma of defeat and revolution in 1918 produced a highly unstable political situation. However, in neither Italy nor Germany did fascist groups seize power through civil war or a coup (Hitler's attempt to do so in 1923 was a pathetic failure). Everywhere existing state institutions, even when badly weakened by a crisis of legitimacy as in the Weimar Republic, were strong enough to resist such attempts. Nor was it possible to take power by obtaining a majority in parliament – existing parties remained strong and the 38 per cent of the vote obtained by the Nazis in 1932 was their high point in truly democratic elections. The route to power, in both Italy and Germany, lay through coalitions with other conservative groups and then the exploitation of opportunities to seize power. In countries where existing parties were able to keep control of the political system such an avenue was not open and fascist parties failed.

Fascism first appeared in Italy in 1919, although at that stage it bore little relation to what later became typical of the doctrine. It was developed by Mussolini who, before the First World War, had been a leader of the radical socialist party. In 1912, when the moderates in the party were expelled for supporting the war with the Ottomans to seize Libya, Mussolini became editor of the party journal *Avanti*, where he argued 'the Arab and Turkish proletarians are our brothers' and 'the national flag is a rag to be planted on a dunghill'. Following the collapse of working-class solidarity in August 1914, when socialist parties across Europe generally supported the war, he rapidly became convinced that the proletariat would never be revolutionary and that the differences within countries were less than the differences between them. During the war and in its immediate aftermath Mussolini gradually evolved a new set of ideas, which drew on a multitude of disparate sources popular at the time. From the revolutionary syndicalists he adopted the idea of direct action, the use of violence to attain political ends and the mobilization of the masses. The 'Futurists' influenced Mussolini through their belief in the positive effects of violence and their idealization of all things new. Much of the style of the fascist movement was taken from the nationalists, and corporatists such as D'Annunzio and De Ambris, who attempted to seize Fiume for Italy as part of the peace settlement. In Fiume De Ambris drafted the Carta del Carnaro, a constitution which attempted to combine democracy and corporatism. While in Fiume D'Annunzio invented many of the symbols that were later associated with fascism – the legionaries (recalling Rome), the use of black shirts and the so-called 'Roman salute', which had been invented for a 1914 film.

The Fasci Italiani di Combattimento were founded in Milan in March 1919. The programme they advocated had nothing to do with what is conventionally regarded as fascism and much more to do with radical socialism. They stood for a republic, a radically decentralized government, the end of conscription, general disarmament, the closure of arms factories, suppression of joint-stock companies, confiscation of church property, distribution of land to the peasants, management of industry by syndicates of workers and technicians, abolition of secret diplomacy and a federation of nations. The party was a failure – in the 1919 elections not a single deputy of theirs was elected and even in Milan they received only 5,000 of the 275,000 votes cast. Over the next three years the ideas and composition of the party and even its name were transformed by Mussolini, during a period of general political instability stemming from the economic and social dislocation at the end of the war and the impact of a growing 'red scare'. By late 1919 antiimperialism had been dropped from the party programme; within another two years it was replaced by imperialism and acceptance of the monarchy. Fascism developed into a radical nationalism whilst dropping any ideas of social revolution. In October 1921, when it had a quarter of a million members, the party changed its name to the Italian National Fascist Party.

In the 1919–22 period Italian politics was deadlocked. Political violence was common on the streets, coming not just from the fascist *squadristi* and the 'legionaries' of the right-wing Nationalist Association but also from the left and the Communists. The two main parties in the Assembly – the Socialists with 156 seats out of 508 and the Catholic-based Italian Popular Party with 100 seats – refused to co-operate or join with others in a coalition. The government was therefore weak and indecisive and by the summer of 1922 some of the fascist *squadristi* were taking power in the cities and leaders such as Italo Balbo in Ferrara and Dino Grandi in Bologna were slipping out of Mussolini's control. The fascists had won about 15 per cent of the vote in the 1921 elections and had thirty-five seats, so they could only take power as part of a coalition. That coalition came about in late October 1922 as fascists continued to seize power locally and the government in Rome temporized and seemed unwilling to declare martial law. Mussolini was near the Swiss border in case he needed to flee. Later mythology, designed to fit in with the fascist idea of 'action', emphasized the so-called 'March on Rome' to seize power. In fact there was no march and Mussolini travelled from Milan by train. Although he first met the king wearing the symbolic black shirt, on the next occasion, after the formation of his government, he wore the normal morning dress. Mussolini's position was weak. Even after amalgamation with the nationalists he still controlled only fifty seats in the Assembly and ten out of the fourteen ministers in the new government were not fascists.

Mussolini was temperamentally opposed to working out coherent plans and the fascist party's rapid rise to power made this difficult anyway. The result was that for the first three years the coalition led by Mussolini adopted an ad hoc policy. Its main emphasis, after a crackdown on the Communists and D'Annunzio's nationalists, was on controlling the fascist movement and ensuring the supremacy of the government. A Fascist Grand Council was established, but state prefects were given supremacy over local party chiefs and within three months of taking office the *squadristi* were transformed into a state militia. As part of a growing emphasis on symbolism, especially that supposedly derived from ancient Rome, the militia was staffed by consuls, centurions and legionaries. Mussolini became Il Duce and Labour Day was replaced by 'Birth of Rome Day'. In a conscious imitation of the French Revolution, 1922 became Anno Primo. The elections held in April 1924 were rigged and gave the coalition government nearly three-quarters of the seats. In June, following the murder of a minor fascist functionary by the opposition, the Socialist deputy Giacomo Matteotti was murdered by the *squadristi*.

These events led into the next phase of Mussolini's government. The period from 1925 to 1929 saw the construction of a dictatorship. Major influences within the government were the corporatists and the syndicalists, with the latter wanting a radical break with the past and the construction of a new type of state. By the mid-1920s the Socialist and Catholic trade unions had collapsed and been replaced by a fascist confederation, which expanded to over 2 million members, three times bigger than the party itself. The leader of the unions, Edmondo Rossoni, was given a monopoly of labour representation and secured compulsory arbitration across industry. However, corporatism remained limited in its impact. Although by the mid-1930s twenty-two corporations were established to regulate the economy, their membership was confined to industrialists and organized labour was excluded. No coherent or integrated economic policy was adopted. Direct state intervention only began in 1933 as an emergency response to the depression, although by the end of the decade the state owned nearly a fifth of Italian industry (the second largest proportion in the world). Nevertheless Italy remained a semi-industrialized country whose economic performance was unspectacular.

The dominant group within the government was the conservative nationalists. The Fascist Grand Council became the chief organ of government in 1928 and elections to the Assembly were made indirect. The fascist party expanded (it had over 2·5 million members by the late 1930s), but it became increasingly bureaucratic, representing mainly state employees. The party remained strictly subordinate to the state structure. After 1925 Mussolini and the main theoretician of the new regime called the system *totalitario*. In practice, despite the grandiose rhetoric, a semi-pluralistic structure survived. King Victor Emmanuel III was still head of state, industry and the armed forces remained largely autonomous and the police were a state not a party function. Although a political police force (OVRA) was established in 1932 the number of political prisoners numbered only a few thousand at most. The fascist government was not particularly oppressive and no more unpopular than most governments. No propaganda and culture ministry was set up until 1936. From the start the government paid particular attention to the position of the Catholic Church. In November 1922 religious education was reintroduced into primary schools and display of the crucifix in all public buildings was made compulsory. The climax came in 1929 with the Lateran pacts, which for the first time since the establishment of the Italian state nearly sixty years earlier concluded an agreement between the Church and the government.

Despite the reality of a generally conservative, nationalist and authoritarian government, Italy was portrayed, and seen in some quarters, as a dynamic state, a role model for other aspiring dictatorships with a 'philosophy' for the future. The superficial trappings of the regime – the blackshirted fascist militia, the 'Roman' salute, the parades and the impression of great efficiency and modernity – impressed many. In practice by the early 1930s Mussolini's government was no longer dynamic. It had settled into near torpor at home and was drifting towards a more adventurous foreign policy as a way of continuing the activist image. Until the mid-1930s Italy remained generally close to its old wartime allies, Britain and France. It was particularly suspicious of the new Nazi regime in Germany and concerned about the future of Austria, which Italy wished to see remain independent. The attempt in 1935 to revive imperial Roman glory and avenge the 1896 defeat at Adowa by attacking Abyssinia ran foul of the League of Nations. The British and French could not decide whether to appease Mussolini and so keep him as an ally, or use the League to invoke sanctions, bring down the government and end the aggression. They finished up applying neither policy properly. Their botched diplomacy and Mussolini's success drew Italy into an alliance with Germany.

The result was a semi-Nazification of policy at home. The goose-step was introduced (it was called the *passo romano*) and racism and anti-Semitism became more explicit. Fascism in Italy originally had no racist overtones and as late as 1938 there were over 10,000 Jewish members of the fascist party (a higher proportion than their representation in the Italian population as a whole). Mussolini's fatal mistake was to join what he thought was the winning side in June 1940. In alliance with Germany he expected to make major gains. This misjudgement was compounded by military failure in Greece and North Africa in late 1940. The result was dependence on Germany and by the summer of 1943 the loss of Sicily and a likely invasion of the mainland. Mussolini was ousted from power by an ad hoc coalition of the old right: the monarchy, the army and some moderate fascists. He was restored to a semblance of power by the German occupying forces in the north of Italy. In this short-lived collaborationist regime Mussolini, surrounded by the more radical fascists, reverted to the earlier beliefs of the movement. Policy was closer to syndicalism and corporatism, backed up by a much more repressive regime. He was eventually killed by the resistance in April 1945.

Mussolini formed a government about three years after the formation of the fascist party. In Germany, despite the much greater economic, social and political disintegration after the First World War, it took Adolf Hitler fourteen years to gain power. When he did so it was in very different circumstances from those of the immediate post-war period. Unlike Mussolini, Hitler had no political background when in early 1919 he was sent by the army to monitor a minor right-wing political party in Munich during the chaotic period following the collapse of the imperial regime. Eventually he became a fringe politician and leader of the National Socialist German Worker's Party (NSDAP). Its programme bore a strong resemblance to that of the early fascist party in Italy with its combination of socialism and nationalism. It demanded state socialism through control of major companies and financial institutions, but also the encouragement of small-scale ownership, with the army being replaced by a people's militia. Like Hitler, but unlike the fascists in Italy, the rest of the party leadership was relatively new. The party was not well organized and drew little support, despite post-war chaos, the fear of left-wing revolution, French occupation of the Ruhr and unprecedented hyper-inflation. The NSDAP found that there were numerous other nationalist, right-wing groups in politics, many of whom were able to draw on deeper levels of support from the German political elite and from pre-war nationalist and conservative movements. The attempt to recreate the 'March on Rome' through the Beer Hall Putsch in Munich in November 1923 ended in humiliating failure within hours. Hitler was sent to jail.

By the late 1920s Hitler had established a position of dominance within the Nazi Party that was never obtained by Mussolini. However, the ideology of the movement remained confused. It was different from fascism in that it was based on Hitler's own worldview, which he had set out in *Mein Kampf*, written during his time in jail. He emphasized a racial nationalism based on a crude social

Darwinist view of the world and a popular anti-Semitism, which he had adopted during his time in Vienna before the First World War. Any remaining 'socialist' ideas were dropped as the party moved closer to business and elite groups, although Hitler never showed much interest in economic policy. The Nazi Party remained an unimportant movement on the fringes of politics – it obtained less than 3 per cent of the vote in the 1928 elections. Its prospects were transformed by the onset of economic depression and the gradual collapse of the Weimar Republic under the strains this produced.

The Nazi programme was imprecise, but its emphasis on action and national revival proved attractive. Most Germans were never reconciled to the peace terms imposed at Versailles, especially the clause allocating to them the sole guilt for the war and the desire for a political and military status commensurate with German economic power remained strong. The unparalleled period of turmoil and national disorientation after November 1918 left a lasting impression on society and politics in a country where democracy lacked a substantive base and where the temptation to shift to authoritarian solutions was strong. Most support for the Nazis came not from the middle class in the cities but from farmers, people in small towns and the urban upper class. It was relatively weak among women voters and the working class. The latter remained loyal to the Social Democrats (SDP) and the Communists. The Nazis were pre-eminently the party of youth. By 1932 over 40 per cent of its members were aged under thirty compared with less than half that proportion in the SDP.

The Nazis gained support rapidly as the depression began to bite. From just under 20 per cent of the vote in 1930, their share rose to over 30 per cent in early 1932, reached a peak of nearly 40 per cent in July 1932 and then slipped back to 33 per cent in the November elections. This fall in support reflected a defection among rural voters and disillusion in areas such as Brunswick and Thuringia, where the Nazis had taken power as part of coalitions. Many who joined the party after the first electoral success in the autumn of 1930 left. The Nazis remained excluded from power, distrusted by figures such as President Hindenburg and elite groups such as nationalist politicians and senior army officers. However, after 1930 the Weimar Republic began to break down. The constitution was effectively suspended and the government ruled by presidential decree. Governments changed rapidly and were increasingly composed of authoritarian figures from the right and the army. The key to Nazi success was not electoral support but manoeuvrings within the political and military elite. It was at the moment when Nazi fortunes were on the wane in the autumn and winter of 1932–3 that these groups decided that Hitler, as the leader of the largest political force in Germany, would have to be brought into government, even though he insisted he would only join as chancellor. Despite this precondition, the conservative elite believed that they would be able to keep Hitler under control in a coalition in which the Nazis would provide little more than the popular element in a government dominated by authoritarian groups. On 30 January 1933 Hitler became chancellor in a coalition made up largely of established conservative forces.

Hitler was able to exploit the political situation and a set of fortuitous circumstances to attain almost complete power within three months. The Nazis used their position in government to mount a number of propaganda drives, which developed a sense of momentum behind what was seen as a new departure in German politics and national fortunes. Hitler convinced his coalition partners to call an election in early March, something they had at first vehemently opposed. The burning down of the Reichstag by a lone Communist gave the excuse for the first security clampdown. Even so, at the March election the Nazis received just under 44 per cent of the vote and obtained a smaller proportion of seats than the SPD in 1919. They could only obtain a majority with the support of the nationalist DNVP. Goebbels was made Minister of Public Enlightenment and Propaganda and an Enabling Bill was put to the Reichstag to give full powers to the government. With the Communists excluded, only the SPD opposed the legislation, which was supported by all the other political groups including the Catholic Zentrum. It was passed by the Reichstag in April. By July 1933 all parties except the Nazis were either banned or had dissolved themselves. The Nazis dominated the government but continued to rule in conjunction with existing institutions, especially the army, which was appeased by the clampdown on the party militia (the SA) in June 1934. In August 1934 Hindenburg died and Hitler assumed the joint office of chancellor and president as Führer.

The Nazi state was in constant flux until its destruction in 1945. It was an administrative shambles because Hitler disliked bureaucratic decision-taking, cultivated institutional conflict in order to strengthen his own position and rarely took decisions in writing. The Nazi Party was generally excluded from the state except at the local level, where the party officials (Gauleiter) became state officials (the opposite of what happened in Italy). The army was brought under control in early 1938 when Hitler was able to install a compliant leadership. There was no clear economic policy and Hitler rejected both corporatism and the reactionary policy of some of the Prussian agrarian groups. A generally conservative policy with limited state regulation and priority for economic recovery prevailed. There was no social revolution, although the trade unions were abolished. Some groups and individuals such as the Five-Year Plan administration under Göring were influential for a while and then declined. Only the SS under Himmler became increasingly powerful. By the last years of the war it had become a huge empire involved in running elite combat units in the army, massive industrial enterprises and the concentration and death camps. Existing institutions either adapted or lost any influence they might have. The aims of the Nazi Party, and Hitler in particular, were either so grandiose as to be unattainable or so ill-defined as to be incoherent. A series of improvisations both at home and abroad brought a stunning series of successes until the winter of 1941–2. Then disintegration set in, leading to total collapse as the Allied armies neared Germany. The self-destructive elements in Nazism became dominant. In the last resort, as a convinced social Darwinist, Hitler believed that Germany had failed him. In March 1945 he told his armaments minister, Albert Speer, that the war was lost: 'The nation has proved itself weak, and the future belongs solely to the stronger Eastern nation. Besides those who remain after battle are of little value; for the good have fallen.' New orders were issued that the war was to be continued 'without consideration for the German people'.

Italian fascism and German Nazism are often lumped together as a similar phenomenon, partly because they were contemporaneous and on the same side in the Second World War. There were, however, despite the similarities in style and form, significant differences between them. Fascism was essentially syncretic, incorporating as it did elements of liberalism, nationalism, conservatism and socialism in what it believed was a new political synthesis. Nazism was more exclusive and racial – anti-Semitism was central to Nazism but not to fascism. Germany became a complex dictatorship of largely one-man rule with few legal constraints, whereas Italy remained a semi-plural state with a formal legal basis and a constitution that eventually provided the mechanism for Mussolini's overthrow. Italian foreign policy was relatively traditional, based on colonial expansion and a limited war in the Mediterranean. Although Nazi foreign policy had much in common with earlier German aspirations (for example the programme drawn up by the Chancellor Bethmann-Hollweg when Germany seemed on the verge of victory in September 1914) it developed into a racial restructuring of eastern Europe. The Poles and Slavs were turned into sub-human slave labourers, the Jews were exterminated and the areas they vacated were to be populated by German peasant farmers. Nazism gained power in one of the most advanced industrial states of the core. Fascism, as in Italy, gained most of its support in the weaker states of the European semi-periphery. There were some rather pathetic imitators of Nazism, particularly in the occupied states of western Europe during the Second World War, but it was the Italian fascist model that had the widest appeal.

There were some immediate imitators of Mussolini, such as the Romanian fascist party and the British fascisti, both founded in 1923. None had any impact. After 1923, as the immediate post-war crisis ended and a degree of economic and social stability returned to Europe, politics too began to stabilize. Although parliamentary government broke down in many countries, it was generally replaced by traditional, authoritarian regimes and not by groups with specifically fascist ideas. There was little reason to believe that Italy was pointing the way ahead for the rest of Europe. Fascism became much more popular in the 1930s under the pressures stemming from the depression. To some fascism did seem the wave of the future. With liberal democracy in retreat it offered a way of organizing a modern society and resisting Communism. It was only in two states, Hungary and Romania, that fascist groups gained any significant support. Hungary was a strongly revisionist state after the losses imposed in the peace treaties of 1919–20. It had also experienced a brief period of Communist rule under Bela Kun in 1919. It was controlled by a conservative, authoritarian, land-owning elite under Admiral Horthy. The leader of the fascist radical right, Gyula Gombos, was made prime minister in 1932, but unlike Hitler in Germany he was kept under control by the elite. A new fascist group, the Arrow Cross, which had a strongly racist programme, gained about a fifth of the vote in the 1939 elections. However, Horthy kept control throughout the war until late 1944, when the Germans established a puppet government of the Arrow Cross. Unlike Hungary, Romania was a victorious power in 1918 but its fascist movement was very similar to the Arrow Cross. The

Iron Guard, formally the Legion of the Archangel Michael, was founded in 1927 by Corneliu Codreanu. It was anti-Semitic and aimed at the religious rescue of the Romanian 'race' through a cultural revolution which would create the *Omul nou* – the 'new man'. Like the Arrow Cross its route to power was blocked by right-wing authoritarianism, in this case the royal dictatorship of King Carol. Its maximum support was about a sixth of the vote in the 1937 elections. The dismemberment of Romania in the summer of 1940 led to a new fascist-style regime under the king, with the Iron Guard as part of the coalition. An attempted coup by the Iron Guard in early 1941 was put down, and it was destroyed as an organization with Hitler's full consent.

In the rest of eastern and central Europe fascism was notable mainly by its absence. There were no movements of any importance in Greece, Bulgaria and Yugoslavia. In Czechoslovakia, although there were two fascist movements – the National Fascist Community founded in 1926 and Vlajka in the 1930s – neither was of any importance. In Poland the government was highly authoritarian after 1936, but it kept its distance from the Falanja, the only semi-fascist party. The situation was much the same in northern Europe. In no state did the fascists receive more than about 2 per cent of the vote, except in Finland in 1936 and the Netherlands in 1935 and 1937 when they obtained about 8 per cent. The Dutch movement was called 'National Socialist', but it was much closer to Italian fascism with its corporatist beliefs, advocacy of religious freedom and its acceptance of Jewish members. In Belgium the Christus Rex movement and the Flemish VNV gained slightly under a fifth of the vote in 1936, but neither were really fascist at this stage. Only in 1938 did the VNV under Staf de Clerq and the Catholic, corporatist Rexist movement under Leon Degrelle become fascist and their vote immediately fell. Both movements eventually collaborated with the Germans during the war.

In France, despite the existence of a wide variety of groups, fascism never received more than about 2 per cent of the vote. This was despite the fact that many of the ideas of fascism and Nazism such syndicalism and racism first emerged in France. The most influential movement intellectually was Action Française, but it was not interested in social and political activism. A breakaway group – Le Faisceau – was formed in 1925 and probably had about 50,000 members at its peak, but it was in decline by the end of the 1920s. In the mid-1930s an authoritarian nationalism was far more popular than fascism, although there were two fascist parties, both formed by politicians of the left. In 1934 the Socialist Party of France (PSF) was founded by Marcel Déat, a rising star of the Socialist Party in the early 1930s. Within three years it had over 600,000 members. In 1935 Jacques Doriot broke with the Communist Party and founded the Parti Populaire Français which consisted mainly of ex-Communists. The PPF had a genuine working-class base and about 300,000 members, but took little interest in electoral politics, preferring instead to concentrate on reducing the power of the Communist-led trade unions by strike breaking. Both parties only became truly fascist in 1941 when Déat and Doriot embarked on rival careers of outright collaboration with the German occupying authorities.

In neighbouring Spain fascism emerged in the mid-1930s when José Antonio Primo de Rivera, the eldest son of the dictator of the 1920s, founded Falanga Espanola (Spanish Phalanx) with its twenty-seven point programme to establish a fully corporatist state. Although politically it was anti-clerical, the Falange, with its corporatism, did have strong Catholic overtones (as did its name-sake in Poland). However, it had little public support, gaining less than 1 per cent of the vote in the 1936 elections and it was suppressed in the spring of that year. It grew rapidly during the first year of the civil war and in April 1937 it was taken over by General Franco, when he decided to form a state party from the disparate elements of the Falange, the Carlists and other right-wing groups. However, Franco, who was looking for some sort of political programme in an attempt to avoid the odium of purely military rule, made it clear that the Falange programme would be merely a point of departure for his government. The new party – the Falange Espanola Tradicionalista (FET) – was not controlled by the old Falange and Franco ensured that it remained a minority within his government, which was a traditional, authoritarian, conservative, military dictatorship. Despite the pressures of the war and previous support for Franco from both Germany and Italy, Spain did not become a fascist state. The FET became a faction, and a subordinate one, within the government. By the 1950s it had become the Movimiento Nacional. After a last attempt by the old Falangists to shift the government in their direction in 1957, the old programme of twenty-seven points was dropped and replaced by an anodyne collection of ten principles. The Falange was finally dissolved during Spain's democratization process in the late 1970s.

In Portugal the Salazar dictatorship was even more determined to ensure that there was no separate fascist movement. Only briefly in 1934–5 was the 'Blueshirt' movement of the National Syndicalists under Rolao Preto important, but he was exiled and an attempted coup was easily put down.

In Britain the Imperial Fascist League was set up by the anti-Semitic, eugenicist Arnold Leese in 1929, but remained no more than a fringe movement. The main fascist movement eventually sprang out of the maverick political career of Oswald Mosley. A member of a wealthy family, he became a Conservative MP in 1918 at the age of twenty-one, but in 1926 defected to the Labour Party and joined the cabinet of the minority Labour government in 1929. He argued for a more radical economic programme than the government favoured, before resigning and forming the New Party in 1931. It was overwhelmingly defeated in the elections of September that year. In October Mosley, still dissatisfied by his exclusion from politics, founded the British Union of Fascists, expecting it to be the wave of the future. Its programme 'The Greater Britain', advocating imperial autarky together with a corporate framework for private enterprise, was one of the most explicit fascist programmes ever produced. The BUF gained considerable support among the elite, especially from Lord Rothermere, publisher of the *Daily Mail*, which proclaimed in January 1934 'Hurrah for the Blackshirts'. By June 1934 there were about 50,000 members (including some Jews), but this support soon drifted away. The BUF had no electoral base and after 1936 when it became more openly anti-Semitic its membership fell to less than 5,000. Long before the outbreak of the war Mosley was an insignificant political figure.

Fascism remained a European phenomenon. Although during the war and by some commentators afterwards Japan was portrayed as a fascist state, this was not the case. Japan was not subject to the same intellectual and political influences as Europe in the first two decades of the century. It was an authoritarian state by the 1930s, but its traditional institutions remained intact and the fact that it was militaristic and expansionist and eventually fought on the same side as Germany and Italy did not make it fascist. The European state it most closely resembled was imperial Germany before 1914 rather than fascist Italy and Nazi Germany.

South America produced a few synthetic imitators of fascism, but they remained insignificant. The largest – the Açao Integralista Brasiliera – was founded in 1932 by Plinio Salgado and directly inspired by Italian fascism, although it was strongly Catholic in orientation. Its attempted coup in 1938 was easily put down. Chile even produced a replica of the Nazi Party – the National Socialist Movement founded in 1932 by Gonzalez von Marees (who was of German descent). In 1937 he criticized Hitler for being a tyrant and turned his party into a democratic organization and finally admitted that there was no 'Jewish problem' in Chile. He won 3 per cent of the vote at elections and then attempted a coup which was a failure.

Fascism did not die with the defeat of Germany and Italy in 1945. In 1949 an opinion poll in West Germany found that nearly six out of ten people thought that Nazism was a good idea but it had been badly implemented. In the elections that year over 10 per cent voted for conservative and nationalist groups drawn from the old DNVP, which had joined Hitler's first cabinet in January 1933. Two years later the Socialist Reich Party, run by ex-Nazi Party members, gained 11 per cent of the vote in Lower Saxony. In general these groups remained on the fringe of politics until the 1960s and the formation of the National Democratic Party (NPD), which argued for the expulsion of all foreign troops and workers and the establishment of a more authoritarian government. By 1968 it had 28,000 members, although it never gained more than 4 per cent of the vote and therefore no seats in the Bundestag. The NPD faded away, although a network of neo-Nazi groups remained. In 1983 the Republican Party (one of whose founders was an ex-member of the Waffen-SS) took over the neo-Nazi mantle. It argued for the reunification of Germany on the old 1937 boundaries (which implied the take-over of large parts of Poland) and rejected Hitler's 'singular guilt' for the Second World War. Its highest level of support came in the 1989 elections to the European parliament when it gained 7 per cent of the vote, although it never gained enough support to obtain seats in the Bundestag. Despite the lack of electoral support for the neo-Nazi parties, there was still considerable sympathy in Germany for Nazi aims. It came from the gangs who beat up and in some cases killed immigrants and the four out of ten Germans who in 1989 thought that, but for the 'persecution' of the Jews, Hitler could be counted among the country's top statesmen.

In France the corporatist and authoritarian views of Action Française reappeared in the late 1940s when its journal *Aspects de France*, edited by Xavier Vallat, the commissioner for Jewish affairs in the Vichy government, was published again. In the mid-1950s a new political phenomenon emerged, 'Poujadisme'. It was named after Pierre Poujade, an ex-member of Doriot's PPF who later fought with the Free French. His French Union and Fraternity (UFF) advocated corporatism, a new constitution and an attack on 'the enemy within' (especially the Jews). It was essentially a protest movement of small shopkeepers and similar groups. In the January 1956 elections, when it ran under the slogan 'Kick the Old Gang Out', it won nearly 12 per cent of the vote and fifty-two seats. It collapsed rapidly following the demise of the Fourth Republic and the triumph of de Gaulle in 1958. The strongest successor to Poujadisme was the National Front (FN) founded in 1972 by Jean-Marie Le Pen, an ex-Poujadist deputy. At first it was very weak – in 1974 it gained less than 1 per cent of the vote and in 1981 Le Pen could not even obtain the necessary 500 signatures to enable him to run as a presidential candidate. Nevertheless, within a couple of years the FN was transformed as it concentrated on an anti-immigrant campaign and won a sixth of the vote at Dreux in local elections. From 1984 the FN consistently obtained about 10 to 14 per cent of the vote at national elections and became more corporatist in the 1990s. In Britain, on the other hand, similar anti-immigration campaigns run by the National Front and other neo-Nazi groups were relatively ineffective, partly because the Conservative Party and government were perceived as having very strong policies in this area.

The most successful of the post-war fascist movements was in Italy. After 1945 many ex-fascists joined the Christian Democrats. This was especially the case after 1947, when the Communists were removed from the governing coalition and a strongly anti-communist programme and rhetoric were adopted. The Italian Social Movement (MSI) was founded in 1946 by Giorgio Pini, a junior minister in Mussolini's collaborationist government after 1943, and Giorgio Almirante, the editor of the main fascist party racist publication. After 1950 the party was led by Augusto de Marsanich, an old fascist who had remained loyal to Mussolini in 1943. The party was linked to the monarchists and plagued by arguments and splits. It rarely gained more than about 6 per cent of the vote and twenty or thirty seats in parliament. There was, however, a violent wing of the fascist movement. Two coups by fascist supporters were attempted in 1964 and 1970 and a terrorist network carried out numerous bombings, the worst of which was at Bologna railway station in August 1980 when 85 people were killed and over 200 injured. The fascist movement also seemed to be linked to the powerful but shadowy P2 masonic lodge and the Gladio network of anti-Communist resistance groups.

Even under its new leader, Gianfranco Fini, the MSI continued to gain only about 5 per cent of the vote in the late 1980s. The collapse of the post-war political system in the early 1990s gave the fascists a major opportunity. They began to gain control of local authorities and Fini himself won nearly half the vote in the contest for mayor of Rome. In January 1994 the MSI became the National Alliance (AN), supporting a strong president, a Europe of nation-states, 'Catholic values' and a border revision with Yugoslavia. It joined forces with Forza Italia, run by the millionaire businessman Silvio Berlusconi, and the Northern League to form the 'Freedom Alliance'. The AN gained over 13 per cent of the vote and 107 deputies in the 1994 elections. It took five posts in the government formed by Berlusconi, the first fascists to be in power in Europe since 1945. They left office when the Berlusconi government collapsed at the end of 1994. Fini claimed that the National Alliance had become a 'post-fascist' party and more 'Gaullist' in its philosophy, but most commentators felt that it had not really changed and was still essentially fascist.

15 DICTATORSHIP

THE MOST common form of government in the twentieth century was dictatorship. The exceptions were the core states which, apart from the Nazi period in Germany and wartime occupation, maintained varying degrees of representative government: even the traditional regimes before 1918 had strong representative elements. Elsewhere in the world unrepresentative dictatorships were the norm, only occasionally punctuated by democratic or semi-democratic phases. For much of the century large parts of the world were ruled by imperial powers, which imposed dictatorial rule except for brief periods immediately before independence. Outside the colonial empires there were two major periods in which dictatorships flourished. The first was in the late 1920s through to the 1940s and occurred in the European semi-periphery, especially in the new states created at Versailles, and in Latin America. The second came in the 1960s and 1970s in the newly independent states and in Latin America. Outside these two periods there was some greater degree of representative government. However, many states, especially those in Central America and most of Africa, never experienced any form of government apart from dictatorship. The one exception to this general pattern in the periphery came in the world's second most populous state, India. After independence in 1947, apart from a brief period of authoritarian rule under Indira Gandhi in the mid-1970s, India was able to maintain a democratic system.

Dictatorship was nothing new. In Latin America, which had been independent since the 1820s, even semi-democratic structures were the exception and rule by dictators was the norm. What was new in the twentieth century was the spread of dictatorship across the globe and the more 'sophisticated' variants which emerged after 1920. These new forms of dictatorship often embodied an 'ideology' about the development and industrialization of the nation in the face of the core states' power. As a form of rule it included both military and civilian dictators, and in both these forms a political party to support their aims and to semi-mobilize the population was often found. In some regimes state-supported 'opposition' parties were encouraged and financed to provide what it was hoped would be a mantle of legitimacy. In some cases military rulers even tried to transform their regimes into civilian rule through the use of such parties. This type of authoritarian government first emerged in the 1920s in states such as Turkey after the end of Ottoman rule, China under the Kuomintang, and Mexico after the revolution of 1911–20, as they all attempted to 'modernize'. In other cases the social and economic strains created by industrialization and economic growth, especially in the states of the semi-periphery, produced pressures that tended to lead to dictatorship. If workers began to demand greater rights and higher pay this was threatening to governing elites and they were often tempted to support authoritarian, usually military, rule in order to maintain their position. Such moves, especially after 1950, could usually be presented as suppressing 'Communism' and therefore, particularly in Latin America, they normally had the support of the United States. Across the world there was an almost endless succession of coups to install military and civilian dictators. With the sole exception of Czechoslovakia in 1948, coups against democracy came from the right of politics. Coups by the left were against dictatorial regimes.

One distinguishing characteristic of twentieth-century dictatorships was the predominance of military regimes and the high level of intervention by the military in politics. Even the core states found it difficult to exclude the military completely from politics. In Germany before 1914 they held a special place in the constitution and were largely outside the control of the civilian government. In the 1920s and early 1930s, although Generals Seeckt and Schleicher, the leaders of the army, kept to the constitutional formalities, they were barely under civilian control. They were essentially 'political' generals, deeply involved in political manoeuvring and the formation of new governments. The army was not brought under full civilian control in Germany until Hitler's changes in early 1938 and then the consequences were catastrophic. In France a partial mutiny by the army in 1958 ended the Fourth Republic and brought General de Gaulle to power as president of a new republic. Within three years he too had to defeat a full-scale revolt by the army in Algeria over his policy of independence for the country. In 1914 the

British government similarly found itself facing a mutiny when parts of the army refused to coerce Ulster into a united Ireland. The United States had a long tradition of military presidents dating back to George Washington and his numerous successors in the nineteenth century. The tradition was continued by the election of General Eisenhower in 1952. Eisenhower's predecessor, Truman, had to sack General MacArthur for insubordination during the Korean War.

In the core states intervention by the military in politics was, however, regarded as an aberration. In the semi-periphery and the periphery this was not the case. In these states the military often represented one of the few genuinely national and integrative forces in society and were a major contributor to social mobility. They could, with some plausibility, portray themselves as embodying the 'national interest' against the claims of factional politicians, who represented no more than the interests of some group within the elite or one particular region within the country. In these circumstances, particularly in Latin America, the military did not 'interfere' in politics, rather they were an integral part of the historical and political process. Neither were these societies particularly 'militaristic' – Latin America was one of the most peaceful regions of the world in terms of inter-state conflicts. Many interventions by the military were highly popular. The coup in Argentina in 1930 was welcomed as the only way of removing the Radical Party government, which was determined to stay in power. Again in 1943 the removal of President Castillo, who was attempting to keep a small group in power and nominate his successor, was, at least initially, equally popular. Similarly the military in Brazil intervened in 1955 to ensure that a democratically elected president and vice-president were installed in power. In Turkey, a state largely created by the army in the early 1920s, the military saw themselves as its 'guardians'. The 1960 coup to remove the repressive regime of Adnan Menderes, who was trying to keep the Democratic Party in power, was highly popular. It led to the writing of a new, highly liberal, constitution and the almost immediate handing back of power to an elected civilian government. Similarly, in Pakistan the military came to see themselves as representing the national interest against the claims of unrepresentative, factional and often corrupt politicians. Failure to support a government could be just as effective as a coup in some circumstances. In South Korea in 1960 rigged elections, which gave President Syngman Rhee a fourth term in office, led to riots in which over a hundred people were killed. The army chief General Song Yo Chan made it clear that the army would not support the police in any new riots and this forced Rhee to resign.

In many cases, however, the military could not claim such a degree of legitimacy. Often they too only represented one part of the state. In Spain in the first half of the century the army was dominated by groups from Andalucia and Castille. In Yugoslavia between 1919 and 1941 the army was almost entirely Serbian (they provided 161 out of the 165 generals in 1938) and in Venezuela between 1889 and 1945 the army was similarly composed almost entirely of groups from the Andean region. Military governments always faced major problems in legitimizing their rule. Very few were able to adopt the tactics of General Odria in Peru in the late 1940s. He overthrew the elected government in 1948 and suspended Congress, although he claimed, like so many other military governments, that this was purely a transitional measure. In 1950 Odria resigned as president in favour of his vice-president and then ran as candidate for president in the elections. The opposition party was proscribed and his main opponent prevented from standing. Not surprisingly he was elected as the 'constitutional' president. Most of the hundreds of military coups in the twentieth century were carried out by only a very small group within the armed forces. They relied on others not to interfere and risk splitting the military. If the group lacked support then there was usually a counter-coup later – in Bolivia Colonel Alberto Natusch lasted just seventeen days in power in 1979 before he was overthrown by another group from the army. Events like this illustrate another major problem for military governments in gaining legitimacy. Once one part of the military had taken power, others felt that they had an equal right to do the same and there was no legitimate reason why they should not. The result could be a succession of coups. For example, between 1946 and 1970 there were 229 military coups in 59 countries. However, these were not evenly spread. Bolivia and Venezuela had 18 each, Argentina 16 and Ecuador 12. Outside Latin America there were 14 in Syria and 11 in Iraq. After 1970 there were a succession of coups in many states in Africa.

Although the twentieth century saw many dictatorial regimes claiming they were based on a particular 'philosophy', one of the most common forms of dictatorship remained that of the personal rule of one man. Under these dictatorships, known in Latin America as rule by the *caudillo*, government was largely personal and familial. Remarkably such regimes could be highly stable once a flourishing system of corruption had been established and enough powerful groups co-opted into the governing elite. In some cases power was passed on through the *caudillo*'s family. One of the most remarkable examples of the family-run state was Nicaragua from 1936 until 1979 under the Somozas. The dynasty was founded by Anastasio Somoza, head of the National Guard which was established under American guidance in the 1920s. In 1933 the Guard was used to kill the radical leader Augusto Sandino and three years later Somoza seized power from President Juan Sacasa. Anastasio was assassinated in 1956 but replaced by his son Luis, who was, in turn, replaced in 1967 by his younger brother, also called Anastasio. Only for short periods in 1947 and 1963 were other close colleagues allowed to rule, although the family retained effective control. By 1979 the Somoza family was worth about $600 million. It owned a fifth of all the cultivable land in Nicaragua together with the twenty-six largest industrial companies and the national airline. It also had a monopoly on alcohol production and car imports. The army and National Guard were always controlled personally by the Somozas and their main purpose was to operate a series of protection rackets. Opposition was contained, although it gained ground after nearly all the international aid provided after a devastating earthquake in 1972 was stolen by the Somozas. The family regime survived until the United States, always its strongest supporter, withdrew its backing in late 1978. Elsewhere in Latin America *caudillo*-type regimes similarly survived for decades and were handed on from father to son, as in Haiti under the Duvaliers.

Paraguay had a slightly more 'modern' form of *caudillo* rule from 1954 to 1989 under General Alfredo Stroessner (nicknamed 'El Tiranosauro'). Following a civil war in 1947 the faction fighting within the ruling Colorado Party was only ended by Stroessner's coup in May 1954. His rule initially had some popular base in the Colorado Party, but the party was rapidly brought under the control of the army. The army gradually took control of the country, as what Stroessner called 'the price of peace'. The system was institutionalized by a decree which allowed the army to undertake private business interests – equipment was requisitioned and conscripts provided free labour. The domestic airline was taken over and used for smuggling, by the late 1980s about half of all Paraguay's trade was 'unregistered'. The system was based on large-scale corruption. The government sold residence permits to criminals, including war criminals such as Joseph Mengele. The vicious Croatian Ustasha were used to train Stroessner's bodyguard (the Escolta Battalion) and the Urban Guard, which kept control of the cities. Fake end-user certificates were sold to countries such as Iran, South Africa and the United States, which wanted to avoid arms sanctions. About a fifth of the government's total wage bill was credited to staff who did not exist. In 1986 the state cement company built a new plant, which had a capacity three times the level of domestic consumption. It was immediately mothballed. Of the total cost of $341 million about $125 million went 'missing' and finished up in the bank accounts of various ministers and officials. At the same time most people lived in poverty and even the government admitted that fewer than one in fourteen of the population had access to a sewage system. Stroessner was eventually ousted in February 1989 by General Andres Rodriguez, who represented a faction in the Colorado Party and the army which did not want one of Stroessner's sons to succeed him.

Caudillo-type regimes were also found outside Latin America, especially in Africa after 1960. The sudden granting of independence left most states without any established civic and political culture and politics rapidly degenerated, as in many parts of Latin America, into a private struggle for power between various civilian and military groups. Once the legitimacy of the immediate post-colonial rulers was broken, any group could equally well claim the right to rule. None of these groups, civilian or military, had any real popular links, instead power and influence were distributed through networks of patrons, clients and supporters. Apart from a few short-lived Marxist states, most of the authoritarian states in Africa were liberal about freedom of religion, property and the operation of the free market, but very restrictive on political rights. However, as long as the networks of power, patronage and clientèlism worked well, such regimes could survive for long periods. Restraints on power were mainly personal – the rulers' need to deal with other powerful people. Only a few declined into the crude and unrestrained violence that characterized Uganda under Idi Amin and Equatorial Guinea under Francisco Nguema or into the megalomania of President, later Emperor, Bokassa of the Central African Republic (later Empire).

In the Middle East there were also *caudillo* regimes, such as Iraq under Saddam Hussein. He rose through the faction-ridden and violent politics of the Ba'ath Party. In 1979, following a deliberately bloody and brutal coup, he took power. His rule was based on his family and people from the town of Tikrit, where he grew up. Tikrit was at the heart of the Sunni triangle of central Iraq, which, despite the fact that it was a small minority of Iraq's population, had long provided the country's rulers. By the early 1990s Tikrit (which had a population of about 25,000) provided, apart from Saddam Hussein himself, the vice-president, both the defence and foreign ministers, the mayor of Baghdad, the commander of the Baghdad garrison and the commander of the elite Republican Guard. By 1995 Saddam's son, Uday, held twenty-nine official positions including head of the National Olympic Committee, head of the National Lottery and he also ran the regime's 'praetorian guard' – the 'Fedayeen of Saddam'. Saddam's family was badly divided between the Majids (the descendants of Saddam's paternal uncle) and the descendants of Hassan Ibrahim ('Hassan the Liar'), Saddam's stepfather. Uday, however, was detested by them all. In the last resort the family, and the other families from Tikrit, were held together by fear within the regime itself and, more importantly, by fear of what would happen to them if the regime was overthrown.

Most dictatorial governments were able to establish a wider basis for rule than a single man's immediate family and friends. They were often based on the armed forces, the bureaucracy and the social and economic elite, in situations in which such groups wanted to hold on to power and avoid radical reforms which might damage their position. Such developments were particularly apparent in the semi-periphery in the 1920s and 1930s. In both Latin America and eastern, central and southern Europe, states with only a limited level of industrialization and with a strong peasant class were dominated by narrow oligarchies, which depended on patronage and corruption to stay in power. Most of these states were dependent on agricultural exports, and the worldwide depression after 1929, linked to a dramatic fall in commodity prices and the withdrawal of credits by the core states, severely damaged their economies. Economic collapse was followed by political collapse. In Latin America only Chile survived as a loosely democratic regime. Elsewhere on the continent military and other dictatorial groups took power often on nominally 'populist' programmes of support for greater industrialization.

One of the most remarkable of these populist regimes emerged in Argentina in the mid-1940s after a succession of army coups. Within a year of the June 1943 coup Colonel Juan Perón, originally Minister for War, became vice-president and secretary of labour and welfare. He began building support among the workers and trade unions through a programme of paid holidays, medical insurance and pensions, together with security from arbitrary dismissal. In October 1945 he was able to use trade-union support to block an attempt to remove him and in February 1946 he was elected president with strong support from the public and the army. For a few years 'Perónism' was no more than a collection of slogans such as 'social justice' and 'economic independence'. Then Perón began to work out an ideology of *justicialismo*, which he believed struck a middle position between collectivism and individualism. In his 1952 book *Conduccion Politica*, he set out his idea of the 'conductor', who would be more than a mere *caudillo* since he would be 'a creator as well as a leader, an artist more than a technician'. There would be no need for a 'formal' democracy because the 'conductor' would be in contact with his followers and able to divine their needs. In 1946 Perón formed the Partido Unico de la Revolucion to replace the old three-party coalition which supported the military government. This soon became the Partido Perónista. Gerrymandering of elections meant that in 1951 the Perónistas won twice as many votes as the Radicals but ten times as many seats. From 1951 a state of 'internal warfare' was declared, the opposition was jailed or exiled and newspapers were closed down. Nevertheless, Perón remained popular, partly because of his pro-labour policies but more because of his wife, Eva Perón. Eva founded and ran the Feminino side of the Partido Perónista. She was also informal head of the trade union wing as well as head of the Eva Perón Welfare Foundation, which built (with state money) schools and hospitals. She was the focus of a personality cult even greater than the one round Perón himself and was beatified as 'The Mother of the Innocents' and 'The Lady of Hope'. Eva's death in July 1952 marked the beginning of the regime's end. Growing unpopularity and resistance within the armed forces to increasing politicization led to a coup in September 1954 and the installation of a military government. Nevertheless Perónism remained important in Argentine politics for decades – Perón himself returned briefly to power in 1973 and, after his death in July 1974, was succeeded by his second wife until the military took power again in 1976.

The strongest, most widespread and most important backlash against 'democratic' regimes in the 1920s and 1930s occurred in the

European semi-periphery. One of the first countries to experience this reaction was Portugal, a highly rural, isolated and Catholic country. The republic created by the 1910 revolution was anti-clerical and highly unstable: in the sixteen years after the revolution there were forty-four governments and an average of two coups a year. A lay Christian Democratic movement – the Portuguese Catholic Centre – was founded in 1912 but because it remained close to the monarchy until 1922 it was politically isolated. Then, under the influence of António de Oliveira Salazar, a professor of economics at Coimbra University, it effectively accepted the republic. Salazar was deeply influenced by French conservative and Catholic thinkers such as Maurras and elaborated a programme of 'Nation, Family, Authority and Hierarchy'. He declared, 'Let us protect the state before we look after the poor and the weak.' A military coup in 1926 brought Salazar into government; by 1932 he was prime minister and embarking on the civilianization of the authoritarian regime, based on support for his supposedly 'non-ideological' policies. In 1932 the Estado Novo was established as a corporative republic. There was an assembly made up of people hand-picked by Salazar, who were 'elected' by fewer than one in twelve of the adult population – no opposition candidate ever won a seat. The assembly had no powers anyway and corporatism was little more than a façade for state-directed capitalism. In practice much of the new state's 'philosophy' was made up by Salazar as he went along. While remaining a strong anti-Communist, he was also deeply opposed to both Hitler and Mussolini, their ideologies and their policies. There was no attempt to create a state party to support the government, but there was highly effective internal repression through the secret police, the PVDE (PIDE after 1945). The government was extremely conservative on social matters, content to see Portugal as a mainly rural nation with high levels of illiteracy, isolated from much of the rest of Europe but determined to hold on to its empire as a symbol of past greatness. The regime established in 1926 proved to be one of the most stable in Europe and survived almost unchanged, even after the death of Salazar, until the revolution of 1974.

In neighbouring Spain a similar economic and social situation in the early twentieth century was combined with a more complex political situation, partly because of the survival of the monarchy but also because of deep political divisions dating back into the nineteenth century. In 1923 General Miguel Primo de Rivera rebelled but was then appointed prime minister by the King. Unlike Italy under Mussolini the constitution was suspended and a military directory established. A military junta became the effective government, martial law was imposed and the military even ran local government. After 1925 there was some civilianization of the regime and de Rivera began to develop vague ideas about the 'regeneration' of Spain. This was to be achieved through a strongly anti-Communist and highly Catholic policy, combined with centralization and an attack on *caciquismo* – the corrupt political system dominated by strong local political bosses. The Union Patriotica became the government party, although others were allowed to exist. Membership of the Union was compulsory for state employees, but it had no real political role because elections were not allowed even at local level. The regime collapsed in January 1930 as de Rivera lost support in the military and the depression caused growing economic problems. Although the de Rivera episode was relatively short-lived, it provided a training ground for many later Spanish authoritarians and was part of the growing political breakdown that led to the civil war of 1936–9.

After de Rivera, the fall of the monarchy and the establishment of the Second Republic in 1931, there was a radical government of left-wing republicans and socialists who were intent on transforming Spanish society. This in turn had a major impact on Spanish conservatism. In particular, corporate Catholicism grew more powerful under both Gil Robles and CEDA (a semi-Christian Democratic party), which became the largest party in the Cortes in November 1933. The army coup against the Popular Front government in July 1936 failed and led to nearly three years of civil war. General Franco became the overall military leader and head of state in September. In early 1937 he merged the various traditionalist movements and the fascist Falange into a single FET (Falange Espanola Tradicionalista) with himself as head. Membership was obligatory in the army and civil service, but the FET had little political role because little 'politics' was allowed under the Franco government once it had established full control over Spain in early 1939. The military remained central to the new regime. Martial law was not ended until April 1947 and until then all political and labour opposition was treated as 'military rebellion' and tried in military courts. The military held about a third of all civil service posts, they also controlled the three service ministries and the Ministry of the Interior until 1969.

Franco was the most senior military officer and much of his government was a matter of personal rule – he even adopted the title of *caudillo*. In 1939 the Law of Head of State gave him all governmental powers and in 1947 by the Law of Succession, when Spain nominally became a monarchy again, he was made regent for life and head of state. He combined both offices until 1973 when, at the age of eighty-one, he handed over the post of head of government to Admiral Carrero Blanco. Prince Juan Carlos (the grandson of the deposed King Alfonso XIII) was designated as Franco's successor in 1969. Franco ran an intensely conservative government, in which he was able to keep the conflicting groups that supported the regime under control. The Ministry of Education was always run by strong Catholics and the Carlists headed the Ministry of Justice until 1973. Until the mid-1940s the Falangists set much of the ideological tone of the regime, but their influence over policy-making was much more restricted. After 1945, with the defeat of Hitler and Mussolini, the ex-CEDA groups, which had originally been tarred by their association with the Second Republic, became more powerful and from the late 1950s conservative technocrats keen on modernization were highly influential. The Franco regime only began to lose its grip over a rapidly changing country in the early 1970s. Franco's death in 1975 was followed by a rapid transformation to a democratic system.

Like Portugal and Spain, Greece was a largely rural, peasant society with a fractured political system, but one in which the monarchy came to play a highly controversial role. The major political divisions in Greece dated from 1915 and centred around the dominating figure of Eleuthérios Venizelos, leader of the Liberal Party, who took the Allied side in the war against the policy of the king and the conservative groups. He drew most of his support from the 'new lands' Greece had gained at the end of the nineteenth century (Crete, Macedonia and Thrace), whereas anti-Venizelist and pro-monarchy groups dominated the south and west. In 1924 Venizelos abolished the monarchy, but it was restored after the anti-Venizelists gained power in 1932. By the mid-1930s the depression had heightened the problems of a deeply divided political system which lacked legitimacy. The army was badly split, with leading generals siding with different political groups. A Venizelist coup failed in 1935 and the king appointed General John Metaxas (a highly political general since the early 1920s) as premier. The Metaxas regime was a royal, bureaucratic dictatorship (much like its contemporaries in Yugoslavia, Bulgaria and Romania). Parliament and civil liberties were suspended, local government was replaced by appointed officials and politicians were largely excluded from government. The Orthodox Church was regarded as part of the state and attendance was enforced by the police. The regime did not have its own political party, although it did have its own youth movement, the Neolaia. The Metaxas regime was not fascist (it was strongly opposed to Hitler); in outlook it was probably closest to the Salazar government in Portugal and the Vichy government in France.

Metaxas died in early 1941 and no replacement political system emerged before the German and Italian occupation in April that year. One of the major disputes between Greek politicians in exile during the war was over the future of the monarchy, which most of them saw as highly tainted by its association with Metaxas. Eventually after 1945 the British and the Americans forced through a restoration of the monarchy, in alliance with highly conservative groups and army leaders such as General Plastiras and Marshal Papagos. The latter were prepared to fight a bitter civil war against the more radical groups which had emerged in the resistance during the war. By the early 1950s the 'Greek Rally' under Marshal Papagos was in power (after winning highly undemocratic elections in November 1952). A conservative regime kept all opposition under strict control – a certificate of 'civil reliability' was required for even the most simple task, such as obtaining a hunting licence. In the early 1960s under the pressure of increasing urbanization and economic development the post-war system began to break down. Support for George Papandreou (an old Liberal politician and head of the nominally socialist PASOK party) rose sharply. In response the wartime right-wing IDEA group in the army (the Sacred Bond of Greek Officers) and the more activist EENA (Union of Young Greek Officers) under General Papadopoulos were both revived. The army managed to rig the 1961 elections, but was unable to stop Papandreou gaining power as prime minister in 1963. However, the king was not prepared to allow Papandreou to control the army and dismissed him in 1965. A series of unrepresentative governments and the possibility of new elections produced a coup in April 1967, led by Papadopoulos and the younger officers of EENA, with the full support of the United States. It was the consequence of the long-term politics of the army in Greece, its association with an increasingly discredited monarchy and the failure to establish a political system which had widespread support. The highly repressive army regime lasted until 1974 when the Turkish invasion of Cyprus led to its collapse. Only after the mid-1970s did a stable, generally conservative but reasonably democratic regime establish itself in Greece.

In addition to the establishment of the civilian Salazar regime in 1926 and the military regimes of Franco and Metaxas in 1935–6, there was a general trend towards dictatorship in the semi-periphery of Europe in the 1920s and 1930s. Long-established states such as Romania and Bulgaria, as well as nearly all the new states created at Versailles in 1918–19, succumbed to dictatorships. Romania nearly doubled its population between 1912 and 1918 through annexation. The overwhelming majority of the people were illiterate peasants and the country was split between the Regat, the old kingdom, and the new territories. Major land reform in the ten years after 1917 broke the power of the old, conservative groups of large landowners which had supported the Central Powers in the First World War. However, the political parties were little more than coalitions of important families and factions. The dominant National Liberals were controlled by the Bratianu family of the Regat, who ensured that most public money (derived from the oil production of the Ploesti region) was spent here (the rest was siphoned off by corrupt politicians). The strongly anti-Liberal King Carol was exiled and excluded from the throne in 1926, but was called back by the National Peasant Party in 1930. After his return from exile King Carol, from a position of great weakness, gradually established a royal dictatorship. Between 1930 and 1933 he exploited the factions within the National Peasant Party to splinter it and then did the same to the National Liberals in the four years up to 1937. During the 1930s governments were only fleetingly in power. King Carol appointed eighteen different premiers (and one of them lasted four years) and twenty-five different cabinets. After the relatively free but indecisive election of December 1937 he set up a full dictatorship under the ultra-nationalist Orthodox patriarch, Miron Cristea, with a corporatist constitution under which all political parties were dissolved. In December 1938 the king set up his own regime party – the Front of National Resistance – and in 1940, under the pressure of German victories in the war, the system became even more authoritarian.

In Bulgaria defeat in the First World War led to the removal of Tsar Ferdinand in favour of his son Boris. In the aftermath of the war the old bourgeois parties (there were over forty), which were little more than factions created by government ministers to support them personally, collapsed. Politics was dominated by Alexander Stambolski, leader of the Peasant Party and its 'Orange Guard' militia. In June 1923 the old nationalist elite, especially the military and the IMRO terrorist group which claimed Macedonia as part of Bulgaria, overthrew Stambolski's government and set up a government of 'National Concord', which included the old bourgeois parties. This group kept power until 1931 when slightly more liberal groups replaced it. They only lasted until May 1934, when there was an army coup. However, the army government was so incompetent that in January 1935 Tsar Boris took power himself. The 1879 constitution was suspended, political parties were prohibited, the cabinet was made responsible only to the tsar and parliament was selected by the government. Boris was able to rule through various civilian and military figureheads until his death in August 1943.

The creation of Yugoslavia produced a highly fractured and unstable state dominated by a Serb elite. In the ten years after 1918 there were over thirteen parties represented in parliament, most of them purely ethnic in membership, twenty-four governments (only one of which was not led by a Serb) and all but one of which fell as a result of internal manoeuvrings. The dominant party was the Radicals, which had controlled Serbian politics since 1903 and Yugoslavia was run as a 'Greater Serbia', with most other groups being excluded from power. In June 1928 the Croatian parliamentary leader, Stjepan Radic, was shot. Six months later King Alexander set up a centralized royal dictatorship and divided the country into nine governorships which deliberately cut across ethnic boundaries. An attempt was also made to reorganize political parties along non-ethnic lines. The government party of the new dictatorship – the Yugoslav National Party – remained unpopular as did the new constitution promulgated in 1932. Alexander was assassinated in October 1934 during a visit to France. The centralized dictatorship continued under a regent for the young king, headed by Milan Stojadinovic, a protégé of Nikola Pasic who had led the Serbian Radical Party for decades. Parliament remained powerless, elections were rigged and despite general lack of support the dictatorship continued until the German invasion in the spring of 1941.

Unlike Romania, Bulgaria and Yugoslavia, a royal dictatorship was not an option in Hungary because the Allies refused to allow a

Habsburg restoration. In the year after the collapse of the Habsburg empire in 1918 Hungary was in a state of political confusion, but by August 1919 the old aristocratic, land-owning elite was re-established in power. Six months later Admiral Miklos Horthy (the last commander of the Austro-Hungarian navy) was elected regent. Hungary nominally remained a kingdom in order to maintain its claim to the extensive territories lost under the peace treaties. Horthy dominated Hungary as head of a deeply conservative regime which bore many similarities to other contemporary European dictatorships, such as those of Salazar, Franco and Metaxas. During the 1920s politics was controlled by the Government Party, which was an alliance of the Legitimist Christian National Union and the Smallholders Party (which represented not the peasants but the small landowners). The governing elite ensured that the huge aristocratic estates were maintained and in 1922 they restored the pre-1914 restricted voting system, which also ensured that peasants had to cast their votes openly under the supervision of their landlords. The Government Party kept power throughout the 1920s until the depression badly affected an economy dominated by agricultural exports. The post-1919 system collapsed in 1932 when Gyula Gombos, leader of the more radical, semi-fascist right, took power. He was the first foreign leader to visit Hitler, but unlike the German leader he was kept under control by Horthy and the old elite. Gombos died in 1936, and the groups around Horthy maintained power and kept the truly fascist Arrow Cross out of power until the system was finally ended in 1944 following the German occupation.

In Austria, unlike Hungary, a democratic system was established following the fall of the Habsburgs. Although strongly divided between the Social Democrats and the conservative, Catholic and mainly rural Christian Social Union, the system survived through the 1920s, but disintegrated under the pressure of the depression and the rise to power of the Nazis in Germany. In March 1933, when the railway workers called a strike backed by the SDP, the government (dominated by the CSU) took power to rule by decree. The rights to free speech, to strike and to demonstrate were abolished. Two months later Chancellor Engelbert Dollfuss banned the Nazi and Communist Parties and founded the Fatherland Front, which was intended to be all-embracing. In February 1934 the offices of the SDP were attacked and the party banned. Three months later the democratic constitution was formally overturned and replaced by a corporate constitution to create a 'Social, Christian, German state founded upon estates under strong authoritarian leadership'. Parliament was replaced by six councils, all of whose members were appointed and supporters of the Fatherland Front. Only the employers' association and the Catholic Church retained any independence. In practice the corporate system existed more on paper than in reality, but it survived until the *Anschluss* with Germany in early 1938.

The Polish state created in 1918 faced a multitude of problems. The frontiers were ill-defined, there was a major war with the Soviet Union in 1919–20 and the borders eventually established meant that a third of the population were not Polish. The minority were excluded from the strongly centralized, Catholic, anti-Semitic and culturally exclusive state. Between November 1918 and May 1926 there was political instability, with fourteen governments, an unrepresentative Constituent Assembly holding on to power until the end of 1922 and a very weak presidency. The last was specifically designed by its opponents to restrict the potential power of Josef Pilsudski, the head of state and commander-in-chief between 1918 and 1922. An economic crisis in the spring of 1926 was followed by a coup led by Pilsudski, which split the army and only succeeded because the railway workers stopped the movement of opposition troops. Pilsudski kept the façade of a 'semi-democratic' system – he was minister for war rather than president and the parliament continued to function, although the powers of the president were increased. With elections due, the government constructed the 'Nonpartisan Bloc for Co-operation with the Government' (BBWR) as a party to keep Pilsudski in power. This it did until 1930 when, under increasing pressure from the economic and social strains caused by the depression, opposition leaders were arrested. Repression was increased and in November 1930 the BBWR was able to gain a parliamentary majority through blatant intimidation. The government could now rule more or less as it pleased, although it was not until 1935 that a new authoritarian constitution giving greatly increased powers to the president came into effect. Pilsudski died shortly afterwards, but his successors manipulated the electoral system to ensure that the government always won. The BBWR was abolished in order to establish a parliament and government that were formally non-party. The authoritarian, nationalist government was heavily influenced by the military and drifted steadily to the right and a corporatist system. The system survived until the

German conquest of September 1939.

Poland's neighbours in the Baltic were affected by a similar pattern of events. After independence in 1918 each was organized as a highly democratic republic with a unicameral sovereign legislature elected every three years and extensive referenda and initiatives. In practice all suffered from extreme political instability and succumbed to coups. The first was in Lithuania in 1926 (soon after Pilsudski's coup in Poland) and in 1934 Latvia and Estonia also became dictatorial regimes. In each case the coup was largely pre-emptive and carried out by a hero of the battles for independence with the support of conservative groups, in order to avoid any more radical solution. None of the regimes established was extreme, highly repressive or strongly ideological. The only new state established at Versailles to avoid outright dictatorship was the most advanced economically and industrially – Czechoslovakia.

By the mid-1930s dictatorships of the authoritarian right in various guises were the most common form of government in Europe. Apart from the Nazis in Germany, they were found in the semi-periphery of the Iberian peninsula, the Mediterranean, the Balkans and east and central Europe. None of these states had been able to establish the necessary civil society and political culture to support functioning democratic systems. They all fell under the rule of right-wing, conservative, nationalistic dictatorships which generally protected the interests of the social, economic and political elites. Across central and eastern Europe and the Balkans after 1945 authoritarian dictatorships of the right were replaced by Communist regimes. Elsewhere, in particular in Portugal and Spain, the governments established in the 1920s and 1930s survived into the mid-1970s, and Greece was hardly democratic until the last quarter of the century. Even after the collapse of Communism in the late 1980s, few of the states of eastern and central Europe became full democracies. In some such as Romania, Bulgaria, the Ukraine and Belorussia large parts of the Communist elite kept power in authoritarian systems.

In Latin America another wave of dictatorial, mainly military regimes, started with Brazil in the mid-1960s. These developments took place not in the poorest, least developed countries such as Nicaragua, Paraguay, El Salvador and Haiti, which tended to retain *caudillo*-style regimes, but in more economically developed states which were undergoing the strains of industrialization and urbanization. In these states social and economic changes threatened

the position of the established elites through demands for greater
equality and the 'inclusion' of groups such as industrial workers and
peasants. The new regimes that emerged in Brazil (1964–85),
Argentina (1966–73 and 1976–83), Uruguay (1973–85), Bolivia
(1971–8) and Chile (1973 to the early 1990s) were described as
'bureaucratic-authoritarian'. Although the military were in formal
control, they were much more sophisticated regimes than the
relatively crude types of military rule found earlier in the century.
They were committed to ruling in association with existing elites
and promoting development and economic growth through foreign
investment. Chile, under General Pinochet, after 1973 carried these
policies to an extreme of free market liberalization, under guidance
from American academic economists, whereas Brazil retained a very
strong state sector and in Argentina the military still controlled an
extensive range of economic assets. All the regimes were highly
repressive, limited popular participation and political rights (Brazil
kept a nominal party system, but it was completely remoulded by
the military) and suppressed trade unions and the limited workers'
rights that existed previously. All received extensive American
support and were able to portray themselves as 'anti-Communist' in
dealing with internal discontent. Military rule eventually broke
down in all these states during the 1980s. However, the military
ensured that they handed over power to governments that accepted
the broad policy base they had established since the 1960s.

The link between economic development and dictatorial regimes
in the periphery was even more apparent in Asia. The exemplar for
many of these states was Turkey. The modernization of the
Ottoman empire, which had begun with the Young Turks in 1908,
was only fully realized after the collapse of the empire in 1918. The
Turkish state which emerged by 1923 from a battle to establish itself
against the Allied powers of France, Britain and Greece was the first
non-Communist, ideological, one-party state anywhere in the
world. It was also a model in being a monolithic, repressive
dictatorship which allowed little dissent over its general policy of
national modernization. General Mustafa Kemal, the military leader
of the Turkish forces in Anatolia, was elected president in 1923 and
retained the office until his death in 1938. However, from the start
Kemal saw himself as a civilian leader – there was no military junta
as such. He was head of the Society for the Defence of the Rights of
Anatolia and Rumelia until it was transformed in 1923 into the
Republican People's Party (RPP), of which he became permanent

leader. (Kemal had the informal title 'Great Leader', but was given the name Ataturk in 1934 when the law on the adoption of western-style surnames was passed.) Opposition parties were only tolerated for two brief periods in 1924 and 1930. The RPP had a legal monopoly and was elitist, disciplined and highly centralized, although debate about policy was allowed within limits. Its main role was to select the candidates to be elected to the national assembly. Despite rule by a civilian leader and the existence of the RPP, the army retained a key role in the new state and saw itself as a guardian of the new order, a role it exercised again in the 1960s and 1980s. The basic fact remained that Kemal established his position of leadership from his military role and did not retire from the army until 1927, by which time he had removed most of his military rivals. Kemal's deputy and Prime Minister Ismet Inonu similarly did not leave the army until 1927 and the military continued to supply about a quarter of the cabinet and a fifth of the national assembly until the early 1940s.

The new state did not undertake a programme of full economic and social revolution. Modernization and 'westernization' took place in an evolutionary and generally conservative way. Kemal did not provide any 'sacred texts' to guide his followers, but in 1931 the 'Six Principles' were adopted by the RPP and incorporated as Article 2 of the 1937 constitution as the aim of the state not just the party. They were: Secularism, Republicanism, Nationalism, Populism, Revolutionism and Etatism. All these terms had a peculiarly Turkish interpretation. Secularism meant the total separation of religion and the state, especially in education. Religious courts were abolished in 1924, as were all titles, brotherhoods and orders. The Islamic calendar was replaced by the western one and the weekly day of rest moved from Friday to Sunday. Republicanism involved the abolition of the Sultanate and Caliphate in the early 1920s but not the institution of any democratic alternative. Both political activity and freedom of expression were tightly controlled. Nationalism was based on a Turkish linguistic and cultural identity and, although it might incorporate Christians, it did not accommodate groups such as the Armenians and Kurds. Populism was a highly ambiguous concept that certainly did not imply sovereignty of the people. Instead it meant the welfare of the people achieved through social, not class solidarity and the rule of the RPP. Revolutionism meant change carried out by the RPP with order and method, for example the decision in 1928 to adopt the

Latin rather than the Arabic script for Turkish. Finally, Etatism was about the state's role in directing the economy, as in the industrialization drive of the 1930s. However, there was no state monopoly, no collectivization, no significant land reform and although there was a limited reform of labour law in 1936 strikes remained illegal.

By his death in 1938 Ataturk had been able to set out a clear path for the new Turkish state. Numerous problems, in particular the sluggish pace of economic development, remained, but the major problem was political. Once the initial structural reforms were completed it was difficult to justify the continuance of a single party dictatorship but even more difficult to find the basis for a stable system that would still meet the overriding objective of the Turkish state. Inonu succeeded Ataturk and in 1946 allowed both the first direct elections for the National Assembly and the creation of a true opposition – the Democratic Party – which won about a sixth of the seats in very repressive circumstances. In the reasonably fair elections of 1950 the Democrats won a landslide victory, entrenched themselves in power and became increasingly repressive. By the end of the decade it was clear that they were determined to hang on to power whatever the consequences. In 1960 the armed forces intervened and they did so again in 1971 and 1980. On the first occasion the coup was by younger officers (in the tradition of the Young Turks in 1908) to remove the Democrats and impose a more liberal constitution. On the next two occasions the coups were directed by the military high command and were repressive, anti-liberal and resulted in an attack on trade unions, the purging of universities and the exclusion of a number of politicians. Each intervention was relatively short, but after the restoration of semi-civilian rule in 1983 military supervision of politics remained. It was not until 1989 that the first civilian president since 1960 took office. By the mid-1990s the main threat to the established consensus in Turkey came from the rise of Islamic fundamentalism, both socially and politically, and its demands to alter the basis on which the state had been constructed in the 1920s and 1930s.

The success of the reformers in Turkey in beginning a process of 'modernization' was an example to similar groups in other states, in particular China. However, although there was a civilian reform party (the Kuomintang), in some ways similar to the Turkish RPP, it was unable to secure a solid base for civilian rule and, unlike Turkey, it drifted fairly rapidly into military rule. The problems the

Kuomintang faced were far greater than the RPP in Turkey, partly because of China's vast size and partly because of the much greater degree of disintegration the Kuomintang inherited. This was the result of the power of internal 'warlords' and external pressure from the western powers. The Kuomintang (National People's Party) was founded in 1912 by the first president of the new Chinese republic, Sun Yat-sen. It was forcibly dissolved a year later but re-emerged in the early 1920s. By this time it was clear that the 1911 revolution and the end of the imperial regime had failed to produce a strong central government. China seemed to be breaking down still further as various regional warlords asserted their power. At its congress in Canton in January 1924 the Kuomintang agreed its basic policies – the establishment of a strong government able to revise the unequal treaties with the western powers, control the militarists in China and impose universal suffrage and state control of large industry. Sun Yat-sen died in March 1925, but he left a large body of writings which in 1928 the Kuomintang declared had the force of law. The essence of his philosophy was the Three People's Principles. The first – nationalism – was, by the 1920s, strongly anti-western, but also included ideas of national revival and an affirmation of Chinese national identity. The second – people's rights and power – (often mistranslated as democracy) was about participation but not western-style democracy. Sun Yat-sen was clear that for some time there would be a phase of 'tutelage' by the Kuomintang, as the only party which recognized China's true interests. The third principle – people's livelihood – (often mistranslated as socialism) was a vague concept, but was built around a state capitalism which would lead the private sector into expansion and modernization. In 1924 the Kuomintang adopted the Leninist principle of 'democratic centralism', strict control from the top of the party. After Sun's death there was a short period of collective leadership, but by early 1926 the dominant figure within the party was Chiang Kai-shek, the commander of the army. In the two years after 1926 the Kuomintang was able to gain control of large parts of China including Peking, turn on its Communist allies and in 1927 defeat them politically and militarily.

On taking power the Kuomintang proclaimed a period of 'tutelage', which it optimistically claimed would end in 1935. The party itself went through an evolution very similar to that of the Communists in the Soviet Union. The Central Executive Committee was too large to exercise effective control, so power was concentrated first in a standing committee set up in 1924 and then, after 1928, in the Political Council (the equivalent of the Soviet Politburo). Eventually even the Political Council became too large and split into various functional committees, with the key Organization Department controlling not just the party but also appointments within the civil service. In 1931 all other political parties were banned and formal one-party rule established. In practice, almost from the beginning, the military were the basis for Kuomintang rule and party control of the military through commissars was abolished in 1927. The party remained relatively small – fewer than 300,000 members in 1930 – and less than half of China's provinces even had a party committee. Much of the Kuomintang's influence was exercised through a confederation of regional military regimes which accepted varying degrees of central control. The extension of direct Kuomintang control in the early 1930s was largely the result of an extension of military, not party control. In the long guerrilla war with the Communists, extensive 'Bandit Suppression Zones' were declared in which authority was handed over to the National Military Council. This in turn rapidly developed its own administrative network, exercising power over both the state and party. By the mid-1930s most provinces were ruled by the military command based at Chunking rather than the party apparatus, which was centred on Nanking.

As head of the Kuomintang military Chiang Kai-shek became the predominant influence in the government. At first he shared power with Hu Han-min, the head of the legislature, and for a time in 1931 Wang Ching-wei. However, as chairman of the National Military Council, his position was crucial and China drifted towards military dictatorship. Chiang was also able to develop a network within the key Organization Committee which supported him. In 1932 he founded (though he always denied this in public) the 'Blue Shirts' (technically the 'Restoration Society'), a quasi-fascist elite of some 10,000 men fanatically loyal to Chiang himself. By 1935 Chiang's domination was finally recognized when he became head of government as well as head of the Military Committee. However, any chance the Kuomintang under Chiang Kai-shek might have had of constructing a modernized China (and there were few signs of progress along this path in the early 1930s) ended with the Japanese attack in mid-1937. The Kuomintang lost control of much of the country, especially the richest cities, and the Communist guerrillas in Yunan became increasingly powerful. The pressure of the

Japanese invasion and attempted Chinese mobilization proved too great for the fragile Kuomintang government. By 1945 they were too weak to resist the Communists; they were defeated in the civil war and fled to Taiwan in 1949. Here they ruled using the same government structure of military domination combined with a nationalist party structured along Leninist lines.

The newly independent states created after the Second World War faced many of the same problems as Turkey and China. There was a clear need, accepted by the small political elite which took power on independence, for national regeneration, economic growth and 'modernization'. The problem was that, as states of the periphery, they had to start from a highly subordinate position within the world economy. Change also had to be achieved in circumstances where colonial rule or, as for example in Iran and Thailand, strong external influence, had produced weak political structures with little sense of an inherited political culture and legitimacy. The democratic structures of the core states depended on strong civic structures, so it was hardly surprising that democratic systems imposed by the imperial powers, often at the last moment and with no developed social, economic and political infrastructure, were ill-adapted to cope with all these problems. The new states fairly rapidly became one-party states with strong leaders, military dictatorships or combinations of the two. In most cases power was held initially by the leaders of the struggle for independence, but only a few of them survived for long. Many of these leaders tried to develop their own 'philosophies' to define and explain what they were trying to achieve, but they were usually ill thought out and little more than justifications for one-man or one-party rule.

Burma and Indonesia were two of the first new independent states. In Burma the Anti-Fascist People's Freedom League, which led the struggle for independence, was able to win elections through lack of opposition and manipulation. However, in 1958 a split in the party led to a coup by head of the army, General Ne Win, who installed himself as prime minister. Four years later there was a full coup: the 1947 constitution was abrogated, parliament was dissolved and a military junta headed by Ne Win and sixteen officers took over all legislative and government functions. The military established a one-party state, but developed what they argued was a distinctive philosophy for Burma. In 1963 they published *The System of Correlation of Man and His Environment: The Philosophy of the Burma Socialist Programme Party*. Military rule was seen as transitional to eventual rule by the BSPP. The military adopted state control of industry and agricultural marketing (but not collectivization or land reform) together with self-sufficiency and import substitution. The BSPP was an elitist vanguard party, in 1966 it had just twenty full members, nearly all of them military. In 1972, when the military decided it was to become a 'people's party', it had 73,000 members, half of whom were from the military. Between 1972 and 1974 all Burma's leaders theoretically resigned from the army and the government became 'civilian'. In practice by the early 1980s the entire government was made up of retired officers and Ne Win still commanded the loyalty of the army because of his personal power. The system collapsed in the late 1980s under economic strain and after Ne Win's retirement. In September 1988 the military staged a coup and established the State Law and Order Restoration Council, which was separate from the BSPP. The coup was proclaimed as a move towards democracy and away from the one-party state of the BSPP, but the military leaders refused to accept the results of the 1990 elections and instead adopted straightforward, non-ideological military rule.

In Indonesia the independence leader Achmed Sukarno directed what was described as a 'guided democracy'. This was based on the 'Pancasila' – the Five Principles of nationalism, internationalism, consultative democracy, social justice and belief in one God – formulated by Sukarno in 1942 and incorporated into the first constitution. Sukarno ruled in collaboration with the army and the Indonesian Communist Party. The post-independence system survived slightly longer than in Burma – until an army coup in March 1966 led by General Suharto. Even before the coup the army had developed the concept of *dwifungsi* or 'dual mandate', under which the army was both a military force and a social and political force. The army also established what, after 1966, became the state party, the Golkar. All civil servants and their families were forced to campaign for Golkar and in the early 1980s all village headmen were designated civil servants. After 1971 the opposition was forced to merge into two parties, the Muslim PPP and the nationalist PPI. Neither received any state funding, unlike Golkar, and the government had power to disbar any of their candidates. In practice the PPP and the PPI developed into minority wings of Golkar. The military were able to keep control in a less open manner than in Burma. About 100 seats in the National Assembly were reserved for the military and they controlled Golkar through a series of supervisory committees. The military also developed a unique *karyawan* or 'civic mission' system under which some 16,000 officers held civilian posts in the government but reported to the military command not the civilian hierarchy. The system remained stable but authoritarian and repressive for more than thirty years, with an unusual degree of merging between civilian and military rule.

One-party rule followed a roughly similar evolution in Egypt, with a complex intertwining of military and civilian. In July 1952 a coup by the Society of Free Officers overthrew the corrupt and decadent monarchy and the 'parliamentary system'. Military rule through a Revolutionary Command Council was imposed and within a couple of years Colonel Nasser emerged as leader. His prestige was greatly increased by the successful nationalization of the Suez Canal and failure of the Anglo-French invasion in 1956. In 1953 Nasser published *The Philosophy of the Revolution*, arguing that the military must initially rule and then have a vanguard role. After at first promoting Arab nationalism, Nasser decided in 1961 to concentrate on Arab socialism. He argued that this form of socialism was both 'scientific' and 'humane', unlike Communism and capitalism, and in conformity with a deep Arab tradition. In reaching these aims Egypt was unusual in having two successive regime parties. In 1952 the military banned all political parties, but in 1957 set up the National Union (NU). All adults were regarded as members, although there was an elite of active members who had to pass special tests. The NU was organized both territorially, with the lowest rung in every village, and by occupation. Nasser appointed himself as head of the NU and then selected the remaining leaders. It achieved very little and in 1961 Nasser decided it should be replaced by the Arab Socialist Union (ASU). As with the NU, all adults could join (by 1964 about one in five had done so) but only one in fifty were allowed to become 'active' members. In addition there was a super elite of fewer than 20,000 at the top of the party. The ASU lacked a governing role – its main activity was choosing candidates for the one candidate elections to all 'representative' bodies in Egypt. The ASU was dominated by the military: they provided the majority of the ASU Supreme Executive Committee and controlled the key ministries, provincial governorships and the top of the civil service. After Nasser's death in 1970 the system drifted into one-party bureaucratic, authoritarian rule, under which the military were simply one of the key elements in the state structure.

In Africa nearly all the initial rulers under independence were civilians (the military were generally very weak in the immediate post-colonial period) but few survived for long. One of the most influential of the early leaders was Kwame Nkrumah, the first head of a newly independent black African state – Ghana. Nkrumah developed his own philosophy called 'Consciencism', which was a mixture of Christianity, Marxism, Socialism, Anti-Imperialism and Pan-Africanism. It was set out in his book *Africa Must Unite*, published in 1963, and was intended to be developed by the Kwame Nkrumah Institute of Ideology, which was established in the following year. Ghana was a one-party state after 1958, although this was only formalized in 1964. The Convention People's Party (CPP), founded by Nkrumah in 1949, created a series of supplementary organizations – the National Council of Ghana Women, the Young Pioneers, the United Ghana Farmers Council – and a massive bureaucracy, in which party regional leaders became the effective local government. Nkrumah also established his own military unit, the President's Own Guard Regiment, as part of a National Security Service established in 1963 and separate from the army. In practice the CPP did not control the state apparatus – the civil service remained independent and Nkrumah's attempt to politicize the army was one of the major factors that led to the coup against him in 1966. For most of the rest of the century Ghana was ruled by a succession of military regimes.

One of the longest lived of the post-independence regimes was in Guinea under Sekou Touré. After independence in 1958 Guinea became an ideological one-party state which was much more repressive than Ghana. By 1970 Sekou Touré had produced seventeen volumes of his ideology, although they were formally described as the works of the party he founded in 1947, the Parti Democratique de Guinée (PDG). Sekou Touré advocated a 'national democracy' which in practice was little different from the 'people's democracies' of eastern Europe. The PDG was 'the definer of the general interest, the custodian of the popular will, and the incarnation of the collective thought of the whole Guinean people'. Formally Guinea was not a one-party state, although in practice opposition was not allowed. Those individuals who were thought to oppose the regime became either political prisoners or were killed after show trials. In 1962 membership of the PDG became automatic for all tax-payers because subscriptions were collected by the tax authorities. The PDG formally adopted 'democratic centralism', and the regional party organization was kept under strict control (unlike many other African states). Policy-making took place in the Politburo not the cabinet, the colonial trained army was disbanded and a 'popular' army, with elected party committees and commissars established. Most of the old military leadership were killed after a failed coup in 1970 and the party militia was expanded to over 300,000 compared with an army of just 13,000. In 1964 Sekou Touré decided to embrace 'socialism' and established a state monopoly over foreign trade and commerce. Industrialization was to be achieved through state-owned enterprises, except in the lucrative bauxite industry, where foreign investment was required and allowed. There was a 'cultural revolution' in 1967 (a poor relation of the one in China), but agriculture was not collectivized. By the late 1960s Sekou Touré was the 'Supreme Leader of the Revolution', the 'Father of Guinea' and the 'Terror of International Imperialism, of Colonialism and Neo-Colonialism'. It was a personality cult unrivalled even in Africa. By the late 1970s it was obvious that 'socialism' was not working and the level of discontent was increasingly difficult to suppress. Sekou Touré therefore suddenly shifted to a new policy of embracing the capitalist world and supporting Islam rather than persecuting it. Government degenerated into personal and family rule, very similar to a *caudillo*-type regime before its final collapse in 1984.

In general the Communist states of the semi-periphery and periphery avoided military coups and maintained party control of the armed forces. The partial exception was Cuba under Fidel Castro. However, in many respects this was not a Communist regime. Castro took power in January 1959 from the corrupt regime of President Batista after a long guerrilla war. He seemed a typical *caudillo* and became head of the armed forces and prime minister. However, the rhetoric of the new regime, combined with its programme of land reform and state intervention, led the United States to see him as a dangerous radical. A deterioration in relations, followed by a botched American attempt to launch a counter-revolution using Cuban exiles at the Bay of Pigs landings in April 1961, saw Castro drift towards the Soviet Union. It was one of the few powers prepared to offer him support. In December 1961 Castro declared himself to be a Marxist-Leninist. The first regime party – the ORI – was dissolved in 1962 and replaced by the United Party of the Socialist Revolution, which was itself replaced in 1965 by the Communist Party of Cuba. Castro developed his own ideological variant, Fidelismo, in which socialism and Communism were developed in parallel rather than consecutively as in traditional Marxism. In addition, based on Latin American experience, the role of guerrillas in bringing about the revolution was emphasized. However, the Cuban government was much closer to the normal one-party state of the periphery rather than a Communist state. Castro was commander-in-chief, president and leader of the party and his brother Raul was Minister of Defence. The Communist Party was kept small until the mid-1970s (its first Congress did not take place until 1975), commissars were not allowed in the army and the key group in the government remained the members of the original guerrilla band that took power in 1959. A very strong level of support for Castro remained and he retained power in the 1990s, even as the nominally Communist system was slowly dismantled.

The only unambiguous case of the military taking power in a Communist state was in Poland in the 1980s, when an incompetent and corrupt party elite produced economic and social stagnation combined with rising opposition. The party leader, Edward Gierek, was removed from office in 1980 and this allowed the rise of a highly popular grassroots workers' and intellectuals' movement – Solidarity. It had a major impact within the party. At the Party Congress in July 1981 there was a revolt by the delegates and only a small fraction of the Politburo and Central Committee was re-elected – an unheard-of event in Communist states. The conservative wing of the party, General Jaruzelski (Defence Minister since 1968) and the Soviet Union were alarmed at the direction events were taking. In February 1981 Jaruzelski became prime minister. In October 1981, after the party leader Kania refused to use force against Solidarity, Jaruzelski became party leader too. On 13 December 1981 martial law was declared and Solidarity suppressed. Jaruzelski claimed that 'the Polish soldier-patriot has been compelled to act to save the nation from fratricidal conflict'. It was the same claim that the military regularly made in other states to justify their political interventions. Poland had, like so many other countries, succumbed to a military coup. A Military Council of National Salvation (WRON) composed of the twenty senior military commanders took formal power and a National Defence Committee chaired by Jaruzelski became the effective government. The military took over as provincial governors, all employees in major factories were placed under military discipline and could therefore be tried in military courts for disobeying instructions. The

Communist Party was left with an advisory role on policy. In 1983 both martial law and the formal role of the junta ended, but Jaruzelski still held all the key posts – prime minister, head of the party, head of the National Defence Committee, Minister of Defence and de facto head of the army. Military officers also held other key posts such as the Interior ministry.

By the end of the twentieth century the majority of states in the world were either under military rule, personal dictatorships, or one-party governments. Excluding the former and remaining Communist states, over forty countries, most of them in Africa, had military rulers, twenty-two (such as Turkey, Thailand, South Korea, Taiwan, the Philippines and Indonesia) had militarized party systems, in which the military retained a central, defining role. Just under thirty were one-party states and in many this situation was formalized in the constitution. The overwhelming majority of the world's people had no say in how they were governed.

16 REVOLUTION

THROUGHOUT THE twentieth century every society in the world was characterized by massive inequality. In the states of the periphery and the semi-periphery, there were huge differences in income and wealth between the elite and the mass of peasants and labourers. Even in the core states, where there was a major rise in living standards for all citizens over the course of the century, significant poverty and large-scale inequality remained. During the second half of the nineteenth century many people, not just Marxists, socialists and revolutionaries, believed that the long-term survival of such glaringly unequal societies was doubtful. They thought that the disadvantaged and the poor would inevitably revolt against such degradation and try to create a new society with a more egalitarian social, economic and political structure. One of the strangest phenomena of the twentieth century was the lack of revolution, the survival of traditional structures and the acceptance of inequality.

During the twentieth century none of the core states experienced social and economic revolution. There were a number of reasons for this. First, industrial workers, who in theory should have been the most radical group because of the scale on which they were exploited, never constituted a majority in any society. Second, such workers were divided among themselves; in particular there were very strong differences of interest, between the skilled and unskilled. In addition, many industrial communities were introverted and isolated from each other. Third, most workers were mainly interested in specific improvements to their living and working conditions. In the core states such improvements were achieved, partly through trade union pressure. The governments of the core states also slowly constructed welfare systems of pensions, insurance and healthcare which not only improved the conditions of the workers but also gave them a stake, even though very small, in the continuation of the existing society. Dreams of international solidarity faded in August 1914 when the workers in each of the European core states demonstrated that they placed nationalism above any generalized working-class unity.

The most significant examples of the revolution that did not happen came in Germany and Austria in 1918–19. Both were highly developed industrialized countries with a large working class and were exactly the kind of state in which Marx predicted revolution would occur. Both also suffered catastrophic military defeat and political failure in the autumn of 1918. As Allied armies moved north through the Balkans, the Austro-Hungarian empire collapsed and effectively ceased to exist on 21 October, when the German-speaking area decided to form its own Austrian state and the remainder of the empire seceded. In the same month the resignation of the military leadership marked the stage at which the old German order tried to wash its hands of responsibility for national defeat. On 9 November a new social democratic government took control in Berlin to agree the armistice terms. In both countries mutiny in the armed forces and the formation of workers' and soldiers' councils seemed to mark the onset of social revolution. In practice most of the existing social, economic and political structure survived. In both countries the strong social democratic movements which had been built up in the decades before 1914 were able to maintain internal discipline and keep control of any tendency towards a revolutionary solution.

In Germany, where the Social Democrats had split in 1917 giving rise to the small left-wing and semi-revolutionary Independent Social Democratic Party, the leaders of the breakaway group realized their limited influence and the likely catastrophic consequences of any attempt to seize power. From the beginning the new social democratic chancellor, Friedrich Ebert, co-operated with the army authorities. This was essential if Germany was to meet the armistice condition that the army be withdrawn to German territory within a few weeks. However, it also provided some support for the new regime during a difficult transitional period. The workers' and soldiers' councils were kept in moderate SPD hands (except briefly in Munich) and at their first national congress in December 1918 they maintained the long-standing party commitment to liberal democracy by deciding in favour of immediate elections for a National Assembly which would draft a new constitution. This was a crucial step. It signified acceptance of the possibility that the bourgeois parties might either obtain a majority in the elections or, as a minimum, the SPD would be forced to work with them, as was the case when the Weimar constitution was drafted. In Germany the old imperial institutions – the army, the civil service and the judiciary – survived the 1918–19 transition almost intact. The limited threat of social revolution was easily contained through the moderation and discipline of the strong social democratic movement. The strength of the conservative forces was demonstrated in the early 1930s when the resurgent right wing, which had never accepted defeat and the post-imperial system, overthrew the Weimar Republic.

Revolution in the twentieth century, when it did occur, was a phenomenon not of the core states but of the primarily peasant societies of the semi-periphery and periphery (in contradiction to Marx's theories). It did not happen as a result of deep-seated social and economic forces; still less as a consequence of the political activities and agitation of the very small revolutionary movements which existed in most countries. The most important factor was the crumbling of existing political structures, following defeat in war, external intervention or civil war. In these circumstances it was possible for radical groups to take advantage of a chaotic situation, gain power, gradually consolidate their position and then begin the construction of a new state. The three key revolutions of the twentieth century occurred in Mexico (1911–20), Russia (1917–21) and China (1935–49), although in every case it took much longer to work out the full consequences of the revolution. (The imposition of Communist rule in the states of the semi-periphery in eastern and central Europe in the late 1940s was the result of occupation by Soviet forces and not the consequence of genuine revolution.) At the time of their revolutions all three countries were primarily agrarian states with fragile links between state power, the landed class and the mass of peasants. All three had a dominant landed class combined with limited commercial and industrial development, based on considerable external investment.

Of the three revolutions Mexico's was by far the least radical. However, it did produce genuine social change and a highly stable demilitarized political system which was able to achieve at least as much in terms of economic development as the roughly comparable states of Turkey, Egypt and Iran. The importance of the Russian Revolution was less the economic transformation that it created (over the course of the century the Russian economy grew more slowly than those of similar countries of the semi-periphery, such as Portugal, which experienced no social revolution) than in the fact that a genuinely revolutionary movement gained power. This could be seen as either a glowing example of the changes that were possible in society or as a dire warning of the catastrophic consequences of any major departure from established social and economic norms. The revolution in China was important because it unified the largest country in the world and was the first in an Asian state.

There were also, of course, important differences between the revolutions. In Mexico a largely ex-Spanish ruling elite was isolated from the majority native and *mestizo* majority. Russia, though a country of the semi-periphery, was attempting to compete in the power politics of the European core states and maintain a colonial empire in Asia. The result was a significant additional burden for a relatively weak state. Disintegration in China had reached a more advanced stage than in Mexico and Russia following the economic and political demands imposed by the western powers in the nineteenth century. This was compounded by the failure of the 1911 Revolution against the imperial system and the political and military collapse of the 1920s. In Mexico and China revolution was essentially a provincial phenomenon: in both cases the central political structures were weak and provincial movements fought to gain control of the country. Although in Russia important trans-formations did take place in the provinces, the course of the revolution was determined far more by events in the capital. The Bolsheviks were able to seize control through a coup in Petrograd (St Petersburg), using a small group of loyal forces against a dramatically weakened government. Only then did they gradually extend their control throughout the country. In Russia the relatively small working class in the cities was important, whereas in Mexico and China this was not the case. In Russia and China there were also relatively strong, ideological revolutionary movements. This was not the case in Mexico, to some extent because the revolution started long before 1917 and was effectively completed by 1920. It was not therefore influenced by the success of the Bolsheviks in Europe. Elsewhere revolutionaries always had the example of the Russian Revolution to follow.

It is possible to analyse the revolutions in Mexico, Russia and China by comparing them in a series of phases: first, the disintegration of well-established political systems; second, the conflict between rival political groups to obtain power; third, civil war and the victory of one of these groups through military conquest; fourth, the consolidation of a new regime and the arguments within the new revolutionary government over 'the fate of the revolution'; finally, the construction of a new, essentially 'conservative', political structure capable of enduring for some decades. Although the stages were broadly similar, the outcomes were very different and reflected the different revolutionary groups involved.

In the 1900s Mexico was ruled by Porfirio Diaz, a military leader in the war against the French in the 1860s who had been in power almost continuously since 1877. Under the Porfiriato, Mexico was a typical country of the semi-periphery. Fairly rapid economic expansion was built upon foreign investment in railway construction and raw material production for export (first minerals and then oil). Manufacturing for the local market was restricted mainly to textiles. No political parties were allowed and the regime was based on an alliance of large landowners and the wealthy elite who made their money mainly by acting as agents for foreign investors. The group excluded from this system was the peasants, the overwhelming majority of the population. Under the Porfiriato there was, with government support, a massive expropriation of communal land by landowners to form huge estates (*haciendas*) to grow crops for export. Local politics was dominated by the landowners and the new railways enabled the government to move the army around to suppress peasant discontent. By 1910 nine out of ten peasants were landless and forced to work on *haciendas*. The resident workers, who were often forbidden to set foot outside the *hacienda*, were usually relatively docile and under tight control. As real wages fell elsewhere, the fact that they received food and accommodation from the *hacienda* left them in a relatively better economic position than some other peasants. Landless labourers, usually only employed for part of the year, were the fastest growing group. The third group, sharecroppers and *peóns* were in decline, except in the south, but the conditions for these peasants were brutal in the extreme. On average, peasant debts were three times annual wages, the debts were inheritable and peasants could be sold by landowners to settle their own debts. In effect, especially in the south, large numbers of peasants lived in conditions of slavery.

The 1900s saw a growing crisis and the eventual collapse of the Porfiriato. There was a huge flood of foreign investment (three times as much as in the previous twenty-five years), which resulted in a steep rise in inflation. The adoption of the Gold Standard, the effects of the 1907–8 depression in Britain and the United States, growing unemployment, the return of migrant workers from the United States together with a massive fall in real wages, all produced a major economic crisis. The government tried to protect the position of its elite supporters by increasing taxes on the middle class and the peasants. By the end of the decade there was a peasant revolt in Morelos state. That was nothing unusual, but the key problem for the elite was the succession to the ailing President Porfirio Diaz. By 1907 many in the northern states of Sonora, Chihuahua and Coahuila were turning against the president. The head of a wealthy land-owning family in Coahuila, Francesco Madero, founded the Anti-Re-electionist party to oppose Diaz in the 1910 elections. The United States was lukewarm in its support for Diaz because he was judged to be too close to British interests in Mexico, in particular the oil company run by Sir Weetman Pearson (later Lord Cowdray).

In June 1910 Madero was arrested just a fortnight before Diaz was declared the winner of the election after massive fraud. Madero escaped to the United States and called for a revolt. The call was ignored in his home state in Coahuila, but a popular revolt, led by Pancho Villa, erupted in Chihuahua. By early 1911 Madero was back in Mexico as the uprising spread across the country. In May Diaz and Madero made a deal aimed at containing the revolts before there were major social and economic changes. Diaz resigned and in interim presidential elections held in October Madero was elected. He had already authorized the army to suppress the peasant rebellion in Morelos under Emiliano Zapata. Madero and his 'liberal' supporters believed that the revolution was now over, after the emergence of their new regime with its promise of a new constitution and a package of limited reforms. They were to be disappointed, Mexico was about to enter a nine-year phase of acute internal conflict.

The economic position of Russia in the early twentieth century was remarkably similar to that of Mexico. State-directed rapid economic growth was built around the export of agricultural products (in particular wheat) and high levels of foreign investment in railways and industry – all the Russian oil industry was foreign owned. This too created strains within society, not just for the peasants but also for the growing, though still relatively small working class employed in the large factories found in some of the major cities. In 1861 the peasants were formally emancipated from serfdom (roughly equivalent to *peónage* in Mexico) but they were still tied to their local communities. They had to make forty-nine years of redemption payments to their landlords as compensation for the end of serfdom and most land was still held and distributed by the *obschina* or village commune. Not until 1907 did the government change its policy of trying to shore up the village commune and shift to a policy of helping the break-up of communal land into individual holdings. By 1917 about half of all the peasants (twice the proportion ten years earlier) owned their own land.

The political situation in Russia was very different from Mexico. After the assassination of Tsar Alexander II in 1881 the long tradition of imperial autocracy had been reasserted. The problem was that an increasingly sophisticated civil society, partly produced by economic development, was denied any civil rights or any meaningful political participation apart from the almost powerless local councils, the *zemstvos*. The problems were made worse by the government's determination to act as a major power, both in Europe and Asia. It was the humiliating defeat by Japan in the war of 1904–5 (the first inflicted on a European country by an Asian state) that brought about revolution. In November 1904 a national *zemstvo* congress demanded civil liberties, legal equality between citizens and a legislative assembly – the standard nineteenth-century liberal demands made across Europe – which would produce a constitutional monarchy. In early January 1905 troops fired on a massive demonstration outside the Winter Palace in St Petersburg. From then on the situation rapidly slipped out of the government's control. As its power weakened, a widespread peasant revolt developed in the Ukraine and Volga areas, where exploitation was at its greatest. Elsewhere there was a wave of strikes and the railways were paralysed. In mid-October 1905 the tsar agreed to the demands for civil liberties and legislative powers for a Duma (parliament) to be elected on a wide franchise. This acceptance of liberal demands was tactically adroit and split the opposition. The liberals (the Kadet Party and the less radical Octobrists) reluctantly accepted the deal, leaving the more radical workers and peasants isolated. Between October and December 1905 there was a rash of mutinies, strikes and peasant disturbances. In St Petersburg the central strike committee became a Soviet with quasi-governmental functions and controlled a militia. However, as the army slowly returned from Asia after the end of the war the government had more power to put down strikes and revolts. In November the St Petersburg Soviet called a general strike which was not fully effective; at the beginning of December the members of the Soviet were arrested and an armed revolt in Moscow was suppressed.

The events of 1905 demonstrated how the strains of even a limited war could bring about near-revolution and that in such circumstances the government had few resources to control the situation. After 1905 the government embarked on a risky policy. The liberals found that the offer of October 1905 was not fully implemented: civil liberties remained restricted, the Duma was indirectly elected on a limited franchise of class and property groups, its powers were minimal and government ministers remained responsible only to the tsar. It is possible that had this system been given time to operate it might have evolved into something close to the contemporaneous quasi-democratic system in Germany. In practice the ingrained assumptions of the elite around the tsar gave the system little chance. The Duma met in April 1906 but was dissolved within two months when the government refused to accept its proposals for major reform. The government then embarked on a programme of limited economic and social reform combined with political repression. In some ways it was probably the only option open to the tsar. An agreement with the liberals would destroy his own power without providing a very firm basis for future government, and a return to complete autocracy (as before 1861) was impossible. Although much has been made of the personal failings of the tsar and his entourage, these had only a marginal effect. After 1906 it was increasingly apparent that Russia had a deadlocked political system which was drifting towards destruction.

To some extent this situation was not very different from the last years of the Porfiriato in Mexico. The significant difference was the development of an ideological revolutionary movement in Russia (and among Russian exiles) based partly upon the emerging intelligentsia. The tsarist system relied upon the small, university-educated elite to run the government and society. However, particularly from the 1860s, many in the intellectual elite became dissatisfied with the all too obvious political, social and economic backwardness of Russia. An increase in the number of graduates and restrictions on the opportunities open to them because of the limits imposed on civil society in Russia, led many into open intellectual and political dissent. A number of groups emerged. Some supported the 'Populist' ideology of Alexander Herzen, which rejected much of the western European road to modernization and idealized the peasant commune. This, they argued, was a primitive form of socialism which would enable Russia to move directly to full socialism and avoid capitalism. Marxism first became important among the Russian intelligentsia in the 1880s. Early adherents like Plekhanov were clear that the country would, as Marx's theory insisted, have to become fully capitalist before it could move to socialism. In 1903 the Social Democratic Party was refounded in Brussels and London but immediately split between the majority (Bolsheviks) and the minority (Mensheviks) over the terms for membership in the party. However, this dispute reflected a deeper split between the Bolsheviks under Lenin, who argued for an elite of highly disciplined activists dedicated to the revolution and the Mensheviks under Martov, who rejected these ideas as institutionalizing a gap between the party and the workers. Co-operation between the two groups continued for some time, but by 1912 the Bolsheviks (who were in fact a minority not a majority) were a fully independent party with their own central committee. Both these Marxist parties began to draw significant support from the workers in Russian cities. Until 1905 most of the local committees and activists came from the intelligentsia, but afterwards the workers became increasingly important. At the 1912 Bolshevik conference in Prague two-thirds of the delegates were workers, although, as with most political parties, the leadership was dominated by the intelligentsia. Despite this growth in support, few people in 1914 would have expected either the Bolsheviks or the Mensheviks to gain power. Indeed, as late as January 1917 Lenin told students in Switzerland, where he was living in exile, that his generation would probably not live to see the revolution.

What changed this situation was Russian collapse in the war against the Central Powers – a reflection of the underlying weaknesses which had already been demonstrated in the war against Japan. Major defeats in the autumn of 1916, combined with growing economic dislocation and repression at home, produced a crisis in St Petersburg even as Lenin was talking to the Swiss students. Demonstrations brought on by fear of bread rationing led, as in 1905, to strikes and the formation of a Menshevik-led Soviet. Within a week the military leadership, fearing that the troops would not act to repress the workers, recommended abdication to the tsar. In an incredibly short period and with little resistance the centuries-long autocracy crumbled. It was replaced, in agreement with the St

Petersburg Soviet, by a Provisional Government under Prince Lvov containing just one socialist member.

After February 1917 the revolutionary situation in Russia was similar to that in Mexico after Madero took power as president. Both revolutions were at the end of their first phase. The questions that now had to be answered were whether a viable government could establish itself in a situation in which the existing state structure was already very weak and, if it did collapse, which political group would take power. In Mexico the split among the elite in 1910–11 allowed peasant revolts, which had often occurred in the past, to spread and become deeply entrenched. The revolt began in the north in 1910, but the centre of the movement was in Morelos state under the leadership of Zapata (who was not a *peón* himself). It was a parochial revolt hardly linked to the wider national conflict. Much of this revolt was about what the peasants saw as 'moral' issues: the loss of land held immemorially by the community, the imposition of commercial agriculture and the harsh discipline and exploitation which accompanied it. From early 1911 *hacienda* lands were taken over and landlords and their agents attacked. In November 1911, with the help of a local schoolmaster Otilio Montano, Zapata drew up the Plan of Ayala to encapsulate peasant demands against Madero, whom he regarded as having sold out the revolution. The peasant demands were moderate: land illegally usurped by the *haciendas* was to be restored to the peasants and a third of the *haciendas* were to be expropriated (with full compensation) to provide land for the landless peasants. The peasants were not demanding a total restructuring of rural society, only a restoration of what they believed was rightfully theirs. By the end of 1911 the Zapatistas controlled all of Morelos apart from the large towns, and in early 1912 they extended their control south into Puebla.

Elsewhere in Mexico the growing revolt had very different origins. In Sonora, which was dominated by mining and commercial interests, it was essentially political. In Sinaloa state there was also a revolt by the Yaqui Indians and other marginal groups. The revolt in the north, led by men like Pancho Villa, was an attack on local political bosses but did not have such deep social roots as in Morelos – Pancho Villa was little more than an old-style *caudillo*. In Mexico City President Madero, attached as he was to old-style liberalism, favoured small landowners and peasants but developed no policy to help them. In general the Madero government lacked power and gradually lost control of the country. The revolts in the north and in

Vera Cruz, were partially suppressed by the army under General Victoriano Huerta. His success led to his coup in February 1913, during which Madero was murdered. It was this coup which led to civil war.

In Russia the February 1917 Revolution led to a rapid breakdown in government. The liberals, in conjunction with the Soviet, held power in St Petersburg. Across the country as the old autocracy collapsed the absence of strong local institutions led to the seizure of power by local Soviets reflecting the interests of soldiers, workers and peasants. At first the Provisional Government seemed reasonably popular, especially after early May when the moderate socialists and the Mensheviks joined the coalition. However, the government was dominated by the Kadet Party, which was highly moderate and attached to Russia's great power status and the maintenance of the Russian empire. A largely peasant army wanted peace and land, but the government decided to stay in the war and postpone the question of land reform until after a Constituent Assembly met to write a new constitution. At the same time it was reluctant to call elections for the assembly, fearing that they would be won by radical groups. Inevitably the peasants took control of events, seized estates and divided them up. Unlike 1905, the government lacked an army to suppress them. Although it is difficult to see on what terms the government could have obtained a separate peace with Germany, the decision to launch an offensive in June 1917 was disastrous. The army was in a poor state and reluctant, like the French army earlier in the year, to do more than oppose any German attacks. The failure of the offensive weakened the Provisional Government seriously. The socialists and Mensheviks in the government were caught in a difficult situation. They believed they had an opportunity to push towards a radical solution. The conservative Kadets blocked these efforts, but the socialists were reluctant to oppose them for fear of provoking a counter-revolutionary coup by conservative elements in the army. By the late summer of 1917 the provisional government was at an impasse, unable to agree on policy. It also lacked the power to implement one even if agreement had been possible.

As initiative and power slipped away from the government, the demands of the peasants, workers and soldiers became more important. They were not manipulated by a small revolutionary clique of Bolsheviks trying to seize power, but were rather articulating long-held and coherent demands. The peasant demand for land had been apparent for decades, if not longer. The workers were not a simple, unified mass but had strongly differing objectives. The skilled workers were, from the beginning, the most radical in calling for a government based on the Soviets. Their aim at first was simply to eradicate some of the worst aspects of the existing industrial system and secure wage increases. However, as the economy became increasingly dislocated they began to argue for control of the factories simply as a way of keeping a job. The soldiers supported land reform because they were nearly all peasants. They also had two other demands. The first, for a more humane system in the army, was reflected in Order Number One, issued by the Petrograd Soviet which gave soldiers' councils effective disciplinary control. Second, they wanted an end to the war. Increasingly during the summer of 1917 the soldiers and workers, and to a lesser extent the peasants, began to believe that a replacement of the Provisional Government was the only way in which they were going to achieve their aims. By October 1917, of the 670 delegates to the Second All-Russian Congress of Soviets, over 500 supported the transfer of all power to the Soviets.

It was in these circumstances that the Bolsheviks were able to increase their support. Party membership rose from about 10,000 in February to over 200,000 in October. Most of the new members were workers, with a substantial minority of soldiers and peasants. Many were ex-Mensheviks or Social Revolutionaries. As new members flooded in and new party groups were founded, the central organization had little control over, or even knowledge about, who joined and what their beliefs might be. In 1917 the Bolsheviks were very far from Lenin's idea of a small, tightly knit group of dedicated revolutionaries. There was considerable openness within the party, internal discipline was limited and its strength came from its ability to respond to demands arising from within society. Many of its policy changes, for example its opposition to the Provisional Government after April, came in response to pressures from below not from Lenin's direction. In some cases the party refused to carry out Lenin's demands, as for example in rejecting the severance of links with the Mensheviks after April and in rejecting a military coup in July.

Lenin's own views in the summer of 1917, as set out in his book *State and Revolution* and in numerous articles, were optimistic. He believed, contrary to the views he expressed in February, that European revolution was now near and that Russia could be an inspiration to the socialists in the west. Russia would be the prologue to a world revolution and socialism would arrive in Russia after this had been achieved. Meanwhile there would be a decentralized and direct democracy, along the lines of the Paris Commune of 1871, which was the only example of a revolutionary state so far. The Bolsheviks would provide ideological leadership but not a strong governmental role. The Soviets with their combined legislative and executive functions would do away with the distinction between governors and the governed. A people's militia would replace the army. There would be wide powers of autonomy for workers, who would control the factories within a framework of government planning. This was clearly a utopian vision, but it lasted until early 1918 when the Bolshevik government had to face the problems brought about by the revolution.

The general aspirations of the soldiers, peasants and workers, together with the Bolsheviks' ability to respond to them were crucial to the seizure of power in October 1917. By the autumn Bolshevik control of local Soviets was growing, especially around Moscow and in the Urals region, in the army on the western front and in the Baltic fleet. The Bolsheviks argued about what to do. Lenin did not have overwhelming support within the Central Committee for a coup. When Zinoviev and Kamenev, who both opposed Lenin, made their arguments public the Committee refused to support Lenin in expelling them from the party. The party knew that support for a coup was limited even among radical groups such as the Red Guard in Petrograd. They therefore decided to operate through the Petrograd Soviet and the Military Revolutionary Committee, where they had a majority, and to act in the name of Soviet power. A handful of troops was enough to disperse the Provisional Government and the Bolsheviks took power. They were clearly a minority in the country, although a powerful one. Their lack of support was reflected in the elections to the Constituent Assembly, which Bolshevik troops dispersed as soon as it met. In the immediate aftermath of their coup the Bolsheviks had a fragile hold on power in St Petersburg, Moscow and in some other areas where they controlled the local Soviets. Whether they could maintain and expand their power would depend on a complex political and social situation as the Russian empire disintegrated and 'white' armies of the right fought both to sustain the empire and remove the Bolsheviks from power.

The result was a bitter four-year long civil war between a multitude of forces. The Bolshevik government was gradually able to build a 4-million-strong Red Army under the leadership of the ex-Menshevik Leon Trotsky out of the remains of the old imperial army. This was possible once they had agreed a compromise peace and signed the humiliating Treaty of Brest-Litovsk with Germany. The principal 'white' armies under Admiral Kolchak in Siberia and General Denikin in the south-west were ill-co-ordinated and unable to deliver a knock-out blow. They were weakened by their determination to restore tsarism and the landed estates, which alienated the peasants, and to restore the Russian empire, which meant they could not build alliances with the nationalist groups. These groups were powerful in every area from the Caucasus, through the Ukraine and Belorussia, to the Baltic states. In addition the main ex-Allied states – Britain, France, the United States and Japan – all intervened, sending troops and supplies to back the anti-Bolshevik forces. In the end, after numerous brutal campaigns and shifting fortunes, the Bolsheviks prevailed and established control over most of the territory of the old imperial Russian state.

The civil war in Mexico was even more prolonged, had as many contestants as in Russia and also its own outside intervention – by the United States. After September 1913 there was open civil war between General Huerta, the leader of the coup against President Madero, and the Governor of Coahuila, Venustiano Carranza, who declared himself leader of the 'constitutionalists', seeking to unite the pro-Madero forces and to restore order by elections. Until early 1914 Huerta controlled most of the country. Then a constitutionalist offensive using US-supplied arms, together with the seizure of Vera Cruz by the Americans, led to the capture of Mexico City in August, Huerta's flight into exile and what was hoped would be the end of the civil war. However, the constitutionalist forces split when Carranza reneged on an agreement to hold a 'convention' to decide the political future of the country. The civil war restarted but with different forces. The northern army under Pancho Villa (now backed by the United States) combined with the Zapatista peasant forces to capture Mexico City. In July 1915 the Carrancista forces, led by General Obregon, recaptured the capital and re-established a limited national government in which effective control remained with the army. The Constitutional Convention now met at Querétaro in November 1916. It consisted almost entirely of members of the old political elite and was dominated by the increasingly powerful war minister, General Obregon. It agreed on a new constitution for Mexico, which provided for a strong

president, state ownership of national resources, no religious
education, a redistribution of land, a guarantee of the right to strike
and the eight-hour day. In the political manoeuvring ahead of the
forthcoming 1920 election, Carranza, increasingly tied to
conservative groups, tried to impose his own candidate against his
two military rivals – Generals Obregon and Gonzales. His attempt
to arrest Obregon in early 1920 led to an open revolt by both
generals, which was supported by Villa and the Zapatistas. Carranza
was captured and killed, as was Zapata. The Obregon forces
triumphed and Gonzales was forced into exile. Obregon was
declared the overwhelming winner of the 1920 election. The election
unexpectedly marked the end of civil war and the emergence of a
new state after ten years of internal conflict.

The first two phases of revolution in China took place in the first
three decades of the century – the disintegration of the old imperial
state and the conflict between different groups to gain power. By the
early 1920s central government was conspicuous mainly by its
absence and two groups sought to gain control of the country. The
Kuomintang rapidly became a military government, a coalition of
regional leaders with some control from Chiang Kai-shek in the
centre. The Chinese Communist Party was founded in 1921 at a
meeting in Shanghai attended by just twelve delegates. It emerged
into a world where China was already disintegrating and on the
verge of civil war, where state power was very limited and where
the party could, unlike its counterpart in Russia before 1917,
immediately take advantage of the situation. In the early 1920s the
Kuomintang and the Communists were allies, both taking aid from
the Soviet Union. Although the Communists gained strength from
the nationalist May the Fourth Movement, they still had fewer than
a thousand members by the end of 1925 and only 58,000 early in
1927. At the end of March 1927 Kuomintang troops entered
Shanghai and three weeks later turned on the Communists in a
vicious purge which effectively eliminated them in urban areas. It
was at this stage that China became involved in a civil war similar to
those in Mexico from 1911 to 1920 and in Russia in the four years
after 1917.

The events of spring 1927 were a major disaster for the
Communists, who were ideologically orthodox in basing their
revolution upon the workers in the cities. The problem was that in
China this provided neither a sufficient level of support nor a
suitable base for operations. After 1927 some of the Communists

found themselves isolated in Kiangsi province, one of the most primitive parts of China. The party here was a collection of a few intellectuals and peasants, which was certainly not the base Marx had envisaged for the socialist revolution. (Marx called the peasants 'the class that represents barbarism within civilization'.) In 1927 one of the Communist leaders, Mao Tse-tung, visited his home province in Hunan and wrote a *Report of an Investigation into the Peasant Movement in Hunan*. It had an elegant simplicity, although ideologically it was absurd and it is unclear how much Marxism Mao really understood. (In 1942 Mao told party intellectuals that dogma was 'less useful than excrement'.) Mao's arguments may have been poor theory, but they were a good political strategy. He argued for a revolution based on the Chinese reality, which was also applicable to all societies in the periphery. Revolution, Mao argued, had to be agrarian. The main force would be the poor peasants and the party would support them and any 'excesses' they might carry out in ending a highly unjust system. Mao was disowned by the party and the Comintern in Moscow, which had little idea of what was going on in a remote mountain range in China. Moscow-trained Communists still controlled the Politburo in the early 1930s and Mao spent much of the period in disgrace.

Although isolated from the party, Mao was one of the few revolutionaries in China with a power base, however limited. In September 1927 he went back to Hunan and led what later became known as the 'Autumn Harvest Uprising'. It was no more than an attack on the city of Changsha by a small group of peasants and it failed after a few days. Mao was captured and only escaped death by buying his release. The next month he set up the first revolutionary peasant base in the mountains along the border between Hunan and Kiangsi. He was joined by about 10,000 men – the remnants of the Communists who had been defeated in the cities and a defecting Kuomintang army – most of the men were in rags and they had roughly one rifle for every five soldiers. For three years the main priority was survival. A land-redistribution scheme was started and the size of the army slowly increased to over 60,000. In November 1931 a Chinese Soviet Republic was formally created with Mao as president – it controlled a few areas in the middle and upper Yangtse valley. The party's base was, however, clear. When the second Congress of Soviets was held in January 1934 there were just eight urban workers out of 821 delegates. In the eighteen months after April 1933 the Soviet Republic was subjected to a series of increasingly effective Kuomintang offensives. In October 1934 Mao decided to retreat. He embarked upon what became the great symbolic moment in Chinese Communism, an event which established him as undisputed leader – the Long March. It was a year-long epic on a continental scale involving a march of over 10,000 kilometres along a convoluted route across China to the remote area of northern Shanshi province in the far north-west of the country. About 100,000 people started on the march, but fewer than 10,000 reached its destination.

Once the Communists had recovered from the Long March, their political position was transformed by the Japanese attack in mid-1937. Although Kuomintang popularity increased initially, the Communists joined a 'popular front' and took on the mantle of the nationalist struggle. In order to fight the Japanese the Communists mobilized the peasantry, introduced land reform and steadily increased their area of control. There was little the Kuomintang could do to stop them; they had lost most of their areas of support and had to devote their efforts to fighting both Japanese and the Communists. By 1945 the areas under Communist control included Shanshi, Hopei and Shantung with a population of nearly 100 million (ten years earlier they had controlled under a million people). In the four years after the end of the Second World War there was full-scale civil war in China. The Kuomintang regained control of the cities with US help and the Soviet Union ensured that the Communists took control of Manchuria. By July 1946 there was open fighting between the People's Liberation Army and the Kuomintang forces. For the first eighteen months the Kuomintang were reasonably successful, but in 1948 they suffered major defeats. In January 1949 Communist troops entered Peking and then expanded their control southwards. After the fall of Shanghai, the Kuomintang moved to Taiwan and the People's Republic of China was formally declared at the beginning of October 1949.

By 1920 in Mexico and the Soviet Union and by 1949 in China, new revolutionary regimes were in power. They faced the task of consolidating their power and deciding how to construct a new social, economic and political order. In the early 1920s the Mexican state, which was run by the victors in the civil war from the north-west of the country under General Obregon, was weak and its new rulers knew little about the rest of the country. Much of the old Porfirian system survived and the new Mexico was not the liberal democracy envisaged by Madero. The 1920s saw the gradual emergence of a strong semi-corporatist state based upon a new consensus incorporating previously excluded groups. The government supported CROM (Confederación Regional Obrera Mexicana) as representing the workers and made deals with the peasants, in particular a party led by one of Zapata's secretaries. A unifying feature was the new nationalism, in particular an emphasis on pre-Columbian culture, which attempted to identify with Mexico's native rather than its Spanish roots. There was also a major education programme which, for the first time, incorporated Indian communities and rapidly improved literacy rates. The new state education programme was just one aspect of the attack on the Catholic Church, which resulted in it rapidly becoming one of the main opponents of the new regime.

The construction of a new, stable political order took a considerable time. In 1923 Obregon nominated his minister of the interior, Plutarch Calles, who also came from the north-west, to succeed him. This produced a military revolt, in which all the leaders were shot and one of the last survivors of the civil war leadership, Pancho Villa, was murdered. Calles took office in 1924, but had to deal with Obregon as the power behind the throne. The Calles government was strongly anti-clerical and in July 1926 the Church suspended all its services as a protest against the attack on its interests. By early 1927 there was a major rebellion by the Cristeros, peasants in the west and centre of the country seeking to protect the Church. A vicious guerrilla war continued for another two years. In Mexico City Obregon was determined to regain office under a constitutional amendment, which allowed him to stand again for a new six-year term as president. He was assassinated by a Catholic mystic on the day after his election. The result was a new election in 1929, won by the unknown Ortiz Rubio, with Calles this time acting as the power behind the throne. The end of the 1920s marked an important departure in the construction of the new order. In 1928 Calles founded the Partido Nacional Revolucionario (PNR), the forerunner of the PRI (Partido Revolucionario Institucional), the permanent governing party of the new state. The new party marked the end of an uncertain period, institutionalized the new regime and confirmed its civilianization. In the last it was successful: Mexico was the only country in Latin America after 1920 not to experience a successful military coup.

The regime in Mexico between 1920 and 1934 was, to a large extent, essentially conservative. A new group of politicians and generals gained power and enriched themselves, but structural changes were limited apart from the education and anti-clerical programmes. At the most fundamental level the revolution was not able to alter the structural dependence of the Mexican economy and its position in the semi-periphery of the world economy. Financial policy was highly conservative, the railways were denationalized and the countryside was little altered, as agriculture still concentrated on production for export from the *haciendas*. Although Obregon recognized the land seizures made by the Zapatistas in Morelos and neighbouring states, there was no land-reform programme. By 1934 less than a tenth of the agricultural land had been redistributed to the peasants. Calles, both as president and as the real power in the early 1930s, argued that agrarian reform was over and that, in the face of the economic disruption caused by the depression, Mexico should adopt a conservative policy based on capitalist development and agricultural production for export. However, by the early 1930s new groups were gaining power within the regime, which supported many of the ideas of the 1910 popular revolution which had still not been implemented. A power struggle within the PNR led to a radical candidate, Lazaro Cardenas, the governor of Michoacan, being nominated and elected president in 1934. Throughout 1935 he was engaged in a power struggle with Calles, which was not resolved until Calles was sent into exile in the spring of 1936. The way was clear for a radical departure in Mexico, which ensured that the 'fate of the revolution' was more radical than seemed likely in the 1920s.

Agrarian reform was central to the new policy and made Mexico, once again, unique in Latin America. In the four years after 1936 nearly 20 million hectares of land were redistributed to nearly a million peasants – twice as much as had been achieved in the whole period between 1910 and 1934. The landless population fell by a quarter, output improved and rural wages rose by a third. This was not a process of gradual reform, but a major campaign launched by central government to support the peasants and often involved the seizure of large estates. A major new education drive, which was both radical and anti-Catholic, further increased literacy rates. In the industrial sector there was also a new departure. In 1937 the railways were renationalized, although this was not unusual in Latin America. However, they had received little investment from their overseas owners and the decision to hand them over to the trade unions to run simply passed on their extensive problems to the unions. The most radical departure was in the oil industry, which was almost entirely foreign owned and the source of much of the national wealth and government revenue. There was a major strike in the industry in 1937 and a subsequent government enquiry was highly critical of the oil companies. The rejection of the report by the companies was a direct challenge to the government, which was forced either to take action or face a humiliating climbdown. On 18 March 1938 the government announced the total expropriation of the industry and the establishment of a state-owned company PEMEX (Petroleos Mexicanos). This produced outrage in the foreign companies and their governments but a huge patriotic response among Mexicans. The new company proved easily capable of running the industry and the foreign governments had little option but to accept the situation. In 1941, in order to secure Mexican military and diplomatic co-operation, the US government agreed a deal under which American oil companies received less than 4 per cent of their claims for the expropriation of their assets. The Mexican action was important because it was the first of a series of nationalizations in the oil industry by the states of the periphery and semi-periphery and provided an important example for others to follow. After the radical departures by President Cardenas in the late 1930s, a peaceful transition of power followed in 1940 to a slightly less radical president. However, the new settlement was accepted, as it was again in the 1946 elections and a new stable regime was in power under the one-party rule of the PRI.

In Russia the civil war of 1917–20 marked a profound discontinuity between the essentially popular revolution of 1917 and the highly authoritarian state structure built upon a tightly disciplined Bolshevik Party. In 1917 and early 1918 there were still extensive and open debates within the party about policy. Under the pressure of civil war, external intervention and the almost total disintegration of the Russian state and economy, the new Bolshevik government built its power on the party, the only organization it had available. A standing army with strict discipline was rebuilt, workers' control of industry was replaced by the authority of state managers, political opposition was suppressed, a political police was instituted to carry out 'revolutionary terror', censorship was imposed, the Soviets were weakened and suspended and power was concentrated in the Council of People's Commissars – the Bolshevik government. The party itself was subject to discipline in order to win the civil war – appointments were made from above rather than by election from below. By the end of 1920 the Bolsheviks had won the civil war, but they were isolated both internally and externally: there was no world revolution and they knew that they would have to survive in office by their own efforts. The party rejected any return to the openness and freedom of 1917, which would have involved them losing much of their power. They chose power and reinterpreted their Marxist ideology to justify what they were doing. The symbolic moment came in February 1921 with the rebellion at the Kronstadt naval base near St Petersburg, which called for the restoration of Soviet power and freedom for competing political parties. The rebellion was ruthlessly suppressed and the party moved even further along the road to dictatorship. At the Tenth Party Congress in the month after Kronstadt the party reluctantly accepted Lenin's proposal to ban internal factions. A year later the establishment of a party secretariat (Orgburo) run by Stalin ensured stronger central control of the party.

Under this new system the party not only became the base of the government, but also insisted that it was the only body which could decide what was in the interests of the workers, peasants and society as a whole. This highly authoritarian political system was partly designed to ensure that the old pre-revolutionary society was not recreated in the much more liberal economic system the party had been forced to introduce in early 1921. The 'war communism' of the civil war period, which was little more than a euphemism for forced requisitioning, was replaced by the New Economic Policy (NEP). Under the NEP private ownership of small-scale industry was allowed and the peasants who now effectively owned the land were allowed to rent it out and hire labour. Internal trade and limited profit-making were also permitted. On this basis the economy recovered quickly from the disasters of the civil war, by the late 1920s output was back to 1913 levels. The political situation became highly fluid after December 1922 following Lenin's stroke, from which he never fully recovered. In his last testament of January 1924, which the party subsequently suppressed, Lenin criticized all his potential successors on different grounds. For several years in the second half of the 1920s the Bolshevik leaders – Kamenev, Zinoviev, Stalin, Bukharin and Trotsky – manoeuvred for position and argued about the direction the revolution should take (just as the revolutionary leaders did in Mexico at the same time). Despite the ideological background of the party, three outcomes seemed possible. The first was a form of military-party dictatorship, possibly under Trotsky, the leader of the Red Army. The second was the retention of a mixed NEP-type economy with strong one-party political control, but in a more tolerant system which would not be much stricter than that in Mexico. The third was a move to a highly repressive system with party control of society and the economy and enforced industrialization. The situation was made worse by the fear of factionalism in the party, the limited debates about alternatives this allowed and the bitter rivalries between the leaders.

The Soviet economy was central to all these debates. The Soviet Union was, like Mexico, part of the semi-periphery and therefore the fundamental problem was how to find the capital necessary to industrialize. The social and economic restructuring involved in industrialization could not be made pain-free – the only question was who should bear the price and how large it should be. The new Mexican regime was essentially conservative and prepared, apart from nationalization of the oil industry in the late 1930s, to rely on foreign capital combined with land reform to bring about a steady improvement in the conditions of the peasants. Because of its ideological isolation and the opposition of the capitalist states, the Soviet Union could not rely on foreign capital. In these circumstances there were only two possible ways forward and both were favoured by different groups in the party at different times. The first involved increasing the wealth of the peasantry (the overwhelming majority of the population) so that they would supply plenty of food and buy industrial products. This would have to be a gradual process and was advocated by Bukharin and, for tactical political reasons, by Stalin until 1927. The alternative was to obtain the necessary capital from the peasants through forced collectivization and dispossession of their land so that they provided an industrial labour force. This was originally argued by Trotsky, but was taken up by Stalin after 1927 when he had secured effective control of the party.

The basis of Soviet policy after 1928 was forced industrialization through a series of Five Year Plans. At first the kulaks (supposedly wealthy peasants) were dispossessed and deported. Then land was taken from the peasants through collectivization and they were forced to work for communes, in which the state decided how much food would be taken and the peasants had to survive on what was left. This attack on society's peasant base (the exact opposite of the Mexican revolution) could only be carried through by force and terror. The resulting confusion and food requisitioning led to mass starvation. Equally drastic were the first stages of industrialization, where the emphasis (which had always been apparent in Marxism and, in particular, in Lenin's thinking) was on mass production as the way of building socialism and communism. This policy produced rapid increases in output and massive social mobility as the peasants moved into the new cities and new elites emerged. The Bolsheviks were no longer Lenin's vanguard party of dedicated revolutionaries (although they retained that mythology), but became a bureaucratic party trying to control a revolutionary social situation and plan extensive industrialization. Internal discipline was essential if control was to be maintained. Stalin, however, combined this discipline with a series of ruthless purges designed to eliminate all opposition and ensure his retention of power. At the 1939 Party Congress only 59 of the 2,000 delegates who attended the previous Congress in 1934 still survived and 98 of the 149 members of the 1934 Central Committee had been eliminated, as had all Stalin's rivals – Kamenev, Bukharin and Zinoviev.

By the late 1930s through a system of terror Stalin dominated the Soviet state. The rule of one man and even a 'cult of personality' were not unusual in the dictatorships that flourished around the world. What was different was that the ideology and initial aspirations of the Bolshevik Revolution were radically different from what finally emerged from that Revolution. Although some of the roots of what became known as Stalinism were present under Lenin, there was no automatic line of progression from one to the other. The 'fate of the revolution', as it emerged by the late 1930s, followed from a series of decisions made after 1917 and, in particular, those which followed Lenin's death in 1924. These decisions resulted from not only the ideological preconceptions of the leaders (something that was missing from the Mexican revolution), but also from the situation the new regime faced after it seized power. Some of the policies adopted – growing nationalism, a mass literacy drive, strong anti-clericalism and the attempt to create a new culture – were remarkably similar to those of the Mexican revolution. In the same way the Soviet government's view of itself as encircled by enemies was only a more extreme version of the strong opposition of the Mexican leadership to American intervention during the civil war and economic interference afterwards. What was different in the Soviet Union was the existence of a strong ideological party determined to ensure a monopoly of power.

In China after 1949 the Communist Party had the Soviet Union as an example when it decided how to consolidate its power and build a new society. There was, however, one important difference. The base of the party in China was in the countryside and a major policy aim in the early 1950s was to establish control over the cities and industry. In the Soviet Union the Bolshevik Party had had little contact with the mass of the peasants (they tended to support the Social Revolutionaries), which made it easier for them to turn on the peasants in the late 1920s. Not only was the base of the party different in China, so too was the economy, and this significantly limited the options available to the new government. The Chinese economy in 1949 was far less industrialized than the Soviet Union's in the late 1920s. In these circumstances the Chinese had little alternative but to build upon the peasants before embarking on industrialization. The first stage of this process was the radical land reform programme of the early 1950s, under which land was confiscated and the landlords were forced to pay back rents. This was achieved by so-called 'struggle rallies', with party cadres using poor peasants to lead the movement locally. Probably about 5 million 'landlords' and 'rich peasants' were killed in the process. After 1953 the government decided to move to full collectivization because land reform had produced neither large increases in output nor capital accumulation for industrialization. At first co-operatives were introduced followed by full collectivization, with the peasants working in communes. By 1957 over 90 per cent of the rural population was living in communes. However, this was generally achieved by co-operating with the peasants rather than attacking them as in the Soviet Union.

By the late 1950s it seemed that with the party in control of China (it had over 13 million members compared with a third of that number at the start of the decade) and with agriculture collectivized, the way was open to industrialization. In practice for twenty years after the late 1950s the party was unable to agree on a way forward and numerous changes of policy and bouts of radicalism achieved little. Not until the late 1970s was 'the fate of the revolution' finally decided. In 1958 the party decided on a radical departure under the slogan of the 'Three Red Banners'. There was to be a simultaneous development of agriculture and industry, using both traditional and modern methods. This was to be achieved by a 'Great Leap Forward' and by a comprehensive collectivization of life through the development of People's Communes. The people were promised that 'a life in abundance of food and clothing' would be achieved in two to three years. Within that period the programme collapsed through widespread opposition, economic chaos, starvation and death. The original idea was to have communes each containing about 5,000 households and below them production brigades of about 150 households. Throughout China people would live in a semi-military manner in barracks with canteens. It proved so unpopular that the programme had to be dropped within a year. The subsequent agricultural chaos produced a widespread famine in which probably 30 million people died. The development of industry under the 'Great Leap Forward' was limited and technologically primitive. In 1962 the programme was abandoned and the party was left to argue about the way forward.

From the early 1960s until 1965 the debate inside the Chinese Communist Party about the way forward closely mirrored that in the Soviet Party in the mid-1920s. Nobody advocated political liberalization, but some, like Teng Hsiao-ping, suggested a more market-oriented, pro-peasant line with agriculture being given priority. The main advocate of a more radical line was Mao and he was supported by the People's Liberation Army under Marshal Lin Piao. The PLA abolished all ranks and insignia in May 1965, an action which turned out to be highly symbolic for later developments. By the autumn of 1965 it was clear that the party was badly split. The conservatives controlled much of the party, but the radicals attacked them together with the 'intellectuals' and the prevailing 'culture'. By early 1966 there was talk of a 'cultural revolution' against reactionary elements in the party. Mao backed this line as a way of maintaining his dominance within the party. The movement gathered momentum in the cultural area and then in May 1966 all schools were closed, followed in June by all the universities. Students became one of the main weapons used to terrorize various sections of society. The Chancellor of Wuhan University, Li Ta (a founder member of the party in 1921) was beaten to death for his 'reactionary views'. In July 1966 there was effectively a Maoist coup in Peking, led by the PLA against the existing leadership.

On 8 August 1966 the Central Committee agreed the 'Decision Concerning the Great Proletarian Cultural Revolution'. It was to lead to unprecedented internal violence and the near disintegration of the Chinese state into anarchy. Under the resolution the existing party organization was to be replaced by new groups. The aim was fundamental change of the 'superstructure' of society through violence. Mao and his allies were attempting to use these groups to radicalize and transform the party and its bureaucracy. In some ways the effects were similar to those of the terror under Stalin in the late 1930s. However, in China the process was carried out in a more populist manner and its purpose was only indirectly to maintain the power of one individual. Under the Cultural Revolution education was to be combined with long periods of manual work so that intellectuals experienced the reality of peasant life. A new proletarian ideology and culture would emerge which would totally reject both western and traditional Chinese values. The critics of this policy would experience 'the full harshness of the dictatorship of the proletariat'. The army tried to control the new 'Red Guard' units, but by August 1966 the Red Guards had over 10 million members and were split into rival factions. By January 1967 it was clear that Mao, Lin Piao and Mao's wife, Chiang Ch'ing were in control in Peking. However, across China there was near anarchy as the control structures of the party and state collapsed and local party groups resisted the policy set out by the radical Peking leadership. The PLA was ordered to protect banks, civil aviation and factories from the Red Guards. The PLA effectively took over broadcasting as well. There were street battles across China as both the army and the Red Guards split into rival factions. The situation was near crisis point by the summer of 1967. There was tension on the border with the Soviet Union, Red Guards had taken over some government ministries in Peking and the army in Wuhan had turned on the Red Guards. However, by early 1968 the leadership, relying on the army, was just able to close the lid of the Pandora's box it had opened. Clashes continued (50,000 died in Kwangsi province) but the army 'helped' students back to school. In July 1968 the PLA occupied Peking University and the defeat of the ultra-radicals was clear. However, the PLA was the dominant force in the rebuilding of the party in the early 1970s and its special role was recognized in the constitution. In 1971 Lin Piao was 'purged' in unexplained but suspicious circumstances. In August 1973 the moderate Teng Hsiao-ping was re-elected to the Politburo. There was a further radical period in the mid-1970s after the deaths of Mao and Chou En-lai, but the radicals were defeated and a moderate leadership took control.

By 1940 in Mexico, after the Cardenas presidency, by the early 1950s in the Soviet Union after the death of Stalin and by the late 1970s and the assertion of control by the moderate elements in the party in China, all three revolutionary states entered a period of general stability. The regimes installed by the revolution had created a new but essentially conservative consensus. All three countries shared certain similarities. They were one-party states controlled by a well-entrenched elite, determined on economic development and with strong state support for that programme. There was little toleration of dissent, although the Mexican government was far less repressive than those of China and the Soviet Union. Mexico was a strongly capitalist country, China tolerated quasi-capitalist developments but the Soviet Union remained wedded to state socialism.

In Mexico after 1920 there were no successful military coups and from 1934 the presidential succession was negotiated within the ruling party which controlled the country without a break until the end of the century. The system was authoritarian but generally moderate and not highly repressive, although about 200 demonstrators were shot in 1968 and the Zapatista rebels were a major problem by the mid-1990s. The system coped with a massive rise in population and industrialization. Stability came partly from equilibrium between the various groups incorporated into the system – the peasants, workers, capitalists and bureaucrats. The government aim was capitalist development, but only an elite gained the major benefits. This elite was made up of three parts – the technicians and bureaucrats who ran the system, the politicians who worked their way up through the PRI machine and the 'silent partner' – the army – which provided the final guarantee of stability. The whole system ran in close harmony with the interests of the United States, despite the rhetoric that was sometimes employed. The system was semi-corporatist with its inclusion of rival interest groups within a broad governing consensus, which was represented by the permanent party of government. Inevitably there was corruption in all areas and a steady decline in support for the PRI. In the 1988 elections President Salinas was elected with just over half the vote against the son of the former President Cardenas, who ran on a radical anti-PRI ticket. The government victory was achieved by massive vote-rigging. The system staggered into the 1990s, but seemed just strong enough to retain control.

After the death of Stalin in March 1953 there was a brief, peaceful struggle for power in the Soviet Union in which party control over the secret police was reasserted. By 1955 Khrushchev was in effective control. His denunciation of Stalin at the Twentieth Party Congress in 1956 was, in effect, a call to return to the ideals of a Leninist party. Change and even discussion were still to be controlled by those at the top, although a large proportion of those

incarcerated in labour camps were released and the worst excesses of
Stalinism ended. However, Khrushchev remained an optimist,
believing that the full potential of the Soviet system could still be
realized. At the Party Congress in 1961 he argued that full socialism
could be built in twenty years and that by 1980 the Soviet Union
would be wealthier than the United States. In practice the growth of
the Soviet economy was slowing down. It never successfully
managed the transition from concentrating on heavy industrial
production (at which it was quite efficient) to the production of high
levels of high-quality consumer goods. Khrushchev was removed
from power peacefully in 1964 mainly because of the failure of his
agricultural policy and doubts about his erratic handling of foreign
affairs.

After 1965 a highly conservative collective leadership dominated
the Soviet Union. The country was a major international power, its
economy grew steadily but slowly and it had little interest in
changing the status quo. The party bureaucracy (the *nomenklatura*),
which had long dominated all aspects of society and the economy
became even more entrenched. Economic planning through huge
ministries continued, even though increasingly they represented the
various interests within the state they were supposed to supervise.
Ideas of economic reform were buried by the late 1960s. In the
republics local party groups entrenched themselves in power.
Corruption was apparent everywhere. From the late 1960s a cloak of
caution was thrown over every policy. The power of the party and
its internal discipline ensured there was little, if any, debate about
alternatives. The exact purpose of the party was unclear except that
it remained the only route available for the ambitious to climb to
places of power. The price they paid was attendance at endless party
meetings and rallies, where they listened to long rhetorical addresses
which bore little relation to reality and certainly fired no enthusiasm
among the general public. Leonid Brezhnev dominated the system,
as party secretary (and president after 1977), but there was a
collective leadership and no return to the brutalities of the Stalin era.
Brezhnev stayed in power until his death in 1982, despite being
seriously ill and hardly capable of carrying out his duties. He was
replaced by the already sick Andropov, who, in a brief period of
power, tried to start an anti-corruption campaign. He died in
February 1984 and was replaced by Chernenko, who died just over
a year later. The period of uninspiring leadership by old and sick
men, which left the political, economic and social system highly

sclerotic ended in March 1985 with Mikhail Gorbachev's election as head of the party. His attempts to reform the system (especially by ending the absolute control of the party) unleashed the forces which, within little more than six years, destroyed the Soviet Union.

The establishment of the non-radicals in power in China in the late 1970s initiated a period of reform for which they had argued since the early 1960s. Absolute political control remained in the hands of the party and no dissent was allowed. The destruction of the student demonstrations in Tienanmen Square in Peking in 1989 demonstrated that, although the party leadership was willing to consider economic reform, political pluralism would not be tolerated. Economic reform began in the peasant sector in 1978. The rural communes were transformed into 'townships', decisions were decentralized and sale of peasant produce on the open market was allowed. In the 1980s these freedoms were extended into urban areas and factories were given much greater power to act as capitalist companies. These reforms were carried through to their greatest extent in the 'special economic zones' in the south of the country, where foreign investment and production for export were encouraged. The Chinese leadership, which remained highly stable after the late 1970s, chose to adopt a policy very similar to that of the Soviet Union in the 1920s under the New Economic Policy. Strict political control was maintained, but a kind of 'market socialism' prevailed, with state planning at a macro-economic level and quasi-capitalism at the micro-economic level. By the late 1990s the large-scale sale of state assets became party policy. It was a combination which produced very high growth rates. Despite the huge social disruption caused by such rapid economic growth, the party seemed able to keep control politically and the system appeared to be highly stable. In some ways it was not greatly dissimilar to the systems found in other Asian industrializing countries such as South Korea, Indonesia, the Philippines and, ironically, Taiwan.

17   DEMOCRACY

DURING THE twentieth century only a small minority of the world's people lived in democratic countries. At the beginning of the century no state was fully democratic. Only a handful allowed all their adult male citizens to vote and women were almost completely excluded. Before the First World War there was little change, but in 1918 the states of western Europe became more democratic. Democratic states were established across central and eastern Europe but within little more than a decade these new states were dictatorships and by 1939 there were only about a dozen democracies in the world. The number expanded again in the late 1940s with the restoration of democracy in Germany and Italy and with the creation of the newly independent states of India, Israel and Ceylon. As the former colonial states of Asia and Africa became independent in the late 1950s and early 1960s there was another increase, but none of the new democracies survived for more than a short period. The collapse of the Communist states of eastern Europe in the late 1980s increased the number of democracies, as did the establishment of majority rule in South Africa in the mid-1990s. A few of the ex-Communist states were democratic but many became semi-authoritarian fairly rapidly. During the second half of the century only twenty-one states in the world were continuously democratic. Even among this category some caveats about their democratic credentials are necessary. Switzerland denied the vote to women until 1971 and few blacks could vote in the United States until the late 1960s.

In general, throughout the century democracy was limited to the core states and here there were only rare breakdowns in the system, as in Germany in the 1930s. In the semi-periphery democracy was not a permanent feature and in the periphery it was very rare. It might seem therefore that democracy was closely associated with capitalism, the form of economic and social organization which characterized the industrialized and prosperous core states. However, capitalism also flourished in predominantly non-democratic states such as South Korea, Taiwan, Brazil and Chile. Although capitalism tended to strengthen the position of middle-class managers and professionals and, to some extent, the working class against the landed upper class, this did not automatically lead to democracy. In Latin America the middle-class group often allied with the elite in supporting dictatorships which excluded the working class and peasants rather than accept a more inclusive democratic system. There was no simple equation between capitalism and democracy. The relative stability of democracy in the core states was the result of the conjunction of a number of factors. It was the position of the core states in the global economy, rather than just their capitalist structure, which provided one of the major bases for democracy. The prosperity generated in the core states (at the expense of the rest of the world) meant that it was possible to share at least part of that wealth among the various groups in society. Stark inequalities remained, but enough of the wealth was distributed down the social hierarchy, either directly through higher incomes or indirectly through state welfare programmes, to give all groups a stake in preserving the existing society and, in most circumstances, the political status quo too. (Only in extreme circumstances, such as Germany after 1918, did other grievances and issues override these factors.) In addition the democratic systems of the core states were deeply embedded in a complex civil society with wide-ranging interests which stemmed from industrialization, growing wealth and economic and social diversification. None of the core states set out to design democracy, it emerged as the consequence of the complex interplay of a variety of social and political processes over a considerable period. Those states which set out to create democracy from the top down, often following independence or revolution and in circumstances in which there was no tradition of democracy, usually produced an unstable structure. This meant that democracy was unlikely to survive the economic and social stresses which were always much more apparent in the states of the semi-periphery and periphery than in the core.

Even in the core states democracy was not accompanied by major changes in the power structure. Elites and powerful interest groups were able to maintain their positions. In addition none of these states, with the possible exception of Switzerland, managed to produce systems which provided for broad-based decision-taking.

Many crucial decisions in these societies were still taken within the increasingly complex systems of state administration or in courts of law. Generally both proved fairly impervious to democratic influences. Nor did the development of mass political parties seeking votes among all adult citizens produce greater citizen involvement. As many commentators forecast at the beginning of the century, the development of mass parties led to a concentration of power among a small group of increasingly professionalized politicians, who were able to control the parties and through them dictate much of the political agenda. In addition democracies rarely produced governments which represented a majority of voters. In the period between 1945 and 1968 there were 337 elections in the twenty-one democratic countries. Only twenty-three of them produced a vote of more than half for one party and six of those were in New Zealand. After 1968 this proportion became even smaller.

Democratic states had to undertake a number of difficult tasks. They had to reconcile a number of social and economic cleavages within their societies which often cut across each other in a complex fashion. These included class and sectional interests stemming from the structure of the economic system, religious differences, geographical differences between the centre and peripheral regions, in some cases ethnic and language divisions and in a few instances, for example the Weimar Republic, significant groups which denied the legitimacy of the regime. Even if these problems were resolved, further questions arose. What status should minority groups have, how should public opinion be brought to bear on government, what were the restraints on the exercise of power and what rights should be guaranteed? In practice no modern state, even in the core, could be fully democratic and participatory. What in practice they did achieve was a strong restraint on government because of the need for re-election. At best they produced governments whose actions were fairly close to the wishes of a large proportion of citizens over a relatively long period.

In 1900 only a few of the core states allowed all adult males to vote. In some cases such as France, Norway, Switzerland and Denmark the proportion who could vote was high (over 80 per cent) but in others it was very low – about a quarter in Sweden and a half in the Netherlands. Most were therefore only quasi-democratic. In Britain, for example, the government was responsible to an elected parliament, there was a fairly open discussion of issues together with solid individual rights and limited state authority. However, the overwhelming majority of adults could not vote. All women were denied the franchise and about four out of ten men were also excluded from voting. In the United States the process of removing the vote from most black males was drawing to a successful close. In some states voters were also excluded by a multitude of wealth and income tests or, as in Italy and many states in the United States, a literacy test. In Italy this meant that only about a quarter of men were allowed to vote. Indeed, the prime minister, Francesco Crispi, told parliament in 1896 that the common people were 'corrupted by ignorance, gnawed by envy and ingratitude, and should not be allowed any say in politics'. In most states the voting age was high. In Sweden, when the wealth-based suffrage qualification was slightly eased in 1909, the voting age was actually raised from twenty-one to twenty-five. Some states also allowed the wealthy and educated to vote more than once. In Britain about 10 per cent of the electorate had more than one vote and university graduates were allowed at least two votes until 1950. In Sweden plural voting in rural districts was widespread. Before 1909 it was possible for a single landlord to cast up to 5,000 votes, but in the reforms of 1909 this was 'limited' to only 40 votes.

Other states, such as Prussia and Austria, had glaringly unequal voting systems. In Prussia voters were divided into one of three classes according to the amount of tax they paid, so the bottom 80 per cent of the population elected the same number of representatives as the top 3 per cent. In 10 per cent of electoral districts there was only one elector in the top group – for example, the head of the Krupp family in Essen. In Austria there were 253 seats in the lower house of parliament with male voters divided into four classes. The result was that the 5,000 noble landlords elected 85 deputies and the 500 members of the Chambers of Commerce elected 21 members. In nearly every core state the proportion of people able to vote in local elections was even more restricted and normally depended on the payment of local taxes, which was made by landlords and house owners rather than tenants. In London only one in eight of the adult population could vote for the members of the local authority.

These were not the last of the impediments to democracy in 1900. In states such as Germany, which allowed nearly all males to vote for members of the Reichstag, the government was removed from democratic control by being accountable to the Kaiser not parliament. In addition all the core states had upper houses of parliament which shared legislative power and which were not democratically elected. In Germany, the Netherlands and Switzerland, the upper chamber was elected by the provincial governments; in Belgium half of the members were elected, half chosen by the provinces. Britain was unusual in having an upper house almost entirely composed of the hereditary aristocracy, but in many other states such as Italy, Austria, Finland, Portugal and Spain the upper house was composed of nobles, those chosen by the monarch or those who held their position because of their role in the state bureaucracy. All these bodies were prepared to use their power to defend their privileged positions. Switzerland was the only exception in Europe to this model of restricted democracy. By 1900 all the features of the highly participatory Swiss system were in operation – male suffrage, referendums on constitutional changes, the optional referendum and popular initiative.

The major change in the level of democracy in most of the core states came immediately after the First World War. All states allowed adult males to vote (except for nearly all blacks in the United States and Aborigines in Australia) and most also allowed women to vote: the exceptions were Britain, where all women could not vote until 1928, as well as France, Italy and Japan, where they had to wait until new constitutions were written after the Second World War. These changes made an enormous difference to the size of the electorate. For example, in Britain in 1910 about 7 million people were entitled to vote, whereas at the next election in 1918 over 21 million could do so and by 1929 the electorate totalled nearly 30 million. The only other change for the rest of the century was a reduction in the age at which people could vote. In general until the 1960s the age was twenty-one, although in some countries it was twenty-five until 1945. By the late 1970s this had generally been reduced to eighteen. In the semi-periphery when elections did take place, the size of the electorate varied considerably. In most of the European semi-periphery all males could vote after 1920, but the vote was not extended to women in Spain until 1931, Greece until 1956 and Portugal until 1974 after the fall of the Salazar regime. In Latin America electorates remained much smaller until the second half of the century. In Argentina, even after the electoral reforms of 1916, only about a third of adults could vote and all women and immigrants were excluded. In Chile as late as 1949 fewer than one in five adults could vote. In general women were not given the vote in Latin America until the 1950s.

In the core states about twenty countries were democracies of various types for most of the twentieth century. They had certain basic principles in common. They allowed considerable, but not total, freedom of expression. There was a general freedom to join organizations, though again this was not absolute – the United States, Australia, Finland and West Germany at various times banned the Communist Party – and they allowed a wide range of information sources, although the media were never completely free. These democracies, however, differed greatly in the way in which they were organized both in terms of the structure of government and the way the electoral system operated.

In general they fell into two types, majoritarian and consensus. The majoritarian model was mainly British in origin, although its most highly developed form was found in New Zealand until the major changes of the mid-1990s. In this system there was a concentration of executive power and one party normally formed the government. There was a near-total fusion of executive and legislative powers because the executive was able to dominate the legislature through party control and discipline. The legislature had two houses, although the upper house was not normally very powerful. The party system normally represented a left–right cleavage. Power was generally strongly centralized with little independent power for local government except in the federal systems of Canada and Australia. The problem with majoritarian systems was that they could become exclusionary and eliminate the minority from any effective power. This was the case in Northern Ireland between 1922 and 1972, where the state was run on religious lines with the Protestant majority deliberately discriminating against the Catholic minority. There were similar problems in Canada from the 1960s onwards with the French Canadian community in Quebec.

Consensus systems were constructed in a very different way. They were intended to represent a wide variety of the cleavages within society and provide a limitation on the exercise of majority power. In some cases, for example in Switzerland and in Belgium after 1970, there was agreement that the government should represent all major groups. Most governments in these states were coalitions and the electoral system ensured that no party could achieve an outright majority.

About half of all the core democracies were constitutional monarchies, although the power of the monarch was usually only symbolic. Only three had popularly elected presidents – the United

States, France under the Fifth Republic and Finland – and only in the first two did the president have any effective power. In the other republican states, such as Ireland and West Germany, the president's powers were largely symbolic. Nearly all the democracies were parliamentary in nature, that is the government depended on a majority in parliament to stay in power. The exceptions were the United States and Switzerland, which had its own unique hybrid system. In all but the United States and Norway, the executive was allowed to dissolve the legislature and call for new elections. In all but the United States and France under the Fifth Republic, the legislature could vote to end the life of the government, although in Germany after 1949 it was necessary to have a 'constructive' vote to name a successor. In the United States, France and Switzerland, members of the executive were not allowed to sit in the legislature and in the Netherlands, Luxemburg and Norway, they could participate in debates but they were not allowed to vote. Elsewhere it was a prerequisite for members of the government to have seats in the legislature. Most legislatures had two houses, the upper usually being smaller and elected for a longer term.

The upper houses were usually unrepresentative. In the United States, even though the Senate was popularly elected, 5 per cent of the population chose nearly a third of the total because there were two senators from each state regardless of population. In most countries the lower house held most power. In only four states were their powers formally equal – Belgium, Switzerland, Italy and the United States. In the last many would argue that the Senate was the more powerful. In both West Germany and the Netherlands the upper house was very powerful even though it was indirectly elected by the provincial governments. Only Britain retained an upper chamber with no elected element, it was made up of hereditary peers until 1957 and of hereditary peers and government appointees after that date. Six states had no upper house at all – Finland, Luxemburg, Israel, New Zealand, Denmark and Sweden – the last three all abolished their upper houses in the second half of the century.

Only seven of the main democracies were federal states, the United States, Switzerland, West Germany, Canada, Australia, Belgium and Austria. Only Canada, Belgium and Switzerland showed any significant ethnic or religious fragmentation at the national or provincial level which might account for this diffusion of power. The other federal systems had their origins in past experience, especially the existence of separate states before a national constitution was established (as in the United States and Australia), or in an overriding desire to decentralize power, as in West Germany following the Nazi period. Three of the main democracies had no formal written constitution – Britain, New Zealand and Israel. Of those that did have a constitution only four allowed for amendment by referendum, the rest had to be changed by a variety of complex schemes involving special majorities and minority vetos, as in the United States, with its mixture of legislative and state approval.

In general, the democracies remained solidly representative with very little direct democracy. At some time during the twentieth century nearly half of all the core democracies used referendums at a national level, but three of them (Britain, Belgium and Austria) did so only once and Norway only twice. Nine states had none at all after 1945, even though they had held them earlier in the century. Nearly all these referendums were 'constitutional' in nature, but they were tightly controlled in that the government decided the exact question to be asked, expected to win and normally did so. Overwhelmingly referendums as a method of government were restricted to Switzerland – in the thirty-five years after 1945 there were 169 national referendums and many others at canton and city levels. The ability of individual citizens to force referendums through initiatives was even more limited. At a national level this was only allowed in Switzerland and Italy and at a lower level in Swiss cantons and some states of the United States. Primaries for the selection of party candidates were notable mainly by their absence outside the United States. Even here they did not apply in all states, although the number where this was possible increased during the century.

The systems used by states to elect members to parliament varied considerably. They reflected the different types of democracy and they had a major impact on both political parties and citizens. Electoral systems tended to reflect existing party divisions, indeed they were often designed to meet the interests of particular parties and groups. None of them could resolve one of the fundamental problems of democracies, that minorities were bound to lose. The only question electoral systems could settle was how big the losing minority was to be and what level of influence it might have after an election. Broadly the systems fell into three categories. First, there were single-member constituencies in which a candidate only needed to gain the largest number of votes, not a majority, to win.

This system was only found in Britain and in states with a strong British influence, the white dominions of the empire and the United States. It was not used in any western European democracy. Second, were single-member constituencies in which a majority of the total vote was required for election; this was normally obtained, if needed, through a second ballot. This system was often used in France. The third type involved proportional systems of representation through a variety of mechanisms, such as a transferable vote within a multi-member constituency or by using a party list, with the latter being common in western Europe. Proportional systems were introduced in two main phases. The first wave before 1914 was designed to protect the interests of minorities, as in Belgium. In the second phase after 1918 the main aim was to contain the rise of socialist parties and ensure that they could not obtain a majority in parliament. Some countries also imposed thresholds for representation – these might be very low (less than 1 per cent in the Netherlands) but significant in others (4 or 5 per cent in Sweden and West Germany).

Some of these electoral systems were of long standing (established well before the end of the nineteenth century) and in the United States and Britain did not alter when full democracy was introduced. Others were frequently changed to try and obtain party advantage, as in France. Single-member districts were abolished three times and restored three times. In twenty out of twenty-eight French elections in the twentieth century there was a second ballot, although the conditions varied considerably from one election to another. Various forms of proportional representation were also tried at different times. Other systems were devised at the time a constitution was written, for example in West Germany in 1949. Here the very high threshold for minority parties (designed to exclude extremists) meant that the two main blocs of the Christian Democrats and Social Democrats were over-represented and only the minority Free Democrats regularly gained representation. In Italy, on the other hand, the post-war constitution and electoral system was a very pure proportional system which favoured small parties. It also gave strong control to party organizations and enabled the Christian Democrats to maintain their position as the largest party in a highly fragmented system. The Japanese system after 1945 was unique and was carefully designed to reinforce traditional styles of electioneering and voting. Voters had a single vote, but it was cast in a multi-member constituency. This encouraged candidate-centred mobilization of the vote based on influence and favours. It also tended to fragment opposition parties and allowed the ruling Liberal Democratic Party to continue in its highly factional form, yet still elect a majority in parliament through its strong party organization.

All these electoral systems had their own particular problems. The single-member constituency, with only a plurality of votes required for election, tended to produce governments which had large majorities in parliament despite the fact that they had the support of far less than half of those who voted. In Britain, no government after 1935 obtained a majority of the votes cast. In Canada, the Liberals dominated politics and government yet did not receive a majority of the votes after 1908. The system was also capable of producing the wrong result. In Britain in 1951 and Australia in 1954 the Labour parties won most votes, but they did not win more seats than their main rivals, who after the election formed the new government. One of the most spectacular examples of the 'wrong' result was in South Africa in the whites-only election of 1948. The Nationalists won 42 per cent of the vote but gained 79 seats and the United Party, which won 52 per cent of the vote, obtained 71 seats. It was on this 'democratic' basis that the Nationalists claimed a mandate to construct the full apartheid system. This type of electoral system also discriminated against small- to medium-sized parties which had their support fairly evenly distributed across the country. In Britain, for example, the Liberals regularly received about 20 per cent of the vote after 1974, but gained less than 2 per cent of the seats in the House of Commons, a result almost exactly duplicated by the Social Credit Party in New Zealand in 1981. However, the second ballot system, designed to ensure that the winner did receive a majority of the votes, also had important side-effects. It encouraged existing parties to form alliances and trade support to keep out some other parties; in France it was normally operated in this way against the Communists. The problem with proportional systems was that, because they reflected the relative stability of voting patterns within societies, they tended to produce almost the same result at every election. Party list systems also strengthened the power of the party organization, by making it responsible for the selection of those candidates who would be successful.

In many democracies voting was also distorted by highly unequal voting areas designed to over-represent one particular group, usually the rural, conservative sections of society. In Germany before 1914 the constituencies still reflected the population distribution in 1871 before the onset of major industrialization and urbanization. Berlin, despite its population of over 1 million returned only 8 members to the Reichstag. One constituency in the city had 247,000 voters, compared with an electorate of 9,500 in the rural area of Schaumburg-Lippe. The result was that in the 1912 election a Conservative in East Prussia was elected with 7,900 votes whereas in Bochum the Social Democratic candidate who gained nearly 65,000 votes was not elected. Similarly Atlanta, the state capital of Georgia, contained a fifth of the state's population, yet it elected just one of the state's 35 senators and only 7 out of 106 representatives. One of the most corrupt electoral systems was in Northern Ireland after 1922 as the Unionists sought to ensure their control over the nationalist, Catholic minority by gerrymandering constituency boundaries. In Londonderry, which had a Catholic majority, the Unionists redrew the boundaries so that there were only 3 constituencies. Each of them followed the divisions of the highly segregated housing and left the Unionists controlling 2 out of the 3. The result was that about 10,000 Catholic voters returned 8 councillors and the 7,500 Unionists returned 12.

Within this highly variable democratic framework political parties competed for support and power. In the divided societies that characterized the core, political parties developed a dual function. The first was to articulate the interests of some groups against others, and the second to integrate these interests into the overall state structure. The cleavages in the core societies were usually along lines of class, religion, ethnicity and region. However, which of these cleavages were dominant in society and which were represented in the different party systems, varied both from country to country and over time. In Britain, a division between the interests of the state and the Church was largely absent. To some extent before 1918 the Liberals tended to represent the interests of the Nonconformists against those of the established Church, but this political division rapidly faded. On the other hand, the religious cleavage was very important in the Netherlands, Germany and Switzerland, where there were strong Catholic minorities (as was also the case in Ireland, as the British knew to their cost before 1922). All states had parties representing the working class even before all of them were allowed to vote. Regional parties were of no importance in Britain before the 1960s, or in Italy before the late 1980s, whereas in Spain they were fundamental and in Germany the conservative party in largely Catholic Bavaria remained formally separate from the Christian Democrats. Agrarian parties were rare and only emerged in very specific circumstances. They were found primarily in Scandinavia, the Protestant parts of Switzerland and in parts of Austria. These were places where industrial and urban areas were still relatively weak when all males finally gained the vote. In addition, agriculture was still dominated by smallholding peasants, there were large cultural differences between the cities and the countryside and the Catholic Church was not strong. In some states, such as Switzerland and Ireland, the ideological differences between the parties was always minimal: the Irish had their own unique party system based on the divisions within the nationalist movement in the early 1920s.

In the core states party systems were established long before all males could vote, let alone females. Once parties were established, they developed very strong roots in society and were very difficult to dislodge by any new movements that arose. In general, by the early 1920s the main lines of social and political cleavage within the core states were settled and these were the ones that were represented in the differing party systems. There was very little change after this period, despite the rise of fascism and Nazism, the Second World War and foreign occupation. The main change was the emergence of Christian Democratic parties in West Germany and Italy (although at the first West German election of 1949 the proportion of the vote won by the conservative parties and the Social Democrats almost exactly reflected their support in the 1920s) and the rise of Gaullism in France. Not until the late 1970s did the first signs of disintegration in the existing party systems begin to emerge. Some states showed very high degrees of stability. In the Netherlands in the fifty years after all males were allowed to vote in 1917 the left regularly gained about a quarter of the vote, the three confessional parties of the centre about half and the small right-wing Liberals about 10 per cent. This meant that the confessional parties normally formed the government either on their own or with the right, as was the norm between 1917 and 1940, or with the left, as happened between 1945 and 1958. During the long economic boom in western Europe after 1945, the differing party systems appeared to be highly stable – variations in party strength were normally less than 5 per cent of the vote. The only exception was in France. There the Gaullists saw their vote increase from less than 2 per cent in 1946 to just over 46 per cent in 1968, and even smaller parties such as the

Poujadists could gain 12 per cent of the vote in 1956 but then disappear from the political scene. After the early 1970s there was greater instability with the rise of regional parties in many countries, new parties such as the Greens and a general trend towards greater volatility in voting patterns. Throughout the twentieth century in most national party systems one party had a hegemonic position, winning elections and being in power more frequently than its opponents. In Britain this was the Conservatives, in Germany and Italy the Christian Democrats and in Sweden the Social Democrats. Even though most parties stood little chance of gaining power, they still continued to exist and attracted substantial support. The Communist Parties failed to secure power anywhere in western Europe, except for a brief period in coalition governments after 1945 and in the early 1980s in France, yet they flourished for decades. Other smaller parties also continued. The Liberals in Britain split in 1916 and after the early 1920s never stood a realistic chance of gaining power. By the 1950s they were reduced to just six members of parliament. However, they had a determined but small base. They built up their support to over a fifth of the voters by the 1970s, but they were still far from gaining any political power except at a local level.

The major exception to this party pattern in the core countries was the United States, which had its own unique, essentially two-party system – a number of other parties such as the Socialists in 1912, the Progressives in 1924 and 1948 and separate southern Democrats in 1948 and 1968 made brief appearances but then disappeared. However, the parties were much weaker than in any other political system found in the core states. Given the highly diverse union of the United States and its huge geographical extent, political parties became coalitions of different interests, some of which were deeply incompatible. As a consequence the parties had very little ideological content. The lack of any major religious differences meant that the most important problem was the racial question and that was kept off the political agenda until the early 1950s. The American system began to diverge widely from that of the other core states in the 1890s, with the failure of a socialist party to become established and with the elimination of party competition at a national and to some extent at a state level too. Between 1896 and the late 1920s the party system in the United States showed an extreme degree of sectionalism with a Democratic-controlled south, and Republican-controlled north and north-east. In the west with its semi-colonial economy, occasional protest movements against the system emerged. Between 1896 and 1928 over 85 per cent of the total presidential electoral vote for the Democrats came from the south and the border states. The Democrats won 97 per cent of the elections for governor in the states of the south and the Republicans over 80 per cent of those in the north. In most areas therefore elections became a formality. Attention was concentrated on the party primary to select the candidate in the states where these were held. In other states, party machines effectively selected the candidate who would be successful in the election.

After 1928 the Democrats began to build their strength in the cities of the north and this became the basis of the governing New Deal coalition until the early 1950s. Between 1932 and 1966 the Democrats still won 98 per cent of all the contests for governor in the southern and border states. The main change was that they won just over 40 per cent of the contests in the Midwest and north-east too. From the early 1950s the Republicans became more dominant in the national political system. This trend was massively reinforced from the mid-1960s as, for the first time in almost a century, they established control over the politics of the south. This followed the decision of the Democratic Kennedy and Johnson administrations to enforce civil rights for the black population.

Throughout the twentieth century two factors tended to decrease the importance of the party system in the United States. Party programmes always had a minimal ideological content, but increasingly politicians and parties were influenced by lobby groups acting on behalf of particular interests in society. Second, politics became focused on the candidate rather than the party. Candidates increasingly had to raise substantial sums of money, usually from the special interest groups, and campaign at great expense through the media, especially using television advertising, in order to gain support. National trends and political parties became even less important in determining the outcome of elections. In 1920 only 4 per cent of districts split their vote between the party candidates for president and the House of Representatives. By 1972 this was happening in 45 per cent of districts and by the 1980s nearly two-thirds of voters were failing to vote for all of one party's candidates in national elections. At the same time, party voting in Congress was also in decline. In the House of Representatives in the 1930s about 60 per cent of votes followed party lines (although this was already very low by the standards of other core democracies), but by the

1970s this figure had fallen to below 40 per cent.

The democracies of the semi-periphery (Latin America, southern Europe and the Balkans) were very different from those of the core. They had weak foundations within society, were subject to enormous economic strains and faced the threat (often carried out) of overthrow by authoritarian regimes. In the early twentieth century they were dominated by oligarchies which derived their power from their role in the export of raw materials and food, the limited degree of industrialization that had taken place and extensive landholdings. Political parties were little more than clubs to link a few politicians in the capital with local elites and they relied on both legal and illegal manipulation of the electorates to gain and retain power. The social and economic control of powerful landlords and representatives of the central government was relatively easily transferred into control of the electorate because of the high levels of illiteracy. Between 1860 and 1913 government parties did not lose a single election in Romania, Italy, Spain or Portugal – changes in government took place by agreement between the monarch and the party leaders. In Spain, despite the granting of full male suffrage in the 1890s, the political system remained in the control of local bosses – *caciques* – who, operating with the provincial governors and the Ministry of the Interior, delivered majorities for whichever political group was favoured in Madrid. In the 1890s the parties agreed on a *turno pacifico*, under which they alternated in power in order to share the benefits derived from the extensive corruption. In Latin America political parties were also built on patron–client relationships, in which office and power were used to build personal political machines and blocs of support. In countries such as Colombia and Uruguay, the parties which dominated the twentieth century had their roots in the immediate post-independence phase in the nineteenth century. Over that long period they constructed deep foundations in particular regions and among certain interest groups in society. Although each party was a collection of personal factions (rather like the Japanese Liberal Democratic Party) they were, because of their foundations, highly stable and easily capable of surviving periods of authoritarian rule.

All these democratic systems were based on widespread electoral fraud. For example, in one electoral district in Spain in 1918, 124 voters managed to return 9,015 votes for the official candidate. Shifting alliances between elite groups could produce farcical differences in election results depending on which party was in government and able to manipulate the system. In Romania the Liberal Party won 17 seats in 1920, 260 in 1922, 16 in 1926, 298 a year later and 13 the year after that. In 1955 the right-wing government in Greece invented an electoral system of Byzantine complexity in order to maintain itself in power. The boundaries for seats were drawn using the 1940 census, to bias the system in favour of the rural areas. In 26 seats a simple plurality was all that was required for election, in 183 seats there was a mixed majority and proportional system and in 91 seats there was a pure proportional system, although only the two largest political alliances could participate in this 'redistribution' of representation. In these democracies, since political parties stood for very little, they tended to multiply rapidly. By 1926, just seven years after independence 31 parties were represented in the Polish parliament. In the eleven years after 1920, 44 parties participated in the Latvian elections, although this may have been related to the fact that a party could be set up with just 100 signatures and was then guaranteed state financial support. In Greece 44 parties contested the 1950 election.

In the European semi-periphery and Latin America, oligarchic political systems began to break down in the 1920s under pressure from the world depression after 1929, which was especially severe in these economies. In Europe the semi-periphery slipped into dictatorship of various sorts, but in Latin America a new 'populism' emerged, typified by leaders such as Getulio Vargas in Brazil and movements such as Acción Democratica in Venezuela and Movimento Nacionalista Revolucionario in Bolivia. In practice much of the language of populism turned out to be mere rhetoric. It was nationalist, statist and elitist and still saw the masses as something to be controlled and manipulated. These regimes concentrated their efforts on greater industrialization and import substitution. However, it proved to be very difficult to build any solid political base that could incorporate both the demands of the workers for greater share in the national wealth and the interests of the existing elites. These populist systems broke down after the late 1950s and were replaced by a wave of authoritarian, military dictatorships. In Brazil, the military forced through their own changes to the party system after 1964, maintaining a tradition of building parties from the top down. In turn these dictatorships lost power in the 1980s and were replaced by nominally democratic regimes. However, the social and economic base for the democracies of Latin America remained highly fragile, given the severe economic and social

divisions within these countries. On the other hand, in parts of the European semi-periphery – Portugal, Spain and Greece – the end of dictatorships in the 1970s did seem to mark a new departure. Membership of the European Community, together with increasing economic development which brought these states closer to the core economies, produced circumstances which appeared to favour a transition to a new social and economic base which would support democracy. In eastern and central Europe the transition to democracy after the fall of Communism in 1989 remained much more fragile. Economic conditions were still poor and democratic traditions were weak. In many countries, most of the old Communist ruling elite survived in power, though under slightly different political labels.

In the periphery democracy was notable mainly by its absence in the twentieth century. In Africa there was only one example of a peaceful transition from one-party rule to an alternative democratically elected government (Zambia in the early 1990s). India was the only state with a relatively continuous democratic tradition after independence. This was not based on any inheritance from the long period of British rule, which was essentially authoritarian, with only brief periods when Indian politicians were allowed some local and provincial power. Congress, founded in 1885, was an uneasy coalition between a leadership drawn from the small middle-class elite and the popular support for independence mobilized by Gandhi. There was always a tension between the essential moral demands of Gandhi and his followers and the much more limited and conventional aims of politicians such as Jawaharlal Nehru. The leadership were strong advocates of western institutions, which they saw as necessary for the 'modernization' of India. Congress was not an ideological party (apart from the demand for independence), nor was it a class party or directly a religious one, although de facto it became mainly Hindu after the formation of the Muslim League. It was an integrationist party which tried to represent as many different interests as possible in what was a highly diverse society. Politics within Congress was about the building of alliances from local to state, to regional and ultimately to national level. Faction leaders acted very much like *caciques* in the politics of the Latin American and Spanish semi-periphery: they were brokers to wield power, but also to integrate what would otherwise be a mass of conflicting interests. In the north Congress was built on the dominant land-owning castes and only in a few states (Karnataka and Gujarat) was its base in the lower castes, although it always had strong support from the lower social groups across the country. The dominance of the Congress Party lasted with little challenge, except in a few areas at local level, until the late 1960s and the passing of the generation which had secured independence. Under the leadership of Indira Gandhi in the early 1970s, increasing authoritarianism culminated in the suspension of the constitution in June 1975. Although Gandhi lost power in early 1977, she subsequently split the old Congress Party and regained power with the support of most of the old party power-brokers. However, Congress became increasingly dependent on the attractions of the remaining members of the Nehru–Gandhi dynasty. After the assassinations of both Indira and her son Rajiv, Congress found it increasingly difficult to maintain its support.

India used the British system of voting in single-member constituencies with only a plurality required for election. This exaggerated the level of support for Congress – it never obtained the majority of votes cast and kept power because the opposition was fragmented. In 1971 Congress won 44 per cent of the vote but over two-thirds of the seats in parliament. Other parties, such as the Communists in West Bengal, were allowed to control some states, but the central government was also prepared to declare a state of emergency and remove them from power when necessary. In other states such as Tamil Nadu and Andhra Pradesh ex-film stars matched and even exceeded the personal appeal and charisma of the Gandhi dynasty. Other parties represented particular interests – Akali Dal (the Sikhs), Jharkhand (the tribal communities) – but the most important development was the rise of the BJP (Bharatiya Janata Party) a strongly Hindu religious nationalist party. This challenged the very basis on which the Indian state had been constructed in 1947, namely secularism. Until the late 1980s the BJP was of little significance, but in 1991 it gained a fifth of the vote and took power in a number of states. At the same time Indian politics entered a new phase, with the end of Congress domination and the rise of coalition politics, as a vast range of parties attempted to find a stable basis for government. Whether Indian democracy would be able to withstand a multitude of strains following the demise of Congress with its strongly integrating role remained an open question.

By the last two decades of the twentieth century across the core states there were clear signs of growing disillusion with the performance of democracy, even though no one seriously suggested replacing it. The disenchantment was the result of a number of factors. There was an increasing level of discontent with party politics. The major political parties did not disappear and they continued to control the political system even though their membership levels dropped dramatically. Citizens found that single-interest lobby and campaigning groups were more attractive. Environmental groups such as Greenpeace and Friends of the Earth, women's groups, animal rights groups, peace groups, anti-abortion groups – all seemed able to deliver changes and articulate individual concerns better than the political parties. This was partly because parties necessarily had to appeal to a wide range of opinions and offer a policy mix across the political spectrum. Opinion polls and election results also showed that people became less attached to any one particular party, more neutral about all the parties and more willing to change their vote. The massive increase in education levels in the core states did not produce greater political knowledge and interest. In the United States in 1980 fewer than one in six of the population knew which party controlled the House of Representatives. A survey in Britain in 1996 showed that half the adult population was 'not interested' in politics, and three-quarters thought politicians were out of touch with ordinary people and would put the interests of their party above those of the nation. Less than 10 per cent trusted politicians to tell the truth if they were in trouble. In Japan opinion polls from the mid-1950s showed a steady decline in the number of people who thought the House of Representatives represented 'the will of the people'.

One consequence of this trend was a significant fall in voter participation. To some extent this was a problem throughout the twentieth century, especially in areas that were effectively one-party states. In the south of the United States the series of measures taken to stop blacks voting also reduced the white electorate and the consolidation of a one-party system further reduced interest in elections. In Texas the number of whites bothering to vote fell from 80 per cent in 1890 to less than 30 per cent in 1910 and it did not rise above 50 per cent until after 1950. In Virginia the electorate was so small that state employees and office-holders cast a third of all the votes. This ensured that state politics was controlled by the Byrd family and their political machine. Similarly in Northern Ireland, where the Unionist Party was guaranteed a majority in every election, many seats were never contested – more than 40 per cent of the total at the 1938 election for example. This phenomenon became more widespread in the latter part of the century. Voter turnout was high in western Europe immediately after the Second World War, but then declined. In Switzerland participation in national elections fell on every occasion after 1955 from just over 70 per cent to less than 50 per cent by the early 1980s. Even the mass of referendums available did not prove very attractive: turnout fell from an average of 60 per cent before 1940 to less than 40 per cent by the early 1980s. The lowest levels of voter participation in the core democracies were in the United States: less than half the electorate bothered to vote in most presidential elections and in the mid-term elections it was usually less than a third. In Britain, about seven out of ten electors voted in general elections but fewer than three out of ten voted at local elections and in those for the European parliament.

Another consequence of growing voter disillusionment was the rise of 'anti-system' parties, which stood on a platform attacking the existing system and all those who ran it. Some movements such as the Poujadists in France in the mid-1950s incorporated this appeal, but the first to be openly 'anti-system' was the Progress Party in Denmark. It was founded by a tax lawyer Mogens Glistrup and attacked taxes, bureaucracy and the welfare system, together with the 'conspiratorial' politics of the old parties. Its defence policy was a tape-recording in English and Russian to be played in the event of invasion, announcing that Denmark had surrendered. In the 1973 elections it received 16 per cent of the vote and became the third largest party. It remained an outcast in the system and gradually faded away. Similar protest parties could be found in states such as Sweden, Britain (the Monster Raving Loony Party) and the United States where the presidential campaigns of Ross Perot in 1992 and 1996 attempted to tap the same vein of disillusion with politics. With the disintegration of the Italian political system in the early 1990s the businessman Silvio Berlusconi decided to enter politics and set up his own party, Forza Italia. The methods adopted illustrate both the strength of anti-system feeling but also some of the realities of late-twentieth-century democratic politics. Six months before a formal decision was announced, Berlusconi's public relations firm Publitalia set up a network of 14,000 'supporters' clubs of which the firm's local representative became chairman. Forza Italia was not a political party in the accepted sense of the term. It was created artificially from the top down to support the ambition of one man. Officials were appointed not elected, committees were named not chosen. All the staff came from Berlusconi's firms. Its policies were developed not by the party members but by the executives of his main firm, Fininvest. No party congress was ever held, it had no agreed programme and no elected leadership. Support was built through the television stations which Berlusconi owned. Yet it was successful in the short term simply because it seemed to offer a solution to the problems of Italian democracy.

Another cause of disillusion among the electorate was the increasingly widespread belief that much of democratic politics was corrupt. To a large extent politics had always been about the trading of favours between politicians and political parties on the one hand and various interest groups, in particular industry, on the other. American politics was characterized by the strong party machines in the inner cities. These dated from the mid-nineteenth century, with the Tweed regime in New York, for example, and existed through to the 1960s, with the Daley machine in Chicago. All of them had close links to organized crime and were associated with high levels of corruption. Politics was based on these urban political machines, one-party control in many other areas and the need for politicians to raise money to finance their political campaigns. In return for campaign contributions there was the expectation that state contracts and favours would flow in the other direction. This process enriched numerous politicians, such as Lyndon Johnson, who rose from being a member of a poor family in rural Texas to being a multi-millionaire all, theoretically, financed by his salary as a professional politician.

The system of institutionalized corruption was deeply ingrained in Japan with its close links between the ruling Liberal Democratic Party and businessmen. This linkage was vital because of the need for politicians, especially the faction leaders within the party, to finance campaigns when the voters often expected tangible rewards for their votes. Direct bribery in return for contracts, especially defence contracts, was common in numerous countries from Belgium, the Netherlands and Japan to India. In Japan the prime minister from 1972–4, Tanaka Kakuei, accepted a $1.8 million bribe from the American Lockheed Corporation, and in India numerous politicians were implicated in the 'Bofors affair', involving bribes from the Swedish company in the mid-1980s. In 1996 it was also discovered that the Indian businessman S.K. Jain had 115 politicians and officials on his payroll, including the leader of the BJP party

(L.K. Advarni) and six cabinet members, with bribes totalling £12 million.

In other countries, such as Britain, direct corruption was less common. Instead businessmen and others could buy honours and titles, and achieve respectability in a deeply status-conscious society, through contributions to party funds. Normally the details were kept away from the public and surfaced only occasionally. They did so in the early 1920s when Lloyd George as prime minister and leader of one faction of the Liberal Party was openly selling honours to build up his campaign fund. All that was unusual in this operation was its scale and the open price list for each honour, depending on status. Equally worrying for many electors was the corruption of power; the suspicion that politicians were prepared to use the power of the offices they held for party and personal ends. The clearest example was the illegal actions and the abuse of power demonstrated by President Nixon in the Watergate scandal.

Perhaps the most devastating exposure of corruption in a modern democracy came in Italy in the early 1990s; it led to the collapse of the political system which had existed since the Second World War. By 1995 over 200 deputies, 5 ex-party leaders, 4 ex-prime ministers and 3,000 other senior figures were either charged with, or under investigation for, corruption. Giulio Andreotti, who had been prime minister on seven occasions, was on trial accused of collaboration with the Mafia and acting to protect their interests while in government. The post-war system was built on the Christian Democrats' permanent occupation of office, no matter what happened to their vote. This was deemed necessary in order to exclude the second largest party, the Communists. Although governments changed regularly, the political system was highly stable (Italy only had the same number of post-war elections as the other major west European states). The governmental changes were merely slight adjustments between the ruling coalition parties or within the Christian Democrats. Like the Liberal Democrats in Japan and Congress in India, the Christian Democrats split into factions to promote various interests and groupings: for example, one was based around the old southern ruling class and another on the newer groups from the industrial areas of the north. Given the stability of the political system there were really only two coalitions possible in Italy. Either centrism (which tended to apply until the early 1960s) through an alliance of the Christian Democrats with the Liberals and republicans, or a centre-left grouping including the PSI 'socialists' instead of the Liberals, which applied until the mid-1970s. From the mid-1970s, with the Liberals in decline, a *pentapartito* including both Liberals and the PSI was the norm. Between 1945 and 1981 every prime minister was a Christian Democrat and they continuously controlled defence and foreign affairs. In permanent office they built a huge bureaucracy of patronage using public money. From the early 1980s the PSI was incorporated into the system when its leader Bettino Craxi became prime minister.

In the 1980s the system of organized 'kleptocracy' began to collapse under its own weight. The Christian Democrats had long done deals with the criminal groups in the south. Criminals dominated much of local government and, in return for large amounts of public money, organized large-scale ballot fraud to ensure the Christian Democrats maintained political control. The scale of the misuse of public funds was immense. For example, by the mid-1980s the Calabrian forestry service employed over 30,000 people, even though the area was almost barren of trees. In the small Calabrian town of Taurianova both politics and crime were controlled by the local criminal boss and head of the Christian Democratic Party, Don Francesco Macri. Out of a total population of 16,000 over 2,000 worked for the local health authority and another 3,500 lived on state disability benefit. The town also had a murder rate twice that of the worst inner-city area in the United States.

Such corruption was normal in the south but it was in the north, particularly Milan, that the system began to unravel. The problems started in February 1992 when the PSI head of a local charitable trust, Mario Chiesa, a close friend of Craxi, was caught taking a bribe. It was found that he was worth over $9 million and paying 10 per cent of the bribes to the PSI. It rapidly became clear that the contracts for the railway system, tramway and sports stadia in Milan all included large bribes to the political parties. As investigations spread, a system of highly organized corruption was revealed. Thousands of public works contracts had no purpose other than to generate bribes for politicians, probably involving several billion dollars. These bribes were split between all the parties (in some cases including the Communists) and this was often done in proportion to the vote each party received at the elections. The PSI went even further by forcing businessmen to pay contributions to party funds to allow them to join a list which enabled them to compete for state contracts on which further bribes then had to be paid. Estimates suggested that the PSI was getting about $20 million a year in bribes and the Christian Democrats more. Much of the money also went personally to the politicians – by the late 1980s Craxi was the owner of a luxury flat in Milan, a house on Lake Como and a private villa in Tunisia (where he eventually fled into exile when he was charged with corruption).

Investigations also turned to the role of the state-owned companies, especially the nationalized holding company ENI. It was discovered that the company paid over $1 billion to the political parties in the 1970s alone and that was before really serious corruption began. State money too was used to benefit the parties directly. In 1990 the state bought out, on generous terms, the Ferruzzi group's stake in a public-sector chemical company and in return Ferruzzi paid the parties $100 million. As the investigations continued the whole political system and the parties that had flourished with it for the previous fifty years collapsed in ignominy and public hatred. One of the first replacements – the businessman, Silvio Berlusconi – was also forced from office when it became clear he too had paid numerous bribes in the previous decade, though it was difficult to see how his business empire could have survived without doing the same as every other corporation.

Another factor in the increasing disillusionment with and lack of interest in politics in the core states was the feeling that governments were losing their power to wider and more impersonal economic forces. In this respect, democratic governments were no different from others around the world. The problem was that the claims of the political parties to be able to provide prosperity, rising living standards and jobs were increasingly out of line with reality. All governments found that the international financial system and international capitalism, in which large transnational corporations wielded substantial power, often left them with little ability to control their own destinies. To some extent this had always been the case. As early as 1931 the Labour government in Britain had been forced to cut public expenditure, in particular social spending, in order to meet the demands of the major international banks whose support was required to maintain the value of sterling. Governments found that the alternatives available to deal with the decline in industrial employment in the core states in the late twentieth century were problematic. If they intervened to provide subsidies, these tended to escalate to unmanageable proportions. If they stood aside and allowed the forces of the free market to operate, then they were still left with a major bill in terms of unemployment pay and increasing social problems. In these circumstances, electorates began to suspect that many problems were beyond the power of mere politicians to solve and that party politics was increasingly irrelevant.

18 SOCIALISM

REVOLUTIONARY GROUPS attracted little support in the core democracies. By the early twentieth century nearly all the members of socialist movements in the core countries were prepared to operate within the limits set by liberal democracy in a capitalist state in order to achieve a more just and egalitarian social and economic order. Democracy might seem an odd route to power for socialists to adopt. Many socialist leaders in the latter half of the nineteenth and the early part of the twentieth centuries were schooled in Marxism. If they believed, as Marx did, that capitalism as a form of social organization was doomed and that it would eventually be replaced by socialism, then there was little point in participating in liberal democratic politics and seeking to reform capitalism. Indeed such action, if successful, would merely ameliorate social and economic conditions, thereby postponing the rise of revolutionary feeling in the working class. Perhaps the working class would be better advised to organize itself and await the inevitable downfall of capitalism. The Anarchist congress at Chaud-de-Fronds in 1870 declared: 'All workers' participation in bourgeois governmental politics cannot have other results than the consolidation of the existing state of affairs.' The problem for socialists, particularly those of a Marxist persuasion, was that the capitalist system showed few indications of behaving as Marx had predicted. By the late nineteenth century there were few, if any, signs of breakdown. Indeed, in many respects capitalism seemed not only more stable but able to deliver rising living standards for most workers. Eduard Bernstein, a leading member of the German SPD and former secretary to Friedrich Engels, scribbled a note setting out his doubts: 'Peasants do not sink; middle class does not disappear; crises do not grow ever larger; misery and serfdom do not increase.' In these circumstances perhaps the revolution forecast by Marx would not happen.

Despite widespread doubts about the imminence of capitalist collapse and revolution, participation in electoral politics remained a contentious issue among socialists for decades. New social democratic parties were founded in the 1880s and within a decade the first socialists were elected to the parliaments of the western European states. However, they were not really participants in liberal democracy. At first many parties such as the SPD in Germany and the Social Democrats in Sweden were involved in politics merely as part of their propaganda drive. In 1898 a survey of the leaders of the Second International (the organization of socialists from many countries) found that a fifth of them thought socialist parties should never participate in government, nearly 40 per cent thought that they could but only in very exceptional circumstances and only a minority thought such participation was desirable. Nevertheless many socialist leaders continued to advocate participation. In 1892 Karl Kautsky argued in *The Class Struggle* that socialism would transform parliamentary democracy and not vice versa: 'Whenever the proletariat engages in parliamentary activity as a self-conscious class, parliamentarism begins to change its character. It ceases to be a mere tool in the hands of the bourgeoisie . . . The proletariat has therefore no reason to distrust parliamentary action.' Bernstein, in *Evolutionary Socialism* in 1899, explicitly abandoned a Marxist analysis and argued that because capitalism was ameliorative then socialism would have to build a broad alliance in order to achieve power.

The majority of socialists were convinced that they were bound to gain office under liberal democracy and that then they would be able to use their political power to reach their economic and social goals. A series of reforms would gradually accumulate until full socialism was achieved. This argument seemed to be supported by the rapid rise in support for socialist parties. The German SPD gained just 125,000 votes in 1871, yet by 1890 it gained nearly 1·5 million and by 1912, when it was overwhelmingly the strongest party, over 4 million votes. In the Netherlands the socialist vote rose from 3 per cent of the total in 1895 to nearly 20 per cent by 1913. As industrial output continued to expand, the number of industrial workers increased. It seemed inevitable that the working class would eventually be the majority in society and vote for the socialist parties, who would then take power. The early socialist parties therefore retained in their programmes radical aims intended to bring about a major restructuring of society. The first programme of the Swedish Social Democrats stated, 'Social Democracy differs from other parties in that it aspires to completely transform the economic organization of bourgeois society and bring about the social liberation of the working class.' In 1918 the new constitution for the Labour Party in Britain stated the party's aims as being the 'common ownership of the means of production, distribution and exchange'. If this was carried out, it would be completely incompatible with capitalism.

A more sophisticated analysis might have suggested certain problems with these arguments. The flaws began to be apparent in the first decades of the twentieth century and it gradually became clear that optimistic assumptions about the inevitable triumph of socialism were sadly misplaced. The growth in electoral support for socialist parties, which seemed so strong early in the century, slowed and nowhere did it reach over half the vote. The maximum was well over 40 per cent in the two decades after the Second World War in Austria, Norway, Sweden and Britain. (Democracies rarely gave any single party a majority of the vote in the twentieth century.) The problem for the social democratic parties was that the workers – defined as the manual working class engaged in mining, manufacturing, construction and transport – never became a majority in any society. The economic and social changes in the core states during the twentieth century, in particular the relative decline of heavy industry and the growth of service industries, meant that the working class rarely made up more than a third of the total population. The socialist parties always recognized that a fundamental prerequisite to obtaining a majority was the gaining of the vote by all adult males. When this was finally granted it was counterbalanced by women also gaining the vote, which reduced the proportion of manual workers in the electorate. In general women were less likely to vote for the socialist parties. Neither was the working class united in voting for the socialists. Before 1914 only in Germany did a majority of workers vote for a socialist party – in Britain most still voted Liberal even after the setting up of a separate Labour Party.

Although the proportion of the working class voting for the social democratic parties generally rose significantly after 1918, there was still a substantial percentage, at least a third and sometimes more, who voted for the 'bourgeois' parties. Nor were the interests of the working class always harmonious and this produced problems for social democratic parties. The interests of skilled and unskilled workers were often different and there was a deep gulf between the employed and the unemployed. The decision to operate within the existing liberal democratic order brought other fundamental problems. Under liberal democracy economic and political organization did not coincide, the different classes and interests within society operated in politics as individuals. Social democratic parties found that they had to accept the prevailing ethos of a basic harmony of interests between the citizens of a state, even if they sought their own self-interest on particular issues. Parliaments were fora in which there was a consensus about the need to pursue the common good of society (not merely one group within it). Once they took part in parliamentary politics, the leaders of the social democratic parties were incorporated into the values and manoeuvrings of bourgeois politics.

In these circumstances the options open to social democratic parties were limited. If they accepted the constitutional route to power under liberal democracy then they had to forgo the alternative of mass industrial action. This may not have been a great loss, since general strikes turned out to be unproductive, as the trade unions discovered in Belgium in 1902, Sweden in 1909, France in 1920 and Britain in 1926. As the chairman of the Labour Party in Britain, John McGurk, told the annual conference in 1919:

> We are either constitutionalists or we are not constitutionalists. If we are constitutionalists, if we believe in the efficacy of the political weapon (and we do, or why do we have a Labour Party?) then it is both unwise and undemocratic because we fail to get a majority at the polls to turn around and demand that we should substitute industrial action.

One alternative was to remain a party that only represented the interests of the working class. This was the strategy adopted by the SPD in Germany before 1914 and to a large extent up until 1933. The party could develop very strong institutions and deep roots within the working class, but it could not achieve a majority and it could only govern as part of a coalition with the bourgeois parties. In 1912 the British Labour Party (which was always closely based on membership by trade unions as a whole rather than by individuals) specifically refused to grant membership to 'managers, foremen and persons engaged in commercial pursuits on their own account'. The alternative strategy was to try to build support in areas outside the traditional working class. But this was equally problematic. In the

1890s the French socialists tried to develop a programme designed to appeal to small businessmen, shopkeepers and small peasant farmers. The SPD in Germany refused to have such a programme until 1927. In 1918 the Labour Party in Britain tried to widen its support by opening membership to 'workers by brain' and by appealing to 'the people', 'all producers' and 'the entire working population'. The only group excluded were 'the idlers who live upon the income from investments'. However, the decision by socialist parties to adopt this strategy meant that their policies had to be adapted to appeal to other groups in society. Socialism was therefore bound to be diluted into a generally reformist stance. The social democratic parties were usually reluctant to go too far down this road – they regarded their base in the working class as vital and, in addition, they were often dominated by working-class institutions such as trade unions and co-operative movements. In some countries, such as France, Germany before 1933 and Italy, the danger in widening their appeal too much was that it would enable the strong Communist Parties to increase their strength to the left of the socialists. On the other hand, failure to widen their appeal could mean that social democratic parties were doomed to long-term structural decline.

Although the first half of the twentieth century was the time when the industrial working class was at its peak in terms of numbers, it was also the time when the social democratic parties had little impact on the political scene. Although it was clear that the social democratic parties had broken with any idea of revolution, it was unclear what they had to offer in its place. After the First World War they achieved power for the first time, but nearly always as minority governments or as part of a coalition. In Britain Labour, which replaced the Liberals as the main opposition party during the 1920s, formed two minority governments in 1924 and 1929–31, there were three socialist governments in Sweden in the 1920s, the SPD was reasonably strong in Germany as were the Social Democrats in Austria and in 1936 there was a short-lived Popular Front government in France. The only major achievement was in Sweden, where the Social Democrats gained power as a majority government in 1932. All these governments had to cope with the problems the core economies experienced in the 1920s and 1930s, when it was unclear how socialist remedies, such as common ownership, would deal with these problems. Most socialist governments turned out to be highly conventional in their economic policies, supporting traditional financial policies and introducing a few limited social reforms which were usually little different from those other reforming parties supported. The only advance came in Sweden, where Ernst Wigfoss, the party's main theoretician, advocated Keynesian economic policies to stimulate recovery (something the Labour government of 1929–31 in Britain specifically rejected). In 1938 he set out what was to become, after 1945, a compromise adopted by most of the social democratic parties in Europe: 'Neither the working-class movement nor private capitalists could hope to suppress the other altogether, that they should recognise this fact, and should co-operate to achieve their common interest – increased efficiency in production.'

After 1945 social democratic parties gained power occasionally in western Europe. They lacked any clear 'socialist' ideology, but they had clear programmes that offered partial solutions to immediate problems. For a time the idea of 'planning', which had been in vogue in the 1930s and during the Second World War, was seen as a way of imposing some control over capitalism, but it rapidly passed out of fashion after the late 1940s. A major policy instrument for social democratic governments became 'nationalization' or public ownership of key industries. This was only partly based on any theory of how a 'socialist' economy (whatever that was) might operate, but owed more to an attempt to provide at least some levers of power within a broadly capitalist economy. The difficulties involved were made painfully apparent under the post-war Labour government in Britain. State ownership of industries was nothing new: the pre-war Conservative governments had established a state-controlled airline, publicly owned underground transport in London and a state system for electricity distribution. After 1945 basic industries such as coal, energy, railways and iron and steel were nationalized by the Labour government. The problem was that, except in the last case, they were unprofitable in the private sector yet they had to be kept in being for the sake of the economy as a whole. This rescue of failing industries involved a major cost to governments over long periods of time yet produced few tangible benefits in terms of improving economic performance. The options open to social democratic governments were therefore limited. They were restricted to attempts to 'regulate' the economy through general economic policy and taxation and the introduction of welfare policies. However, this was even further from any evolutionary road to socialism, particularly because governments depended on continued economic growth in the private sector to fund increases in public spending on welfare measures. There were, therefore, inherent and unavoidable tensions between policies designed to ensure that the private sector operated efficiently and the need to fund welfare programmes aimed at mitigating some of the social effects produced by the operation of the market economy, especially as it began to operate on a global scale.

Under American pressure through the Marshall Aid programme and from the realities they faced in operating within a capitalist economy, social democratic parties accepted capitalism. The most they now hoped to do was make it marginally more just socially. In many countries this acceptance of market economies was marked by the formal rejection of any Marxist heritage. The Bad Godesberg programme adopted by the SPD in West Germany in 1959 and roughly contemporaneous actions in the Netherlands and Austria were typical of this change. Remarkably it was the British Labour Party, probably the least influenced by Marxism of any of the west European social democratic parties, that refused to formally jettison its commitment to complete state ownership. In practice it adopted the reformism advocated by Anthony Crosland in *The Future of Socialism*, published in 1956. Crosland argued that the widespread adoption of Keynesian economics, together with the wealth produced by the long post-war economic boom made possible a gradual redistribution of this new wealth through taxation and benefits so as to achieve greater equality. The formal commitment to total state ownership was not dropped by the Labour Party until 1995. In France there was little revisionist thinking, but the socialists remained a relatively small minority until they became a general reformist party in the 1970s. In Italy any remaining radicalism in the socialist parties was ditched in the 1950s. In 1963 the social democrats joined the Christian Democratic coalition.

Outside Scandinavia the social democratic parties remained weak. Although in Britain the Labour Party regularly gained over 40 per cent of the vote, it was out of power between 1951 and 1964, having lost the key election just before the long post-war economic boom began. In France the socialists were a marginal political force in the 1950s, as they were in the Netherlands, where the confessional parties remained strong. Unexpectedly the SPD in Germany were unable to match their best performances before the rise of Nazism and remained out of power until the 1960s. After the early 1960s there was a brief revival for the social democratic parties. In part this reflected rising concern about the performance of some of the core economies, especially in Britain, which produced renewed emphasis on 'modernization' and 'planning' as a way of increasing growth. The social democratic parties retained a commitment to 'equality', although they had little precise idea of what this meant in practice or how to achieve it. In Britain the Labour Party was in power from 1964 to 1970 but achieved little. The SPD gained power in West Germany in 1966, though as part of a 'grand coalition' with the Christian Democrats. It went on to dominate German politics in the 1970s and Labour was again in power in Britain between 1974 and 1979. In both countries these social democratic governments could achieve little more than crisis management in the face of the problems caused by the end of the long post-war boom in 1973 and the major increase in oil prices.

Social democracy did achieve a major success in Scandinavia apart from in Finland, which had a very different political history from its neighbours following the attempted revolution and 'white' reaction after 1917. At the beginning of the twentieth century these countries seemed the least likely candidates to be strongly social democratic. They still had economies with large rural sectors and were very much on the periphery of western Europe. However, relatively late industrialization (never very extensive in Denmark) took place in conditions of semi-democracy, where the independent peasantry (the land-owning aristocracy was weak) allied itself with the growing working class to demand universal suffrage. These states also had the advantage of not having extensive overseas empires or strong military traditions and all avoided war until 1940. In the 1920s politics was unstable in all these countries, but this period was followed by a merging of the social democratic and peasants' parties into general 'people's parties', in Denmark in 1929, Sweden in 1932 and Norway in 1935. This fusion was built upon agreement to wide-ranging agricultural subsidies by the social democratic parties.

The social democratic parties in Scandinavia developed their own unique brand of socialist thought which believed that cumulative reforms could have a revolutionary impact. Unlike the British Labour Party, they did not place the nationalization of industries at the centre of their programmes. The primary aim was seen as obtaining political power and then using that power to provide the working class with a greater share of the national wealth. This was done by creating an extensive welfare state that incorporated benefits not just for the poor but also for major and powerful groups in society. Their intention was to build a wide coalition that benefited from the welfare state and therefore had an interest in maintaining it. This policy had the consequence politically of shifting the consensus in society towards the left and making the social democrats the natural party to run the system they had devised. However, these parties did not follow Crosland in believing that Keynesianism and a limited welfare state was sufficient. Although in the Scandinavian system there was no need for extensive nationalization, social democratic governments gradually established an extensive regulation of capitalism through centralized wage bargaining and pressure from the government for industry to meet certain social and economic goals.

Outside Scandinavia, failure to incorporate the middle class extensively into the welfare state produced a limited base for the social democratic parties. The result was that the decline of the industrial working class as a major element in society, and the emergence of new occupational structures, worked against their long-term interests. Across western Europe social democratic parties were in decline in the last third of the century. In Britain, the Labour Party's vote peaked in 1951 at nearly 50 per cent, but declined fairly steadily thereafter to 37 per cent by 1979 and to just over 27 per cent in 1983. The major rise in support in 1997 followed the abandonment of most of the Labour Party's historic beliefs and its transformation into no more than a moderately reformist party. By the late 1980s support for the SPD in Germany was back to its low point in the late 1950s. In Austria the party lost a fifth of its support in a decade. Only in Greece, Spain and Portugal did the socialist parties do well. But these parties were hardly social democratic in their policies and projected little more than a general reformist image, if that.

Decline in support for social democratic parties was also reflected in the declining importance of trade unions in the core states. At the beginning of the century they were the epitome of working-class organization, with a determination to improve their conditions of life and work. However, they owed little to socialist theory. It was not the most downtrodden and oppressed who organized themselves, but rather the skilled workers, who created the most effective trade unions and went on strike the most often, usually at times of high employment when their bargaining position was greatest. They did so for better conditions and higher wages and only rarely were their actions ever linked to a commitment to socialism or to achieve political ends. Most trade union members were not highly committed politically. The most heavily borrowed books from the SPD and trade union libraries in Germany at the start of the century were not the classics of socialist literature but escapist fiction, adventure stories and romances. Only in a few countries, in particular Russia, where demands for better conditions were regarded as revolutionary, were the workers and trade unions driven towards greater radicalism and even revolution as the only way of securing their demands. Until after the First World War the growth in trade unions was limited and in many countries rivals to the avowedly socialist unions were started by the churches and other political parties. The main period of growth came in the 1920s – in Germany membership was three times the pre-war level and new, widely based, primarily unskilled unions such as the Transport and General Workers in Britain, grew in importance. Organization among workers in the new service industries proved much more problematic.

After 1945 the general trend was towards de-coupling the trade unions from the social democratic parties. This was not difficult in countries such as France, where the Communists controlled the major unions. The closest relations between the trade unions and the party were in Scandinavia, especially Sweden. There the trade union confederation (LO) was very strong. Nine out of ten manual workers were organized into twenty-three streamlined industrial unions, strongly controlled from the centre and able to deliver agreements in the tripartite negotiations between government, employers and unions which began in 1938. The LO was probably as important as the Social Democratic Party, and indeed many of the party's and the government's economic policies were first developed by the unions. In Austria and Germany the trade unions were equally strong, but they were not so close either to the party or the government. The position in Britain was unique and represented the worst of both worlds. The trade unions were formally affiliated to the Labour Party, they were major contributors to its funding, they sponsored many members of parliament and were deeply involved in party policy-making at all levels, indeed they could normally control the party conference through use of their block vote. However, the unions were highly fragmented and not controlled by the Trades Union Congress. Relations between the party and the unions were reasonably harmonious until the mid-1950s, but then they became increasingly acrimonious. The Labour governments of the 1960s and 1970s tried to reach agreements with the trade unions over wages policy, accompanied by trade-offs in terms of greater benefits. The government found that the agreements were not kept for any significant period because of the fragmentation in the union movement. In practice, association with the unions was a disadvantage to the party, especially given the fact that a considerable number of union members did not vote Labour and many Labour voters were not members of trade unions.

Throughout the twentieth century the social democratic parties of western Europe always worked within the ground rules laid down by liberal, capitalist democracy. This meant that the changes they advocated and occasionally carried out were limited and incremental. They were in essence little different from other reformist parties. The realization that this was the case often took years to achieve, as many members of the parties continued to advocate more radical changes, which were not practical politics given the realities of the power structures in the liberal democracies and the power of strong vested interests. The eventual realization of the limits on action came late in the century, not till the mid-1990s for the Labour Party in Britain. By then the parties would have been almost unrecognizable to the socialists of the early twentieth century with their high hopes and idealism about what democratic socialism could achieve.

It is difficult to see what real difference the social democratic parties made to the course of development over the century. The creation of a state-owned sector in the economy was not a specifically social democratic response. It took place in every western European state and was the result of specific problems, often the failure of certain industries and companies in the private sector. Governments judged that these activities were essential and that the state would, in the wider national interest, have to step in and rescue the failures of capitalism. Neither was the creation of a welfare state a specifically social democratic policy. Greater welfare provision in the twentieth century was common to all the core states and some of the most developed systems were found in the states normally run by conservative or Christian Democratic governments. The trend towards some greater income equality was common in all the core states until the 1980s and was not the result of specifically social democratic policies. The contribution of the social democratic parties, especially in Scandinavia, was that the state took a higher proportion of national wealth than in other countries and the welfare systems had a wider scope than the more 'liberal' variants found in France, Italy and Germany and the mixed system in Britain. They were fundamentally different from those found in Japan and the United States.

Social democracy as an effective political force was almost entirely confined to western Europe. Why were the United States and Japan so different from the other industrialized core states? Early in the twentieth century the United States had a socialist movement that was at least as influential and well developed as any in western Europe. The American socialists had many of the same arguments as their European counterparts about whether to participate in the existing political system; they also arrived at the conclusion that they should do so, if only for the propaganda opportunities this would provide. By 1912 the Socialist Party had nearly 120,000 members and over a thousand were elected members of local government. The leader of the party, Eugene Debs, stood in the 1912 presidential election and gained almost a million votes. This was about 6 per cent of the total and was relatively high compared with the levels of support for social democratic parties in other countries. In practice this turned out to be the high-water mark of socialism in the United States. The reasons why are complex.

In the American political system it was difficult for any party to make a breakthrough against the two major parties. This was not just because of the electoral system, but also because the two main parties were coalitions of widely varying (indeed at times almost incompatible) interests. The Republicans and Democrats, usually with strong support from local businesses, were prepared when necessary to combine at a local level on 'fusion' tickets to defeat the socialists. The trade unions in the United States were also weak and divided and not closely linked to the Socialist Party. The American Federation of Labor was led by Samuel Gompers, a moderate who was prepared to play a subordinate role and not challenge the existing industrial system. Gompers was widely distrusted within the Socialist Party, but so also were the anarcho-syndicalist International Workers of the World. The IWW (or 'Wobblies') were radical and therefore subject to high levels of repression from government and employers' organizations at both national and state levels. The degree of government repression in the United States was such that the emergence of a strong working-class movement proved very difficult. Occasionally the socialists could score a limited success – in 1913 the party still had over thirty mayors and a similar number of state legislators and could gain a third of the vote when running against the Republicans and Democrats in Chicago. The movement split over American participation in the First World War (as did some other social democratic movements in western Europe). Gompers supported the war, Debs did not. Nevertheless Debs still gained nearly a million votes in the 1920 presidential election while still in jail for his anti-war activities. A crucial factor in the socialists' decline was heavy government repression during the 'Red Scare' after the First World War. The movement split again over its attitude to the Russian Revolution. During the 1920s its organization across the country crumbled. Debs was still highly popular, but he did not run in the 1924 elections. Instead the Socialists were part of the progressive coalition backing Robert La Follette. The coalition was dominated by La Follette's Farmer-Labor party from Minnesota and although it gained nearly 5 million votes there was no space for a third party in the American political system. The socialists did run for the presidency in 1932, when Norman Thomas gained almost 900,000 votes, but the party split again two years later and degenerated into no more than a fringe political organization.

In Japan a Social Democratic Party was formed in 1901, but it was immediately banned by the government. In the period before 1945 the semi-democratic imperial political system was dominated by conservative groups and social democratic parties were notable by their absence. Trade unions were weak: their membership was never more than about one in twelve of factory workers. They had to face major police harassment and the use of large numbers of transient female and rural workers, which reduced the importance of skilled workers who were normally the main organizational base of trade unions. The trade unions also had to counter a strong campaign from the major companies, which created their own limited welfare systems to stop their skilled workers joining unions. In 1938 the government forced the unions in each factory to convert themselves into associations which were part of the Industrial Patriotic Movement, designed to support the expansionist aims of the government. Only after the Second World War was the Japan Socialist Party (JSP) formed through the amalgamation of numerous small groups. Within five years three groups – a centrist party, a neo-Buddhist party and a Communist Party – split from the party. The rump of the JSP saw its share of the vote decline to about a fifth of the total and it became heavily dependent on the support of unions in the public sector. A gradual revival following numerous scandals in the ruling Liberal Democrats saw the JSP achieve power for a brief period in the early 1990s. Like its counterparts in western Europe, it achieved little and found that it could not act as much more than a general reformist party.

19   REPRESSION

ONE OF the characteristic features of the twentieth century was the worldwide increase in the power of the state. Governments took greater responsibility for economic development and industrial policy, they created welfare systems and they introduced policies and regulations affecting activities in almost every part of society. There was, however, a darker side to this expansion of the state. In every country the state's power to control its own citizens increased, as did its ability to deal with those whom it thought posed a threat to its interests. The democracies of the core states were no exception. However, the actions they took were completely different from those of the dictatorships of the semi-periphery and periphery, let alone the highly developed repressive system of the Soviet Union and the barbarism of Cambodia under Pol Pot in the late 1970s. There was a gradation in government action, from restrictions on free expression and monitoring of certain activities by security agencies, to the banning of certain organizations and imprisonment without trial. The democratic states generally did not go beyond this point. Elsewhere in the world people were subject to arbitrary arrest, torture, death or slave labour for long periods in conditions where death was often a merciful release. In the most extensively repressive systems millions of people worked in these 'empires of slavery' and millions were deliberately killed for various 'crimes' against the regime.

The problem for the individual was that it was not simply state violence that was a threat, it was also the climate of fear that this induced. Who was a government agent and informer? What sort of action or unguarded comment might prove fatal? Once governments built huge repressive structures and organizations, they found them difficult to control. Often these organizations carried out their own policies, not those of the government. Even the democracies faced this problem. In discussing repression, the concept of 'legality' is not useful. The highly repressive apartheid system in South Africa was constructed legally by passing the necessary legislation through the whites-only parliament, and much of the Soviet system of repression was 'legal' under the 1936 constitution. On the other hand, in Britain there was no legal basis for the activities of the intelligence agencies until the late 1980s, except for the vague concept that they could act under the residual powers of the monarch.

Some trends worked against the power of the state especially in the last quarter of the century. Governments could, if they wanted, control much of the flow of information within a country. However, they faced increasing problems from technological developments and the global transmission of information. States could usually stop newspapers entering a country. Radio transmissions could be jammed and in only a few cases, such as West German broadcasts into East Germany, did terrestrial television have the range to cause problems for repressive states. The introduction of satellite broadcasting left governments unable to control much of the information coming into their countries. The only possible response, adopted by some states in the Middle East such as Iran and Saudi Arabia, was to ban the use of satellite dish receivers. The development of fax communications, portable phones, electronic mail and the worldwide computer web meant that information could be transmitted around the globe in ways that were beyond the control of any government.

In the later part of the nineteenth century it was generally assumed in the core countries, as part of their widespread optimism about the future, that their societies were becoming more liberal and tolerant, that individual freedom was increasing and that the power of the state would remain limited. From the mid-nineteenth century most of the core states ended their control over newspapers and allowed relatively free expression of opinion, though the British retained state censorship of the theatre until 1968. The core states also relaxed their restrictions on meetings and assemblies. There were a few limited exceptions to this general trend. The British found that dealing with organizations demanding Home Rule or independence for Ireland drove them to create special police units and give extra power to the security organizations in Ireland.

In 1898 an international conference was held in Rome to coordinate, for the first time, an international response to the anarchist movement. The main outcome was that over twenty countries agreed to treat anarchists as criminals rather than political offenders. This meant that they could be extradited and it was agreed that any attempt on the life of a monarch, head of state or their immediate family became automatic grounds for extradition. In 1903 the United States went further. They banned immigration by anyone who did not believe in organized government. Some states in the United States went further still. In 1902–3, three states, including New York, made it a criminal offence to advocate anarchism. These were the first laws in American history that made it a criminal offence simply to belong to a group. Five years later the federal government banned anarchist material from the mails, the first time such a ban had been imposed on political grounds.

In most core states it was the activities of trade unions that brought the most repressive response. Most states legalized trade unions and strikes in the second half of the nineteenth century, although in Britain only with legislation in 1906 and 1911 was their legal position finally resolved. Even when union activities were legalized, there were often strict limitations on what they could do. In Sweden a law passed in 1899 made peaceful picketing or arguing with strike-breakers punishable by two years in jail. In the ten years after 1902 legal strikes on the railways in Italy, Hungary, Bulgaria, France and Spain were all ended by conscripting workers into the army and threatening them with court martial unless they returned to work. In the early twentieth century the most repressive democratic state in its attitudes to trade unions and labour organizations was undoubtedly the United States. Only highly moderate unions like the AFL were tolerated and strong campaigns were mounted by state governments and employers against more radical groups. Disputes were characterized by high levels of violence by workers against property and by the state and companies (using private police and 'armies') against workers. In general local politics was dominated by business interests and in many places, especially company towns, they controlled the police and were also able to recruit their own private forces. In 1919 during the steel strike in Pennsylvania 25,000 company workers were enrolled as police deputies and joined with a special Coal and Iron Police, which was chosen, paid and armed by the companies. State militia and federal troops were also used against strikers. In Colorado, when the Western Federation of Miners called a strike in 1903 to secure an eight-hour day, martial law was declared, the state militia arrested the union leaders, held them in military detention and refused to obey a court order to release them. Over 400 union leaders were deported from the state. In 1912 during a garment workers' strike in Lawrence, Massachusetts, all public meetings were declared illegal, the strike leaders were jailed for ten months without charge and a fifteen-year-old boy was bayoneted to death. When the strike leaders sent their children out of the town the local police refused to allow the train to leave. They then beat and clubbed the women and children on the train and had fourteen of the children sent to state institutions by the local juvenile courts, even though they had committed no offence. A year later during another miners' strike in Colorado the National Guard was mobilized and sent into the area. Together with the local militia they attacked the striker settlement, killing eleven children and two women. Three union leaders were taken prisoner and shot.

All countries saw a growth in their police forces during the nineteenth century, but they remained relatively weak. In general their powers were limited and not strongly enforced: Victor Adler, the Austrian socialist leader, characterized the Habsburg empire as 'absolutism tempered by slovenliness'. The major exception to this trend was Russia, an absolute monarchy which was only slightly less slovenly than the Habsburgs. The Russian government tried hard to suppress certain publications but with only limited success. In the five years after 1905 administrative penalties were imposed on over 4,000 periodicals and over 1,000 were suppressed. This might seem an impressive achievement, but in practice the government was unable to stem the flood of information. In the two years before the outbreak of war in August 1914 the Bolshevik newspaper *Pravda* published 645 issues, but less than a quarter were stopped by the authorities. Troops were used regularly to suppress meetings and demonstrations, but it was difficult to know where to stop because in Russia almost any criticism of the government was regarded as potentially revolutionary. In January 1904 the police closed down a conference in St Petersburg of over 3,000 delegates to the Third Congress of Activists in the Field of Technical Education. In 1906 a lecture on 'Tuberculosis and Its Social Causes' was forbidden and in 1912 a lecture by the historian Paul Miliukov was stopped after he stated 'nationalism has become the banner of the liberal movement'.

Russia had a secret police force – the Okhrana – which took its modern form in 1880. By the early twentieth century it was about 15,000 strong and it had had some 'successes'. For five years after 1903 Yevno Azef was both the head of the terrorist section of the

Socialist Revolutionaries and a police agent who killed his own superior, the minister of the interior. The secret police were also able to place two agents on the editorial board of *Pravda*. One was Roman Malinovsky, the main spokesman for the Bolsheviks in the Duma, a member of the Central Committee and treasurer of *Pravda*. He sought, on police instructions, to widen the split between the Bolsheviks and the Mensheviks, turned over the subscription lists for *Pravda* and used police funds to support the newspaper (they were recovered later through fines). In 1908 the ludicrous position was reached where four out of five members of the Bolshevik committee in St Petersburg were police agents. However, when revolutionaries were jailed or exiled their living conditions were hardly strict. Stalin and Trotsky twice escaped from custody, as did others such as Dzerzhinski (later head of the Soviet secret police) and Pilsudski (later leader of Poland). When Trotsky was imprisoned in the Peter and Paul jail, he found his cell was 'perfect for intellectual work'. He received all the books he wanted, including Marx's *Capital*. He smuggled out articles for publication and was allowed twice-weekly visits from his lover.

A major change in attitudes in the core states came immediately after the First World War. The triumph of the Bolsheviks in Russia, the collapse of the German and Austro-Hungarian monarchies, a short-lived Communist republic in Hungary and the move of Soviet troops westwards into Poland were all combined with high levels of industrial unrest in the chaotic post-war economic conditions. Many members of the core states' governments convinced themselves they too were facing revolution. In Britain in early 1919 the government deployed troops and tanks on the streets of Glasgow to defeat a strike demanding a forty-hour working week. The strike was smashed and its leaders imprisoned. A special intelligence organization was set up to monitor all activities that might be considered potentially revolutionary. Throughout 1919 the government saw every strike, particularly the threat of the 'Triple Alliance' of miners, railwaymen and transport workers, as potentially revolutionary. In September over 23,000 troops were deployed during a rail strike to protect property and drive food lorries. In January 1920 the government committee planning the response to strikes concluded:

> the country would have to face in the near future an organised attempt at seizing the reins of government in some of the large cities, such as

Glasgow, London and Liverpool . . . It was not unlikely that the next
strike would commence with sabotage on an extensive scale.

Troops were maintained on alert, emergency powers were taken and
the government changed the law so that they could issue arms to
'loyal' civilians.

In the United States even more extensive measures were taken.
During 1919 twenty-seven states passed laws banning the display of
red flags and the federal government established a new General
Intelligence Division under J. Edgar Hoover, with the sole function
of collecting information on 'radical' activities. Towards the end of
1919 the government began rounding up aliens for deportation. A
Socialist Party member, Victor Berger, was barred from taking his
seat in Congress and two socialist representatives in New York City
and five others in New York State were permanently barred. Early
in 1920 the attorney-general, A. Mitchell Palmer, authorized a series
of police raids in thirty cities across the country. About 10,000
people were arrested (all but a small proportion of them without
warrants), many of whom were American citizens not aliens. The
arrests were made in what the police believed to be 'radical' bars and
cafés, although the audience at a Ukrainian play and one at an
accordion concert were included in the sweep. Those caught by the
police were usually deported even though most had nothing to do
with 'radical' activities. Palmer described those captured as 'alien
filth . . . [with] sly and crafty eyes, lopsided faces, sloping brows and
misshapen features'.

By the summer of 1920 industrial disputes declined, the advance
of the Bolshevik armies in Poland was halted and reversed and the
'Red Scare' in the core states faded. In a generally conservative
atmosphere in the 1920s only a few cases rumbled on. In the United
States two Italian anarchists, Sacco and Vanzetti, were finally
executed in 1927 for an armed robbery and double murder they
almost certainly had not committed seven years earlier. What is
certain is that they did not receive a fair trial and that their execution
was largely about the determination of the authorities to make an
example of them.

In the 1930s, despite high unemployment, there seemed little
danger of revolution. The British government monitored the
activities of the unemployed associations closely and in Washington
unemployed veterans (the 'Bonus Army') were dispersed by troops
using tanks and tear gas. By the late 1930s the mood in the United

States was beginning to change. In May 1938 the House of Representatives created a committee on 'Un-American' Activities (a concept that would have been alien to nearly every other democracy). It began by targeting Nazi groups, but soon switched to the more congenial task of investigating 'Communists', 'subversives' and 'radicals'. A year later the Hatch Act extended, for the first time, restrictions aimed at aliens to American citizens. It banned from federal employment anyone who was a member of an organization which aimed to overthrow any government in the United States. By 1940 it was illegal to advocate or teach any such ideas or help circulate them in print and any group could be designated by the government, forced to register and disclose lists of its officers, publications and meetings. President Roosevelt also 'authorized' illegal phone-tapping and the opening of mail by the Federal Bureau of Investigations, which was run by the old scourge of the 'radicals', J. Edgar Hoover. In 1941 the attorney-general even authorized a phone tap on the Los Angeles Chamber of Commerce on the grounds that they were 'persons suspected of subversive activities'.

The major expansion of this programme to counter 'Un-American activities' came after the end of the Second World War. It ushered in a period of internal repression unequalled in any core democracy. A growing wave of conservatism was apparent in the 1944 elections and the anti-trade union legislation which followed a series of major strikes in 1946. The main driving force, however, was increasing American animosity towards, and fear of, the Soviet Union. Increasingly, Republicans, scenting power after more than a decade in opposition and an increasingly popular issue, made accusations of 'infiltration' of the government by 'Communists'. Exactly who was a 'Communist' could be very widely defined. Albert Canwell, a representative from California who went on to be chairman of the state Un-American Activities Committee, stated: 'If someone insists there is discrimination against Negroes in this country, or that there is inequality of wealth, there is every reason to believe that person is a communist.'

In March 1947, in order to head off Republican criticism, President Truman instituted a 'loyalty programme' for government employees. They could now lose their job for membership, affiliation or 'sympathetic association' with groups or individuals deemed to be 'Communist'. For the first time a person's assumed beliefs were enough for them to be sacked. People accused were entitled to a hearing before one of the 500 'loyalty boards' that were set up, but the evidence against them did not have to be disclosed. People could be charged more than once if they changed their job or when the loyalty standards were toughened in 1951 and again in 1953. In 1949 the loyalty programme was extended to all defence contractors, involving an extra 3 million people. Many of the 'offences' people were charged with were not against the law. For example, people were told, 'You have during most of your life been under the influence of your father, who was an active member of the Communist Party,' or that they favoured 'peace and civil rights', advocated 'equal rights for all races and classes' or that they allowed 'Negroes' to visit them at home. Inevitably much of the 'evidence' was based on unsubstantiated gossip from informers.

Increasing hysteria about subversion and infiltration was fuelled by Republicans such as Richard Nixon, with his campaign against the diplomat Alger Hiss, and Senator McCarthy, with his constantly changing lists of 'known Communists' in government. Truman was equally prepared to smear his opponents and ex-colleagues. In 1948 he branded his predecessor as vice-president, Henry Wallace, now heading the Progressive Party, as a Communist. He suggested that he should go to the Soviet Union and 'help them against his own country if that's the way he feels'. Wallace and his vice-presidential candidate Senator Glen Taylor were banned from speaking at the Universities of Cincinnati, Iowa State, Missouri, California and Michigan. Taylor was also arrested for refusing to hold a segregated meeting in Alabama. In early 1951 dismissal under the loyalty programme was made easier by the Truman administration – the standard required was reduced from there being 'reasonable grounds' to one where loyalty boards need only have 'reasonable doubts' about a person's loyalty. All people previously cleared had their cases re-opened. In 1953 the new Eisenhower administration gave all government agencies the power of summary dismissal. Now employees could only keep a government job on the grounds that it was 'clearly consistent with the interests of national security'. Over 500 staff in the State Department were fired without being given any hearing at all.

Anti-Communist hysteria spread into other areas of American life. In July 1947 the House Un-American Activities Committee (HUAC) began investigating Hollywood and jailed ten people for contempt for refusing to answer questions about their political beliefs. The Hollywood authorities then announced that only people who publicly renounced Communism would be employed in the film industry. The Hollywood blacklist was followed in 1950 by a similar one for radio and television. Most universities regarded membership of the Communist Party as grounds for refusing employment or sacking those already employed. One academic at Oregon State College was fired simply for defending the (mistaken) arguments of the Soviet geneticist Lysenko. Lawyers often refused to act for those accused, and those who did could be summoned before HUAC and forced to defend themselves. The American Bar Association supported a loyalty oath for all lawyers. Overall a fifth of the American workforce was subjected to the loyalty programme. No spy was ever uncovered, but 3,900 people were sacked from government jobs, 5,400 from private employment and over 1,000 from state and local governments. A huge number resigned when faced with accusations, knowing that whatever happened their lives were permanently blighted. Many, such as the film directors Jules Dassin and Carl Foreman and the musician Larry Adler, moved abroad. Blacklists, which lasted into the late 1960s, ensured that thousands could not work in their chosen profession. Hundreds of thousands of lives were affected by the climate of fear and accusation.

The loyalty programme was only the first step in what became a wave of demands that people should take an oath of loyalty to the United States before they could do certain things. A loyalty oath was required in New York before a permit to fish in the city reservoirs was issued. It was also required in order to sell pianos in Washington DC, to be paid unemployment benefit in Ohio, to vote in Alabama, to live in public housing in California or to be a member of staff or a student at a state college in Texas. The last state went even further and required a loyalty oath from the authors of all books used in state schools. For those authors who were dead, such as Shakespeare and Homer, the publisher had to take the oath on their behalf. Official oaths were supplemented by private organizations requiring similar 'evidence' of loyalty. When an oath of loyalty was imposed by the Regents of the University of California thirty-six academics resigned. In Maryland Quakers were fired from state employment for refusing on religious grounds to take an oath. It was not until 1967 that the Supreme Court ruled that state loyalty oaths were unconstitutional. Twelve states also set up their own 'Un-American Activities' Committees between 1947 and 1955. In California critics of the committee, such as Gregory Peck, Katharine Hepburn and Frank Sinatra, were publicly denounced as 'Stalinists'.

The federal government took further action. People were barred from entering the United States, including Pablo Picasso and Josef Krips, the conductor of the Vienna State Opera, who had made the mistake of conducting concerts in the Soviet Union. Journals and books deemed to be foreign Communist propaganda were seized on entry. They included *Pravda* and also Lenin's *State and Revolution*, which was for use in a course at Brown University. More extra-ordinarily it included the right-wing *Economist*, published in London. Over fifty people a year were deported by the American government on political grounds in the early 1950s. The evidence against them was often flimsy and many had lived in the United States for decades. In the late 1940s the government began denying US citizens a passport to travel abroad. In February 1948 Con-gressman Leo Isaacson of the Progressive Party was not allowed to attend a conference in Greece and the singer Paul Robeson was stopped from undertaking a concert tour in Europe. In February 1951 the State Department formalized the policy. Passports were to be denied to people it was thought might be members of a Communist organization or on the even wider grounds that their 'conduct abroad is likely to be contrary to the best interests of the United States'. Hundreds of people were caught by the refusal to issue a passport, including the eminent scientist Linus Pauling, although his right to travel abroad was hurriedly restored when he won the Nobel Prize.

During the early 1950s the search for internal 'subversives' reached a peak. Although Senator McCarthy led the way, he was not alone. In 1953–4 Congress undertook fifty-one separate investigations of 'Communism' – none had any legislative intent and they were simply designed to 'expose' people, who were denied any fair hearing. Unfriendly witnesses were normally fired by their employers. Twenty-five states passed legislation outlawing Communist and 'subversive' organizations, six required them to register and over thirty states barred them from the ballot. In July 1950 it was made illegal to remain within the city of Birmingham, Alabama if a person was found in 'any secret or non-public place in voluntary association or communication with any person or persons established to be or to have been' a member of the Communist Party. The legislation was widely copied in other cities. At President Eisenhower's inauguration in 1953 a piece of music by Aaron Copland was removed from the programme because he had supported 'leftist groups'. The Voice of America radio station refused to play music by another eminent composer Roy Harris because in 1943 he had dedicated a symphony to the Soviet Union. It also banned a number of speakers, including a cousin of the Secretary of State, John Foster Dulles, and Walter White, the head of the moderate National Association for the Advancement of Colored People. The International Information Administration, which was responsible for running libraries abroad, burned eleven books by 'suspect' authors. Not until 1954 did the wave of intolerance begin to subside. The Eisenhower administration turned on McCarthy as his increasingly wild and unsubstantiated claims of Communist infiltration broadened to include the army. Eventually at the end of 1954 the Senate censured McCarthy for his activities, with a considerable number of Republicans voting against their colleague. It was a symbolic moment and although strong anti-Communism remained a central feature of American political life, the worst of the post-war 'Red Scare' was over.

Elsewhere in the core democracies anti-Communist hysteria was generally kept under control. In 1948 the British government, under pressure from the United States, began its own, less draconian, loyalty programme. Over the next seven years 135 civil servants were investigated, of whom just over half either resigned or were dismissed and the remainder were transferred to non-security jobs. In West Germany the Constitutional Court banned the Communist Party in 1956. Six years earlier the two main parties had agreed the so-called 'Adenauer Decree', which listed thirteen organizations as opponents of the federal republic – support for them meant dismissal from public service. The listed groups included the Communist Party, but also the League of Victims of the Nazi Regime. In 1957 and 1964 the process, known as *Berufsverbot*, was extended throughout the state sector to include teachers and even postal workers. State workers were required to demonstrate that their 'whole behaviour' showed 'attachment to and desire to protect the free democratic order'. In practice these regulations were only used against left-wing groups and not against the former Nazis who continued to hold high office in West Germany. Most civil servants who had worked under the Nazi regime kept their jobs and were promoted – by the early 1960s sixty German ambassadors were ex-members of the Nazi Party and four of them had been in the elite SS. The definition of anti-state activities had to be used very carefully in the case of lawyers because so many had held office under the Nazis. Indeed the head of the Federal Office for the Protection of the

Constitution was headed by an ex-Nazi, Herbert Schrubbers. Under this system, thousands of people with 'leftist' sympathies were denied employment or sacked. France, on the other hand, took a much more liberal line. It had no rules against the employment of Communists – about a quarter of the Communist Party membership worked in the public sector.

During the twentieth century all the core democracies established intelligence agencies to gather information about so-called 'subversive' organizations. Some states had organizations dating back to the mid-nineteenth century but even Britain, supposedly one of the most liberal, moved in the same direction. The Special Branch of the Metropolitan Police was set up in 1887 to monitor the activities of Irish nationalists. Gradually power was accrued by special government agencies, which had few legal controls over their activities. Special Branch extended its surveillance to other groups such as Indian nationalists and the suffragettes demanding the vote for women. In 1909 the government decided to set up a Secret Service Bureau, which rapidly divided into two bodies, one for foreign intelligence (MI6) and one for internal intelligence (MI5). After failing to pass legislation to give itself the power to censor the press, the government introduced a system of 'voluntary' guidance on stories the press should not print (which covered far more than sensitive defence matters). In 1911 the government passed the Official Secrets Act, which made it a criminal offence to disclose any government information without approval. The government abandoned the idea, adopted in the liberal 1840s, that it should not open people's mail and also started tapping telephones. Apart from the Official Secrets Act, all this was done without legal authority and without any public debate. The intelligence agencies expanded after 1918 when they concentrated on a new role, monitoring internal 'revolutionary' activity. Despite the fact that the Communist Party never had more than two MPs and a membership of a few thousand, it was the focus of intense surveillance, as were other 'radicals' in the labour movement. MI5 more than tripled in size and began compiling an extensive register of 'subversives'. Other groups joined in the hunt for 'subversives' including the Economic League (run by business and designed to keep 'undesirables' out of jobs), the Anti-Socialist Union and the Liberty League. Later many from the British Union of Fascists found employment in MI5. Every democratic state established similar institutions to monitor both Communist activities and internal dissent.

The problem all the democracies faced was how to control the activities of these intelligence agencies. Keeping an eye on foreign spies was relatively straightforward, but what counted as domestic 'subversion' and which groups and individuals were to be subject to surveillance? The people who worked in these agencies tended to be highly conservative, if not reactionary, and saw almost any criticism of existing society as 'subversive'. In Britain the activities of MI5 were supposed to be controlled by an informal government directive of 1952, which banned its involvement in party political activities. In practice, suspicions were strong, particularly in the 1970s, that the intelligence agencies were being used to discredit the Labour government and the Prime Minister, Harold Wilson. The problems of controlling the activities of these agencies were even clearer in the United States, where the FBI under Hoover became effectively autonomous and not subject to any political control. In July 1943 the attorney-general, Francis Biddle, instructed Hoover that there was 'no statutory authorization or other justification' for retaining the 'custodial detention' list of American citizens which the FBI had started in 1939. Hoover ignored the instruction, renamed the list the Security Index and ordered the FBI to 'prepare and maintain' lists of 'dangerous and potentially dangerous individuals'. At the same time the government discovered that the FBI had routinely been carrying out phone tapping in criminal cases in violation of the Federal Communications Act of 1934 and two Supreme Court rulings of 1937 and 1939. In 1956 the FBI launched its own COINTELPRO operation, nominally to disrupt 'Communist' activities but in practice to disrupt any group that dissented from any aspect of American policy. In the early 1960s the FBI began investigating the civil rights movement and, in particular, Martin Luther King because Hoover believed that they were all Communist influenced.

The United States found similar problems in controlling other intelligence agencies. After the end of the Second World War the Central Intelligence Agency was set up with the task of external intelligence gathering; it was specifically prohibited from operating within the United States. Yet within a few years it had begun its own programme to read the mail of prominent Americans such as Ted Kennedy, Hubert Humphrey and the chairman of the Federal Reserve Bank, Arthur Burns. In twenty years over 200,000 pieces of mail were read in New York alone. By 1967, at the height of the Vietnam War, the CIA began infiltrating agents into anti-war groups across the country and reading the mail of prominent Quakers. At its height the CIA held detailed files on 7,200 American citizens, over 100 organizations and also maintained a list of 'suspect' individuals which covered over 300,000 people. For thirty years after 1945 all international message traffic was read by the government even though there was no legal authority for this interception. The National Security Agency (established to intercept and decode Soviet signals) also decided to read 150,000 messages a month sent to American citizens and kept files on 75,000 individuals. In 1968 the army decided to set up its own domestic surveillance organization. It used 1,500 agents and kept information on 100,000 people and 750,000 organizations and 'incidents'. These included moderate black groups such as the NAACP and the Urban League, civil rights leaders and politicians such as Adlai Stevenson, twice Democratic candidate for president and a former ambassador to the UN. The army infiltrated agents into a coalition of church youth groups and on one occasion a Hallowe'en party for elementary school children because it thought a local 'dissident' might be present.

Such intelligence organizations could also be used for personal and political purposes. Hoover kept his own files on the activities of leading politicians, which was the main reason he remained head of the FBI for over forty years. Occasionally he would tell presidents interesting gossip about their opponents. He reported to Eisenhower on the social contacts of Eleanor Roosevelt and the liberal Supreme Court Justice, William O. Douglas. In 1964 President Johnson used the FBI to monitor the activities of his rivals in the Democratic Party and, later in the campaign, those of his Republican opponent Barry Goldwater. A year later he instructed the FBI to 'monitor' the civil rights movement (something they were doing anyway without approval) and shortly afterwards he turned on the opposition to the Vietnam War. The FBI was asked to compile files on prominent journalists such as David Brinkley and Joseph Kraft, who were critical of the war. Johnson and his successor Richard Nixon also instructed the CIA to monitor 'dissidents' in the United States to see if they were in contact with outside bodies. Eventually Nixon decided to establish his own private bugging and surveillance unit, 'the plumbers'. It was their activities in breaking into Democratic Party headquarters in 1972 that led to the Watergate scandal and Nixon's downfall.

South Africa between 1948 and the early 1990s was a remarkable example of a highly repressive regime. It was created legally under the guise of a quasi-democratic regime modelled on the core democracies. The implications of the election of the Nationalist Party government in 1948 were made chillingly clear by the party leader, J.G. Strijdom: 'Anybody who purposely tried to upset the government's plans to put into operation its apartheid policy or who failed to do their duty towards the realisation of that aim would be guilty of treason.' The government proceeded on two fronts, the control of information and opinion and the draconian suppression of dissent. The nationalists were able to use legislation dating from 1931 to censor and ban films on the grounds that they included 'scenes containing reference to controversial or international politics' or 'scenes of intermingling of Europeans and non-Europeans'. Legislation also allowed bans on the importation of books. By 1968 over 11,000 titles were banned, including *I Claudius* by Robert Graves, a biography of Marilyn Monroe, *Why I am Not a Christian* by Bertrand Russell and the highly subversive *Black Beauty* by Anna Sewell. In 1960 the Prime Minister Dr Verwoerd declared 'a politically nonconformist press will not be tolerated'. The resulting Publications and Entertainments Act of 1963 allowed the government to prohibit the circulation of books and newspapers and close art exhibitions and stage and film shows on the grounds that they were 'offensive to the religious convictions of any group', that they brought any group of people 'into ridicule or contempt' or were 'harmful to the relations between any sections' of the people in South Africa. In 1968 newspapers were forced to introduce a code under which 'comment should take due cognisance of the complex racial problems of South Africa' and the 'general good and the safety of the country and its peoples'. The government-controlled radio had a monopoly and was hardly likely to be critical, given its director-general's view that 'no useful purpose can be served by causing the public to distrust our leader's policies'. Television was not allowed until 1976 and was then subject to strict government control.

More important were the measures taken to stop criticism of the government's racial policies. The Suppression of Communism Act of 1950 made the Communist Party illegal (it had already dissolved itself). It allowed the government to ban organizations, their publications and attendance at their meetings, to remove members of such organizations from public office, place them under house arrest and limit their movements. The definition of 'Communism' in the act was given a peculiarly South African meaning and a scope so wide as to embrace almost any activity. Communism was any doctrine which 'aims at bringing about any political, industrial, social or economic change . . . by the promotion of disturbance or disorder' or which 'aims at the encouragement of feelings of hostility between the European and non-European races'. After the deliberate shooting of black demonstrators at Sharpeville in 1960 both the African National Congress and the Pan-African Congress were banned under this legislation and the minister for justice stated that 'rights were getting out of hand'. The government response was the Sabotage Act of 1962. Once again this included a remarkable definition of sabotage, which was so wide-ranging that it included putting up posters and trespass. Accused people had to prove they were innocent of any charge. In addition the government could ban people and force them to report daily to the police. The reporting of any statement by a banned person was prohibited. By 1968 over 600 people were subject to banning orders.

In parallel the government passed legislation to give itself the power to detain people at will. In 1963 legislation allowed individuals to be arrested without a warrant and detained for ninety days without access to a lawyer. No court was able to order their release and police torture became routine. In 1965 the period of detention was extended to 180 days and widened to include not just 'suspects' but also witnesses. A year later any attempt to leave South Africa without the appropriate travel documents became an act of sabotage. The full system of state repression came into force with the Terrorism Act of 1967. Once again this contained a unique South African definition of terrorism, namely 'causing feelings of hostility between whites and non-whites' and 'embarrassing the administration of the affairs of the state'. The burden of proof was placed on defendants to demonstrate their innocence. Anyone 'suspected of terrorism', or having any information about it, could now be detained indefinitely without access to a lawyer or the courts having any say in the case. In effect the state had given itself the power, perfectly legally under the constitution, to incarcerate anybody it chose for any period and torture them without them having any judicial redress.

Such actions by state authorities across the world were not unusual by the mid-twentieth century; most, though, did not bother to go through the formal process of passing legislation to give themselves such powers. Most of the world's people throughout the twentieth century lived under regimes which repressed their own citizens. The colonial empires which spanned the globe until the late 1950s rarely allowed free expression of opinion. In the last resort, they were prepared to ban political and other organizations, imprison without trial and send people into exile, as Indian leaders such as Nehru and Gandhi found from the 1920s onwards. Ultimately force was used to put down demonstrations of opinion that challenged the rule of the colonial power. In the states of the periphery and semi-periphery independence brought little change, except in a few such as India, which remained broadly tolerant in the second half of the century. Most newly independent countries joined the majority of states which ruled by force, repressed opposition, both actual and potential, and treated human rights lightly. By the 1980s a survey of countries outside the core states showed that three-quarters of them, affecting over 3 billion people, used violence against their own citizens in the form of torture, brutality, summary executions and the use of 'death squads'. The attitude of many governments was well summed up by two presidents of Guatemala. In 1944 Jorge Ubico declared, 'While I am President I will not grant liberty of the press nor of association because the people of Guatemala are not prepared for democracy and need a strong hand.' Twenty-five years later Carlos Arana was even blunter when he announced, 'If it is necessary to turn the country into a cemetery in order to pacify it, I will not hesitate to do so.'

Latin America was an area where governments traditionally paid only limited respect to the views of their citizens. However, repression was not universal and permanent. Some states such as Chile and Uruguay until the early 1970s and Costa Rica after the 1940s were generally tolerant. Most of the repressive regimes in Latin America came from the right; only a few such as Cuba under Castro and Nicaragua under the Sandinistas in the early 1980s were from the left. Other states, such as Paraguay after the middle of the century, Nicaragua under the Somoza dynasty and the Dominican Republic under Trujillo, existed under constant repression and brutality. In the twenty years after 1975 about 25,000 people in Guatemala were killed by unofficial groups (the 'White Hand', the 'Purple Rose' and the 'Secret Anti-Communist Army') supported by the ruling elite. It was a period of random terror directed mainly against peasants, peasant leaders, intellectuals, priests and opposition Christian Democrat politicians. The campaign had the tacit and occasionally open, support of the army and police. In El Salvador after the military coup in 1979 the army, strongly supported by the ruling elite, fought a small-scale war against a guerrilla 'army' which may have totalled 6,000 people. During the fighting the state was responsible for 20–30,000 deaths including labour and peasant leaders, church leaders, reform politicians and members of the media.

One of the most carefully documented phases of repression in Latin America occurred under the military junta in Argentina between 1976 and 1983, although in scale it was more restricted than the contemporaneous Pinochet regime in Chile. The military seized power in Argentina from a decaying Perónist government which seemed unable to deal with the threat from a very small 'urban guerrilla' movement – the Monteneros. This gave the military an excuse to crack down on all forms of opposition. One of the leaders of the junta, General Videla, explained: 'A terrorist is not just someone with a gun or a bomb; he can also be someone who spreads ideas that are contrary to Western and Christian civilization.' Altogether about 11,000 people 'disappeared' and were tortured and killed by various units in the armed forces. The campaign was directed by the main security agency, SIDE (Service of State Information), but it was run by small units who kidnapped whoever they wanted. Prisoners were taken to innocuously named military establishments – one of the worst was the Navy Mechanics School – or even to premises owned by the state oil company. What happened next was explained by witnesses who gave evidence to the National Commission on Disappeared Persons established after the fall of the junta in 1983. Mrs A.Z., a lawyer, was kidnapped in November 1976 and taken to a place where people were

> put in ditches which had been previously dug, and buried up to the neck, sometimes for four days or more . . . They were kept without food or water, exposed to the elements. When they were dug out they were covered with insect bites; they had been buried naked. They were then taken to the torture chambers.

The types of torture and the techniques used were typical of all repressive regimes in the second half of the century as the technology available 'improved' and became more 'sophisticated'. Old-fashioned techniques such as beatings on the soles of the feet and palms of the hands, pumping people full of water and burning them with cigarettes, hot plates and wire grids, remained common. Newer methods were also used, as described by another witness to the commission:

the *picana* [electric prod] was stronger, and they forced it really violently into your anus, while they put electrodes on to your teeth. It seemed like a bolt of lightning which struck you from head to foot . . . and they put a string of pellets in my mouth which were difficult to swallow . . . each pellet was an electrode and when the current was turned on, it felt as though a thousand pieces of glass were breaking inside me.

Many of those who did not die under torture were shot or thrown alive out of aircraft over the Atlantic.

Across Asia similar repressive regimes were common during the twentieth century. One of the most brutal was the Chinese nationalist regime under Chiang Kai-shek. During their battles to control the country, the nationalists killed a million people in Kiangsi province and almost as many in Hupei. During the war with Japan after 1937 probably 3 million nationalist soldiers died of neglect and brutality rather than in action. Another million people died and 4 million lost their homes when the government deliberately destroyed the Yellow River dykes in 1938, flooding vast areas of the countryside. In the areas regained from Japanese occupation in 1945 over a million were killed by nationalist forces in a wave of repression designed to eliminate 'Communists'. Equally brutal were the Kuomintang actions on Formosa after it was regained from Japan at the end of the war. The repression of the native population was far harsher than under Japanese colonial rule and over 50,000 were murdered in a wave of killings following demonstrations against nationalist rule in February 1947.

Other states were typified by continuing low-level repression, as in the Philippines under President Marcos after martial law was declared in 1972. The military were given the power to arrest and detain anybody and to judge 'national security' cases before military tribunals. In five years about 60,000 people were arrested, of whom several hundred a year 'disappeared'. In Indonesia the military coup in 1965 led to a massive onslaught on supposed 'Communists'. This was not high-technology killing and torture. The army rounded up 'suspects' and then handed them over to civilian groups, who stabbed and beat them to death, often after mutilating their victims. Many of the killings were the result of local feuds between different Muslim groups or between Hindus and others. In total between 500,000 and 1 million people were killed in the six months after the coup and another million were held in squalid conditions in army camps. It was years before those who survived began to be slowly released.

Dictatorships in Asia, Africa and the Middle East allowed little or no freedom of expression; any sign of dissent was ruthlessly stamped out by a variety of methods, ranging from detention and imprisonment to torture and killings. However, their capabilities varied enormously. Many African states were repressive, but they often lacked the necessary infrastructure to carry this out in an 'efficient' and 'modern' way. After 1965 Zaire under General Mobutu was a highly corrupt, despotic regime – a secret police force was established in 1969, but its effectiveness was limited. In 1973 the government introduced a new exploitative measure – *salongo* – which was supposed to be a traditional form of labour, described as 'collective work in the public interest'. In practice it was just forced labour. People had to work on roads and bridges and cultivate land owned by various state institutions (which often turned out to be owned by the Mobutu family). The main oppressors were the army and the gendarmerie, who were poorly and irregularly paid by the state. In order to survive they raided villages, stole food and money, demanded payment if people had 'irregular' documents and generally terrorized the population. Similarly Uganda under Idi Amin suffered from a general, crudely applied terror, characterized by its randomness and brutality.

A much more sophisticated system of repression operated in Iran under the shah between 1953 and his overthrow in 1979. The key institution was SAVAK (the National Security and Information Organization), which was established in 1957 with the help of the CIA, the FBI and the Israelis. Only two political parties, both of which supported the shah, were allowed and the press was state controlled through censorship guidelines laid down by SAVAK. Books were only censored after publication, but because publishers had to pay all the costs of any action they were left effectively to censor themselves. The sermons of religious leaders, who were one of the main sources of opposition to the regime, were also closely monitored. SAVAK had a network of agents in the trade unions, universities, civil service and large industrial plants and all people joining these organizations were vetted. Only the landed and merchant class (strong supporters of the shah) were exempted from this treatment. At its height SAVAK had about 5,000 full-time staff. The shah also established the Imperial Inspectorate, headed by a childhood friend, whose role was to monitor SAVAK, investigate military conspiracies and report on the financial dealings of wealthy families. To complete the circle, the J2 military intelligence unit kept watch on both SAVAK and the Imperial Inspectorate. At the height of the shah's rule in 1975 Amnesty International reported, 'No country in the world has a worse record in human rights than Iran.' Arrest and detention by SAVAK were arbitrary, absolute and subject to no legal control. Political trials were held in secret before military or SAVAK tribunals and no defence witnesses were allowed. Political prisoners were held in special prisons and confession followed by recantation of previous beliefs was essential before release could be considered. Torture was routine both before and after 'trial'.

The dictatorships of the European semi-periphery established in the 1920s and 1930s were repressive, often highly so in the immediate aftermath of civil war or attempted revolution. But they usually had a significant degree of support in society and fairly quickly could settle down to a low level of repression that kept dissent under control. In Portugal under the Salazar government the secret police (PIDE) were small – less than 3,000 strong in the early 1970s. It was effective against African nationalist leaders, killing, with book bombs, both Eduardo Mondlane the leader of FRELIMO in Mozambique and Amilcar Cabral the nationalist leader in Guinea-Bissau. Internally the main crackdown was on labour leaders in the 1930s; most were sent to a prison camp on Tarrafel, a barren island in the Cape Verde group and did not return. In other areas PIDE was far from effective. The oligarchy of the twenty or so richest families who supported the regime was left alone, as was the army. All three of the leading anti-regime figures, Alvaro Cunhal, Henrique Galvao and Herminio Inacio, escaped from prison. PIDE also appears to have had no advance warning of the coup in April 1974, despite its network of about 20,000 informers.

During the Spanish civil war about 140,000 executions and reprisals were carried out by both sides, about the same as the total number of direct military casualties. Once the Franco government was firmly in power in early 1939 the prison population tripled and political offences were made retrospective back to 1934. Martial law remained in force and political crimes were tried in military courts. About 30,000 people were executed in the six years after Franco took power. Many of the prosecutions took place under a 1940 law for the 'suppression of masonry and communism'. Freemasonry was seen as the chief source of spiritual and cultural subversion and membership of a masonic lodge or a left-liberal political party was automatic grounds for prosecution. From September 1939 a system of 'militarized labour camps' for political prisoners was established to undertake reconstruction projects. Inmates had to undergo 're-education' by Catholic priests (or nuns if they were in a female camp) and attend compulsory religious services. The gradual release of political prisoners began in 1940 and about half of all death sentences were commuted. Five years after victory in the civil war the new government probably held about 20,000 political prisoners. After this date repression was firm but not murderous. Protestants were not allowed to worship in public, but censorship was gradually relaxed as the economy and society were opened up through tourism. It was not finally abolished until 1974.

In its actions towards German non-Jewish citizens the Nazi government, for much of its existence, bore more relation to the repressive systems in Spain, Portugal and Italy under Mussolini than the large-scale violence and slave labour of the Soviet Union. The Nazis could also rely on a high level of support among the population. Within a month of taking power at the end of January 1933, and the day after the Reichstag fire, the new government passed an emergency decree which suspended the personal freedoms guaranteed by the Weimer constitution, abolished freedom of the press and allowed the police to hold suspects in 'protective custody'. In mid-March Heinrich Himmler, then police chief in Munich, set up the first concentration camp in the grounds of an old gunpowder factory at Dachau near the city. In the months following, there was much independent action by various units in the Nazi Party, but by the summer, when about 27,000 people were being held, the system was regularized. About 100,000 people were held in concentration camps at some time in the first four years of the Nazi government, of whom about 500 were killed. Some degree of legality remained: in June 1933 the commandant of Dachau was charged with the murder of a prisoner and, although he was not tried, Himmler was forced to dismiss him. In early 1935 over twenty members of the SA were given short prison terms for maltreating prisoners. The number of prisoners fell to just over 7,000 by the winter of 1936–7 and many of the temporary camps established in 1933–4 were closed.

The Nazis established a new secret police, the Gestapo. It was founded in Prussia in April 1933 by Hermann Göring, the interior minister, as part of a drive against Communists and to build up Göring's position as part of the internal power struggles within the Nazi hierarchy. By late 1933 it had extended its activities to the whole of Germany. Most of the people who manned it were not previously connected to the Nazis and were either career policemen or from conservative and nationalist groups. The formal role of the Gestapo was set down in 1936: 'to investigate and suppress all anti-State tendencies'. Although a climate of fear was carefully cultivated, in practice the capabilities of the Gestapo were quite limited. Even at its height in 1944 there were only 50,000 security police for the whole of Germany and for most of the time there were far fewer. Dusseldorf, with a population of 500,000, had 126 Gestapo personnel; Essen, which had a population of 650,000, had only 43. Wurzburg had 22 Gestapo officials to cover the whole of Lower Franconia, which had a population of nearly 850,000. Many small towns and nearly all rural areas had no Gestapo presence at all. In these circumstances the Gestapo had to rely not just on a few informers (nearly all of whom were volunteers) but on denunciations by members of the public. Estimates suggest that at least a third of all Gestapo cases started with a denunciation and in some areas, such as 'friendship with Jews' or 'racial defilement', the proportion was probably nearer two-thirds. Even the Gestapo and senior Nazis, including Hitler and Göring, were worried by the level of denunciations and considered ways of trying to curb such activities. The widespread practice of denunciation only reinforces the impression that Nazi policies in general and their racial policies in particular, including the persecution of the Jews and the widespread use of slave labour from Eastern Europe, could not have worked without a high level of consent and co-operation among the population. Denunciations reached a peak in 1941 and only as the war became unpopular after 1943 did the level drop.

There was, however, a significant change in Nazi repressive policies around 1936–7 when Himmler, the commander of the elite SS, took control of all police and security matters. Himmler set out the role of the police in the Nazi state in 1937:

> to carry out the will of the State leadership [its] powers are therefore necessarily based, not upon detailed laws but the realities of the National Socialist Führer state [and] cannot therefore be restricted by formal regulations . . . the police can act only in accordance with the orders of the leadership and not according to laws.

New camps such as Sachsenhausen and Buchenwald were constructed, but until the summer of 1938 there were still only four concentration camps in Germany. Dachau was overwhelmingly the 'political' camp and at Sachsenhausen the majority were 'anti-social elements' – homosexuals, Jehovah's Witnesses and criminals (an increasingly important category in the camps after 1937). In January 1938 'protective custody' was applied to all those 'whose behaviour endangers the existence and security of the people and the state'. Later in the year the category of 'anti-socials' was widened and forced labour became central to the system with the founding of the SS firm (DEST), which began by operating brickworks and quarries from the new camps at Flossenbürg and Mauthausen. Although the camp population increased in 1938 after the takeover of Austria, by the outbreak of war it had fallen back again to about 25,000.

As in so many other areas, it was war which radicalized the Nazi state. Hitler and Himmler issued instructions that the camp inmates could be 'brutally liquidated' if necessary. By 1942 the number of people in the concentration camps had risen to about 100,000 and the level of arrests to about 10,000 a month in Germany (ten times the level of the mid-1930s). However, the majority of camp inmates came from territories occupied by Germany. Increasingly, as the power of the SS expanded, the camps became reservoirs of slave labour for the various SS-controlled enterprises. New camps were established at Auschwitz (intended to have over 200,000 slaves) for the construction of an IG Farben factory to manufacture synthetic rubber. As the inmates were exploited more brutally the death toll rose rapidly: in the last six months of 1942 well over half the total camp population of 120,000 died. In 1943 the number of inmates rose more rapidly still as Poles and Russians were crammed in; by the autumn of 1943 there were about 225,000 in the camps (a third of them in the Auschwitz complex). The last available statistics from January 1945 show that over 700,000 people were in the SS-run concentration and labour camps, including the huge underground aircraft and rocket factories. It is impossible to calculate exactly how many died here, the best estimate suggests about 1 million people.

Even while this exploitation and suffering was going on Goebbels could write in his diary:

> The leaders of the Reich certainly don't need to know whenever someone living in the back of beyond unburdens his anguished heart. Just as the Führer need not know if somewhere in some company people complain about the way the war is run, it is unnecessary for the political

leaders to know if here or there someone damns the war or curses it or vents his spleen.

In general until the attempt to assassinate Hitler in July 1944 the regime was willing to tolerate a low level of dissent and opposition. It was only in the last few months as imminent defeat loomed and the leading Nazis became even more irrational that widespread slaughter of the opposition took place.

The behaviour Goebbels described was exactly that which would guarantee a long sentence and probable death in the Gulag in the Soviet Union. It was the Bolsheviks who, during the Russian Revolution, first developed widespread 'revolutionary terror' and later instituted one of the most repressive of all regimes. The Soviet security police went through a number of different guises (Cheka, GPU, OGPU, NKVD, KGB), but remained essentially the same. The Cheka was established within a month of the Bolsheviks seizing power when a mass strike in the public sector seemed likely. The instructions for the Cheka (the All-Russia Extraordinary Commission for Combating Counter-Revolution and Sabotage) were 'to suppress and liquidate all attempts and acts of counter-revolution and sabotage throughout Russia'. Its head until his death in 1926 was Felix Dzerzhinsky, a Pole who had spent eleven years in prison and exile under the tsars. The Cheka's aim was to help the Bolsheviks hold on to power when they were surrounded by enemies. In February 1918 Lenin told a fellow revolutionary, 'You do not imagine that we shall be victorious without applying the most cruel revolutionary terror?' The next day the Cheka announced publicly that there was 'no alternative to annihilating mercilessly on the scene of their crime all counter-revolutionaries, spies, speculators, thugs, hooligans, saboteurs and other parasites'. Until July 1918 most shootings were of 'criminals' rather than political opponents ('counter-revolutionaries') mainly because the Left Social Revolutionaries were still part of the Bolshevik government coalition. After the attempted coup in July and the attempt to assassinate Lenin at the end of August 1918 the Left Social Revolutionaries were some of the first to be shot. The Cheka rapidly became one of the central instruments of Bolshevik rule. Its strength rose to about 150,000 (excluding the frontier troops under its control) and the shooting of hostages started in September 1918.

In parallel with the Cheka a new system of courts was established by the Bolsheviks. At the local level were the people's courts and

revolutionary tribunals. In July 1918 the tribunals were given the power to sentence people to death; as the Commissar for Justice put it, they were not 'courts in the real sense of the word, but special organizations for the fight against the counter-revolution'. In April 1919 compulsory labour mobilization was introduced and forced labour camps were established. They were originally intended for workers who broke regulations and their regime was not therefore particularly harsh. By October 1922 there were over 130 camps with about 60,000 inmates, only a fifth of whom were 'politicals'. This was partly because the Cheka ran its own network of camps. In early 1922 this had about 25,000 inmates (although there were plenty of massacres to reduce the population). A few special camps, such as the old monastery on the Solovetskii Islands on the White Sea coast near Archangel where the conditions were especially harsh, were established for the 'counter-revolutionaries' and those guilty of 'anti-Soviet activities'. Although the end of the civil war and the institution of the NEP brought about a degree of economic liberalization, this was not reflected in the political sphere, where the remaining opposition socialist parties were eliminated. Exactly how many were killed during the establishment of Soviet rule, apart from in the fighting of the civil war, will never be known. Estimates suggest there were about 200,000 victims of 'revolutionary terror', of whom about two-thirds were killed by the Cheka. The total number of deaths during the civil war period was about 3 million, the overwhelming majority of whom died during the large-scale famine.

With Stalin's establishment in power from 1928 rising paranoia about foreign espionage and sabotage, in a country which saw itself as surrounded by enemies (which it was), grew rapidly. However, far more important, and the biggest single cause of death under the Soviet government, was the collectivization of agriculture. The attack on the kulaks, the so-called rich peasants, followed by the forcible collectivization of peasant agriculture produced massive suffering. From early 1929 kulaks were subject to increasingly stiff quotas to provide the state with grain. Failure to meet the quota meant the forced sale of their property and exile. About 5 million people were deported on crowded trains. Many died en route because of the lack of sanitation and water. On arrival in Siberia they were either taken to labour camps or dumped in the countryside and told to construct a new village. Probably about 1 million people died as a result of this policy. Collectivization was even more catastrophic. The peasants slaughtered their animals rather than hand them over to the new collective farms (four out of ten cows and two-thirds of the sheep in the country were killed). A short pause in the summer of 1930, when conditions were at their worst and revolts had broken out across the Ukraine, Crimea and Azerbaijan, was followed by an intensified drive. In the five years after 1929 roughly 20 million family farms were replaced by 240,000 collective farms, which controlled almost all the agricultural land in the Soviet Union. The disruption caused by this process was made worse by government policies. The level of requisitioning by the state was doubled, a fifth of the crop was also taken by the state-controlled machine tractor stations for their help and private trade was only allowed once all government quotas were fulfilled. Any 'hoarding' of food or eating of 'state property' was punishable by ten years in jail.

The situation was worst in the Ukraine, where by mid-1932 about 3 million people were trying to leave the countryside for the cities in the hope of finding food. By the winter, when only about two-thirds of the state quota had been delivered, villages and whole districts were blockaded, in the belief that they held food which the peasants were refusing to release. No goods from the towns were allowed through the blockade. In the spring of 1933 deaths on a large scale started. Even stricter rationing was imposed in cities such as Kiev and carts carried the dead away during the night. Probably about one in ten of the urban population died, but in the countryside it was nearer to one in four. The government finally relaxed its policy, temporarily ended requisitioning and allowed some trading in grain and the importation of seed for the next crop. Army food reserves were released to feed the starving. Exactly how many died in the collectivization and subsequent famine was carefully hidden by the Soviet authorities. The compilers of the 1937 census were shot when their draft figures revealed the extent of the disaster. When access to the 1937 census data was finally allowed in the early 1990s it confirmed the worst unofficial estimates. In 1933 the population of the Soviet Union actually fell by nearly 6 million. Some of this was the result of a lower than normal birth rate in the countryside, but the death rate rose substantially. In the Ukraine it tripled in 1933 compared with the previous year and that figure was already higher than normal. In addition, account has to be taken of the 2 million or so 'refugees' in central Asia who are supposed, according to the official version, to have fled the Soviet Union. Almost certainly they died in the famine. In total, taking account of the kulak deaths from transportation and exile, the death toll from the Soviet-imposed collectivization of agriculture was probably about 8 million people.

Collectivization was not the only disaster to be imposed on the Soviet people in the 1930s. There was also a massive increase in the level of repression, affecting in particular the Bolshevik Party and the higher echelons of the Red Army but also the population as a whole. Although this process was dominated by Stalin, what happened cannot be explained solely by his psychology or as his attempt to set up a 'totalitarian' system. There is no doubt that the party did face huge problems in managing the widespread social and economic changes of the early 1930s. It was still not monolithic and relations between the centre and the local parties were often chaotic. There were still debates about how to implement the party's general line, even if arguments about what that line should be were no longer allowed. The events of the 1930s were not a simple process that can be embraced by a single term – the 'Great Terror'. The membership purges in the party in 1933–6 were very different from the general terror under Yezhov in 1937–8. As late as June 1935 the central committee had to issue an instruction that too many party members were being expelled. Most of those who were expelled were charged not with ideological offences but with abusing their position and violating party discipline. Nor did Stalin always get his own way. In 1932 an old Bolshevik and a party secretary in Moscow, Martimian Ryutin, was arrested and charged with anti-Soviet agitation for taking part in a genuine conspiracy to remove Stalin as party leader. Stalin demanded the death penalty for all the conspirators, but the Politburo refused to agree. Instead they were expelled from the party. Most were eventually shot in 1937–8, but some survived the labour camps and one, Sergei Kavtaradze, was even rehabilitated by Stalin and made a deputy foreign minister.

A key turning point in the institution of widespread terror came on 1 December 1934 when Sergei Kirov, the Leningrad party boss, was shot in his office by Leonid Nikolayev. Exactly what lay behind the shooting is still an unresolved and contentious question. Was it arranged by Stalin, who was concerned at Kirov's popularity in the party, to provide an excuse for a widespread purge? That was the view of many Soviet exiles and western writers during the Cold War. However, although Kirov was a rising star in the party, he was hardly the 'liberal' portrayed by the exiles. There is also considerable evidence to implicate the police, who arrested Nikolayev while he was carrying a gun and a map of Kirov's route to work but released him. Nikolayev died in a car 'accident' on his way to be interviewed by Stalin and the Politburo. The permutations of the possible conspiracies that could be involved are almost endless. What is clear is that the shooting of Kirov did not lead to an immediate and well-orchestrated purge. A fortnight later the old Bolsheviks, Zinoviev and Kamenev, who had fallen out with Stalin years before and been removed from the party leadership, were arrested. They seemed likely to face exile until it was announced in the middle of January 1935 that they would be put on trial. Even then it was not until 1936 and their second trial that other old Bolsheviks such as Piatakov, Radek, Bukharin and Rykov were also arrested. This was the start of the series of show trials in 1936–8 when most of the old leadership of the party confessed to numerous and highly improbable crimes against the revolution. Even the most powerful in the party were affected – leaders such as Molotov, Kalinin and Poskrebyshev found that their wives were arrested.

The widespread purges and terror began in June 1937 under the new head of the secret police, Yezhov. He replaced Yagoda, who was subsequently tried and shot. Across the country people were arrested and tortured until they confessed to various offences against the Soviet Union; in the process they were usually forced to implicate others, who were then subjected to the same process. There was little or no rationale as to who was arrested and any suspicion, denunciation, false confession or event from the past could lead either to death or, more likely, a long sentence in a forced labour camp. One of the most widespread purges was in the Red Army. It is unclear whether the 'evidence' that started the process was deliberately planted by the NKVD, whether it came from the Germans and Czechs (who did pass some information to the Soviet government about activities in the Red Army), or whether it was a genuine conspiracy. Whatever the origins, the results were catastrophic. In June 1937 Marshal Tukachevsky, a hero of the civil war, was arrested and shot. By the end of the process three out of five marshals of the Soviet Union, fifteen out of sixteen army commanders, sixty out of sixty-seven corps commanders and three-quarters of the divisional commanders were either dead or in labour camps. In addition, 37,000 officers were discharged. Some were reinstated later – in 1941 Marshal Rossokovsky was taken from the camps, restored to command and became a hero of the 'Great Patriotic War'.

The worst of the terror ended with the removal of Yezhov (who was shot probably because Stalin thought he was gaining too much power) and his replacement by Beria. After 1939 the system settled down to a lower level of steady and harsh repression, where even the slightest critical remark could lead to a long sentence in a labour camp. There were still a number of short, vicious purges of particular areas – the Leningrad leadership (again) in 1949, the anti-Semitic purges of the late 1940s and the so-called 'doctors' plot' of early 1953 shortly before Stalin's death. In the years after Stalin's death a more bureaucratic form of repression emerged. The number of people in the labour camps was reduced drastically and the type of 'crimes' likely to result in arrest and punishment was narrowed. Party control over the secret police was emphasized with Beria's shooting. In 1958 a party professional, Ivan Serov, who was not a career secret policeman, was made head of a restructured KGB. From the 1960s, although there were still very strict limits on expression, the techniques and attitudes of the secret police were very different from the 1930s. Violence was limited and they concentrated instead on a few prominent dissidents rather than instituting a broad wave of terror throughout society. New psychological techniques were used and about twenty people a year were sent for political reasons to mental hospitals, where they were given large doses of drugs.

Exactly how many people passed through the extensive network of about 500 labour camps (the Gulags) run by the secret police and how many died there is a matter of acute historical debate. During the Cold War, based on estimates from exiles and very fragmentary evidence, some high figures were suggested – a maximum population in the Gulags of about 8 million in the 1940s with about 12 million people passing through the system. These estimates are certainly too high. Forced labour did play a major part in the Soviet construction industry in the 1930s and 1940s. This was a major 'benefit' to the Soviet economy because it enabled scarce capital equipment to be concentrated in heavy industry and arms production. In 1940 the NKVD undertook 13 per cent of all the capital work in the Soviet economy and at the giant Magnitogorsk metalworks roughly a third of the workforce (about 40,000 people, nearly all of them ex-kulaks) were slave labourers. Since the late 1980s some work has been done in the Soviet archives and, although this information needs to be analysed with caution, it suggests that the population of the Gulags at its height was about 4 million people. On average about 10 per cent of those arrested, in total about 1 million people, were shot before they reached the camps. (Mass graves were discovered by the Germans at Vannitsa in the Ukraine in 1943, where about 9,000 bodies were found, all shot in the back of the head. Other massacre sites were revealed after the fall of the Soviet Union.) The death rate in the camps was about 10 per cent a year; higher in the terrible north Siberian camps of Kolyma and during the early years of the war when food rations were drastically cut and work norms increased. If the population of the Gulag at any one time was between 3 and 4 million and the death rate was about 10 per cent a year, then it seems likely that between the mid-1930s and the early 1950s about 8 million people passed through the camp system and of those about 4 million died. Together with those shot, this would give a minimum death toll at the height of the Soviet system of terror and forced labour of about 5 million people.

The total number who died under the Soviet regime was much higher. Account also has to be taken of deportations during the Second World War and its immediate aftermath. This involved various minority groups such as the Volga Germans, the Crimean Tartars and smaller minorities, such as the Chechen, Karachai, Kalmyks and Ingush who were deemed to have either collaborated with the Germans or to be a danger to national security. Altogether about 2·5 million people were deported in horrendous conditions to Siberia. About 500,000 of them died immediately or in the Gulag. In addition the death toll in the camps outside the main period of repression between 1935 and 1953 has to be taken into account. This would add about another 3 million deaths. When those who died during collectivization (8 million) are added to the deaths in the camps and during deportations (8 to 9 million), it is clear that the Soviet regime directly caused the death of about 17 million of its own citizens.

The Soviet occupation of eastern Europe after 1943 and the establishment of Communist governments was a far less bloody process. In most countries in the first years of Communist rule the security forces were dominated by Soviet officials, but they were gradually replaced by locals, often recruited from the pre-war internal security forces. In Yugoslavia probably about 100,000 were killed in the immediate aftermath of the war. The quarrel with the Soviet Union from the late 1940s led to about another 50,000 people from the top echelons of the party being sent through the detention camp on Goli Otok island off the Dalmatian coast, with perhaps another 1 million lower-ranking officials being subject to various forms of investigation. From the early 1950s the labour camps were wound down and by the early 1960s the level of repression was relatively mild and the regime seemed little different from that in any other authoritarian government. Much the same trends were apparent in other countries. The biggest wave of show trials took place in Czechoslovakia in the late 1940s. Those accused were supposedly pro-Tito elements, although there were also anti-Semitic overtones in the trials of Rudolph Slansky, the Slovak party leader, and Bedrich Reicin, the head of military intelligence. In Hungary there were some trials, but in Poland, despite divisions within the leadership, no major leader was ever put on trial and shot. In Hungary after 1956, Czechoslovakia after 1968 and Poland in the early 1980s, there were waves of repression but in general they were not bloody. Like Yugoslavia all these regimes drifted towards an authoritarian stance with little freedom of expression and a climate of fear, but no outright wave of terror.

The collapse of East Germany in 1989–90 led to the capture, almost intact, of the secret police archives. They make it possible to see how the regime operated and the level of day-to-day repression. East Germany, like West Germany, was an artificial creation of the Cold War. It was occupied by about 300,000 Soviet troops, its most symbolic act was the construction of the Berlin Wall in August 1961 and it had little internal legitimacy. Yet it was reasonably prosperous – it was the richest country in the Soviet bloc. After the workers' disturbances of 1953 there was no political instability, even though the official trade union files reveal a very high level of workplace discontent. The ruling Socialist Unity Party, formed in 1946 through the compulsory unification of the Social Democrats and the Communists in the Soviet zone, remained united and controlled by the Moscow-trained elite, first under Walter Ulricht and then, after 1971, by his supporter Erich Honecker. The Christian Democrats and other parties, such as the Peasants, were allowed formal independence in order to incorporate as many different groups in society as possible, although they were all under strict government control. Only in the 1980s were a few truly independent groups – environmentalists and in the churches – able to establish themselves. The secret police – Staatssicherheitdienst (the 'Stasi') – was established in February 1950 and originally employed about 4,000 people. By 1989 it was 100,000 strong, employed at least 200,000 informers at any one time and kept files on about 6 million people. It was therefore on a completely different scale from its Nazi predecessor, the Gestapo. Stasi activities penetrated every part of society and it recruited as informers many who were thought at the time to be opponents of the regime. These included Wolfgang Schnur, a lawyer who defended dissidents and later founded the conservative Democratic Awakening, Manfred Stolpe, the head of the evangelical church, and, almost certainly, Lothar de Maiziere, the first and last democratically elected head of East Germany after the collapse of Communism. The detailed records of the Stasi and the number of people recruited, willingly or unwillingly, to act as informers demonstrate many of the problems of life under a repressive regime. People could not know who was likely to be an informer. Every action and comment had to be judged with care. However, it was also very difficult to make any clear-cut stand against the regime. Unless people wanted to be branded as outright dissenters, which resulted in very clear penalties, then they were forced to reach some accommodation with the authorities and accept a degree of collaboration with the regime.

The Communist regimes of Asia were probably more repressive than the Soviet Union, although detailed information is even sparser than for the USSR. After taking power in 1949, the Chinese Communists established a detailed system for monitoring the population. By 1953 there were already 4 million party propagandists, each responsible for a hundred peasants or ten workers. In the cities there were street secretaries and street offices with 'resident's committees', which supervised a few hundred households, and below them 'resident's groups' of between fifteen and forty families to transmit party directives and gather information about the political and social behaviour of individuals. 'Re-education' and 'struggle' meetings were used against those judged to be ideologically unsound. In 1960 political education classes took up two hours a day, although this was later reduced to about three hours a week. In 1949 a security police was established, which within three years had set up a local network in factories, schools and residential districts.

In the aftermath of the revolution forced labour camps were set up in remote areas, with the nominal task of 're-education'. Their exact population is unknown, although in October 1952 a party official admitted that there were over 10 million prisoners working on water projects alone. By the mid-1950s the best estimates suggest a total population in the labour camps of about 20 million. How many died in the camps is unknown. In addition, there was a campaign for the 'mass liquidation' of 'counter-revolutionaries'. The government admitted that over 1 million were killed during the first year of the new regime, with at least as many again being killed in the next campaign in 1951–2. The redistribution of land campaign probably resulted in another 5 million being killed. Casualties during the first decade of the new revolutionary government probably amounted to a minimum of 15 million, possibly 20 million. In addition, account has to be taken of the great famine of the late 1950s and early 1960s, brought about by the disastrous attempt to simultaneously collectivize life and to industrialize. This led to the deaths of about 27 million people. Apart from the shootings, torture and labour camps, there was also a purge of intellectuals, writers and the universities. In 1951 over 300,000 people were denounced as 'unreliable' and had their civil rights withdrawn and in Canton alone over 16,000 books were burnt. The brief moments of relaxation such as the 'Hundred Flowers' movement of 1957 merely served to illustrate the depth of the opposition. Within months the government introduced indefinite forced labour for 'vagabonds and loafers', people who broke police regulations and 'counter-revolutionaries and reactionaries' even though they had committed no crime. The Cultural Revolution was simply another phase of disruption and terror for many in the population. Undisciplined Red Guards selected their victims on a variety of grounds and probably 400,000 died in the first wave of action in the summer and autumn of 1966. In the near anarchy of the period the total casualties were almost certainly close to 2 million. In the last couple of decades of the century China settled down to a lower level of repression, although this was especially brutal in areas such as Tibet and the labour camps continued on an extensive scale. The government also showed with the shootings in Tienanmen Square in 1989 that it was not prepared to tolerate any political dissent. The exact number who died as a result of government policy and repression in China after 1949 is unknown, but it is unlikely to be fewer than 50 million and may be more.

Other regimes were just as repressive. In Vietnam the elimination of opponents and the land reform campaign of the Communist government in the north from the late 1940s was matched by repression in the south under the authoritarian and corrupt Diem government. After reunification in 1975 a massive system of 're-education' camps was set up, which had a total of about 2·5 million inmates. In total the various governments of Vietnam probably killed, apart from the direct casualties of the thirty-year-long war, about 1 million people. Exactly what happened in North Korea under the isolationist and highly repressive regime of Kim Il-sung and his son is unclear. The level of repression and control of information were as strict as any in the world although North Korea was, in many ways, closer to a modern *caudillo* dictator state, than a true Communist regime. It is likely that about 4 million people were identified as potentially hostile on class grounds and subject to hard labour in special camps. There were another 150,000 specifically political prisoners. The death toll is unknown, but probably somewhere near 2 million people.

The most barbaric regime in the twentieth century, not in terms of absolute numbers killed but in proportion to the population, was that of the Cambodian Communists during the late 1970s. Before 1970 Cambodia was ruled by a moderately corrupt but not particularly repressive regime, in a society where wealth was concentrated in the elite and the peasants were badly exploited. The overspill of the fighting in Vietnam, largely as a result of American policy, brought a military regime to power, increased corruption, began a civil war and led to an eventual Communist victory. What was unusual about the new regime was its strong, doctrinaire determination to build a completely new society and its highly puritanical policies. When the Khmer Rouge captured the capital Phnom Penh in late April 1975, almost immediately they forced all the inhabitants to leave carrying just a few possessions (the rest were 'confiscated'), with even the hospitals being cleared of patients. The aim was to rebuild society from the foundations. The 1 million or so urban dwellers (who were regarded as parasites) would be turned into peasants. In the new society the population was divided into three categories. Full rights were accorded only to poor peasants and workers. Candidate status was give to middle and upper peasants and the poorer members of the bourgeoisie. Only the former could speak and vote in meetings, candidates could only speak. The rest of the population had no rights.

The attempt to settle about a million people on the land without tools and seed, when the best land was already occupied, predictably led to starvation. This was worsened by the purges carried out by local party officials. Large numbers of people were executed and others sent to labour camps. The slightest infringement of government rules could lead to death. Many others died through the destruction of nearly all medical facilities and the killing of about half of all the doctors in the country. Industry was run down and the workers were sent off to the countryside to be re-educated.

Education above elementary level was abolished and even that was combined with work in the fields. To appear educated was highly dangerous and likely to lead to death. No religious activities were tolerated. All the major Buddhist leaders were executed and monks were forced to become peasants. The Christian cathedral in Phnom Penh was demolished. Marriage required party authorization and the couple had to come from the same class. From 1977 communal dining was imposed on the whole country in an attempt to hoard food for the approaching war with Vietnam. Apart from these attempts to remake society, there were incessant conflicts within the Khmer Rouge itself. Ideological conflict was rampant, with the losers being demoted to peasant status. There were strict rules on sexual relations between party cadres and infringement led to death. The secret police, the Nokorbal, were mainly concerned with party control and running the Tuol Sleung prison in Phnom Penh, where dissident party members were imprisoned, tortured and shot. About 20,000 probably died here. The original leader Pol Pot seems to have lost power in 1976, but regained it two years later. He then purged the party of all its pre-1960 members (they were regarded as supporters of Vietnam), executed ten members of the Politburo and built the party around the group that had gone into exile with him in 1963.

Exactly how many died in Cambodia under the Khmer Rouge will never be known. One problem is that the population can only be estimated because no census was taken after 1962. The best estimate is that there were just over 7 million people in Cambodia when the Khmer Rouge took power. Taking account of the evidence from the mass graves discovered after the overthrow of the Pol Pot government and other information, the total death toll is likely to have been a minimum of 2 million, probably slightly higher. In other words the Khmer Rouge government killed a third of the population of Cambodia in four years. This was the most barbaric government repression of the twentieth century.

How many of their own citizens did governments kill through repression in the twentieth century? In absolute terms the worst was Communist China (50 million), followed by the Soviet Union (17 million) and the Nationalist Chinese (10 million). The other Communist regimes of Asia added about 4 million and the other repressive regimes of Asia such as Indonesia and in the Middle East perhaps another 2 million. Although Africa after independence and Latin America gained a reputation for vicious repression, the actual death toll there was not more than 3 million. The Nazi treatment of its own citizens apart from the Jews would add another 1 million. In total therefore, and on a conservative estimate, governments killed about 100 million of their own people. This terrible statistic is only one measure of the effect of repression. For every person killed there were many more who had their lives blighted by long periods in forced labour camps. Even more lived under the continual threat of denunciation, arrest and torture, never knowing whether they or their family would be the next to suffer. When repression was at its height in the middle of the century, perhaps as many as a half of the world's population lived such lives.

20 DISCRIMINATION

MOST STATES in the world in the twentieth century were multi-racial and few of them were free from prejudice or discrimination against different groups on grounds of colour, ethnic origin, religion or a mixture of all three. Most discrimination was on the basis of race or colour. In these circumstances it was not the presence of objective physical differences that created 'races', but the social and political belief that such differences were significant and a basis on which separate and highly unequal treatment could be justified. The most highly developed systems of discrimination were found in the European and ex-European settlement colonies of the United States, South Africa, Southern Rhodesia, Australia, New Zealand and Canada. In these states there was major discrimination against the native peoples, those whom the Europeans had enslaved and those who might emigrate to these countries and threaten European exclusivity.

In creating these systems of discrimination Europeans and their descendants drew on a long-established view of the world. From at least the fifteenth century, when the Portuguese and Spaniards ventured into the Atlantic and along the African coast, Europeans saw colour as a mark of inferiority. They regarded themselves as superior and entitled on both religious and moral grounds to enslave their inferiors. The native people of the Atlantic islands, the Caribbean and South America were enslaved. When they died out under the harsh treatment and exposure to previously unknown diseases they were replaced by slaves brought from Africa. In the nineteenth century social Darwinist thinking strengthened these long-held beliefs. Human history was seen as a struggle between the races. Even more importantly, it was seen as essential to keep races 'pure' and separate if they were to flourish. The mixing of races would merely cause a decline in racial strength through deleterious cross-breeding. By the early twentieth century the dominant way of thinking in the western world saw the human population as divided into unchanging natural types which were recognizable by physical features. Mental, moral and political behaviour were closely linked to racial type and were transmitted between generations. The various human races were believed to form a carefully graded hierarchy with the white, and in particular Anglo-Saxon, races at the top. Beneath them were the Mediterranean and eastern European races, followed by the races of the Middle East, China and India. At the bottom of the hierarchy was the African. Indigenous races like the Aborigines were hardly allowed into the hierarchy. It followed from this way of thinking that races did not have equal rights. In general, only the whites were fit to govern themselves and some of the lesser white races were not really suited to democracy.

The two states which had the most highly developed systems of discrimination in the early twentieth century were the United States and South Africa. Both became far more discriminatory. In the United States this process lasted until the 1940s, when official discrimination began to be reduced, whereas in South Africa discrimination intensified until apartheid was finally dismantled in the late 1980s and early 1990s. In both countries the key element was segregation – whites and blacks lived apart as far as possible. Although there were clear similarities between the steps taken in each country to enforce inequality, there were also significant differences. In the United States, blacks were about a tenth of the population, although they were a majority in parts of the south and in some inner urban areas in the north after 1920. In South Africa, whites were never more than about a fifth of the population. Discrimination was explicit in the 1910 Union constitution, which was devised by the British and the white South Africans after the Boer War. In the United States, the constitutional amendments passed in the immediate aftermath of the civil war (the Fourteenth and Fifteenth Amendments) explicitly prohibited the denial of civil and political rights. Until the 1890s the civil rights of the black population were given minimal protection, but then the Supreme Court dismantled the constitutional protections in a series of decisions marked by legal sophistry.

A further crucial difference between the two states was their labour systems. Until 1910 nine out of ten black Americans lived in the south, where they were agricultural labourers enmeshed in a system of tenant farming and sharecropping which was, in many ways, little different from slavery. The labour for industrialization was provided in the north by European immigrants; it was not until after 1910 that blacks became part of the industrial labour force. That movement produced chronic racial antagonism and conflict in the north. South Africa had its own unique labour system, based on a relatively low level of white immigration. The whites were the farmers and managers. Mass labour was provided by Indian and Chinese indentured labour and then by the Africans. Strong restrictions on African peasant farming ensured a constant supply of labour under contract. African labourers were controlled by a pass law system and forced to live in compounds where they were denied any rights. The final difference was that the definition of who was a 'black' or 'Negro' in the United States was much stricter than in any other country in the world. Most southern states worked on the basis that any known black blood made a person black. On the other hand, in South Africa there was an extensive 'Coloured' mixed-race class from which it was even possible to pass into the white category.

The 'philosophy' of segregation was clearly set out by Senator James K. Vardaman of Mississippi when he was elected in 1912. He spoke of the need 'to save this country from the black race' and explained:

> I unhesitatingly assert that political equality for the colored race leads to social equality. Social equality leads to race amalgamation, and race amalgamation to deterioration and disintegration . . . I favour . . . the enactment of laws that will make perfect the social and political segregation of the white and colored races. We cannot follow the idea of Lincoln and send the colored man away to a country of his own. The next best thing, therefore, is to bring about complete segregation.

His words would have found a sympathetic hearing among most whites and not just in the United States. Discrimination against free blacks in the north had been widespread since the eighteenth century. The reassertion of control by southern whites following the withdrawal of federal troops in the 1870s saw the imposition of increasing de facto segregation and discrimination. The key legal decision, which was to dominate American society for the next sixty years, was Plessy v. Ferguson in 1896. The Supreme Court had to rule on the legality of the Louisiana Railway Accommodations Act of 1890, which enforced separate but theoretically equal accommodation for whites and blacks. The Supreme Court upheld the Act in a judgement of almost unparalleled casuistry. Their problem was to square the legislation with the Fourteenth Amendment, which provided for equal protection under the law and gave the right to declare void any state actions which impaired the privileges and immunities of American citizens. Justice Brown admitted that the amendment was designed 'to enforce the absolute equality of the two races before the law'. However, he went on, 'a statute which implies merely a legal distinction between the white and colored races . . . has no tendency to destroy the legal equality of the two races'. He added, 'It could not have been intended to abolish distinctions based upon color or to enforce social, as distinguished from political equality.' His conclusion was, 'If one race be inferior to the other socially, the Constitution of the United States cannot put them upon the same plane.'

The decision in Plessy v. Ferguson on the legality of 'separate but equal' provisions was the green light for a vast extension of segregation in every area of social life, much of which was sanctioned by the Supreme Court in further cases. Little attempt was made to discover whether the 'separate' facilities were in practice 'equal'. In 1899 the Supreme Court allowed separate schools and in 1908 accepted the right of states to impose segregation in private schools. The consequences were predictable. By 1910 in Wilcox County, Alabama, the 2,285 white pupils each received on average $28,000 of state spending and the 10,745 black pupils less than $4,000 each. Before 1899 only three states in the south had separate railway waiting rooms, by 1910 all did. In 1900 only Georgia had segregated streetcars, within seven years this practice had spread to all southern states. In 1915 South Carolina passed a law segregating textile factories, under which separate workrooms, entrances, pay windows, exits, doorways, stairways, lavatories, drinking water, cups and glasses had to be provided. In the same year Oklahoma insisted on separate telephone booths and a year earlier Louisiana had enforced segregated circuses in which whites and blacks had to sit a minimum of twenty-five feet apart. Between 1910 and 1917 many southern cities such as St Louis, Atlanta, Baltimore and New Orleans passed residential segregation ordinances prohibiting white and black from living in the same block. These were ruled illegal by the Supreme Court, not on the grounds that they were discriminatory but because they interfered with property rights. Much the same results were achieved by informal pressure instead. By 1920 Mississippi, Alabama, Louisiana, North Carolina and South

Carolina provided for separate hospitals, in which nurses could only treat patients from the same race. In other states similar rules were imposed without formal legislation. Thirteen states had segregated mental hospitals and ten had segregated prisons and homes for the aged, orphans, blind and deaf. In order to avoid possible contamination, North Carolina and Florida provided separate school books for each race, which also had to be stored separately. In many cities separate Bibles were provided in court.

After 1920 segregation continued to be extended. In Atlanta in 1926 black barbers were prohibited from cutting the hair of white women and children. Six years later the city insisted that amateur baseball teams of different races had to play at least two blocks apart. Most states and cities passed laws to ensure separate taxis and long-distance buses. In 1944 the development of air travel led Virginia to legislate for separate waiting areas at airports. Texas banned 'Caucasians' and 'Africans' from boxing and wrestling together, Arkansas insisted on separate betting facilities at racetracks and Birmingham in Alabama stopped mixed-race dominoes and checkers. By 1930 twenty-nine of the forty-eight states of the union outlawed marriages between whites and blacks (something which was not ruled illegal by the Supreme Court until 1967).

Equally important was the removal of the right to vote from blacks in the southern states from the mid-1890s. The scale and speed with which it occurred was phenomenal. In 1896 just over 130,000 blacks voted in Louisiana and they made up slightly over half the total electorate. Eight years later only 1,342 voted. The move to restrict voting rights began in Mississippi in 1890, when the new constitution of the state made voting depend on the voters' ability to understand the constitution. This was judged by a local registrar, who was easily able to pass uneducated whites and reject educated blacks. These clauses were supplemented by literacy tests, the requirement to pay property and poll taxes and so-called 'grandfather' clauses. The last restricted the ballot to people whose grandfathers had voted in the state, which naturally excluded all blacks. These qualifications were accepted as legal by the Supreme Court in 1898 and spread rapidly through all the southern states. At the same time the Democratic Party instituted white-only primaries across the south to select their candidates. Since the south was effectively a one-party state, the white-only primary elections decided who was to be elected at local, state and federal levels. In 1921 the Supreme Court decided that Congress did not have the power to regulate primaries and banned state interference too.

Just as important as the decisions of the Supreme Court and the actions of city and state governments were the attitudes of the federal government. Until the 1890s the Republicans, who usually controlled the federal government, still appointed blacks (who supported them as the party which had freed the slaves), to numerous posts such as postmasters and customs officers across the southern states. Federal policy began to change because black appointments became increasingly unacceptable in the south and too dangerous for their incumbents. In 1898 at Lake City in South Carolina, when a black postmaster was appointed a white mob burned him alive in his house and shot all his family as they tried to flee the fire. In the early twentieth century the federal government began to implement a policy of increasing discrimination. In 1908 the Census Bureau changed its rules so that people were only interviewed by members of their own race. The real changes, though, came after 1912 under President Wilson, the first southerner to be elected president since the civil war. Like most of his compatriots, he was a racist and as head of Princeton University had barred blacks from entry. Under Wilson the federal government introduced segregation in the Treasury and Post Office, with separate workrooms, lunchrooms and lavatories. One particular aim was to ensure that blacks did not supervise white women. All the remaining black appointees in the south were removed and all new federal buildings in the south were built with segregated facilities. In the 1920s segregation was extended to the Navy Department and the Department of the Interior. The early days of the New Deal under Roosevelt were similarly discriminatory. Until the late 1940s the Federal Housing Authority actively recommended restricted housing covenants to exclude blacks and the various federal loan organizations effectively shut off housing loans to blacks. One of the centrepieces of the New Deal, the Tennessee Valley Authority, only recruited blacks as unskilled labour and refused to train them. The US armed forces were also strictly segregated. No blacks were allowed in the Marines, in the navy they were only allowed in the all-black messmen and servants' branch and in the army there were only small segregated black units. This pattern of strict segregation was maintained throughout the Second World War. It was general policy that no black could be superior in rank to a white in the same unit, so nearly all officers were white, although only the worst were sent to black units. With the approval of the Red Cross, the

American services also insisted that blood donors and the use of plasma should be rigidly segregated so that whites were not 'contaminated' by being given black products.

Segregation and discrimination were enforced not just through legislation but also by social pressure, particularly in the north. In 1900 eighteen northern states had civil rights legislation prohibiting public discrimination, but it was mainly symbolic and its enforcement was sporadic. Much depended on the willingness of blacks to bring expensive civil action through the courts. Before the 1940s only thirteen states had laws on employment discrimination and none had any on housing. The move of black people to the north after 1910 (the black population of Detroit increased seven-fold between 1910 and 1920) produced major changes. Before 1910 the small black population of the north lived widely scattered in the cities. Within little more than twenty years most of the far larger black population was concentrated in inner-city ghettos. This was partly the result of people moving to where they had family or community links, just as the European immigrants did. However, the black ghettos were very different from those of the immigrant communities, where people passed through before being slowly absorbed into American society. In the case of the blacks the ghettos were enforced through the use of 'Improvement Associations', under which white communities banded together to keep out blacks through massive social pressure on residents selling their homes and on local estate agents. An opinion poll in 1942 found that more than eight out of ten white Americans thought there should be separate sections in cities for blacks. The rapid rise in black immigration resulted in widespread violence by whites. During 1919 there were twenty-six race riots in northern cities. In July and early August a riot in Chicago, which started with an alleged black violation of a tacit racial boundary on a beach, lasted intermittently for nearly a fortnight. The most vulnerable people were blacks travelling to work in white areas (nearly two-thirds of blacks were employed as servants) – many were trapped and killed in streetcars. Altogether 38 people were killed, over 500 were injured and more than 1,000 people were made homeless as black houses were firebombed.

In the southern states such violence against blacks remained an everyday fact of life. Blacks were forced to adopt a submissive attitude, were referred to as 'boy' regardless of their age and any infringement of the unwritten code of behaviour imposed by the whites was likely to result in whippings, beatings and lynchings. On average in the first three decades of the century there were about 140 lynchings a year in the southern states. Many of these resulted from the white obsession with miscegenation and in particular the violation of white women. As the *Winston-Salem Journal* of North Carolina put it in 1932, 'in the South it has been traditional . . . that its white womanhood shall be held inviolate by an inferior race'. Any accusation of rape normally led to a lynching involving mutilation and then death by slow strangulation rather than by hanging. In the 1890s in Paris, Texas when a black, Henry Smith, was accused of raping a white child, he was held while special trains were laid on to bring in thousands who wanted to witness the outcome. Over ten thousand watched as first the flesh on Smith's feet was burned off with white hot irons, his tongue was burnt out and then his eyes were put out. Much of the work was done by a fifteen-year-old white boy. Smith was still conscious when he was finally soaked in oil and burnt alive. The number of lynchings fell in the 1920s but doubled again in the 1930s. Under outside pressure the whites increasingly realized that it was just as easy to use the biased legal system which they controlled to obtain the same ends and unofficial killings declined.

Racism in the United States did not just apply to blacks. Equally important, especially in the states of the west, was the 'threat' posed by Chinese and Japanese immigration. The Chinese arrived in California during the gold rush of the 1850s, but immigration was stopped in the 1880s and unregistered Chinese were expelled. Only those Chinese born in the United States were allowed to become citizens. However, together with all other Asians, they were classified as 'non-white' by the Supreme Court in 1927 and therefore subject to the same segregation measures as blacks. Although Chinese immigration was banned, the small Japanese community in California was still growing. In 1905 the Asiatic Exclusion League was formed to stop contamination from an 'unassimilable and inferior race' – within three years it had 110,000 members in California alone. In 1907 the California School Board decided to impose segregated schooling. Japanese government protests resulted in an agreement with the American government. Japan would stop the flow of immigrants, but in return the United States would not impose segregation. The leaders of the United States were clear what was at stake. President Teddy Roosevelt wrote: 'This is a race question, and race questions stand by themselves . . . the important point is that the Japanese should, as a race, be excluded from becoming permanent inhabitants of our territory.' Woodrow Wilson stated during the 1912 presidential campaign: 'I stand for the national policy of exclusion. The whole question is one of assimilation of diverse races.' It was not possible, he added, to make 'a homogeneous population out of a people who do not blend with the Caucasian race'.

Although formal segregation was limited, California did pass the Anti-Alien Land Act in 1913 to stop the Japanese from owning any more agricultural land and competing with white-run farms. As the State Board of Control wrote in its 1922 report: 'The people of California are determined to repress a developing Japanese community within our midst.' Assimilation was impossible, 'just as the thought of intermarriage of whites and blacks would be impossible'. The United States was one of the white countries to reject the Japanese request that a clause outlawing racial discrimination be included in the Charter of the League of Nations. Growing pressure from around the United States produced new legislation which effectively ended non-white immigration. The 1924 Immigration Act was deliberately designed to be both racist and discriminatory. The very low level of black immigration was ended altogether by removing the 'descendants of slave immigrants' (sic) from the population base on which the quotas for admission under the Act were based. Also removed were 'aliens ineligible for citizenship'. This stopped other non-white immigration because since 1790 only whites could become naturalized American citizens. Finally, the Act discriminated against immigrants from southern and eastern Europe by taking the 1890 census, before the wave of immigration from this area, as the basis for the allocation of country quotas.

The greatest act of discrimination against the Japanese and their descendants came during the Second World War. The United States had nearly a million German and Italian aliens living in the country, but fewer than 10,000, nearly all of them hardline Nazi and fascist sympathizers, were interned. No action was taken against American citizens of German or Italian descent. Policy towards the 47,000 Japanese aliens and the 80,000 American citizens of Japanese descent was very different. From February 1942, following pressure from the military and anti-Japanese organizations, President Roosevelt ordered all people who were either Japanese or American citizens of Japanese descent to be moved to special camps guarded by the army. People who had been born as American citizens were, like the Japanese aliens, expected to sell all their property except for clothing, bedding and cooking utensils before they moved. Overall they lost property worth about $350 million. The internees were forced to live in communal barracks and were not allowed to practise their religion. The Supreme Court upheld their illegal imprisonment until 1945 when many, on their eventual release, emigrated to Japan. It took those who remained behind nearly forty years to obtain compensation for the American government's actions.

Equally discriminatory was American policy towards native Americans. The history of European settlement in North America was one of slow extermination of the native people as they were driven further westward. By the late nineteenth century native Americans were confined to a series of reservations in the west, but the process did not end there. When Oklahoma was opened for white settlement at the turn of the century, the Indians were removed to even worse land and by 1934 they had lost two-thirds of their remaining land (over 80 million acres). Like the Aborigines in Australia, they were driven to the margin of society, subjected to the rule of authoritarian and corrupt government agents who ran the 'reserves' and denied many rights in white American society. Despite some improvements in the 1930s and later, the Indians were left as a depressed minority in the United States, suffering from a very low standard of living, high infant mortality and heavily dependent on federal government welfare programmes. Even a reassertion of pride in the Indian heritage from the 1960s made little impact after centuries of discrimination.

Extensive discrimination in South Africa was prevalent in both the British- and Boer-controlled areas throughout the nineteenth century. However, there were some significant differences. In the Boer-controlled Transvaal and Orange Free State, only whites had political rights and the Transvaal constitution specifically prohibited racial equality. In the British-controlled Cape colony a small group of 'coloureds' were allowed to vote if they passed what became increasingly stiff income and educational tests. Only about 8,000 people did so, but the provision was of symbolic importance. In the British colony of Natal, although in theory there was no colour bar for voting, over 23,000 whites could vote, 150 Indians, 50 coloureds and 6 Africans. When the Boers finally surrendered at the end of the war, they insisted on a provision in the Treaty of Vereeniging which stated that the question of whether to give the vote to 'natives' would not be decided until after self-government for the former Boer republics was granted. This left the Boers in control of the issue and there was no doubt about what their decision would be. In practice the British shared their views and had, for example, refused to use Indian or 'native' troops during the war so as not to offend Boer susceptibilities. The British High Commissioner, Lord Milner, made the position clear:

> A political equality of white and black is impossible. The white man must rule because he is elevated by many, many steps above the black man; steps which it will take the latter centuries to climb and which it is quite possible that the vast bulk of the black population may never be able to climb at all.

During the drafting of the constitution for the new Union of South Africa, in which discussions no Africans, Indians or Coloureds were allowed to participate, a 'compromise' was reached. Africans and Coloureds were still allowed to vote in the Cape if they passed the tough qualification test, but that right could be removed by the Union parliament on a two-thirds vote. Elsewhere only whites could vote and only whites could be members of the Union parliament. The implications of white control rapidly became clear after 1910. The Africans were turned into helots to work for the whites. In 1913 the country was formally divided up by the Natives' Land Act. The Africans, who made up nearly three-quarters of the total population, were confined to the 'native reserves' which made up less than 10 per cent of the total land, nearly all of it of very poor quality. Families who had farmed land for centuries were uprooted and people were crowded into the reserves. Africans were not allowed to buy land in 'white' areas.

As the whites expected, the Africans were forced out of the reserves where there was no work and migrated to the cities to find jobs. There they were subject to even stricter controls. Under an Act of 1923 the Africans legally became residents of the reserves and were only allowed to settle in the cities (in segregated areas) to work. Their right to move and work was regulated by the passbook they had to carry with them at all times. In 1930 these controls were extended to women. If there was no work Africans had to return to the reserves. As the Transvaal Local Government Commission put it in 1922, the African should leave the city 'when he ceases to minister to the needs of the white man'. In 1937 workers from the reserves were allowed a fortnight to find work and the police were given the power forcibly to remove any African in a city who did not have a job. In many cases Africans were recruited en masse as low-paid labourers particularly in the mines. They were forced to live in barrack-like compounds separated from their families, who legally could only live in the reserves. Under a series of acts passed between 1911 and 1924 the Africans were relegated to the lowest-paid, most menial jobs. They were barred from apprenticeships, from being mine managers, overseers, mechanical engineers and from any job that might require them to supervise whites. They were excluded from any form of collective bargaining and strikes by natives were illegal.

Social segregation was left to local authorities and individuals. Separate hospitals and cemeteries were the rule and the railways had separate facilities. On buses and trams Johannesburg had separate vehicles but elsewhere, except in Cape Town, there were separate areas on the same vehicle. Most hotels and restaurants barred blacks. Residential segregation was strictly enforced. In 1927 'immorality' between Europeans and Africans was made a criminal offence. Nearly all whites were agreed on the policy set out by Jan Smuts, prime minister of South Africa and close confidant of numerous British governments. In a speech in London in 1917 he stated, 'there must be no intermixture of blood between the two colours'. He continued, 'Instead of mixing up black and white in the old haphazard way, which instead of lifting up the black degraded the white, we are now trying to lay down a policy of keeping them apart as much as possible.' The position of the black in this situation was made clear in a speech he made in 1942: '[he is] the beast of burden; he is the worker'.

Throughout the 1930s and early 1940s the sense of crisis increased in South Africa. Nearly two-thirds of Africans lived in European-designated areas and they outnumbered the whites in urban areas. This reflected the simple fact that because the Africans were required to work in the white-dominated economy or as servants to the whites then they had to live in the cities. It was seen as a developing 'black peril'. In 1946 the political rights of the Indians were reduced and their right to buy land was severely limited to stop them moving into white areas. This merely brought down on South Africa its first international condemnation by the United Nations. A parting of the ways was approaching rapidly. The United Party under Smuts appeared to have no answer, although it was firmly committed to continuing segregation. The more extreme Afrikaaners in the Nationalist Party wanted to go further and construct a system, apartheid, in which white domination would be permanently enshrined through a full separation of the races. One of the proponents of apartheid, Dr Geoff Cronje of the University of Pretoria, set out its position in his 1945 book *Home for Posterity*:

> The more consistently the policy of apartheid could be applied, the greater would be the security for the purity of our blood and the surer our unadulterated European racial survival . . . total racial separation . . . is the most consistent application of the Afrikaner idea of racial apartheid.

Such ideas were backed by many leaders of the Dutch Reformed Church, who thought Africans were inferior on the basis of the Bible. The Nationalists portrayed the 1948 election as a choice between 'integration and national suicide' or the implementation of apartheid and the preservation of 'a pure white race'. Over-representation of rural areas ensured that the Nationalists won a majority in parliament, even though they gained little more than 40 per cent of the votes.

The implementation of apartheid proceeded on two fronts: the removal of what little remained of non-white political power and the imposition of much more severe social legislation. The Cape Coloureds were removed from the common voting roll and given separate representation (by whites) and finally in 1968 even that representation was removed. In the same year inter-racial political parties were made illegal. In 1959 the small number of whites in parliament who were supposed to represent African 'interests' were removed. At the same time the 260 small, scattered African reserves were grouped into a series of 'homelands', one for each major ethnic group, from which whites, Coloureds, Indians and all Africans not of that tribal group were barred. This was designed to split the Africans and encourage industry to move to the 'border' areas, to avoid the need for blacks to reside in white cities. The long-term project was to partition the country on a highly unequal basis. The homelands first became self-governing and finally in the 1970s 'independent'. No other government recognized such a transparent fiction since South Africa kept control of every important aspect of government. The homelands were poor, had few resources and only a few in the African elite benefited from the new 'government' jobs. The attraction of the policy for the whites was that the Africans became citizens of the new homelands and therefore lost their South

African citizenship, even though most still lived in South Africa. They became 'foreign' migrant workers with no rights at all. In 1983 the white government imposed a new constitution designed to incorporate Coloureds and Indians into the system in a highly dependent position. These groups were given their own largely powerless houses in a restructured parliament which the whites (about one in six of the population) continued to control. The Africans (over 70 per cent of the population) were excluded altogether.

The social legislation introduced by the new Nationalist government during its first ten years in office was designed to fill any gaps in the existing discriminatory legislation and then build what it saw as a coherent racial structure. In 1949 inter-racial marriages were prohibited and the next year the Immorality Amendment Act prohibited sexual intercourse between whites and all non-whites. In 1953 all public premises and vehicles had to be reserved solely for the use of one race, but it was not necessary to provide facilities for all races. The measure was essentially symbolic, given the level of discrimination already in force. Before 1959 most universities were for whites and the few that were multi-racial had strictly segregated facilities. In that year it was made a criminal offence for any non-white student to register at these previously 'mixed' universities, the multi-racial Hare university was turned into a Xhosa tribal college and the subjects that could be taught in the African colleges were heavily restricted. By 1970 only one in twenty African children went to secondary school and each white child had, on average, over thirty times more spent on his or her education than an African. In 1950 the Group Areas Act created racial areas for the ownership and occupation of land. As a result whole African communities were uprooted – in Johannesburg 60,000 people were removed from Sophiatown to create a white suburb which was suitably named 'Triomf'. The key piece of legislation was the Population Registration Act of 1950, which created a racial register of three groups – European, Coloured and African – on the basis of 'appearance, general acceptance and repute'. The lives of individuals and families were determined by how they were placed in this classification and some existing families were broken up because they crossed the now forbidden racial barriers. African labour was regulated even more strictly after 1952. All employers were forced to use labour bureaux, which regulated migrant labour, decided where each African could work and for how long. No African could be in an urban area for more than three days without a permit. Those Africans 'surplus' to requirements (i.e. unemployed) were subject to removal. The onus was placed on Africans to prove that they were in an urban area legally. By the 1960s 400,000 Africans a year were being convicted of offences under the pass laws and labour regulations. They were sent to the homelands, even though many had never been there before, subjected to forced agricultural labour or sent to remote 'resettlement camps'.

The theoreticians of apartheid were clear about their aims in this the most highly developed system of European racial thinking. One of the most rigid ideologues was Hendrik Verwoerd, the minister for native affairs and prime minister after 1958. He was not an Afrikaner, having been born in the Netherlands, but with all the fervour of a convert he believed in the total separation of black and white through the homelands policy. He made it clear that as far as the African was concerned, 'there is no place for him in the European community above the level of certain forms of labour'. He also explained that the purpose of the government control contained in the 1953 Bantu Education Act was to ensure 'natives will be taught from childhood to realize that equality with Europeans is not for them'. By the 1960s the elaborate system of apartheid was almost complete. Whether it could work in an increasingly complex economy and when the whites were such a small and increasingly embattled minority was another question. In the last result the whites were determined to hang on to their highly privileged positions and keep those whom they saw as their racial inferiors in a subordinate position. In April 1955 Verwoerd's predecessor as prime minister, Johannes Strijdom, told parliament, in what he admitted was a 'blunt' speech: 'Either the White man dominates or the Black takes over . . . The only way the Europeans can maintain supremacy is by domination . . . And the only way they can maintain domination is by withholding the votes from non-Europeans.'

The United States and South Africa were not the only countries to have highly discriminatory racial policies and immigration rules which were designed to keep out 'undesirable' racial elements. To the north of South Africa the separate colony of Southern Rhodesia developed a system of segregation that was very similar to that in the larger dominion. The problem for the whites was that they were an even smaller proportion of the population than in South Africa, never more than one in twenty-five. As in other colonies, the

Africans were seen as no more than a cheap labour force. A poll tax forced them to work in mines and on white farms and the whites ensured that they took all the good land for themselves. This system reached its apogee with the 1931 Land Apportionment Act, which divided up the country. In total over 1 million Africans were given 28 million acres, whereas the 50,000 whites controlled 48 million acres (over half the land), with the remainder being left either unallocated or as game reserve. The whites had so much land that they were never able to occupy, let alone farm, all of it. All urban areas were white and Africans were prohibited from buying land in these areas. However, because the whites were so dependent on cheap African labour, blacks had to be 'temporary residents' in the cities, where they lived in squalid townships with few facilities. As workers they were not allowed to join trade unions and were restricted to unskilled jobs. All facilities were rigidly segregated and education was free for whites but not for blacks. Even the so-called 'relaxation' of some rules in the 1950s simply demonstrated their real nature – for example, the decision that the handful of African university graduates should be allowed to consume alcohol. The nature of inter-racial relations was demonstrated by the 1903 Immorality Suppression Ordinance. This made sexual intercourse between a black man and a white woman illegal (rape was a capital offence), but similar relations between a white man and a black woman were not illegal.

British refusal from the late 1950s to allow independence unless there were some minimal provisions which would theoretically allow eventual majority rule by the Africans merely drove the Rhodesian whites to greater extremism. The rise of the Rhodesian Front, committed to seizing independence, aligned the country with the apartheid regime in South Africa. In 1962 one of its MPs explained, 'If the European is ousted from his pride of place it could only be done by an intelligent race – a requirement that precludes the African.' The whites declared independence unilaterally in 1965 and by the end of the decade had implemented a new constitution designed to entrench white supremacy for ever.

The British settlement colonies of Australia, New Zealand and Canada faced a different problem. Their racial policy was not about how to control and exploit a native labour force – they did not have one – but instead how to keep out cheap labour, especially from Asia, which would undercut white wages and threaten white exclusivity. Racial policy in Australia operated on two separate but linked fronts, immigration and the status of the Aborigines. The first restrictions on Asian immigration were imposed by a number of Australian colonies in the 1850s and only very small numbers had arrived by the end of the century. Nevertheless, the Australians saw themselves as a white outpost in the Far East surrounded by a mass of 'yellow' races who would, without controls, swamp the country. In 1896 each colony passed legislation prohibiting the immigration of all Asians, Africans and Polynesians. Britain, as the imperial power, used its residual authority to veto the legislation. It did so not because of opposition to the racist nature of the legislation but only because it openly discriminated against citizens of the empire. It suggested the colonies should instead adopt the same measures as Natal by imposing a literacy and dictation test in a European language for all immigrants. (The language used could be varied to ensure no non-white could pass.)

The new federal union of Australia, created at the beginning of the twentieth century, was based upon a consensus between all the parties about a white Australia. In 1903 the Prime Minister, Deakin stated, 'The white Australia policy goes to the roots of our national existence.' The Labour Party candidates in the first federal election of March 1901 campaigned on saving Australia from 'the coloured curse' so as to avoid becoming 'a mongrel nation torn with racial dissension'. This was important because Australia was 'the last chance of the white race'. In 1905 the party adopted as its aim the cultivation of 'an Australian sentiment, based upon the maintenance of racial purity'. Deakin also spoke of 'the desire we should be one people, and remain one people without the admixture of other races [because] a united race means that its members can intermarry and associate without degradation'.

The small number of Asians in the country were subject to considerable discrimination. Queensland and Western Australia banned people of Asian descent born in Australia from voting. In 1903 Western Australia prohibited Asians from owning or working in a factory and in the 1930s Queensland barred them from owning land and restricted them to working in a limited range of industries. The federal government reinforced this policy. In 1904 it banned the import of indentured labour from the Pacific islands to work in the plantations of Queensland and two years later the existing workers were forcibly repatriated. No federal subsidy was available to any mail service that employed coloured workers and resident Asians were denied old-age pensions. The white Australia policy was maintained unaltered until 1966, when there were just 40,000 non-Europeans in the country (less than a third of 1 per cent of the total population), nearly all of them temporary Asian students. In March 1966 the government decided to admit a very limited number of highly skilled non-Europeans and allow them permanent residency after five rather than the normal fifteen years. However, the cabinet insisted that 'the basic principles of Australia's immigration policy' and 'the fundamental soundness of a policy directed towards social homogenity [are] not in question'. The 'white Australia' policy was not finally abandoned until the late 1970s.

A 'white Australia' policy could only make sense on the assumption that the Aborigines did not exist. This was the prevailing view, so they were excluded from the 1901 constitution and not counted in the national census. Australia was based on a long tradition of brutality to the Aborigines – in the nineteenth century they had been driven off the land, killed, denied all rights and worked in conditions of near and actual slavery. The basis of policy in the twentieth century was that the Aborigines were incapable of existing in a modern society. They could therefore be denied legal rights. Aborigines could reside legally only in reserves, unless they were lawfully employed or married to a white, which, like all Aboriginal marriages, required a government permit. The government also issued permits to employers to employ Aborigines (Asians could not have such permits), although there was no provision that wages had to be paid. If they were paid, they would go into a trust account which was controlled by the police or the Chief Protector. The latter could take over the property (and sell it) of any Aborigine. The police had powers to remove Aborigines from cities at any time without needing a reason. It was assumed that half-castes would eventually be absorbed into the white population, whereas full Aborigines would die out. In the 1930s the Australian parliament discussed speeding up the process by sterilizing all Aborigines and all part-Aborigine women. As part of government policy, Aborigine and part-Aborigine children were taken from their parents, placed in institutions, mission schools or with white parents, where they could be brought up away from parental and tribal influence. In addition there was large-scale official and un-official violence towards Aborigines. In November 1928 the police deliberately killed seventeen Aborigines on suspicion that they might have murdered a white – the police faced no charges and their actions were widely supported. Until the late 1940s Aborigine witnesses in Western Australia were neck-chained together. In 1963 the same state made it possible to prosecute Aborigines on reserves for 'insubordination or unseemly behaviour or use of obscene language'. The result of this policy of massive discrimination was that the Aborigines lived in poverty, largely without education, on the fringes of Australian society, subjected to violence and degrading treatment and denied the most basic human rights. A few changes were made in the last part of the twentieth century – Aborigines were finally allowed to vote – but their social conditions remained little changed.

The neighbouring dominion of New Zealand had a similar immigration policy to that of Australia, based on highly discriminatory literacy and dictation tests designed to keep out Asians and other undesirables. Internally the white settlers faced much more advanced and determined opposition from the native Maori population than the Aborigines had put up in Australia. From the beginning British policy was based on integration rather than confinement to reserves. The mythology of New Zealand in the twentieth century was that there was no discrimination. It was certainly the case that the open segregation and discrimination which characterized the United States, South Africa, Rhodesia and Australia were not present. Nevertheless, there was unofficial segregation in housing and hotels until the 1970s and intermarriage was generally frowned on. Although the All Blacks rugby team adopted the Maori *haka* for its pre-match intimidation of opponents, it was also willing, until 1965, to exclude Maoris from its tours to South Africa. Towards the end of the century there was a reassertion of Maori culture and identity, a demand for the return of their land confiscated in the nineteenth century and a growing rejection of assimilation into white (*paheka*) culture.

Canada also excluded non-white immigrants. American blacks were turned back at the border, there was a high poll tax on the Chinese, an agreement with the Japanese government to restrict immigration and a ban on Indian immigration. Along the Pacific coast in British Columbia there was a very strong movement (similar to that in California) to exclude Asian immigrants. Racial discrimination probably reached a peak in Canada in the 1930s and during the Second World War. The openly racist prime minister, Mackenzie King, was determined to follow the American lead and insisted on the forcible removal of 20,000 Canadians of Japanese descent from the Pacific coast into camps, despite the advice of the military that they were no threat to Canadian security. All their assets were confiscated and after the war they were offered the choice of 'repatriation' to Japan or forced settlement east of the Rockies. The 1952 Immigration Act was racist in that it allowed refusal of entry to be based on nationality, ethnic group, occupation or class, so that in practice only Europeans were admitted. The Act was not modified until 1966 and there remained little recognition of the ethnic diversity within Canada, apart from the British-French split. Unofficial discrimination against Asian immigrants and the native peoples of the north continued.

The imperial power, Britain, also had its own system of low-level discrimination in the first two-thirds of the century. Black immigration was very low and largely confined to the seaports, though this could still bring about race riots as in Cardiff in 1919. The government took power to exclude aliens, especially coloured seamen – Asian seamen could be compulsorily repatriated under 1894 legislation. In 1919 legislation legalized differential pay rates at sea according to race and in 1925 all coloured seamen landing in Britain were forced to register with the police. The armed forces maintained segregated units and 'persons not of pure European descent' could not become officers. Before 1940 no coloured people could join the civil service and although after that date coloured servicemen were allowed, until 1969 they were subject to a quota to keep their numbers at minimal levels. Immigration into Britain from the empire was unrestricted. However, the moment large numbers of people from the Caribbean and Africa began to arrive from the mid-1940s onwards there were immediate demands for restrictions. In 1949 the Royal Commission on Population reported that although there was a shortage of workers colonial immigrants would be undesirable because of a multitude of problems. It argued that they could only be accepted 'into a fully established society like ours . . . if the immigrants were of good human stock and were not prevented by their religion or race from intermarrying with the host population and becoming merged with it'. Although people from Ireland were entering the country at thirty times the rate of the black and Asian immigrants, this was not seen as a problem because, as a report to the cabinet in 1955 noted, 'the outstanding difference is that the Irish are not a different race'. Controls on immigration were instituted in 1962 and steadily tightened over the next thirty years. These controls were racially based: for example, in 1968 they were imposed on those who held British passports unless they had at least one grandparent born in Britain. Discrimination within Britain was widespread and anti-discrimination legislation, beginning in 1965, had only a limited impact.

The European colonies that stemmed mainly from British settlement were not the only ones to experience discrimination, but their history was distinctive. A very different evolution of race relations occurred in Brazil. Until the early twentieth century European immigration to Brazil was very low and the overwhelming majority of the population was coloured, the descendants of the huge numbers of slaves brought from Africa to work on the plantations. Although the conditions for the slaves were little different from those in the United States and slavery was not abolished until 1888, Brazil was not characterized by the fear of blacks, in particular free blacks, that was so widespread in the United States. The key to the difference was the emergence of a very broad category of *mulatto* people in Brazil. In the United States people were either black or white and even the slightest 'taint' of 'Negro' blood made someone black. In Brazil there were perhaps as many as twelve gradations from *preto* (black) through *mulatto*, *pardo* and *moreno*, to *brancos de terra* who had some black blood but were treated as whites. The result was that the racial system was never as harsh as in the United States, mainly because the *mulatto* group offered an escape route to blacks and produced a multitude of different racial categories.

Throughout the twentieth century the carefully cultivated mythology of Brazil was that because of this mix of racial categories there was no discrimination. Formally that was certainly the case: there was no system of segregation, the 1946 constitution explicitly prohibited discrimination and legislation in 1951 provided heavy penalties for any discrimination in public places. In practice, although there was a high degree of racial tolerance, there was considerable social segregation. This was partly along class lines because blacks tended to occupy the lowest positions, especially in employment, and the whites the highest. It was also geographical in that the north-eastern states such as Bahia, with the highest proportion of blacks, also had the highest levels of racial mixing, whereas further south, especially south of Rio de Janeiro and around São Paulo there were much higher levels of social segregation. Throughout the country the poor were, as in the United States, overwhelmingly black. In Bahia in 1936 nine out of ten people in the professions were white, while the same proportion of porters and stevedores were black. The same pattern was true of education: in Rio in 1968 blacks made up about a quarter of the population but only 2 per cent of the secondary school population. This inevitably affected access to elite jobs: in 1968 four out of five government employees were white, 2 per cent were black and there was only one black diplomat. Mixed marriages remained unusual, but the overall trend was towards a 'mixed race' society – by the middle of the century a third of the population were officially classified as *mulatto*. However, this trend and the belief that discrimination did not exist, made it much more difficult for blacks to organize and for programmes to be developed that would alleviate their low social status.

The remaining European settlement colony to practise discrimination was Israel. The state established in 1948 was not a normal state in the accepted sense of the term – Israel was defined as the 'sovereign state of the Jewish people' and therefore excluded the Arab population of the country by definition. Under the Law of Return (1950) and the Israeli Nationality Act (1952) any Jew anywhere in the world was entitled to Israeli citizenship. There was no such right for the Arabs, who had lived in Palestine for centuries and no 'right of return' for the 700,000 people expelled in 1948 or their descendants. The right to own land was also discriminatory. Under Zionist regulations Jewish-held land could not be sold to non-Jews. However, Arab land was confiscated if the owner was deemed to be absentee. This was defined as not living in the same place as in 1947 and therefore applied not just to those Arabs who either fled or were expelled from the new state. Other areas of the country were declared to be 'closed military areas', where land could not be owned or used by the original inhabitants and was taken over by Jewish organizations. Altogether between 80 and 90 per cent of Israeli territory was either held by Jews or designated as only for Jewish settlement. Arabs were also effectively excluded from other areas of the state. They could not serve in the armed forces and they made up only 1 per cent of the civil service and even then they were restricted to working in the Arab sections of ministries.

The result of this policy was to turn roughly one in six of the population of Israel into an underclass. The Arabs were transformed from peasants into landless agricultural labourers, sharecroppers, migratory workers and basic labourers in jobs such as construction. On average they were paid half the rate of an Israeli for the same job and were excluded from many of the benefits of Israeli society.

Because child allowances, subsidized mortgages and immediate unemployment benefit were paid under the Discharged Soldiers Act, they were not available to Arabs. A third of all Arab children in 1973 received no schooling. Of the available irrigation water, all but 2 per cent went to Jewish settlements and farmers. Jewish attitudes to the Arabs in Israel remained extremely hostile, reflecting decades of prejudice. In the early 1970s four out of five Israelis agreed with the statement that 'Arabs will not reach the level of progress of Jews' and a roughly similar proportion were extremely worried by any idea of intermarriage or even friendship between Arab and Jewish children.

The second half of the twentieth century witnessed a fundamental change in levels of discrimination, with the end of formal discrimination in the United States and South Africa. The process began at a very measured pace with the federal government in the United States in the 1940s. In 1941–3 President Roosevelt issued executive orders which required non-discrimination in all defence contracts, defence industries and within the federal government itself. In February 1948 his successor, Truman, sent the first-ever message to Congress on civil rights. A major part of his argument was 'the United States is not so strong . . . that we can ignore what the world thinks of our record'. In less coded terms he meant that because the United States saw itself as engaged in a battle with Communism for control of the world it could hardly counter Communist propaganda or gain support in Asia and Africa while it continued to discriminate so badly against a large group of its own citizens.

The key turning point was the unanimous Supreme Court ruling in May 1954 in Brown v. Board of Education, Topeka, Kansas. It overthrew more than half a century of contrary rulings and declared that segregation, even when theoretically equal facilities were provided, was bound to lead to inequality and therefore breach the Fourteenth Amendment. In the next two years it produced similar rulings on segregation in public facilities and state and city legislation which required segregation. The problem was how to implement these rulings and bring about fundamental changes in American society, particularly in the south. There was widespread and fundamental opposition to any change. In 1948 some southern Democrats left the party and ran their own candidates in protest over the inclusion of a civil rights plank in the party platform. In the mid-1950s a movement of white Citizen's Councils spread across the south arguing that integration was 'nothing more and nothing less [than] a strategic campaign of the world communist movement'. The Mississippi association announced it was 'the South's answer to the mongrelisers. We will not be integrated! We are proud of our white blood and white heritage of sixty centuries.' Southern members of Congress issued a manifesto to try to reverse the Supreme Court decision, oppose its implementation as contrary to the constitution and prevent force being used. A meeting of southern governors in 1956 promised 'not to comply voluntarily with the Supreme Court's decision'. The whites were prepared to use pressure and the threat of violence against moderates and actual violence against blacks to retain the existing position. In May 1955 Emmett Till, a fourteen-year-old black boy from Chicago who was staying in Mississippi, was accused of having 'wolf-whistled' at a white woman. He was taken from his grandfather's home at night by a gang of white vigilantes, pistol-whipped, stripped naked, tied with barbed wire to a cotton gin, shot in the head and dumped in the local river.

In 1955 the Supreme Court ruled that desegregation must be implemented 'with all deliberate speed'. The emphasis, however, seemed to be on the deliberate rather than the speed. The federal government under Eisenhower showed a marked lack of determination to speed up the very slow progress of desegregation. He refused to use federal troops in Alabama in early 1956, but did so a year later at Little Rock, Arkansas. He did so less because of a desire to end discrimination and more because the governor of the state, Orval Faubus, called out the National Guard to stop enforcement of a federal court order to integrate schools. This was defiance of the authority of the federal government and after three weeks of inactivity Eisenhower federalized the National Guard and ordered federal troops to enforce the court order. At the same time he appeared to sympathize with the action of local whites, saying that their resistance stemmed from seeing a future 'mongrelization of the race'. Rather than integrate, many states chose to legislate to end their legal duty to provide a state education system. Mississippi did so and Georgia tried to lease out its whole system. Others such as North Carolina, South Carolina and Virginia gave grants to parents so they could send their children to private white-only schools. Overall the delaying tactics worked. By 1964 less than 1 per cent of black pupils in the public schools of the eleven states of the old Confederacy was attending an integrated school.

The result of this inactivity and resistance was that the pressure for change came from a widespread movement among the blacks themselves. Long-established organizations such as the National Association for the Advancement of Coloured People (NAACP), founded in 1909, were left behind by new movements that grew out of the black churches in the south. People developed a new self-confidence, an unwillingness to suffer what they had suffered for decades and a belief after 1954 that, for the first time, the law was on their side. The first signs of this change came in 1955 in one of the most segregated and prejudiced cities in the country – Birmingham, Alabama. A year-long bus boycott led by the Reverend Martin Luther King, involving ad hoc tactics (based on Gandhi's non-violent tactics against the British in India) and community mobilization eventually succeeded, in the face of considerable violence from the white population, in securing integrated buses. Similar pressure and boycotts produced results in other cities. In January 1957 the Southern Christian Leadership Conference was founded in Atlanta to co-ordinate a major campaign against segregation and insist on implementation of the Supreme Court rulings. Other organizations sprang up. In February 1960 a sit-in at a segregated lunch-counter in Greensboro, North Carolina spread rapidly, with similar action at beaches, libraries, churches and theatres led by students of the Student Non-Violent Co-ordinating Committee. In May 1961 the 'Freedom Ride' organized by the Congress of Racial Equality saw thirteen people leave Washington to ride on inter-state buses through the south and challenge the segregation of facilities. It was a major radicalizing experience as the passengers were attacked and the buses burned by white vigilante groups.

The climax of the civil rights movement came in 1963. In Birmingham a long-prepared campaign to secure desegregation was initiated by King. The full panoply of sit-ins, boycotts and demonstrations, with high school students and undergraduates at the forefront, led to the arrest of hundreds of demonstrators including King and his main assistant Ralph Abernathy. White violence followed with the bombing of King's home. The local police chief, Bull Connor, then turned pressure hoses and dogs on to women and children in full view of national and international television cameras. Eventually, under pressure from the federal government and the threat of the use of the army, desegregation was achieved. The first attempt to desegregate the schools in Birmingham led to the bombing of a black church in which four children were killed. In Mississippi similar protests led to even greater white violence. The leader of the NAACP in the state, Medgar Evers, was murdered by whites who were never prosecuted and the police used electric cattle prods on demonstrators. There was a brief moment of unity on the March for Jobs and Freedom in Washington in August, when 250,000 demonstrators (about a quarter of them white) gathered at the Lincoln Memorial to hear King make his inspiring 'I have a dream' speech. The next summer a voter-registration drive in Mississippi (where less than 6 per cent of blacks were registered to vote) led to the murder of three civil rights workers, together with the killing of a number of local blacks, the bombing of thirty homes and thirty-five churches. The drive was a failure. In March 1965 a march in Selma, Alabama to present a petition calling for equal voting rights led to police violence, the clubbing of demonstrators and the use of tear gas. In response the federal government moved slowly to enforce civil rights. There was some moral support from President Kennedy, the National Guard was used to ensure that court orders were obeyed, but there was no effective legislation until 1964. The Civil Rights Act of that year forced desegregation in all institutions and activities supported by public and state sources and in all federally assisted programmes. The Voting Rights Act of 1965 outlawed all tests for the right to vote and finally allowed the federal government to maintain voter lists and force states to accept them. In the next seven years a million new black voters were registered in the seven states of the deep south.

By the mid-1960s the civil rights coalition was breaking down. American society had, with little real cost, ended formal segregation and the denial of the right to vote. The crucial remaining problem was how to deal with the consequences of generations of discrimination and exploitation and the resulting poverty, poor health and lack of education. This was no longer an issue just for the south, but involved the whole country. Now that the whites outside the south were forced to make major concessions by ending discrimination in housing, education and employment, increasingly they felt that black rights had gone far enough. At the same time blacks felt that the whole of society was discriminatory and prejudiced and that the possibility of progress was limited. The demands for 'black power', the emergence of more radical groups such as the Black Panthers and Black Muslims, together with riots in the northern cities, only made many whites more resistant to change. By the end of the twentieth century, more than thirty years after the formal ending of segregation, progress in removing informal discrimination and dealing with its consequences was still very slow. Blacks lived overwhelmingly in inner-city ghettos – three-quarters of all blacks lived in areas that were more than half black. Their unemployment rate was twice that of whites and their average income was little more than half that of whites. Inner-city child-mortality rates were more than double the national average and more than half of all black children left education before completing high school. About half of black youngsters were unemployed, blacks were seven times more likely to be killed by the police and they made up half the prison population, despite being only one in eight of the population. Surveys showed that half of all whites thought that equal rights had been pushed too far and two-thirds still thought white people had the right to keep blacks out of their neighbourhood.

In South Africa, the majority black population resisted discrimination from the beginning of the century (the predecessor of the African National Congress was founded in 1912) but with no success. By the 1940s, with the drift of even more blacks into the cities, the rise of black trade unions and the impact of the propaganda the Allies used in the war about fighting for freedom and democracy, there was a rise in African determination to resist the massive discrimination which characterized South African society. On Easter Sunday 1944 at the Bantu Men's Social Centre in Johannesburg the African Congress Youth League was founded to give a more radical impetus to the ANC. The leader, Anton Lembede, died in 1947 but the others – Nelson Mandela, Oliver Tambo, Walter Sisulu and Robert Sobukwe – formed the new generation who were to lead the ANC fight against apartheid for the next forty years. Their programme was not radical: 'We . . . realize that the different racial groups have come to stay', but they argued for the 'abandonment of white domination' and 'a change in the basic structure of South African society' to eliminate 'exploitation and human misery'. They were determined on an African-led movement and were hostile to the Communist Party, although the party was represented on the ANC executive.

In 1949, in response to the Nationalist Party election victory, the ANC adopted a programme of civil disobedience, boycotts and strikes. What happened over the next decades starkly illustrated the differences between South Africa and the United States. The South African authorities were even more determined than those in the south of the United States. They also wielded far more power, controlled the government and were prepared to defy international opinion. In 1952, over 8,000 people were imprisoned for breaking the apartheid laws. The leaders were subject to banning orders for promoting Communism. In 1955 the Freedom Charter (a moderate, idealistic programme) was approved by a 'Congress of the People' composed of the ANC, trade unions and some left-wing groups. The government's response was to start a series of treason trials involving 156 people, including the ANC leadership, and twenty-three whites, including Joe Slovo and Ruth First, who were both ex-members of the Communist Party. By 1961 all the cases had either been dropped or those involved had been acquitted. As the rest of Black Africa became independent the pressure on the South African government mounted and Sobukwe broke from the ANC to set up the Pan-African Congress as a more radical and aggressive body. The defining moment for the African movements and the white government came in early 1960. In March the PAC mounted an anti-pass-law campaign. During a demonstration at Sharpeville (a township built for workers at the Vereeniging steel plant) the police shot 69 people (most of them in the back) and wounded 186 others. A state of emergency was declared, 18,000 people were arrested and both the ANC and PAC were made illegal organizations.

The South African government was determined on a path of outright repression and the majority black population had little power to stop them. A general strike and a low-level sabotage campaign had little impact and the African leadership was imprisoned. In August 1962 Mandela was captured, charged with inciting people to strike and leaving the country without permission and sentenced to five years' hard labour on Robben Island. A year later, with other ANC leaders, he was put on trial charged with treason. In June 1964 they were sentenced to life imprisonment. For the next ten years African resistance was kept under control until the rise of the 'black consciousness' movement under Steve Biko. He was banned in 1973, but a government attempt three years later to impose Afrikaans as the major teaching language in the African townships led to rioting and a school boycott. By the end of 1976 over 600 people had been killed and another 1,000 wounded. In September 1977 Biko was murdered whilst in police custody: the minister of justice, James Kruger, remarked, 'It leaves me cold.' The ANC had some presence outside South Africa in the newly independent Angola and Mozambique, but it was badly divided and had little influence inside South Africa. Resistance to the new apartheid constitution of 1983 was led by a coloured priest, Allan Boesak and the United Democratic Front. The Front was able to engineer an effective boycott of the new government councils set up to run the townships, but there seemed to be no sign of any break in the determination of the white leaders to enforce their supremacy, even though a state of emergency had to be imposed after 1986 and in February 1988 seventeen anti-apartheid organizations, including the UDF, were banned.

Beneath the surface, however, growing social and economic changes were undermining both apartheid and the white government's ability to control the situation. Until the early 1970s white domination of the economy and control of African labour was maintained. Between 1948 and 1973 white wages rose over 400 per cent, black wages by 36 per cent. African agricultural wages were at 1866 levels. However, the problem was that the whites were a small minority of the population. A modern complex economy could not function without skilled labour and only Africans could fill this role. More Africans came into the cities, making the homelands policy a farce, and more were allowed into skilled and semi-skilled jobs, which meant higher wages and increased training and education. In the 1970s African wages in the mining industry quadrupled, while white wages hardly rose at all. Some areas of social apartheid were beginning to fray at the edges. Africans were allowed to live in some new urban areas and bring in their families, some townships were reprieved from destruction and Africans were allowed to join their own trade unions, which immediately became centres for the struggle against apartheid.

During the mid-1980s under both internal economic pressure and external pressure from the growing level of boycotts and sanctions, the government began to make concessions. A few symbolic gestures were made: the ban on inter-racial sex and inter-racial political parties was ended and citizens of the homelands were allowed South African citizenship even while living in 'white areas'. Eventually the pass laws and influx control legislation were scrapped and African urbanization accepted. However, no African leader of any standing would negotiate with the government on the basis of these minimal changes. Gradually during the late 1980s the white government was driven to recognize that apartheid could not be maintained and that negotiations with the African leaders were essential to avoid a bloody and chaotic disintegration of white rule.

In the last resort negotiation to maintain as much as possible of the white social and economic, if not political, privilege was the only way forward. The symbolic moment came with the release of Nelson Mandela, which was essential if Africans were to begin to negotiate with the whites. By 1995 an ANC-dominated government was in power. It faced the herculean task of dealing with the ingrained legacy of centuries of discrimination and gross inequality in circumstances where the white elite retained major economic power.

Racism in the twentieth century was not confined to Europeans and their descendants. Similar beliefs were found across the globe. The Chinese had very strong feelings of superiority over non-Chinese and during the Second World War protested to the British government when they sent Indian troops to China and to the American government when they sent black troops. Like the Chinese, the Japanese valued a white skin and saw themselves as white not 'yellow' and certainly whiter than the Spanish and Portuguese. On their first contacts with black people they described them as 'uncivilized and vicious in nature' and thought they looked 'like devils depicted in pictures' or monkeys. In particular they disliked curly hair. The Japanese also disliked Caucasians. A deep study of Japanese attitudes carried out in the 1960s reported widespread agreement with views such as the following: 'I feel that they are basically different beings from us. Certainly they are humans but I don't feel they are the same creatures as we are . . . they belong to a different world . . . they are somehow connected with something animal-like.' In India too a light skin colour was seen as desirable, especially in the case of brides, as the matrimonial columns of the national newspapers showed. Indians who settled in Africa as traders and merchants certainly saw themselves as different from, and more advanced than, the Africans. In South Africa at the beginning of the century Gandhi worked for Indian, not African, rights. In North Africa, which had long dominated West Africa, the descendants of the slaves brought north were left as a minority at the bottom of the social scale. Although there was no formal segregation, an informal system was rife. The most common word for 'black' in Arabic was *abd*, which meant slave and in Berber it was 'dumb' or 'unintelligible'. In Liberia and Sierra Leone there were very strong differences between the ruling elite of freed slaves from America and the majority local African population.

As in Brazil, a lighter skin colour remained the most desirable in the rest of Latin America and there was often a strong anti-black prejudice. In the 1964 Panamanian elections ex-President Arnulfo Arias came second on a platform of exterminating the Negroes, though in Panama this referred to people of Jamaican descent who had been imported to build the canal and who kept both their English language and their Protestantism as a sign of distinction. Acute awareness of skin type produced a multitude of different terms, which varied from country to country, to describe various combinations. Highland Peru had *indio, cholo, mestizo* and *blanco* and elsewhere there were even more. Mexico was obsessed by the minutiae of appearance and colour and had a special term for every possible crossing of Indian, European and African over three generations.

The introduction of indentured labour by the colonial authorities, in particular the British, left behind a legacy of racial conflict. This was particularly the case with Indians, who kept a separate culture and tended not to marry into the local white and black population. In Guyana all political parties were organized along racial lines – the PPP led by Cheddi Jagan was the Indian party, the PNC led by Forbes Burnham was the black party and the United Front represented the Portuguese-Creole groups. The situation was the same in neighbouring Surinam. In Fiji the descendants of Indian labourers came to outnumber the native Fijians, although the native Fijians retained control of the country through various forms of discrimination. In Malaysia there were strong racial tensions between the native Malays (about half the population) and the descendants of immigrant Chinese and Indians. In 1938, a decade before independence, the Indian government banned the further emigration of Indians to Malaya because of the discrimination against them. Much of the internal conflict in the late 1940s and early 1950s was along racial lines (there were race riots in Penang in the early 1950s) and political parties were similarly divided. Singapore, with its overwhelmingly Chinese population, left the Malaysian federation and became independent in 1965.

One of the most complex systems of social discrimination in the world was the caste system in India, in particular in its treatment of the 'scheduled' castes (the untouchables). This discrimination was based not on racial characteristics but on the ritual and religious prohibition of certain activities such as tanning, cobbling and oil pressing. These tasks were essential to society, but those who carried them out were doctrinally not part of Hindu society. They were regarded as both polluted and polluting to different degrees, depending on the caste to which they belonged. The number of people involved varied from area to area – it was generally highest in the north – but probably involved between a sixth and a fifth of the total population of India. The scheduled castes were subject to various types of discrimination: they were excluded from temples, cremation grounds, from the use of wells, roads and other public utilities. In the south of India they were not allowed to live in brick and tile houses and were forced to live at least half a mile from any village, in an area which no Brahmin (high-caste Hindu) would enter. In addition individual discrimination was enforced by social pressure – they were excluded from barbers' shops, restaurants and hotels. In 1932 there were even reports of a Purada Vannan caste, which was so defiling that mere sight of them would pollute a Hindu and so they were only allowed out of their houses at night. Although the British made some effort to reduce the discrimination against the scheduled castes, there is considerable evidence that many practices were expanding as late as the 1930s. In December 1930 Hindus in Ramnad set out new clothing and other restrictions: the untouchables were not to wear gold and silver, males could not wear coats, shirts, sandals or use umbrellas. The women could not wear flowers, they could only use earthenware vessels and they were not allowed to cut their hair. Six months later the restrictions were expanded further to prohibit literacy and the use of Indian music. In general, although some untouchables such as the leather workers might be economically secure, they were all poor and their children were condemned to the same sort of existence.

By the 1930s the question of the scheduled castes was a major political issue. Gandhi wanted to 'reform' Hinduism and incorporate the untouchables so that Congress could speak for all India. Many Hindus and many others in the minorities rejected such an approach, preferring to emphasize their separate identities. The leader of the untouchables, Dr B.R. Ambedkar was more inclined to an anti-Hindu stance (he started the movement for the conversion of untouchables to Buddhism) and wanted a separate electorate for them. Following independence, the Indian government embarked on a system of preferential treatment which remained unequalled in its scope and extent. The 1950 constitution declared all citizens equal, banned discrimination and the Untouchability (Offences) Act of 1955 made the practice of untouchability illegal. However, the government recognized that this policy would not be enough to counter centuries of extreme discrimination. The untouchables were grouped with the 'Scheduled tribes' and given reserved seats in the central and state legislatures, a quota of roughly one in eight of higher level civil service posts and one member of the group normally sat in the cabinet. In addition, the scheduled castes (about 80 million people in the 1970s) and the scheduled tribes (about 40 million) were grouped with 'other backward classes' of other very low-caste Hindus and some other minorities (about 60 million) and given preference on a communal basis. They were exempt from the payment of education fees, given hostel accommodation and scholarships (the number rose from 114 in 1944 to over 350,000 thirty years later), special land allotments, access to housing, health care and legal aid. In general, these programmes secured a high degree of support except from those just above the scheduled castes. In practice the reservation of places in education had little impact because of the low level of education – in the early 1960s the scheduled caste literacy rate was still only a third of the average for India. In practice, progress in removing discrimination, despite the government's open identification with the scheme, was slow. The scheduled castes continued to work in agriculture and the lowest occupations, although the routes to advancement were open, particularly through politics. Violence between castes and informal discrimination remained widespread.

Roughly similar groups of 'untouchables' undertaking certain polluting occupations (usually associated with animals) were found in Korea, Tibet and Sri Lanka. One of the most extensive were the *eta* of Japan (the word means 'full of filth'), who numbered about a million at the end of the nineteenth century. This group, later known as *burakumin*, were indistinguishable physically from the majority of Japanese, but were believed to be the descendants of a less human race and subjected to segregation and discrimination in housing, employment and education. In the 1920s they were still unable to use public bath houses and barbers' shops, rent houses outside their own ghettos or work in factories. Although conscripted into the armed forces, they were confined to the most menial jobs. At many village primary schools *buraku* pupils were not allowed to sit in the same rooms as the other children, they had to clean the classroom after school and use separate cups and pails. The new post-war constitution, like the Indian constitution, contained a clause providing equality before the law and making it illegal to discriminate on any grounds whatsoever. However, the

Japanese government, unlike the Indian, went no further and did not institute any form of compensatory discrimination. Efforts were directed instead towards assimilation, though these met with little success. The *buraku* community, nearly 2 million people, continued to live in separate areas, mainly around the major towns, and continued to suffer major discrimination.

In one part of the core democracies there was substantial discrimination on religious grounds. The very existence of Northern Ireland as a separate area within the United Kingdom with its own parliament was based on religion and the refusal of Ulster Protestants to be part of a united Ireland dominated by Catholics. Northern Ireland was a single-party state, and it was run for the fifty years after it came into existence in 1922 almost exclusively for the benefit of its majority population. As Lord Graigavon, the first prime minister, declared, 'We are a Protestant Parliament and a Protestant state.' A draconian Special Powers Act, backed up by a Protestant police militia known as the 'B specials', ensured that the Catholic community was kept subordinate.

Although the Catholics made up nearly a third of the population and an even higher proportion in the border areas, they were systematically excluded from power. In the early 1920s when, on British insistence, a short-lived proportional system of representation was in place, the Catholics controlled a number of local authorities. Within less than a decade following major government gerrymandering of the twenty-four local government areas with a Catholic majority, the overwhelming majority were controlled by the Protestants. This enabled them to determine housing policy, particularly the allocation of scarce council housing. This was done not on the basis of need but in order to keep political control of particular areas. Housing was therefore allocated on a sectarian basis and the Catholic community was confined increasingly to a series of ghettos. Education was similarly divided. In 1925 the government legislated to ensure that Protestant religious education was compulsory in state-funded schools and that teachers could be compelled to teach such lessons. By the 1930s the state schools were controlled by the Protestant community and the government stated its aim 'to make the schools safe for Protestant children'. The Catholic religious hierarchy made the situation worse by preferring their own denominational schools to any non-sectarian system. Discrimination in employment was intense. The higher grades of the civil service, especially the security sections of the Home Affairs

Ministry, were made up exclusively of Protestants, as were all public bodies. At a local level the Protestant-controlled councils generally refused to employ Catholics except as low-paid manual workers. The largest employer in Belfast, the Harland and Wolf shipyard, was entirely Protestant. Government policy on the location of industry favoured the Protestant areas in the east of the province, not just to benefit their own community, but also to encourage Catholic emigration through high unemployment and reduce the long-term threat from the Catholics' higher birth rate. Overall the policy worked. By the time the British resumed control of the province in 1972 the Catholic unemployment rate was two-and-a-half times greater than the Protestant. As in so many other areas of the world which suffered from discrimination in many forms, the British government found that the removal of formal discrimination and the implementation of equality programmes only marginally affected a deeply rooted social, economic and political situation which had developed over a long period of time.

21 GENOCIDE

DISCRIMINATION, SEGREGATION and persecution of minorities during the twentieth century were not new in human history. Nor was the mass destruction of people in war, although the twentieth century brought this to new heights of barbarism, with mass bombing and nuclear weapons. The deliberate killing of whole groups of people because of their ethnic or religious origin was new. Such actions were to reach a peak of unparalleled, industrialized barbarity with the killing of millions of Jews by the Germans in the Holocaust.

After the Second World War the definition of a new crime – genocide – was agreed in the United Nations Convention on Genocide, which was adopted in December 1948. Genocide was defined as acts intended 'to destroy, in whole or in part, a national, ethnical, racial or religious group'. Although full of holes and ambiguities, this remained the only internationally agreed definition. Under this definition genocide did not apply to political groups and social classes, mass bombing of civilians or the threat of a nuclear strike (although some international lawyers disagreed on the last point). The actions of many governments, especially acts of internal repression against their own citizens, were excluded. The Soviet regime could claim that its actions in incarcerating millions of people in the Gulag were only directed against those it accused of breaking the law, even though the end result was death on a greater scale than the number of Jews killed in the Holocaust. Others might argue that some of the actions of the Soviet government, particularly against some of the minority groups in the country such as the Chechens, the Volga Germans, Tartars and Meskhetians among others, were very close to genocide. Similarly Chinese actions in Tibet after 1950 were on the borderline between repression and genocide.

The twentieth century opened with the European powers

engaged in genocidal campaigns against some of the last surviving tribal peoples in the world. This was nothing new. The Europeans had been killing such people for the previous five centuries. The German conquest of South-west Africa was one of the most brutal, especially following the revolt of the Herreros in 1904. General Lothar von Trotha, the commander sent to put down the uprising, made his aims clear from the start: 'It was and remains my policy to apply force by unmitigated terrorism and even cruelty. I shall destroy the rebellious tribes by shedding rivers of blood.' However, this could not be accomplished simply by defeating the Herreros in battle, which would be relatively straightforward given the technological superiority of the German army. German aims could only be accomplished by killing the women and children too. When the two sides met at the Battle of Waterberg, von Trotha deliberately left very light forces to the south-east so that the defeated Herreros, including the women and children could escape. Their escape route, however, led them into the Omaheke desert. Before the battle a German army study remarked:

> If, however, the Herrero were to break through, such an outcome of the battle could only be even more desirable in the eyes of the German command because the enemy would then seal his own fate, being doomed to die of thirst in the arid sandveld.

After the escape of the Herreros the German army continued to push the Herreros into the desert and then sealed off the whole area for a year. They reported, 'The arid Omaheke was to complete what the German army had begun: the extermination of the Herrero nation.' In 1904, at the beginning of the revolt, there were over 80,000 Herreros. By the end of the decade fewer than 15,000 were left alive. Across the world other, smaller scale, genocides continued. In Paraguay the Ache Indians were almost eliminated. In neighbouring Brazil throughout the century the settlers pushing out into the Amazon forest killed tens of thousands of tribal Indians.

The first of the deliberate, ideologically motivated twentieth-century genocides occurred during the First World War in the Turkish empire. The antipathy between the Turks and Armenians was of long historical standing but came to a head in the 1890s. Probably over 100,000 Armenians were killed during a series of massacres in 1895–6. In the first decade of the century smaller scale killings took place at Adana in 1905 and across Cilicia three years

later. Each time about 20,000 Armenians were killed. The entry of
Turkey into the First World War in the autumn of 1914 and the start
of fighting with Russia radically transformed the situation. The
Turkish authorities decided that the Armenians, as Christians, were
likely to side with the Russians and were potential traitors as well as
ethnic and religious enemies. In February 1915 a decree was issued
disarming all Armenian soldiers in the Turkish army and all
Armenian civilians. This was the first stage in ensuring that the
Armenian population was unable to resist the Turks. The Armenians
in the army were used as labourers, kept in appalling conditions and
given little food. Moving from area to area in a carefully phased
operation, the Turkish authorities then arrested and deported the
Armenian elite. This was followed by a series of massacres in the
border areas near Russia. (As Armenian troops in the Russian armies
advanced briefly into Turkey they probably killed about 100,000
Turks and Kurds.)

At this stage the Turkish government ordered the deportation of
the rest of the Armenian community. As they were rounded up,
most of the men were killed. Women were normally offered
conversion to Islam, marriage and giving up their children to be
raised as Muslims. If they refused, as most did, they were deported
on foot to the Syrian desert and Mesopotamia. A few were forced
into overcrowded cattle trucks and taken by rail. None was given
sufficient food and water and many were attacked by their military
escorts and the local population. The few who survived were left in
the desert or some other wasteland without shelter and food. The
exact death toll will never be known. The most accurate estimate is
that of the 1·5 million Armenians who were deported, probably only
about one in ten survived. Four years later the Turkish republican
armies were at war with the new republic of Armenia which
emerged, for a brief period, out of the wreckage of the Russian and
Ottoman empires. During the Turkish occupation of parts of the
republic probably about 250,000 Armenians were killed. In total it
is likely that about 1·7 million Armenians were killed by the Turks
in the period 1915–20. The establishment of the new Turkish
republic also led to the expulsion of the Greek population from
Anatolia and the coastal cities – probably about 250,000 died in the
various massacres, especially during the destruction of Smyrna
(modern Izmir).

The emergence of newly independent nations and states across the
world led to similar massacres, sometimes on an even bigger scale.

The partition of India in 1947 resulted in a huge outburst of communal violence, a form of 'ethnic cleansing' in which probably about 500,000 people died. Similarly, during the violence that led up to the Nigerian civil war in 1966, the Ibos of the north were killed in an outburst of communal violence. However, the killings in India and Nigeria (and many similar ones across the globe) were not genocide because they lacked the essential element of deliberate state-directed policy. This was apparent in a number of other episodes in newly independent states. In Sudan a civil war between the Muslim north and the largely Christian south began soon after independence in 1956 and lasted on a large scale until 1972. Sudanese army operations in the south created over 1 million refugees (about a third of the population). About 500,000 people were deliberately killed by the army. The collapse of the Portuguese empire led to a declaration of independence by East Timor in November 1975 and invasion by Indonesia (with American support and little condemnation from the UN) a month later. What followed could be described as state repression if the Indonesian takeover was regarded as legal, genocide if it was not. The army campaign, the deliberate restriction of food supplies to create famine and the killing of civilians led to the deaths of about 200,000 people, about a quarter of the total population.

The creation in 1947 of a Pakistan divided into East and West, separated by hundreds of miles of Indian territory, was bound to produce a highly divided country. The new state was dominated from the start by the west. The east was almost entirely Bengali and less than 2 per cent of the population spoke Urdu, the language of the west and the official language of Pakistan. In 1970 the Awami League, standing on a platform of the maximum autonomy possible short of independence, gained nearly all the seats in the national assembly allocated to the east. In March 1971 the federal government intervened with troops to take control of East Pakistan. The army engaged in a massive campaign of terror against the local population and the 12 million Hindus in particular. Awami League activists and leaders were tortured and killed. Collective reprisals were instituted as resistance mounted and special camps were established where many of the local population were killed. What may have begun as state repression rapidly turned into genocide as ethnic violence mounted and the army turned on the local population. By the time the massacres were stopped, following the intervention of the Indian army in December 1971, about 10 million refugees had fled into India, over 1 million houses had been destroyed and about 3 million people had been killed.

The worst legacy of the colonial period, leading to one of the largest modern genocides, came in the former Belgian colonies of Burundi and Rwanda. The majority population (more than four out of five) were Hutu, who before European occupation had been ruled by the minority Tutsi, who made up just over a tenth of the population. There was also a very small population of Twa (pygmies). The Belgians took over the colonies from the Germans in 1919 and had very clear views about the different groups. An official government report in 1925 gave a description of the 'races' of the area. The Twa were 'a worn-out and quickly disappearing race . . . with a monkey-like flat face and huge nose . . . quite similar to the apes whom [they] chase through the forest'. The majority Hutu 'display very typical Bantu features . . . generally short and thick set with a big head, a wide nose and enormous lips. They are extroverts who like to laugh and lead a simple life'. However, the minority Tutsi 'had nothing of the negro, apart from his colour . . . his features are very fine . . . gifted with a vivacious intelligence, the Tutsi displays a refinement of feelings which is rare among primitive people. He is a natural-born leader, capable of extreme self-control and of calculated goodwill.' The Belgians were convinced that the Tutsi could not possibly be local and were probably an aristocratic group from outside. Indeed, such were their qualities that the Belgians thought they were Caucasian in origin and came from India or Tibet. These divisions were almost entirely a European invention. There were no clear divisions between the Hutu and Tutsi (people were easily able to move from one group to another) and any distinctions were merely those between the rulers (Tutsi) and the ruled (Hutu). Belgian policy was to emphasize the 'racial' differences and unashamedly to favour the Tutsi. By the late 1950s they provided 43 out of the 45 major chiefs and 549 out of the 559 sub-chiefs. The Hutu were removed from their traditional areas of control, especially over land. The Tutsi, as the local elite, were given preference in education by the Catholic Church. Gradually the Africans came to accept the 'racial' divisions imposed by the Belgians, partly because they reflected the local division of power.

Burundi became a kingdom on independence, but within four years an army coup installed the minority Tutsi as rulers. A series of Hutu uprisings was put down. In 1972 unco-ordinated ethnic violence merged with a government programme to eliminate leading

Hutus from all areas of public life. Those targeted were the small educated minority in the civil service and army, and wealthy Hutus. The exact number killed is unknown. The Tutsi remained in control until the late 1980s when 'democratization' of the country produced rule by the majority Hutu. In Rwanda the Hutu took power on independence. Within three years there were over 130,000 Tutsi refugees outside the country fleeing persecution. A quota policy was introduced to ensure that the Hutu retained control of all key posts. Tensions rose in 1972 following the killings in Burundi and ethnic violence led to another 300,000 Tutsi refugees leaving the country. A military regime took power after a coup in 1973. It was relatively mild and popular with the Hutu because of institutionalized discrimination against the Tutsi – they had just one officer in the army and two members of parliament. It was not until the late 1980s that the system began to disintegrate through the social strains imposed by a rapidly rising population, shortage of land, increasing corruption and growing competition within the elite for the remaining assets and privileges in a decaying state structure.

The major problem for the Rwandan regime was the existence of over 700,000 mainly Tutsi refugees outside the country, who were controlled by the Rwandese Patriotic Front and the Rwandese Patriotic Army. In October 1990 the RPF/RPA launched an attack into Rwanda and began a long civil war, although they were unable to secure control in more than the border areas. The result was a series of local massacres, encouraged by the government, against 'rebels' (i.e. any Tutsi) and the growth of private militias controlled by Hutu extremists. Even more refugees fled the country, including, for the first time, large numbers of Hutu. In August 1993 a worthless 'peace agreement' was concluded between the Hutu government and the Tutsi forces, which in theory was to lead to a provisional government and the integration of the RPA into the Hutu army. There was never any chance it would be implemented. In April 1994 President Habyarimana, who had been head of state for over twenty years, died when his plane crashed. It was almost certainly shot down by Hutu extremists convinced that he was going to hand Rwanda over to the Tutsis in the peace agreement.

The death of President Habyarimana was followed by the seizure of power by extremist Hutus. They instigated genocide. The new government, using the presidential guard and the Hutu private militias, organized a wave of killings in the capital, Kigali. Those eliminated were 'liberal' and 'opposition' Hutus and any Tutsi unwise enough still to be living there. Over 60,000 bodies were collected by local garbage trucks and two-thirds of them were dumped into Lake Victoria. Outside the capital the killings were started by local representatives of the government, but the situation soon disintegrated into anarchy, with waves of killings carried out by local peasants. The people killed were Tutsi, those who had lost their identity cards, those who were thought to be members of the opposition or those who looked too much like Tutsi. About 800,000 men, women and children died during the wave of killings. After little more than three months there were probably no more than 100,000 Tutsi left alive and they were all in exile. Having unleashed the killings, the Hutu extremists found that they could no longer control the country. The Tutsi RPA advanced on the capital Kigali and captured it in July 1994. This was followed by a massacre of Hutus and an exodus of Hutu refugees. Over 2 million people (almost a third of the total population) fled. Having driven many of the Hutu out of the country, the RPA/RPF instigated more low-level massacres designed to dissuade the Hutu from returning. The two government-induced genocides of 1994 in Rwanda by the Hutus and Tutsis were the major constituent in a death toll amounting to about 1 million people from the ethnic conflicts in Burundi and Rwanda in the thirty years after independence.

At the same time as the Rwandan genocide was taking place, another on a much smaller scale was under way in Yugoslavia. The ethnic and religious differences in this artificial state spilled over into conflict and genocide on two occasions after its foundation in 1919 – in the Second World War and during the disintegration of the country in the early 1990s. These conflicts reflected deep historical differences and the clash of rival nationalisms between the Catholic Croats, the Orthodox Serbs and the Muslims of Bosnia dating back to the medieval period and the later Turkish occupation. The establishment of an independent Serbia and the smaller Serbian Montenegro in the late nineteenth century resulted in the forcible conversion or expulsion of the Muslim population. It also led to demands for a Greater Serbia, incorporating areas that were not ethnically Serb. The creation of Yugoslavia after the First World War resulted in a state dominated by the Serbs, with the other groups, in particular the Croats, kept in a permanently inferior position. Defeat in the spring of 1941 and occupation by the Germans and Italians created an unprecedented situation. The major partisan movement – the Chetniks – was Serb dominated and controlled by the ex-minister of war in the pre-war Belgrade government, Draza Mihailovic. In December 1941 he drafted plans for a Greater Serbia to be created at the end of the war, which incorporated Bosnia-Herzegovina, Montenegro, Macedonia, Kosovo, Vojvodina, most of Croatia and parts of Bulgaria and Hungary. In such a state the Serbs would be in a minority in most areas except the core of Serbia and Montenegro. The aim would therefore be 'to cleanse the state territory of all national minorities and anti-national elements'. As he explained to his commanders, 'No one except Serbs will be left in Serbian lands.'

The dissolution of Yugoslavia was followed within four days by the establishment of a separate Croatian state under Axis occupation. In 1869 the so-called 'father of the Croatian nation', Ante Starcevic, spoke of the Serbs:

> They are the race of slaves, beasts worse than any. There are three levels of human perfection: that of the animal, that of comprehension and that of reason. Slavo-Serbs have not quite reached the first level and cannot rise above it.

The new Croatian state was dominated by the extremist and semi-fascist Ustasha led by Ante Pavelic. The policy of the new regime was to create an ethnically pure Catholic state from a situation in which the Croats only just constituted a majority. Policy towards the Serbs was run by the 'State Directorate of Renewal'. It began with persecution – banning Orthodox schools and use of the Cyrillic script – and was followed by forcible conversion. Mile Budak, the minister of education, spoke of killing a third of the Serbs, expelling a third and converting the rest. He concluded, 'Thus our new Croatia will get rid of all Serbs in our midst in order to become one hundred per cent Catholic within ten years.' However, there was a much darker side to Croat policy, which amounted to state-directed genocide. Ante Pavelic declared, 'A good Ustasha is one who can use his knife to cut a child from the womb of its mother.' Within a few weeks of taking power the Ustasha turned on the Serbs. Orthodox priests had their throats cut and were hung up on display in butchers' shops. Concentration camps run by Franciscan priests were established at Jasenovic and Alipasin Most. At others such as Zemun, where 50,000 of the 70,000 inmates died within a few weeks through lack of food and sanitation, the conditions shocked even the German SS. By the end of the summer of

1941 over 350,000 Serbs were dead. Two years later the total had risen to over 700,000. In addition, the Croats implemented German anti-Semitic and other racial polices, killing about 30,000 Jews and the same number of gypsies. This slaughter was supported by the Catholic Church, in particular the leader of the Croatian Church, Cardinal Stepinac. Ante Pavelic was received by the pope with the honours due to a head of state and described as 'a much maligned man'.

The establishment of the Communist government under Tito in 1945 led to forty years of stability in Yugoslavia. After his death, as the state collapsed in the late 1980s, there was a strong revival of Serbian nationalism, the Orthodox Church and ideas about creating the 'Greater Serbia' described by Mihailovic during the Second World War. This inevitably came into conflict with both the Croats (who set up their own state) and the Muslims, who were the largest group in Bosnia-Herzegovina. During the war with Croatia, the Serbs began the process of 'ethnic cleansing' around Vukovar and did so on an even greater scale during their invasion of Bosnia. Over a wide area the Muslims were forced out of their homes through military pressure and persecution. Concentration camps were set up, although the conditions were not as bad as in the Croatian camps fifty years earlier. When the Croats invaded Bosnia and during the Muslim offensives in 1994–5, similar tactics were employed to expel the Serb population. During the fighting of the early 1990s about 750,000 people fled as refugees and about 200,000 were killed. In the twentieth century national conflicts and genocides in Yugoslavia probably killed about 1 million people.

All the other twentieth-century genocides pale into insignificance compared with the German extermination of around 6 million Jews during the Second World War. This genocide was qualitatively different not just because of the scale on which the killings were carried out, but because of the construction of camps and facilities that had no purpose other than to kill people on a massive scale. Anti-Semitism was nothing new in European history. Its roots went back to persecutions of the medieval period directed by the Catholic Church and the centuries of deep-seated distrust and dislike between Christian and Jewish communities. During the nineteenth century, as part of the liberalism that characterized many western European societies, the civic disabilities that had been imposed on the Jews for centuries were gradually removed. By 1900 only a handful of European states still denied full civic rights to Jews. These were granted during the revolutions in Portugal (1910) and Russia (1917) and in Spain in the 1920s.

Because of the Holocaust there has been a tendency to look back into German history to find the roots of Nazism and anti-Semitism in particular. German history has been viewed as in some way different from that of the rest of Europe and leading almost inevitably to the Nazi catastrophe and the Holocaust. This was not the case. German Jews were formally emancipated in 1867–9 and although some anti-Semitic feeling remained, especially among conservative groups, this was not unusual in western Europe. Germany was unusual in that much anti-Semitic activity was concentrated in the Reichstag and a series of anti-Semitic parties, beginning with the Christian Social Worker's Party of 1879. In 1893 anti-Semitic parties won about 3 per cent of the total vote in the Reichstag elections and gained sixteen seats. The Conservative Party, which had a wider agenda, also contained a large number of anti-Semites and gained about 400,000 votes and seven members. This turned out to be their best electoral performance. Overall the anti-Semitic parties failed badly – only seven anti-Semitic pieces of legislation were even debated before 1914 and none stood the slightest chance of becoming law. In the last imperial elections held in 1912, they only put up fifteen candidates (less than a third of the number in 1893) and gained only 130,000 votes (0·6 per cent of the total).

In Germany the Jews were highly assimilated and were overwhelmingly urban, middle class and commercial. About a third of them married outside their faith. Although there was a degree of social prejudice and discrimination (typical of most European countries), assimilation seemed to be the main danger facing the Jewish community in Germany. In western Europe in 1900 the most anti-Semitic country was probably France. Politics and national opinion were still heavily divided by the unresolved Dreyfus affair in which a Jewish officer was framed as a spy by high-ranking colleagues, who were then supported by the army hierarchy. The most virulent anti-Semitism was found in eastern Europe, especially Poland, Romania and Russia, where four out of five European Jews lived. In Romania Jewish children were largely excluded from schools, adults were barred from business and the professions and there were regular pogroms and riots during election campaigns. About 5 million Jews lived in Russia (compared with 0·5 million in Germany), but they were not permitted to live within forty miles of the western frontier and only about 200,000 of the richest were

allowed to live in the major cities of St Petersburg, Moscow and
Kiev. Most Russian Jews lived in abject poverty and were denied
equal access to many parts of society, in particular the universities,
which operated a strict quota system. They were, however, over-
represented in the call-up to the army, where conscripts were forced
to serve for twenty-five years and Jews were not allowed to practise
their religion. From the 1880s there was a series of pogroms across
western Russia and Poland. One of the worst episodes occurred
during the turmoil of the 1905 revolution when nearly a thousand
Jews were killed. Overall, probably about 3,000 were killed between
1900 and the revolution of 1917. In these conditions it was hardly
surprising that between 1900 and the outbreak of the First World
War about 1·3 million Jews emigrated from Russia. During the civil
war 'white' forces carried out numerous pogroms, resulting in the
death of about 100,000 Jews.

Anti-Semitism became more widespread in Germany after
November 1918 following defeat, the end of the empire and the
establishment of the Weimar Republic. Only a few months earlier
Germany had seemed to be on the point of victory following the
separate peace with Russia at the Treaty of Brest-Litovsk, which
secured the widespread German war aims in the east, and the initial
success of the spring offensives in the west. Many asked themselves
who had been responsible for such a catastrophic change in fortunes
and why the war ended, following the 'stab-in-the-back' in Berlin,
when the army was still fighting outside the borders of Germany.
They thought that the revolution in Russia was a Jewish conspiracy
because of the high proportion of Jews in the Bolshevik Party, and
the Jews became one of the scapegoats for German defeat. The
number of anti-Semitic parties, of which the Nazi Party, then largely
confined to Bavaria, was only one, increased. In this fervid
atmosphere a new document emerged – the *Protocols of the Elders of
Zion*. They purported to be the lecture notes of a member of a secret
Jewish government ('The Elders of Zion') setting out their plot to
achieve world domination. The plot had supposedly been in
existence for a long time, but had still not reached fruition. The Jews
supposedly supported liberalism, the overthrow of monarchy and
the aristocracy, backed economic monopolies, caused wars and
argued for the overthrow of morality. Out of this chaos would come
Jewish world domination. The *Protocols* were first published in
Russia in 1903 and were promoted by the right-wing supporters of
the pogroms and during the civil war by the whites. White officers

took them to the west, where they were rapidly taken up – 120,000 copies were sold in Germany in 1920 alone. They subsequently formed part of Nazi racial theories. The Nazis, in particular Hitler, saw Bolshevism as just another example of the Jewish plot in action. The *Protocols* were actually a forgery, created in 1897–8 in Paris at the height of the Dreyfus affair and based on an anti-Napoleon III book published in the 1860s. They were almost certainly written by a right-wing Russian close to the Okhrana and were part of a general attack on all aspects of 'modernism', which was seen as a threat to tsarist autocracy and traditional society and which could be blamed on the Jews.

In Germany until the late 1920s the Nazis made little progress and although their anti-Semitic propaganda was strong it did not make much impact. After Hitler became chancellor at the end of January 1933, the Nazis had little idea what anti-Jewish policy to adopt apart from general discrimination and the removal of some rights. During the first months of their seizure of power, the defeat of opposition parties was their main objective. In early March 1933 the SA launched its own anti-Jewish campaign, including a boycott of Jewish enterprises, but it had little central direction and was stopped by Hitler, who was worried about its impact. Eventually on 26 March Hitler agreed to a one-day boycott on 1 April to be enforced by the SA, but it was only patchily successful. Even so the pressure on the Jewish community was immense. It was increased by the first anti-Semitic legislation in April 1933. This was aimed at Jewish professionals, but was carefully drafted so as not to be specifically anti-Semitic because the Nazis were unable to define a Jew. The legislation was therefore written in racial terms as applying to non-Aryans. The Law for Restoration of the Professional Civil Service was ostensibly about procedures for dismissal. It only applied at senior levels (where there were few Jews) and, on President Hindenburg's insistence, veterans were exempt. Other laws applied to lawyers and doctors and also restricted Jewish children's access to schools. These had a much greater effect and about a third of Jewish doctors and lawyers were barred from practising. Five months later Jews were banned from agriculture and owning land, although few of what was a highly urbanized group were affected. In many ways this legislation was less discriminatory than the contemporary racial legislation in the United States and South Africa and the levels of violence in Germany were probably no greater. However, despite the limited nature of the initial legislation, an important threshold had been crossed. For the first time a modern, advanced, industrial western European state specifically discriminated against a group of its own citizens. It also allowed and encouraged others to embark on a programme of boycotts and violence.

After the initial burst of legislation, intimidation and boycotts (especially in the cultural sphere) the situation stabilized. In June 1933 Hitler agreed to use government money to rescue a major Jewish-owned department store, Hermann Tietz, from bankruptcy in order to save the jobs of 14,000 workers. The defeat of the SA in the Night of the Long Knives in June 1934 also seemed to be a stabilizing measure. By early 1935 there was even a net inflow of Jews back into Germany. The next discriminatory step was taken under pressure from Hitler at the Nuremberg party rally in September 1935. He demanded a Law for the Protection of German Blood and Honour. Marriages between Germans and Jews were prohibited, as were extra-marital relations. It was also made unlawful for a Jew to employ a German housemaid aged under forty-five. The legislation required the civil servants involved to define a Jew – something the Nazis had not previously done. They found that a racial definition, as favoured by Nazi thinking, was impossible and they therefore relied on religion as the key factor. Anyone with three or four Jewish grandparents was 'Jewish' regardless of their religion. A person with two Jewish grandparents was Jewish if they practised their religion or were married to a Jew. A half-Jew who did not practise Judaism and was not married to a Jew was a *mischling*. A quarter-Jew was only regarded as Jewish if he or she practised Judaism. In practice these definitions left about a third of those who the Nazis regarded as Jewish as non-Jews and produced major problems, especially with the *mischling* category. The intention of the legislation was clear – over time the *mischling* would disappear leaving only 'racially pure' Aryans and Jews. Another consequence of the legislation was that 'Aryans' had to be able to prove their racial ancestry for ordinary purposes in their day-to-day lives. (For special units such as the SS it was necessary to prove pure Aryan ancestry back to 1750.) This legislation had strong support. The Catholic Archbishop of Freiburg wrote of the Nuremberg laws, 'The right to safeguard the purity of the race, and to devise measures necessary to that end, can be denied to no one.'

Although there was no further legislation after 1935, apart from subsidiary decrees, action against the Jews was now concentrated in other areas. One solution to what the Nazis defined as the 'Jewish question' was emigration. This was supported by various groups in the Nazi regime in the 1930s (including the SS) and a number of meetings were held with Zionist groups and vague schemes involving Syria, Ecuador and Madagascar were discussed. Jewish emigrants who did leave Germany were allowed to take no property with them and only a minimal amount of foreign currency. They then had to pay an emigration tax, although the treatment of those going to Palestine was more generous. Even so, between 1933 and 1938 150,000 Jews left Germany. Those who stayed behind were subjected not just to increasing discrimination but to a growing process of 'Aryanization' – the takeover of Jewish businesses for nominal amounts. Until November 1938 such takeovers were voluntary and despite local campaigns the government, which gave priority to rearmament and exports, tried to restrain local activists and even gave a few contracts to Jewish firms. In April 1938 there were still 40,000 Jewish firms operating, although the pressure from large firms such as Krupp, I.G. Farben and families such as the Thyssens for cheap takeovers was mounting.

From early 1938 onwards there was a much more active anti-Jewish policy and far less restraint was placed on the party radicals. In January a Jewish firm was defined for the first time and Jewish firms were excluded from government contracts, except for rearmament and exports. Jews were also required to register their wealth. Within a year nine out of ten Jewish firms had ceased to exist and their assets had been taken over for minimal sums by 'Aryans'. At the end of October 1938 the anti-Semitic Polish government (where discriminatory policies very similar to those in Germany were in force) attempted to revoke the passports of Polish Jews living abroad and dump their families over the border into Germany. The Nazi government refused to take them and on 7 November a Polish Jew shot a member of the German embassy in Paris. The result was a 'spontaneous', though in practice long-prepared, attack on Jews throughout Germany in the *Kristallnacht* of 9–10 November. There was huge destruction of Jewish property, and synagogues in particular. The Jewish community was made to pay a huge fine, their insurance payments were appropriated by the government and any remaining Jewish organizations and newspapers were closed down. This outburst of violence was not repeated and Nazi policy against the Jews appeared to have reached an impasse. Emigration seemed an unlikely option and the Nazi leadership was undecided about what should be done next.

The situation was radically altered by the German attack on Poland on 1 September 1939 and the rapid occupation of the western and central parts of the country. The Nazis now found they had to decide policy not just for the relatively small and well-integrated Jewish communities of Germany and Austria, where some minimal attention had to be paid to the attitudes of the non-Jewish population, but for the nearly 2 million Polish Jews now under their control. Here there was no attempt to go through the legal niceties of defining a Jew – anybody thought to be a Jew, or, as was often the case, denounced as such by the local Polish population, was treated as a Jew. After the initial violence associated with the military conquest the SS came up with a plan to concentrate the Jewish population in cities and near railways, as a first stage in what was still intended to be a policy of forced emigration. On grounds of racial purity, all those Jews living in the western part of Poland, which was to be incorporated into Germany, would be moved to central Poland – the General Government – adjacent to the Soviet zone of occupation. This began in December 1939 and the plan was to move over 600,000 people at a rate of 10,000 a day. Property had to be left behind by those forced to move. At the same time all Jews living in Poland were subject to forced labour. By the end of the year the Jewish councils, which the Germans had forced the Jewish communities to set up, agreed to organize the system and provide the labour the Germans demanded. From mid-1940 labour camps were created, where the conditions were brutal in the extreme, with little food, heavy labour and random killings by the German guards. Outside the camps, under a savage occupation regime, the Jews were placed below even the Polish population, subjected to killings on the streets and provided with even less food than the Poles.

The forced movement of hundreds of thousands of Jews into the major cities of central Poland created new problems as far as the Germans were concerned. Without a coherent policy, local German rulers revived the old medieval ghetto and began concentrating the Jews into the poorest parts of the city. The first ghetto was set up in Lodz in April 1940, Warsaw followed in October and Lublin in April 1941. The process was not complete across Poland until well into 1941. In the ghettos the Jews were cut off from any access to food supplies other than those the Germans chose to provide and, as before, they always came at the bottom of the priority list. In every ghetto about six months after it was set up there was a similar crisis – thousands of Jews were dying of starvation. This did not greatly concern the German authorities but, with no central decision having been taken on what to do with the Jews, it was decided that the inhabitants of the ghettos would have to work in order to earn minimal rations to survive on. The exact position varied from ghetto to ghetto and depended partly on how the local Jewish authorities reacted. They were in an impossible position, since they had no realistic means of resistance. The best policy seemed to be to try to meet some demands in order to postpone any drastic decisions by the Germans and in the hope of saving as many people as possible. In some ghettos private enterprise continued, with a few Jews exploiting the many; in others the Jewish council organized community schemes and conscripted labour. Everywhere conditions in the ghettos continued to deteriorate. Tens of thousands of people were crammed into grossly overcrowded conditions, with many families forced to share a single house. Food was scarce, sanitation systems collapsed and there were outbreaks of disease. By March 1942 about 5,000 people a month were dying in the Warsaw ghetto. In Lodz one in five of those incarcerated in the ghetto died in the two years after it was established in April 1940. In total, it is likely that about 600,000 Polish Jews died in the ghettos and labour camps, about one in five of those alive in 1939.

A major development in German policy came with the decision to attack the Soviet Union. During the planning stage of what the Nazis saw as an ideological and racial war, the army commanders enthusiastically endorsed Nazi aims. In the first weeks of the campaign General von Reichenau told his troops that it was an attack on 'the Jewish-Bolshevik system' and its aim was 'the complete destruction of the sources of power and the eradication of the Asiatic influence on the European cultural sphere'. The German soldier was 'the carrier of an inexorable racial concept' and 'the avenger of all bestialities inflicted upon the Germans'; he therefore had to understand 'the necessity of harsh, but just measures against Jewish sub-humanity'. A year later the High Command issued an order to all officers on the eastern front that they 'must have an unambiguous, completely uncompromising position regarding the Jewish question. There is no difference between the so-called decent Jews and others.' In orders issued before the start of the campaign in June 1941 the army was instructed to co-operate with and assist the Einsatzgruppen. These were four small units (about 3,000 strong in June rapidly rising to some 20,000) attached to each Army Group. Without the assistance of the army, they would not have been able to carry out their task of killing the Communist leadership and as many Jews as possible in western Russia as soon as areas were occupied.

The first Einsatzgruppen operations took place near the front line, but in the autumn a second sweep of areas under German control took place, this time using more systematic methods and larger forces, including the SS and police units. Nearly everywhere there was a standardized killing operation. The Jews in a town were rounded up, taken to an open grave in the countryside (an anti-tank ditch, a shell crater or a trench dug by the Jews themselves), forced to hand over their valuables and clothing and then shot in batches. Many were still alive when the graves were covered over. Some of the survivors crawled out later, although most of them were caught and shot. These mass killings were semi-public with army units and some of the local population, who often co-operated enthusiastic-ally with the Germans, watching the slaughter. What happened in the Ukrainian town of Uman in mid-September 1941 was typical of these operations. A German army officer, Lieutenant Erwin Bingel, later wrote down what he saw. An order was posted in Uman and the local area that Jews 'of all ages' were to assemble so that 'an exact census of the Jewish population' could be carried out.

The result of this proclamation was, of course, that all persons concerned appeared as ordered . . . One row of Jews was ordered to move forward and was then allocated to the different tables, where they had to undress completely and hand over everything they wore and carried . . . Then, having taken off all their clothes, they were made to stand in line in front of the ditches, irrespective of their sex. The commandos then marched in behind the line . . . with automatic pistols . . . these men mowed down the line with such zealous intent that one could have supposed this activity to have been their life work. Even women carrying children a fortnight to three weeks old, sucking at their breasts, were not spared this horrible ordeal.

Nor were mothers spared the terrible sight of their children being gripped by their little legs and put to death with one stroke of the pistol-butt or club, thereafter to be thrown on the heap of human bodies in the ditch, some of which were not quite dead.

The people in the first row thus having been killed in the most inhuman manner, those in the second row were now ordered to step forward. The men in this row were ordered to step out and were handed shovels with which to heap chloride of lime upon the still partly moving bodies in the ditch. Thereafter they returned to the tables and undressed.

After that they had to set out on the same last walk as their murdered brethren, with one exception – this time the men of the alternative firing squad surpassed each other in cruelty, lest they lag behind their predecessors. The air resounded with the cries of the children and the tortured.

By the autumn of 1941 the four main Einsatzgruppen reported that they had killed about 300,000 Jews and the police forces, who were operating further behind the front line than these units, had probably killed at least another 100,000. The second, and more comprehensive, sweep during the late autumn of 1941 was on a much larger scale and probably killed about 900,000 Jews. In total, allowing for other killings by police units and those which were not reported, it is likely that this wave of slaughter killed about 1,400,000 people. In June 1942 the Germans set up a special unit to go over the entire area of the occupied Soviet Union and erase all traces of the killings. This unit returned to the sites of the massacres, dug up the graves and burnt the bodies in massive funeral pyres.

Extensive as these killings were, there were still millions of Jews alive in eastern Europe, Germany and the occupied countries of western Europe. German policy on what the Nazi leadership saw as the 'Jewish question' was still undecided in the summer and autumn of 1941, although there were a number of developments which suggested that an even more barbaric policy was about to be implemented. At the end of January 1939 Hitler told the Reichstag:

> If international-finance Jewry inside and outside of Europe should succeed once more in plunging nations into another world war, the consequence will not be the Bolshevization of the earth and thereby the victory of Jewry, but the annihilation of the Jewish race in Europe.

The speech illustrates that to Hitler, Jews and Bolsheviks were identical but it does not reveal exactly what the Nazi leadership planned. Until well into 1941 no firm plans were made. Göring's instructions to Heydrich at the end of July 1941, to make all the necessary organizational and financial preparations 'for bringing about a complete solution of the Jewish question in the German sphere of influence in Europe', probably refer to the deportation of the Jews into the vast areas to be conquered from the Soviet Union. In the same month Hitler was still talking about sending all the Jews to Siberia or Madagascar.

However, convinced because of their racial and anti-Semitic views that a 'Jewish question' existed, the Nazis decided that a 'solution' had to be found. German policy changed in the autumn of 1941 when it became clear that the war would be prolonged and that mass deportation from western and central Europe to the east would not be possible while the war with the Soviet Union continued. Already some killing centres were operating where Jews were being killed on a large scale. At the end of November 1941 invitations were issued for a conference on the 'remaining work' on the 'final solution' of the 'Jewish question'. After some postponements it took place at Wannsee in Berlin on 20 January 1942. The conference was chaired by Heydrich and included representatives of all the government departments which would be involved in the programme, including the occupation authorities in Poland and the Interior and Foreign Ministries. The record of the meeting was careful not to set out clearly and unambiguously that it was intended to exterminate millions of Jews. The conclusions were that there would be mass transportation to the east, and forced labour for those capable of it. Most would die, but the survivors would have to be subject to 'appropriate treatment' as the most dangerous (i.e. strongest) Jews. No document has been found giving Hitler's authorization for this programme. However, such a policy could not have been adopted without his approval and a formal order was neither required nor in conformity with his usual method of working. Clearly Hitler was aware of what was going on and as one of the most fanatical anti-Semites in the Nazi government he ensured that the policy was carried through. In a speech at the end of September 1942, he referred to his speech of 1939 and predicted that he would be right in his prophecy about the Jews. At the end of March 1942, as the early stages of the 'final solution' were under way in Poland, Goebbels, who had just heard about what was decided at Wannsee, wrote in his diary, 'Here, once again, the Führer is the undismayed champion of a radical solution.' Within the German government, as defeat loomed, the extermination of the Jews became the real war – it was to be furthered as quickly as possible and it was seen as a war which could be won even if Germany was defeated militarily.

The construction of killing centres to murder as many Jews as possible as quickly as possible was related to, and to some extent grew out of, an earlier German programme for the killing of the mentally and genetically unfit. Such a programme was a barbaric extension of the common European and American concern about eugenics and the 'fitness of the race' that had been apparent since the beginning of the century. In other countries, in particular the United States, people were forcibly sterilized to stop race deterioration. The programme was not adopted in Germany until July 1933 with the Law for the Prevention of Hereditarily Diseased Progeny. In February 1936 all mental institutions and hospitals were ordered to establish detailed hereditary records for each inmate and a year later all German coloured children were forcibly sterilized. Altogether between 1934 and the end of the war about 400,000 people were sterilized.

When the German army moved through Poland in September 1939, SS units killed about 6,500 inmates of Polish mental asylums so as to clear space for barracks. On the outbreak of war Hitler issued instructions allowing the killing of incurable patients in Germany. This programme was only possible because of wide-spread public agreement with its aims and the active co-operation of doctors, who compiled false death certificates, scientific experts and even the clergy, who ran many of the asylums. A major survey of the patients in German mental hospitals was carried out and doctors identified about 75,000 people, a quarter of the total, as suitable for death. A special organization known as T-4 was set up to carry out the programme, which began in January 1940 using carbon monoxide gas chambers to kill the patients. Most of the 75,000 had been killed by September 1941. The killings continued after this date, but they were done on a more covert basis by asylum staff, using starvation diets and the lethal injection of sedatives. From 1943 foreign workers in Germany were also killed if they were deemed to be suffering from 'psychological problems'. The programme was still continuing as the war ended – of the 3,948 patients admitted to the Obrawalde asylum in 1944, 3,814 were dead by the spring of 1945, nearly all of them killed by lethal injection. In total probably about 100,000 patients in German mental hospitals were killed.

The programme changed in the autumn of 1941 because the staff of T-4 moved on to work on the initial stages of the 'final solution'. Many of the techniques they had developed to kill mental patients – the use of gas chambers, crematoria and the robbing of the dead for gold teeth and other useful materials – were developed on an industrial scale for use against the Jews. T-4 staff gave advice on the operation of the first killing centre at Chelmno. Here, because of the numbers involved, the Jews were killed using carbon monoxide from diesel engines rather than by the pure gas provided by the chemical company I.G. Farben which had been used to kill German mental patients. The last part of the killing process was developed in the autumn of 1941. On 3 September 1941 about 900 Soviet prisoners of war were killed at Auschwitz, using Zyklon B gas (hydrogen cyanide) also provided by I.G. Farben. During 1941 killings were carried out using mobile gas vans, but by December 1941 the first killing centre (Chelmno) was in operation, to be joined in the first months of 1942 by four others – Auschwitz, Belsen, Majdanek, Sobibor – and by the last, Treblinka, in July 1942.

These characteristics of the Holocaust differentiate it from the other twentieth-century genocides. The slaughter of the Armenians by the Turks and the ethnic killings in Rwanda were essentially 'primitive', they could have taken place in any century. The Holocaust was a specifically modern, twentieth-century phenomenon. Its origins were deeply embedded in the European history of anti-Semitism, but were magnified by nineteenth-century concepts of racism and eugenics. It depended upon industrial 'progress', the development of technology that made possible the gas chambers and mass crematoria. It also relied on another specifically twentieth-century phenomenon – the growth of bureaucracy. The Holocaust required 'rational', ordered organizations that could identify, process and transport people to the killing centres without themselves being directly involved in the killing process.

The first task the Germans carried out was to select and then transport the victims to the killing centres. The Germans could act on their own in Germany and Austria (though with some circumspection here) and far more ruthlessly in the occupied territories of Poland and the western Soviet Union. Elsewhere the Germans needed the co-operation of either their allies or the authorities in the occupied countries of western Europe. One ally, Finland, refused to co-operate and Italy did not support German policy until it was occupied in September 1943. Similarly, the Jews of Hungary were protected until German troops took over in March 1944. The small Jewish populations in Norway and Denmark survived relatively unscathed. Although 770 Jews were deported from Norway to their deaths, over 900 found sanctuary in neutral Sweden. When the Germans tried to round up the Danish Jews following their total takeover of the country in September 1943, they were foiled by an unprecedented act of mass resistance. Over 7,300 Jews were secretly moved across the country to a fleet of trawlers, which took them to Sweden. Jewish hospital patients were 'discharged' and reregistered under different names without moving from their beds. Only 2 per cent of the Jewish population, mainly the old, were caught by the Germans. They were sent to the Theresienstadt concentration camp, but the king of Denmark insisted that they be treated well and under considerable pressure the German authorities allowed Danish and Red Cross representatives to visit the camp and provide supplies. The overwhelming majority of these Danish Jews survived the war.

On the other hand Romania enthusiastically supported the German policy. Indeed the killing of over 60,000 Jews when Romanian troops occupied Odessa in October 1941 was the biggest single massacre on the eastern front. The Vichy government, which controlled a considerable part of the country until November 1942, also collaborated willingly. Without any prompting by the German authorities, it introduced its own anti-Jewish policies. In August 1940 the law against slandering or libelling any racial or religious group was repealed. Two months later French Jews (defined as those who had two Jewish grandparents or who practised Judaism) were excluded from all elected and public functions and were not allowed to serve in the army, the media or as magistrates. A quota was set for admission to universities and the professions. Businesses were taken over by non-Jews. In the spring of 1941, 40,000 foreign Jews were interned in special camps in the south of France. In December 1941 a special tax was imposed on the Jewish community. In May 1942 Jews were required to wear the yellow star, were excluded from public places and were only allowed to shop in the afternoons when most food had already been sold. The French authorities co-operated fully with the Germans over arrangements for the deportation to the killing centres of the foreign Jews whom they held. The biggest deportations from western Europe came from the Netherlands (about 110,000) and France (about 90,000). In total about 250,000 Jews were deported to the killing centres from western Europe (about four out of ten of those alive in 1939) and only a handful of them survived. However, this was only a small part of those killed by the Germans; overwhelmingly those who died came from central and eastern Europe. In the end only military occupation and defeat stopped the deportations. The last regular train from the French internment centre at Drancy left on 31 July 1944, a month before Allied forces entered Paris. The last transport from Italy to Auschwitz departed on 24 October 1944 just six

months before the end of the war. The last five Jews were sent from
Berlin to Auschwitz in January 1945.

Jews were not the only people to be sent to the killing centres. The
forgotten victims of the Holocaust were the gypsies (or Sinti and
Roma) and homosexuals. Gypsies, following a long European
history of suspicion and antagonism, were first seen as a problem in
Germany in the late nineteenth century. Like the Jews and the
mentally and physically infirm, they were excluded by the Nazis
from their definition of the German 'Volk'. Under the Nuremberg
laws of 1935 they were banned from marrying Germans. The 'gypsy
problem' was seen in racial not social terms and in 1936 the Reich
Central Office for the Combating of the Gypsy Nuisance was
established. The definition of a gypsy was drawn up by scientists on
a racial basis and gypsies were forced into separate camps. As early
as March 1936 the German bureaucracy was describing the anti-
gypsy programme as a 'total solution of the gypsy problem'. On 21
September 1939 a government conference on the 'gypsy question'
agreed on the removal of 30,000 gypsies to Poland and the
confinement of all the rest in special camps. They were deported in
separate trucks attached to the trains of the Jewish deportees. In the
summer of 1941 the Einsatzgruppen army and police units began
shooting Roma and Sinti in Poland, the Soviet Union and the
Balkans. In the next couple of years others were rounded up and
sent to the killing centres.

Homosexuals were subject to very strong legislation in Nazi
Germany, especially after the establishment of the Reich Central
Office for the Combating of Homosexuality and Abortion. The two
were linked because they both stopped the increase and improvement in the 'stock' of the 'German race'. Offenders convicted of
homosexual offences were sent to concentration camps after they
had served a prison sentence. There were about 10–15,000 in the
camps, forced to wear a pink star rather than the Jewish yellow star.

The victims of German policy were rounded up from the ghettos
and towns of eastern Europe. Each time there would be a 'selection'
of those Jews to go, and often the Jewish Councils were forced to
take part in the exercise. People were herded together, marched off
to the railway station and told to leave their belongings behind as
they would be forwarded later. (They were ransacked as soon as the
train left.) Men, women and children were then forced on to the
trains and transported to the killing centres in terrible conditions.
They spent days, often weeks, in grossly overcrowded cattle trucks

(usually there was no more than standing room) with little or no food and water and no sanitation. Any attempting to escape were shot. Tens, possibly hundreds, of thousands died before they even reached the camps.

On 27 August 1942 the several thousand Jews of the Galician town of Czortkow were rounded up and assembled in the town square. One of them, Zonka Pollack, recalled seeing 'children being shot to death in their mothers' hands and thrown from the balconies'. The Jews were then lined up and marched into the prison yard for the night. In her account Zonka Pollack described the scene with 'many wounded people with bloody injuries from having been beaten, children without parents, separated families'. The next morning they were left without food and water:

> we quench our thirst with rain water in the nearby barrels. Hours are passing with the heat becoming unbearable. We are like animals destined for slaughter and kept in a cage; but for those animals they spare neither water nor food. Everybody is hungry and forgets even the feeling of shame, making his ordure in public.

Eventually in the early afternoon they were marched off to the railway station:

> we are split up in groups of 120 and more, and packaged off into freight cars. The doors of the cars are shut. It is dark and tense, impossible to stretch out your arms, absolutely no air to breathe. Everybody strangles and chokes and you feel as if a rope were tied around your neck and such a terrible heat, as if a fire had been set under the car.
>
> About ten people from our group are placed near the door; whoever has hairpins, nails, fasteners, starts to bore between the boards to get a little bit of air. People behind us are in a much worse plight. They take off their clothes and look as if obsessed by bestiality and madness. They are choking and driven to the utmost despair ... after a long waiting, the train is in motion, a sigh of relief emanates from those still alive. They hope that now more air will find its way into the carriage, or it will start raining and a few drops will penetrate through the clefts. But none of these miracles happen.
>
> I notice that in our carriage there is more and more free space. People die and we are seated on their dead bodies. The remaining are raving and wild, mad from suffering, quarrel between themselves about water; mothers hand their children urine to still their thirst.

During the night the train stopped and Zonka Pollack managed to escape undetected. Those who were still alive when they arrived at Belzec were killed within hours.

What happened when the trains arrived at the killing centres varied only slightly. The Jews were forced out of the trains surrounded by guards. At Auschwitz and Majdanek there were a series of 'selections', from which a number of Jews were chosen to work in the factories attached to the camps. They were given numbers, which were tattooed on their arms. Once they were no longer required or became too weak to work they were killed. Some were taken for so-called medical experiments, involving simulation of high-altitude conditions without oxygen, revival of the half-frozen, anti-typhus treatments, sterilization by X-rays and drugs, experiments on twins and studies of the 'racial' characteristics of skulls. The number of workers held at Auschwitz varied considerably, there were 140,000 in December 1943 but less than half this number four months later. Generally only those sent to Auschwitz late in the war survived this temporary avoidance of death. At the other killing centres only a few hundred Jews were required to carry out the most revolting tasks. These Sonderkommando were killed on a regular basis and replaced by men from the next trainload to arrive. Since they were already condemned to death, they were regarded as totally disposable, subject to torture, beatings, attacks by dogs and were killed at the slightest whim of the guards. Only a handful of the millions who were transported to these camps survived.

The Germans were careful to avoid mass panic among those chosen for immediate death. They were told that they were being given baths and showers before being taken to work. All were forced to take off their clothes. All men and those women with short hair were separated from the rest and taken straight to the gas chambers. The remaining women and children were taken to separate rooms, where Jewish barbers cut off their hair (it was later used to make boots for U-boat crews). At Treblinka the Germans found that the children cried too much during this process and they were separated, taken to ditches and shot before being thrown on to funeral pyres. Women who objected to being separated from their children found that the German guards took the children and smashed them against the wall until they were dead. The women were then required to hold the bloody remains of their children. The process of hair cutting continued while the men were dying in the gas chambers. Then the women went to the gas chambers.

The naked men and women were pushed at bayonet point, about 750 at a time, into the gas chambers. At Auschwitz the killing was relatively quick once the Zyklon B gas pellets sublimated on the floor of the chamber. After a terrible struggle to breathe the gas-free air at the top, within about four minutes all the occupants were dead. Half an hour later the chambers were opened to reveal a mass of bodies turned pink with green spots, some had bled through the nose, many had foamed at the mouth. At the other killing centres carbon monoxide was used in the gas chambers. This took far longer to kill everybody – often up to three hours. The Sonderkommando then entered the chambers, dragged out the dead, pulled out any gold teeth and dragged the bodies to the mass graves. Chelmno operated a bone-crushing machine, but at Belzec and Sobibor the bodies were burned in open pits. Auschwitz had specially con- structed crematoria capable of burning 12,000 bodies a day, but this was less than the rate at which the gas chambers were killing people (often 20,000 a day). Auschwitz also had eight open pits, sixty yards long and four yards wide, where the bodies were burned. The Sonderkommando were expected to collect the human fat which accumulated at the bottom and pour it back into the fire in order to speed up the burning process.

The killing centres operated rapidly. Chelmno was effectively closed after March 1943 and Treblinka, Sobibor and Belzec were evacuated and the facilities destroyed in the autumn of 1943. Majdanek was overrun by the Red Army in July 1944. After this date only Auschwitz was operational, but it was used to kill the maximum possible number of Hungarian Jews. Himmler ordered its closure in November 1944 and it was evacuated in January 1945 – 58,000 of its inmates were sent on a forced march westwards during which most died. Some 6,000 of the ill and dying were left behind to be liberated by Soviet troops. The exact number who died at the killing centres will never be known. The most accurate estimate is about 4 million people, of whom about half were killed at Auschwitz. To this figure has to be added the approximately 600,000 who died in the ghettos and the 1,400,000 killed in the mobile operations by the Einsatzkommando, the army and the police. In total the Germans killed about 6 million Jews during the Holocaust. About 500,000 gypsies were also killed. The total death toll in all the genocides of the twentieth century was about 14 million people.

Part Five

RETROSPECT AND PROSPECT

WHEN GUSTAV FLAUBERT died in May 1880 he left his great
novel *Bouvard et Pecuchet* unfinished. It told the story of two
Parisian clerks, one of whom inherits a large sum of money. They
retire to the countryside and begin to explore every field of human
knowledge. They abandon each one disillusioned. On his death
Flaubert left an outline of how the novel, which he had long planned
as his attack on human and especially bourgeois stupidity, was to
conclude. Bouvard and Pecuchet were to give up their quest for
knowledge and become clerks again. Before they reached their
apotheosis they were to discuss the future of humanity. Flaubert's
sketch sets out one prediction:

> Bouvard takes a rosy view of future of mankind. Modern man is
> progressing.
> Europe will be regenerated by Asia . . . two branches of mankind will
> finally be merged.
> Future inventions; means of travel. Balloon. Submarine boat with
> windows . . .
> Animals tamed – All kinds of cultivation.
> Future sciences – Control magnetic pull.
> Paris a winter-garden – fruit espaliers on the boulevards.
> Evil will disappear as want disappears. Philosophy will be a religion.
> Communion of all peoples. Public holidays.
> There will be travel to the stars – and when the earth is used up mankind
> will move over to the stars.

Bouvard's view represents the optimistic, liberal, rational thinking
typical of mid-nineteenth-century Europe. Human history was the
story of progress which had reached its height with these newly
industrialized societies. The evidence for progress was apparent
everywhere in the mass of new inventions and with the achievement
of higher living standards for all. As humanity progressed, war and

conflict would be a thing of the past. All problems could be resolved by rational discussion and agreement.

Flaubert sets out an alternative vision:

> Pecuchet takes a gloomy view of the future of mankind.
> Modern man has been diminished and has become a machine.
> Final anarchy of the human race.
> Impossibility of peace.
> Barbarity caused by excessive individualism and ravings of science.
> Three hypotheses: 1. pantheistic radicalism will break every link with the past, and inhuman despotism will result; 2. if theistic absolutism triumphs, the liberalism which has pervaded mankind since the Reformation will collapse, everything is overturned; 3. if the convulsions existing since the Revolution of 1789 continue endlessly between two outcomes, these oscillations will carry us away with their own strength. There will be no more ideal, religion, morality.
> America will have conquered the world.
> Universal vulgarity. There will be nothing left but a vast working-class spree.
> End of the world because heat runs out.

Pecuchet's bleaker view is based on the understanding that the dominant mid-nineteenth-century belief in progress overlaid much deeper, darker forces and ideas in European history which would, over time, show that Bouvard's optimism was naïve. The rise of industrial production would condemn people to more monotonous work and insecurity. Intolerant ideologies and more powerful states would create modern barbarisms, which would wreck people's lives.

From the vantage point of the late 1990s it is clear that Bouvard's and Pecuchet's visions were not mutually exclusive. The twentieth century demonstrated that progress and barbarism could exist alongside each other. If Bouvard and Pecuchet were able to look back over the history of this century, what evidence could they find to support their rival predictions? Bouvard would search for signs of progress and could find much to support his arguments. By the end of the century, everywhere in the world, people lived longer than their predecessors did in 1900. All of them were less likely to die from infectious diseases, especially in childhood. By the 1990s the world's production of food had increased to levels that would have been unimaginable in 1900, and the majority of the world's people were reasonably fed, even though there were four times as many of them as in 1900. At the same time, there was an even greater increase in industrial production. However, it was not the sheer volume of production that mattered, even though that far surpassed anything previously seen in human history. The key was the development of a vast range of new technologies and products. One of the most fundamental was electricity. Without the development of this crucial industry and the technology to distribute electricity to homes and factories, all the secondary developments – consumer goods industries, radio, television, computers and communications – would have been impossible. The lives of people who had access to these products, and over the course of the century an increasing number did, were transformed. They gave people access to a far wider range of experiences and allowed time to be spent in more productive ways. The second key industry was vehicle production, which became the driving force behind much of the industrial expansion in the first two-thirds of the century. Like electricity it transformed the way people lived. Overall, everywhere in the world people benefited, to some extent, from technological progress. Bouvard might add that the first stage of 'travel to the stars' began with the landing of men on the moon in 1969.

He could also point to progress in a number of key social changes. During the twentieth century, for the first time in human history, a majority of the world's people became literate. Even though for the majority educational opportunities remained limited, this was a fundamental change, making a significant difference to the way in which people could experience the world around them and the knowledge that they could acquire. The status of women was also greatly improved, particularly in the core states. This was not just a question of finally recognizing legal equality between the sexes, but also of providing greater opportunities at work and greater social freedom. The increasing availability of easy forms of contraception gave women much greater control over their lives. In addition many states in the world built welfare and health care systems which provided people with greater security.

On the other hand, the pessimistic Pecuchet would find much from the history of the twentieth century to support his views. He could argue that much of the progress seen by Bouvard only affected a small minority of the world's population, the 20 per cent who lived in the rich countries of the core. Throughout the century the greatest barbarism was that the world was characterized by huge and growing inequalities between the overwhelming majority, who were very poor, and the small minority, who were rich. These differences

affected every facet of life. In the periphery, tens of billions of people
suffered from malnutrition, at times half the people alive in the
world were affected. Tens of millions of people died every year
because they could not obtain enough food. Although the health of
those living in the periphery improved, by the end of the century life
expectancy for some was still half that of people living in the core
states and infant mortality rates were thirty times higher. There were
also growing signs of a revival of infectious diseases, some of which
were immune to treatment with the antibiotic drugs developed in
mid-century.

Bouvard's view that the massive increases in agricultural and
industrial output constituted 'progress' could be opposed by
Pecuchet pointing out that they were catastrophic for the world's
environment. This barbarism involved not just the destruction of
animals and natural habitats but, perhaps even more importantly,
increasing pollution. Although there were some localized environmental improvements, by the 1990s pollution had become a major
global problem. The output of carbon dioxide from the burning of
fossil fuels, in particular from vehicles, threatened irreversible
damage to the world's climatic systems. Global warming might
produce winter gardens in Paris as Bouvard forecast, but its overall
impact was likely to be catastrophic.

Pecuchet would argue that although the new technologies
eulogized by Bouvard brought many products that changed
people's lives, in the most fundamental respect their lives changed
very little. Work continued to dominate their time and long grinding
hours of monotonous toil in factory or field were the norm. The idea
of more leisure time proved to be illusory. For the workers in the
core states the century ended in the middle of a fundamental
transition. The prospect of a lifetime of secure employment, which
seemed assured in the middle of the century, was rapidly disappearing as jobs became part-time and short-term. In the periphery
insecurity remained the norm. At the same time all societies
remained highly unequal, with the opportunities available to individuals still largely determined by the group into which they were
born. Despite the changes of the twentieth century, women,
especially in the periphery, still remained in a subordinate and
exploited position. By the end of the century, for the first time in
human history, a majority of the world's population lived in cities.
Although cities could provide greater access to an improved quality
of life, overwhelmingly they remained sprawling, polluted, crime-

ridden and anonymous places in which to live.

Pecuchet would have even stronger arguments to support his pessimism in the century's wider political developments. Just as Bouvard's optimism about the ending of want turned out to be false so too did his belief that evil would disappear. Pecuchet could argue that the twentieth century was characterized by unparalleled evil. The European empires were built on exploitation of the native people. Yet their disintegration and the achievement of freedom meant little because power passed to small, unrepresentative elites who continued to exploit the people, in alliance with the powerful economic and political interests of the core states. The decline of Europe was paralleled, as Pecuchet forecast, by American domination of the world. The expression of national sentiment, especially in eastern and central Europe, brought untold suffering in terms of violence, civil war, the creation of millions of refugees, 'ethnic cleansing' and the creation of excluded and persecuted minorities. As Pecuchet forecast, peace did seem impossible. Over 150 million people were killed in the century's wars and even more were wounded or became refugees. Warfare became ever more barbarous and increasingly civilians were regarded as legitimate targets. This process reached its apogee with the deployment of nuclear weapons, whose sole purpose was to kill tens of millions of people and turn vast areas into uninhabitable radioactive wastelands.

In the twentieth century only a very small handful of the world's people lived in democracies. The overwhelming majority lived under authoritarian dictatorships, few of which even went through the pretence of seeking popular endorsement. The two great projects to reform society – Communism and social democracy (both born from the optimistic world of the nineteenth century) – failed. In the democracies, attempts by social democrats to create greater equality by democratic means had little impact. The revolutionary Marxist states were only partially successful economically and they too were ruled by small elites and remained highly unequal societies. Even more importantly, they were the most repressive states the world had ever seen. But it was not just Pecuchet's 'pantheistic radicalism' that created human despotism. Across the world increasingly repressive states turned on their own citizens, killing at least 100 million people and blighting the lives of hundreds of millions more. The only original twentieth-century ideologies – fascism and Nazism – simply combined all the worst aspects of European anti-liberalism. The systems of formal racial discrimination, established by Europeans across the world, increased in scope until the middle of the century and even their decay, not completed until the end of white-minority rule in South Africa in the mid-1990s, left high levels of informal discrimination stemming from deep-seated racial prejudices. Perhaps the greatest barbarities of the twentieth century were the mass killing of people simply because they had a different identity. They began with the Turkish attack on the Armenians but culminated in the Holocaust – the construction of death camps whose sole purpose was the mass murder of people and the deliberate killing of 6 million Jews by one of the supposedly advanced states of the core. The Holocaust called into question the very nature of European 'civilization' and the idea of 'progress'. Indeed it was the very 'progress' of the core states – industrialization and mass production, railways and the development of anonymous state bureaucracies – that made possible such an act of unparalleled barbarism.

How we interpret the twentieth century is therefore, to some extent, dependent on how we view the world. Optimists such as Bouvard could find much to support their views; so too could the pessimists such as Pecuchet. Progress and barbarism co-existed side by side throughout the century. The balance between them for each person was largely determined by where and when they were born. Overwhelmingly individuals had a better chance of seeing some of the fruits of progress if they were one of the minority who lived in the core states. However, even within the core states experiences differed widely. Citizens of the United States enjoyed the highest material standard of living across the century: they made up about 5 per cent of the world's people yet they were responsible every year for between 30 and 40 per cent of the world's total consumption of resources. At the same time, they experienced little of the suffering of the other core states. Their experience of war was limited – their death toll was comparatively small and no conflict took place on their soil. The other core states experienced war, defeat, occupation and much higher casualty rates.

Outside the core states, levels of human suffering were far greater. People faced lives of great uncertainty, often subject to war, civil war, repression and random brutality. By the end of the century the world was an even more unequal place than it was in 1900. By the 1990s the richest fifth of the world's people, those who lived in the core states, received over 80 per cent of the world's total income. The poorest fifth received less than 2 per cent. Of the roughly 6 billion people alive at the end of the century, over 1 billion had no access to safe drinking water, 880 million adults could not read or write, 770 million did not receive sufficient food to sustain an active working life, more than 1 billion lacked the basic necessities of life. Every year about 18 million people, most of them children, died from poverty and hunger. For all these people the idea of progress was not even a distant dream. For most of the people who lived in the twentieth century there is little doubt that the signs of progress were outweighed by the sheer barbarism of everyday life.

The scale of the destruction of human life in the twentieth century was unprecedented. Hundreds of millions starved to death because of the permanent maldistribution of the available food in the world. In addition, about 100 million died in the great famines of the century. This compares with the perhaps 10 million who died in natural disasters and the 25 million killed by motor vehicles. War killed another 150 million, government repression about 100 million. The total of 14 million who died in the century's genocides was, on this scale, comparatively small, but they were the victims of the greatest acts of deliberate murder.

Although the world appeared to be driven by technological change, one of the major features of twentieth-century economic history was just how little changed. The general structure of the world economy, with the core, semi-periphery and periphery, remained the same and few countries changed their position significantly. The United States remained the dominant economy and only Japan moved unambiguously into the core. The rise of Japan was almost exactly mirrored by the relative decline of Britain. A few minor economies such as Singapore and Hong Kong and small states with huge oil revenues such as Kuwait and the Emirates of the Gulf, became very wealthy, but this was not a route open to the majority of countries. Some such as China and Brazil were large economies simply because of their geographical scale and the size of their population, but in terms of wealth per head they lagged far behind the wealthy states of the core. Alternative routes of development to the capitalist norm, such as that adopted in the Soviet Union, proved of little utility – overall growth rates were no better than similar capitalist economies in the semi-periphery. It is this overall structure that helps to explain why the fall of Communism in the late 1980s made so little difference to the world economy.

In international political history there was one very clear trend. In the longest historical context the twentieth century saw the beginning of the end of the long 'Atlantic' dominance of the world which had begun in the sixteenth century. European predominance reached its greatest physical extent in the early 1920s with the final division of the Ottoman empire. The decline of Europe was evident with the fall of the European empires by the 1960s and the parallel demise of Britain and France as world powers. Although there was a major power struggle (the 'Cold War') between the United States and the Soviet Union, it was matched by the one between the United States on the one hand and Britain and France on the other. Twice the last two powers needed American help to defeat Germany and it was largely as a result of these struggles that the United States emerged as the one global military power by the middle of the century. After 1945 the United States quickly replaced Britain and France as the dominant 'Atlantic' power in the world. However, it was never able to expand its influence into areas not previously under European control. Indeed, the major problem for the United States was not only to supplant Britain and France, but also to maintain the spheres of influence it had already established. In this it was only partly successful and political control over large areas such as Indo-China together with parts of Africa and the Middle East was effectively lost after 1950.

The counterpart of this trend was the revival of those parts of the world outside of the control of the 'Atlantic' powers. Up to the 1930s the crucial development was the ability of Turkey, Iran and most importantly China to preserve their independence. Perhaps the most significant event of the century was the re-unification of China under a strong government after 1949. Continued industrial expansion, a high growth rate and the adoption of a semi-capitalist economic system by the 1980s were signs of the growing economic strength of the largest country in the world. This could be seen as the first sign of a gradual return to the more usual pattern of world history, with China playing a crucial role. This tilt towards a 'Pacific' rather than an 'Atlantic' focus in the world was reflected in the growing economic power of Japan and the shift of the United States away from an 'Atlantic' orientation, with the growing importance of California within the United States and of intra-Pacific trade.

During the twentieth century the number of independent states in the world rose five-fold. At the same time the nature and role of the state changed significantly. All states took on more functions in terms of regulating society, providing state welfare schemes and controlling their own citizens. For a period in mid-century many became much more interventionist economically and, in some cases, took control of key industries. By the last quarter of the century a number of trends stemming from two sources – the changing nature of the world economy and pressures leading to the disintegration of the nation state – were becoming apparent. These trends called into question the very nature of the state as it had developed earlier in the century and raised significant doubts about whether the state, especially the core states, could continue to carry out what had earlier been assumed to be its key functions.

By the latter part of the century the growing integration of the world economy, the development of global financial markets and the rising importance of transnational corporations were significantly affecting the role of states. By the 1990s of the hundred biggest 'economies' in the world (judged in terms of turnover), half were states and half were corporations. Transnational corporations, encouraged by and demanding further liberalization of world trade, were to a large extent beyond the control of any state. Their ability to shift production around the world according to their own priorities had major effects on all national economies, which governments were largely unable to control. Indeed states became competitors for the favours of the transnational corporations and attempted to attract them by various subsidies and grants. The increasing scale of international financial flows and foreign exchange dealings was beyond the control of any individual state. Throughout the century the states of the periphery and the semi-periphery found that they were able to exercise little control over their own economies because of the demands of the world economy. By the latter part of the century the states of the core were finding increasingly that they too were in the same position. Although they all subscribed to the prevailing orthodoxy of free trade and economic liberalization, and though institutions such as the IMF and World Bank tried to ensure that the states of the periphery and semi-periphery adopted similar policies, they found that their own economic independence was being rapidly circumscribed. At the same time the core states reduced their own functions by selling off state assets and moving towards greater private provision of those services which earlier in the century had been regarded as the state's responsibility. The dominant economic liberalism of the core countries left the state weaker and with a reduced role in many social areas. However, the social stresses created by such liberalization meant that the state had to become stronger in order to contain them. This meant more police, stiffer penalties for criminals and more people in jail. Internationally states found the preservation of their security increasingly difficult. Many faced civil wars and internal violence, but equally problematic was the threat from terrorism, which states could contain but not eliminate.

The rise in the number of states in the world was the result not just of the fall of the colonial empires but also of the disintegration of many states, in particular the Soviet Union, Yugoslavia and Czechoslovakia in Europe. The demands of ethnic and regional groups for autonomy and independence reflected two trends. As states became weaker economically, there seemed less reason to remain within the larger identities. Small states might be weak but no less so than large units. Indeed, many of the smaller states were among the most prosperous in the world. One of the main sources of national feeling had always been the search for, and assertion of, a separate cultural identity. By the end of the twentieth century the increasing globalization of culture, which even the strongest states seemed unable to resist, created more pressure for the protection of cultural differences through the promotion of separate national identities. In some cases the disintegration of the state was even more fundamental, with the collapse of its authority even within its own boundaries. States such as Colombia were unable to control the large-scale criminal groups running the drugs trade (a situation not dissimilar to the problems caused by the Mafia in southern Italy for much of the century). In Africa countries such as Somalia, Sierra Leone and Liberia collapsed into virtual anarchy after years of coups and civil wars.

The world seemed to be moving towards a 'new medievalism', based on a complex structure of overlapping economic and political power and with weak state boundaries. Increasingly states were not the only powerful institutions in the world, as they had been earlier in the century. Political and economic power no longer coincided and many states were far weaker and exercised much less political and economic power than non-sovereign bodies such as trans-national corporations and international institutions. States were not even the only institutions to wield force – something which had long been claimed as their exclusive prerogative. Internally private security organizations were increasingly important. Externally small terrorist groups were powerful and in some instances transnational corporations were hiring their own armed forces to defend their investments in some of the weaker countries in the world. The core states were not immune to these developments. Many crucial economic decisions, affecting the livelihoods of millions of people, were no longer taken by governments. Often they could do no more than adapt their policies to what were seen as 'economic realities' and attempt to ameliorate the social consequences. In many international negotiations governments spoke for the interests of powerful economic groups, equating them with the national interest. In areas like western Europe, governments were giving authority to supra-national institutions such as the European Union where, on some issues, they could be forced to accept policies with which they did not agree. By the end of the century the distribution of power in the world was far more complex than it had been a century earlier.

Long-term speculation is a futile business. If we imagine writing a book in the late 1890s and trying to identify what might happen in the twentieth century, there is much that could not possibly have been forecast correctly. Some of the technologies developed would have been incomprehensible, some ideas would have been beyond belief. Many might have guessed that the United States would become more powerful, but few would have forecast the end of all the European empires within seventy years. Surely no one would have suggested that one of the most civilized of the European states would deliberately murder 6 million people using, in part, specially constructed death camps. The same problem faces anyone trying to look into the twenty-first century. However, although this is a work of history it is worth considering where some of the trends already apparent in the late twentieth century might be leading over the next few decades without trying to forecast developments over the next hundred years.

Projections of population have some accuracy. The United Nations forecasts that if human fertility falls across the world to the replacement level of 2·1 births per woman by 2035 then world population would stabilize at about 10 billion by the end of the twenty-first century. However, these projections are probably too optimistic because they are based on an average fall in fertility of 40 per cent from current levels, which implies far greater falls in parts of the periphery. Evidence in the late twentieth century suggests that the decline in fertility visible in the 1960s and 1970s has slowed down markedly, almost certainly because access to contraception remains limited. Unless fertility continues to fall rapidly, the more realistic forecast is that the world's population will reach about 14 billion by 2040, about two and a half times its current level.

There must, however, be doubts about whether in practice world population will reach this level. The first problem is whether world food production and distribution will be capable of feeding this number of people. Unless there are radical changes to the current position, in which the 20 per cent of the world's people who live in the core states eat two-thirds of the world's food, then massive increases in food output will be required. Current output would have to double even if there were more equal access to food. Any such increase in world food production faces two problems. First, the amount of land suitable for agriculture in the world is limited. Second, it is not clear that enough resources and techniques exist or can be developed to continue the rapid rise in agricultural productivity found in the second half of the twentieth century. During that time the harvested area in the world expanded by a quarter, but rapid population growth meant that the amount of agricultural land per head fell by half. Increases in output were mainly obtained through a ten-fold increase in fertilizer use. There are limits to the productivity grains from greater fertilizer, pesticide and herbicide use and they may have been reached. After 1984 the average 3 per cent a year increase in world harvests of the previous thirty years fell away to less than 1 per cent a year, far below the population growth rate. This meant that output per head fell steadily.

Even if enough food can be found, two further questions remain. First, can the resurgence of infectious diseases be contained? If this can be done, is there enough work available for all these extra people? It is already clear that in the periphery there will be an extra 700 million people in the labour force by 2010, about half of whom will be in Africa. In total this is roughly twice the current workforce of Europe. It is extremely hard to see how these people will be able to find work to buy enough food in order to survive. This is particularly the case because most of the population growth will take place in the cities. By 2025 about 4 billion people will live in the cities of the periphery (roughly two and half times the current level). At the end of the twentieth century the population density of cities such as Lagos and Jakarta was already ten times that of New York and they were centres of social collapse and poverty. It is unclear how they will be able to cope with population growth on the levels projected.

The structure of the world economy is unlikely to change. It will remain dominated by the core economies, with those of the semi-periphery and periphery in a subordinate position. World trade will continue to be mainly between the core states, although it is likely to be increasingly regionalized. If the trends apparent in the last two decades of the twentieth century continue for the first ten years of the twenty-first century then by 2010 China will be the largest economy in the world. The United States will still be one of the richest countries in the world, its income per head would be about five times greater than that of China. However, Japan will be almost as rich as the United States, confirming its phenomenal economic rise in the twentieth century – in 1900 its wealth per head was less than a quarter of US levels. The relative decline of Britain will be even more apparent since it will be overtaken by Italy, which in 1900 had an income per head less than half that of Britain.

There seems no reason why industrial output should not continue to expand at a rapid rate as new technologies are developed. The problem will be whether the resources exist to support such growth. In the early 1970s the Club of Rome published an influential book, *Limits to Growth*, which argued that the world faced catastrophe because resources would run out early in the twenty-first century. Those forecasts did not take account of the slow-down in world growth after 1973 and the computer models on which the projections were made were over-simplistic in the extreme. It is unlikely that the world will run out of any major resources in the first half of the twenty-first century. Experience over the last century or more suggests that no major mineral will become exhausted and that recycling and substitution can be massively extended. Technological developments will also enable lower grades of ore to be utilized – between 1850 and the end of the twentieth century the grade of mined copper ores fell ten-fold yet the real cost of copper remained roughly the same. The problem is that this trend, together with other industrial processes and increasing electricity use, will involve continued massive increases in energy consumption.

In the last half of the twentieth century the world became about one-third more efficient in its use of energy. Even so, there is still major scope for improving energy efficiency in industry, homes and vehicles. However, increasing demand for energy is likely to outstrip any efficiency gains. At 1990 levels of consumption there are enough known reserves of coal to last for 220 years. Even with major increases in use, especially from Chinese industrialization, there will be enough coal for the whole of the twenty-first century.

At the end of the twentieth century, oil reserves were sufficient to last twenty years. However, the world has only had twenty years of known reserves since the mid-twentieth century – oil companies do not bother, for obvious cost reasons, to try and discover more oil than this. World consumption of oil was roughly steady in the twenty years after 1980. Even at this rate of consumption and with increasing use of lower-grade reserves, it is unlikely that oil reserves will last far beyond the middle of the next century. On the other hand, natural gas will almost certainly outlast oil.

The most crucial problem posed by increasing energy use is the effect it will have on climate. Levels of carbon dioxide in the atmosphere rose at an increasing rate throughout the twentieth century and by the mid-1990s scientists were agreed that it was having a discernible impact on the world's climate. Further carbon dioxide output will only speed up the process, bringing about major, unpredictable climatic changes, shifts in vegetation and crop belts, rising sea levels and major social and economic costs. International negotiations seem unlikely to produce more than stabilization or a very limited reduction in output, which will not be sufficient to make any significant difference to the rate of climate change. At the same time other major environmental problems will have to be resolved. World paper production rose more than five-fold in the latter half of the twentieth century, so that by the 1990s over 4 billion trees were being cut down every year, enough to cover an area equivalent to the whole of England. Combined with the pressures to create more cropland out of the tropical forests, it seems likely that substantial areas of the world's forests, especially in the tropics, will be destroyed in the early twenty-first century with unpredictable climatic consequences. The world is also likely to face a major water shortage in the twenty-first century. By the end of the twentieth century humans were already using a quarter of all the non-salt water on the planet. In the late 1990s per capita supplies were one-third lower than in 1970, a situation which will worsen as population continues to rise and more water is used in agriculture. At the end of the twentieth century over 300 million people in Africa (a third of the total population) lived in water-scarce countries and the situation was probably worse in the Middle East. China, which had nearly a quarter of the world's population, had less than a tenth of its fresh water.

In 1992 a joint report by the United States National Academy of Sciences and the Royal Society in Britain concluded:

If current predictions of population growth prove accurate and patterns of human activity on the planet remain unchanged, science and technology may not be able to prevent either irreversible degradation of the environment or continued poverty for much of the world.

Although some might question whether science and technology are part of the solution or part of the problem, it is clear that the manifold social, economic and environmental problems of the early twenty-first century will occur in a highly unequal world. It will be a world where wealth, economic power and political power are held, as in the past, by a small minority of the world's people. In the twentieth century the world became far more unequal and there is no sign of any reversal of that trend. In the 1990s the average American used forty-six times more electricity than a person living in India and ate fifty-two times more meat every year. The official report to the United Nations' review conference on Environment and Development in 1997 was blunt in its analysis:

> Too many countries have seen economic conditions worsen, public services deteriorate; and the total number of people in the world living in poverty has increased. The gap between the least developed countries and the other countries has grown rapidly in recent years.

Little attempt was being made to alter these huge differences and, given the distribution of economic and political power in the world, there seemed no way in which they could be altered. Even in the highly unlikely event of the political authorities in the core states deciding on a major redistribution of resources, it is unlikely that they would have enough power to implement such a policy. The relatively autonomous world economy seemed to be incapable of operating in a radically different manner from the way in which it had functioned for centuries. Equally important, it is unlikely that any major increase in consumption and wealth for the majority of the world's population could be sustained environmentally. If the population of the world at the end of the twentieth century (just over 6 billion people) were to live at western European (not American) standards of living, it would require a 140-fold increase in the consumption of resources and energy. This would not be sustainable in resource terms and the environmental consequences, particularly in terms of increased global warming, would almost certainly be catastrophic.

Given the way the world evolved in the twentieth century and the distribution of economic and political power at the end of the century, it seems likely that, as in the past, the world will, over the next few decades, continue to be characterized by progress for a minority and barbarism for the overwhelming majority.

CHRONOLOGY

AFRICA

1902   Treaty of Vereeniging ends Boer War

1904   Herrero uprising in German South-west Africa

1905   Maji-Maji uprising in German East Africa

1907   Indian immigration restricted in Transvaal Gandhi begins civil disobedience campaign

1908   First aerial bombing by Italians in North Africa

1910   Union of South Africa established

1911   Italo–Turkish war in North Africa

1913   Nationalist party founded in South Africa

1915   South African conquest of German South-west Africa

1918   Wafd party founded in Egypt

1921   Nationalist riots in Egypt Uprising in Morocco

1922   Southern Rhodesia established as self-governing colony

1935   Italian invasion of Ethiopia

1936   Anglo–Egyptian treaty on eventual withdrawal of British forces

1941   Allied re-conquest of Ethiopia

1948   Nationalist government in South Africa

1949   Convention People's Party established in Gold Coast by Kwame Nkrumah

1952   Nationalist army coup in Egypt State of emergency in Kenya. Nationalist leader Jomo Kenyatta arrested

1953   Central African Federation established

1954   Start of nationalist uprising in Algeria

1956   Sudan and Tunisia become independent Spanish and French Morocco united Egyptian nationalization of the Suez Canal Joint Anglo–French–Israeli attack on Egypt

1957   Ghana independent

1960   Independence for French West African states, Nigeria and Belgian Congo

1961   South Africa becomes a republic Sharpeville massacre

1962   Algerian independence agreed

1964   Nelson Mandela sentenced to life imprisonment in South Africa

1965   Rhodesian declaration of UDI

1967   Start of Nigerian Civil War

1974   Mozambique independent

1975   Soweto uprising in South Africa

1980   Rhodesia independent as Zimbabwe

1984   About one million people die in Ethiopian famine

1990   Release of Nelson Mandela

Namibia (last colony on the continent) becomes independent

1991 Last apartheid laws repealed

1994 First non-racial elections in South Africa. Nelson Mandela becomes President

AMERICAS

1901 President McKinley shot

1903 US sponsored revolution in Panama. US gains rights to Panama Canal

1904 President Roosevelt claims right for US to intervene in Latin America

1906 UK troops leave Canada

1907 US limits Japanese immigration

1909 National Association for the Advancement of Colored People founded

1910 Start of Mexican Revolution

1912 US intervention in Nicaragua

1913 Direct election of US Senators

1914 Panama Canal opened. US intervention in Haiti

1917 US declares war on Germany

1920 'Red Scare' and Prohibition in US

1924 New restrictive immigration policy in the US

1926 Clerical uprising in Mexico

1927 Guerrilla resistance to US occupation of Nicaragua

1930 Getulio Vargas President of Brazil

1932 Bolivia–Paraguay war over Chaco

Franklin Roosevelt elected President of US

1933 Prohibition ends in US. Start of 'New Deal'

1934 Cardenas elected President of Mexico. Economic/social reforms

1938 Mexican nationalization of oil industry

1946 Perón elected President of Argentina

1954 School segregation ruled illegal by US Supreme Court

US intervention in Guatemala

1955 Perón exiled from Argentina

1957 'Papa Doc' Duvalier becomes President of Haiti

1959 Castro seizes power in Cuba

1961 Failed US-backed invasion of Cuba

1962 Cuban missile crisis

1963 President Kennedy assassinated

1964 Military regime takes power in Brazil

1968 Martin Luther King and Senator Robert Kennedy assassinated

1973 Military coup in Chile led by General Pinochet against Allende government

1974 Resignation of President Nixon over Watergate scandal

1976 Military coup in Argentina

1977 Panama Canal treaties restore Panamanian sovereignty by 1999

1979 Sandinistas overthrow Somozo government in Nicaragua

1982 Falklands/Malvinas war between Britain and Argentina

1983 US invasion of Grenada

1988 US-backed coup in Panama

1989 Democratic elections in Argentina

ASIA/OCEANIA

1900	'Boxer' nationalist uprising in China
1901	New state of Australia created
1902	Anglo–Japanese alliance
1904	Russo–Japanese war
1905	Japanese sink Russian fleet. Treaty of Portsmouth ends war
1906	Muslim League founded in India
	Revolution in Persia leads to first parliament
1908	Young Turk revolution
	Nationalist cultural society Budi Utomo founded in Indonesia
1911	Revolution in China ends Manchu dynasty and establishes republic
1914	Turkey enters First World War on the side of the Central Powers
	German colonies in Asia/Pacific captured by Allied powers
1915	Allied attack on Dardanelles fails
	Japanese Twenty-One demands on China
	Armenian genocide in Turkey
1916	Arab revolt against Turkey
1917	Balfour declaration on Jewish homeland in Palestine
1919	Amritsar massacre in India
	Nationalist revolution in Turkey under Mustafa Kemal
	Division of Ottoman empire between Britain and France
1920	Congress party of India adopts Gandhi's programme of non-co-operation
1922	Gandhi sentenced to six years in jail

1923	Turkish republic established
1925	Sun Yat-sen dies in China
1926	Ibn Saud declares himself ruler of Arabia
	Pahlev dynasty established in Persia
1927	Indonesian nationalist party founded
1930	Start of major civil disobedience campaign by Gandhi
1931	Japanese occupation of Manchuria
1934	Start of Chinese Communist Long March from Kiangsi to Shensi
1936	Arab rebellion in Palestine over Jewish immigration
1940	Japanese occupation of northern Indochina
1941	Anglo–Soviet occupation of Iran
	Japanese attack on Pearl Harbour and European colonies in Asia
1942	Japanese occupation of Indochina, Hong Kong, Philippines, Dutch East Indies, Malaya & Burma
	'Quit India' resolution of Congress Party. Nationalist movement suppressed
1945	First use of A-bomb at Hiroshima. Japanese surrender
	Nationalist uprisings in Indochina and Dutch East Indies
1946	Start of Jewish terrorist campaign in Palestine
	Independent Philippine republic established
1947	India/Pakistan independent
1948	Gandhi murdered by Hindu extremist
	Ceylon independent
	Israel established
	Arab–Israeli war

1949	Chinese People's Republic established	1997	Hong Kong returned to China
	Indonesian independence		
1950	Outbreak of Korean war		EUROPE
	Chinese occupation of Tibet	1902	Sinn Fein Irish nationalist party founded
1951	Nationalization of Iranian oil industry	1903	Russian Social Democratic Party splits into Menshevik and Bolshevik factions
1953	Armistice in Korean war		
	Re-establishment of Shah in Iran		
1954	Geneva agreements end French rule in Indochina	1904	Anglo–French Entente
		1905	Failed revolution in Russia
	SEATO established		Norway declares independence from Sweden
1957	Malaya independent		
1958	'Great Leap Forward' starts in China	1907	World's first women MPs elected in Finland
1959	Nationalist uprising in Tibet	1908	Austria-Hungary annexes Bosnia-Herzegovina from Turkey
1960	Military coup in Turkey		
1965	Start of full-scale US intervention in Vietnam	1910	Revolution in Portugal establishes republic
	Start of 'Cultural Revolution' in China	1912	First Balkan war
		1913	Second Balkan war
1967	Arab–Israeli 'Six Day War'	1914	Assassination of Archduke Ferdinand. Outbreak of First World War
1970	US bombing of Cambodia		
1973	'Yom Kippur' Arab–Israeli war		
		1915	Italy joins Allies
	Final withdrawal of US troops from Vietnam	1916	Battles of Verdun and the Somme
1974	Start of Lebanese civil war	1917	Revolution in Russia and overthrow of the Tsar
1975	Khmer Rouge seize power in Cambodia		Bolsheviks seize power
	Reunification of Vietnam	1918	Treaty of Brest-Litovsk
1976	Death of Mao Tse-Tung		Revolution in Germany and Austria-Hungary establishes republics
1979	USSR invasion of Afghanistan		
	Revolution in Iran and exile of Shah. Religious regime established		Armistice ends First World War
		1919	Irish republic declared. Nationalist uprising
	Israel–Egypt peace treaty		Italian Fascist Party founded
1980	Outbreak of Iran–Iraq war		
1982	Israeli invasion of Lebanon		Treaty of Versailles
1988	Iran–Iraq cease-fire	1921	New Economic Policy in Soviet Union
	'Intifada' begins in Palestine		
1989	Student demonstration suppressed in Tienanmen Square, Peking	1922	Creation of USSR
			Mussolini Prime Minister of Italy
1990	Iraq invades Kuwait		
1991	Gulf war		Irish Free State Established

1997 Hong Kong returned to
          China

EUROPE
1902 Sinn Fein Irish nationalist
          party founded
1903 Russian Social Democratic
          Party splits into
          Menshevik and Bolshevik
          factions
1904 Anglo–French Entente
1905 Failed revolution in Russia
          Norway declares
          independence from
          Sweden
1907 World's first women MPs
          elected in Finland
1908 Austria-Hungary annexes
          Bosnia-Herzegovina
          from Turkey
1910 Revolution in Portugal
          establishes republic
1912 First Balkan war
1913 Second Balkan war
1914 Assassination of Archduke
          Ferdinand. Outbreak of
          First World War
1915 Italy joins Allies
1916 Battles of Verdun and the
          Somme
1917 Revolution in Russia and
          overthrow of the Tsar
          Bolsheviks seize power
1918 Treaty of Brest-Litovsk
          Revolution in Germany and
          Austria-Hungary
          establishes republics
          Armistice ends First World
          War
1919 Irish republic declared.
          Nationalist uprising
          Italian Fascist Party
          founded
          Treaty of Versailles
1921 New Economic Policy in
          Soviet Union
1922 Creation of USSR
          Mussolini Prime Minister
          of Italy
          Irish Free State Established

1923 French and Belgian occupation of the Ruhr
Failed coup in Munich by Adolf Hitler
1924 Death of Lenin
1925 Locarno Pact
1926 Military coup in Poland by Pilsudski
1928 First Five-Year Plan in USSR
1929 Royal dictatorship established in Yugoslavia
Lateran Treaty between Italy and the Papacy
1931 Spanish republic established
1932 Nazis largest party in German elections (May)
1933 Hitler becomes German Chancellor. Dictatorship established
1935 German rearmament announced. Anti-Semitic Nuremberg laws
1936 German re-militarization of the Rhineland
Metaxas dictatorship in Greece
Start of Spanish civil war
1938 German–Austrian 'Anschluss'
Munich agreement on the division of Czechoslovakia
1939 German–USSR non-aggression pact
German invasion of Poland
Start of Second World War
USSR invasion of Finland
1940 German occupation of Norway, Denmark, Belgium, Luxemburg and the Netherlands
Armistice with France. Italy enters the war.
1941 German invasion of the USSR
1942 Battle of Stalingrad
Wannsee Conference starts final stage of Jewish holocaust

1943 Italian surrender and fall of Mussolini
1944 Liberation of most of Western Europe
1945 German surrender. Suicide of Hitler
1946 Start of Greek civil war
1947 Benelux customs union established
'Marshall Aid' plan
1948 Berlin airlift. Communist coup in Czechoslovakia
Tito split with USSR
1949 NATO established
1951 European Coal and Steel Community established
1953 Death of Stalin
1955 West Germany joins NATO
Warsaw Pact established
1956 Anti-Stalin speech by Khruschev at Soviet Party Congress
Hungarian uprising suppressed by Soviet troops
1957 Treaty of Rome establishes European Economic Community
1958 Fifth French Republic established by General de Gaulle
1961 Berlin wall built
1967 Military coup in Greece
1968 Warsaw Pact military intervention in Czechoslovakia
1973 UK, Denmark and Ireland join the EEC
1974 Coup in Portugal
1975 Death of Franco
Helsinki Treaty
1980 Death of Tito
Beginnings of Solidarity movement in Poland
1981 Martial law in Poland
1982 Death of President Brezhnev (USSR)
1985 Mikhail Gorbachev General Secretary of Communist

Party in USSR

1989 Partial democratic elections
in Poland

Berlin wall demolished

1990 Communist Party
monopoly of power in
USSR ended

Reunification of Germany

Warsaw Pact dissolved

1991 Failed Communist hardline
coup in USSR

Disintegration of
Yugoslavia

Dissolution of USSR

1992 Dissolution of
Czechoslovakia

1996 Expansion of European
Union to fifteen states

SOCIAL

1900 American Federation of
Labour founded in the
US

1901 First Nobel prizes awarded

1902 Nine-hour maximum work
day for miners in France

1903 General strike in the
Netherlands suppressed
by the military

1906 Free school meals started in
the UK

1907 Boy Scouts founded

Bubonic plague kills one
million people in India

1909 Old age pensions
introduced in the UK and
Australia

1911 Unemployment insurance
started in the UK

1913 16th Amendment in the US
allows federal income tax

1916 Eight-hour work day
established in the US

1918 About 21 million people die
in world-wide influenza
epidemic

1919 Eight-hour work day
introduced in France, the
Netherlands and Spain

1920 Abortion legalized in the

USSR but made illegal in
France

1921 Capital punishment
abolished in Sweden

First birth-control clinic in
London

1922 First radio adverts in US

First out-of-town shopping
centre, Kansas City, USA

1925 State of Tennessee bans the
teaching of evolution

The world population
exceeds 2 billion

1933 First gas chamber execution
in US

1934 Durex condoms first
produced

1936 Tampax Inc. founded in the
US to manufacture
tampons

1938 State medical service
established in New
Zealand

Instant coffee first
produced by Nestlé in
Switzerland

1947 Monosodium glutamate
marketed for the first
time

1954 Divorce legalized in
Argentina

1956 Oral vaccine for polio
developed

1959 South African government
refuses to allow television

1960 World population exceeds 3
billion

First use of aluminium cans
for food and drinks

1963 Valium first produced

1964 First official report linking
tobacco smoking and
cancer (US)

1967 Birth control legalized in
France

First human heart-
transplant

1968 Pope Paul VI declares any
form of artificial birth
control a violation of

Divine Will
1975 World population exceeds 4 billion
1981 France abolishes the guillotine
1984 AIDS virus identified
1987 World population exceeds 5 billion
1996 World population exceeds 6 billion

WORLD
1902 First decision by International Court of Arbitration at The Hague
1907 Hague Peace Conference
1919 International Labour Organization founded
1920 First full meeting of the League of Nations in Geneva
1922 Washington Conference on naval limitation
     International Court of Justice established
1928 Kellogg–Briand pact renouncing war
1930 London Conference on naval limitation
1931 Statute of Westminster formally establishes British dominions as autonomous states
1932 Disarmament conference, Geneva
1943 Teheran Conference
1945 Yalta/Potsdam Conferences. Establishment of United Nations
1946 UNESCO/UNICEF established
1947 Universal Declaration of Human Rights
1955 Bandung Conference of Non-Aligned Nations
1959 Antarctic Treaty signed
1963 Partial Nuclear Test Ban Treaty
1969 Nuclear Non-Proliferation

Treaty
1972 SALT Treaty
1989 Chemical Weapons Treaty
1992 UN Conference on Environment and Development (Rio de Janeiro)
1996 Comprehensive Test Ban Treaty

ECONOMIC/FINANCIAL
1900 Gold dollar sole official currency of USA
1908 Gold standard established in Germany
1913 Federal Reserve established in US
1918 US major creditor/financial nation in the world
1921 Final agreement on level of German reparations
1923 German hyperinflation
1924 Dawes plan on German reparations
     Introduction of Reichsmark
1925 Restoration of gold standard in UK and Germany
1929 Wall Street Crash
1930 Bank for International Settlements established
1931 UK abandons gold standard. Austrian Kreditanstalt Bank bankrupt
1932 Final abandonment of Free Trade by UK
1933 US abandons gold standard Failure of World Economic Conference in London
1934 US establishes gold price at $35 an ounce
1936 Devaluation of French, Swiss and Italian currencies
     Tripartite Monetary Agreement (USA, UK and France)
1941 USA Lend-Lease legislation
1944 Bretton Woods Conference

discusses IMF/World Bank

1945 IMF/World Bank established

1946 Nationalization of Bank of England

1947 GATT signed

1948 Deutschmark established
Marshall Plan begins operating
OEEC established

1949 Devaluation of Sterling, the Franc, Deutschmark and most European currencies
COMECON established for USSR and Eastern Europe

1950 European Payments Union established

1954 London gold market re-opens

1958 West European currencies convertible

1960 OEEC becomes OECD when USA and Canada join

1964 First UNCTAD meeting

1967 Sterling devalued
Conclusion of Kennedy round of GATT negotiations

1971 First US trade deficit since 1894
Suspension of dollar convertibility

1973 Devaluation/flotation of the US dollar. End of post-war financial system
OPEC raises oil price four-fold

1979 Further oil price increases
European Monetary System introduced

1981 European Currency Unit introduced

1986 Single European Act signed to enable establishment of a single market in the EEC

1993 GATT Uruguay Round concluded

1995 World Trade Organization established

SCIENCE/TECHNOLOGY

1900 First flight of an airship
'Box Brownie' camera introduced by Kodak

1901 First radio communication across the Atlantic

1903 First powered flight by the Wright Brothers
Artificial silk produced

1904 Teabags first produced

1905 Einstein's relativity, $E = MC^2$

1909 Louis Blériot flies across the Channel

1910 Fluorescent light tube invented

1913 Typhoid vaccine discovered

1914 First demonstration of colour photographic film

1915 First 'tank' using caterpillar tracks

1917 Synthetic petrol produced from coal

1919 First transatlantic flight

1920 First regular radio broadcasts (Pittsburgh)

1925 Michelson measures the speed of light

1926 First demonstration of television
Wireless telephone link between London and New York established

1927 Production of synthetic rubber in the US
Lindberg's solo trans-Atlantic flight

1934 Start of 'Dust Bowl' in mid-west US

1935 Continuous steel casting in the US and USSR
Radar tested

1936 First diesel car production in Germany
First helicopter constructed

1937 Invention of nylon
1939 DDT first produced
     First transatlantic passenger
       flight
1942 First guided rocket flight
1945 A-bomb tested and used
1946 First commercial computer
1947 Invention of photocopier
1948 Invention of transistor
1951 First colour television
       broadcasts in the US
     H-bomb tested
1954 First nuclear powered
       submarine launched (USS
       Nautilus)
     Solar cells invented
     First nuclear generated
       electricity
1955 Fibre optics developed
     Salk polio vaccine
1956 First telephone cable from
       the US to Europe
1957 Sputnik I, first satellite,
       launched
1958 Invention of the laser
1960 First contraceptive pill
       marketed in the US
1961 First manned space flight
       (Vostok I with Yuri
       Gagarin)

1962 Telstar satellite beams first
       TV pictures across the
       Atlantic
     First industrial robots
       installed by General
       Motors
1965 First commercial satellite
       for TV transmission
1969 First silicon microprocessor
     Manned landing on the
       moon
1970 First flight of Boeing 747
1972 DDT banned in US
1976 Viking spacecraft lands on
       Mars
1978 Demonstration of the
       compact disc
1981 Space shuttle 'Columbia'
       launched
1986 Chernobyl nuclear
       explosion
1987 Start of work on the
       Channel Tunnel
     First agreement on limiting
       CFC production to
       protect ozone layer
1997 First cloning of an animal

SUGGESTIONS FOR FURTHER READING

The literature on the twentieth century is so vast that nobody could read even a small part of it in a lifetime. The list below is therefore no more than a guide to a few of the books that take further some of the arguments set out in the main chapters.

2 People

Castles, S., and Miller, M., *The Age of Migration: International Population Movements in the Modern World* (London, Macmillan, 1993).

Grigg, D., *The World Food Problem, 1950–80* (Oxford, Blackwell, 1985).

3 Production

Bairoch, P., *The Economic Development of the Third World Since 1900* (London, Methuen, 1975).

Clark, J., *The Political Economy of World Energy: A Twentieth-century Perspective* (London, Harvester-Wheatsheaf, 1990).

Hughes, T., *Networks of Power: Electrification in Western Society, 1880–1930* (Baltimore, Johns Hopkins University Press, 1983).

Maddison, A., *The World Economy in the Twentieth Century* (Paris, OECD, 1989).

——*Dynamic Forces in Capitalist Development: A Long-run Comparative View* (New York, Oxford University Press, 1991).

4 Environment

Ponting, C., *A Green History of the World* (New York, St. Martin's Press, 1992).

5 Globalization

Dicken, P., *Global Shift: The Internationalization of Economic Activity* (New York, Guilford Press, 1998).

Waters, M., *Globalization* (New York, Routledge, 1995).

6 Economies

Amsden, A., *Asia's Next Giant: South Korea and Late Industrialization* (Oxford, Oxford University Press, 1989).

Rostow, W., *The World Economy: History and Prospect* (Austin, University of Texas Press, 1980).

7 Societies

Berry, B., *Comparative Urbanization: Divergent Paths in the Twentieth Century* (London, Macmillan, 1981).

Cross, G., *Time and Money: The Making of Consumer Culture* (London, Routledge, 1993).

Edwards, R., *Contested Terrain: The Transformation of the Workplace in the Twentieth Century* (New York, Basic Books, 1979).

Esping-Andersen, G., *The Three Worlds of Welfare Capitalism* (Princeton, Princeton University Press, 1990).

Flora, P., and Heidenheimer, A.,

The Development of Welfare States in Europe and America (London, Transaction, 1987).

Pahl, R. (ed.), *On Work: Historical, Comparative and Theoretical Approaches* (Oxford, Blackwell, 1988).

Rifkin, J., *The End of Work: The Decline of the Global Labor Force and the Dawning of the Post-Market Era* (New York, Putnam, 1995).

Shorter, E., *The Making of the Modern Family* (New York, Basic Books, 1975).

8 Empires

August, T., *The Selling of the Empire: British and French Imperialist Propaganda, 1890–1940* (Westport, Greenwood Press, 1985).

Beasley, W., *Japanese Imperialism* (Oxford, Oxford University Press, 1987).

Clarence-Smith, G., *The Third Portuguese Empire, 1825–1975* (Manchester, Manchester University Press, 1985).

Fieldhouse, D., *The Colonial Empires: A Comparative Survey from the Eighteenth Century* 2nd ed. (London, Macmillan, 1982).

Pratt, J., *America's Colonial Experiment* (Gloucester, Peter Smith, 1964).

von Albertini, R., *European Colonial Rule, 1880–1940: The Impact of the West on India, South-east Asia and Africa* (Oxford, Clio Press, 1982).

9 Freedom

Ansprenger, A., *The Dissolution of the Colonial Empires* (London, Routledge, 1989).

Darwin, J., *Britain and Decolonization: The Retreat from Empire in the Post-War World* (New York, St. Martin's Press, 1988).

Holland, R., *European Decolonization, 1918–81* (London, Macmillan, 1985).

Gifford, P., and Louis, W., *The Transfer of Power in Africa: Decolonization, 1940–60* (New Haven, Yale University Press, 1982).

——*Decolonization and African Independence: The Transfers of Power, 1960–80* (New Haven, Yale University Press, 1988).

Mommsen, W., and Osterhammel, J., *Imperialism and After: Continuities and Discontinuities* (London, Allen & Unwin, 1986).

10 Nations

Keating, M., *State and Regional Nationalism: Territorial Politics and the European State* (Hemel Hempstead, Harvester, 1988).

Pearson, R., *National Minorities in Eastern Europe, 1848–1945* (London, Macmillan, 1983).

Simon, G., *Nationalism and Policy Towards the Nationalities in the Soviet Union* (Boulder, Westview, 1991).

Suny, R., *The Revenge of the Past: Nationalism, Revolution and the Collapse of the Soviet Union* (Stanford, Stanford University Press, 1993).

11 Power

Jacobsen, C., *Strategic Power: USA/USSR* (New York, St. Martin's Press, 1990).

Kennedy, P., *The Rise and Fall of the Great Powers: Economic Change and Military Conflict from 1500 to 2000* (New York, Vintage, 1989).

Venn, F., *Oil Diplomacy in the Twentieth Century* (New York, St. Martin's Press, 1986).

12 Conflict

Terraine, J., *White Heat: The New Warfare, 1914–18* (London, Sidgwick & Jackson, 1982).

13 Tradition

Blinkhorn, M., *Fascists and Conservatives: The Radical Right and the Establishment in Twentieth-century Europe* (London, Unwin Hyman, 1990).

Dale, P., *The Myth of Japanese Uniqueness* (New York, St. Martin's Press, 1986).

Girvin, B., *The Right in the Twentieth Century: Conservatism and Democracy* (London, Pinter, 1994).

Hobsbawm, E., and Ranger, T., *The Invention of Tradition* (Cambridge, Cambridge University Press, 1983).

Mayer, A., *The Persistence of the Old Regime: Europe to the Great War* (London, Croom Helm, 1981).

14 Fascism

Eatwell, R., *Fascism: A History* (New York, Penguin, 1997).

O'Sullivan, N., *Fascism* (London, Dent, 1983).

Payne, S., *Fascism: Comparison and Definition* (Madison, University of Wisconsin Press, 1980).

15 Dictatorship

Brooker, P., *Twentieth-century Dictatorships: The Ideological One-party States* (New York, New York University Press, 1996).

Finer, S., *The Man on Horseback: The Role of the Military in Politics* (London, Pall Mall, 1962).

Perlmutter, A., *The Military and Politics in Modern Times* (New Haven, Yale University Press, 1977).

16 Revolution

Acton, E., *Rethinking the Russian Revolution* (London, Edward Arnold, 1990).

Bianco, L., *The Origins of the Chinese Revolution, 1915–49* (Stanford, Stanford University Press, 1971).

Carsten, F., *Revolution in Central Europe, 1918–19* (London, Temple Smith, 1972).

Knight, A., *The Mexican Revolution*, 2 vols (Lincoln, University of Nebraska Press, 1990).

Mommsen, W., and Hirshfeld, G., *Social Protest, Violence and Terror in Nineteenth- and Twentieth-century Europe* (London, Macmillan, 1982).

Skocpol, T., *States and Social Revolutions: A Comparative Analysis of France, Russia and China* (Cambridge, Cambridge University Press, 1979).

17 Democracy

Lijphart, A., *Democracies: Patterns of Majoritarian and Consensus Government in Twenty-one Countries* (New Haven, Yale University Press, 1984).

Mouzelis, N., *Politics in the Semi-Periphery: Early Parliamentarianism and Late Industrialization in the Balkans and Latin America* (London, Macmillan, 1986).

Rueschemeyer, D., Stevens, E., and Stevens, J., *Capitalist Development and Democracy* (Oxford, Polity, 1992).

18 Socialism

Esping-Andersen, G., *Politics Against Markets: The Social Democratic Road to Power* (Princeton, Princeton University

Press, 1985).

Padgett, S., and Paterson, W., *A History of Social Democracy in Postwar Europe* (London, Longman, 1991).

Przeworski, A., and Sprague, J., *Paper Stones: A History of Electoral Socialism* (Chicago, Chicago University Press, 1986).

19 Repression

Conquest, R., *The Great Terror: Stalin's Purge of the Thirties* (New York, Oxford University Press, 1991).

——*The Harvest of Sorrow: Soviet Collectivization and the Terror-Famine* (New York, Oxford University Press, 1986).

Fulbrook, M., *Anatomy of a Dictatorship: Inside the GDR, 1949–89* (Oxford, Oxford University Press, 1995).

Gellately, R., *The Gestapo and German Society: Enforcing Racial Policy, 1933–45* (New York, Oxford University Press, 1990).

Getty, J., *Origins of the Great Purges: The Soviet Communist Party Reconsidered, 1933–8* (Cambridge, Cambridge University Press, 1985).

Goldstein, R., *Political Repression in Modern America: From 1870 to the Present* (Cambridge, Schenkman, 1978).

Thurlow, R., *The Secret State: British Internal Security in the Twentieth Century* (Oxford, Blackwell, 1994).

20 Discrimination

Degler, C., *Neither Black nor White: Slavery and Race Relations in Brazil and the United States* (New York, Macmillan, 1971).

Franklin, J., *Color and Race* (Boston, Houghton Mifflin, 1968).

Frederickson, G., *White Supremacy: A Comparative Study in American and South African History* (New York, Oxford University Press, 1981).

Ringer, B., *'We the People' and Others: Duality and America's Treatment of Its Racial Minorities* (New York, Tavistock, 1985).

Zureik, E., *The Palestinians and Israel: A Study in Internal Colonialism* (London, Routledge, 1979).

21 Genocide

Chalk, F., and Jonassohn, K., *The History and Sociology of Genocide: Analysis and Case Studies* (New Haven, Yale University Press, 1990).

Hilberg, R., *The Destruction of the European Jews* (Chicago, Chicago University Press, 1961).

Hirschfeld, G., *The Policies of Genocide: Jews and Soviet Prisoners of War in Nazi Germany* (London, Macmillan, 1986).

Kuper, L., *Genocide: Its Political Use in the Twentieth Century* (London, Penguin, 1981).

Prunier, G., *The Rwanda Crisis, 1959–94: History of a Genocide* (London, Hurst & Co. 1995).

Rummel, R., *Death by Government* (London, Transaction Books, 1994).

22 2000

Brown, L. (et al.), *Vital Signs: The Trends that Are Shaping Our Future* (London, Earthscan, 1993).

Horsman, M., and Marshall, A., *After the Nation-State: Citizens, Tribalism and the New World Disorder* (London, HarperCollins, 1994).

INDEX